# Asian American Politics

# THE SPECTRUM SERIES

## Race and Ethnicity in National and Global Politics

### Series Editors

**Paula D. McClain**
*Duke University*

**Joseph Stewart Jr.**
*University of New Mexico*

The sociopolitical dynamics of race and ethnicity are apparent everywhere. In the United States, racial politics underlie everything from representation to affirmative action to welfare policymaking. Early in the twenty-first century, Anglos in America will become only a plurality, as Latino and Asian American populations continue to grow. Issues of racial/ethnic conflict and cooperation are prominent across the globe. Diversity, identity, and cultural plurality are watchwords of empowerment as well as of injustice.

This new series offers textbook supplements, readers, and core texts addressing various aspects of race and ethnicity in politics, broadly defined. Meant to be useful in a wide range of courses in all kinds of academic programs, these books will be multidisciplinary as well as multiracial/ethnic in their appeal.

### SERIES TITLES INCLUDE

*American Indian Politics and the American Political System* by David E. Wilkins
*Asian American Politics: Law, Participation, and Policy* edited by Don T. Nakanishi and
James S. Lai

### FORTHCOMING TITLES

*Latino Politics* by John A. Garcia
*Media & Minorities* by Stephanie Greco Larson

# Asian American Politics

## Law, Participation, and Policy

Edited by
Don T. Nakanishi and James S. Lai

ROWMAN & LITTLEFIELD PUBLISHERS, INC.
*Lanham • Boulder • New York • Oxford*

ROWMAN & LITTLEFIELD PUBLISHERS, INC.

Published in the United States of America
by Rowman & Littlefield Publishers, Inc.
A Member of the Rowman & Littlefield Publishing Group
4720 Boston Way, Lanham, Maryland 20706
www.rowmanlittlefield.com

PO Box 317
Oxford
OX2 9RU, UK

British Library Cataloguing in Publication Information Available

**Library of Congress Cataloging-in-Publication Data**

Asian American politics : law, participation, and policy / edited by Don T. Nakanishi and
    James S. Lai.
        p. cm. — (Spectrum series)
    Includes bibliographical references and index.
    ISBN 0-7425-1849-3 (cloth : alk. paper) — ISBN 0-7425-1850-7 (pbk : alk. paper)
    1. Asian Americans—Politics and government. I. Nakanishi, Don T. II. Lai, James
S. III. Series

    E184.O6 A84145 2002                                                2002009334

Printed in the United States of America.

♾™ The paper used in this publication meets the minimum requirements of American
National Standard for Information Sciences—Permanence of Paper for Printed Library
Materials, ANSI/NISO Z39.48-1992.

# Contents

〰〰〰〰〰〰〰〰〰〰〰〰〰〰〰〰〰〰〰〰〰〰〰

# Figures, Illustrations, and Photographs

$\diagdown\diagdown\diagdown\diagdown\diagdown\diagdown\diagdown\diagdown\diagdown\diagdown\diagdown\diagdown\diagdown\diagdown\diagdown\diagdown$

## FIGURES

## ILLUSTRATIONS AND PHOTOGRAPHS

# Boxes and Tables

~~~~~~~~~~~~~~~~~~~~~~~~~~~~~~~~~~~~~~~~~~~~~~~~~~~~~~~~~~~~~~~~

## BOXES

## TABLES

# Preface

~~~~~~~~~~~~~~~~~~~~~~~~~~~~~~~~~~~~~~~~~~~~~~~~~~~~~~~~~~~~~~

The idea for this volume began eight years ago during a meeting on the campus of the University of California, Los Angeles (UCLA). The conversation centered around the need for a book aimed at scholars, students, and community members on Asian American politics in the discipline of American politics. Despite the 150-year history of Asians and Pacific Islanders in the United States, very few compilations existed on their political participation. This volume is an attempt to bring together a wide array of literature on Asian American politics to serve this need.

As the title of this volume suggests, we decided to focus on three areas of Asian American politics: law, participation, and policy. We realize it is impossible to include every topic on Asian American politics, but we felt these three areas would provide readers a solid overview of some of their key political issues and movements. Many of the contributing scholars are renowned or emerging stars in their own respective fields of study. We hope that this volume will provide students, scholars, and community members a better understanding about the complex historical and contemporary phenomena of Asian Americans and American politics.

Our deepest gratitude must first be extended to Paula McClain and Joseph Stewart Jr., the series editors, for their faith and support in compiling a volume on Asian American politics. Special thanks must also be extended to Jennifer Knerr, the political science editor at Rowman & Littlefield Publishing Group, and her assistant, Renee Legatt, for their constant support and assistance throughout the manuscript development process. Without Jennifer's professional support during the preliminary stages, we know that this volume would not have become a reality.

Professor James Lai also thanks his wife, Florence, for her steadfast emotional support during the entire publication process. She endured not only morning sickness with their son Ethan but also his many trials and tribulations in putting this manuscript together. Professor Don Nakanishi thanks his wife, Dr. Marsha Hirano-Nakanishi, for her continued commitment to his research and policy interests in relation to Asian American politics. He also thanks his son, Thomas, who achieved in an exemplary and independent manner and is now a student at Yale University.

Many thanks to Lorie Valdez, a Santa Clara University undergraduate, for her assistance with research, manuscript compilation, and photo selection during the production stages, as well as to the staff and faculty of the UCLA Asian American Studies Center. And finally, thanks to all the contributing authors and photographers who helped make this book possible. While the actual void in the American politics literature cannot be filled by this one publication, we hope it will mark the beginning of many publications in the field. Asian American politics is a growing academic discipline. Within these pages, we have assembled some of its brightest shining stars.

# Understanding Asian American Politics

*Don T. Nakanishi and James S. Lai*

Secretary of Transportation Norman Y. Mineta Recites His Oath of Office. Joined by President George W. Bush, second from left, in the Oval Office at the White House, Secretary of Transportation Norman Y. Mineta, right, recites his oath of office during a ceremonial swearing in, Thursday, February 8, 2001. Vice President Dick Cheney, left, read the oath for the secretary as his wife Danielia Mineta holds the Bible. *Courtesy of AP/Wide World Photos*

## THE GROWING ASIAN AND PACIFIC ISLANDER POLITICAL PARTICIPATION

Large-scale immigration from Asia and the Pacific Islands since the enactment of the Immigration Act of 1965 has had a dramatic impact on many states and regions across the United States. From a predominantly U.S.-born group of 1.5 million in 1970, this diverse group became a largely immigrant and refugee population of nearly 12 million by 2000. Projections estimate that it will continue to increase to approximately 20 million by 2020 (Ong and Hee 1993). The term "Asian Pacific American" reflects the diversity of this ethnic population, connoting a more contemporary, broader political identity than does "Asian American" by including both Asian and Pacific Islander ethnic groups in the United States. Scholars and activists frequently use the term "Asian Pacific American" interchangeably with or in place of "Asian American," and we follow this convention.

In recent years, a number of political scientists and commentators have speculated about whether Asian Pacific Americans will become an influential new force in American electoral politics, perhaps akin to American Jews, because of their dramatic demographic growth and concentration in certain key electoral states like California, New York, Texas, and New Jersey. Many believe that if Asian Pacific Americans, like American Jewish voters, come to represent a segment of the electorate that is comparable to, if not greater than, their share of the total population, they may become a highly influential "swing vote" in critical local, state, and presidential elections. In California, for example, there are over 4 million Asian Pacific Americans, accounting for one in eight residents of the state. If they also become one in eight California voters—who will continue to control the nation's largest number of congressional seats and Electoral College votes—then they could play a strategically important role in national and local elections. Indeed, their voting potential coupled with other attractive dimensions of their political infrastructure (e.g., their campaign fund-raising capabilities) could elevate Asian Pacific Americans to the status of important new actors in American electoral politics.

During the past two decades, there has been an unmistakable increase in the representation of Asian Pacific Americans in electoral politics. In 1978, for example, when the first edition of the *Asian Pacific American Political Almanac* was published, it listed several hundred elected officials who held offices primarily in Hawaii, California, and Washington (Nakanishi 1978). Almost all were second- and third-generation Asian Pacific Americans, with the vast majority being Japanese Americans. In contrast, the tenth edition of the political almanac, published in 2001, lists over two thousand Asian Pacific American elected and major appointed officials in thirty-three different states and the federal government (Nakanishi and Lai 2001). Although most continue to be of the second or third generation, like Hawaii Governor

Ben Cayetano and Washington Governor Gary Locke, a growing number of recently elected politicians have been immigrants and refugees. Former Franklin Township, New Jersey, Mayor Upendra J. Chivukula became the first Asian Pacific American and Indian American elected to the New Jersey State Assembly; city Councilman Tony Lam of Westminster, California, was the first Vietnamese American elected to public office.

These increasing levels of electoral participation and representation are all the more remarkable when they are considered in the context of the historical legacy of disenfranchisement of Asian Pacific Americans in relation to the American electoral system. Early Asian Pacific immigrants in the nineteenth and twentieth centuries were disenfranchised and excluded from fully participating in key sectors of American life because of a plethora of discriminatory laws and policies ranging from the Chinese Exclusion Act of 1882 to *Ozawa v. United States* (1922). The latter forbade Asian immigrants from becoming naturalized citizens. These legal barriers prevented early immigrants from participating in electoral politics of any form—whether the machine politics practiced by waves of European immigrants in the cities of the Atlantic and Midwest states or simply voting for their preferences in a local or presidential election—and substantially delayed the development of electoral involvement and representation by Asian Pacific Americans until the second and subsequent generations during the post–World War II period, over a hundred years after their initial period of immigration. However, this did not mean that the early immigrants did not engage in political activities. They often exhibited strong political resistance to the hostility and discrimination they encountered in the United States. Charles McClain, a scholar of early Chinese Americans, wrote:

> The conventional wisdom concerning Chinese and their supposed political backwardness needs to be stood on its head. The nineteenth-century Chinese American community may, because of language, have been more isolated from mainstream society than other immigrant groups in certain respects, but lack of political consciousness was not one of its distinguishing characteristics. There is abundant evidence that the leaders were thoroughly familiar with American governmental institutions, the courts in particular, and knew how to use those institutions to protect themselves (McClain 1994, 3).

McClain's observations are applicable to other Asian immigrants of the nineteenth and twentieth centuries who were politically aware and pursued various forms of civic engagement. These forms were usually limited to those that were afforded to noncitizens at that time, especially legal challenges.

Until recently, Asian Pacific American politics received limited scholarly and media attention. Early works such as Morton Grodzins's *Americans Betrayed* (1949) and Roger Daniels's *Politics of Prejudice* (1968) focused on how American political institutions, especially the major political parties and West Coast state legislatures, had a decisive impact on creating and maintaining a system of exclusion and discrimination against Asian Pacific Americans. There were few studies on the flip side of that structural condition—how Asian Pacific Americans responded to such treatment and, more generally, how they pursued a variety of political activities in both the domestic and nondomestic arenas during the course of their historical experiences.

This book introduces the burgeoning field of study and policy analysis dealing with the historical and contemporary dimensions of Asian Pacific American politics. It presents significant legal decisions, public policy commentaries, personal reflections by leading Asian Pacific American elected officials, and a comprehensive array of "classic" founding works along with new pathbreaking articles to capture the growing presence of Asian Pacific Americans in the nation's political processes. Although the readings are drawn predominantly from political science, also represented are cultural studies, ethnic and gender studies, public policy research, anthropology, and sociology, which have all contributed theoretical insights and empirical findings on the politics of Asian Pacific Americans.

## ORGANIZATION OF THE BOOK

This volume consists of four parts. In part 1, "Historical Forms of Civic Engagement and Protest," some of the major forms of discrimination and exclusion that early immigrant and second-generation Asian Pacific Americans encountered during the nineteenth and twentieth centuries—and how they challenged them—are presented. Included in this section are several significant U.S. Supreme Court decisions involving Asian Pacific Americans that set legal precedents and had an impact on their rights of naturalization (*Ozawa v. U.S.* [1922] and *U.S. v. Thind* [1923]) and equal protection (*Yick Wo v. Hopkins* [1886] and *Korematsu v. U.S.* [1944]).[1] These cases also serve to illustrate how Asian Pacific Americans, like other racial minorities, have had a long history of seeking social justice and equal treatment through the courts system.

Part 2, "The Impact of Immigration Laws on Asian Pacific America," examines how two of the most wide-ranging changes in immigration laws during the twentieth century influenced the demographic characteristics of the Asian Pacific American population. Lee A. Makela analyzes the Immigration Act of 1924, which represents one of the darkest chapters in the immigration history of Asian Pacific Americans because it essentially ended immigration from Asia for nearly forty years. Immigration from Asia was not placed on an equal footing with immigration from Europe until 1965 (Chan 1991). In "Making and Remaking Asian Pacific America: Immigration Policy," legal scholar Bill Ong Hing analyzes how the Immigration Act of 1965 contributed to the explosive growth and diversification of Asian Pacific Americans during the past three and a half decades, which in turn has led to new opportunities, resources, and challenges for their political organizations and leaders.

Part 3, "The Period of Political Incorporation (1965 to Present)," focuses on how the contemporary Asian Pacific American population, spurred by the African American Civil Rights Movement of the 1960s, is pursuing an array of electoral and nonelectoral strategies to enhance their political presence in the nation's political institutions and to confront social issues damaging to their group interests. Along with studies that examine their voting behavior, this section contains works on the involvement of Asian Pacific Americans in transnational political networks, labor and protest movements, and pan-ethnic coalitions. It also features extensive readings on the topics of elected leadership and politics, media, and racial profiling, where Asian Pacific Americans have witnessed diametrically opposite gains and setbacks in recent years.

The selections on elected leadership examine the factors that have contributed to the growing numbers of Asian Pacific American candidates and elected officials, along with personal commentaries by several current Asian Pacific American elected and major appointed officials like Secretary of Labor Elaine Chao, Secretary of Transportation Norman Mineta, Washington Governor Gary Locke, and Oregon Congressman David Wu. The readings on politics, media, and racial profiling examine two of the most controversial episodes of racial profiling that have had adverse effects on the political participation of Asian Pacific Americans: the 1996 campaign finance scandal involving the Democratic National Committee and alleged illegal foreign contributions from Asian nationals and the trial of Dr. Wen Ho Lee, a Chinese American nuclear scientist at the Los Alamos National Laboratories, who was charged with security violations and jailed for nine months.

In part 4, "Contemporary Public Policy Issues in the New Millennium," many of the most compelling public policy issues that Asian Pacific American organizations and leaders have pursued in recent years are examined. The readings include research studies and policy commentaries on affirmative action, Japanese American redress and reparations, labor organizing, race relations and urban unrest, and political redistricting. These policy concerns underscore the fact that despite their popular characterization as the "model minority," Asian Pacific Americans continue to face a number of significant institutional and individual-level challenges to their full participation in American politics and society.

## THE GROWING POPULATION AND DIVERSITY OF ASIAN PACIFIC AMERICANS

According to the 2000 U.S. Census, the term "Asian and Pacific Islanders" encompasses over twenty-five different ethnic groups, all with their unique cultures and histories of migration and settlement in the United States.

As illustrated in table 1, the expansion of immigration quotas through the 1965 amendments to the Immigration and Naturalization Act had an

**Table 1  National Immigration of Asian Americans**

| Period | From Asia | Asian Pacific, % of Total Immigration | Chinese | Japanese | Asian Pacific Indian | Korean | Filipino | Vietnamese |
|---|---|---|---|---|---|---|---|---|
| 1851–1860 | 41,571 | 1.6 | 41,397 | 0 | 43 | 0 | 0 | 0 |
| 1861–1870 | 64,815 | 2.8 | 64,301 | 186 | 69 | 0 | 0 | 0 |
| 1871–1880 | 123,736 | 4.4 | 123,201 | 149 | 163 | 0 | 0 | 0 |
| 1881–1890 | 68,206 | 1.3 | 61,711 | 2,270 | 269 | 0 | 0 | 0 |
| 1891–1900 | 73,751 | 2 | 14,799 | 25,942 | 68 | 0 | 0 | 0 |
| 1901–1910 | 325,430 | 3.7 | 20,605 | 129,797 | 4,713 | 7,697 | 0 | 0 |
| 1911–1920 | 246,640 | 4.3 | 21,278 | 83,837 | 2,082 | 1,049 | 869 | 0 |
| 1921–1930 | 110,895 | 2.7 | 29,907 | 33,462 | 1,886 | 598 | 54,747 | 0 |
| 1931–1940 | 15,853 | 3 | 4,928 | 1,948 | 496 | 60 | 6,159 | 0 |
| 1941–1950 | 32,086 | 3.1 | 16,709 | 1,555 | 1,761 | 0 | 4,691 | 0 |
| 1951–1960 | 153,444 | 6.1 | 25,201 | 46,250 | 1,973 | 6,231 | 19,307 | 0 |
| 1961–1970 | 428,496 | 12.9 | 109,771 | 39,988 | 27,189 | 34,526 | 98,376 | 3,788 |
| 1971–1980 | 1,586,140 | 35.3 | 237,793 | 49,775 | 164,134 | 271,956 | 360,216 | 179,681 |
| 1981–1990 | 2,817,391 | 38.4 | 446,000 | 44,800 | 261,900 | 338,800 | 495,300 | 401,400 |
| 1991–1994 | 1,356,447 | 31.4 | 282,900 | 28,995 | 154,587 | 79,435 | 239,465 | 233,992 |

*Source:* Larry Shinagawa, "The Impact of Immigration on the Demography of Asian Pacific Americans," Table 4.

unprecedented impact on the growth of the Asian Pacific American population. Asian Pacific Americans grew eightfold, from 1.5 million in 1970 to
nearly 12 million in 2000. At the same time, the population became predominantly foreign born, with approximately two-thirds being born abroad by
1990 (Ong and Hee 1993b; Shinagawa 1996; Wong 1999).

With the emergence of Asian Pacific Americans as one of the fastest growing groups in the nation (2000 U.S. Census), it is important to realize that this
is not an ethnically and racially homogeneous population. Tables 2 and 3
illustrate the racial and ethnic diversity that exists among Asian Pacific
Americans, which is due to not only the number of different countries of origin but also the large percentage of individuals from interethnic and interracial marriages and backgrounds. In 2000, more than 2 million Asian Pacific
Americans were biracial or multiracial.

As multiracial and multiethnic Asian Pacific Americans become more
politically involved, one of the primary challenges facing Asian Pacific American organizations will be to develop inclusive structures and issue agendas
that can represent the diverse interests of Asian Pacific Americans, as well as
reach out and build viable coalitions with other communities. Underlying
this challenge is the shift from the traditional biracial black–white paradigm,
which has historically defined American race relations, to a multiracial one
that includes Latinos and Asian Pacific Americans (Oh 2000; Ong 2000). For
Asian Pacific Americans, a political coalition based on a collective group
identity (e.g., Asian Pacific American identity) may become increasingly difficult to achieve based on common interests, ideology, and leadership, particularly due to the emergence of multiracial and ethnic-specific identities. The
traditional coalition partners that defined minority struggles for political

**Table 2    Asian Pacific Population for the United States (2000)**

| Race | Number | Percent of Total Population |
|---|---|---|
| **Total Population** | **281,421,906** | **100.0** |
| Asian Pacific alone | 10,242,998 | 3.6 |
| Asian Pacific in combination with one or more other races | 1,655,830 | 0.6 |
| Asian Pacific; White | 868,395 | 0.3 |
| Asian Pacific; Native Hawaiian and Other Pacific Islander | 138,802 | — |
| Asian Pacific; Black or African American | 106,782 | — |
| Asian Pacific; Native Hawaiian or Other Pacific Islander; White | 89,611 | — |
| All other combinations including Asian Pacific | 452,240 | 0.2 |
| Asian Pacific alone or in combination with one or more other races | 11,898,828 | 4.2 |

*Note:* The racial group Asian Pacifics consists of the following ethnic groups (2000 U.S. population): Chinese (2,432,585), Filipino (1,850,314), Asian Pacific Indian (1,678,765), Vietnamese (1,122,528), Korean
(1,076,872), Japanese (796,700), Other Asian Pacifics)—Category includes Cambodian, Hmong,
Bangladeshi, Burmese, Indonesian, Pakistani, and Sri Lankans—(1,285,234).
*Source:* U.S. Census Bureau, Census 2000 Redistricting (Public Law 94-171). Summary File, Table PL1.

**Table 3    Native Hawaiian and Other Pacific Islander Population for the United States (2000)**

| Race | Number | Percent of Total Population |
|------|--------|----------------------------|
| **Total Population** | **281,421,906** | **100.0** |
| Native Hawaiian and Other Pacific Islander alone | 398,835 | 0.1 |
| Native Hawaiian and Other Pacific Islander in combination with one or more other races | 475,579 | 0.2 |
| Native Hawaiian and Other Pacific Islander; Asian Pacific | 138,802 | — |
| Native Hawaiian and Other Pacific Islander; White | 112,964 | — |
| Native Hawaiian and Other Pacific Islander; Asian Pacific; White | 89,611 | — |
| Native Hawaiian and Other Pacific Islander; Black or African American | 29,876 | — |
| All other combinations including Native Hawaiian and Other Pacific Islander | 104,326 | — |
| Native Hawaiian and Other Pacific Islander alone or in combination with one or more other races | 874,414 | 0.3 |

Note: The racial group Pacific Islanders consists of the following ethnic groups (2000 U.S. population): Native Hawaiian and Pacific Islander (398,835), Native Hawaiian (140,652), Samoan (91,029), Guamanian or Chamorro (58,240), and Other Pacific Islanders—category includes Tongan Tahitian, Northern Mariana Islander, Paulauan, Fijian, Melanesian, Micronesian, and Polynesian—(108,914).
Source: U.S. Census Bureau, Census 2000 Redistricting (Public Law 94-171). Summary File, Table PL1.

incorporation in the past will inevitably be challenged in the future. New political alignments between and among minority and mainstream groups will likely emerge in local and state politics that transcend traditional notions of minority politics. Asian Pacific Americans will likely be key actors. As one political pundit of California minority politics observed:

> But, because of their heterogeneity, Asian Pacific Americans are not likely to make any ideological difference in American politics, at least not in the way that other powerful ethnic groups have. Their most lasting contribution may be their unique ability to transcend traditional ethnic fault lines; indeed, the political maturation of Asian Pacific Americans may signal a new era in racial politics. (Rodriguez 1998, 22)

For the political maturation of Asian Pacific Americans to signal a new era in racial politics, the group will have to overcome at least two major challenges. First, Asian Pacific Americans have comparatively low voter registration and turnout rates (Nakanishi 1991; Field Institute Poll 1994; Ong and Nakanishi 1996; Asian Pacific American Legal Center of Southern California 1996; Nakanishi 1998). Second, they are the most geographically dispersed and residentially integrated minority group (Rodriquez 1998). Both of these conditions have tended to diminish the impact that their recent population increases might suggest. On the other hand, the rapid population growth of Asian Pacific Americans during the decade of the 1990s has laid the foundation for increased representation, particularly in the formation of political districts with substantial Asian Pacific American populations. According to the Democratic National Committee, for instance, congressional districts with an Asian Pacific American population of 5 percent or more increased from sixty-three districts in 1990 to ninety-six districts in 2000. It was further projected that by the year 2000, there could be at least ten districts in California and Hawaii that will have Asian Pacific American populations ranging from 20 percent to 60 percent. Moreover, this population growth occurred in states such as New Jersey, Minnesota, Oregon, Nevada, and Pennsylvania. In New Jersey, during the 1990s, the number of congressional districts with an Asian Pacific American population of 5 percent or more increased from one to eight (Office of Asian Pacific American Outreach, Democratic National Committee Press Release, October 13, 1999). As a result, Asian Pacific American voters have the potential to play a greater role in future state and federal politics on the U.S. mainland in the new millennium, and it is likely that more Asian Pacific American candidates will also emerge.

## FINDING TIES THAT BIND: THE CHALLENGES OF CONSTRUCTING AND MAINTAINING PAN-ETHNIC COALITIONS

Political barriers exist within the Asian Pacific American community due to its rapid population growth and ethnic diversity. One recent political strategy of Asian Pacific American political leaders and community activists on the U.S. mainland has been to build pan-ethnic coalitions within this ethnically diverse population. The perspective of Asian Pacific American pan-ethnicity dates from the late 1960s, during a period of social strife in urban cities across the nation, as racial minority groups protested their lack of political incorporation and injustices. Its goal was to unify diverse groups based on their common racial categorization rather than solely their ethnic heritage. A pan-ethnic strategy represents a very important strategy among Asian Pacific American political activists because of the lack of Asian Pacific majority districts and an increasingly diverse Asian Pacific and Pacific Islander population (Espiritu 1992).

The challenges to constructing and maintaining such political coalitions are many. One such challenge is the salience of race and ethnicity in today's political arenas. In regard to ethnic salience, one contemporary trend in the politics of the state of California, where nearly 40 percent of the nation's Asian Pacific Americans reside, is for ethnic groups to "go it alone" (Cain 1991). This is particularly the case among recent immigrant Asian Pacific ethnic groups (post-1965) who do not necessarily identify with issues that marked the political struggles of more established Asian Pacific American groups during the 1960s. As a result, pan-ethnic coalitions among Asian Pacific Americans, often difficult to construct, have tended to be short-lived.

At the same time, other factors have diminished the potential for a pan-Asian Pacific identity among recent Asian Pacific immigrants, including variations in socioeconomic background such as education and income, generation issues, and homeland politics (Espiritu 1992; Wei 1993; Espiritu and Ong 1994; Lien 1997).

## GROWING NUMBERS OF ASIAN PACIFIC AMERICAN ELECTED OFFICIALS

The number of Asian Pacific Americans elected to local, state, and congressional positions across the nation has continually increased in recent years. Table 4 illustrates the growing numbers of Asian Pacific American elected officials. In 2000, 309 Asian Pacific American held elected offices representing thirty-three states ranging from city school board member to U.S. senator (Nakanishi and Lai 2001). Among them were twenty-five state senators in five states (Colorado, Minnesota, Oregon, Washington, and Hawaii); forty-two state representatives in five states (California, Maryland, West Virginia, Washington, and Hawaii); and fifteen city mayors in seven states (California, Colorado, Illinois, New Mexico, Texas, Washington, and Hawaii).

During the twenty-year period between 1978 and 1998, the greatest increase in Asian Pacific American elected representation on the U.S. mainland occurred at the state and local levels. While Hawaii currently remains the state with the largest number of Asian Pacific American elected officials at all governmental levels, mainland states such as California, Washington, Oregon, and Texas have significantly increased numbers of Asian Pacific Americans in key elected and major appointed posi-

**Table 4    Total Number of Asian Pacific Americans Elected Officials in Key Federal, State, and Local Positions**

| Year | Federal | State | City | Total |
|------|---------|-------|------|-------|
| 1978 | 5 | 63 | 52 | 120 |
| 1979 | 6 | 68 | 69 | 149 |
| 1980 | 6 | 69 | 98 | 173 |
| 1982 | 6 | 59 | 109 | 174 |
| 1984 | 5 | 59 | 109 | 173 |
| 1990 | 2 | 111 | 185 | 298 |
| 1995 | 8 | 66 | 157 | 231 |
| 1996 | 7 | 66 | 181 | 254 |
| 1998 | 7 | 67 | 187 | 261 |
| 2000 | 8 | 70 | 231 | 309 |

*Source:* Compiled by author from the *National Asian Pacific American Political Almanac,* First to Eighth Editions.

tions (*National Asian Pacific American Political Almanac,* 2001–2002). For example, Gary Locke became the first Asian Pacific American elected governor of a mainland state in 1996 in Washington. Governor Locke's acceptance speech is featured in part 3. Another example of the positive growth in elected representation for state-level elected positions has been in California, where a record four Asian Pacific Americans currently serve in the state assembly.[2]

The number of states in which Asian Pacific Americans have been elected has increased substantially. In 1978 less than a dozen states had Asian Pacific American elected positions, compared with thirty-three states in 2000. Those who are running and winning elections are beginning to reflect the ethnic diversity of the population. Despite the recent growth in elected representation, however, Asian Pacific Americans are still underrepresented in comparison to other racial minority groups and to their share of the population. In California, for example, where Asian Pacific Americans make up one in every eight residents, they would need to increase their representation from four to fifteen of the 120-member California legislature (forty in the Senate and eighty in the Assembly) to reach a hypothetical parity with their proportion of the state's population.

## POLITICAL DIFFERENCES BETWEEN HAWAII AND THE U.S. MAINLAND

Many differences exist in regard to the political experiences of Asian Pacific American elected officials on the U.S. mainland compared with those in Hawaii, where Asian Pacific Americans have historically attained the greatest elected representation. The first major difference is that, in comparison with Asian Pacific American elected officials in Hawaii, there is a lack of direct representation between Asian Pacific American elected officials and Asian Pacific American constituents on the U.S. mainland. Given the lack of Asian Pacific American majority districts on the U.S. mainland, it would be an unwise political strategy for any Asian Pacific candidate to rely solely on the group's bloc vote. However, Asian Pacific American elected officials and candidates who strategically target Asian Pacific American resources within and outside of their own district can benefit greatly from their political resources, particularly campaign contributions. Therefore, a second difference is that Asian Pacific American elected officials and candidates on the U.S. mainland tend to rely more heavily than their Hawaiian counterparts for support by Asian Pacific American community-based organization leaders, community activists, and the ethnic media for access to political resources. One of the most important resources is campaign contributions, which Asian Pacific Americans have long provided in substantial amounts in local, state, and presidential campaigns (Tachibana 1986; Nakanishi 1991; Nakanishi 1998).

A third difference is that Asian Pacific American elected officials and candidates on the U.S. mainland must rely on different political strategies and resources in order to compensate for the lack of Asian Pacific majority districts than those in Hawaii, where Asian Pacific Americans represent the majority population and hold a majority of the local and state elected positions. In contrast, Asian Pacific American candidates and elected officials on the U.S. mainland may pursue a mainstream campaign strategy (e.g., running as a mainstream candidate who happens to be Asian Pacific American) or a multiracial campaign strategy (e.g., one who builds coalitions between mainstream and minority groups). Asian Pacific American elected officials and candidates on the U.S. mainland may seek to target community leaders (i.e., labor union leaders or community-based organization leaders) who can provide them with access to resources within their ethnic communities. These resources range from providing a mass number of volunteers during get-out-the vote (GOTV) drives to financial contributions. This strategy is optional, depending on the type of campaign strategy pursued by the Asian Pacific American elected official or candidate. Although this political network does not exist for the Asian Pacific American community alone, it has become a key strategy for many Asian Pacific American candidates on the U.S. mainland.

The experiences of Asian Pacific American elected officials on the U.S. mainland are also different from African American and Latino elected officials in one important aspect: they tend to be nonethnic representatives (Cain, Kiewiet, and Uhlaner 1986). In short, Asian Pacific American elected officials on the U.S. mainland emerge from non-Asian Pacific districts that are either heavily white or multiracial. African American and Latino elected officials at the local, state, and congressional levels tend to emerge from political districts in which they represent the majority or a substantial portion of the total population (Browning, Marshall, and Tabb 1990). At the federal level, twenty-three of thirty-nine African American U.S. congresspersons represented districts in 1998 in which the African American voting-age population was 50 percent or more of the population (Bositis 1998). For Latinos, seventeen of nineteen members of Congress were in districts where the Latino population was at least 50 percent (*Capitol Advantage* 2001). In contrast, Asian Pacific American elected officials on the U.S. mainland represent non-Asian Pacific majority districts where Asian Pacific constituents are a minority or are nonexistent. For example, the two congressional seats held by Asian Pacific Americans on the mainland are overwhelmingly non-Asian Pacific majority districts. Therefore, in the absence of elected representation districts with a substantial Asian American population, are there any political agents, at the local level, who represent their interests? The next section addresses the political roles of Asian Pacific American community-based organizations in local governance, particularly in the absence of elected representation.

## FILLING THE ELECTORAL VOID: ASIAN PACIFIC AMERICAN COMMUNITY-BASED ORGANIZATIONS AND LOCAL GOVERNANCE

Asian Pacific American community-based organizations and other community leaders undertake a variety of roles during group political mobilization. Such roles have been heightened due to the fact that the majority of Asian Pacific American candidates on the U.S. mainland represent non-Asian Pacific districts in contrast to elected officials in Hawaii. For example, U.S. Representative David Wu (D-OR) represents a constituency that has less than 3 percent Asian Pacific Americans. During the 105th Congress, only two of the top fifty congressional districts on the U.S. mainland with the largest Asian Pacific American populations were represented by an Asian Pacific American (*National Directory of Asian Pacific American Organizations* 1997–1998).[3] For Asian Pacific Americans on the U.S. mainland, the lack of ethnic representation from their largest districts has led to a political void. During the past two decades, Asian Pacific American community leaders, organizations, and activists have played a significant role in helping to fill this electoral void at the local levels.

Asian Pacific American community-based groups can act as a conduit with mainstream elected officials and institutions. For example, in Los Angeles's Koreatown, the commercial and organizational focal point for the largest population of Korean Americans in the nation, Korean American community-based organizations have provided their substantial ethnic community with a political voice in expressing their concerns to mainstream elected representatives and institutions. One such organization is the Korean American Coalition (KAC), a nonprofit, nonpartisan organization representing the interests of more than 500,000 Korean Americans living in Southern California. During the past five years, KAC has conducted an annual legislative luncheon in Southern California with local and statewide elected officials and legislative aides who are invited to Koreatown to meet with Korean American community leaders/organizations. At the fifth annual legislative luncheon on November 12, 1999, five Korean American community-based organizations (Korean American Family Service Center, Korean American Museum, Korean Health Education Information and Research Center, and Korean Youth and Community Center) made presentations to a large non-Korean American legislative group. In the past, the elected officials who have been invited to their legislative luncheons included California Governor Gray Davis, former Governor Pete Wilson, U.S. Senator Barbara Boxer, U.S. Congressman Xavier Bacerra, and Los Angeles Mayor Richard Riordan. Their luncheons have served as a forum to present and discuss issues affecting Korean Americans in Southern California.

Community-based organizations can help recruit and train potential Asian Pacific American candidates. At the local level, the Japanese American

Citizen's League chapter in Los Angeles has held candidate training workshops led by Asian Pacific American elected officials who worked hand in hand toward the goal of increasing elected representation. These workshops usually feature current and past Asian Pacific American elected officials, campaign strategists, and political researchers. At the national level, the Asian Pacific American Institute for Congressional Studies, the only national Asian Pacific American public policy institute in Washington, D.C., and the University of California at Los Angeles Asian American Studies Center, a leading research center on Asian Pacific Americans, annually cosponsor a National Leadership Academy for Asian Pacific American Elected Officials in Washington, D.C. Various Asian Pacific American candidates and elected official participants from across the country attend the three-day workshops.[4] According to the Leadership Academy's 1999 press release: "Fifteen outstanding elected officials—Democratic, Republican, and Independent, from Massachusetts to Hawaii, representing many different ethnic groups—have been selected to attend this intensive training program. During the program, these elected officials will develop the skills they need to advance in their careers and to prepare for higher office."[5] This three-day event includes various training sessions with current and former Asian Pacific American elected officials, congressional staffers, political and public relations consultants, fund-raisers, and print and broadcast journalists.[6]

The success of the inaugural 1999 Leadership Academy resulted in the formation of the Asian Pacific American Political Education Institute in California. The cosponsors of this political education institute were two of the most visible Asian Pacific American community and academic organizations in Los Angeles County—the Chinese Americans United for Self-Empowerment (CAUSE) and the University of California at Los Angeles's Asian American Studies Center. According to their press release, the mission of the institute was "to gather top notch political consultants, elected officials, community leaders, and media together with individuals who are interested in seeking elected offices for two days of interactive panel discussions and training. . . . Through this institute we strive to enhance the success rate of the Asian Pacific American candidates by discussing issues facing these candidates . . . and provide our community with a better understanding of the mechanics of political campaigns" (Asian Pacific American Political Education Institute 1999).

Another important Asian Pacific American community resource on the U.S. mainland is the ethnic media, which can provide candidates with important media exposure to a large segment of Asian Pacific foreign-born, bilingual population of potential voters and donors. The vast majority of Asian Pacific American ethnic newspapers and television shows cater to them. In Los Angeles and Orange Counties during 1998–1999, there were nearly two hundred different Asian Pacific and Pacific Islander media outlets, ranging from newspapers and journals to radio and television programs (*Asian Pacific and Pacific Islander*

*Community Directory for Los Angeles and Orange Counties,* 1998–1999). Given their strong influence in reaching the Asian Pacific and Pacific Islander foreign-born population, it was no surprise that high-profile candidates such as Republican Matt Fong, a Chinese American and son of former California State Secretary March Fong-Eu, targeted the Chinese American print media in order to get his message out to prospective Chinese American voters and contributors during his closely contested 1998 bid in California for the U.S. Senate against incumbent Senator Barbara Boxer.

The advantage of targeting the ethnic media was that it provided Fong a cost-effective medium to advertise his campaign to potential Asian Pacific American voters and contributors, who could tip the balance of a close election in his favor. During the Republican primary election, Fong's principal challenger, Darrell Issa, spent $2 million dollars in radio advertisements alone. While Fong targeted the mainstream media during his campaign, he also focused his limited resources on the Asian Pacific ethnic media. The cost-effectiveness of advertising in Asian Pacific ethnic print media versus mainstream print media can be seen in the following: a full-page advertisement in the *San Francisco Chronicle* costs $55,000, compared with $1,200 for a full-page advertisement in *Sing Tao,* a Bay Area Chinese language newspaper with a national circulation of sixty thousand. Fong utilized the Chinese American print media to his advantage and even credited them with helping him win his Republican primary election (Lin and Galbraith 1998).

## CONCLUSION

The present and future potential of Asian Pacific Americans and American politics is deeply rooted in historic immigration laws. From the National Origins Act of 1924 to the Immigration Act of 1965, the face of Asian Pacific America has been shaped and reshaped by immigration laws enacted by the U.S. Congress. For example, by allowing Asian Pacific immigration to resume to the United States in 1965, after over forty years of complete exclusion, the Asian Pacific American community represents one of the youngest and fastest growing racial populations in the United States (2001 U.S. Census).

Conceptualizing Asian Pacific American politics requires researchers and students to go beyond customary ways of viewing political participation, such as voting and running for office, and to include myriad other forms of nonelectoral and nondomestic political activities that Asian Pacific Americans have long pursued. However, recent trends strongly suggest that more and more Asian Pacific Americans, especially immigrants and refugees, will register to vote, cast ballots, and run for elected office as they become naturalized (Aoki and Nakanishi 2001).

With their political potential lies future challenges for Asian Pacific Americans such as whether they will be completely integrated into mainstream American institutions. A recent national survey entitled "American Attitudes toward Chinese Americans and Asian Americans," commissioned by the Committee of 100, a Chinese American leadership group, found that other Americans felt uneasy toward Asian Americans in the aftermath of the Wen Ho Lee trial and 1996 campaign finance scandal. In this survey, Asian Americans were viewed as "clannish" and "less likely to be full participants in the entire community as other Americans." Asian American respondents believed that other Americans view them as "permanent aliens," and this perception has contributed to their lack of interest in American politics (Committee of 100 Survey Findings 2001). For Asian Americans, these future challenges of complete incorporation into mainstream American institutions represent the next step that this group must address.

All of the above political behaviors, perceptions, and struggles are vividly captured and reflected in the articles within this anthology. We hope that these articles will stimulate class discussion and encourage future political studies on Asian Pacific American politics. Political scientists in American politics have long neglected this growing and increasingly influential group, and it is our hope that this volume will generate new research questions and a comprehensive understanding of their distinct political history.

## NOTES

1.  Although the selected articles focus on federal laws, legal historians have noted that many similar lawsuits were filed in state supreme courts.

2.  In 2001 the four Asian American members in the California State Assembly are Wilma Chan (D-16), Judy Chu (D-49), Carol Liu (D-44), and George Nakano (D-53). This represents the largest number of Asian American members to serve at one time in the California State Assembly. One previous assembly member, Mike Honda, was elected to the U.S. House of Representatives that same year. Prior to this year, no Asian American woman had been elected to the California Assembly since March Fong-Eu in the late 1970s. After March Fong-Eu, Paul Bannai, Floyd Mori, Nao Takasugi, and Mike Honda served in the California Assembly before the current group of four were elected.

3.  At the time, two Asian American members of Congress from the U.S. mainland were Robert T. Matsui (D-CA) and Jay Kim (R-CA).

4.  The following thirteen elected officials attended the Leadership Academy for Asian American Elected Officials (May 20–22, 1999): Jon Amores (a Filipino American member of the West Virginia House of Delegates); Kumar P. Barve (an Asian Indian American delegate in the Maryland House of Delegates); Michael Gin (a Chinese American mayor pro tem of the city of Redondo Beach, Calif.); Solomon P. Kaho'ohalahala (a native Hawaiian state representative); Conrad Lee (a Chinese American city council member in the city of Bellevue, Wash.); Joaquin Lim (a Chinese American mayor pro tem of the city of Walnut, Calif.); Karyl Matsumoto (a Japanese American vice mayor of the city of South San Francisco); Hermina Morita (a Japanese American Hawaii state representative); Michael Park (deputy mayor in the city of Federal Way, Wash.); Amy Mah Sangiolo (a Chinese American alderman at large in the city of Newton, Mass.); Paul Shin (a Korean

American senator in the Washington state senate); Benjamin Wong (a Chinese American city council member in the West Covina, Calif.); and Martha J. Wong (a Chinese American city council member in Houston).

5. Leadership Academy for Asian American Elected Officials, press release, May 20–22, 1999, Washington, D.C.

6. Among the elected officials and political experts who participated in the training panels were the following: Representatives Robert T. Matsui (D-CA) and Patsy T. Mink (D-HI); U.S. Delegate Robert A. Underwood (D-Guam); former Representative Norman Y. Mineta, then with Lockheed Martin Corporation; former California Secretary of State Matt Fong, then with the Leadership for America Foundation; Geoffrey Becker, Tarrance Group; Eric K. Federing, KPMG LLP; Scott Gail, Fundraising Management Group; John Jameson, Winning Connections; Samuel T. Mok, International Technology and Trade Associates; Teri Okita, WUSA-TV; Maeley Tom, Cassidy & Associates; John Yang, *Washington Post*; and Judy Yu, AsiaNet.

## REFERENCES

*Asian and Pacific Islander Community Directory for Los Angeles and Orange Counties.* 1998–1999. 8th ed. Los Angeles: UCLA Asian American Studies Center Press.

Asian Pacific American Legal Center of Southern California. 2000. *November 2000 Southern California Voter Survey.*

———. *1996 Southern California Asian Pacific American Exit Poll Report: An Analysis of APA Voter Behavior and Opinions*, 1996.

Browning, Rufus P., Dale R. Marshall, and David H. Tabb. 1984. *Protest Is Not Enough: The Struggle of Blacks and Hispanics for Equality in Urban Politics.* Berkeley: University of California Press.

———. 1997. "Mobilization, Incorporation, and Policy in Ten California Cities." In *Racial Politics in American Cities*, 14–37. 2d ed. New York: Longman.

Cain, Bruce E. 1991. "The Contemporary Context of Ethnic and Racial Politics in California." In Byran O. Jackson and Michael B. Preston, eds., *Racial and Ethnic Politics in California*, 1:9–24. Berkeley: Institute of Governmental Studies Press.

Cain, Bruce E., and Roderick Kiewiet. 1986. "Minorities in California." Proceedings of a public symposium, Pasadena, Calif., March 5.

Cain, Bruce E., Roderick Kiewiet, and Carole J. Uhlaner. 1991. "The Acquisition of Partisanship by Latinos and Asian Americans." *American Journal of Political Science* 35(2): 390–422.

Chan, Sucheng. 1991. *Asian Americans: An Interpretive History.* Boston: Twayne.

Democratic National Committee. 1999. "Political Power of Asian Pacific Americans Increases due to Projected Population Growth." Press release, October 13.

Espiritu, Yen Le. 1992. *Asian American Panethnicity: Bridging Institutions and Identities.* Philadelphia: Temple University Press.

Espiritu, Yen Le, and Paul M. Ong. 1994. "Class Constraints on Racial Solidarity among Asian Americans." In Paul M. Ong, Edna Bonacich, and Lucie Cheng, eds., *The New Asian Immigration in Los Angeles and Global Restructuring*, 395–422. Philadelphia: Temple University Press.

Field Institute Poll. 1994. In Don T. Nakanishi and James S. Lai, eds., *1996 National Asian Pacific American Political Almanac*, 187–88. 7th ed. Los Angeles: UCLA Asian American Studies Center Press.

Guerra, Fernando J. 1990. "Ethnic Politics in Los Angeles: The Emergence of Black, Jewish, Latino, and Asian Officeholders, 1960–1989." Ph.D. diss., University of Michigan.

———. 1991. "The Emergence of Ethnic Officeholders in California." In Byran O. Jackson and Michael B. Preston, eds., *Racial and Ethnic Politics in California*, 1: 117–32. Berkeley, Calif.: Institute of Governmental Studies Press.

Hing, Bill Ong. 1993. *Making and Remaking Asian America Through Immigration Policy, 1850–1990.* Stanford, Calif.: Stanford University Press.

Lai, James S. 2000. "Asian Pacific Americans and the Pan-Ethnic Question." In Richard A. Keiser and Katherine Underwood, eds., *Minority Politics at the Millennium,* 203–26. New York: Garland.

Lien, Pei-Te. 1997. *The Political Participation of Asian Americans: Voting Behavior in Southern California.* New York: Garland.

Lin, Sam Chu, and Bob Galbraith. 1998. "Fong Wins First Round: What His Victory Means for Boxer, for Asian Americans, for GOP." *AsianWeek* 19(42).

Louie, Steve, and Glenn Omatsu. 2001. *Asian Americans: The Movement and the Moment.* Los Angeles: UCLA Asian American Studies Press.

Maki, Mitchell T., Harry H.L. Kitano, and S. Megan Berthold. 1999. *Achieving the Impossible Dream: How the Japanese Americans Obtained Redress.* Urbana: University of Illinois Press.

McClain, Charles J. 1994. *In Search of Equality: The Chinese Struggle against Discrimination in Nineteenth-Century America.* Berkeley: University of California Press.

Nakanishi, Don T. 1991. "The Next Swing Vote? Asian Pacific Americans and California Politics." In Byran O. Jackson and Michael B. Preston, eds., *Racial and Ethnic Politics in California*, 1: 25–54. Berkeley, Calif.: Institute of Governmental Studies Press.

Nakanishi, Don T. 1998. "When Numbers Do Not Add Up: Asian Pacific Americans and California Politics." In M. B. Preston, B. E. Cain, and S. Bass, eds., *Racial and Ethnic Politics in California*, 2:3–43. Berkeley, Calif.: Institute of Governmental Studies Press.

*National Asian Pacific American Political Almanac.* 1st ed. (1978); 2d ed. (1979); 3d ed. (1980); 4th ed. (1982); 5th ed. (1984); 6th ed. (1995); 7th ed. (1996); 8th ed. (1998–1999); 9th ed. (2000–2001); 10th ed. (2001–2002). Los Angeles: UCLA Asian American Studies Center Press.

Oh, Angela. 2000. "The Future of Race Relations: Diversity, Balance, and a New Frontier." In Don T. Nakanishi and James S. Lai, eds., *National Asian Pacific American Political Almanac, 2000–01*, 1–3. Los Angeles: Asian American Studies Center Press.

Ong, Paul M. 2000. "The Affirmative Action Divide." In Paul M. Ong, ed., *Transforming Race Relations*, 313–61. Los Angeles: LEAP Public Policy Institute and UCLA Asian American Studies Center.

Ong, Paul M., and Tania Azores. 1991. *Asian Pacific Americans in Los Angeles: A Demographic Profile.* Los Angeles: LEAP Public Policy Institute/UCLA Asian American Studies Center.

Rodriguez, Gregory. 1998. "Minority Leader: Matt Fong and the Asian American Voter." *New Republic* (October 19): 21–24.

Shinagawa, Larry H. 1996. "The Impact of Immigration on the Demography of Asian Pacific Americans." In Bill Ong Hing and Ronald Lee, eds., *Reframing the Immigration Debate*, 59–130. Los Angeles: LEAP Public Policy Institute/UCLA Asian American Studies Center.

Sonenshein, Raphael J. 1993. *Politics in Black and White: Race and Power in Los Angeles.* Princeton: Princeton University Press.

Tachibana, Judy. 1986. "California's Asians: Power from a Growing Population." *California Journal* 17: 534–43.

Takaki, Ronald. 1989. *Strangers from a Different Shore: A History of Asian Americans.* Boston: Little, Brown.

Wei, William. 1993. *The Asian American Movement.* Philadelphia: Temple University Press.

# Part I

# Historical Forms of
# Civic Engagement and Protest
## Selected United States Supreme Court Cases

Where Both Platforms Agree. *Courtesy of Phillip P. Choy*

## EARLY LEGAL BATTLES FOR U.S.
## NATURALIZATION AND EQUAL PROTECTION RIGHTS

The history of Asian and Pacific Islanders in the United States is long and rich, encompassing nearly 150 years, beginning with the arrival of the first wave of Chinese gold miners to California in 1848 (Takaki 1989; Chan 1991). Since this period, many political events have affected their citizenship and political rights in the United States. Early Asians in America were not "political" in the traditional sense of voting and running for elected office because they were never afforded basic constitutional rights such as the ability to naturalize, to vote, and to hold elected office. However, they did practice civic engagement, particularly nonvoting forms, in order to protect themselves against various discriminatory laws. The U.S. court system represented a political institution that allowed the first Asians in America to challenge the legality of such discriminatory laws.

Part 1 focuses on the use of the highest court in the nation, the United States Supreme Court. It contains several significant United States Supreme Court rulings that illustrate the broader forms of civic engagement that were practiced by the late-nineteenth- and early-twentieth-century Asians in America. The two largest Asian immigrant groups prior to 1965 were from China and Japan. Both groups represent the primary focus of this section. Chinese immigrants in the United States during the nineteenth century had been typically viewed as outsiders to mainstream political institutions since they could neither vote nor testify in court due to their legal inability to become U.S. naturalized citizens. Nevertheless, early Chinese community leaders utilized, among other available avenues, the U.S. court system with the help of progressive American lawyers to contest for constitutional rights such as equal protection under the Fourteenth Amendment. Many of the late-nineteenth-century Chinese leaders arose from merchant and clan associations such as the Chinese Consolidated Benevolent Association (CCBA), also known as the Chinese Six Companies in San Francisco. In 1886, the U.S. Supreme Court deliberated over the case of *Yick Wo v. Hopkins*. The majority ruled that the San Francisco ordinance requiring wood laundry facilities to obtain permits unfairly discriminated against Chinese businesses and therefore was a violation of their Fourteenth Amendment equal protection status. This case still stands and is often cited as precedent. The significance of the *Yick Wo* case is that it illustrates one historical instance in which the early Chinese in America challenged discriminatory laws through the U.S. court system to protect themselves. Moreover, it demonstrates that early Asians in America were politically aware despite their lack of basic constitutional rights. Although they could not become naturalized U.S. citizens, they would challenge discriminatory laws with help from U.S. citizens to fight for these basic civil rights protections. This form of political consciousness and activity was practiced not only among early Chinese in America but among other Asian American groups as well.

Japanese community leaders, like their Chinese cohorts, struggled and fought for basic U.S. constitutional rights and protections. One of the most controversial cases deliberated by the United States Supreme Court was the World War II internment case *Korematsu v. U.S.* (1944). The U.S. Supreme Court used the strict scrutiny standard for the first time in addressing whether a Fourteenth Amendment equal protection violation had occurred against Japanese Americans. At issue was President Franklin Delano Roosevelt's Executive Order 9066, which required "all persons of Japanese ancestry" to report to evacuation centers along the West Coast. The U.S. Supreme Court's majority eventually decided that Executive Order 9066 did not violate Japanese Americans' equal protection rights. Almost fifty years later, President Reagan signed the Civil Liberties Act of 1988, which issued a formal apology to former Japanese American internees along with a sum of $20,000 to all survivors. This act resulted from the unrelenting efforts of Japanese American national and local leaders and organizations lobbying to rectify this past civil rights injustice.

The issue of naturalization rights and whether Asians could become naturalized U.S. citizens represented a key issue within the early-twentieth-century

Positively No Filipinos Allowed. *Courtesy of Visual Communications*

Asian communities. Without the ability to naturalize, the early Asians in America were second-class citizens who lacked have basic constitutional rights and protections. During this period, only free white persons were allowed to become naturalized U.S. citizens. Two of the most controversial decisions by the United States Supreme Court on this legal issue are included in this section. Both the *Takao Ozawa v. U.S.* (1922) and the *U.S. v. Thind* (1923) cases reveal the racist doctrine that justified the majority's decisions. In the *Ozawa* case, Takao Ozawa, an individual of Japanese descent who was born in Hawaii and educated on the U.S. mainland, attempted to argue that he was white in the cultural sense in aspects such as language, education, and religion. The United States Supreme Court majority ruled that Ozawa was not white in the traditional understanding of this racial category and was denied the right to naturalize. The United States Supreme Court majority would change this rationale when Bhagat Thind, an Asian Indian, attempted to argue that Asian Indians possessed ancestral linkages to European Americans a year after *Ozawa*. Here, the United States Supreme Court majority ruled that Thind was not white in the common sense of what that was understood to be for this racial category, despite his historical arguments. In the end, the majority of the Court ruled that Thind could not become a naturalized citizen. Despite their creative arguments, many early-twentieth-century Asians in America were denied the crucial right to become naturalized U.S. citizens.

### REFERENCES

Chan, Sucheng. 1991. *Asian Americans: An Interpretive History*. Boston: Twayne.
Takaki, Ronald. 1989. *Strangers from a Different Shore: A History of Asian Americans*. Boston: Little, Brown.

# 1.1

# *Yick Wo v. Hopkins*, 118 U.S. 356 (1886)

These two cases were argued as one, and depend upon precisely the same state of facts; the first coming here upon a writ of error to the supreme court of the state of California, the second on appeal from the circuit court of the United States for that district.

The plaintiff in error, Yick Wo, on August 24, 1885, petitioned the supreme court of California for the writ of habeas corpus, alleging that he was illegally deprived of his personal [118 U.S. 356, 357] liberty by the defendant as sheriff of the city and county of San Francisco. The sheriff made return to the writ that he held the petitioner in custody by virtue of a sentence of the police judge's court No. 2 of the city and county of San Francisco, whereby he was found guilty of a violation of certain ordinances of the board of supervisors of that county, and adjudged to pay a fine of $10, and, in default of payment, be imprisoned in the county jail at the rate of one day for each dollar of fine until said fine should be satisfied; and a commitment in consequence of non-payment of said fine.

The ordinances for the violation of which he had been found guilty are set out as follow:

Order No. 1,569, passed May 26, 1880, prescribing the kind of buildings in which laundries may located.

'The people of the city and county of San Francisco do ordain as follows:

'Section 1. It shall be unlawful, from and after the passage of this order, for any person or persons to establish, maintain, or carry on a laundry, within the corporate limits of the city and county of San Francisco, without having first obtained the consent of the board of supervisors, except the same be located in a building constructed either of brick or stone.

'Sec. 2. It shall be unlawful for any person to erect, build, or maintain, or cause to be erected, built, or maintained, over or upon the roof of any building now erected, or which may hereafter be erected, within the limits of said city and county, any scaffolding, without first obtaining the written permission of the board of supervisors, which permit shall state fully for what purpose said scaffolding is to be erected and used, and such scaffolding shall not be used for any other purpose than that designated in such permit.

'Sec. 3. Any person who violate any of the provisions of this order shall be deemed guilty of a misdemeanor, and upon conviction thereof shall be punished by a fine of not more than on thousand dollars, or by imprisonment in the county jail not more than six months, or by both such fine and imprisonment.' [118 U.S. 356, 358] Order No. 1,587, passed July 28, 1880, the following section:

'Sec. 68. It shall be unlawful, from and after the passage of this order, for any person or persons to establish, maintain, or carry on a laundry within the corporate limits of the city and county of San Francisco without having first obtained the consent of the board of supervisor, except the same be located in a building constructed either of brick or stone.'

The following facts are also admitted on the record: That petitioner is a native of China, and came to California in 1861, and is still a subject of the emperor of China; that he has been engaged in the laundry business in the same premises and building for 22 years last past; that he had a license from the board of fire-wardens, dated March 3, 1884, from which it appeared 'that the above-described premises have been inspected by the board of fire-wardens, and upon such inspection said board found all proper arrangements for carrying on the business; that the stoves, washing and drying apparatus, and the appliances for heating smoothing-irons, are in good condition, and that their use is not dangerous to the surrounding property from fire, and that all proper precautions have been taken to comply with the provisions of order No. 1,617, defining 'the fire limits of the city and county of San Francisco, and making regulations concerning the erection and use of building in said city and country,' and of order No. 1,670, 'prohibiting the kindling, maintenance, and use of open fires in houses'; that he had a certificate from the health officer that the same premises had been inspected by him, and that he found that they were properly and sufficiently drained, and that all proper arrangements for carrying on the business of a laundry, without injury to the sanitary condition of the neighborhood, had been complied with;

that the city license of the petitioner was in force, and expired October 1, 1885; and that the petitioner applied to the board of supervisors, June 1, 1885, for consent of said board to maintain and carry on his laundry, but that said board, on July 1, 1885, refused said consent.' It is also admitted to be true, as alleged in the petition, that on February 24, 1880, 'there were about 320 laundries in the city and county of San Francisco, of which [118 U.S. 356, 359] about 240 were owned and conducted by subjects of China, and of the whole number, viz., 320, about 310 were constructed of wood, the same material that constitutes nine-tenths of the houses in the city of San Francisco. The capital thus invested by the subjects of China was not less than two hundred thousand dollars, and they paid annually for rent, license, taxes, gas, and water about one hundred and eighty thousand dollars.' It is alleged in the petition that 'your petitioner, and more than one hundred and fifty of his countrymen, have been arrested upon the charge of carrying on business without having such special consent, while those who are not subjects of China, and who are conducting eighty odd laundries under similar conditions, are left unmolested, and free to enjoy the enhanced trade and profits arising from this hurtful and unfair discrimination. The business of your petitioners, and of those of his countrymen similarly situated, is greatly impaired, and in many cases practically ruined, by this system of oppression to one kind of men, and favoritism to all others.'

The statement therein contained as to the arrest, etc., is admitted to be true, with the qualification only that the 80-odd laundries referred to are in wooden buildings without scaffolds on the roofs. It is also admitted 'that petitioner and 200 of his countrymen similarly situated petitioned the board of supervisors for permission to continue their business in the various houses which they had been occupying and using for laundries for more than twenty years, and such petitions were denied, and all the petitions of those who were not Chinese, with one exception of Mrs. Mary Meagles, were granted.'

By section 11 of article 11 of the constitution of California it is provided that 'any county, city, town, or township may make and enforce with its limits all such local, police, sanitary, and other regulation as are not in conflict with general laws.' By section 74 of the act of April 19, 1856, usually known as the 'Consolidation Act,' the board of supervisors in empowered, among other things, 'to provide by regulation for the prevention and summary removal of nuisances to public health, the [118 U.S. 356, 360] prevention of contagious disease; . . . to prohibit the erection of wooden buildings within any fixed limit where the streets shall have been established and graded; . . . to regulated the sale, storage, and use of gunpowder, or other explosive or combustible materials and substances, and make all needful regulations for protections against fire; to make such regulation concerning the erection and use of buildings as may be necessary for the safety of the inhabitants.'

The supreme court of California, in the opinion pronouncing the judgment in this case, said: 'The board of supervisors, under the several statutes conferring authority upon them, has the power to prohibit or regulate all occupations which are against good morals, contrary to public order and decency, or dangerous to the public safety. Clothes washing is certainly not opposed to good morals, or subversive of public order or decency, but when conducted in given localities it may be highly dangerous to the public safety. Of this fact the supervisors are made the judges, and, having taken action in the premises, we do not find that they have prohibited the establishment of laundries, but they have, as they well might do, regulated the places at which they should be established, the character of the buildings in which they re to be maintained, etc. The process of washing is not prohibited by thus regulating the places at which and the surroundings by which it must be exercised. The order No. 1,569 and section 68 of order No. 1,587 are not in contravention of common right, or unjust, unequal, partial, or oppressive, in such

sense as authorizes us in this proceeding to pronounce them invalid.' After answering the position taken in behalf of the petitioner, that the ordinances in question had been repealed, the court adds: 'We have not deemed it necessary to discuss the question in the light of supposed infringement of petitioner's rights under the constitution of the United States, for the reason that we think the principles upon which contention the that head can be based have in effect been set at rest by the cases of *Barbier v. Connolly*, 113 U.S. 27, S. C. 5 Sup. Ct. Rep. 357, and *Soon Hing v. Crowley*, 113 U.S. 703, S. C. Sup. Ct. Rep. 730.' The writ was accordingly discharged, and the prisoner remanded. [118 U.S. 356, 361] In the other case, the appellant, Wo Lee, petitioned for his discharge from an alleged illegal imprisonment, upon a state of facts, shown upon the record, precisely similar to that in the Case of Yick Wo. In disposing of the application, the learned Circuit Judge Sawyer, in his opinion, (26 Fed. Rep. 471,) after quoting the ordinance in question, proceeded at length as follows:

'Thus, in a territory some ten miles wide by fifteen or more miles long, much of it still occupied as ere farming and pasturage land, and much of it unoccupied sand banks, in many places without a building within a quarter or half a mile of each other, including the isolated and almost wholly unoccupied Goat island, the right to carry on this, when properly guarded, harmless and necessary occupation, in a wooden building, is not made to depend upon any prescribed conditions giving a right to anybody complying with them, but upon the consent or arbitrary will of the board of supervisor. In three-fourths of the territory covered by the ordinance there is no more need of prohibiting or regulating laundries than if they were located in any portion of the farming regions of the state. Hitherto the regulation of laundries has been limited to the thickly settled portions of the city. Why this unnecessary extension of the limits is affected, if not designed to prevent the establishment of laundries, after a compulsory removal from their present locations, within practicable reach of the customers or their proprietors? And the uncontradicted petition shows that all Chinese applications are, in fact, denied, and those of Caucasians granted; thus, in fact, making the discriminations in the administration of the ordinance which its terms permits. The fact that the right to give consent is reserved in the ordinance shows that carrying on the laundry business in wooden buildings is not deemed of itself necessarily dangerous. It must be apparent to every well-informed mind that a fire, properly guarded, for laundry purposes, in a wooden building, is just as necessary, and no more dangerous, than a fire for cooking purposes or for warming a house. If the ordinance under consideration is valid, then the board of supervisors can pass a valid ordinance preventing the maintenance, in a wooden [118 U.S. 356, 362] building, of a cooking-stove, heating apparatus, or a restaurant, within the boundaries of the city and country of San Francisco, without the consent of that body, arbitrarily given or withheld, as their prejudices or other motives may dictate. If it is competent for the board of supervisors to pass a valid ordinance prohibiting the inhabitants of San Francisco from following any ordinary, proper, and necessary calling within the limits of the city and county, except at its arbitrary and unregulated discretion and special consent,—and it can do so if this ordinance is valid,— then it seems to us that there has been a wide departure from the principles that have heretofore been supposed to guard and protect the rights, property, and liberties of the American people. And if by an ordinance general in its terms and form, like the one in question, by reserving an arbitrary discretion in the enacting body to grant or deny permission to engage in a proper and necessary calling, a discrimination against any class can be made in its execution, thereby evading and in effect nullifying the provisions of the national constitution, then the insertion of provisions to guard the right of every class and person in that instrument was a vain and futile act.

'The effect of the execution of this ordinance in the manner indicated in the record would seem to be necessarily to close up the many Chinese laundries now existing, or compel their owners to pull down their present buildings and reconstruct of brick or stone, or to drive them outside the city and county of San Francisco, to the adjoining counties, beyond the convenient reach of customers, either of which results would be little short of absolute confiscation of the large amount of property shown to be now, and to have been for a long time, invested in these occupations. If this would not be depriving such parties of their property without due process of law, it would be difficult to say what would effect that prohibited result. The necessary tendency, if not the specific purpose, of this ordinance, and of enforcing it in the manner indicated in the record, is to drive out of business all the numerous small laundries, especially those owned by Chinese, and give a monopoly of the business to the large institutions established and carried on by means of large associated Caucasian capital. If the facts appearing on the face [118 U.S. 356, 363] of the ordinance, on the petition and return, and admitted in the case, and shown by the notorious public and municipal history of the times, indicate a purpose to drive out the Chinese laundrymen, and not merely to regulate the business for the public safety, does it not disclose a case of violation of the provisions of the fourteenth amendment to the national constitution, and of the treaty between the United States and China, in more than one particular? . . . If this means prohibition of the occupation, and a destruction of the business and property, of the Chinese laundrymen in San Francisco,—as it seems to us this must be the effects of executing the ordinance,—and not merely the proper regulation of the business, then there is discrimination, and a violation of other highly important rights secured by the fourteenth amendment and the treaty. That it does mean prohibition, as to the Chinese, it seems to us must be apparent to every citizen of San Francisco who has been here long enough to be familiar with the course of an active and aggressive branch of public opinion and of public notorious events. Can a court be blind to what must be necessarily known to every intelligent person in the state? See *Ah Kow v. Nunan,* 5 Sawy. 560; *Sparrow v. Strong,* 3 Wall. 104; *Brown v. Piper,* 91 U.S. 42.'

But, in deference to the decision of the supreme court of California in the Case of Yick Wo, and contrary to his own opinion as thus expressed, the circuit judge discharged the writ and remanded the prisoner.

# 1.2

# *Korematsu v. United States,* 323 U.S. 214 (1994)

Mr. Justice Black delivered the opinion of the Court.

The petitioner, an American citizen of Japanese descent, was convicted in a federal district court for remaining in San Leandro, California, a "Military Area," contrary to Civilian Exclusion Order No. 34 of the Commanding General of the Western Command, U.S. Army, which directed that after May 9, 1942, all persons of Japanese ancestry should be excluded from that area. No question was raised as to petitioner's loyalty of the United States. The Circuit Court of Appeals affirmed, and the importance of the constitutional question involved caused us to grant certiorari.

It should be noted, to begin with, that all legal restrictions which curtail the civil rights of a single racial group are immediately suspect. That is not to say that all such restrictions are unconstitutional. It is to say that courts must subject them to the most rigid scrutiny. Pressing public necessity may sometimes justify the existence of such restrictions; racial antagonism never can. [ . . .]

Exclusion Order No. 34, which the petitioner knowingly and admittedly violated, was one of a number of military orders and proclamations, . . . issued after we were at

war with Japan, declaring that "the successful prosecution of the war requires every possible protection against espionage and against sabotage to national-defense materials, national-defense premises, and national-defense utilities. . . ."

One of the series of orders and proclamations, a curfew order, which like the exclusion order here . . . , subjected all persons of Japanese ancestry in prescribed West Coast military areas to remain in their residences from 8 p.m. to 6 a.m. As is the case with the exclusion order here, that prior curfew order was designed as a "protection against espionage and against sabotage.' In *Hirabayashi v. United States*, 320 U.S. 81, we sustained a conviction obtained for violation of the curfew order. The Hirabayashi conviction and this one thus rest on the same 1942 Congressional Act and the same basic executive and military orders, all of which orders were aimed at the twin dangers of espionage and sabotage.

[ . . .] We upheld the curfew order as an exercise of the power of the government to take steps necessary to prevent espionage and sabotage in an area threatened by Japanese attack.

In the light of the principles we announced in the Hirabayashi case, we are unable to conclude that it was beyond the war power of Congress and the Executive to exclude those of Japanese ancestry from the West Coast war area at the time they did. True, exclusion from the area in which one's home is located is a far greater deprivation than constant confinement to the home from 8 p.m. to 6 a.m. Nothing short of apprehension by the proper military authorities of the gravest imminent danger to the public safety can constitutionally justify either. But exclusion from a threatened area, no less than curfew, has a definite and close relationship to the prevention of espionage and sabotage. The military authorities, charged with the primary responsibility of defending our shores, concluded that curfew provided inadequate protection and ordered exclusion. They did so, as pointed out in our Hirabayashi opinion, in accordance with Congressional authority to the military to say who should, and who should not, remain in the threatened areas.

In this case the petitioner challenges the assumptions upon which we rested our conclusions in the Hirabayashi case. He also urges that by May 1942, when Order No. 34 was promulgated, all danger of Japanese invasion of the West Coast had disappeared. After careful consideration of these contentions we are compelled to reject them.

Here, as in the Hirabayashi case, ". . . we cannot reject as unfounded the judgment of the military authorities and of Congress that there were disloyal members of that population, whose number and strength could not be precisely and quickly ascertained. We cannot say that the war-making branches of the Government did not have ground for believing that in a critical hour such persons could not readily be isolated and separately dealt with, and constituted a menace to the national defense and safety, which demanded that prompt and adequate measures be taken to guard against it."

Like curfew, exclusion of those of Japanese origin was deemed necessary because of the presence of an unascertained number of disloyal members of the group, most of whom we have no doubt were loyal to this country. It was because we could not reject the finding of the military authorities that it was impossible to bring about an immediate segregation of the disloyal from the loyal that we sustained the validity of the curfew order as applying to the whole group. In the instant case, temporary exclusion of the entire group was rested by the military on the same ground. The judgment that exclusion of the whole group was for the same reason a military imperative answers the contention that the exclusion was in the nature of group punishment based on antagonism to those of Japanese origin. That there were members of the group who retained loyalties to Japan has been confirmed by investigations made subsequent to the exclusion. Approximately five thousand American citizens of Japanese ancestry refused to swear unqualified allegiance to the United States and to renounce allegiance to the Japanese Emperor, and several thousand evacuees requested repatriation to Japan.

We uphold the exclusion order as of the time it was made and when the petitioner violated it. [ . . .] In doing so, we are not unmindful of the hardships imposed by it upon a large group of American citizens. [ . . . ] But hardships are part of war, and war is an aggregation of hardships. All citizens alike, both in and out of uniform, feel the impact of war in greater or lesser measure. Citizenship has its responsibilities as well as its privileges, and in time of war the burden is always heavier. Compulsory exclusion of large groups of citizens from their homes, except under circumstances of direst emergency and peril, is inconsistent with out basic governmental institutions. But when under conditions of modern warfare our shores are threatened by hostile forces, the power to protect must be commensurate with the threatened danger.

It is argued that on May 30, 1942, the date the petitioner was charged with remaining in the prohibited area, there were conflicting orders outstanding, forbidding him both to leave the area and to remain there. Of course, a person cannot be convicted for doing the very thing which it is a crime to fail to do. But the outstanding orders here contained no such contradictory commands.

Since the petitioner has not been convicted of failing to report or to remain in an assembly or relocation center, we cannot in this case determine the validity of those separate provisions of the order. It is sufficient here for us to pass upon the order which the petitioner violated. To do more would be to go beyond the issues raised, and to decide momentous questions not contained within the framework of the pleadings or the evidence in this case. It will be time enough to decide the serious constitutional issues which petitioner seeks to raise when an assembly or relocation order is applied or is certain to be applied to him, and we have its terms before us.

Some of the members of the Court are of the view that evacuation and detention in an Assembly Center were inseparable. After May 3, 1942, the date of Exclusion Order No. 34, Korematsu was under compulsion to leave the area not as he would choose but via an Assembly Center. The Assembly Center was conceived as part of the machinery for group evacuation. The power to exclude includes the power to do it by force if necessary. And any forcible measure must necessarily entail some degree of detention or restraint whatever method of removal is selected. But whichever view is taken, it results in holding that the order under which petitioner was convicted was valid.

It is said that we are dealing here with the case of imprisonment of a citizen in a concentration camp solely because of his ancestry, without evidence or inquiry concerning his loyalty and good disposition towards the United States. Our case would be simple, our duty clear, were this a case involving the imprisonment of a loyal citizen in a concentration camp because of racial prejudice. Regardless of the true nature of the assembly and relocation centers—and we deem it unjustifiable to call them concentration camps with all the ugly connotations that term implies—we are dealing specifically with nothing but an exclusion order. To cast this case into outlines of racial prejudice, without reference to the real military dangers which were presented, merely confuses the issue. Korematsu was not excluded from the Military Area because of hostility to him or his race. He was excluded because we are at war with Japanese Empire, because the properly constituted military authorities feared an invasion of our West Coast and felt constrained to take proper security measures, because they decided that the military urgency of the situation demanded that all citizens of Japanese ancestry be segregated from the West Coast temporarily, and finally, because Congress, reposing its confidence in this time of war in our military leaders—as inevitably it must—determined that they should have the power to do just this. There was evidence of disloyalty on the part of some, the military authorities considered that the need for actions was great, and time was short. We cannot—by availing ourselves of the calm perspective of hindsight—now say that at the time these actions were unjustified. [ . . .]

Mr. Justice Murphy, dissenting.

This exclusion of "all persons of Japanese ancestry, both alien and non-alien," from the Pacific Coast area on a plea of military necessity in the absence of martial law ought not to be approved. Such exclusion goes over "the very brink of constitutional power" and falls into the ugly abyss of racism.

In dealing with matters relating to the prosecution and progress of a war, we must accord great respect and consideration to the judgments of the military authorities who are on the scene and who have full knowledge of the military facts. The scope of their discretion must, as a matter of necessity and common sense, be wide. And their judgments ought not to be overruled lightly by those whose training and duties ill-equip them to deal intelligently with matters so vital to the physical security of the nation.

At the same time, however, it is essential that there be definite limits to military discretion, especially where martial law has not been declared. Individuals must not be left impoverished of their constitutional rights on a plea of military necessity that has neither substance nor support. Thus, like other claims conflicting with the asserted constitutional rights of the individual, the military claim must subject itself to the judicial process of having its reasonableness determined and its conflicts with other interests reconciled. [ . . .]

The judicial test of whether the Government, on a plea of military necessity, can validly deprive an individual of any of his constitutional rights is whether the deprivation is reasonably related to a public danger that is so "immediate, imminent, and impending" as not to admit of delay and not to permit the intervention of ordinary constitutional processes to alleviate the danger. [ . . .] Civilian Exclusion Order No. 34, banishing from a prescribed area of the Pacific Coast "all persons of Japanese ancestry, both alien and non-alien," clearly does not meet that test. Being an obvious racial discrimination, the order deprives all those within its scope of the equal protection of the laws as guaranteed by the Fifth Amendment. It further deprives these individuals of their constitutional rights to live and work where they will, to establish a home where they choose and to move about freely. In excommunicating them without benefit of hearings, this order also deprives them of all their constitutional rights to procedural due process. Yet no reasonable relation to an "immediate, imminent, and impending" public danger is evident to support this racial restriction which is one of the most sweeping and complete deprivations of constitutional rights in the history of this nation in the absence of martial law. [ . . .]

That this forced exclusion was the result in good measure of this erroneous assumption of racial guilt rather than bona fide military necessity is evidenced by the Commanding General's Final Report on the evacuation from the Pacific Coast area. In it he refers to all individuals of Japanese descent as "subversive," as belonging to "an enemy race" whose "racial strains are undiluted," and as constituting "over 112,000 potential enemies . . . at large

today" along the Pacific Coast. In support of this blanket condemnation of all persons of Japanese descent, however, no reliable evidence is cited to show that such individuals were generally disloyal, or had generally so conducted themselves in this area as to constitute a special menace to defense installations or war industries, or had otherwise by their behavior furnished reasonable ground for their exclusion as a group.

Justification for the exclusion is sought, instead, mainly upon questionable racial and sociological grounds not ordinarily within the realm of expert military judgment, supplemented by certain semi-military conclusions drawn from an unwarranted use of circumstantial evidence. Individuals of Japanese ancestry are condemned because they are said to be "a large, unassimilated, tightly knit racial group, bound to an enemy nation by strong ties of race, culture, custom and religion." They are claimed to be given "emperor worshipping ceremonies" and to "dual citizenship." Japanese language schools and allegedly pro-Japanese organizations are cited as evidence of possible group disloyalty, together with facts as to certain persons being educated and residing at length in Japan. It is intimated that many of these individuals deliberately resided "adjacent to strategic points," thus enabling them "to carry into execution a tremendous program of sabotage on a mass scale should any considerable number of them have been inclined to do so." The need for protective custody is also asserted. The report refers without identity to "numerous incidents of violence" as well as to other admittedly unverified or cumulative incidents. From this, plus certain other events not shown to have been connected with the Japanese Americans, it is concluded that the "situation was fraught with danger to the Japanese population itself" and that the general public "was ready to take matters into its own hands." Finally, it is intimated, though not directly charged or proved, that persons of Japanese ancestry were responsible for three minor isolated shellings and bombings of the Pacific Coast area, as well as for unidentified radio transmissions and night signaling.

The main reasons relied upon by those responsible for the forced evacuation, therefore, do not prove a reasonable relation between the group characteristics of Japanese Americans and the dangers of invasion, sabotage and espionage. The reasons appear, instead, to be largely an accumulation of much of the misinformation, half-truths and insinuations that for years have been directed against Japanese Americans by people with racial and economic prejudices—the same people who have been among the foremost advocates of the evacuation. A military judgment based upon such racial and sociological considerations is not entitled to the great weight ordinarily given the judgments based upon strictly military considerations. Especially is this so when every charge relative to race, religion, culture, geographical location, and legal and economic status has been substantially discredited by independent studies made by experts in these matters.

The military necessity which is essential to the validity of the evacuation order thus resolves itself into a few intimations that certain individuals actively aided the enemy, from which it is inferred that the entire group of Japanese Americans could not be trusted to be or remain loyal to the United States. No one denies, of course, that there were some disloyal persons of Japanese descent on the Pacific Coast who did all in their power to aid their ancestral land. Similar disloyal activities have been engaged in by many persons of German, Italian and even more pioneer stock in our country. But to infer that examples of individual disloyalty prove group disloyalty and justify discriminatory action against the entire group is to deny that under our system of law individual guilt is the sole basis for deprivation of rights. Moreover, this inference, which is at the very heart of the evacuation orders, has been used in support of the abhorrent and despicable treatment of minority groups by the dictatorial tyrannies which this nation is now pledged to destroy. To give constitutional sanction to that inference in this cases, however well-intentioned may have been the military command on the Pacific Coast, is to adopt one of the cruelest of the rationales used by our enemies to destroy the dignity of the individual and to encourage and open the door to discriminatory actions against other minority groups in the passions of tomorrow.

No adequate reason is given for the failure to treat these Japanese Americans on an individual basis by holding investigations and hearings to separate the loyal from the disloyal, as was done in the case of persons of German and Italian ancestry. [ . . .] It is asserted merely that the loyalties of this group "were unknown and time was of the essence." Yet nearly four months elapsed after Pearl Harbor before the first exclusion order was issued; nearly eight months went by until the last order was issued; and the last of these "subversive" persons was not actually removed until almost eleven months had elapsed. Leisure and deliberation seem to have been more of the essence than speed. And the fact that conditions were not such as to warrant a declaration of martial law adds strength to the belief that the factors of time and military necessity were not as urgent as they have been represented to be.

Moreover, there was no adequate proof that the Federal Bureau of Investigation and the military and naval intelligence services did not have the espionage and sabotage situation well in hand during this long period. Nor is there any denial of the fact that not one person of Japanese ancestry was accused or convicted of espionage or sabotage after Pearl Harbor while they were still free, a fact which is some evidence of the loyalty of the vast majority of these individuals and of the effectiveness of the established methods of combating these evils. It seems incredible that under these circumstance it would have been impossible to hold loyalty hearings for the mere 112,000 persons involved—or at least for the 70,000 American citizens—especially when a large part of this number represented children and elderly men and women. Any inconvenience that may have accompanied an attempt to conform to procedural due process cannot be said to justify violations of constitutional rights of individuals.

I dissent, therefore, from this legalization of racism. Racial discrimination in any form and in any degree has no justifiable part whatever in our democratic way of life. It is unattractive in any setting but it is utterly revolting among a free people who have embraced the principles set forth in the Constitution of the United States. All residents of the nation are kin in some way by blood or culture to a foreign land. Yet they are primarily and necessarily a part of the new and distinct civilization of the United States. They must accordingly be treated at all times as the heirs of the American experiment and as entitled to all the rights and freedoms guaranteed by the Constitution.

# 1.3

# *Takao Ozawa v. United States,* 260 U.S. 178 (1922)

∿∿∿∿∿∿∿∿∿∿∿∿∿∿∿∿∿∿∿∿∿∿∿∿∿∿∿∿∿∿∿∿∿

Mr. Justice Sutherland delivered the opinion of the Court.

The appellant is a person of the Japanese race born in Japan. He applied, on October 16, 1914, to the United States District Court for the Territory of Hawaii to be admitted as a citizen of the United States. His petition was opposed by the United States District Attorney for the District of Hawaii. Including the period of his residence in Hawaii appellant had continuously resided in the United States for twenty years. He was a graduate of the Berkeley, California, high school, had been nearly three years a student in the University of California, had educated his children in American schools, his family had attended American churches and he had maintained the use of the English language in his home. That he was well qualified by character and education for citizenship is conceded.

The District Court of Hawaii, however, held that, having been born in Japan and being of the Japanese race, [260 U.S. 178, 190] he was not eligible to naturalization under section 2169 of the Revised Statutes (Comp. St. 4358), and denied the petition. Thereupon the appellant brought the cause to the Circuit Courts of Appeals for the Ninth Circuit and that court has certified the following questions, upon which it desires to be instructed:

'1. Is the act of June 29, 1906 (34 Stats. At Large, pt. 1, p. 596), providing 'for a uniform rule for the naturalization of aliens' complete itself, or is it limited by section 2169 of the Revised Statutes of the United States?

'2. Is one who is of the Japanese race and born in Japan eligible to citizenship under the naturalization laws?

'3. If said act of June 29, 1906, is limited by section 2169 and naturalization is limited to aliens being free white persons and to aliens of African nativity and to persons of African descent, is one of the Japanese race, born in Japan, under any circumstances eligible to naturalization?'

These questions for purposes of discussion may be briefly restated:

1. Is the Naturalization Act of June 29, 1906, (Comp. St. 4351 et seq.), limited by the provisions of section 2169 of the Revised Statutes of the United States?
2. If so limited, is the appellant eligible to naturalization under that section?

First, Section 2169 is found in title XXX of the Revised Statutes, under the heading 'Naturalization,' and reads as follows:

'The provisions of this title shall apply to aliens, being free white persons and to aliens of African nativity and to persons of African descent.'

The act of June 29, 1906, entitled 'An act to establish a Bureau of Immigration and Naturalization, and to provide for a uniform rule for the naturalization of aliens [260 U.S. 178, 191] throughout the United States,' consists of thirty-one sections and deals primarily with the subject of procedure. There is nothing in the circumstance leading up to or accompanying the passage of the act which suggest that any modification of section 2169, or of its application, was contemplated.

The report of the House Committee on Naturalization Immigration, recommending its passage, contains this statement;

'It is the opinion of your committee that the frauds and crimes which have been committed in regard to naturalization have resulted more from a lack of any uniform system of procedure in such matters than from any radical defect in the fundamental principles of existing law governing in such matters. The two changes which the committee has recommended in the principles controlling in naturalization matters and which are embodied in the bill submitted herewith are as follows: First, the requirement that before an alien can be naturalized he must be able to read, either in his own language or in the English language and to speak or understand the English language; and, second, that the alien must intend to reside permanently in the Unites States before he shall be entitled to naturalization.'

This seems to make it quite clear that no change of the fundamental character here involved was in mind.

Section 26 of the Act (Comp. St. 4381) expressly repeals sections of 2165, 2167, 2168, 2173 of title XXX, the subject matter thereof being covered by new provisions. The sections of title XXX remaining without repeal are: Section 2166, relating to honorably discharged soldiers; section 2169 (Comp. St. 4358), now under consideration; section 2170 (section 4360). Requiring five years' residence prior to admission; section 2171 (section 4352 [260 U.S. 178, 11] ), forbidding the admission of alien enemies; section 2172 (section 4367), relating to the status of children of naturalized persons; and section 2174 (section 4352 [260 U.S. 178, 8] ), making special provision in respect of the naturalization of seamen.

[260 U.S. 78, 192] There is nothing in section 2169 which is repugnant to anything in the act of 1906.

Both may stand and be given effect. It is clear, therefore, that there is no repeal by implication.

But it is insisted by appellant that section 2169, by its terms is made applicable only to the provisions of title XXX, and that it will not admit of being construed as a restriction upon the act of 1906. Since section 2169, it is in effect argued, declares that 'the provisions of this title shall apply to aliens being free white persons, . . . ' it should be confined to the classes provided for in the unrepealed sections of that title, leaving the act of 1906 to govern in respect of all other aliens, without any restriction except such as may be imposed by that act itself.

It is contended that, thus construed, the act of 1906 confers the privilege of naturalization without limitation as to race, since the general introductory words of section 4 (Comp. St. 4352) are:

'That an alien may be admitted to become a citizen of the United States in the following manner, and not otherwise.'

But obviously, this clause does not relate to the subject of eligibility but to the 'manner,' that is, the procedure, to be followed.

Exactly the same words are used to introduce the similar provisions contained in section 2165 of the Revised Statutes. In 1790 the first naturalization act provided that—

'Any alien being a free white person . . . may be admitted to become a citizen. . . . ' 1 Stat. 103. c. 3.

This was subsequently enlarged to include aliens of African nativity and persons of African descent. These provisions were restated in the Revised Statutes, so that section 2165 included only the procedural portion, while the substantive parts were carried into a separate section (2169) and the words 'An alien' substituted for the words 'Any alien.'

In all of the naturalization acts from 1790 to 1906 the privilege of naturalization was confined to white persons [260 U.S. 178, 193] (with the addition in 1870 of those of African nativity and descent), although the exact wording of the various statutes was not always the same. If Congress in 1906 desired to alter a rule so well and so long established it may be assumed that its purpose would have been definitely disclosed and its legislation to that end put in unmistakable terms.

The argument that, because section 2169 is in terms made applicable only to the title in which it is found, it should now be confined to the unrepealed sections of that title, is not convincing. The persons entitled to naturalization under these unrepealed sections include only honorably discharged soldiers and seamen who have served three years on board an American vessel, both of whom were entitled from the beginning to admission on more generous terms than were accorded to other aliens. It is not conceivable that Congress would deliberately have allowed the racial limitation to continue as to soldiers and seamen to whom the statute had accorded an especially favored status, and have removed it as to all other aliens. Such a construction cannot be adopted unless it be unavoidable.

The division of the Revised Statutes into titles and chapters is chiefly a matter of convenience, and reference to a given title or chapter is simply a ready method of identifying the particular provisions which are meant. The provisions of title XXX affected by the limitation of section 2169, originally embraced the whole subject of naturalization of aliens. The generality of the words in section 2165, 'An alien may be admitted, . . . ' was restricted by section 2169 in common with the other provisions of the title. The words 'this title' were used for the purpose of identifying that provision (and others), but it was the provision which was restricted. That provision having been amended and carried into the act of 1906, section 2169 being left intact and unrepealed, it will require something [260 U.S. 178, 194] more persuasive than a narrowly literal reading of the identifying words 'this title' to justify the conclusion that Congress intended the restriction to be no longer applicable to the provision.

It is the duty of this Court to give effect to the intent of Congress. Primarily this intent is ascertained by giving the words their natural significance, but if this leads to an unreasonable result plainly at variance with the policy of the legislation as a whole, we must examine the matter further. We may then look to the reason of the enactment and inquire into is antecedent history and give it effect in accordance with its design and purpose, sacrificing, if necessary, the literal meaning in order that the purpose may not fail. See *Church of the Holy Trinity v. United States*, 143 U.S. 457, 12 Sup. Ct. 511; *Heydenfeldt v. Daney Gold, et., Co.*, 93 U.S. 634, 638. We are asked to conclude that Congress, without the consideration of recommendation of any committee, without a suggestion as to the effect, or a word of debate as to the desirability, of so fundamental a change, nevertheless, by failing to alter the identifying words of section 2169, which section we may assume was continued for some serious purpose, has radically modified a statute always theretofore maintained and considered as of great importance. It is inconceivable that a rule in force from the beginning of the government, a part of our history as well as our law, welded into the structure of our national polity by a century of legislative and administrative acts and judicial decisions, would have been deprived of its force in such dubious and casual fashion. We are, therefore, constrained to hold that the act of 1906 is limited by the provisions of the section 2169 of the Revised Statutes.

Second. This brings us to inquire whether, under section 2169, the appellant is eligible to naturalization. The language of the naturalization laws from 1790 to 1870 had been uniformly such as to deny the privilege of [260 U.S. 178, 195] naturalization to an alien unless he came within the description 'free white person.' By section 7 of the act of July 14, 1870 (16 Stat. 254, 256 [Comp. St. 4358]), the naturalization laws were 'extended to aliens of African nativity and to persons of African descent.' Section 2169 of the Revised Statutes, as already pointed out, restricts the privilege to the same classes of person, viz. 'to aliens [being free white persons, an to aliens] of African nativity and to persons of African descent.' It is true that in the first edition of the Revised Statutes of 1873 the words in brackets, 'being free white persons, and to aliens' were omitted, but this was clearly an error of the compilers and was corrected by the subsequent legislation of 1875 918 Stat. 316, 318). Is appellant, therefore, a 'free white person,' within the meaning of that phrase as found in the statute?

On behalf of the appellant it is urged that we should give to this phrase the meaning which it had in the minds of its original framers in 1790 and that it was employed by them for the sole purpose of excluding the black or African race and the Indians then inhabiting this country. It may be true that those two races were alone thought of as being excluded, but to say that they were the only ones within the intent of the statute would be to ignore the affirmative form of the legislation. The provision is not that Negroes and Indians shall be excluded,

but it is, in effect, that only free white persons shall be included. The intention was to confer the privilege of citizenship upon that class of person whom the framers knew as white, and to deny it to all who could not be classified. It is not enough to say that the framers did not have in mind the brown or yellow races of Asia. It is necessary to go farther and be able to say that had these particular races been suggested the language of the act would have been so varied as to include them within its privileges. As said by Chief Justice Marshall in *Dartmouth College* [260 U.S. 178, 196] *v. Woodward*, 4 Wheat. 518, 644 (4 L. Ed. 629), in deciding a question of constitutional construction:

'It is not enough to say that this particular case was not in the mind of the convention, when the article was framed, nor of the American people, when it was adopted. It is necessary to go farther, and to say that, had this particular case been suggested, the language would have been so varied, as to exclude it, or it would have been made a special exception. The case, being within the words of the rule, must be within its operation likewise, unless there be something in the literal construction so obviously absurd, or mischievous, or repugnant to the general spirit of the instrument, as to justify those who expound the Constitution in making it an exception.'

If it be assumed that the opinion of the framers was that the only persons who would fall outside the designation 'white' were Negroes and Indians, this would go no farther than to demonstrate their lack of sufficient information to enable them to foresee precisely who would be excluded by that term in the subsequent administration of the statute. It is not important in construing their words to consider the extent of their ethnological knowledge or whether they thought that under the statute the only persons who would be denied naturalization would be Negroes and Indians. It is sufficient to ascertain whom they intended to include and having ascertained that it follows, as a necessary corollary, that all others are to be excluded,

The question then is: Who are comprehended within the phrase 'free white persons?' Undoubtedly the word 'free' was originally used in recognition of the fact that slavery then existed and that some white persons occupied that status. The word, however, has long since ceased to have any practical significance and may now be disregarded.

We have been furnished with elaborate briefs in which the meaning of the words 'white person' is discussed [260 U.S. 178, 197] with ability and at length, both from the standpoint of judicial decision and from that of the science of ethnology. It does not seem to us necessary, however, to follow counsel in their extensive researches in these fields. It is sufficient to note the fact that these decisions are, in substance, to the effect that the words import a racial and not an individual test, and with this conclusion, fortified as it is by reason and authority, we entirely agree. Manifestly the test afforded by the mere color of the skin of each individual is impracticable, as that differs greatly among persons of the same race, even among Anglo-Saxons, ranging by imperceptible gradations from the fair blond to the swarthy brunette, the latter being darker than many of the lighter hued persons of the brown or yellow races. Hence to adopt the color test alone would result in a confused overlapping of races and a gradual merging of one into the other, without any practical line of separation. Beginning with the decision of Circuit Judge Sawyer, in Re Ah Yup, 5 Sawy. 155, Fed. Cas. No. 104 (1878), the federal and state courts, in an almost unbroken line, have held that the words 'white person' were meant to indicate only a person of what is popularly known as the Caucasian race. Among these decisions, see, for example: In re Camille (C. C.) 96 Fed. 256; In re Saito (C. C.) 62 Fed. 126; In re Nian, 6 Utah, 259, 21 Pac. 993, 4 L. R. A. 726; In re Kumagai (D. C.) 163 Fed. 922; In re

Yamashita, 30 Wash. 234, 237, 70 Pac. 482, 94 Am. St. Rep. 860; In re Ellis (D. C.) 179 Fed. 1002; In re Mozumdar (D. C.) 207 Fed. 115, 117; In re Singh (D. C.) 257 Fed. 209, 211, 212; and In re Charr (D. C.) 273 Fed. 207. With the conclusion reached in these decisions we see no reason to differ. Moreover, that conclusion has become so well established by judicial and executive concurrence and legislative acquiescence that we should not at this late day feel at liberty to disturb it, in the absence of reasons far more cogent than any that have been suggested. *United States v. Midwest Oil Co.,* 236 U.S. 459, 472, 35 S. Sup. Ct. 309[260 U.S. 178, 198]. The determination that the words 'white person' are synonymous with the words 'a person of the Caucasian race' simplifies the problem, although it does not entirely dispose of it. Controversies have arisen and will no doubt arise again in respect of the proper classification of individuals in borderline cases. The effect of the conclusion that the words 'white person' means a Caucasian is not to establish a sharp line of demarcation between those who are entitled and those who are not entitled to naturalization, but rather a zone of more or less debatable ground outside of which, upon the one hand, are those clearly eligible, and outside of which, upon the other hands, are those clearly ineligible for citizenship. Individual cases falling within this zone must be determined as they arise from time by what this court has called, in another connection (*Davidson v. New Orleans,* 96 U.S. 97, 104), 'the gradual process of judicial inclusion and exclusion.'

The appellant, in the case now under consideration, however, is clearly of a race which is not Caucasian and therefore belongs entirely outside the zone on the negative side. A large number of the federal and state courts have so decided and we find no reported cases definitely to the contrary. These decisions are sustained by numerous scientific authorities, which we do not deem it necessary to review. We think these decisions are right and so hold.

The briefs filed on behalf of appellant refer in complimentary terms to the culture and enlightenment of the Japanese people, and with this estimate we have no reason to disagree; but these are matter which cannot enter into our consideration of the questions here at issue. We have no function in the matter other than to ascertain the will of Congress and declare it. Of course there is not implied—either in the legislation or in our interpretation of it—any suggestion of individual unworthiness or racial inferiority. These considerations are in no manner involved. [260 U.S. 178, 199] The questions submitted are therefore answered as follows:

Question No. 1. The act of June 29, 1906, is not complete in itself, but is limited by section 2169 of the Revised Statutes of the United States.
Question No. 2. No.
Question No. 3. No.

It will be so certified.

# 1.4

# *United States v. Bhagat Singh Thind,* 261 U.S. 204 (1923)

〰〰〰〰〰〰〰〰〰〰〰〰〰〰〰〰〰〰〰〰〰〰〰〰

Mr. Justice Sutherland delivered the opinion of the Court.

This cause is here upon a certificate from the Circuit Court of appeals requesting the instruction of this Court in respect of the following questions:

'1. Is a high-caste Hindu, of full Indian blood, born at Amritsar, Punjab, India, a white person within the meaning of section 2169, Revised Statutes? [261 U. S. 204, 207]

'2. Does the Act of February 5, 1917 (39 Stat. 875, 3), disqualify from naturalization as citizens those Hindus now barred by that act, who had lawfully entered the United States prior to the passage of said act?'

The appellee was granted a certificate of citizenship by the District Court of the United States for the District of Oregon, over the objection of the Naturalization Examiner for the United States. A bill in equity was then filed by the United States, seeking a cancellation of the certificate on the ground that the appellee was not a white person and therefore not lawfully entitled to naturalization. The District Court, on motion, dismissed the bill (In re Bhagat Thind, 268 Fed. 683), and an appeal was taken to the Circuit Court of Appeals. No question is made in respect of the individual qualifications of the appellee. The sole question is whether he falls within the class designated by Congress as eligible.

Section 2169, Revised Statutes (Comp. St. 4358), provides that the provisions of the Naturalization Act 'shall apply to aliens being free white persons and to aliens of African nativity and to persons of African descent.'

If the applicant is a white person, within the meaning of this section, he is entitled to naturalization; otherwise not. In *Ozawa v. United States*, 260 U.S. 178, 43 Sup. Ct. 65, 67 L. Ed.—, decided November 13, 1922, we had occasion to consider the application of these words to the case of a cultivated Japanese and were constrained to hold that he was not within their meaning. As there pointed out, the provision is not that any particular class of persons shall be excluded, but it is, in effect, that only white persons shall be included within the privilege of the statute. 'The intention was to confer the privilege of citizenship upon that class of persons whom the fathers knew as white, and to deny it to all who could not be so classified. It is not enough to say that the framers did not have in mind the brown or yellow races of Asia. It is necessary to go farther and be able to say that had these particular [261 U.S. 204, 208] races been suggested the language of the act would have been so varied as to include them within its privileges'—citing *Dartmouth College v. Woodward*, 4 Wheat. 518, 644. Following a long line of decisions of the lower Federal courts, we held that the words imported a racial and not an individual test and were meant to indicate only persons of what is popularly known as the Caucasian race. But, as there pointed out, the conclusion that the phrase 'white persons' and the word 'Caucasian' are synonymous does not end the matter. It enabled us to dispose of the problem as it was there presented, since the applicant for citizenship clearly fell outside the zone of debatable ground on the negative side; but the decision still left the question to be dealt with, in doubtful and different cases, by the 'process of judicial inclusion and exclusion.' Mere ability on the part of an applicant for naturalization to establish a line of descent from a Caucasian ancestor will not ipso facto to and necessarily conclude the inquiry. 'Caucasian' is a conventional word of much flexibility, as a study of the literature dealing with racial questions will disclose, and while it and the words 'white persons' are treated as synonymous for the purposes of that case, they are not of identical meaning, idem per idem.

In the endeavor to ascertain the meaning of the statute we must not fail to keep in mind that it does not employ the word 'Caucasian,' but the words 'white persons,' and these are words of common speech and not of scientific origin. The meaning of the word 'Caucasian,' is not clear, and the use of it in its scientific form is probably wholly unfamiliar to the original framers of the statute in 1790. When we employ it, we do so as an aid to the ascertainment of the legislative intent and not as an invariable substitute for the statutory words. Indeed, as used in the science of ethnology, the connotation of the word is by no means clear, and the use of it in its scientific sense as an equivalent [261 U.S. 204, 209] for the words

of the statute, other considerations aside, would simply mean the substitution of one perplexity for another. But in this country, during the last half century especially, the word by common usage has acquired a popular meaning, not clearly defined to be sure, but sufficiently so to enable us to say that its popular as distinguished from its scientific application is of appreciably narrower scope. It is in the popular sense of the word, therefore, that we employ is as an aid to the construction of the statute, for it would be obviously illogical to convert words of common speech used in a statute into words of scientific terminology when neither the latter nor the science for whose purposes they were coined was within the contemplation of the framers of the statute or of the people from whom it was framed. The words of the statute are to be interpreted in accordance with the understanding of the common man from whose vocabulary they were taken. See *Maillard v. Lawrence*, 16 How. 251, 261.

They imply, as we have said, a racial test; but the term 'race' is one which, for the practical purposes of the statute, must be applied to a group of living persons now possessing in common the requisite characteristics, not to groups of persons who are supposed to be or really are descended from some remote, common ancestor, but who, whether they both resemble him to a greater or less extent, have, at any rate, ceased altogether to resemble one another. It may be true that the blond Scandinavian and the brown Hindu have a common ancestor in the dim reaches of antiquity, but the average man knows perfectly well that there are unmistakable and profound differences between them today; and it is not impossible, if that common ancestor could be materialized in the flesh, that we should discover that he was himself sufficiently differentiated from both of his descendants to preclude his racial classification with either. The question for determination [261 U.S. 204, 210] is not, therefore, whether by the speculative processes of ethnological reasoning we may present a probability to the scientific mind that they have the same origin, but whether we can satisfy the common understanding that they are now the same or sufficiently the same to justify the interpreters of a statute—written in the words of common speech, for common understanding, by unscientific men—in classifying them together in the statutory category as white persons. In 1790 the Adamite theory of creation—which gave a common ancestor to all mankind—was generally accepted, and it is not at all probable that it was intended by the legislators of that day to submit the question of the application of the words 'white person' to the mere test of an indefinitely remote common ancestry, without regard to the extent of the subsequent divergence of the various branches from such common ancestry or from one another.

The eligibility of this applicant for citizenship is based on the sole fact that he is of high-caste Hindu stock, born in Punjab, one of the extreme northwestern districts of India, and classified by certain scientific authorities as of the Caucasian or Aryan theory as a racial basis seems to be discredited by most, if not all, modern writers on the subject of ethnology. A review of their contentions would serve no useful purpose. It is enough to refer to the works of Deniker (*Races of Man*, 317), Keane (*Man: Past and Present*, 445, 446), and Huxley (*Man's Place in Nature*, 278) and to the *Dictionary of Races*, Senate Document 662, 61st Congress, 3d Sess. 1910–1911, p. 17.

The term 'Aryan' has to do with linguistic, and not at all with physical, characteristics, and it would seem reasonably clear that mere resemblance in language, indicating a common linguistic root buried in remotely ancient soil, is altogether inadequate to prove common racial origin. There is, and can be, no assurance that the so-called [261 U.S. 204, 211] Aryan language was not spoken by a variety of races living in proximity to one another. Our own history has witnessed the adoption of the English tongue by millions of negroes, whose descendants can never be classified racially with the descendants of white persons, notwithstanding both may speak a common root language.

The word 'Caucasian' is in scarcely better repute.[1] It is at best a conventional term, with an altogether fortuitous origin,[2] which under scientific manipulation, has come to include far more than the unscientific mind suspects. According to Keane, for example (*The World's Peoples*, 24, 28, 307, et seq.) it includes not only the Hindu, but some of the Polynesians[3] (that is, the Maori, Tahitians, Samoans, Hawaiians, and others), the Hamites of Africa, upon the ground of the Caucasic cast of their features, though in color they range from brown to black. We venture to think that the average well informed white American would learn with some degree of astonishment that the race to which he belongs is made up of such heterogeneous elements.[4] [261 U.S. 204, 212] The various authorities are in irreconcilable disagreement as to what constitutes a proper racial division. For instance, Blumenbach has 5 races; Keane following Linaeus, 4; Deniker, 29.[5] The explanation probably is that 'the innumerable varieties of mankind run into one another by insensible degrees,'[6] and to arrange them in sharply bounded divisions is an undertaking of such uncertainty that common agreement is practically impossible.

It may be, therefore, that a given group cannot be properly assigned to any of the enumerated grand racial divisions. The type may have been so changed by intermixture of blood as to justify an intermediate classification. Something very like this has actually taken place in India. Thus, in Hindustan and Berar there was such an intermixture of the 'Aryan' invader with the dark-skinned Dravidian.[7]

In the Punjab and Rajputana, while the invaders seem to have met with more success in the effort to preserve [261 U.S. 204, 213] their racial purity,[8] intermarriages did occur producing an intermingling of the two and destroying to a greater or less degree the purity of the 'Aryan' blood. The rules of caste, while calculated to prevent this intermixture, seem not to have been entirely successful.[9]

It does not seem necessary to pursue the matter of scientific classification further. We are unable to agree with the District Court, or with other lower federal courts, in the conclusion that a native Hindu is eligible for naturalization under section 2169. The words of familiar speech, which were used by the original framers of the law, were intended to include only the type of man whom they knew as white. The immigration of that day was almost exclusively from the British Isles and Northwestern Europe, whence they and their forebears had come. When they extended the privilege of American citizenship to 'any alien being a free white person' it was these immigrants—bone of their bone and flesh of their flesh—and their kind whom they must have had affirmatively in mind. The succeeding years brought immigrants from Eastern, Southern and Middle Europe, among them the Slav and the dark-eyed, swarthy people of Alpine and Mediterranean stock, and these were received as unquestionably akin to those already here and readily amalgamated with them. It was the descendants of these, and [261 U.S. 204, 214] other immigrants of like origin, who constituted the white population of the country when section 2169, re-enacting the naturalization test of 1790, was adopted, and, there is no reason to doubt, with like intent and meaning.

What, if any, people of primarily Asiatic stock come within the words of the section we do not deem it necessary now to decide. There is much in the origin and historic development of the statute to suggest that no Asiatic whatever was included. The debates in Congress, during the consideration of the subject in 1870 and 1875, are persuasively of this character. In 1873, for example, the words 'free white person' were unintentionally omitted from the compilation of the Revised Statutes. This omission was supplied in 1875 by the act to correct errors and supply omissions. (18 Stat. C. 80, p. 318). When this act was under consideration by Congress efforts were made to strike out the words quoted, and it was insisted upon the one hand and conceded upon the other, that the effect of their retention was to exclude Asiatics generally from citizenship. While what was said upon that occasion, to be sure, furnishes no basis for judicial construction of the statute, it is, nevertheless, an important historic incident, which may not be altogether ignored in the search for the true meaning of words which are themselves historic. That question, however, may well be left for final determination until the details have been more completely disclosed by the consideration of particular cases, as they from time to time arise. The words of the statute, it must be conceded, do not readily yield to exact interpretation, and it is probably better to leave them as they are than to risk undue extension or undue limitation of their meaning by any general paraphrase at this time.

What we now hold is that the words 'free white person' are words of common speech, to be interpreted in accordance with the understanding of the common man, synonymous with the word 'Caucasian' only as the [261 U.S. 204, 215] word is popularly understood. As so understood and used, whatever may be the speculation of the ethnologist, it does not include the body of people to whom the appellee belongs. It is a matter of familiar observation and knowledge that the physical group characteristics of the Hindus render them readily distinguishable from the various groups of persons in this country commonly recognized as white. The children of English, French, German, Italian, Scandinavian, and other European parentage, quickly merge into the mass of our population and lose the distinctive hallmarks of the European origin. On the other hand, it cannot be doubted that the children born in this country of Hindu parents would retain indefinitely the clear evidence of their ancestry. It is very far from our thought to suggest the slightest question of racial superiority or inferiority. What we suggest is merely racial difference, and it is of such character and extent that the great body of our people instinctively recognize it and reject the thought of assimilation.

It is not without significance in this connection that Congress, by the Act of February 5, 1917, 39 Stat. 874, c. 29, 3 (Comp. St. 1918, Comp. St. Ann. Supp. 1919, 4289 1/4b), has now excluded from admission into this country all natives of Asia within designated limits of latitude and longitude, including the whole of India. This not only constitutes conclusive evidence of the congressional attitude of opposition of Asiatic immigration generally, but is persuasive of similar attitude toward Asiatic naturalization as well, since it is not likely that Congress would be willing to accept as citizens a class of persons whom it rejects as immigrants.

It follows that a negative answer must be given to the first question, which disposes of the case and renders an answer to the second question unnecessary, and it will be so certified.

Answer to question No. 1, No.

### NOTES

1. *Dictionary of Races.* Senate Document 662, 61st Congress, 3d Sess. 1910–1911, 31.

2. 1 *Encyclopaedia Britannica* (11th ed.), 113: 'The ill-chose name of Caucasian, invented by Blumenbach in allusion to a South Caucasian skull of specially typical proportions, and applied by him to the so-called white races, is still current; it brings into one race peoples such as the Arabs and Swedes, although these are scarcely less different that the Americans and Malays, who are set down as two distinct races. Again, two of the best marked varieties of mankind are the Australians and the Bushmen, neither of whom, however, seems to have a natural place in Blumenbach's series.'

3. The United States Bureau of Immigration classifies all Pacific Islanders as belonging to the 'Mongolic grand division.' *Dictionary of Races*, 102.

4. Keane himself says that the Caucasic division of the human family is 'in point of fact the most debatable field in the whole range of anthropological studies.' Keane, *Man: Past and Present*, 444.

And again: 'Hence it seems to require a strong mental effort to sweep into a single category, however elastic, so many different peoples—Europeans, North Africans, West Asiatics, Iranians, and others all the way to the indo-Gangetic plans an uplands, whose complexion presents every shade of color, except yellow, from white to the deepest brown or even black.

'But they are grouped together in a single division, because their essential properties are one, . . . their substantial uniformity speaks to the eye that sees below the surface . . . we recognize a common racial stamp in the facial expression, the structure of the hair, partly also the bodily proportions, in all of which points they agree more with each other than with the other main divisions. Even in the case of certain black or very dark races, such as the Bejas, Somali, and a few other Eastern Hamites, we are reminded instinctively more of Europeans or Berbers, thanks to their more regular features and brighter expression.' Keane, Man: *Past and Present,* 448.

5. *Dictionary of Races*, 6. See, generally. 2 Encyclopedia Britannica (11th ed.), 113.

6. 2 *Encyclopedia Britannica* (11th ed.), 113.

7. 13 *Encyclopedia Britannica* (11th ed.), 502.

8. 13 *Encyclopedia Britannica* (11th ed.), 502

9. 13 *Encyclopedia Britannica*, 503. 'In spite, however, of the artificial restrictions placed on the intermarrying of the castes, the mingling of the two races seems to have proceeded at a tolerably rapid rate. Indeed, the paucity of women of the Aryan stock would probably render these mixed unions almost a necessity from the very outset; and the vaunted purity of blood which the caste rules were calculated to perpetuate can scarcely have remained of more than a relative degree even in the case of the Brahman caste.'

And see the observations of Keane, *Man: Past and Present*, 561, as to the doubtful origin and effect of caste.

# Part II

# The Impact of Immigration Laws on Asian America

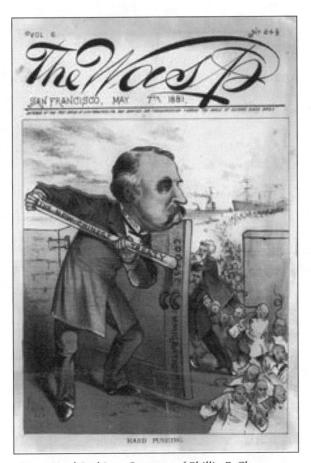

Hard Pushing. *Courtesy of Phillip P. Choy*

## CLOSING AND OPENING THE GOLDEN DOOR:
## THE MAKING OF CONTEMPORARY ASIAN AMERICA

Perhaps the most important U.S. congressional act to influence the development of contemporary Asian America is the 1965 Amendments to the Immigration and Naturalization Act. For Asians and Pacific Islanders, immigration policies since their arrival in the United States in the late nineteenth century have served to make and shape this community into its current state. Early examples of such policies in U.S. history are the Immigration Acts of 1882 and 1884, which limited the number of skilled Chinese laborers entering the United States. The Gentleman's Agreement of 1909, a political accord between the United States and Japan in which the latter agreed to limit the issuance of passports to Japanese skilled laborers, brought an end to Japanese skilled immigration. Eventually, the National Origins Act of 1924, passed by the U.S. Congress, closed the door to a majority of Asian immigrants for over forty years, while European immigration was allowed to continue during this period (Chan 1991). It was not until the U.S. Congress passed the 1965 Amendments to the Immigration Act that Asian immigration was put on even footing with European immigration. According to the provisions of the 1965 Immigration Act, Asian immigration was set at twenty thousand per country with a total of 170,000 visas granted from the Eastern Hemisphere. In comparison, European immigration had no quota per country, with a total of 120,000 visas granted from the Western Hemisphere (Chan 1991). Perhaps the most important aspect of the 1965 Immigration Act was that it essentially reorganized the immigration system to favor family reunification in two ways. First, it provided 80 percent of visas to family relatives of U.S. citizens or to those of permanent residents. Second, parents of U.S. citizens became exempt from numerical limitations that previously existed. This privilege was previously extended only to spouses and children of U.S. citizens (Ong and Liu 1994).

The impact of the Immigration Act of 1965 on Asian Pacific Americans cannot be denied. During the period between 1921 and 1960, Asian immigration constituted less than 4 percent of total U.S. immigration. After the Immigration Act of 1965, Asians represented 35 percent of the total U.S. immigration from 1971 to 1980 and 42 percent from 1981 to 1989. The immigration of Asians and Pacific Islanders during this period came primarily from China (Hong Kong), Taiwan, Korea, India, the Philippines, and Vietnam. Nearly 4 million Asian Pacific Americans arrived between 1970 and 1990 (Ong and Liu 1994). The sudden large flux of immigration as a result of the Immigration Act of 1965 had a profound impact on Asian Pacific American political participation and potential. For example, given the large influx of Asian and Pacific Islander immigration between 1970 to 1990, one general characteristic of the national Asian Pacific American population is that it is predominantly foreign-born. In Los Angeles County, where the largest concentration of Asian Pacific Americans in the United States resides, approximately 70 percent are foreign born (Ong and Azores 1991). This general characteristic has had a lasting impact on Asian Pacific American political participation, as this community has traditionally relied on other forms of political participation beyond voting (e.g., campaign contributions) to exert its political influence.

### REFERENCES

Chan, Sucheng. 1991. *Asian Americans: An Interpretive History*. Boston: Twayne, 1991.

Ong, Paul, and Tania Azores. 1991. *Asian Pacific Americans in Los Angeles: A Demographic Profile*. Los Angeles: UCLA Asian American Studies Center/LEAP Asian American Public Policy Institute.

Ong, Paul, and John M. Liu. 1994. "U.S. Immigration Policies and Asian Migration." In Paul Ong, Edna Bonacich, and Lucie Cheng, eds., *The New Asian Immigration in Los Angeles and Global Restructuring*, 45–73. Philadelphia: Temple University Press.

The Pigtail Has Got to Go. *Courtesy of Phillip P. Choy*

# 2.1

# The Immigration Act of 1924

*Lee A. Makela*

‿‿‿‿‿‿‿‿‿‿‿‿‿‿‿‿‿‿‿‿‿‿‿‿‿‿‿‿‿‿‿‿‿‿‿‿‿‿‿‿‿‿‿‿‿‿

The Immigration Act of 1924 reluctantly signed into law May 26, 1924, by President Calvin Coolidge is usually considered by immigration historians in the context of growing American Nativistic concern with the rising tide of immigration emanating from Southern Europe and the Mediterranean. The Act is generally portrayed as a tightening and narrowing of earlier legislation approved in 1921, which had first established he notion of immigration quota limitations based on census data. It is represented primarily as both a purposeful attempt to further restrict the numbers of newcomers entering the United States in general, and a move to limit immigrants largely to those from preferred population sources in Northern Europe and the British Isles.[1]

The Immigration Act of 1924 was much more than that, however; it was also the most influential pieces of immigration legislation ever passed in the United States

with respect to its influences on the course of future relationships between the United States and Japan and, internally, between Japanese immigrants and their (largely Caucasian) American neighbors. In fact, it represents the only major pieces of legislation acted upon at the national level prior to 1965 concerning itself directly with immigration from Japan to the United States.

To be sure, the subject of Japanese immigration had surfaced in a number of setting over the years. Localized legislative activity, treaty negotiations, and diplomatic agreements—as well as Supreme Court considerations thereof—all predated this particular congressional action.[2] Yet none of these earlier measures can be considered representative of the collective national consensus regarding immigration from Japan; that remains the province of the Immigration Act debated and passed by both houses of Congress in the spring of 1924.

To the casual observer, the centrality of the Immigration Act of 1924 as a reflection of prevailing American attitudes toward Japanese immigration is not immediately apparent. Indeed, the act itself contains not one direct mention of the Japanese. Among

Makela, Lee A. "The Immigration Act of 1924." In Hyung-Chan Kim, ed., *Asian Americans and Congress: A Documented History*, (Westport, Conn.: Greenwood, 1996), 225–31; 239–52. Reprinted with permission.

its provisions, however, the legislation does incorporate a clause prohibiting the immigration of the United States of any "alien ineligible to citizenship." This wording, in turn, represents a legalistic euphemism meant to designate "emigrants from Asia"—Asians being the only racial group defined by a series of Supreme Court rulings as ineligible to naturalization rights. Furthermore, the majority of indigenous Asian populations had already been formally excluded from the specific right to immigrate to the United States by prior restrictions acts.[3] The Japanese alone had escaped—and that exemption had been accomplished by Japanese government action (under the terms of the Gentlemen's Agreement of 1908).[4] Hence the presence of the phrase "aliens ineligible to citizenship" in the Immigration Act of 1924 clearly and unequivocally was meant to refer solely to the Japanese, the only Asian immigrant community "ineligible to citizenship" still nominally permitted unrestricted immigration access to the Untied States.

In 1924, of course, the use of such diplomatically neutral language to disguise the intentions behind the action being undertaken by U.S. Congress did not go unnoticed, either in Japan or among the Japanese immigrant community resident in the United States. In fact, although not primarily a product of anti-Japanese agitation nor a reflection of anti-Japanese sentiment in the United States, the passage of the Immigration Act of 1924 markedly influenced the course of future Japanese-American interactions and the fate of the Japanese immigrant community in the United States. Abroad, passage of the Immigration Act of 1924 further encouraged those in Japan promoting self-sufficiency in the international arena at the expense of those seeking adherence to Wilsonian principles.[5] Within the diplomatic community, passage of the Immigration Act of 1924 severely inhibited American attempts to maintain Japanese-American relations on an even keel; in the United States itself, passage of the Immigration Act of 1924 significantly influenced a shift within the Japanese immigrant population as American resident aliens away from dependency of the Japanese government to protect community interests toward a subsequent emphasis on low-profile assimilation into the prevalent American cultural nexus.

In Japan, as we shall see, the American action was viewed as a major diplomatic affront, an insult to Japan's national honor, a setback in that nation's quest for acceptance as a major power on the international scene, and a threat to her ability to survive as an independent nation state. This analysis in turn rested on a Japanese interpretation of a historically patterned sequence of events and wide-ranging set of prior assumptions.

For decades Japan had been obsessed with protecting her own interests both at home and abroad. She had long pursued *bunmei-kaika* ("civilization and enlightenment"), a policy of accelerated modernization following imported Western models in the quest for *fukoku-kyohei* ("a strong nation and a powerful army.") In her attempts not to become a victim of imperialism, Japan had become herself an imperialist nation, acquiring several overseas colonial possessions and proprietary interests in large parts of China and Manchuria.[6] She also had come to see herself increasingly as meriting admittance into the international community as an equal partner with the nations of Europe and the United States.

In fact, Japan had come to sit at the Paris Peace Conference ending the World War I in 1919 as one of five great powers during treaty negotiations, however, she had faced a series of major diplomatic defeats suggesting that successes enjoyed in the last decade of the nineteenth century and the opening years of the twentieth century might prove illusory indications of her acceptance on the basis of equality in the international arena. At Versailles, Tokyo not only was denied recognition of her claim to exalted great power status but was also forced to accept League of Nation Mandate status for her newly acquired Pacific possessions (inherited from the Germans) and to witness the defeat of a clause guaranteeing racial equality in the proposed charter for the League of Nations.

Having previously suffered a number of similar diplomatic setbacks in the course of acquiring her overseas possessions,[7] the Japanese were well aware that issues of perceived diplomatic inequality inhibited attempts to assure Japan's survival as an independent and powerful nation state. In the aftermath of this recent round of failed negotiations, then, as Japan entered the 1920s, she warily watched American exclusionist efforts directed against Japanese immigration as a troublesome sign that her continuing quest for international acceptance as an equal (and the related ability to assure national survival) rested on shaky rounds indeed.[8]

On a related front, Japan was also concerned with maintaining a sense of national distinctiveness, a claim to a unique cultural identity not to be confused with that of any other nation, Asian or otherwise.[9] Whatever their specific attitudes toward their Asian neighbors might be, in their relationship with the United States, the Japanese were acutely aware that Japanese immigrants in 1924 enjoyed a "unique" immigration status as citizens of the only Asian nation whose nationals were not expressly forbidden the right to immigrate as a result of long-standing U.S. legislation; and, just as clearly, the government in Tokyo sought diligently to maintain this special status as an indication of Japan's superior position among the nations of Asia.[10]

Japan's reaction to passage of the Immigration Act of 1924 in light of these premises appears logical and inherently justifiable. Ultimately, as history demonstrates, Japanese government attempts to deal effectively with American willingness to discriminate against Japanese immigrants per se (and all this came to portend in Japanese eyes) led first to attempts to carve out an independent, self-sufficient Japanese empire (the Greater East Asia Co-Prosperity Sphere) in Asia and then to war with the United States and the debacle of World War II.[11]

In the 1920s, however, that future remained unknown. At that time the diplomatic community in the United States and the executive branch of government in Washington, well aware of Japanese needlessly being targets of discrimination, consistently sought to work through diplomatic channels to ameliorate relations between Tokyo and Washington. During 1911 treaty negotiations, for instance, American diplomats willingly acceded to maintaining the informal ban on Japanese emigration guaranteed informally by the Gentlemen's Agreement despite calls at home for outright exclusion. The American negotiators ultimately rejected as well a clause permitting the United States to exclude Japanese laborers, choosing to seek to reconcile anti-Japanese forces in the United States to their adopted position rather than risk worsening relations with Japan.

In so doing, the self-important tendency to overplay the influence of the State Department and the White House in settling matters of international dispute—and successes enjoyed in negotiations surrounding the Gentlemen's Agreement of 1908, the 1911 treaty with Japan and the Washington and London naval disarmament conferences—led many American diplomats and State Department officials to downplay potential problems such as that represented by the Congressional debate over passage of the Immigration Act in 1924. That is to say, the American diplomatic community tended to assure the Japanese government that the matter was not as serious a threat as it might have seemed—followed by pledges that the American diplomatic and executive communities would handle the matter expeditiously without unnecessary Japanese involvement in internal American political affairs.

Unfortunately, not only had the State Department and the White House overestimated their prowess in this particular instance, they also failed to carry the battle to victory because of a lack of firm conviction that what they were seeking on behalf of the Japanese government ultimately was in the best interests of the United States. Surely avoidance of armed conflict with

Japan was an important policy objective; however, few Americans involved in the diplomatic maneuvering associated with opposition to passage of the Immigration Act were themselves free from the ingrained racism prevalent among Americans of the time that saw Asians as both inferior and ultimately "unassimilable." Privately, from President Coolidge on down the ladder of administrative authority, racist remarks present to implied in the written record demonstrated an underlying lack of conviction in seeking to assuage Japanese fears that the West was unwilling to grant Japan "equal status" in the international community.[12]

While the diplomatic community and the executive branch in the United States saw Japan as a power to be reckoned with on the international scene, at home the American public remained largely indifferent. If anything, the average citizen tended toward restriction due to lingering negative associations originally engendered in the course of the much earlier debate over Chinese exclusion in the 1880s and 1890s. Essentially anti-Chinese rhetoric used to accomplish that earlier end was easily transferred in the popular imagination to the Japanese case as argued in 1924.

Pervasive racist interpretations of the threat represented by immigration from Japan (fostered by a burgeoning of Nativistic sentiment throughout the United States) also were encouraged to some degree by Japan's recent international successes. In the 1890s, for example, a similar attempt to ban Japanese immigration outright had failed principally because Japan itself was not then seen as a threat to American security; by 1924, however, Japan had become a much more prominent member of the international community and as a result more attention was paid her emigrant population as well.

It also is important to remember that the battle for passage of the Immigration Act was not fought over exclusion alone. Many members of Congress, particularly those representing urban and industrialized constituencies composed of later immigrant populations, sought to focus on the question of which decade's census data to utilize in determining the quotas the Immigration Act would impose on those seeking immigration rights. In such a debate the questions of excluding "aliens ineligible to citizenship" took a back seat. Political rivalries within Republican ranks between the executive and congressional branches of the party in an election year had a profound effect as well on the ultimate passage of the Immigration Act, as did the political ambition of Senator Hiram W. Johnson (R-CA). The diplomatic community, then—however concerned it might be with maintaining cordial relations with Japan—was in no position, acting independently, to influence significantly the course of the congressional debate over the Immigration Act of 1924 and its ultimate outcome.

Just as international repercussions of passage of the Immigration Act of 1924 can be seen as far-reaching, so, too, internal ramifications of the Act's passage can be traced through time. Darrel Montero, in his seminal study *Japanese Americans: Changing Patterns of Ethnic Affiliation Over Three Generations*, suggests that Nisei (second generation Japanese Americans) have become more acculturated because of increased educational opportunities and the need to leave local ethnic communities in search of opportunities to practice their chosen professions.[13] "Another salient factor," he asserts, "that contributes to the assimilation of the Nisei is that they do not consider themselves sojourners as did their parents, the Issei."[14] I would contend that discriminatory attitudes surfacing in the events leading to passage of the 1924 United States Immigration Act contributed to this shift in emphasis among the Japanese American community resident in the United States toward both the value of education and the desirability of assimilation.

"When the first generation immigrants, the Issei, arrived in the United States, they sought (and found) security within the ethnic enclave. Regarding themselves a sojourners, they came to the United States in search of financial security, and planned to return to their homeland once they had made their fortunes."[15] These new Asian arrivals not surprisingly tended to settle in ghettos, enclaves of Japanese, mostly rural, where they were comforted by the similarity of language, custom, and culture. Recalling their roots, they organized in these communities according to prefecture of origin; many also formed ethnic institutions as systems of mutual aid and support, such as rotating credit associations.[16] Most joined Japanese Associations designed to assure continued support from the homeland Japanese government and through which they could organize return visits to Japan and, after 1907, arrange the issuance of marriage-related immigration visas.[17]

The perception of these tightly organized ethnic communities by the surrounding Anglo majority population as representative of worrisome concentrations of "unassimilable aliens" contributed in no small measure to agitation on the West Coast for the banning of Japanese immigration. Generally self-isolated from the majority community around them, the Issei, unintentionally perhaps, opened themselves to charges that their goals and intentions countered the expectations of their "Americanized" neighbors while the tendency to cling to and maintain their Japanese cultural and linguistic heritage undercut, in the eyes of the Anglo majority, any claims they might have made concerning a willingness and ability to assimilate into the surrounding culture.

All this changed rapidly beginning in 1924. Thereafter, although many continued to enjoy great economic success within the smaller context of the ethnic community itself, those who did not or could not find suitable employment within the ethnic economy increasingly were forced to branch out into the larger Anglo society in search of success. Like it or not, individual Japanese immigrants "had to learn the language, customs, habits, and practices of the host society in order to make headway and gain an economic foothold in their newly adopted society." Once they made a determined effort to do so, and aided by hard

work, perseverance, and a value system "compatible with that of the American middle class," the Japanese immigrant community made quick strides toward acculturation and acceptance.[18] Although the ultimate success of these assimilation efforts is due to both compatible value systems and an ingrained willingness to adapt the customs of a perceivably advanced culture in order to achieve valued success, in the end it was surely prompted to some degree as well by pragmatic reaction to the anti-Japanese bias evident in the 1924 debate over exclusion and by an understanding that anti-Japanese bias in the United States was rooted in the question of "assimilability."

Our extended discussion of the Immigration Act and its effect on internal, diplomatic, and international affairs involving the United States, Japan, and the Japanese immigrant community resident in the United States begins with a consideration of the political process by the which the proposed legislation became law. An analysis of the variety of political, diplomatic, social, and cultural influences affecting passage of the bill follows, attempting to clarify some of the significant reasons behind approval of the legislation. The chapter concludes with a discussion of the impact of the act's passage in historical perspective, considering both internal ramifications among the resident Japanese immigrant population and international influences exerted on Japanese attitudes toward the United States.

## THE POLITICAL PROCESS: ENACTING THE IMMIGRATION ACT

The time period between February and May 1924—between the initial introduction of the Immigration Act of 1924 and its eventual approval by President Coolidge—encompasses an apt illustration of the mechanisms and maneuvering typical of the progress of a bill through the legislative branch of the U.S. government. The process involved illustrates as well the myriad influences likely to impact the course of any piece of important legislation as it works its way toward becoming law. In this particular instance, in the case of the Immigration Act, we can also see how little impact rational analysis of the bill's content and of its international ramifications had on the course of events. The passage of the Immigration Act of 1924 was, in fact, more the product of internal domestic political considerations than of deliberate debate over the actual content of the legislation itself.

The process began February 9, 1924, with the formal introduction of the bill into the House of Representatives by vote of the House Committee on Immigration and Naturalization. A similar bill had been presented to the preceding 67th Session of Congress year earlier but had died before being taken up in either chamber, the result of a crowded legislative docket.[19] The bill came to the full House with the endorsement of Committee Chair Albert Johnson (R-WA) and the majority of committee members, most of whom hailed from Southern and Western constituencies known to be hostile to unfettered immigration.

The intent of the newly introduced legislation was clearly to maintain the United States as a "Nordic" preserve by severely limiting the right of immigration of those considered "alien," described in the accompanying report as those with "but a slight knowledge of America and American institutions" who represented "a great undigested mass of alien thought, alien sympathy, and alien purpose [and] . . . a menace to the social, political, and economic life of the country."[20] A secondary economic purpose was to slow the arrival of additional unskilled labor whose presence was assumed to depress wages.[21]

In pursuit of this end, the proposed legislation included a clause denying the right of immigration entirely to what the bill described as "aliens ineligible to citizenship," a group taken to represent only those of Asian origins. A series of interpretations by the Supreme Court of various Naturalization Acts passed by the United States

Congress between 1790 and 1906 (most recently in *Ozawa v. U.S.* which had extended its application to Japanese immigrants) had denied resident Asians the right to become naturalized citizens of the United States. Past domestic legislation, as mentioned earlier, had already narrowed this definition significantly through the denial of immigration rights specifically to Chinese and most other Asians through the Chinese exclusion laws and the Asiatic Barred Zone Act (both of which were to remain in force).[22] In the debate over exclusion, then, the phrase was commonly taken to apply only to those of Japanese origin. Japanese immigration, thus, was to be prohibited entirely. If the proposed legislation were to become the law of the land, thereafter no "alien ineligible to citizenship," that is, no citizen of Japan, was to be admitted to the United States "save diplomatic staff, tourists, students, seamen, and persons on temporary business."[23]

All other nationalities were to be admitted to the United States as immigrants on the basis of the number of foreign-born nationals in this country at the time of the 1890 census, only 2 percent of that number permitted to each year. In the House debate that followed beginning April 5, 1924, these provisions became the focus of concern as representatives from the urban, industrialized areas of the nation contended that the census base ought to be shifted from 1890 to 1910, the latter more reflective of a rising tide of immigration from other than England, Germany, and Scandinavian nations. Just as in this debated the basic notion of imposing strict immigration quotas was never seriously challenged, so, too, the House debate never questioned the appropriateness of imposing Asian exclusion in its consideration of the provisions of the Immigration Act.

Not that the issue of exclusion went completely unremarked upon during this initial period of the bill's consideration by the House. Secretary of State Charles Evans Hughes, in a letter to Albert Johnson in mid-March, put forth the executive branch position opposing the incorporation of the exclusion clause. Hughes' memorandum indicated that, while he tended to agree with the House Committee on Immigration and Naturalization opinion that the Japanese represented a group of undesirable immigrants, he (and, by extension, President Coolidge) disagreed with the method of halting such immigration.[24] Hughes pointed out that the proposed legislation conflicted with Article I of the Treaty of 1911 with Japan, which guaranteed Japanese the "liberty to enter, travel, and reside [in the United States] . . . carry on trade, wholesale and retail, to own or lease and occupy houses, manufactories and shops [and] . . . to lease land for residential and commercial purposes."[25] The secretary of state also pointed out that Japanese resentment over exclusion would undermine relations with the United States, relations which had been improving as of late due to the results of the Washington Naval Conference and the outpouring of American relief to Japan following the disastrous Great Kanto Earthquake of September 1923. Indeed, to Hughes, the exclusion clause was not needed at all, since, although not formally barred from the right to immigrate to the United States, Japanese emigrants leaving Japan were prevented from coming to the United States under provision contained in the Gentlemen's Agreement of 1908.[26]

As a result of the Hughes comments, the bill was briefly returned to committee and revised so as to accommodate the provision of the 1911 treaty. To accomplish this, the revised version created an exempt class of aliens—"an alien entitled to enter the Untied States solely to carry on trade under and in pursuance of the provisions of a present existing treaty of commerce and navigation."[27]

The Hughes letter, however, perhaps unintentionally, opened discussion among House members on another issue, the legality of the Gentlemen's Agreement. In the debate over the revised version of the immigration bill, the Gentlemen's Agreement was declared not a legal treaty, because it had never been granted the requisite congressional approval. Furthermore, it was seen not to be an example of Wilsonian "open covenant openly arrived at" since it had been negotiated secretly in 1908 between the executive branch and the Japanese government, its provisions never publicly disseminated and discussed. To House members, always jealous of their constitutional prerogatives, to be reminded of the Gentlemen's Agreement was to recall an historical instance in which the Congress surrendered to the executive branch its responsibility for international treaty negotiations. Many also asserted that the Gentlemen's Agreement itself represented a surrender of an internal American prerogative, the right to control immigration within its borders, to a foreign power, the government of Japan. The debate over the exclusion clause thus became mired in "matters of principle."[28]

The debate over the exclusion clause also pointed out that the Gentlemen's Agreement had not succeeded in its intention in that Japanese immigrants continued to come to the United States, most often as the wives of male Japanese immigrant residents. Those seeking to impose exclusion pointed out that the resident Japanese population had increased substantially since 1908, a clear indication that the intention of the Gentlemen's Agreement was being thwarted.[29]

Other points made in the debated noted that not to exclude Japanese (and other Asian) immigrants would bring the new law into conflict with existing naturalization law as interpreted by the Supreme Court. Further, since existing immigration regulations already effectively barred all other Asian immigration, to not include the Japanese would amount to unwarranted discrimination![30]

Some attempt was also made in the debate to place the exclusion clause in the frame of Japanese international expansionism and to intimate that, by doing nothing, the United States ran the risk of permitting Japan to establish political control of the entire Pacific Basin. Since Japanese immigrants were not permitted to become

American citizens through naturalization, they remained technically subjects of the Japanese empire. This not only precluded assimilation but established a "fifth column" presence among an immigrant group which continued to owe allegiance to a foreign government in the United States, a group primed to aid Japan in her expansionist frenzy.[31]

This aside having been considered, however, the focus of the debate returned to Europe with the exclusion clause considered an unquestioned and integral feature of the pending legislation. Gradually opposition to the inclusion of the exclusion clause came to be regarded as an act of political "suicide."[32] By the conclusion of the debate "not only was the bill as a whole assured of passage but . . . the Pacific Coast had inextricably fastened Japanese exclusion to the same flagpole from which the banner of general immigration restriction was flyings."[33]

Still the administration's opposing voice would not be quieted. Its concern with the Japanese reaction to the inclusion of the exclusion clause in the pending bill pushed them to make a second attempt to influence the course of the House discussion. On April 12, 1924, Theodore E. Burton (R-OH), a spokesperson for the administration, rose in the chamber to voice disapproval of the continued inclusion of the exclusion clause. "His speech, which opponents of exclusion have since come to regard as a classic, was more than anything else a formal registering for the record of the Administration's disapproval."[34] Again, as in the past, this objection came more out of concern with the means employed rather than to question the end result accomplished. The speech went unheralded and was followed, almost at once, by passage of the proposed bill by a vote of 326 to 71.

Opposition to the legislation, primarily from representatives of urban and industrial areas, was remarkably nonpartisan with thirty-three Republicans and thirty-seven Democrats opposed to passage;[35] all, however, were essentially protesting the legislation's use of the 1890 census as the base on which European immigration quotas were to be figured. No one opposed the bill because of the incorporation of the clause excluding those ineligible to citizenship from the right to immigrate to the United States.[36]

During the first week in April 1924, debate on a similar immigration restriction measure began in the Senate. The Senate version, however, contained some significant differences. The initial version of the Senate bill, for example, shifted the basis for quota restrictions from 1890 to 1910. Tacit recognition of provisions of the Gentlemen's Agreement was also included in the bill's definition of the term "immigrant" which explicitly excluded from the category "any alien entitled to enter the United States under the provision of a treaty or an agreement relating solely to immigration."[37] Japanese merchants (together with members of the diplomatic staff) thus were permitted residence status under terms of the 1911 treaty while the Gentlemen's Agreement extended similar rights to nonlaborers and the "parents, wives, or children or residents" as well as "settled agriculturists" returning to the United States from periods of residence abroad.

These provisions are evidence that the Senate Committee on Immigration was less provincial than its committee counterpart in the House; the members of the Senate committee were willing to expand quota restrictions placed on European immigrants and were less inclined to purposefully cause affront to the Japanese.[38] The change in the census base also seemingly assured that this provision would become the focus of the Senate debate, leaving the question of exclusion to be dealt with in the joint House-Senate committee convened to consider areas of disagreement between the two versions of the immigration legislation once both had been passed by their respective memberships.

Other considerations boded well for the fate of the exclusion issue in the Senate debates. The foremost proponent for exclusion in the Senate, Hiram W. Johnson

(R-CA), was absent as the debate opened, busily campaigning against the incumbent for the Republican nomination for the presidency of the United States. His California colleague, Republican Senator Samuel M. Shortridge had little of Johnson's considerable prestige and influence and enjoyed much less support from fellow members of the Committee on Immigration than Albert Johnson had in the House of Representatives.[39] The overall leadership of David A. Reed (R-PA) also was uncertain, especially in light of a division among the committee members on which provisions ought to be included in the version of the bill presented to the Senate for debate. When, early on in the debate, Joseph T. Robinson (D-AR) indicated some concern with the willingness of the House to provoke an international crisis rather than continue an existing arrangement accomplishing the same ends,[40] the odds seemed to favor a different outcome from that in the House on the issue of exclusion.

The initial questioning of the need to include the exclusion provision in the Immigration Act in fact continued for some time during the early hours of the Senate debate, led by Southerners using the political opportunity afforded by this bill to counter Shortridges's long-standing support for anti-lynching legislation.[41] One major revelation during this portion of the debate brought the admission that "the net gain of Japanese aliens admitted to this country over those departed during the previous fiscal ear was only 399."[42] Senator Reed refocused the debate once again by voicing support for the alternative proposed by Secretary of State Hughes allowing the current arrangement with Japan concerning emigration to stand unaltered.[43]

This point served to return the Gentlemen's Agreement to center stage. At this juncture, Hiram Johnson, temporarily abandoning the campaign trail, returned to the fray, assuming leadership of the exclusionist cause. In his opening speech on the pending legislation, he asserted that the Gentlemen's Agreement represented not only an infringement of American sovereignty but also a secret agreement that he saw as an executive invasion of congressional prerogative.[44] Even Johnson, however, admitted to only a hazy understanding of the contents of the Gentlemen's Agreement, the provisions of which had never been subject to congressional debate or public scrutiny.

The growing concentration on the reputed contents of the Gentlemen's Agreement led Secretary of State Hughes to urge an explication of the understanding initially reached decades earlier in 1908. He turned to the Japanese ambassador to the United States, Hanihara Masanao, to clarify the contents of the Gentlemen's Agreement. This Ambassador Hanihara did in a letter that proved the turning point in the entire debate over the pending legislation.

The Hanihara letter represented the end product of an extended series of visits, letters, and memoranda on the exclusion issue that had been exchanged between Hughes and the Japanese ambassador over the weeks since the introduction of the Immigration Act before Congress. As early as December 13, 1923, one week after the introduction of the original bill (which was to reintroduced in March of 1924), Hanihara called on Secretary Hughes to object to the inclusion therein of the exclusion provision. A formal written memorandum followed in January of 1924 with an additional note forthcoming in February. These prompted Hughes' original letter to House leadership.

In early April, as the debate in the Senate came increasingly to center on the provisions of the Gentlemen's Agreement itself, Hanihara requested an official memorandum on the agreement from Hughes; and April 8, 1924, State Department memorandum to Hanihara followed with Hanihara's letter to Hughes of April 10, 1924, detailing the Japanese interpretation thereof. The following day, a copy of the exchanges was forwarded to Congress where it was read into the *Congressional Record;* copies of the letters were also released to the press.[45]

The Hanihara letter, in many ways, represented a masterful reading of the situation at hand. Great care was taken by the Japanese ambassador to avoid the appearance of interfering in the internal affairs of the United States.[46] Circumspectly, the letter not only sought to confirm the content of the Gentlemen's Agreement but also to point out the care with which the Japanese had sought to confirm the content of the Gentlemen's Agreement and to point out the care with which the Japanese had sought its effective implementation. The Japanese government in 1922, for example, had halted the common practice of permitting the emigration of "picture brides" to the United States when so requested; likewise, the Japanese willingly had extended the provisions of the agreement to Hawaii and sought to control as well the emigration of laborers to territories adjacent to the continental United States. To better monitor the situation, the Japanese government willingly had shared information on its immigration practices with the United States on a regular basis.[47]

Unfortunately, despite intentions, the Hanihara letter provoked an unexpected reaction, first in the American press and eventually in the Senate. In its concluding paragraph, the letter alluded to the "grave consequences" that might attend any inclusion of an exclusion clause in the pending Immigration Act. This use of the phrase "grave consequences" came to be deemed a veiled threat of retaliation against the United States should the Congress enact any legislation containing an exclusion clause.[48] Later a rumor circulated in London diplomatic circles that the Japanese ambassador had shown the American secretary of state a copy of his intended letter and "it was decided to insert the words 'grave consequences.' It was reported that Secretary Hughes agreed to the insertion, in the hope it would frighten the Senate and prevent passage of the measure."[49] The letter had exactly the opposite effect: it ensured passage instead.

Although the Hanihara letter was read into the *Congressional Record* on April 10 1924, it failed until April 14 to generate a reaction from members of the Senate. The reaction by the Senate was preceded by editorial comment in a number of newspapers across the nation that regarded the phrase "grave consequences" as "very strong" diplomatic language.[50]

Undoubtedly, the strong press reaction was not lost on Senators debating the immigration bill; but other, more overtly political, motivations appear to have prompted the utilization of the "veiled threat" contained in the Japanese ambassador's letter to prompt precipitous action on both the exclusion clause and the larger piece of legislation of which it was an integral part.

A Republican Party caucus was held the morning of April 14, 1924, to discuss the legislation currently before the Congress in light of the ongoing political campaign for the upcoming presidential election scheduled for November. At the time, the Teapot Dome scandal was widening, for the first time implicating a prominent member of the Coolidge cabinet, Andrew W. Mellon, the secretary of the treasury.[51] Democratic members of the Senate, in fact, recently had approved the hiring of a "special counsel" (paid from private funds) to investigate the growing evidence of impropriety, purposefully tweaking the nose of the president whose reaction had been to declare Congress should keep it nose out of matters not concerning it.[52]

In the face of this challenge to Republican power, members of the Republican Senate delegation felt the need to shore up party unity. Central to this plan was the recognized need to regain the support of alienated members from the Pacific Coast. The immediate future held the prospects of a major primary election in California, a contest in which Hiram Johnson figured prominently; although Coolidge was seemingly assured renomination, a Johnson victory (prompted, perhaps, by defeat of the exclusion clause in the immigration bill) might well increase Pacific Coast desertion from party ranks.[53] To quell this possibility—and to distance itself from any close association with foreign protest over Senate actions—the caucus meeting determined to assume a unified congressional stance against the executive branch and its support of the Gentlemen's Agreement alternative to the exclusion clause (even though both were of the same political party affiliation). In doing so, the Republicans realized they were likely to feel little public backlash, to rouse little pro-Japanese response from among the electorate at large.[54]

An extraordinary session of the Senate was then convened almost immediately, a session in which the abrupt turn around of numerous Republicans was readily demonstrated. Henry Cabot Lodge, for example, the Republican floor leader and Chair of the Foreign Relations Committee, exclaimed that he, too, saw the "veiled threat" inherent in the Hanihara letter. Despite the fact that he had been instrumental in suggesting the negotiations leading to the original Gentlemen's Agreement, Lodge now stood with those opposed to recognizing its provisions:

I have always been very friendly to the Japanese people . . . But, Mr. President, the question of immigration . . . is perhaps the greatest of fundamental sovereign right . . . I regret to say that the letter addressed to our State Department by the Ambassador from Japan seems to me improper to be addressed by the representative of one great country to another friendly country. It contains, I regret much to say, a veiled threat.[55]

Although his stance echoes that adopted at the time of the debate over the League of Nations (in which he opposed the League as an unacceptable limitation on national sovereignty), Lodge's shift clearly indicates the primacy attached to party unity in the face of growing external political pressure on the Republican chances for success in the approaching elections. Senator Reed's reversal was similarly remarkable; he attributed his change of heart entirely to the Hanihara letter and the question of national prestige invoked thereby.[56]

The only discordant note was struck by Senator Tom Heflin of Alabama, who with his usual lack of respect for political conventions and courtesies declared that

"it is genuinely refreshing to see Republican leaders back off completely from the position taken on this question last week . . . The Senators from California . . . were fighting on the other side against the Republican-Jap deal almost single handed. The progressives were with us in the fight, and the whole Democratic side stood for American rights in the matter. When Republican leaders discovered that they were whipped, and whipped to a frazzle, they had a hurried conference, had it this morning, and now they come in and say that they take offense at something that a Jap ambassador has written."[57]

The vote that followed to replace the exclusion clause with the provisions of the Gentlemen's Agreement was roundly defeated by a vote of 76 to 2 with 18 not voting.[58] The finalized Senate version, with the exclusion clause intact, was then approved April 16, 1924, and sent to a joint Senate-House committee for reconciliation with the House version.

The Coolidge administration thereafter initiated one last attempt to forestall implementation of the exclusion provision. Initially Coolidge even had hinted at a veto; Ambassador Hanihara, however, had indicated a willingness to negotiate a replacement treaty. Coolidge, therefore, instead prevailed upon the congressional joint committee to allow such negotiations to proceed. Eventually this led to a formal request by the administration to postpone implementation of the Immigration Act long enough to permit negotiations to be undertaken between the two nations in order to redefine the understanding reached in the now-defunct Gentlemen's Agreement to the satisfaction of both parties involved.[59] Once again, political opposition surfaced, however, forcing the administration to abandon this alternative strategy by early May.[60]

By this juncture "Coolidge had accepted the movement for domestic control of Japanese immigration but he had not abandoned his desire to make the break less abrupt by throwing a diplomatic sop to Japan."[61] Final passage of the reconciled legislation became a party matter when members of the Senate discovered the extent of these (essentially secret) diplomatic maneuvers.[62] Coolidge then reluctantly signed the measure into law on May 26, 1924, the measure included to become effective from July 1, 1924.[63]

## ANALYSIS: REASONS BEHIND PASSAGE OF THE IMMIGRATION ACT OF 1924

The convoluted path followed by the Immigration Act as it made its way through Congress in the early months of 1924 was the result of a number of intersecting patterns. In earlier debates over Asian immigration, economic concerns over cheap labor and alien agricultural land ownership often had predominated. In 1924, however, the intersecting patterns determining the nature of the debate emerged instead from a wider variety of political, diplomatic, social, and cultural considerations. Economic concerns played only a minor role.

Politically speaking, as we have seen, the country was in the midst of a major domestic presidential election campaign. Moreover, within the decidedly narrower context of Washington politics, both houses of Congress sensed the time was ripe to attempt to advance their own relative power over and against that of the executive branch of government. Within the ranks of the Republican Party, furthermore, Pacific Coast exclusionists, taking advantage of the politically charged atmosphere, capitalized on the chance provided by the immigration bill to push anew calls for the prohibition of Asian immigration altogether. In the end, these factors all coalesced in prompting the actions we have seen taken with regard to the passage of the Immigration Act of 1924.

Domestic concern with Japan as a rising power on the international scene also clearly colored congressional and popular fears of Japanese emigration among those seeking to include an exclusion clause in the Immigration Act of 1924. State Department officials, the diplomatic community, and the executive branch of government in Washington, however, while similarly concerned with Japan's increased international stature, sought other means to capitalize on a growing sense of *rapproachmant* with Japan following the London and Washington Naval Limitation Conferences and the outpouring of humanitarian aid in the aftermath of the Great Kanto Earthquake. They, too, saw the rising threat of Japan internationally but sought not to limit the opportunity for expansionism per se, but rather to placate the Japanese so as to avoid a confrontation. However, although seeking to avoid ruffling sensitive Japanese feathers, the diplomatic community and the executive branch, in attempting to appease the Japanese, in the end failed to convey to the Japanese government adequately the depth of anti-Japanese sentiment in the United States.

The Japanese thus were misled by American condescension and failed to mount an effective counterattack, not offering, for example, to renegotiate the Gentlemen's Agreement until well after the Senate had acted to void it entirely. Even the force of Japanese public opinion was muted due to a sense that the issue was best left to diplomatic negotiation between governments rather than discussion in the public press.[64] Too long the Japanese allowed the United States to mollify their concerns, convinced that the Americans had their best interests at heart, failing to realize the inherent fear of Japanese expansionism that undergirded their interactions with Japan during this entire period. Though the two diplomatic communities worked together on addressing issues raised in the congressional debate in an attempt to short-circuit American objections to Japanese immigration, never once were the Japanese made aware of the true gravity of the situation (perhaps unrecognized even among the American proxies) nor of the underlying racism shared by all Americans, whatever their political persuasion.

The Japanese in reality were left "out of the loop" on matters critical to an effective diplomatic counterattack. Furthermore, the arrogance with which the executive branch and the diplomatic community approached the debate with Congress left little room for compromise and exhibited no willingness whatsoever to concede anything to the exclusionist stance eventually carrying the day in Congress. Had the American State Department and the executive branch been willing to consult with the Japanese honestly and had both been willing to offer concessions to Congress (as eventually the Japanese independently demonstrated a willingness to do), the situation might have resulted in a facesaving compromise accomplishing exactly what both sides sought: an end to Japanese immigration in such a manner as to preserve Japan's sense of international acceptance as the diplomatic equal of other advanced nation states and the preservation of her unique international position as the only Asian nation not excluded from American immigration privileges. American diplomatic concerns with being branded a "covenant-breaker" on the international scene could also thereby have been avoided.

The long-standing Japanese inability to make common cause with Asians also weakened Japan's bargaining position in diplomatic negotiations over exclusions. Not that the Americans would have likely regarded such a coalition as anything but a greater threat to American sovereignty and prestige, but the unwillingness of the Japanese to counter the American prejudice against Asians in general at any earlier point in the long history of anti-Asian agitation in the United States eventually came home to roost as arguments raised against other Asian communities came to be directed against Japan. Japan's own ingrained racism and her sense of superiority vis-a-vis other Asian nations thereby obviated the possibility of effectively combating racism directed at Japan by the United States.[65]

Negative images and attitudes towards the Japanese, some buttressed by pseudoscientific rationalizations, also played a major role in determining the fate of the legislation before Congress. A generalized indifference in many parts of the United States, areas unaffected by the issues raised by exclusionists, coupled with a general antipathy towards those of another race, remnants from earlier experiences with African slave and Chinese immigrant populations, undoubtedly permitted such rationalizations to carry the day relatively unchallenged.[66]

In the aftermath of the Great War, the United States confronted a remarkably altered international landscape. The world community, in partial reaction to the disarray of the war, had eventually embraced Wilson's principles for international accord. In the United States, however, the reaction to the Great War served to highlight the disadvantages of being drawn into the problems and conflicts of "Old World" Europe. Many Americans came to evidence a preference for withdrawal over involvement as a result, and their opinion came to prevail even in Congress, as shown by the ultimate rejection of the League of Nations.[67]

To many Americans, the world was becoming an increasingly dangerous place. Witness the rise of socialism, communism, syndicalism, and anarchy as political alternatives to the democratic experiment, which until so recently had seemed the wave of the future. American uncertainty in the face of such challenges, an uncertainty arising from a feeling of vulnerability and an underlying lack of faith in the ability of democratic institution to withstand the onslaught of "alien" ideologies, led many to champion withdrawal from the international arena into the relative safety of "American" values and institutions.[68]

This fear of the consequences of involvement in internal European affairs came increasingly to be coupled with an awareness that the United States was vulnerable as well to the transfer from Europe, Asia, and Africa of the problems plaguing "the Old World," problems which, in turn, would inevitably lead to the "importation" of radical solutions also emergent in these Old World settings. The need to protect the United States internally from both the problems of the Old World and their contemporary alternative philosophical agendas for change led inevitably to the wholesale adoption in almost every strata of American society and politics of the recognized need to limit immigration, an issue of particular concern during the 1920s and throughout the nation among those increasingly identifiable as "nativists," be they Progressives, conservative Republicans, or Socialists.[69]

Earlier concerns with the influx of immigrant populations had been in many ways based on economic considerations and fears. Europeans and Chinese immigrants willing to work for minimal salaries depressed wages; the diligence of those seeking to capitalize on the opportunities present in American agriculture competed with established agricultural populations, drove down prices, and captured market share with quality products. Slave labor from Africa gave an advantage to Southern farmers not available in the North. Labor unions and agribusiness interests were among the earliest and strongest advocates of immigration restriction efforts as a result.[70]

But the post-war world was much more attuned to the cultural and philosophical challenges presented by the world at large in the 1920s. Americans no longer seemed as convinced of the universal applicability of the model that had matured in the United States since the Revolutionary War. Where once they had confidently watched as Europe and Asia sought to emulate the American political and philosophical alternatives represented by the democratic impulse, many Americans now saw instead challenges from abroad mounted against an uncertain champion. The need to preserve the American experiment held more persuasive power than did a concern with low

wages and agricultural competition. As a result, these alternative issues were only infrequently raised in the 1924 debates over immigration restriction and played a remarkably small role in the arguments raised in favor of exclusion.

In place of the economic emphasis evident in earlier debates over immigration limitations, the debates in 1924 centered much more on the question of the ability to assimilate—"assimilability." Social Darwinian concepts postulated by Herbert Spencer and others had gained widespread currency in an era increasingly dominated by the search for scientifically foreordained perfectibility.[71] Competition as the primary means of interaction between and among social groups, cultural and national entities, for many, became an accepted frame within which to view the advancement of civilization in the international arena.

Those who had thrown their lot in with the forces of democracy, in light of this overall orientation, knew they had to take steps to preserve that cultural, political, and philosophical entity with which they had identified themselves and their future. Even American socialists and others of a more radical bent agreed that the United States represented a unique cultural and political entity worth preserving; they, too, argued against keeping the door open for whomever might appear on the threshold. To do otherwise was nothing short of irresponsible.[72]

Americans were very conscious as well of the role race played in conceptions associated with Social Darwinian theory. Race mixing through intermarriage was a sure way to weaken the gene pool and to undercut the ability of the larger group to survive the competition with "alien" entities. Since most Americans were themselves Caucasian and accepted as well their innate racial superiority, this proved yet another basis on which to limit immigration rights in the interest of cultural self-preservation.

"Assimilability" essentially was recognized during the 1920s as "the faculty of merging into the population, becoming an integral part of the nation, without causing friction or antagonism." It was seen to entail a far-reaching consideration of such matters as "[c]ustoms and traditions, both social and political, standards of living, color, and intermarriage."[73] The Japanese, particularly, failed to fit into American expectations in these areas due both to racial differences and to "great disparity in customs."

Even the common awareness that the Japanese had followed a program of Westernization in quest of modernization in Japan itself failed to convince many that assimilation was even remotely possible; most Americans aware of such advances dismissed Japanese successes in this regard as merely a manifestation of surface change, a superficial adaptation to American manners and more which, if anything, hinted at the extent to which Japan would go to infiltrate the West Coast of the United States with immigrants acting as colonization agents for their homeland government masters.[74]

In fact, many Americans, examining Japan's growing list of colonial possessions, were all too aware that Japanese immigrants in the United States, denied the right to become naturalized citizens, remained subjects of the Japanese emperor, intimately involved with a potentially hostile and competitive foreign power intent on continuing a foreign policy of active overseas colonization in the Pacific Basin and elsewhere.[75]

Stereotypes played a major role in setting the collective Caucasian mind against those of Japanese descent becoming assimilated into the American mainstream. There has existed from the earliest days of American interactions with Asia a set of positive and negatives images and attitudes trotted out as needed to justify American interactions with nations and peoples in Asia. The basic tendency with respect to East Asians has been to divide the image into two categories—positive and negative images—and to apply each subset in turn to either the Japanese or the Chinese. That is, whenever Americans were favorably disposed toward China, they applied the subset of positive images in their Oriental repertoire to the Chinese, seeing them in the 1920s, for example, as victims of imperialism, potential converts to Christianity, and diligent students of Western culture and civilization.[76] The negative set of images in such a situation seemed inevitably to identify the "other East Asians," in this case the Japanese, who in the 1920s inherited the set of attitudes earlier associated with the Yellow Peril, a particularly virulent threat in an era all too well aware of Japan's growing imperialist appetite.

Interestingly, as Dennis Ogawa has pointed out in his assessment of these stereotypes in *From Japs to Japanese: An Evolution of Japanese American Stereotypes*, these unflattering images were not based on direct knowledge or experience but instead inevitably reflected the negation of those traits seen as particularly characteristic of the ideal American—just as the "good images" reflected those characteristics favored among true (Anglo) Americans. Hence, when Japanese immigrants are viewed as lazy, untrustworthy, and dishonest, as "bandy-legged, bugaboos, miserable, craven, simian, degenerated, rotten little devils,"[77] this assessment emerged more from a willingness to portray an unknown ethnic immigrant group in as negative a light as possible rather than from any attempt to accurately portray the Japanese or to depict with insight aspects of Japanese social, political, or cultural mores. The ultimate result was to make assimilation appear an even more remote possibility.

In this respect, the tendency of Japanese immigrant groups to congregate in a few concentrated areas, particularly in California, worked to the ultimate disadvantage of the immigrant group as a whole. Only a few Americans came into sustained and intimate contract with Japanese immigrants, who in the early 1920s constituted only a small number of the total immigrant tide; most lived in a six-county block in rural California, engaged in either interethnic enterprises serving the Japanese community or in agriculture. This meant only a relatively few Americans, most (because of a fear of economic competition) with an inherent willingness to portray the Japanese in a negative light, came into contact with Japanese immigrants. These few Americans framed the discourse that emphasized the inability of this immigrant community to assimilate successfully into the American mainstream.

The emergent image stressed racial differences and what were portrayed as innate cultural distinctions. Skin color and slanted eyes, small stature together with differences in diet, language, and religion were frequently cited as evidence that the Japanese immigrant represented essentially an unassimilable alien community. Even their admittedly positive virtues were seen to instill unbecoming cockiness and arrogant pride among the "bucktoothed and bespeckled" minority while their struggle to learn and communicate in English left them open to ridicule directed toward their peculiar patterns of speech. Family and group solidarity were similarly subject to negative evaluation as undercutting the American devotion to individualism and self-sufficiency. Their "clannish" behavior left them open to charges that they sought to evade established laws and would remain forever aloof from the political processes associated with the workings of democracy.[78]

Those who interacted directly with the Japanese portrayed them as careless in their work, filthy and ignorant of habits of personal hygiene, tricky, and sly. Japanese were pictured as disloyal, immoral, and sexually promiscuous and as products of "a low standard of civilization, living, and wages."[79] Few objective observers would associate the majority of these characterization with the Japanese; these images represented instead negative aspects of those positive characteristics most frequently associated with ideal American values and traits.

Exclusionist propaganda played on innate American fears surfacing during the 1920s reflecting a growing unease with respect to the ability of the American Dream to flourish in the face of advancing foreign alternatives, and the crisis of spirit led many to lend credence to those calling for the elimination of internal threats to American homogeneity in order to keep the existing nation state and its political, social, religious, and cultural system intact even among those with no contact whatsoever with the Japanese immigrant group being so branded as unassimilable.[80]

Based on ignorance or a misreading of observed traits, reflecting exaggerations and prejudgements centered on an unwarranted negation of widely held views of positive traits shared by "real Americans," frequently buttressed by intellectual or pseudoscientific rationalization, the Japanese immigrants in the 1920s were subsequently seen as "highly un-American, inferior citizens sexually aggressive and part of an international menace."[81] Their geographical concentration in the West and the prior American experience with the Chinese also worked against the Japanese immigrant community, giving rise to organized campaigns and fears of the Yellow Peril in the press, in political circles, among labor groups, and within such fraternal and patriotic organizations as the American Legion and the Native Sons of the Golden West.

In the light of the growing presence of such a negative set of stereotypes, that earlier attempts to halt immigration from Japan through the Gentlemen's Agreement could be portrayed as a failure added fuel to the flame of the exclusionist argument. In fact, the Japanese immigrant community with the seeming connivance of the Japanese government had managed to circumvent many of the restrictions imposed on their activities in the United States.[82] Alien Land Laws, too, had been circumvented by the formation of corporate entities, by the registration of land in the name of citizen children, and by collective entities seen to operate outside the intent of the law.

An example of ways in which Japanese immigrants were perceived to be working hand in glove with the Japanese government to circumvent the intention of the American government and diplomatic community can be discerned in the way in which Japanese immigrants handled marriage arrangements after 1907. The Gentlemen's Agreement of 1908 to end emigration from Japan to the United States had seen the basic threat as emergent from transient Japanese labor; therefore, the ban had not been extended to the wives and families of Japanese (male) laborers who might decide to stay and settle down in the United States. Japanese marriages traditionally have been viewed as transactions uniting families and not as the outgrowth of an established love relationship between two individuals. This pattern came into use among the Japanese immigrant community as a means to allow Japanese immigrant males to establish family units in the United States. Japanese law permitted marriage registrations to occur by proxy; a Japanese male living in the United States, therefore, was able to search out a willing bride "at home," marry her by proxy in Japan, and then have her join him in the United Sates without violating the ban on immigration. These "picture brides" further swelled the Japanese immigrant population by producing children. In this way the inadequate premises of the Gentlemen's Agreement of 1908 contributed to the rising tide of exclusionist fervor on the West Coast and among exclusionists nationwide.

The Japanese government and diplomatic community, throughout the period in question, had shown itself remarkably concerned with the fate of its emigrant communities wherever they were domiciled.[83] Following the British lead in assuming an association between the treatment of emigrants and international status and prestige, Japanese officials carefully evaluated the treatment of overseas Japanese communities, intent on maintaining national prestige at all costs. In fact, even when their actions undercut the rights and privileges of the Japanese immigrant, the government in Japan often took up an issue seeking a resolution that would maintain the international position assumed so important by Japan. In 1922, for example,

the Japanese government informed the United States, in reaction to growing agitation concerning the arrival of "picture brides," that they (the Japanese) would no longer permit such wives to leave Japan if their destination were the United States.[84] Clearly under such circumstances—as shown in the later diplomatic interchanges over the Immigration Act of 1924—it appears likely that the Japanese would have undertaken to satisfy American objections in whatever manner was open to them—had they known the full extent of those objections.

Instead, the American government, governed by an ingrained need to placate an increasingly powerful Pacific threat and confident of its ability to carry off the task successfully, persisted in maintaining that the internal fight over exclusion amounted to little and that, acting as Japan's proxy, the American diplomatic community and the executive branch of government could win out in their objections to the inclusion of exclusionist language in the 1924 immigration bill.

This stance prevailed despite the fact that, privately and in internal communications within the United States, Japan's major proxies—including both Hughes and Coolidge (and many of their predecessors)—harbored racist sentiments closer to those held by exclusionists than they ever let on to in their communications with the Japanese.[85] American proxies for Japan thus were never passionately committed to forestalling exclusion; most supported the end result advocated by exclusionists, disagreeing only on how best to achieve that result. Furthermore, however much the executive branch and the diplomatic community saw the issue in terms of its international ramifications and the need to appease Japan, generally the congressional debate failed to consider the issue as grounded in the international arena; they viewed it essentially as an internal matter, a debate over how best to slow the tide of immigrants not easily assimilated into American culture and civilization. Such a stance seriously undermined any opportunity to mount a well reasoned or truly effective ethical or moral counter-argument against exclusionism per se. As a result, political expediency and an unthinking extremism carried the day against moderation in the politically charged atmosphere of the times.

## EVALUATION OF THE REACTION AMONG JAPANESE RESIDENTS IN THE UNITED STATES TO PASSAGE OF THE IMMIGRATION ACT

In the eyes of the United States Congress—and eventually the executive branch of the government as well—passage of the Immigration Act in 1924 served to establish the important legislative principle that "all immigration into the United States shall be a matter solely for domestic consideration."[86] During the debate over the bill, as we have seen, the Gentlemen's Agreement (which the exclusion provisions of the legislation eventually replaced) had come to be interpreted as the ultimate surrender of national interest and an illegal international agreement rightfully abrogated by the new legislation.[87] Even President Coolidge, one of those most opposed to the original bill when initially introduced before Congress, at the time of his January 1924 inauguration for a second term, saw the new immigration act as a valid defensive action undertaken for national self-protection.[88]

Indeed, passage of the Immigration Act of 1924 simply confirmed in legislative form the general temper of the times concerning the need to limit further immigration into the United States. A canvas of congressional votes taken on April 8, 1924, several days before eventual Senate passage of the legislation, showed fifty-four confirmed votes in favor of exclusion even before the receipt of the Hanihara letter; this support would have proved enough to assure passage of the proposed legislation on its own merits. The letter from the Japanese ambassador, to be sure, allowed a politically expedient "change of heart" among those Senators concerned with congressional party solidarity in an election year; however, others merely used the Hanihara communication to buttress their own previously established leanings acquired well before receipt of the letter threatening "grave consequences."[89]

Even more obviously, the entire process leading to the adoption of the Immigration Act was in retrospect quite clearly "tailored to fit exclusively home needs and wishes."[90]

> In regular order the problem of the Southern vote—its relation to the Dyer anti-lynching bill, the issue of Congressional prerogative, the questions of the senatorial investigations and of party loyalty, the need for thinking of the Pacific Coast's presidential vote, to say nothing of the Pacific Coast's racial future—in regular order those internal points of conflict became the determinants that guided the Senate.[91]

As had been true in the earlier debate over the peace settlement at the conclusion of the World War I, domestic considerations were of notably more importance than questions of foreign policy in opinions voiced during the course of the debate; and short-range, pragmatic, internal political needs far outweighed long-range, altruistic, international, and diplomatic concerns in determining the final outcome.[92]

Judged on this criteria the measure might well be seen as a rousing success: Coolidge did in fact escape Pacific Coast Republican party censure and was elected to a second term in November. There were, however, a multitude of other unforeseen, long-term ramifications of the passage of the Immigration Act in 1924 that lingered for decades, profoundly influencing the course of history, both internal and external, long after initial passage of the original legislation.

Politically, the passage of the Immigration Act, although only a blip in the collective memory of the American public at large, signaled (together with trends visible elsewhere in American life in 1924) a retreat from the priniciple of progressive Wilsonianism into isolationism, discriminatory exclusivity, and cultural protectionism. This retreat occurred in the face of what was perceived by many Americans as an increasingly coercive ideological threat from abroad. Psychological determinants operable at the time reflected these internal Nativistic uncertainties, raised in the face of communism and other radical political philosophies as well as fear engendered by a continuing concern with a "rising tide of color" in a racist society, mattered much more than did any rational confrontation with issues of, say, economic competition or overpopulation. However important many saw the principles established by the new immigration law to be, in fact the issue was carried along more on emotional grounds than on the basis of rational argument.

Some initial American press reaction reflected a measure of chagrin over the resulting (seemingly irrational) actions taken by the two houses of Congress. The *New York Times* on April 15, 1924, for instance, saw passage of the Immigration Act as yet "another example of . . . legislative intemperance." Another extended analysis in the *New York Commercial* felt the entire issue had been bungled badly, giving undue prominence to the unfortunate use of inappropriate diplomatic language in the Japanese ambassador's letter. The *Boston Evening Transcript* (April 15, 1924), however, disagreed, proclaiming the Hanihara letter to be clearly "a veiled threat against our peace."[93]

The general public reaction appears to have taken the middle ground between these two extremes and has been characterized as having "regarded the incident with regret, with a certain amount of bewilderment, but usually with determination."[94] Most Americans appeared to have adopted the position advanced by the *Cincinnati Enquirer*: "the crux of the matter is that the United States, like Canada and Australia, must be kept a white man's country."[95] The Immigration Act, in the eyes of an approving public, had quite clearly established that principle alongside that of asserting congressional control over the immigration process.

The limitations established in 1924 were in fact not revised until 1965; and, as a result, after 1924 "[r]eal immigration . . . [from Japan] almost entirely stopped."[96] Had the exclusion provision been omitted, the Immigration Act would have permitted no more than one hundred new Japanese immigrants per year under the quota system established in the legislation. Hence the impact of exclusion itself on Japanese immigration per se was negligible. Recognizing this, later attempts were made, proposed by the conciliatory California Council of Oriental Relations, to revise the legislation to include Japan under the quota provison.[97] Such a face-saving retreat, however, never materialized, and the exclusion provisions remained in effect unaltered until 1965.

Nativistic exclusionist sentiment continued as well to extend to the treatment of Japanese immigrant residents and their citizen offspring. Early in 1925 some concern was voiced, for example, over the reemergence of "picture brides" in the guise of "tourist brides," Japanese women visiting the United States as tourists who married resident immigrants, then left when their visas expired only to return at a later date, once again on tourist visas, to give birth to "native American citizens."[98] Measures proposed to deal with this issue including permanently banning from citizenship rights those born to parents themselves "aliens ineligible to citizenship." Although such legislation never was approved, for an extended period, second generation Japanese immigrant women (Nisei) born into American citizenship were deprived of that citizenship, should they marry a first generation Japanese immigrant (Issei) himself ineligible to citizenship. The segregation of Nisei school children also continued to be permitted under the provisions of the Supreme Court decision in *Plessy v. Fergeson* establishing the doctrine of "separate but equal," a legal standard not overturned until 1954.[99]

Nativistic sentiment never attempted to assure the assimilation of the Japanese immigrant community already present in the United States into the Anglo-American mainstream; clearly this position was reflective of a conviction that such assimilation was an impossibility. For the larger community, then, the Immigration Act served to define the ongoing legal position and status of the Japanese immigrant minority within American society until World War II. For most Americans, the Japanese immigrant community came to represent both an unassimilated and unassimilable alien presence within the United States. In due course, such an assumption would form the basis upon which incarceration of the immigrant minority community was to be defended during World War II.

Within the Japanese immigrant community itself, the impact of the Immigration Act was much more substantial than in the larger Anglo-American world. One indication of the larger concern with which this issue was considered can be seen in the extensive number of analytical articles inquiring into the meaning to be attached to the actions taken by the Congress which appeared in Japanese-language periodicals published in the United States for the indigenous Japanese immigrant community.[100] This profound and prolonged concern with analysis indicates just how strongly the legislation impacted the attitudes of Japanese immigrants resident in the United States.

The reactions inspired by this concern in turn led to numerous defensive responses. As a whole, the immigrant community tended to withdraw into itself, creating a defensive perimeter against the obvious prejudice present in the larger surroundings. Over the years, few sought to escape the relative security of the resulting sanctuaries, and, as a result, the concentration of Japanese immigrants in a few Pacific Coast states continued until well into the period of the World War II. These communities, no longer open to an influx of newly arrived residents from Japan, also became more stable and settled than they had been in the past.[101]

Most immigrants likewise kept to established positions in agriculture and petty shopkeeping, unwilling to risk economic adventurism in such a hostile environment. Within these self-contained, quiet, stable communities, Japanese immigrants kept to themselves, content for the most part to avoid confrontation with their racially prejudiced Anglo-American neighbors.

In the years following passage of the Immigration Act, most immigrant families—many of whom had not participated actively for years—withdrew from membership in the Japanese associations, groups whose purpose had been eclipsed by congressional action in passing the Immigration Act. No longer were the associations needed to act as agents for the Japanese government in arranging return visits to the homeland or as sources for the visas needed to assure proper immigration procedures were followed for those seeking to come to the United States from Japan.

As interest in the Japanese Association declined, second generation Japanese Americans, the Nisei, in many instances turned toward assimilation as the requisite response to their precarious position in American society. In the early 1930s this led in turn to the formal founding of the Japanese American Citizens League (JACL). The JACL, which was later to become an important political action committee speaking out on issues of interest and importance to the Japanese American community, was clearly structured in these early years to emphasize the quest for assimilation among Japanese in the immigrant community.

Although the larger Caucasian community held to the position that such assimilation was patently impossible, the Nisei generation nonetheless took up the cause with determination. Their parents had already demonstrated their willingness to throw off centuries of tradition during the Meiji era in Japan (between 1868 and 1912) when the Japanese as a whole showed a remarkable ability to successfully adopt—and adapt—aspects of Western civilization and culture deemed useful in accelerating the transition to an increasingly modern society.[102] Such adjustment on the part of the Japanese were often not recognized by the larger outside world because of ingrained familiarity and a sense that equated "Western" and "modern." The Japanese, however, had mastered the art of selective adaptation of Western ways in pursuit of modernization, and Japanese emigrants carried such skills with them into their new foreign homeland. Nisei inherited these attitudes and skills from the Issei generation and willingly put them to use the United States in a pragmatic reaction to the situation in which they found themselves: if assimilation was what was required, the Nisei would see to its accomplishment.

Numerous values inherent in the Japanese community contributed to the ultimate success of this effort. Many of these basic values were similar to middle-class American values, necessitating minimal alteration in order for the Japanese to fit themselves into the value system of the larger society and move towards successful adaptation to the American demands for assimilation. Education, for example, became an increasingly important conduit for success among second generation Japanese Americans, leading many in this generation to excel academically—or at the very least to come under parental pressure to succeed in school in order to enter to the larger society.

As a result of such determination and because of the settled, concentrated, inward-turning nature of Japanese American community life, it could be reliably reported by outside observers in writings about Japanese Americans that within a few short years that they were "on the road to a life that is conventional in most respects" and that "the obstacles of divided allegiance, language, and customs are disappearing" thus indicating that Japanese Americans were "becoming free of every handicap save color." It was this latter barrier, however, in the view of contemporary observers, which was likely to keep them "a permanently separate group distinct from the main part of the population,"

viewed as innately and inherently inferior, however much that status might be contradicted by the realities of life within the Japanese American community itself.[103] After all, so outside observers held, surface appearances often concealed underlying differences difficult, if not impossible, to overcome.

Another group within the Japanese immigrant community approached the issue of acceptance from a somewhat different perspective. However much these immigrants intended to make their permanent home in the United States, these Japanese immigrants sought to assure that, should the situation in the United States deteriorate further, the intact family unit would be able to return with relatively little inconvenience to resettle in Japan. These families sought to assure a successful resettlement, should it become mandatory, by sending at least one son to Japan during his formative years to receive a Japanese education. Unfortunately, these Japanese-educated Japanese American citizens known as *Kibei*, frequently returned to the United States—especially during the 1930s—quite alienated both from the larger Japanese American community and from mainstream American society as a result of the increasingly patriotic tone of "indoctrination" they were subject to under the Japanese educational system then in place in Japan.

Another defensive reaction also causing a certain amount of friction within the Japanese immigrant community was essentially political, taking the form of active involvement in socialist and other liberal causes. Those involved here were drawn to radical causes as a result of the acceptance in their minds of ideological explanations for American behavior that seemed particularly apt to Japanese immigrants subject to such blatant prejudice and racism as shown during this period and symbolized by passage of the Immigration Act.

Clearly, within the Japanese immigrant community, the most far-reaching effects were to bring the community together in a defensive posture, to induce both stability and community solidarity, to bring into play a dedication to achievement through education, and to motivate a desire for assimilation into the larger surrounding community. However, even in its darkest hour, the community's reaction was far from uniform; some sought, as we have seen, not assimilation, but maintenance of ties to Japan while others became, not withdrawn and fearful, but politically active in socialist circles, determined to oppose racism and prejudice within the majority community.

## THE INTERNATIONAL IMPACT

In Japan the Immigration Act, frequently termed the "Japanese Exclusion Act" in press accounts, "was seen as an unjust and discourteous insult to Japan. It represented an indirect incurred obligations under the terms of the Gentlemen's Agreement. More importantly, by singling out Japan specifically in the exclusion provision, the United States was [seen to be] undermining Japan's international position and maligning her national honor and prestige on racial grounds alone. All this despite the facts that Japan[ese] immigration into the United States had been minimal since 1908 and the Japanese government had adhered scrupulously to the provisions of earlier informal agreements."[104]

Initial Japanese reaction to the introduction of the Immigration Act for congressional consideration in early 1924 had elicited little overt concern at either the government level or in the arena of popular and press opinion. After all, the Japanese government had been assured by its American counterparts that those in the executive branch opposed such legislation as unnecessary; and exclusionist sentiment was assumed to reflect only the opinions of a West Coast minority among Americans.[105] Interationalists held control of the political apparatus in Japan during this period; and this contributed to the benign attitude assumed toward initial word that an exclusionist clause was to be incorporated in the pending legislation.[106] Furthermore, Japanese popular and press opinion had been generally favorable toward the United States since the successful conclusion of the Washington Naval Disarmament Conference of 1922, especially so in the aftermath of the outpouring of largesse following the devastating Great Kanto Earthquake of September 1923. More importantly, perhaps, most Japanese found the issue of less than great moment, if only because under the conditions imposed by the Gentlemen's Agreement, only a very few—those with relatives already in the United States—could hope to take advantage of emigration rights, should they seek to enter the United States.[107] In fact, much of the initial press and public notice given the Immigration Act was not directed toward the United States at all, but rather was taken as yet another illustration of Japanese diplomatic weakness and brought in its wake a critique of Japanese foreign policy, especially regarding matters of emigration.[108]

When optimism aroused by early opposition to exclusion in the American press and at the executive level failed to bring a settlement of the exclusion issue, the Japanese press, once again aroused to watchfulness, began to examine the issues involved more closely. Many emerged from the exercise increasingly convinced of the inevitability of passage, citing an abandonment of democratic principles in the face of inherent racism as a major reason.[109]

"The vast majority recognized that basically the United States had justifiable reasons for the pursuit of her present immigration policies. She did have a right to limit immigration to protect her cultural identity and the basis of her economic livelihood; she also had the right to settle the issue free from international interference—so long as that action had only domestic impact."[110] However, Hori Mitsukame, a Tokyo Commercial University professor, in a speech before the Pan Pacific Club in Tokyo given April 25, 1924, seeking the total exclusion of Japanese immigration while permitting others to enter on a quota basis "would be to take away Japan's position in the world, denying her right to international existence and to the pursuit of her own happiness as a respectable member of the family of nations."[111] This domestic Japanese concern with winning a sense of diplomatic equality on the international scene had long been a goal of the Japanese government; ever since the imposition of the "unequal treaties" in the mid-nineteenth century, Japan had sought to assure her survival as an independent nation state through the quest for international acceptance on the basis of "equality" with the imperialistic nations of the West. Recent events had prompted many in Japan to assume that elusive sense of equality at long last had been achieved: the Japanese had successfully renegotiated the last of the unequal treaties; the Anglo-Japanese Alliance had provided Japan with a powerful Western ally; Japanese forces had contributed to the Allied war effort during World War I; Japanese diplomats had been included in the naval limitation negotiations in London and Washington. The international outpouring of relief following the Great Kanto Earthquake had for many confirmed this newly acquired stature; now, suddenly, actions being taken by the U.S. Congress appeared to threaten these hard-won gains.

The only "reasonable" assumption that could be made concerning the basis for American actions against Japan came to be rooted in charges of an ingrained racism at the heart of American politics and culture. "The activities of the Ku Klux Klan, the lynching of black Americans, the exclusion of Chinese and other Asiatics by earlier immigration laws suddenly assumed a new significance; to *Yorodzu* [a sensational and chauvinistic Tokyo-based newspaper], they indicated that liberty, equality, humanitarianism, and peace existed for Americans 'only in a world of American monopoly."

The peace which the United States advocates is the peace of America and of no other country. The humanity which America insists upon is a

humanity for the exclusive benefit of Americans and the justice which they emphasize is justice for Americans alone.[112]

Having recognized the racist source of the insult represented by passage of the Immigration Act, the Japanese press proved hard-pressed advance any strategy that might reverse the action taken by the U.S Congress. Economically, diplomatically, militarily, Japan was in no position to oppose the American action; a press evaluation of the process leading to passage of the Immigration Act could thus be seen metaphorically follows:

The dispute in regard to the immigration law is a fight between a giant and a dwarf. The giant relies on his strength and his wants to carry his point with a high hand, against which the dwarf protest[s]. The protest enrage[s] the giant, who there upon [strikes] the dwarf with his formidable might.[113]

The Japanese public reaction to passage of the Immigration Act began with a series of rallies, large protest meetings concentrated initially in major metropolitan areas throughout the Empire. Organized by newspaper publishers, patriotic societies, and a variety of religious, educational, labor, fraternal, and social associations, the rallies were intended to expose the public to the issues involved and to stimulate public opposition to exclusion in hopes of prompting a presidential veto in the United States.[114] Rural protests also occurred, leading Frank M. Hedges, a Japan-based correspondent for *The Christian Science Monitor*, to comment at the time, following an extended trip outside the Tokyo area, that "discussion on the train and everywhere with Japanese reveals the fact that they are sorely hurt and disappointed in their belief in American idealism, justice, and altruism. They do not believe Americans capable of such action and still refuse to accept it as the authoritative Voice of the American people."

During June and July, following Coolidge's signing of the Immigration Act, public protests in Japan escalated and other forms of "direct action"—including a proposed boycott of American imports and even a highly publicized *funshi*, or "indignation suicide"—were also undertaken to protest the American action.[116] Although Cyrus Woods, the American ambassador, moved by the sincerity of the suicide, took the note addressed to him home to the United States as a potential weapon in his later attempts to bring about a revision of the Immigration Act, these protests accomplished little in terms of their immediate impact.[117]

The attention given passage of the exclusion act in Japan did, however, serve to initiate a process of reassessment, at both the elite and popular levels, of Japan's international position and of Japan's relationships with the West, particularly the United States. Assumptions of American good will toward Japan increasingly in the years ahead gave way to fears of American power directed against Japan; pan-Asian sentiment grew as the Japanese, increasingly aware of their precarious economic and diplomatic vulnerability, attempted to carve out for themselves a more secure international position.

Japan's assessment of the Immigration Act as unjust and discriminatory led in turn to three important realizations: (1) Japan had not yet achieved true equality in the eyes of the West; (2) Japan was too weak militarily, diplomatically, and (especially) economically to force international recognition of her equality if that equality were challenged or denied; (3) Alliances with Western nations and the good will of European and American governments alone could not guarantee equal international status for Japan.[118]

It is not too difficult to perceive in this reassessment taking place among many in Japan in 1924 the seeds of those thought processes leading eventually to Japan's adventurism on the Asian continent and her involvement in World War II.

## CONCLUSION

Dorothy Borg and Shumpei Okamoto, in their seminal study of *Pearl Harbor as History*, published in 1973, examined the decade of the 1930s through the eyes of both American and Japanese interests and institutions.[119] In their assessment of the lesson learned from this study, they lamented their decision to focus on a single decade:

Frequent allusions to the Triple Intervention of 1895, to the postwar reaction in Japan after 1905, to the memories of the Siberian venture of 1918, to the storm over the Exclusion Act of 1924, and to the civil-military conflict over the London Treaty of 1930—to cite a few examples—revealed the futility of trying to keep within the assigned dates.[120]

Most historians would agree that the road to Pearl Harbor extends back much farther than even historians are sometimes willing to travel. Indeed, the Immigration Act of 1924—known in Japan as the Japanese Exclusion Act of 1924—well might have played a significant role at least as a paving stone in the path leading to the World War II.

Moreover, the impact of this legislation was not confined to its effect on formal diplomatic relations between the United States and Japan; its impress was felt internally within American society among the Japanese immigrant community as well. The nature of the Japanese American immigrant experience seems especially to have been influenced by the decision of the United States Congress in 1924 to officially curtail immigration from Japan, not so much because of the formal end to immigration from Japan it brought about, but rather due to the climate of racial hostility it reflected and the reaction to this fostered within the Japanese American community, one emphasizing the prudence of self-effacing assimilation.

## NOTES

1. See, for example, George Brown Tindall and David E. Shi, *America: A Narrative History* (New York: W.W. Norton, 1993), 679; Mary Beth Norton, et al., *A People and a Nation: A History of the United States* (Boston: Houghton Mifflin, 1990), Vol. II (3rd ed.), 713; Gary B. Nash, et al., *The American People* (New York: HarperCollins, 1990), Vol. II (2nd ed.), 795; and Paul S. Boyer, et al., *The Enduring Vision: A History of the American People* (Lexington, Mass.: D.C. Health and Company, 1993), Vol. II (2nd ed.), 823.

2. The informal Gentlemen's Agreement of 1908 severely limited emigration from Japan to the United States; a treaty signed with Japan in 1911 reconfirmed these restrictions and sought to define the reciprocal rights of both nations' citizens resident in the other country; a series of Alien Land Laws enacted in Western and Pacific Coastal states between 1913 and 1923 affected Japanese immigrants by restricting land ownership and leasing rights to native-born or naturalized citizens; and a legal interpretation formulated by the Supreme Court in *Ozawa v. U.S.* (1922) upheld the intent of these laws by declaring Japanese immigrants "aliens ineligible to citizenship." For an extended discussion of many of these developments, see Teruko Okada Kachi's *The Treaty of 1911 and the Immigration and Alien Land Law Issue between the United States and Japan, 1911–1913* (New York: Arno Press, 1978).

3. As earlier chapters have indicated, the Chinese Exclusion Act of 1882 and the Barred Zone Immigration Act of 1917 had directly excluded not only the Chinese but also South Asian Indians, Southeast Asians, and all others hailing from Asian Pacific Rim nation (excepting those from the Philippines, and American colonial possession); since 1917 none of these groups had enjoyed the right to immigrate to the United States from the Asian homelands.

4. The informal Gentlemen's Agreement between the United States and Japan severely restricted the right of emigration from Japan, should the destination of those who left Japan be the United States, Mexico, Canada, or the territory of Hawaii.

5. During World War I, President Woodrow Wilson sought entry to the conflict on the basis of seeking "a world free from war" to be secured by promoting the self-determination of nations, democratic national autonomy, "open covenants openly arrived at," "freedom of the seas," equality in trade relations, and the formation of a League of Nations. These "fourteen points" later became the basis for negotiations ending the war and for much international diplomacy in the postwar world—especially in Japan where Wilson's ideas inspired the era of Shidehara Diplomacy. See Akira Iriye, *Across the Pacific: An Inner History of American-East Asia Relation* (New York: Harcourt, Brace and World, 1967).

6. Since the late nineteenth century, Japan had acquired an overseas empire consisting of Formosa (Taiwan), the Ryukyu, and Pescadores Island chains in the Pacific and the Korean peninsula.

7. These diplomatic failures led to wars with China (1894) and with Russia (1905) as well as to the forced return of the Liaodong (Liaotung) peninsula to China at the insistence of Russia, Germany, and France at the time of the Triple Intervention in 1895.

8. As was true in Great Britain and elsewhere in Europe, the Japanese government had long interpreted the treatment accorded their immigrant population as a reflection on the status of the nation as a whole. If immigrant populations were badly treated abroad, this reflected negatively on the Japanese at home. Hence the government in Tokyo, particularly sensitive to matters involving attempts at immigration restrictions, always had sought assiduously to curtail or avoid the passage of any such restrictive law wherever and whenever they might emerge.

9. For clarification of the importance attached to "uniqueness" in Japanese society and culture, see Charles A. Moore, ed., *The Japanese Mind* (Honolulu: University of Hawaii Press, 1967); Roy A. Miller, *Japan's Modern Myth* (New York: Weatherhill, 1982); and Carol Gluck, *Japan's Modern Myths: Ideology in the Late Meiji Period* (Princeton, N.J.: Princeton University Press, 1985).

10. This historically ingrained need to maintain a sense of cultural uniqueness may well have prevented the Japanese from seeking a coalition of common interest with other Asian nations when earlier moves were afoot

to ban their citizens from the right to immigrate to the United States. Moreover, most Japanese had long harbored discriminatory views toward their Asian neighbors, seeing them as both culturally and developmentally inferior. Many, indeed, felt that Japan's own unique destiny lay in establishing a measure of Japanese anti-imperialist control over Asia—although among some in Japan these views had been eclipsed by the post–World War I euphoria over Wilsonian principles advocating the "self-determination of nations." See Akira Iriye, *After Imperialism: The Search for a New Order in the Far East* (Cambridge, Mass.: Harvard University Press, 1965).

11. The latter, of course, was to be accompanied by the incarceration of the Japanese immigrant population and their American-citizen children in the United States during the 1940s.

12. Moreover, those carrying the fight against the incorporation of the exclusion clause in the Immigration Act were themselves woefully out of touch with prevailing American popular and political sentiment concerning Japan and the Japanese (to the extent that such sentiment can be demonstrated to have existed at all!). These American diplomatic "apologists" underestimated the volatility of the situation; believing in the ultimate value of rationality and reasonableness, they were taken aback by the reaction to their diplomatic initiatives with regard to the immigration restriction legislation proposed in 1924, underestimating both the reaction to references to the Gentlemen's Agreement in the House debate and later the reaction to attempts to spell out precisely the contents of the Gentlemen's Agreement in the course of the debate in the Senate.

13. Darrel Montero, *Japanese Americans: Changing Patterns of Ethnic Affiliation Over Three Generations* (Boulder, Colo.: Westview Press, 1980), 85–86.

14. Montero, *Japanese Americans,* 86–87, referencing S. Frank Miyamoto, "Social Solidarity among the Japanese in Seattle," *University of Washington Publications in the Social Sciences* 11(2) (December 1939), 57–130.

15. S. Frank Miyamotos's "Social Solidarity among the Japanese in Seattle," *University of Washington Publications in the Social Science* 11 (December 1939), 57–130.

16. Ivan H. Light, *Ethnic Enterprise in America: Business and Welfare among Chinese, Japanese and Blacks* (Berkeley and Los Angeles: University of California Press, 1972), 85.

17. See the discussion in Roger Daniels, *Asian American: Chinese and Japanese in the United States Since 1850* (Seattle: University of Washington Press, 1988), 128–33.

18. Montero, *Japanese Americans,* 87.

19. Rodman W. Paul, *The Abrogation of the Gentlemen's Agreement* (Cambridge, Mass.: Phi Beta Kappa, 1936), 15.

20. Paul, *Abrogation of the Gentlemen's Agreement,* 16; *Congressional Record* 68:1, 3–4.

21. Paul, *Abrogation of the Gentlemen's Agreement,* 17; *Congressional Record* 68:1, 17.

22. William Petersen, *Japanese-Americans: Oppression and Success* (Washington, D.C.: University Press of America, Inc., 1971), 47–48 and n.11.

23. Paul, *Abrogation of the Gentlemen's Agreement,* 16.

24. Paul, *Abrogation of the Gentlemen's Agreement,* 22.

25. Paul, *Abrogation of the Gentlemen's Agreement,* 18, quoting in part *Treaties, Conventions, International Acts, Protocols and Agreements,* etc., 67: 4, Senate Document No. 348 (Washington, D.C., 1923), Vol. III, 2712–17.

26. Paul, *Abrogation of the Gentlemen's Agreement,* 18–19.

27. Paul, *Abrogation of the Gentlemen's Agreement,* 19, quoting *House of Representatives* 68: 1. Report No. 350, 2–3.

28. Paul, *Abrogation of the Gentlemen's Agreement,* 23–24.

29. Official census figures showed the Japanese population resident in the United States in 1910 totaled 72, 157 while in 1920 the total had increased to 111,010 (of which 29,672 were native-born Americans). *Fifteenth Census of the United States,* Vol. 11, 34, tables 4 and 8.

30. Paul, *Abrogation of the Gentlemen's Agreement,* 24.

31. Paul, *Abrogation of the Gentlemen's Agreement,* 17, 29.

32. Paul, *Abrogation of the Gentlemen's Agreement*, 30.

33. Paul, *Abrogation of the Gentlemen's Agreement*, 32.

34. Paul, *Abrogation of the Gentlemen's Agreement*, 32–33; for the contents of Burton's remarks, see *Congressional Record* 68:1, 6249–51.

35. Victor Berger, Socialist from Wisconsin, also cast his vote against the legislation.

36. Paul, *Abrogation of the Gentlemen's Agreement*, 33.

37. Paul, *Abrogation of the Gentlemen's Agreement*, 45; *Congressional Record* 68:1, 5418.

38. Paul, *Abrogation of the Gentlemen's Agreement*, 35–36.

39. Paul, *Abrogation of the Gentlemen's Agreement*, 34, 37.

40. Paul, *Abrogation of the Gentlemen's Agreement*, 39.

41. Paul, *Abrogation of the Gentlemen's Agreement*, 40–43.

42. Paul, *Abrogation of the Gentlemen's Agreement*, 43 and n. 25.

43. Paul, *Abrogation of the Gentlemen's Agreement*, 43–44.

44. Paul, *Abrogation of the Gentlemen's Agreement*, 51.

45. Paul, *Abrogation of the Gentlemen's Agreement*, 58–60. For the text of these diplomatic exchanges and the Hanihara note, see *Congressional Record* 68:1, 6072–74.

46. "It is needless to add that it is not the intention of the Japanese government to question the sovereign right of any country to regulate immigration to its own territories. Nor is it their desire to send their nationals to the countries where they are not wanted . . . To Japan the question is not one of expediency, but of principle," Paul, *Abrogation of the Gentlemen's Agreement*, 64.

47. Paul, *Abrogation of the Gentlemen's Agreement*, 63–64.

48. Paul, *Abrogation of the Gentlemen's Agreement*, 65.

49. Paul, *Abrogation of the Gentlemen's Agreement*, 68, quoting a dispatch from London carried in the *San Francisco Chronicle*, April 20, 1924. See also Paul, *Abrogation of the Gentlemen's Agreement*, 68, n. 13.

50. Paul, *Abrogation of the Gentlemen's Agreement*, 70.

51. During the presidency of Warren G. Harding, Secretary of State Albert Fall leased government-owned oil reserves in the Teapot Dome section of Wyoming to private business interests for several hundred thousand dollars in bribes. Subsequent investigations brought to light other unethical and illegal activities involving the head of the Veterans Administration, the secretary of the Navy, the attorney general, and two close presidential advisors in the Harding administration. Corruption charges carried over into the first Coolidge administration as well. For details, see Burl Noggle, *Teapot Dome: Oil and Politics in the 1920s* (Baton Rouge, La.: Louisiana State University Press 1962).

52. Paul, *Abrogation of the Gentlemen's Agreement*, 71–72.

53. Paul, *Abrogation of the Gentlemen's Agreement*, 74.

54. Paul, *Abrogation of the Gentlemen's Agreement*, 76.

55. Paul, *Abrogation of the Gentlemen's Agreement*, 78.

56. Paul, *Abrogation of the Gentlemen's Agreement*, 79.

57. Paul, *Abrogation of the Gentlemen's Agreement*, 80–81 and n. 36.

58. The following day, April 15, 1924, the Senate passed a domestic measure replacing the provisions of the Gentlemen's Agreement with legislation containing wording similar to that found in the exclusion clause included in the legislation pending before the Senate (an action reaffirmed in a roll call vote of 71 to 4 on April 16). Paul, *Abrogation of the Gentlemen's Agreement*, 82.

59. For details, see Paul, *Abrogation of the Gentlemen's Agreement*, 91–92, 94–95.

60. Paul, *Abrogation of the Gentlemen's Agreement*, 93.

61. Paul, *Abrogation of the Gentlemen's Agreement*, 93–94.

62. Paul, *Abrogation of the Gentlemen's Agreement*, 97.

63. Yuji Ichioka, *The Issei: The World of the First Generation Japanese Immigrants, 1885–1924* (New York: The Free Press, 1988), 245.

64. See the discussion in Lee A. Makela, "Japanese Attitudes towards the United States Immigration Act of 1924," (Ph.D. dissertation, Stanford University, 1973), 57–64.

65. For discussions on Japanese racism and its effects within Japan, see H. Wagatsuma, "The Social Perception of Skin Color in Japan," in Melvin M. Tumin, ed., *Comparative Perceptions on Race Relations* (Boston: Little, Brown, 1969); George A. DeVos, *Social Cohesion and Alienation: Minorities in the United States and Japan* (Boulder, Colo.: Westview Press, 1992); and Michael L. Goldstein, *Minority Status and Radicalism in Japan* (Denver: Center on International Race Relations, University of Denver, 1972). For international ramifications, see bibliographic listings in Note 10 above.

66. For a discussion of eugenics as the basis for a scientific justification of racism, see Elazar Barkan, *Retreat of Scientific Racism: Changing Concepts of Race in Britain and the United States between the World Wars* (Cambridge and New York: Cambridge University Press, 1992).

67. For discussions of broader foreign policy during the 1920s, see N. Gordon Levin Jr., *Woodrow Wilson and World Politics* (New York: Oxford University Press, 1968); Thomas A. Bailey, *Woodrow Wilson And the Lost Peace* (Chicago: Quadrangle Books, Inc. 1963 [1944]); and *Woodrow Wilson and the Great Betrayal* (Chicago: Quadrangle Books, Inc. 1964 [1945]); Ralph A. Stone, *The Irreconcilables: The Fight against the League of Nations* (Lexington: University Press of Kentucky, 1970); and Arthur Walworth, *Wilson and the Peace Makers: American Diplomacy at the Paris Peace Conference* (New York: Norton, 1986).

68. For an extended discussion, see Thomas N. Guinsburg, *The Pursuit of Isolation in the United States from Versailles to Pearl Harbor* (New York: Garland Publications, 1982).

69. The classic account of American nativist sentiment in John Higham, *Stranger in the Land: Patterns of American Nativism, 1860–1925* (New Brunswick, N.J.: Rutgers University Press, 1955).

70. For a discussion on the economic impact on Asian immigrants in general of these economic considerations, see Lucie Cheng and Edna Bonacich, eds., *Labor Immigration under Capitalism: Asian Workers in the United States before World War II* (Berkeley: University of California Press, 1984).

71. The standard account is Richard Hofstadter's *Social Darwinism in American Thought* (New York: G. Braziller, 1959); more recent considerations may be found in Robert C. Bannister, *Social Darwinism: Science and Myth in Anglo-American Social Thought* (Philadelphia: Temple University Press, 1979) and Carl Degler, *In Search of Human Nature: The Decline and Revival of Darwinism in American Social Thought* (New York: Oxford University Press, 1991).

72. See "The Limits of Cultural Laissez-Faire" in Christopher Lasch, *The World of Nations: Reflections on American History, Politics and Culture* (New York: Alfred A. Knopf, 1973).

73. Paul, *Abrogation of the Gentlemen's Agreement*, 6.

74. Valentine S. McClatchy before the United States Senate in 1924 as quoted in Dennis M. Ogawa, *From Japs to Japanese: An Evolution of Japanese-American Stereotypes* (Berkeley: McCutchan Publishing Corporation, 1971), 8–23.

75. See Akira Iriye, *After Imperialism: The Search for a New Order in the Far East* (Cambridge, Mass.: Harvard University Press, 1965).

76. The analytical typography on American images of Asia utilized in this discussion is premised on the work undertaken by Harold R. Isaacs in *Scratches on Our Minds: American Views of China and India* (White Plains, N.Y.: M.E. Sharpe, Inc., 1980).

77. California legislator quoted in Care McWilliams, *Prejudice* (Boston: Little, Brown, 1944), 4.

78. *San Francisco Chronicle,* February 23, 1925.

79. 1910 Asiatic Exclusion League position paper as quoted in Ogawa, *From Japs to Japanese,* 8–23.

80. Homer Lea in *The Valor of Ignorance,* 1909, as quoted in Ogawa, *From Japs to Japanese,* 8–23.

81. Ogawa, *From Japs to Japanese,* 2, 8.

82. The facts and figures involved in this controversy are examined in Yuju Ichioka, *The Issei: The World of he First Generation Japanese Immigrants, 1885–1924* (New York: Free Press, 1988).

83. For a fuller discussion, see Kiyoski Karl Kawakami, *American-Japanese Relations: An Insider's View of Japanese Policies and Purposes* (New York: Fleming H. Revell Co., 1912).

84. Paul, *Abrogation of the Gentlemen's Agreement*, 11; for a discussion of American views of "picture brides," see John B. Trevor, *Japanese Exclusion: A Study of the Policy and the Law* (U.S. Government Printing Office, 1925), 10.

85. For insights into the views held by Hughes and Coolidge, see Paul, *Abrogation of the Gentlemen's Agreement*, 17–22 and 93–94; the earlier perspective of President Theodore Roosevelt on the issue of exclusion also is summarized in Paul, *Abrogation of the Gentlemen's Agreement*, 10.

86. Paul, *Abrogation of the Gentlemen's Agreement*, 98.

87. Paul, *Abrogation of the Gentlemen's Agreement*, 100.

88. Trevor, *Japanese Exclusion*, 2.

89. Paul, *Abrogation of the Gentlemen's Agreement*, 85–86.

90. Paul, *Abrogation of the Gentlemen's Agreement*, 98.

91. Paul, *Abrogation of the Gentlemen's Agreement*, 99.

92. Paul, *Abrogation of the Gentlemen's Agreement*, 99–110.

93. Quoted or paraphrased in Paul, *Abrogation of the Gentlemen's Agreement*, 86–88.

94. Paul, *Abrogation of the Gentlemen's Agreement*, 82–88.

95. Paul, *Abrogation of the Gentlemen's Agreement*, 88.

96. Paul, *Abrogation of the Gentlemen's Agreement*, 101 and n. 5.

97. Paul, *Abrogation of the Gentlemen's Agreement*, 100.

98. Trevor, *Japanese Exclusion*, 37.

99. See Charles A. Lofgren, *The Plessy Case: A Legal-Historical Interpretation* (New York: Oxford University Press, 1987).

100. See, for example, the listing, some eighteen pages of densely packed type, in "Japanese Exclusion Movement" in Yui Ichioka, et al., *A Buried Past: An Annotated Bibliography of the Japanese American Research Project Collection* (Berkeley: University of Los Angeles Press, 1974), 50–68.

101. Paul, *Abrogation of the Gentlemen's Agreement*, 101.

102. For a discussion of the impact of modernization and Westernization in Japan, Marius B. Jansen, ed., *Changing Japanese Attitudes towards Modernization* (Princeton, N.J.: Princeton University Press, 1965); and George B. Sansom, *The Western World and Japan* (New York: Alfred A. Knopf, 1951).

103. Paul, *Abrogation of the Gentlemen's Agreement*, 102.

104. Makela, "Japanese Attitudes," 271.

105. Makela, "Japanese Attitudes," 42.

106. Makela, "Japanese Attitudes," 44.

107. Makela, "Japanese Attitudes," 45.

108. Makela, "Japanese Attitudes," 50–51.

109. Makela, "Japanese Attitudes," 71–74.

110. Makela, "Japanese Attitudes," 98.

111. Quoted in *The Japan Advertiser*, April 26, 1924 and Makela, "Japanese Attitudes," 99.

112. *Yorodzu*, April 24, 1924, quoted in Makela, "Japanese Attitudes," 103.

113. *Chugai shogyo*, April 18, 1924, quoted in Makela, "Japanese Attitudes," 104.

114. Makela, "Japanese Attitudes," 126–27.

115. Quoted in Makela, "Japanese Attitudes," 131.

116. These public protests are described in detail in Makela, "Japanese Attitudes," 159–203.

117. Makela, "Japanese Attitudes," 164.

118. Makela, "Japanese Attitudes," 272–73.

119. Dorothy Borg and Shumpei Okamoto, eds., *Pearl Harbor as History* (New York: Columbia University Press, 1973).

120. Borg and Okamoto, *Pearl Harbor as History*, 22.

# 2.2

# Making and Remaking Asian Pacific America
## Immigration Policy

*Bill Ong Hing*

〰〰〰〰〰〰〰〰〰〰〰〰〰〰〰〰〰〰〰〰〰〰〰〰〰〰〰〰〰

Asian Pacific Americans will continue to be the fastest growing ethnic group in the United States into the next millennium principally because of immigration. The demographic predictions for the year 2020 show that 54 percent of Asian Pacific Americans will be foreign born. This is consistent with census figures in 1980 and 1990 which revealed that except for Japanese Americans, every group was mostly comprised of those born abroad (e.g., Chinese, over 60 percent; Koreans, 80 percent; Asian Indians, 80 percent; Filipinos, over 70 percent; Vietnamese, 90 percent). These predictions also find support from current annual levels of immigration (e.g., Filipinos 60,000, Chinese 55,000, Koreans 30,000, Asian Indians 30,000, Pakistanis 9,700, Thais 8,900). In 1992, 50,000 Southeast Asian refugees were admitted. And a trend in increased immigration from Japan has developed as well. During the 1980s, Asian Pacific immigration totaled about two mil-

lion to help account for the 108 percent increase during the decade (from approximately 3.8 million to 7.3 million).

Beyond numbers, there is every reason to believe that immigration and refugee policies will continue to shape the Asian Pacific American profile in terms of where people live, gender ratios, employment and income profiles, and even social and political life.

## UNDERSTANDING HOW IMMIGRATION POLICY SHAPES ASIAN PACIFIC AMERICA

The 1965 amendments to the Immigration and Nationality Act set the stage for the development of Asian Pacific America as we know it today.[1] Its emphasis on family reunification (ironically not intended to benefit Asian immigration) provided the basis for growth. Family categories offered many more visas (80 percent of all preference and 100 percent of immediate relative, non-quota visas were designated for family reunification) and less stringent visa requirements. A relationship as spouse, parent, child, or sibling is all that was necessary.

Hing, Bill Ong. "Making and Remaking Asian America: Immigration Policy." *State of Asian Pacific America: Policy Issues to the Year 2020.* (Los Angeles: LEAP Asian Pacific American Public Policy Institute and UCLA Asian American Studies Center), 127–40. Reprinted with permission.

In the occupational categories, on the other hand, a certification from the Department of Labor was needed to show that no qualified American worker could fill the position an immigrant was offered. Today, 80 to 90 percent of the immigration from most Asian Pacific nations is in the family categories. But that was not always the case.

Filipinos, Asian Indians, and Koreans are the best examples of how the 1965 amendments were used to transform Asian immigration. In the late 1960s, about 45 percent of Filipino immigrants entered in the professional and 55 percent in the family unity categories. Within a few years, however, family networks developed that enabled naturalized citizens to take advantage of reunification categories. By 1976 Filipino immigration in the occupational categories dropped to about 21 percent. And by 1990, just over 8 percent came from the occupational categories compared to 88 percent in the family categories. About 64 percent of all Koreans entered in family categories in 1969 compared to over 90 percent by 1990. For Asian Indians, the figures were 27 percent in 1969 and about 90 percent in 1990. In the late 1960s and early 1970s, Koreans and Asian Indians also took advantage of the nonpreference investor category. About 12 percent of all Koreans and 27 percent of Asian Indians entered as investors at that time. Investor visas became unavailable in 1978.

Here are some examples of how many Asians eventually used the family categories under the 1965 amendments:

Under the 1965 reforms immigrants essentially were categorized as immediate relatives of U.S. citizens or under the preference system. As immediate relatives they were not subject to quotas or numerical limitations. The category included the spouses and minor, unmarried children of citizens, as well as the parents of adult citizens. The preference system included seven categories. First preference: adult, unmarried sons and daughters of citizens. Second preference: spouses and unmarried sons and daughters of lawful permanent resident aliens. Permanent residents (green card holders) could petition for relatives only through this category. Third preference: members of the professions or those with exceptional ability in the sciences or the arts. Proof from the Department of Labor that the immigrant would not be displacing an available worker was required for third and sixth preference. Fourth preference: married sons and daughters of citizens. Fifth preference: siblings of adult citizens. Sixth preference: skilled or unskilled workers, of which there was a shortage of employable and willing workers in the United States. Seventh preference: persons fleeing from a Communist-dominated country, a country of the Middle East, or who were uprooted by a natural catastrophe. Seventh preference was eliminated in 1980, but not until after about 14,000 Chinese from mainland China entered in the category.

Here are some examples of how the immigration system worked between 1965 and 1990:

- A Korean woman who had married a U.S. serviceman (presumably a citizen) could immigrate in the immediate relative category, thereby becoming a lawful permanent resident of the United States. After three years of marriage, she could apply for naturalization and become a citizen. She could then petition for her parents under the immediate relative category, and also for siblings under the fifth preference. Once her parents immigrated, they, as lawful permanent residents, could petition for other unmarried sons and daughters under the second preference. Married siblings entering under the fifth preference could be accompanied by spouses and minor, unmarried children.
- A doctor or engineer from India could immigrate under the third preference as a professional. He or she could be accompanied by a spouse and unmarried, minor children. After five years of permanent residence, the doctor/engineer could apply for naturalization, and upon obtaining citizenship could petition for parents under the immediate relative

category, siblings under the fifth preference, and married sons and daughters
under the fourth preference (who could
also bring their spouses and minor,
unmarried children). The same scenario
is possible even if the first Indian immigrant in this family had entered as a nonpreference investor when such visas
were available.

- A nurse from the Philippines might be
able to immigrate under the third preference. After qualifying for citizenship five
years later, she could petition for her parents. Her parents could petition for other
unmarried sons and daughters under the
second preference or the nurse could
petition for these siblings under the fifth
preference. If the son or daughter married on a visit to the Philippines, that
spouse could then be petitioned for
under the second preference.
- A Chinese American citizen might
marry a foreign student from Taiwan.
The student would then be able to
become an immigrant under the immediate relative category. After three
years of marriage to a citizen, naturalization opens immigration possibilities
for parents under the immediate relative category and siblings under the
fifth preference.

Gender ratios are affected by immigration as well. Today, more women than men
immigrate from the Philippines, China,
Korea, and Japan. For example, about 60
percent of Filipino and 55 percent of Korean
immigrants in 1990 were women. This has
contributed to census findings that the Chinese, Japanese, Filipino, and Korean American communities are predominantly
female. The Asian Indian community has a
very even gender ratio, in part because
about the same number of men as women
immigrate each year from India.

There is every reason to believe that
many Asian women (particularly Koreans,
Filipinos, and Japanese) immigrate because
they perceive relatively progressive views
on gender equality in the United States.
This is interrelated to the fact that many

women from Korea and the Philippines
were able to qualify for employment categories as nurses and in other medical fields.
Marriages between women and U.S. servicemen in these countries also contributed
to a larger share of immigrant women.

The employment profile of various Asian
Pacific communities also has its roots in
immigration policy. The fifth of the preference visas that were set aside for employment categories under the 1965 amendments provided a window for many Asians
to immigrate who did not have specific relatives in the United States. The proportion
of professionals in every Asian Pacific community increased as a result. And even after
more began using the family categories, the
actual number of immigrants who identified themselves as professionals or managers remained high.

Some observers, who note fewer professionals among Chinese immigrants for
example, contend that after the initial
influx of professionals in the late 1960s and
early 1970s, poorer, working-class Chinese
began entering. But this is only part of the
story. The proportion who enter in professional and occupational categories did
decrease over time in part because a 1976
law required all professionals to first secure
a job offer from an employer. The absolute
number of professionals and executives,
however, has increased. In 1969, for example, a total of 3,499 immigrated from mainland China, Taiwan, and Hong Kong. In
1983 the total had jumped to 8,524. Thus,
the smaller percentage merely reflects the
increased use of family categories. The proportion of those who enter in professional
and occupational categories from Taiwan is
also much higher than for those from mainland China (28 percent to 5 percent in
1989). And though more than twice as
many born in mainland China entered in
1989 (32,272 to 13,974), Taiwan had more
occupational immigrants (3,842 to 1,599).
Large numbers of professionals continue to
enter from the Philippines, Korea, and India
as well. Over 6,500 Indian immigrants who
designate their prior occupation as professionals or managers enter annually.

Immigration policies influence residential preferences as well. Historical recruitment of Asian and Pacific immigrants to work in the fields, on the railroads, and in service industries in the West Coast established a residential pattern that has continued for some time. However, in recent years, more and more Asian immigrants are settling in other parts of the country. Since 1967, New York City has attracted more Chinese immigrants than San Francisco and Oakland combined, and more than 17 percent of Chinese Americans reside in New York State. Almost 23 percent of Korean Americans live in the Northeast, 19.2 percent in the South, and 13.7 percent in the Midwest. Thirty-five percent of Asian Indians live in the Northeast and about 24 percent in the South. Asian Indians and Filipinos are the largest Asian American communities in New Jersey and Illinois. Relatedly, working class immigrants who are able to enter in the family categories have helped to sustain Chinatowns and develop residential enclaves among Koreans, Filipinos, and Asian Indians. Koreans have also established small business enclaves in places like New York, Chicago, Washington, D.C., and, of course, Los Angeles.

The 134.8 percent growth rate of Vietnamese Americans between 1980 and 1990 (261,729 to 614,547) makes them the fastest growing Asian Pacific group. The development of Southeast Asian communities in the United States is related more to refugee policies than to standard immigration admission criteria. Take its current size. Of the 18,000 who immigrated by 1974, many were the spouses of American businessmen and military personnel who had been stationed in Vietnam. But a dramatic upsurge in new arrivals began after 1975, with 125,000 admitted immediately after the troops pulled out of Southeast Asia. By 1980 more than 400,000 additional refugees were welcomed from Vietnam, Laos, and Cambodia, approximately 90 percent of whom were from Vietnam. Although the 1980 Refugee Act established new controls, the flow of refugees continued due to persistent humanitarian pressure on the United States. After a second, sizable wave entered in 1980, the flow of new entries declined steadily. In 1984, 40,604 Vietnamese refugees entered, then the average dropped to about 22,000 until 1988 when 17,626 were admitted. So by 1988, 540,700 Vietnamese refugees had arrived. By October 1991, 18,280 Amerasians (mostly from Vietnam) arrived along with another 44,071 relatives. Eventually as many as 80,000 to 100,000 Amerasians and their relatives may enter. As a result of these entrants, over 90 percent of the Vietnamese population is foreign born, the highest percentage of all Asian American groups.

Refugee policies also affect gender ratios. In 1980 there were 108.5 Vietnamese men per one hundred Vietnamese women, compared to 94.5 per one hundred in the general population. This ratio is not as skewed as those for initial waves of Filipinos and Chinese which were much more male-dominated. The refugee policy that enabled Vietnamese to enter after 1975 under unique circumstances contributed to greater balance. Rather than fleeing individually, those departing Vietnam have done their best to keep their families intact. Roughly 45 percent of recent arrivals are women.

Another policy was to resettle refugees across the country in order to lessen the economic and social impact on just a few areas, and to avoid ghettoization. Although many refugees moved after their initial placement, refugees have become widely dispersed. By 1990, over 54 percent of the Vietnamese resided in the West, but 27.4 percent were in the South, almost 10 percent in the Northeast, and 8.5 percent in the Midwest. More of them lived in the South and Midwest than Filipinos and Japanese.

The goal of preventing ethnic enclaves ignored the dynamics of Vietnamese culture and perhaps even basic psychology. The need for ethnically based social, cultural, and economic support among refugees was either seriously misjudged or coldly ignored. Although enclaves provided an historical means for the mainstream to keep an eye on Asian immigrants, those established by Chinese, Filipino, and Japanese immigrants played key roles in easing their adjustment to American society. The need for a stable support system may be even more crucial for Southeast Asians, whose experience has been profoundly unsettling. Politically persecuted, unexpectedly driven from their homes, their hopes dashed, these refugees not surprisingly turned to the past for sustenance.

In doing so they turned to each other, and despite numerous obstacles have been remarkably successful in developing their own communities. They have, for example, transformed San Francisco's red-light district near Union Square into a bustling hub of Vietnamese hotels, residences, and small businesses. Vietnamese Americans have likewise helped to develop a "booming" wholesale district out of Skid Row in Los Angeles and altered the downtown areas of San Jose and Santa Ana, California, as well as a section of the Washington, D.C., suburb of Arlington, Virginia.

Nationwide, 64 percent of all Southeast Asian households headed by refugees arriving after 1980 are on public assistance, three times the rate of African Americans and four times that of Latinos. Not surprisingly, groups such as the Vietnamese have been accused of developing a welfare mentality, and the government has responded in knee-jerk fashion. Their relatively low rate of labor-force participation has in fact led many Vietnamese refugees to depend on government assistance. But much of this dependency is due to a system that creates disincentives to work. Policy-makers have urged state and local resettlement agencies to expeditiously assist refugees with job placement. Under the 1980 Refugee Act, refugees were given thirty-six-month stipends of special refugee cash, medical assistance programs, and other support services. But in 1982 amendments to the act reduced the stipends to eighteen

months to pressure refugees to become economically independent more quickly. These changes came with the entry of the poorer, less-educated, and more devastated second wave of refugees. After 1982, most programs stressed employment-enhancing services such as vocational, English-language, and job development training. Most refugees are unable to acquire the skills that would qualify them for anything other than minimum-wage jobs in eighteen months. They were, nonetheless, constrained to take these positions in the absence of continued public assistance.

Restrictions on federal assistance thus help to account for increased Vietnamese American concentration in entry-level, minimum-wage jobs requiring little formal education or mastery of English. For many refugees, in fact, these types of jobs and the poverty that results are unavoidable. Indeed, figures show that in 1979, a striking 35.1 percent of Vietnamese families were living below the poverty level. And by 1985 the figure had risen to an astonishing 50 percent for all Southeast Asian refugees.

## Amendments to the Law in 1990

After 1990 reforms, immigration visas are distributed under two preference systems, one for family reunification and the other for employment. The immediate relative category (spouses, unmarried children, and parents of adult citizens) continues to remain unlimited and outside of any of the numerically restricted preference systems. In the family preferences, first preference is for unmarried adult sons and daughters of citizens. Second preference is the only category under which lawful permanent residents of the United States can petition for relatives. There are two subcategories: (1) the 2A category for the spouses and children (unmarried and under twenty-one), and (2) the 2B category for unmarried sons and daughters (age twenty-one and over). Third preference is reserved for the married sons and daughters of United States citizens. And fourth preference is for brothers and sisters of adult citizens. Only United States citizens, not lawful permanent residents or noncitizen nationals, can petition for married sons and daughters and for siblings.

The law now provides several categories for employment-based immigrant visas. First preference is for immigrants with extraordinary ability (such as in the sciences, arts, education, business or athletics), outstanding professors and researchers, and certain executives and managers of multinational companies. Second preference is for members of the professions holding advanced degrees or for those of exceptional ability. Third preference is for skilled workers, professionals, and other workers. Fourth preference is for special immigrants (except returning lawful permanent residents and former citizens). Fifth preference is a category for investors whose investments are to each create at least ten new jobs.

Persons who immigrate to the United States under the preference systems are subject to two types of numerical limitations: a worldwide numerical cap and a country or territorial limit.

At least 226,000 family preference category visas are available annually on a worldwide basis. While in theory the worldwide quota can be increased to a cap of 465,000 annually through 1994, and 480,000 thereafter, the level will not likely be much more than 226,000. This is because the family preference category level is determined by subtracting the number of immediate relative entrants—generally well over 200,000 annually—from the cap (465,000 or 480,000), with an absolute floor of 226,000. Assuming that 226,000 is the operative figure, this means that in a given year, a maximum of 226,000 persons can immigrate to the United States under the first, second, third, and fourth preferences. A separate worldwide numerical limitation of 140,000 is set aside for employment-based immigrants.

In addition to the worldwide numerical limitations, the law also provides an annual limitation of visas per country of 7 percent of the worldwide quotas. Thus, assuming a 226,000 worldwide family visa numerical limitation and 140,000 for employment visas, 7 percent of the total (366,000) is 25,620 for each country. But 75 percent of the visas issued for spouses and children of lawful permanent residents (family second preference "2A") are not counted against each country's quota.

Note that the visa of any immigrant born in a colony or other dependent area of a country is charged to that country. However, Hong Kong, which became part of the People's Republic of China in 1997, is treated as a separate foreign state for purposes of its annual visa allotment (i.e., 25,620), except that through the end of fiscal year 1993 its annual quota was set at 10,000 preference visas.

## CONSIDERATIONS FOR THE FUTURE

The confluence of social, political, and economic conditions in Asia and the Pacific region will continue to drive immigration to the United States for many more decades. And U.S. policies will continue to shape the profiles of Asian and Pacific communities here. As the prospects of immigration during the next several decades are appraised, these are the types of issues that have to be kept in mind:

- *Impact of 1990 reforms.* Asian Pacific immigrants comprise almost half of all legal immigrants today, mostly entering in the family reunification categories. The 1990 reforms did not reduce the number of visas available to family immigrants. In fact it added some numbers for families and added large numbers for employment categories. Asian Pacific immigrants are likely to continue taking advantage of the family preference system. And as in the late 1960s and early 1970s, they will likely use the employment categories and new investor category to create further bases for future family migration.

For example, interest in emigration remains high among Chinese professionals. Taiwan's politically volatile environment has contributed to the desire of the educated class to look for residential options elsewhere, and the stability of the United States and its longstanding anti-Communist philosophy appeals to them. Similarly, the return of Hong Kong to mainland China's jurisdiction in 1997 has provided a strong impetus for its elite to look to the United States. And the Tiananmen Square massacre in June 1989 significantly accelerated emigration from Hong Kong. But there are analogous sociopolitical considerations for Filipinos, Asian Indians, and Koreans. And Japanese have also demonstrated a slow but steady increase in immigration in recent years, particularly among women.

- *Gender ratios.* The special interest in immigration that has been demonstrated by Korean, Filipino, Chinese, and Japanese women is likely to continue, especially because of the increase in employment-based visas and the perception of gender equality in the United States.
- *Working-class immigrants.* A continued influx of working-class and service-class immigrants will also continue to enter in family preference categories. This will continue to impact not only the employment profile of communities, but also such things as the viability of residential enclaves—not only Chinatowns, but also Koreatowns, Little Manilas, and Asian Indian ghettos.
- *Southeast Asians.* In spite of large numbers of refugees that continue to flee Southeast Asia and occupy refugee camps in Asia, the United States has gradually reduced the number of refugee slots to Southeast Asians since the Refugee Act of 1980. The admission of up to 35,000 refugees from Southeast Asia was allocated in 1990, and another 22,000 spots were reserved

for relatives of refugees already in the United States under the Orderly Departure Program. But this is a far cry from the 525,000 that were admitted between 1975 and 1980. Following the pattern set by other Asian Americans, small but increasing numbers of Vietnamese are entering in family reunification categories. In order to take full advantage of these categories, U.S. citizenship is required, and most Vietnamese have been residents long enough to qualify. Some do so to demonstrate allegiance, others recognize that, as citizens, they may petition for more relatives. Though about 38 percent of the first wave of Vietnamese were naturalized by 1984, the rate for the second wave is significantly lower. In 1983 roughly 3,300 entered in the family categories, and by 1988 more than 4,000 had. These figures do not approach those of the other large Asian American communities for family category admissions (with the exception of the Japanese). Nonrefugee admission is likely to remain low because in the absence of normal diplomatic ties between the United States and Vietnam, Vietnamese nationals attempting to obtain exit permits face tremendous difficulties. After an immigration petition is filed by a resident on behalf of a relative in Vietnam, the Vietnamese government must approve it. In 1984 only 3,700 immigrants were allowed under the Orderly Departure Program. More than half a million cases are currently backlogged. As a result, sizable growth of the Vietnamese American community exclusively through existing nonrefugee categories is unlikely.

- *Other Asians.* Aside from the larger Asian Pacific groups mentioned—Chinese, Filipinos, Japanese, Koreans, Vietnamese, and Asian Indians—as well as other groups alluded too, such as Laotians and Cambodians, other Asian Pacific countries send at least a few thousand immigrants to the United

States each year. Annual admissions of Indonesians (3,500), Malaysians (1,800), Pakistanis (9,700), Thais (8,900), Tongans (1,400), and Samoans (700) contribute to growing communities that have become part of the Asian Pacific patchwork.

- *Political backlash.* As always, immigration and refugee policies in the near and distant future will respond to economic and social pressures. The 1990 reforms put into place the concept of a ceiling on preference visas, which could be extended to the immediate relative category given strong xenophobia or nativism. While some might label as extreme the anti-immigrant of color sentiment of someone like presidential candidate Patrick Buchanan, are his views really that different from that of the mainstream's given the popularity of English-Only initiatives across the nation? We also kid ourselves if we think this sentiment is aimed solely at Latin immigration. Consider only the experiences of Chinese in Monterey Park and the widespread upsurge in anti-Asian violence. Public opinion polls reveal that the general population does not hold Asian Americans in very high esteem. In one national survey that ascertained attitudes toward fifteen different ethnic groups, no European ethnic group received lower than 53 percent positive rating, and no Asian group received higher than a 47 positive rating. Conducted before recent Japan bashing, Japanese were considered to be the minority group that had contributed the most (47 percent), followed by African Americans, Chinese, Mexicans, Koreans, Vietnamese, Puerto Ricans, Haitians, and Cubans. In a separate poll that focused on refugees, only 21 percent believed that Southeast Asian refugees should be encouraged to move into their community. Nearly half believed that Southeast Asians should have settled in other Asian countries, and one-fourth believed that "America has too many Asians in its population." Other polls continue to show that much of the public regards Asians as sinister, suspicious, and foreign. Thus, the threat of a serious backlash against Asian Pacific Americans that could negatively impact immigration laws is always real.

Asian Pacific America has been shaped by immigration and refugee policies. The profiles of the communities we know today are reflective of the 1965 amendments and a variety of refugee policies. The reforms in 1990 in all likelihood will continue the opportunities of the past twenty-seven years, particularly in family reunification categories, but also open new doors with the expansion of employment-based numbers and the renewed availability of an investors category. Only if anti-immigrant, or specifically anti-Asian, sentiment carries the day will the course set in 1965 be obstructed.

## NOTE

1. A much more detailed analysis of how immigration and refugee policies shape the demographic and social profiles of various Asian Pacific communities can be found in Bill Ong Hing, *Making and Remaking Asian America Through Immigration Policy* (Stanford: Stanford University Press, 1992).

# Part III

# The Period of Political Incorporation
# (1965 to Present)

Vincent Chen Demonstration, Detroit. *Courtesy of Corky Lee*

At a time when it is being proposed that hundreds of billions be spent to uplift Negroes and other minorities, the nation's 300,000 Chinese-Americans are moving ahead on their own—with no help from anyone else . . . low rate of crime. In crime-ridden cities, Chinese districts turn up as islands of peace and stability.

*(U.S. News and World Report, "Success Story*
*of One Minority Group in the United States."*
December 26, 1966)

## CONTEMPORARY CHALLENGES FOR ASIAN AMERICANS IN THE U.S. POLITIC ARENA

The electoral gains made by racial minority groups during the mid to late 1960s in urban cities across the country, along with the passing of federal legislation such as the Voting Rights Act of 1965, embodied a new era for minority political representation. According to Michael Omi and Howard Winant in their influential book *Racial Formation in the United States: From the 1960s to the 1990s*, the dominant paradigm of race relations that emerged with the civil rights struggles of the mid 1960s and continued to the late 1980s was racial formation theory. Prior to the emergence of racial formation theory, the dominant theoretical paradigm for understanding race relations was the ethnicity paradigm, which defined racial groups as ethnic groups per se (Omi and Winant 1994). In contrast, the racial formation theory paradigm defined race as an uncentered and highly unstable complex of social meanings that is subject to constant change termed the "racial state." As Omi and Winant contend, racial minorities realized that their political influence on public policies and elections depended on their ability to mobilize their interests as a racial bloc. It is this constant struggle between liberals and conservatives, as well as racial minorities and their counterparts, that ultimately determines the social meaning of race and its various public policies.

Coinciding with the emergence of the racial formation theory, the number of minority elected officials increased between the 1960s and the 1980s. The beginning of this period has been characterized for racial minorities as a movement from protests to electoral politics (Browning, Marshall, and Tabb 1984). In 1959, among the 300 most significant elected positions in California, African Americans, Latinos, and Asian Pacific Americans held two, one, and zero positions, respectively. In 1969, African Americans, Latinos, and Asian Pacific Americans held fourteen, two, and six positions, respectively. In 1979, African Americans, Latinos, and Asian Pacific Americans occupied twenty-six, ten, and eleven positions, respectively (Guerra 1991).

The symbolic gains in minority elected officials during the 1970s and 1980s could also be seen outside of California. African Americans in Los Angeles gained their first black elected mayor, Tom Bradley, in 1973; Chicago later elected their first black mayor, Harold Washington, in 1983 (Starks and Preston 1990). The gains in minority elected representation in key political offices at the local level during this decade were parlayed into further representation in other key cities. In 1983, New York City and Atlanta elected their first African American mayors, David Dinkins and Maynard Jackson, respectively (Browning, Marshall, and Tabb 1984). The gains made by African American elected officials in African American majority districts heightened political group consciousness.

For Asian Pacific Americans, the 1960s and 1970s symbolized a period of increased political activity (Wei 1993). This was evident with the emergence of Asian Pacific American elected officials at the federal level, particularly from Hawaii and California. In Hawaii, where Asian Pacific Americans represent the majority population, the first Asian Pacific American federal elected officials were U.S. Senators Spark Matsunaga (D-HI) and Daniel Inouye (D-HI), who were both elected in 1962. Patsy T. Mink (D-HI) was then elected to the U.S. House of Representatives in 1964. Despite the gain in the number of U.S. representatives from Hawaii, Asian Pacific Americans were relatively underrepresented on the U.S. mainland. The majority of the Asian Pacific American federal elected officials on the U.S. mainland came from California. S.I. Hayakawa (R-CA) served as U.S. Senator from 1976 to 1982. Norman Mineta (D-CA) served in the U.S. House of Representatives from 1974 to 1996, and is currently the U.S. secretary of transportation. The current U.S. representative, Robert Matsui (D-CA), was first elected in 1978.

Pan-ethnic Asian Pacific American community-based organizations also began to emerge during the 1960s and 1970s. These organizations attempted to fill the void left by mainstream social welfare organizations in providing adequate social services to the immigrant Asian and Pacific Islander populations. Many of these organizations' leaders were Asian Pacific American activists during the 1960s who sought to provide various types of social services to their communities (Wei 1993). The pursuance of pan-ethnic unity at the local level among Asian Pacific American community-based organizations was especially prevalent in the social welfare and electoral arenas (Espiritu 1992). In the electoral arena, politically oriented Asian Pacific American community-based organizations emphasized the formation of a racial political bloc. These organizations engaged in activities focusing on the political cultivation and education of Asian Pacific Americans. An example in Los Angeles was the Asian Pacific American Legal Center of Southern California, which conducted important political activities such as political education forums, exit polling, advocacy on political issues (e.g., bilingual ballots and redistricting), and "get out the vote" drives. Many of these activities helped build group consciousness among Asian Pacific American citizens and immigrants through their pan-ethnic orientation.

### REFERENCES

Browning, Rufus, Dale Rogers Marshall, and David H. Tabb. 1984. *Protest Is Not Enough: The Struggle of Blacks and Hispanics for Equality in Urban Politics.* Berkeley: University of California Press.

Espiritu, Yen Le. 1992. *Asian American Panethnicity: Bridging Institutions and Identities.* Philadelphia: Temple University Press.

Guerra, Fernando. 1991. "The Emergence of Ethnic Officeholders in California." In Byran O. Jackson and Michael B. Preston, eds., *Racial and Ethnic Politics in California,* 1:117–32. Berkeley, Calif.: Institute of Governmental Studies Press.

Omi, Michael, and Howard Winant. 1994. *Racial Formation in the United States: From the 1960s to the 1990s.* 2d ed. New York: Routledge.

Starks, Robert T., and Michael B. Preston. 1990. "Harold Washington and the Politics of Reform in Chicago: 1983–1987." In Rufus P. Browning, Dale Rogers Marshall, and David H. Tabb, eds., *Racial Politics in American Cities,* 88–107. New York: Longman.

Wei, William. 1993. *The Asian American Movement.* Philadelphia: Temple University Press.

No Vietnamization! *Courtesy of Bob Hsiang*

# 3.1

# Asian American Politics
## An Agenda for Research

*Don T. Nakanishi*

〰〰〰〰〰〰〰〰〰〰〰〰〰〰〰〰〰〰〰〰〰〰〰〰〰

Asian American politics is not a new phenomenon, but it is becoming an increasingly significant focus. Perhaps at no other period have so many individuals and organizations participated in the American political system, and in activities connected with the affairs of Asian countries. Asian Americans have demonstrated that they have the commitment, organizational skills, and fiscal resources to advance their concerns and to confront societal issues that are damaging to their interestes.[1] What has become the routine election of Asian Americans to public office in Hawaii has become less novel on the U.S. mainland with the election and appointment of Asians to federal, state, and local positions.[2]

It would be incorrect, however, to conclude from these recent developments that Asian Americans have become powerful and unified, or that they are now capable of competing equally with other minority groups in realizing their goals. On the other hand, it would be remiss to assert that they are doing noting more than mimicking the styles, agendas, and strategies of other groups, especially Blacks and Chicanos.[3] Asian Americans still have not fully developed the real and symbolic resources that are needed to compete. Their internal diversity—of ethnic origins, generations, social classes, political perspectives, and organizational aims—has ofttimes prevented them from being perceived as a unified actor in articulating their stands on public policy. In several small mainland cities such as Gardena and Monterey Park, and to a much lesser extent in major urban areas like Seattle, San Francisco, and Los Angeles, Asian Americans have become viable participants. In most regions—aside from Hawaii—and at higher levels of state and federal decision-making, they remain largely underrepresented.[4] At best, their impact has been regional and sporadic, and their reputed success as a model minority disguises their lack of representation in the most significant national arenas and institutions.[5]

The roots of contemporary Asian American political activity can be traced to broader societal developments which affected many groups.[6] Their protest activities, for instance, did not simply emerge in the 1960s and 1970s, but have a long history.[7] Similarly, their concerns over events in Asia did not

Nakanishi, Don T. "Asian American Politics: An Agenda for Research," *Amerasian Journal* 12(2): 1–27. Reprinted with permission.

suddenly surface as a result of America's role in Vietnam, because of the resumption of diplomatic relations with the People's Republic of China, the continuing U.S. support of authoritarian regimes, or the influx of new immigrants and refuges. Recent writings by historians indicate that Asian Americans have sustained an interest in Asian affairs since their arrival in the nineteenth century.[8] Finally, the interest which they have shown in electoral politics extends back to the emergence of second-generation Japanese and Chinese Americans during the early twentieth century. Indeed, the Japanese American Citizens League, which is now committed to a non-electoral posture, actively encouraged voting-age Nisei to exercise their right of franchise during much of the pre–World War II period.[9]

In relation to the development of theoretical frameworks and propositions, there is an extreme paucity of analysis. What exists is largely confined to descriptive and historical inquiries in four different areas: (1) Historical works such as Daniels' *The Politics of Prejudice*, as well as much of the literature on the Japanese American Internment, which explore political actors and policies in American society;[10] (2) Research by historians such as Ichioka, Lai, and Low, which uncovers how Asian immigrants responded to discriminatory actions in the United States, as well as to events in their homelands[11] (3), Commentaries by writers such as Okamura, Uyeda, and Wang, which provide case studies of the actions of Asian Americans in relation to issues such as the repeal of Title II of the McCarran Act, the pardoning of Iva Ikuko Toguri D'Aquino ("Tokyo Rose"), and the *Lau y. Nichols* bilingual education case;[12] and (4) Community and organizational studies like those by Kim, Nee and Nee, Kwong, Modell, and Takahashi, which explore the internal dynamics among competing groups such as labor unions, homeland consulate corps, business elites, and leftists in various communities.[13] These four research categories, along with Jo's *Political Participation of Asian Americans*—the sole anthology on the topic—provide an extensive agenda.[14]

The following overview is based on data collected from multiple research strategies and a review of existing literature.[15] It will attempt to analyze conceptual parameters and to suggest major lines of inquiry. Preliminary findings from two empirical case studies on the electoral potential of Asian Americans, a focus of much media attention and little academic inquiry, will be explored. The case studies deal with registered voters in Los Angeles and San Francisco, the two largest communities in the mainland United States.[16] The studies are part of larger research endeavors which are intended to develop a data base for future work, and for ongoing voter registration drives.[17]

## TRADITIONAL PERSPECTIVES

Asian American politics, according to prevailing thinking, should deal with electoral participation,[18] focusing on voting behavior, the monetary and other resources mobilized for campaigns, and on election and appointment to office.[19] In a more provocative vein, it might also analyze the barriers which have prevented Asian Americans from influencing major political parties and legislative and decision-making circles. Studies should also focus on what has been gained from donating sizeable campaign funds to major candidates and how class interests dominate the policy agenda.[20]

Their increased electoral participation has been a remarkable development. Many have been involved as candidates, financial contributors, campaign workers, voters, legislative liaisons, and elected or appointed officials. During each election season, they enhanced their participation by contributing more campaign funds, sought the registration of more voters, and broke new ground in helping to elect candidates. Michael Woo, for example, recently became the first Asian American ever elected to the Los Angeles City Council.

Although electoral politics has been pursued by Asian American leftists, moderates, and rightists alike, it would be premature to exclusively focus on it. Electoral politics is only one activity pursued in order to protect and advance their interests. The study of non-electoral activity shows how the Asian American experience differs from that of other immigrant and minority groups.[21] Empirical, and theoretical studies on electoral participation can be conceptualized in a more integrated manner, utilizing three major approaches. They are: the interplay between domestic and non-domestic activities; micro versus macro lines of inquiry; and electoral versus non-electoral forms of behavior.

## DOMESTIC VERSUS NON-DOMESTIC POLITICAL PHENOMENA

Asian American involvement should not be confined to the domestic scene.[22] At times, non-domestic events, issues, and forces have played an equal or greater role in shaping our communities[23]. The term "non-domestic" includes the following:

1. The transnational activities of Asian Americans in relation to Asia. This involvement, which shares many features with that of other immigrant groups,[24] includes the contributions which practically all the early Asian immigrants provided in support of revolutionary, nationalistic, and independence movements in their homelands,[25] subsequent support of national development,[26] and efforts by recent immigrants and refugees of opposition movements against both right-wing and Communist regimes in countries such as the Philippines, India, Korea, and Vietnam.[27] This also includes the recent activities of Korean Americans in seeking the normalization of relations, and circumventing South Korean government policy by traveling to North Korea.[28]

2. The transnational activities of Asian homeland government and quasi-governmental institutions in local U.S. communities. These activities take the form of seeking to influence both the mass and elite sentiments and activities toward homeland issues; to implement policies regarding the travel, economic behavior, and registration of overseas emigrants; and to support a variety of political socialization programs for youth. Examples include the special relationships that diplomatic corps, and the local consul general have maintained with organizations like the pre–World War III Japanese Association, or the contemporary Korean Association,[29] the intelligence operations of the KCIA or former Marcos government in Koreatowns or Filipino communities,[30] and the complex network of relationships between the Taiwan-based Kuomintang (KMT) and local Chinatown elites.[31] Similarly, homeland governments have supported language schools and other youth-oriented programs in order to maintain linguistic-cultural ties and to politically socialize immigrant children.[32]

3. The impact of bilateral relationships between the United States and Asia on Asian Americans. This ranges from the internment of Japanese Americans during World War II,[33] thwarting leftist activities during various "cold war" periods,[34] reversing long-standing immigration and naturalization policies affecting Chinese Americans as a result of the alliance with China during World War II,[35] or, for Pacific Islanders and Southeast Asians, determining their domestic political-legal status as nationals aliens, refugees, or other designation as a result of United States relationships with their homelands.[36]

4. The manner in which Asian Americans have sought to influence United States-Asia affairs (perhaps with less visible success than other immigrant groups).[37] Examples include lobbying for or against specific U.S. policies as in the case of the KMT's activities on behalf of Taiwan,[38] serving as bilateral

mediators like Japanese American military personnel during the Japanese Occupation[39] and attempting to play a greater role in United States-Pacific Rim affairs through the U.S.-Asia Institute and other organizations, as well as specific bilateral agreements like the United States-Japan Friendship Treaty.[40]

5. The ways in which international processes and policies involving the flow of people, money, goods, and ideas impinge on the political behavior and status of Asian Americans. This includes the impact of capital flight (from both the United States and Asia) on issues such as immigration or community redevelopment projects;[41] migration of political exiles to Asian American communities, and their subsequent efforts to garner support for their opposition movements;[42] the creation of stereotypic media images of Asian Americans in both the United States and Asia as a result of their changing bilateral relationships;[44] and the degree to which Asian nations can defend immigrants from discriminatory legislation through diplomatic procedures.[45]

These non-domestic dimensions are not confined to one historical period or to a specific sector, such as immigrants or those representing certain class interests. These activities reflect not only external constraints but also the ways in which Asian Americans have initiated actions on their own. Testing frameworks like the world systems theory would provide insights on these international linkages. At the same time, many works assume that concern with homeland politics is limited to the immigrant generation, and that involvement declines with succeeding, acculturated generations. This linear approach fails to consider changing conditions. How does one explain, for example, the concern of third-generation Asian Americans toward United States involvement in Vietnam or the resumption of diplomatic relations with the People's Republic of China? Both the second and third generations have increased their interest in Pacific Rim affairs.[46] Asian Americans may identify with the Pacific Rim in order to define their unique niche in American domestic politics, and thus gain symbolic and financial support from politicians and multinational corporate officials.[47] The continued participation of groups, such as Jews, Polish, Greek, blacks, or Chicanos, with homeland issues demonstrates that acculturation does not automatically signal the end of involvement. It remains to be seen whether Asian Americans can achieve significant results either in their ancestral homelands or by lobbying in this nation.[48]

By conceptualizing Asian American politics in terms of both domestic and non-domestic dimensions, our research agenda differs from what is usually undertaken under the rubric of minority politics.[49] A broader view which recognizes the extensive history of protest and non-domestic political activities would prevent us from making unwarranted assumptions about the seemingly low level of past participation in electoral politics. Taking these non-electoral activities into account enables us to understand the structural and legal barriers that prevented other forms of activity. In turn, we would place less emphasis on elements of cultural heritage, or, as Thomas Sowell suggests, prior economic inclinations, which might have dissuaded fuller participation.[50]

## MICRO VERSUS MACRO POLITICAL APPROACHES

What is commonly called the "levels-of-analysis" question, or the dilemma of deciding between micro and macro approaches of inquiry, is a second major issue. In explaining a particular event or phenomenon, do we focus our investigation on the behavior of individuals, groups, organizations, communities, or broader levels such as the relationships between nations or "systems," be they economic, political, or otherwise?[51] The lack of theoretical discussions prevents us from arguing that only one level is more significant, powerful, or parsimonious in explaining political behavior than another. However, the issue can help to delineate both empirical information and theoretical propositions by suggesting lines of inquiry derived from specific disciplines. It also can serve, as I will shortly illustrate with two recent empirical studies on Asian American electoral participation in Los Angeles and San Francisco, as a heuristic device to reveal a range of alternative hypotheses to account for a single phenomenon or issue.

In relation to understanding electoral behavior at the individual level, there are enormous deficiencies. We have much speculative thought, but little empirical or theoretical work, on such basic questions as: What is the likelihood that an Asian American will register and actually vote in elections? What factors—be they social class, level of educational attainment, ethnicity, generation, sex, occupation, or religion—have the greatest influence on an individual's likelihood to register, affiliate with a specific party, or become involved in other activities, such as contributing campaign funds or seeking public office? Which issues are most likely to gain Asian American voters? What political stances or personal qualities of a candidate influence a vote? Aside from such questions, for which much political science research has been developed,[52] other inquiries remain unanswered: To what extent did events such as the Great Depression, internment, or the Civil Rights Era of the 1960s and 1970s influence the political consciousness and efficacy of Asian Americans?[53] In what ways do they identify with positions that other more visible organized minority groups take on immigration reform, voting rights, bilingualism, affirmative action, or social services programs, in which even the most active Asian American political participants are not consulted?[54] Finally, to what extent do recent immigrants and

refugees, like other migrants, undergo political resocialization to acquire values and orientations to participate in the system?[55]

Similarly, the levels-of-analysis issue can guide research on other dimensions. We must recognize the role of internal community politics and undertake more studies utilizing the community as the unit of analysis. Past research has usually focused on community power structures, with their elitist rather than pluralist power arrangements. This is especially apparent in portrayals of Chinatowns, which draw a hierarchical set of relationships between the Six Companies and the Chinatown residents.[56] Much activity also occurs outside the elitist or pluralist model. The intergeneration transfer of power in local communities and also for organizations is important. The Japanese American Citizens League, for example, which many believe took over community leadership from the Issei during World War II, now finds itself engaged in a transfer to the sansei generation.[57] Other neglected areas include the competition and cooperation between traditional community leaders and the growing number of electorally oriented individuals for institutional and agency support. Future studies, akin to research by Ong, should view local communities in the context of specific municipal political systems.[58] Such studies could examine the structural barriers and linkages between community leaders and local elected officials around issues such as redevelopment. Similarly, research should be done on how new refugees and immigrants, who ofttimes have different leaders, information networks, and group interests, place new items on the agenda, augmenting the electoral potential of existing communities, or creating new forms of factionalism. For Korean and Filipino communities, where new immigrants vastly outnumber the American-born sector, it might be revealing to understand how newcomers came to dominate and revamp political and economic concerns.

## ANALYZING ELECTORAL PARTICIPATION: ASIAN PACIFIC AMERICAN VOTERS IN SAN FRANCISCO AND LOS ANGELES

Aside from delineating broad categories, the levels-of-analysis issue can enhance our understanding of a single phenomenon. For example, our knowledge of Asian American electoral behavior is highly preliminary. Current empirical data contains no information on voting preferences in past presidential or major statewide elections, the factors that might influence electoral participation, or the size of this electorate at local or national levels. Speculation is based on either small numbers who were included in larger polling samples, or from simple observation. Grant Din provides an example:[59]

A *San Francisco Examiner* analysis of the analysis of the 1984 California presidential primary discussed the results of the ABC News exit polling in California and New Jersey. According to these results, in California, "Mondale carried the Asian vote with 40%, Hart trailed with 33% (and Jackson had 20%)." A closer examination, however, reveals that only 2% of the 1,125 voters surveyed, or 23, were Asian American. This translates into 9 votes for Mondale, 8 for Hart, and 5 for Jackson! The poll claimed an overall margin of error of 3%, but it must have been higher for such a small population.

Similarly, Mervin Field, who heads the Field Institute, which regularly polls the California electorate, provides a "very rough" estimate of the size and party preferences of Asian American voters. Field estimates that 4 percent of California's 11.5 million registered voters are Asian American (463,000), and that 48.6 percent are Democrats (225,000), 23.8 percent are Republicans (110,000), and 27.6 percent are not affiliated with either party (128,000).[60] These figures, at best, are extrapolations based on either small samples in past Field polls, or from census information.

Two recently completed empirical studies on Asian American registered voters in Los Angeles and San Francisco provide a more detailed glimpse. Both studies identified individuals with Asian surnames from current official voter registration lists, and determined their political party preferences.[61] The San Francisco study, undertaken by Grant Din, identified Chinese and Japanese voters in the city's Chinatown, Richmond, and Sunset districts.[62] The Los Angeles study was performed by a team of researchers of the UCLA Asian Pacific American Voters Project, headed by the author.[63] It identified Chinese, Japanese, Korean, Filipino, Vietnamese, Samoan, and Asian Pacific Americans, as well as the so-called "Asian Corridor" of the City of Los Angeles. The "Asian Corridor" is a contiguous geographic region, which has the largest number and heaviest concentration of Asian Pacific Americans (76,731 of 359,992, or 21.3 percent of the population) and includes the Highland Park, Chinatown, Temple, Silverlake, Los Feliz, East Hollywood, and Koreatown/Uptown neighborhoods.[64] However, it is not a single political entity, and instead is divided among five larger city councilman districts. In both studies, the results were aggregated to the precinct, census tract, neighborhood, or city levels, and comparisons of party preferences and registration rates between Asian Pacific voters and others were undertaken. Both studies also used 1980 Census data to identify areas with significant Asian Pacific populations, and to develop hypotheses to account for differences and similarities in the electoral characteristics of voters.

To identify Asian Pacific voters would have been simpler if individuals were asked to specify ethnicity when they registered, or if a computer-based program were available to identify these surnames. However, neither was the case. The selected methodology involved locating Asian Pacific voters through sight recognition of their surnames. The method could provide the first empirically based estimates of the size and characteristics of this electorate in relation to specific geographic areas. The data also could be later utilized to develop samples for survey analysis, or for in-depth explorations of other electoral issues such as voting trends of selected precincts with high concentrations. Cases in point are the Chinatowns of San Francisco and Los Angeles or the Southland communities of Monterey Park, Gardena, or Torrance where most registered votes are Asian Pacific Americans. The method also was selected for practical purposes, especially in the Los Angeles study, which was designed to maximize the effectiveness of registration drives and political campaigns in the county. For example, the method could yield highly localized information about current and potential registration rates at the precinct or city level, and pinpoint specific areas to undertake registration activities. It also could provide a potential candidate with a gauge of the size and features of the electorate in a particular jurisdiction.

The method has limitations that would generally hold true even if a computer-based program of surnames were available. One involves the identification of Asian women who married non-Asian men and adopted their husbands' surnames. These individuals cannot be identified systematically, although it is possible to locate some who have distinctly Asian first names through sight recognition. Intermarriage is high among some Asian Pacific groups, but it is not possible to estimate the number of those women who have adopted their husbands' surnames, especially in relation to any specific geographic locale.[65] This factor could contribute to an overall undercount of Asian Pacific voters. However, this methodological limitation can also contribute to an overcount in two cases. The first involves non-Asian women who have married Asian men and have adopted their husbands' surnames, and the second concerns the siblings of intermarriages. How to categorize all these individuals is a subjective judgment. In the Los Angeles study, a set of highly conservative decision rules was employed, which probably account for an undercount of Asian Pacific voters. For example, if a woman with a surname of

Smith and a first name of Kimiko was identified by sight recognition, she was counted as a Japanese American voter, but her children were not counted. No attempt was made to determine whether the spouse of an Asian surnamed male was Asian Pacific.

Three additional limitations are also posed by sight recognition. The first involves Asian surnames that are identical to those of non-Asians, like Lee for Chinese and Koreans or Sanchez for Filipinos. The sight recognition of first names allows for some differentiation, but becomes more judgmental for others who have Anglo first names, or those named Mendoza having first names like Emilio, who live in areas with sizeable Hispanic populations. Some Asian surnames are common for more than one group, as in Lee, Young, and Chang for Chinese and Koreans. There is also the issue of ensuring the most reliability in identification, especially when the Los Angeles study involves the sight recognition of Asian surnamed individuals in relation to almost a million registered voters in the areas analyzed.

These limitations were addressed in a systematic and conservative manner. In both studies, tract data from the 1980 Census were used as rough gauges for estimating the size and characteristics of the Asian Pacific population, or a subgroup, in specific geographic areas. For example, the identification of an individual named Lee in a specific locale was determined, first, by the individual's first name, and then by considering the relative size of the Chinese or Korean population in the area in relation to other groups, like blacks or whites, with similar surnames.

In the case of Koreans, a methodological scheme suggested by Yu was also employed. According to Yu, individuals with the surname of Kim almost always are Korean, and they tend to constitute 22.5 percent of that population in a given area.[66] In the Los Angeles study, all registered voters named Kim were systematically identified for each precinct, and this served as an alternative check for the potential size of the electorate, especially in areas with sizeable numbers of

Korean voters. It was less reliable when the population was small, and not altogether accurate in making projections of the political party affiliations of Korean voters in a particular locale. For example, only three Kims, all members of the same household, were identified for the city of San Gabriel, and there were extreme disparities between the projected and actual numbers of Korean voters, as well as their party affiliations. However, the overall aggregate results were amazingly close in terms of both the number of voters and their pattern of affiliations. Yu's method would have projected 2,880 Korean voters based on the identification of 648 voters named Kim, while the study identified 3,089. At the same time, 48.8 percent of the Kims (316) were Democrats, 27.3 percent were Republicans (177), 1.5 percent were affiliated with smaller parties (10), and 22.3 percent were independents (145), while the corresponding results from the Los Angeles study found that 48.5 percent were Democrats (1496), 29.4 percent Republicans (905), 2.0 percent smaller parties (61), and 20.1 percent independents (620).

The reliability of the overall identification process was controlled through the multiple verification of names in which two, and usually three, readers with knowledge of different Asian Pacific surnames verified the same lists. The methodology, despite the above limitations, is unobtrusive, inexpensive, and capable of generating highly localized data, which can be analyzed with tract or block census data, or used in various grassroots mobilization activities.[67] It should be replicated for other areas with sizeable Asian Pacific populations to gain further, empirically based insights.

The Los Angeles and San Francisco studies provide findings that can be explored in relation to various levels-of-analysis. Like many other characteristics of the diverse Asian Pacific population of the 1980s, there are significant differences among the various groups. In both areas, Japanese have the highest registration rate of all groups, based on the proportion of individuals who are eighteen years and older, who were identified as being registered.[68] In San Francisco,

Din found that the overall registration rate for Chinese in the Chinatown, Richmond, and Sunset districts was 30.9 percent, while for Japanese in Richmond and Sunset it was 36.8 percent. The Los Angeles study, on the other hand projected that 43.0 percent of all Japanese were registered, followed by 35.5 percent of Chinese, 28.5 percent of Samoans, 27.0 percent of Filipinos, 16.7 percent Asian Indians, 13.0 percent Koreans, and 4.1 percent Vietnamese.[69] In both locales, all groups have rates which are substantially lower than that of the general electorate, in which approximately 60 percent of all individuals who are eighteen years and older are registered to vote.[70] At the same time, Japanese in both areas, as well as Koreans, Filipinos, Samoans, and Asian Indians in Los Angeles, tend to identify with the Democratic party to a greater extent than Chinese voters in either locale, or Vietnamese in Los Angeles. The most surprising findings of both studies involve the large proportion of independent voters among Chinese, Vietnamese, Korean, and Asian Indians, in which approximately one in five declined to state a party preference. Although recent polls and studies report that a growing number of voters now consider themselves independents, the official registration lists of Los Angeles and San Francisco counties indicate that only ten percent of all voters, like the Japanese, Filipinos, and Samoans in the two studies, decline to specify a party affiliation. Table 3.1a provides the overall aggregate ethnic and political party affiliations for the areas investigated by the two studies.

The two studies also suggest a variety of hypotheses about within-group differences, and their electoral impact on local municipalities. Both studies found that registration rates and, to a certain extent, party affiliations were not uniform for any specific group across the geographic areas examined. Chinese in San Francisco had registration rates which ranged from the Richmond district's 39.9 percent to Chinatown's 23.1 percent. According to Din, "it appears that when the percentage of foreign-born residents go up in an area, the voter registration rate goes

**Table 3.1a    Aggregate Findings of Political Party Affiliations of Asian Pacific American Registered Voters of the San Francisco and Los Angeles Studies**

| Area/ethnic group | Total registered | Democrats (%) | Republicans (%) | Other party (%) | No party (%) |
|---|---|---|---|---|---|
| SF Chinese* | 11,041 | 5,368 (48.6) | 2,360 (21.4) | 187 (1.7) | — |
| SF Japanese* | 1,506 | 1,004 (66.7) | 304 (20.2) | 14 (.9) | — |
| LA Japanese** | 16,747 | 9,191 (54.9) | 5414 (32.3) | 133 (.8) | 2,009 (12.0) |
| LA Chinese** | 13,150 | 5,510 (41.9) | 4,785 (36.4) | 172 (1.3) | 2,683 (20.4) |
| LA Filipinos** | 9,657 | 6,112 (63.3) | 2,206 (22.8) | 213 (2.2) | 1,125 (11.6) |
| LA Koreans** | 3,082 | 1,496 (48.5) | 905 (29.4) | 61 (2.0) | 620 (20.1) |
| LA Samoans*** | 484 | 295 (61.0) | 119 (25.0) | 13 (2.7) | 57 (11.8) |
| LA Vietnamese** | 370 | 148 (40.0) | 133 (35.9) | 13 (3.5) | 76 (20.5) |
| LA Asian Indians*** | 259 | 153 (59.1) | 61 (23.6) | 1 (.4) | 44 (17.0) |

*Notes:* *The identification of Chinese American registered voters in San Francisco was limited to precincts of twenty-eight census tracts of the Chinatown, Richmond, and Sunset districts, while the analysis of Japanese American voters was limited to the Richmond and Sunset areas. Approximately 41.8% of the city's Asian Pacific American population, and 46.5% of the Chinese American population, lived in these twenty-eight tracts according to the 1980 census. Data were derived from the November 1983 lists of official registered voters for precincts of these tracts.

**Japanese, Chinese, Filipino, Korean, and Vietnamese registered voters in the Los Angeles study were identified for the so-called "Asian Corridor" section of the City of Los Angeles, as well as the neighboring cities of Monterey Park, Torrance, Gardena, Cerritos, Carson, Montebello, Glendale, West Covina, Alhambra, Hacienda Heights, Ranchos Palos Verdes, Norwalk, Rosemead, South Pasadena, Hawthorne, San Gabriel, Rowland Heights, El Monte, Covina, and Lomita. In total, these areas included 46.2% of the Asian Pacific American population for Los Angeles County according to the 1980 census. Data were derived from the June, 1984 lists of official registered voters for precincts of these tracts.

***The identification of Samoan registered voters was limited to the cities of Carson, Gardena, Torrance, Lomita, Hawthorne, Cerritos, and Norwalk. In total, these areas included 30.1% of the Samoan American population according to the 1980 census. On the other hand, the identification of Asian Indian voters was limited to the cities of Cerritos, Glendale, West Covina, Monterey Park, and Hacienda Heights, which together accounted for 11.0% of the Asian Indian population in the county according to the 1980 census. Data for both groups were derived from the June 1984 lists of official registered voters in these areas.

down."[71] This somewhat obvious hypothesis is generally supported by the Los Angeles study, in which areas with high foreign-born percentages have the lowest registration rates (e.g., Los Angeles' Asian Corridor with 77.6 percent, Alhambra with 75.7 percent, El Monte with 73.2 percent, or Glendale with 73.2 percent). However, this variable may not serve as a useful baseline in launching activities like voter registration drives because other areas with seemingly higher registration rates have large foreign-born Asian Pacific sectors, e.g. San Francisco's Richmond district (60.1 percent), or West Covina in Los Angeles County which has a comparable registration rate (65.5 percent). Census data on the percentages of foreign-born provide a rough gauge, but not a full and updated enumeration, of the more crucial variable of

percentage of citizens, be they American born or naturalized.[72] More importantly, the single variable of the percentage of foreign-born cannot fully explain why in a city like Gardena, which has the lowest percentage of foreign born at 34.6 percent, Asians do not have the corresponding highest registration rate. Of the twenty cities outside of Los Angeles city, Gardena's Asian Pacific Americans ranked tenth in registration rate at 34.6 percent, a rate lower than that of the Richmond district or West Covina. As Din properly hypothesized there are a host of other factors which must be considered in understanding not only why individuals of the same group do not register at the same rates, but also why Asian Pacific Americans as a whole register at a substantially lower, and usually 50 percent or less, rate than others.

The explanation is multivariate, and can be approached at different levels-of-analysis. Research has consistently found that higher socioeconomic status as reflected in income, educational attainment, occupation, and other related characteristics is strongly correlated with higher rates of political involvement at both the individual and macro levels. The data from the two studies do not allow us to make individual-level generalizations, but it appears that this well-supported explanation of political behavior would require some modifications in its application for Asian Pacific Americans. The most obvious consideration is whether an individual is a citizen and legally eligible to register, no matter how rich or well educated. However, non-citizen status does not preclude participation in other types of electoral activities. As noted earlier, a substantial portion of the funds which are "credited" to Asian Pacific fundraising efforts for major political candidates is derived from non-citizen sources, be they individuals or corporations. Similarly, electoral activities require familiarity with American politics and government, and the English language. Din argues that one possible factor which may account for the differences in registration rates between Japanese Americans, who are predominantly American born, and the general population in San Francisco may be the enduring psychological impact of the internment experience, especially in relation to political efficacy and trust in American politics.[73] For Asian Pacific Americans generally, other factors are lack of English fluency, insufficient resocialization to American political values, the psychological consequences of being a minority, the length of time of political enfranchisement, and the extent of involvement in non-domestic versus domestic issues and events.[74] These variables may intervene in the causal relationship between an individual's socioeconomic standing and electoral participation.

The data from the two studies, along with census information, offer a series of macro-level insights that can serve as hypotheses for subsequent inquiries. The first finding is that of the size of its overall population. In the Los Angeles study the ranking of the total number of Asian Pacific voters for the twenty cities in the county other than the Asian Corridor parallels the ranking of those same cities in terms of their total Asian Pacific populations. The differences in registration rates between those cities, which range from 61.8 percent for Covina to 20.2 percent in Hawthorne, do not appear to have a measurable effect on this relationship when the unit of analysis is the entire Asian Pacific population. The registration rate would matter if we designated the Asian Corridor as a single entity, and hypothetically compared it with an imaginary municipality composed of a comparable number of Asians from the suburban cities. The Asian Corridor, for example, with its 71,297 Asian Pacifics in 1980 would be comparable to the 68,626 Asian Pacifics who resided in Monterey Park, Torrance, Gardena, Carson, and Cerritos. However, the Asian Corridor had half as many registered voters, with 8,969 versus a total of 19,566 for the five cities.

Asian Pacific voters reflect a host of differences and similarities with other voters in their local communities. The general electorates in fifteen cities and all areas of the Asian Corridor have a plurality or majority of Democrats. In contrast, Asian Pacific voters in all cities except South Pasadena and Rancho Palos Verdes, as well as all areas of the Asian Corridor, have a plurality or majority of Democrats. In Democratic strongholds, though, the Asian Pacific proportion is usually less than the electorate as a whole, and also tends to be somewhat higher in the percentage of Republicans. However, in the five cities which have a majority or plurality of Republicans, namely Torrance, Glendale, Rancho Palos Verdes, South Pasadena, and Covina, Asian Pacific Americans are less likely to be Republicans than other voters, and indeed are more likely to be Democrats in Torrance, Glendale, and Covina. There is also more localized data to illustrate the earlier observation about the differences in party preference among the various Asian

Pacific groups in each city. This lack of uniformity, especially among groups of voters in the same city who probably reflect comparable socioeconomic characteristics, suggests that different combinations of factors and regression equations are necessary to explain party affiliation patterns for the groups. It suggests that Asian Pacific voters, despite their aggregate leanings towards the Democratic Party, cannot be viewed as a monolithic bloc of voters in any local community. Their potential electoral impact would be lessened in partisan primaries and the high proportion of independents among certain groups may reflect a more general condition of weak party identification. Finally, none of the areas showed that the proportion of Asian Pacific voters in relation to the general electorate equaled their percentage of the population of those areas. In most cities and areas, like those which Din examined in San Francisco, the percentage of registered voters was less than half of their representation in the population. However, in cities where Asian Pacifics have been successful in winning public office, as well as those where the overall registration rate is extremely low, this disparity is usually much less. Monterey Park, which had two Asian Pacific city council members and a city treasurer, had an electorate which is 29.2 percent Asian Pacific, and in 1980 had an overall population representation of 33.7 percent. In contrast, Asian Pacifics in El Monte accounted for 2.7 percent of the electorate, and 2.8 percent of the total population, but their registration rate was 29.8 percent and only 37.4 percent for the city as a whole.

The contrasts in electoral characteristics and involvement between Asian Pacific Americans and others can be gleamed through a variety of macro-level indicators. Like other regions, Los Angeles County has witnessed a dramatic growth and diversification of its Asian Pacific population in recent years due to increased immigration. Rather than citing the percentage of foreign-born, another census indicator based on the percentage of individuals, five years and older, who resided abroad in 1975 provides a more revealing view of this phenomenon. For example, 29.5 percent (125,545) of all Asian Pacifics, five years and older, in 1980 in the county lived abroad in 1975. This percentage is close to five times more than the total county figure, and Asian Pacific Americans accounted for approximately 30 percent of all individuals who lived abroad. The Asian Pacific populations in half of the twenty suburban cities, as well as the entire Asian Corridor, had percentages of those living abroad which exceeded the county-wide figure for Asian pacific Americans as a whole. All exceeded that of the county's general population. Hawthorne had the highest percentage with 42.7 percent of its Asian Pacifics living abroad, followed by the Asian Corridor with 42.5 percent, Glendale with 40.8 percent, and El Monte with 40.5 percent. Gardena had the lowest percentage at 14.0 percent, almost twice that of both the county and the entire population of the city of Gardena. The recency of their arrival in the United States, and their grater likelihood of not being naturalized, also contributes greatly to lower registration rates. In addition, 26.7 percent of all Asian pacific Americans of voting age in Los Angeles County indicated that they did not speak English well or not at all. In every city or Asian Corridor area, Asian Pacifics had a higher proportion of such individuals than their local communities. In past years, when bilingual ballots were more prevalent in California, only San Francisco was required to provide ballots and other materials in the Chinese language. No area in Los Angeles County has ever had Asian language electoral materials.

Although it appears that the overall voter registration rates for all twenty cities and the areas of the Asian Corridor are highly correlated with commonly used variables such as median family income, percentage of college graduates, and percentage of professionals and managers, the same relationship is much weaker for Asian Pacific Americans. Again, it appears that other group-specific factors aside from socioeconomic characteristics must be taken into account in analyzing electoral participation. Indeed, Asian Pacific Americans may exhibit a group socioeconomic profile that is comparable to that of others in their communities, and yet have other distinguishing features that are negatively correlated with electoral involvement. South Pasadena's Asian Pacific Americans have a higher family median income ($32,077 versus $27,283), a higher proportion of college educated individuals (74.9 percent versus 63.8 percent), and a greater percentage of professionals and managers (46.1 percent versus 41.0 percent) than the city as a whole, but nonetheless have a registration rate of 35.2 percent as opposed to 67.9 percent for the entire population. However, they also are significantly higher on indicators, which would work against electoral involvement. Twenty-six and one-tenth percent of the Asian Pacific Americans versus 5.5 percent of the entire population lived abroad five years ago; 58.0 percent versus 17.0 percent were foreign-born; and, as we will soon discuss, 25.6 percent versus 47.6 percent lived in the same house in 1975 as they did in 1980.

A large number of Asian Pacific Americans in Los Angeles County are recent immigrants, but an ever greater number of both foreign and American born are relative newcomers to their local communities. Their geographic movement—be it from a port-of-entry neighborhood like Koreatown to a secondary one like Glendale, or from one rung of the social mobility ladder like Torrance to another like Rancho Palos Verdes—also is a significant macro-level feature which probably influences electoral participation. For example, Gardena's Asian Pacific Americans who were five years and older in 1980 were the only ones who had a greater proportion of individuals (56.1 percent) who lived in the same house five years previous than the overall city rate (52.7 percent). For all other Asian Pacific populations, the differences in the longevity of residence were quite pronounced, and underscore the fact that most are relatively new settlements in well-established communities. Only 7.9 percent

of the Asian Pacific Americans in Rowland Heights, 14.4 percent in Glendale, 15.8 percent in West Covina, and 17.9 percent in Alhambra lived in the same house versus 40.5 percent, 45.2 percent, and 43.6 percent for the overall populations of those cities, respectively.

All cities and areas experienced dramatic growth, diversification, and movement. Cities that have elected Asian Pacific Americans to public office like Monterey Park, Gardena, Torrance, and Montebello generally have had large, long-standing, and relatively stable Asian Pacific populations, which in recent years grew into a greater proportion of the city's total population. Their local involvement usually has not been recent, although the augmentation of the potential electoral base has clearly enhanced the potential of their own candidates. In contrast, most of the other cities have largely new Asian Pacific populations, which have not been recruited into long-prevalent, local political systems. It is difficult to predict whether they will establish a stable presence in these communities as opposed to treating them as temporary way stations. At the same time, their geographic movement may account for differences in patterns of party preference versus other voters. These differences may result from the cultural, political, or other types of baggage that they carry to new homes, but for whatever reasons are not willing to replace so easily. Asian Pacific voters in Torrance, for example, are largely Democrats, whereas the general electorate has a plurality of Republicans. All things being equal, one factor which may account for this phenomenon may be the continuous movement of Japanese Americans, who represent over half of both Asian Pacific voters and Democrats, from the neighboring, and predominantly Democratic city of Gardena.

In terms of within-group differences and similarities, the UCLA project provides an interesting contrast with the San Francisco study. Din, for example, found that Chinatown's Chinese voters had a slightly higher percentage of Republicans, a lower percentage of Democrats, and a greater proportion of independents than those in the Richmond and Sunset districts. He argued that this less than obvious finding concerning Republican strength among inner city Chinese could be explained by the continued "strong influence of the Kuomintang, or Chinese nationalist Party, and its affiliated family and merchant associations that are headquartered directly in Chinatown."[75] The Los Angeles project came to the opposite conclusion. Republicans were the plurality of Chinese voters in half of the cities in Los Angeles county, but not of the areas of the Asian Corridor. Indeed, all areas of the Asian Corridor, including Chinatown, reflected a plurality of Chinese Democrats, although the percentages of independent voters remained high for both the county and city. The differences may be due to the relative strength of internal community organizations in the two areas, and other group differences between the Chinese populations in San Francisco and Los Angeles. It might be noted that Chinese have never been elected to the ten cities in Los Angeles County that have a plurality of Chinese Republicans.

The within-group differences between those who reside in the Asian Corridor versus suburban communities are not as great for the other groups as Asian Pacific voters. Japanese, Korean, and Vietnamese voters in the Asian Corridor are more Democratic, less Republican, but slightly more independent than their counterparts in the county. Japanese across all geographic areas have a plurality or majority of Democrats, while Korean and Vietnamese exhibit areas of Republican support in the suburbs. Filipino voters, on the other hand, reflect almost no differences between those in the city and county, and tend to be overwhelmingly Democratic.

## ELECTORAL VERSUS NON-ELECTORAL POLITICS

Asian Americans have been involved with, and affected by, the domestic political system in ways that cannot be fully understood by an exclusive preoccupation with electoral politics.

Domestic protest activities, whether they are led by Asian Americans or organized against them, must be viewed as a significant alternative dimension. Recent studies have analyzed the extensive involvement of Asian Americans in labor protests and conflicts;[76] in leftist organizing efforts, as well as the Asian American movement of the 1960s and 1970s;[77] in community challenges to issues such as busing in San Francisco, land development in Hawaii, or urban redevelopment in Los Angeles' Little Tokyo;[78] and in nationally based movement dealing with the repeal of Title II of the McCarran Act and regaining citizenship for Iva Ikuko Toguri D'Aquino.[79] We may see future in-depth treatments of protest activities in relation to the Chol Soo Lee Movement, redress and reparations for the Japanese American Internment, the murder of Vincent Chin, campaigns to designate English as the official language in response to the large influx of Asian immigrants, and studies which combine international and domestic concerns such as local demonstrations over the downing of Korean Air Line's flight 007, or the assassinations of Benigno Aquino, Henry Liu, and Indira Gandhi.[80] Theoretical frameworks on social protest such as Piven and Cloward's controversial thesis on the rise and fall of poor people's movements, which emphasizes the structural preconditions and limitations of these efforts, could be applied to these analyses.[81]

Asian Americans have also been long involved with political activities that transcend internal community politics, and yet fall short of being considered a form of protest, or a straightforward example of electoral involvement. The Japanese American Citizens League, for example, has attempted to steer a middle course and has achieved its greatest success and notoriety from both its federal-level, legislative lobbying efforts and its pursuit of "recognition politics." The latter refers to activities that place greater emphasis on securing symbolic acknowledgement rather than tangible benefits. The JACL's initial reluctance in deciding between seeking a national apology or monetary reparations for the internment reflects these competing orientations. At the same time, it appears that there is an expanding infrastructure involving other interest groups organized around women's issues, educational reform, legal advocacy, or specific professions, which emerged at regional and national levels.[82] These groups are typically organized around the banner of Asian unity, draw members who share a specialized interest or professional training, and engage in policy advocacy activities and recognition politics in narrowly defined issue areas. They usually speak for Asian American interests and are perceived as the representatives of organized ethnic concerns. Although they occasionally channel resources into the most crucial campaigns, the bulk of their activities cannot be labeled as electoral. In many respects, they have embraced the philosophical tenets of the Asian American student movement of the past decade.[83] Yet they largely prefer lobbying to protests; developing networks rather than consciousness-raising—in realizing their maximum worth. However, like the earlier student movement, they maintain a distant nebulous relationship with long-standing community organizations and leaders, although they would be less likely to challenge their presumed authority and status. They also are products of the prevailing single-issue, and highly technical, advocacy in American politics, as well as the increased clustering of Asian Americans in a number of previously restricted fields ranging from law to corporate business. The impact of this emerging infrastructure on the internal community politics and external representation of Asian Americans requires analysis.

Finally, it is important to recognize the normative and ideological dimensions of behavior among Asian Americans. Jere Takahashi, for example, has written an innovative analysis of three major, and yet largely unexamined, pre–World War II generational perspectives of second generation Japanese Americans—serving as a cultural bridge between the United States and Japan, pursuing an unflinching Americanism philosophy, and advancing the cause of the second generation working class—through usage of archival and oral history materials.[84] Similarly, other analyses of the earlier Asian American movement, contemporary Marxist organizations, and major political-literary writers such as Carlos Bulosan and Karl Yoneda have been produced.[85] Additional work would reveal the ideological underpinnings of leaders, writers, and organizations in their struggles to improve their status, to reform or rebel against the status quo, and to realize their vision of a different reality, here and aboard. For example, the often controversial decision to forego involvement in Asian homeland politics and to pursue a domestic orientation is not an automatic one based on increased acculturation, but instead is related to a complex set of beliefs and orientations about a group's interests, the potential for realizing goals, and the dynamics of the political process.

\* \* \*

The parameters I have drawn for the field are intentionally all-encompassing. Individuals may tend to have a limited view of what constitutes Asian American politics, and possess a largely ahistorical understanding of the range of activities which Asian Americans have pursued, as well as the manner in which politics has affected them. I hope this discussion provides a glimpse of the longitudinal significance of politics of the Asian American experience, and some of the theoretical, empirical, and historical issues that can be explored. Electoral politics is a vital part of our lives, and yet it must be understood within broader contexts. By not doing so, we will provide electoral politics with a mandate, which it neither deserves nor has gained in relation to other campaigns.

### NOTES

1. See Milton Morris, *The Politics of Black America* (New York, 1975) for a discussion of resources and structural opportunities that are needed to compete effectively in American politics.

2. See Don T. Nakanishi and Bernie Laforteza, *The National Asian Pacific American Roster, 1984* (Los Angeles, 1984), for a listing of major elected and appointed officials in the United States. Also see Tom Coffman, *Catch a Wave* (Honolulu, 1976), for a journalistic account of the rise of Asian Americans in Hawaiian Politics.

3. See, among others, Yung-Hwan Joe, ed., *Political Participation of Asian Americans: Problems and Strategies* (Chicago, 1980); and Roger Daniels, *Concentration Camps U.S.A.: Japanese Americans and World War II* (Hinsdale, Illinois, 1971), 173.

4. See the various presentations in U.S. Commission on Civil Rights, *Civil Rights Issues of Asian and Pacific Americans: Myths and Realities* (Washington, D.C., 1979).

5. For critical assessments of the model minority thesis, see Bob Suzuki, "Education and Socialization of Asian Americans," *Amerasia Journal* 4 (1977): 23–51; and Ki-Taek Chun, "The Myth of Asian American Success and Its Educational Ramifications," *IRCD Bulletin* 15 (1980): 1–12. However, it should be noted that neither the proponents nor critics of this thesis addresses the issue of Asian American influence and representation in major American political institutions.

6. See Harold Isaacs, *Idols of the Tribe* (New York, 1975).

7. See Karl Yoneda, *Ganbatte: Sixty-Year Struggle of a Kibei Worker* (Los Angeles, 1983), and "One Hundred Years of Japanese Labor in the United States," in Amy Tachiki, et al., eds., *Roots: An Asian American Reader* (Los Angeles, 1971), 138–49; Victor Low, *The Unimpressible Race: A Century of Educational Struggle by the Chinese in San Francisco* (San Francisco, 1982); and Peter Kwong, *Chinatown, New York: Labor and Politics, 1930–1950* (New York, 1981).

8. See Shih-Shan Henry Tsai, "The Emergence of Early Chinese Nationalist Organizations in America," *Amerasia Journal* 8(2) (1981): 121–44; and Kingsley Lyu, "Korean Nationalist Activities in Hawaii and the Continental United States, 1900–1945," Parts I and II, *Amerasia Journal* 4(1–2) (1977).

9. Togo Tanaka, "History of the JACL," unpublished manuscript, Japanese Evacuation and Resettlement Study, Bancroft Library, University of California, Berkeley, n.d.

10. Roger Daniels, *The Politics of Prejudice* (New York, 1968). Also see Audrie Girdner and Anne Loftis, *The Great Betrayal* (New York, 1969); Morton Grodzins, *Americans Betrayed* (Chicago 1949); Michi Weglyn, *Years of Infamy* (New York, 1976); Peter Irons, *Justice at War* (New York, 1983); and Alexander Saxton, *The Indispensable Enemy* (Berkeley, 1971).

11. See Yuji Ichioka, "The Early Japanese Quest for Citizenship: The Background of the 1922 Ozawa Case," *Amerasia Journal* 4(2) (1977): 1–22; Him Mark Lai, "A Historical Survey of the Chinese Left in America," in Emma Gee, ed., *Counterpoint* (Los Angeles, 1976), 63–80; Howard A. DeWitt, "The Filipino Labor Union: The Salinas Lettuce Strike of 1934," *Amerasia Journal* 5(2) (1978): 1–22.

12. Raymond Okamura, "Campaign to Repeal the Emergency Detention Act," *Amerasia Journal* 2(2) (1974): 71–111; Clifford Uyeda, "The Pardoning of 'Tokyo Rose': A Report on the Restoration of American Citizenship to Iva Ikuko Toguri," *Amerasia Journal* 5(2) (1978): 69–94; and Ling-Chi Wang, "Lau v. Nichols: History of a Struggle for Equal and Quality Education," in Gee, *Counterpoint*, 240–63.

13. Illsoo Kim, *New Urban Immigrants* (Princeton, 1981); Victor Nee and Brett Nee, *Longtime Californ'* (Boston, 1974); John Modell, *The Economics and Politics of Racial Accommodations* (Urbana, Illinois, 1977); and Jere Takahashi, "Japanese American Responses to Race Relations: The Formation of Nisei Perspectives," *Amerasia Journal* 9(2) (1982): 29–58.

14. Jo, *Political Participation*. Also see Vincent Parrillo, "Asian Americans in American Politics," in J. Roucek and B. Eisenberg, eds., *America's Ethnic Politics* (Westport, Conn., 1982), 89–112.

15. The discussion is based on interviews with Asian American elected officials and political activists in California; participant-observation studies of Asian American electoral and protest activities; content analysis of Asian American newspapers and publications; and finally, statistical analysis of electoral data on campaign finances, voter registration rates,

and election results. I am especially thankful to my two research assistants, Sam Law and Bernie LaForteza. I also have drawn many observations from my involvement with the Asian America movement, as well as electoral activities such as serving as the interim statewide coordinator for Asian Pacific America affairs during Thomas Bradley's unsuccessful 1982 gubernatorial campaign.

16. The Asian Pacific American population in Los Angeles County, according to 1980 Census, was 434,850. Along with other large populations of Asian Pacific Americans in neighboring counties, especially Orange County, the Southern California region has the largest Asian Pacific American settlement in the mainland states.

17. The Los Angeles study, entitled the *UCLA Asian Pacific American Voters Study*, was sponsored by the Asian Pacific American Legal Center of Southern California, and funded by the Southwest Voter Registration project of San Antonio, Texas and the UCLA Academic Senate.

18. An examination of any Asian American newspaper, especially *Asian Week*, will illustrate the current prominence of electoral politics. Recent stories on Asian American electoral involvement also have appeared in the general media.

19. Jo, *Political Participation of Asian Americans*.

20. Much has been written about the sizeable financial contributions of Asian Americans, especially for Democratic party candidates. An examination of campaign finance disclosure statements for Thomas Bradley's 1982 gubernatorial campaign in California, which was conducted by Sam Law, revealed that Asian Americans gave close to a half-million dollars to his efforts, while providing only token contributions to his Republican rival, George Deukmejian, who eventually won by a very narrow margin.

21. For other treatments of minority and ethnic politics, see Morris, *The Politics of Black America*; Matthew Holden Jr., *The Politics of the Black 'Nation'* (New York, 1973); Lucius Barker and Jesse McCorry, *Black Americans and the Political System* (Cambridge, 1976); Mario Barrera, *Race and Class in the Southwest* (Notre Dame, 1979); and Stephen D. Isaacs,

*Jews and American Politics* (Garden City, 1974).

22. See Don Nakanishi, "In Search of a New Paradigm: Minorities in the Context of International Politics," *Studies in Race and Nations* 6 (1974–1975): 1–29 for a fuller analysis of the international dimensions of minority politics.

23. The broad theoretical perspective on international politics which underlies this discussion draws its insights from Joseph Nye and Robert Keohane, eds., *Transnational Relations and World Politics* (Cambridge, 1971). Also see John F. Stack Jr., ed., *Ethnic Identities in a Transnational World* (Westport, 1981).

24. See Henry L. Feingold, *The Politics of Rescue: The Roosevelt Administration and the Holocaust, 1938–1945* (New Brunswick, 1970); and Lawrence Fuchs, ed., *American Ethnic Politics* (New York, 1968).

25. See Lyu, "Korean Nationalistic Activities"' Tsai, "The Emergence of Early Chinese Nationalistic Organizations"; Alexander Saxton, "The Army of Canton in the High Sierra," *Pacific Historical Review* 35 (1966): 141–152; Mark Juergens-Meyer, "The Ghadar Syndrome: Nationalism in an Immigrant Community," Center for South and *Southeast Asian Studies Review* 1 (1978): 9–13.

26. Lucie Cheng, et al. "Chinese Emigration, the Sunning Railroad, and the Development of Toisan," *Amerasia Journal* 9(1) (1982): 59–74; and Renqui Yu, "Chinese American Contributions to the Educational Development of Toisan, 1910–1940," *Amerasia Journal* 10(1)(1983): 47–72.

27. See H. Brett Melendy, *Asians in America* (Boston, 1977); and "A People's Anger: An Interview with Beth Rosales on the Aquino Assassination," *East Wind* 2 (1983): 8–10.

28. Edward Tea Chang, "The Politics of the Korean Community in Los Angeles Kwangju Uprising and Its Impact." M.A. thesis, University of California, Los Angeles, 1984.

29. See Yuji Ichioka, "Japanese Association and the Japanese Government: Their Special Relationship, 1909–1926," *Pacific Historical Review* 46 (1977): 409–38; and Illsoo Kim, *New Urban Immigrants*, 227–61.

30. See The New Korea, "KCIA Agents All Out to Get New Korea and the Activities of the

South Korean Central Intelligence Agency in the United States," in Gee, *Counterpoint*, 140–45; *Philippine News*, "The Story of Marcos Coercion," in Gee, *Counterpoint*, 134–39; and Chang, *The Politics of the Korean Community*.

31. Lai, "China Politics and United States Chinese Communities," in Gee, *Counterpoint*, 152–59.

32. Raymond Jung. "The Chinese Language School in the United States," *School and Society* 100 (1972): 309–12; and Lai, "China Politics."

33. This does not imply that the war was the sole, or even the most crucial, factor leading to the decision to intern Japanese Americans during World War II. For an analysis of how Nisei were viewing the developing potential for war between the two countries, see Forrett La Violette, "The American-born Japanese and the World Crisis," *Canadian Journal of Economics and Political Science* (1941): 517–27.

34. Lai, "A Historical Survey of the Chinese Left:" Jack Chen, *The Chinese in America* (San Francisco, 1980): 211–18; Yoneda, *Ganbatte*, 172–73; and Sanford Zalburg, *A Spark is Struck! Jack Hall and the ILWU in Hawaii* (Honolulu, 1979).

35. See Chen, *The Chinese in America*, 205–7.

36. U.S. Commission on Civil Rights, Civil Rights Issues, 164–307, provides an overview of these issues.

37. See footnote 24. Also, for an insightful piece on the involvement of Greek Americans in United States foreign policy, see John P. Paul, "The Greek Lobby and American Foreign Policy: A Transnational Perspective," in Stack, *Ethnic Identities*, 47–48.

38. Robert C. Keohane, "The Big Influence of Small Allies," *Foreign Policy* 2 (1971): 161–82.

39. Joseph Harrington, Yankee Samurai (Detroit, 1979); and Tamotsu Shibutani, *The Derelicts of Company K* (Berkeley, 1978).

40. The Washington, D.C.-based U.S.-Asia Institute and its president, Kay Sugahara, are best known for declaring several years back that they would serve as brokers between unspecified Japanese corporations and United States municipalities in providing capital loans totaling over a billion dollars. The loans apparently never materialized. This is only one of a number of groups that is seeking to play a greater role in trade and diplomatic policy issues between the United States and Asian countries. The JACL, on the other hand, has attempted periodically to gain greater representation in the activities of the U.S.-Japan Friendship Treaty, but generally has not been successful. Its top leadership, however, did visit Japan to meet top government, economic, and educational officials, as well as a number of second-generation Nisei, who have lived in Japan since the 1930s and 1940s and have played a vital intermediary role between a number of Japanese and American institutions and corporations.

41. See Lucie Cheng and Edna Bonacich, eds., *Labor Immigration Under Capitalism: Asian Workers in the United States Before World War II* (Berkeley, 1984); Illsoo Kim, *New Urban Immigrants; Little Tokyo Anti-Eviction Task Force*, "Redevelopment in Los Angeles' Little Tokyo," in Gee, Counterpoint, 327–33; and John Wang, "Behind the Boom: Power and Economics in Chinatown, *New York Affairs* 5 (1979): 77–81.

42. See "A People's Anger," *East Wind*.

43. The clearest example involves California's unitary tax law, in which multinational corporations are taxed a percentage of their worldwide earnings rather than the profits they make in the state. Asian, and specifically Japanese, multinational corporations have lobbied vigorously to repeal this law, and have oftimes used politically-active Asian Americans to serve as advocates.

44. Eugene Wong, "On Visual Racism: Asians in American Motion Pictures," Ph.D. dissertation, University of Denver, 1978.

45. See Linda Pomerantz, "The Chinese Bourgeoisie, Commercial Interests, and the Anti-Chinese Movement in the United States," in Nakanishi, "Linkages and Boundaries" (forthcoming); Iriye, "Introduction: Ron Takaki, *Iron Cages* (New York, 1979); and Bailey, *Theodore Roosevelt*.

46. See Odo, "U.S. in Asia"; Marcia Jean Chan and Candice Cynda Chan, eds., *Going Back* (1973); Kalayaan Editorial Collective, "Filipinos: A Fast Growing U.S. Minority-Philippines Revolution," in Tachiki, *Roots*, 312–15.

47. The 1984 presidential primaries and conventions were significant because Asian Americans were well-represented at the national conventions, especially the Democratic, and finally had presidential candidates speak to them about their domestic concerns. In the past, candidates from both parties usually emphasized U.S.-Asia issues in appealing to Asian American voters.

48. There is no question that Asian Americans have received greater media coverage in their responses to major events in Asia, especially with the downing of KAL Flight 007, the assassinations of Benigno Aquino and Indira Gandhi, and the election of Corazon Aquino. However, no work has systematically explored how minority and immigrant groups can be effective in influencing the foreign policy decision-making processes in either the United States or abroad. Most studies tend to be descriptive case studies of a specific group rather than comparative inquiries.

49. Very few works on minority group politics, with the exception of the most recent studies on American Jews, use a dual perspective of both domestic and non-domestic political activities. Although all American immigrant and minority groups have pursued international or homeland issues, most researchers concentrate solely on domestic activities.

50. See Jo, *Political Participation of Asian Americans*; Alfred Song, "Politics and Policies of the oriental Community," in Eugene P. Dvorin and Arthur Misner, eds., *California Politics and Policies* (Pala Alto, 1966): 387–411; and Ralph Bunch, "The Political Orientation of Japanese-Americans," Ph.D. dissertation, University of Oregon, 1968.

51. See, for example, David J. Singer, "The Level-of-Analysis Problem in International Relations," in Knorr Klaus and Sidney Verba, eds., *The International System* (Princeton, 1961), 77–92.

52. See, for example, Norman H. Nie, Sidney Verba, and John Petrocik, *The Changing American Voter* (Cambridge, 1976); and Herbert Asher, "Voting Behavior Research in the 1980s: An Examination of Some Old and New Problem Areas," in Ada W. Finifter, ed., *Political Science: The State of the Discipline* (Washington, D.C., 1983), 339–88.

53. Preliminary work on this question can be found in Jerrold Haruo Takahashi, "Changing Responses to Racial Subordination: An Exploratory Study of Japanese American Political Styles," Ph.D. dissertation, University of California, Berkeley, 1980; and Don T. Nakanishi, "Can It Happen Again? The Impact of the Holocaust and Evacuation on the Political Thinking and Consciousness of American Jewish and Japanese American Leaders," Ph.D. dissertation, Harvard University, 1978.

54. See Ford Kuramoto, "Lessons Learned in the Federal Funding Game," *Social Casework* 57 (1976): 208–18.

55. For an in-depth analysis of the process of political resocialization among new immigrants, see Zvi Gittelman, *Becoming Israelis: Political Resocialization of Soviet and American Immigrants* (New York, 1982). The majority of studies on new Asian immigrants and refugees investigate adaptation mechanism or acculturation processes with very little attention devoted to political resocialization of values and beliefs.

56. In recent years, writers have moved away from describing Chinatown communities in exclusively elitist terms, although most will not claim that they have become entirely pluralist in power competition. For an example of an elitist interpretation, see Stanford Lyman, "Contrasts in the Community Organization of Chinese and Japanese in North America," in his *The Asian in the West* (Reno, 1970), 57–63.

57. For a classic analysis of the issue, see John Burma, "Current Leadership Problems among Japanese Americans," *Sociology and Social Research* (1953): 157–63.

58. Paul Ong, "Chinese Labor in Early San Francisco: Racial Segmentation and Industrial Expansion," *Amerasia Journal* 8(1) (1981): 69–92.

59. Grant Din, "An Analysis of Asian/Pacific American Registration and Voting Patterns in San Francisco," M.A. thesis, Claremont Graduate School, 1984, 51.

60. Din, "Analysis of Registration and Voting Patterns," 49.

61. The UCLA Asian Pacific American Voter Study used the official voter registration lists for the June 1984 primary in Los Angeles County, while the San Francisco study was

based on the November 1983 registration lists for San Francisco County.

62. Din, "Analysis of Registration and Voting Patterns," 63–92.

63. The research assistants for this project were Rani Do, Bernie LaForteza, Susie Ling, Rick Oishi, and Edward Chang, while the advisers were Michael Eng, Stewart Kwoh, and Michael Woo.

64. The term, "Asian Corridor," was coined by the Pacific Asian Consortium on Employment in its research on inner-city Asian Pacific Americans. The area is largely a port-of-entry for Asian Pacific Americans and other groups, but also includes a number of long-standing Asian communities such as Chinatown and the Uptown area, which is now part of Koreatown but has traditionally had a large Japanese American population.

65. See Akemi Kikumura and Harry Kitano, "Interracial Marriages," *Journal of Social Issues* 29 (1973): 570–82.

66. Eui-Young Yu, "Koreans in Los Angeles: Size, Distribution, and Composition," in Eui-Young Yu, et al., eds., *Koreans in Los Angeles* (Los Angeles, 1982), 23–48.

67. See Eugene Webb, *Unobtrusive Measures* (New York, 1966).

68. The two studies used somewhat different indicators to calculate registration rates. The UCLA study used 1980 Census data on the number of individuals sixteen years and older, and assumed that this figure would be closer to the number of age-eligible individuals in 1984, which corresponded with the date of registration lists which were employed. The San Francisco study, on the other hand, used 1980 Census information on the numbers of individuals who were eighteen years and older, and assumed that this was a more reliable indicator for assessing its 1983 registration lists.

69. Registration rates for both studies were calculated by taking the numbers of identified Asian Pacific American registered voters for a particular city or area, and dividing it by the estimated numbers of individuals who were eighteen or sixteen years and older in 1980. See footnote 68. It is highly likely, though, that better estimates of registration rates, as well as the potential size of the Asian Pacific American electorates in both areas, could be obtained by multiple regression equations.

70. Data on overall county registration figures was provided by the Los Angeles County Registrar of voters, as well as through the calculation of voters in each precinct and city that were examined. The calculation of registration rates for cities was consistent with those of Asian Pacific Americans.

71. Din, "Analysis of Registration and Voting Patterns," 83.

72. Micro census data, which is based on a five percent sample of the population, provide data on citizenship. However, the estimation of the numbers of citizens versus non-citizens would probably require other data sources.

73. Din, "Analysis of Registration and Voting Patterns," 85.

74. See, for example, David Schwartz, *Political Alienation and Political Behavior* (Chicago, 1973).

75. Din, "Analysis of Registration and Voting Patterns," 92.

76. See footnote 11. Also see Ethnic Studies Oral History Project, *The 1924 Filipino Strike on Kauai* (Honolulu, Hawaii, 1980).

77. "Personal Reflections of the Asian National Movement," *East Wind* 1 (1982): 25–40; Amy Uyematsu, "The Emergence of Yellow Power in American," in Tachiki, *Roots*, 9–13; and Chester Hartman, "San Francisco's International Hotel: Case Study of a Turf Struggle," *Radical America* 12 (1978): 47–58

78. Philip Lum, "The Creation and Demise of San Francisco Chinatown's Freedom Schools," *Amerasia Journal* 5(1) (1978): 57–74; Kealoha Gard, "Aloha Aina: Native Hawaiians Fight for Survival," *Civil Rights Digest* 9 (1967): 52–57; Little Tokyo Anti-Eviction Task Force, "Redevelopment"; Kenneth Ong, "New York Chinatown: A Community Fights Gentrification," *East Wind* 1 (1982): 10–12; and Hyung-Chan Kim and Nicholas Lai, "Chinese Community Resistance to Urban Renewal," *Journal of Ethnic Studies* 10 (1982): 67–81,

79. See footnote 12.

80. Several works have begun to explore three recent social protest activities such as Rocky Chin et.al, "The Long Road: Japanese Americans Move on Redress," *Bridge* 7 (1981–1982): 11–29; "A People's Anger," *East*

*Wind*; and Derrick Lim, "Learning from the Past: A Retrospective Look at the Chol Soo Lee Movement," M.A. thesis, University of California, Los Angeles, 1985.

81. Francis Fox Piven and Richard A. Cloward, *Poor People's Movements: Why They Succeed, How They Fail* (New York, 1979).

82. See Nakanishi and LaForteza, National Asian Pacific American Roster, for a listing of these new advocacy groups in the Asian American community. No research has been done on this new political infrastructure.

83. These new groups, which tend to be dominated by Asian American white collar and professional workers, have embraced the notion that there is greater political strength through a unification of all the different ethnic groups that compose Asian America. They also, like the earlier Asian American movement, believe that non-Asians perceive and treat all Asian Americans alike, and as a result have been extremely concerned about the growing anti-Asian violence and hostilities in this country. They also believe that Asian Americans have not received their equal share of societal benefits. However, there are clearly a number of fundamental philosophic differences between the two.

84. Takahashi, "Japanese American Responses."

85. See, for example, E. San Juan, *Only By Struggle: Literature and Revolution in the Philippines* (Manfield Depot, Conn., 1980); Yoneda, Ganbatte; and Ron Tanaka, "Culture, Communities, and the Asian Movement in Perspective," *Journal of Ethnic Studies* 4 (1976): 37–52.

# 3.2

# Becoming Citizens, Becoming Voters
## The Naturalization and Political
## Participation of Asian Pacific Immigrants

*Paul M. Ong and Don T. Nakanishi*

≈≈≈≈≈≈≈≈≈≈≈≈≈≈≈≈≈≈≈≈≈≈≈≈≈≈≈≈≈≈≈≈≈≈≈≈

In a 1995 speech at the national conference of the Southwest Voter Registration Project, Vice President Albert Gore stated that naturalization represents the final stage of incorporating an immigrant into American society.[1] Naturalization is not merely a paper change in status, for the passage to citizenship requires a level of acculturation defined by a basic command of the English language, and knowledge of U.S. history and its political institutions. With this act, an immigrant forgoes allegiance to his or her country of origin while pledging loyalty to the United States.

The acquisition of citizenship marks the beginning of full political and social membership in this country. The individual acquires new civil and legal rights, with the opportunity to vote and to participate in the electoral process being perhaps the most important. The stakes are also economic. In today's growing anti-immigrant

climate, citizenship has become a litmus test for inclusion in America's social contract. There is now discussion to make citizenship an eligibility requirement for programs such as SSI (Supplementary Security Income) for the elderly and AFDC (Aid to Families with Dependent Children) for families with children.[2]

Naturalization and political participation have profound implications for groups, as well as individuals. The political strength of an immigrant-dominated population within our electoral system hinges on two interrelated, but distinct processes: first, the group's naturalization rate, that is, the relative proportion of immigrants with citizenship; and second, the rates by which naturalized and native-born citizens both register to vote and actually vote during elections. Low rates of naturalization, voter registration, and voting dilute an immigrant-dominated group's potential electoral power, thus diminishing its influence on legislation and public policy. Moreover, acquiring citizenship and participating in society are seen by the general public as indicators of the ability and willingness of a group to assimilate and to be "Americanized" rather than remaining permanent aliens. While high rates of naturalization

Ong, Paul M., and Don T. Nakanishi. "Becoming Citizens, Becoming Voters: The Naturalization and Political Participation of Asian Pacific Immigrants." In Bill Ong Hing and Ronald Lee, eds., *Reframing the Immigration Debate*, (Los Angeles: LEAP Asian Pacific American Public Policy Institute and UCLA Asian American Studies Center, 1996), 275–305. Reprinted with permission.

and social participation do not guarantee that all members of a group will be fully accepted as equals, low rates foster political isolation and provide fodder for nativist movements.

Although becoming a citizen and becoming a voter are usually viewed as nearly simultaneous processes, they are distinct and temporally distant forms of membership and participation in American life and society. Asian and other immigrants and refugees, especially those who migrated as adults, oftentimes acquired their fundamental political values, attitudes, and behavioral orientations in countries that have sociopolitical systems, traditions, and expectations that are different from those of American politics. Indeed, many came from countries where voting was not permitted, limited to a privileged few, or was widely viewed as being inconsequential because of the dominance of a single political party. As such, they must undergo a process of political acculturation, which goes beyond the rudimentary exposure to the basic facts of American governmental institutions that they receive in preparing for naturalization examinations through citizenship classes. Becoming a voter, and more generally becoming a participant in American electoral politics, is a prolonged and complicated process of social learning for immigrants as much as it is for native-born citizens.

In this report, we empirically examine the rates of naturalization, voter registration, and voting behavior for Asian immigrants and refugees. The first major section explores the overall trends in naturalization between Asian and other groups of immigrants during the past three decades, as well as the factors that have the greatest influence on whether Asian immigrants become naturalized. The second major section analyzes the political participation of immigrant and native-born Asian Americans, with special attention to their voter registration and electoral involvement. Comparisons again are made between Asian Americans and other groups in American society, and the analysis explores the factors that

account for important differences in rates of electoral participation. A concluding section summarizes our major findings, and offers several policy recommendations.

## BECOMING CITIZENS: NATURALIZATION AND ASIAN IMMIGRANTS

Asian Americans, as an immigrant-dominated population, are greatly affected by the rate of naturalization. Since the early 1970s, immigrants have constituted a growing majority of the Asian American adult population, as shown in table 3.2a. The number of foreign-born adults has roughly doubled every decade, mirroring the trend for the total Asian American population. Much of this growth has been driven by large-scale immigration after the enactment of the Immigration Act of 1965. While the number of U.S.-born citizens (including those born abroad to U.S. citizens) doubled between 1970 and 1990, the foreign-born population grew by over eight-fold. As a consequence, the proportion comprised of U.S.-born citizens declined from 52 percent to 21 percent. There was, however, considerable variation across ethnic groups. Throughout this time period, U.S.-born citizens comprised a large majority of the Japanese. On the other hand, newer and rapidly growing groups such as the Southeast Asians, Koreans, and Asian Indians were predominantly foreign-born. Given the recent demographic trends, Asian Americans constituted a racial group wherein naturalization directly and powerfully determined the size of the population eligible to vote, and hence its political future.

This section of the report examines the level of naturalization and determinants of citizenship for Asian immigrants over the age of eighteen, which is one of the criteria for naturalization.[3] The analysis is based on the microdata samples from the decennial census where the units of observation are individuals. The primary advantage of this data source is the large number of observa-

**Table 3.2a    Nativity of Asian Americans, Eighteen Years and Older (1970, 1980, and 1990)**

|  | 1970 | 1980 | 1990 |
|---|---|---|---|
|  | Population (in thousands) | | |
| Total Asian Pacific Americans | 969 | 2,498 | 4,938 |
| U.S.-born citizens | 502 | 741 | 1,022 |
| Immigrants | 468 | 1,758 | 3,916 |
| Percent U.S.-born citizens | 52% | 30% | 21% |
| Distribution by ethnicity |  |  |  |
| Japanese | 411 | 567 | 706 |
| Chinese | 288 | 598 | 1,261 |
| Filipino | 214 | 538 | 1,033 |
| Koreans | 57 | 227 | 548 |
| SE Asians | — | 143 | 592 |
| Asian Indians | — | 274 | 555 |
| Percent U.S.-born citizens |  |  |  |
| Japanese | 73% | 68% | 65% |
| Chinese | 39 | 26 | 19 |
| Filipino | 30 | 19 | 20 |
| Koreans | 43 | 7 | 8 |
| SE Asians | — | 2 | 2 |
| Asian Indians | — | 17 | 6 |

*Notes:* Estimates from Public Use Micro Samples. U.S.-born category includes those born to U.S. citizens.

tions, which allows for detailed tabulations and reasonable estimates of the characteristics of the entire population.[4] While the 1970 sample includes only 1 percent of the total U.S. population, the 1980 and 1990 samples include 5 percent of the population. The census also contains information on nativity, racial and ethnic identity, demographic characteristics, educational attainment, and a host of other variables.

There are limitations with census data. The census does not distinguish between legal immigrants, undocumented aliens, and some foreign visitors. The one group systematically excluded is foreign travelers without an established residence at the time of the enumeration. In other words, those on work and study visas are included, but tourists are not. The immigrant population in the census, then, can be best described as the foreign-born population with an established U.S. residence. The census data are also limited by their cross-sectional nature, that is, the data refer to the characteristics of the sample at one point in time. While we can compare profiles, rates, and other demographic features of populations in 1970, 1980, and 1990, we cannot follow longitudinal changes for individuals.

The census uses five categories to define U.S. citizenship: (1) those born in the United States are citizens by *jus solis*, (2) those who are citizens through birth in a U.S. territory, (3) those born abroad to U.S. citizens are citizens by *jus sanguini*, (4) alien immigrants, and (5) naturalized immigrants.[5] For the purpose of this report, the foreign-born population is comprised of those in the last two categories, and the naturalized population is comprised of those in the last category. The terms "foreign-born" and "immigrant" are used interchangeably.

The major findings are that Asian immigrants are naturalizing at a pace that is at least comparable to that for non-Hispanic white immigrants after accounting for differences in length of time in the United States. The number of years in this nation is the single most important factor in determining naturalization rates. This time-dependent process, along with the underlying acculturation process, appears remarkably stable over the decades. While time is the most important factor, there are other influential factors, such as ethnicity, age, and level of education.

## Overall Pattern of Naturalization

Table 3.2b provides an overview of the naturalization rates for 1970, 1980, and 1990. During this time period, the overall level of citizenship for all immigrants fell by 24 percentage points from 67 percent to 43 percent. Two factors are related to this decline. The first factor is a resumption of large-scale immigration from the early 1960s, which more than doubled the adult immigrant population from less than 8.5 million in 1970 and to over 17.5 million in 1990. Renewed large-scale immigration has dramatically altered the composition of immigrants, counted by number of years they have lived in the United States.[6] A majority (55 percent) of the 1970 adult immigrants had lived in the United States for twenty-one or more years, but two decades later only about a third (35 percent) had lived in the United States for that length of time. This decline in the number of long-term immigrants occurred despite an increase in the absolute number of long-term residents from 4.9 million to 6.2 million. On the other hand, newer immigrants (those in the country for no more than ten years) increased from 25 percent to 39 percent of all adult immigrants. In absolute numbers, their ranks grew from 2.2 million to 6.9 million.

With the shift toward recent immigrants, it is not surprising that the relative number

**Table 3.2b    Naturalization Rates by Years in U.S. and by Race, All Immigrants Eighteen Years and Older (1970, 1980, and 1990)**

|  | 1970 | 1980 | 1990 |
|---|---|---|---|
| All immigrants (in thousands) | 8,468 | 12,423 | 17,612 |
| Distribution by years in U.S. |  |  |  |
| 0–10 years | 25% | 34% | 39% |
| 11–20 years | 19 | 23 | 26 |
| 21 or more years | 55 | 43 | 35 |
| Distribution by race |  |  |  |
| Non-Hispanic whites | 76% | 53% | 37% |
| Blacks | 2 | 5 | 7 |
| Latinos | 16 | 27 | 37 |
| Asians | 6 | 14 | 22 |
| Overall naturalization rates | 67 | 54 | 43 |
| Naturalization rates by years in U.S. |  |  |  |
| 0–10 years | 20% | 20% | 15% |
| 11–20 years | 64 | 49 | 45 |
| 21 or more years | 90 | 85 | 74 |
| Naturalization rates by race |  |  |  |
| Non-Hispanic whites | 77% | 71% | 63% |
| Blacks | 45 | 43 | 36 |
| Latinos | 35 | 31 | 28 |
| Asians | 41 | 36 | 43 |

*Notes:* Estimates from Public Use Micro Samples. Excluding those born abroad to U.S. Citizens.

of citizens among adult immigrants declined from 1970 to 1990. In fact, the recomposition by years of residence in this country accounts for nearly half of the overall decline.[7] The change in the overall naturalization rate can be decomposed with one component being the change between 1970 and 1990 in the composition by years in the United States, holding the rates constant at the level observed for 1970. The calculations indicate the compositional shift accounts for just slightly less than half of the decline—that is, 11.2 of the 23.5 percentage points difference in the naturalization rates for 1970 and 1990.

The second factor, changes in the naturalization rate within groups defined by years in the United States, accounts for slightly more than half of the overall decline. The within-group decline is apparent in all groups. While 20 percent of those who had been in the country for no more than a decade were naturalized in 1970, only 15 percent were in 1990. The comparable figures for those in the country for more than two decades dropped from 90 percent to 74 percent.[8] This decline within cohort is related to changes in the social, cultural, and economic background of the immigrant population, some of which are discussed in the next section.

## Racial Variations

A racial recomposition of the foreign-born population has accompanied the renewal of large-scale immigration.[9] The sources of modern immigration differ dramatically from that of earlier immigration. For the first two-thirds of the century, Europeans dominated flows into the United States. After the elimination of racially biased quotas in 1965, people from Asia and Latin America have dominated. With the change in the source of immigration, the racial composition of immigrants has also changed. Non-Hispanic whites comprised three-quarters of all adult immigrants in 1970 but less than two-fifths in 1990. On the other hand, Latinos and Asians together have increased from less

than a quarter in 1970 to a clear majority in 1990.

The racial recomposition has been toward some populations that have low naturalization rates. Mexicans, for example, are not only the single largest group of recent immigrants, but also a group with a substantially lower than average rate of naturalization (Skerry 1993; Thomas Rivera Center 1994). These new immigrants generally are less educated and less proficient in English, and more likely to maintain ties to their home country through occasional visits. These factors work against becoming citizens. The shift to non-European immigrants, however, is not the sole cause of the drop in naturalization rates. Lower naturalization rates among newer immigrants are also observed for the slower growing non-Hispanic white immigrant population.

Interestingly, the naturalization rates did not decrease for Asian immigrants over three decennial censuses. As shown in table 3.2b, the overall rates fluctuated around the 40 percent level. Non-Hispanic whites exhibited higher overall rates, but this is an artifact of the tremendous differences in years of residence in the United States. As shown in the top half of table 3.2c, long-term residents were dominated by non-Hispanic whites in all three census years, but newer immigrants were predominantly Asians. Compared to the overall decline in naturalization rates, interracial differences are not as great among groups defined by years in the United States. In 1970, the Asian rates were consistently lower for all cohorts, with the largest difference for long-term residents. The substantially lower rate for long-term Asian residents (68 percent versus 92 percent) is a historical legacy. Prior to 1952, most Asian immigrants were ineligible for citizenship (Hing 1993). The historical restrictions not only delayed naturalization for those who wanted to become citizens, but the years of discrimination alienated many other Asian immigrants and dampened their desire to naturalize. However, by 1980, the naturalization rates for non-Hispanic whites declined while those for Asians improved. Asians had a higher rate among those in the country for no more than a decade. By 1990, all Asian rates were at least equal to or considerably higher than those of non-Hispanic whites.

The census understates the level of citizenship of Asian immigrants because the calculated rates do not include those who had emigrated from the United States. In other words, the "true" naturalization rates are lower than those based on census data. Because emigration is more extensive for non-Hispanic whites than for Asians, the bias is greater for non-Hispanic whites (Liang 1994; Jasso and Rosenzweig 1990). An alternative measure used by the Immigration and Naturalization Service, which includes those who emigrated in the calculations, clearly shows that those from Asian countries have the highest rates (INS 1990). The top three Asian nations are Vietnam, China, and the Philippines, with rates of 78 percent, 63 percent, and 63 percent respectively.[10] Among the bottom five

nations are Canada, the United Kingdom, and Italy, with rates of 12 percent, 20 percent, and 23 percent.[11]

## Time-Dependent Acculturation

As the above analysis suggests, time in the United States is a powerful determinant of whether a person naturalizes. This is partly a product of the required waiting period before becoming eligible for naturalization. Currently, there is a three-year waiting period for spouses of citizens, and a five-year waiting period for most other immigrants. Eligibility rules, however, are not the only or even most important constraint on naturalization. Acculturation, the broad process of learning and adopting the language, values, and norms of the host society, is the fundamental factor. Studies have shown a strong correlation between time in the United States and the level of assimilation. The level of economic assimilation, as measured by earnings of immigrants relative to that for their U.S.-

**Table 3.2c  Naturalization Rates, Asian and Non-Hispanic White Immigrants Eighteen Years and Older (1970, 1980, and 1990)**

| Years in U.S. | 1970 | 1980 | 1990 |
|---|---|---|---|
| Non-Hispanic whites | | | |
| 0–10 years | 17% | 16% | 20% |
| 11–20 years | 19 | 18 | 16 |
| over 20 years | 64 | 66 | 64 |
| Asians | | | |
| 0–10 years | 56 | 66 | 54 |
| 11–20 years | 19 | 20 | 32 |
| over 20 years | 25 | 13 | 14 |
| Naturalization rate by years in U.S. | | | |
| Non-Hispanic whites | | | |
| 0–10 years | 20% | 16% | 15% |
| 11–20 years | 69 | 53 | 48 |
| over 20 years | 92 | 89 | 81 |
| Asians | | | |
| 0–10 years | 17 | 19 | 19 |
| 11–20 years | 67 | 67 | 66 |
| over 20 years | 68 | 79 | 81 |

*Note:* Estimates from Public Use Micro Samples.

born ethnic counterparts with similar education and years of work experience, starts from a low point at the time of entry and gradually improves over a fifteen-year period, at which point immigrants reach parity (See Borjas 1990 for summary). There are also improvements over time in terms of understanding the English language and American institutions of the larger society.

Figure 3.2a depicts the naturalization rates of Asian immigrants by time in the United States in five-year increments. The numbers show a remarkably similar pattern for all three censuses.[12] Prior to five years, there are few naturalizations, due in part to the five-year residency requirement for most immigrants.[13] The greatest increase occurs among those in the country between five and fifteen years. By interpolating from the data, we estimate that two-thirds of all naturalizations take place within this range.[14] The naturalization rate continues to increase after more than fifteen years in the United States but in smaller increments. The one exception to the overall pattern is for those who have been in this country for over a quarter century. In 1970, only a third of this cohort were citizens. As we stated earlier, this is due to the legacy of the legal discrimination encountered by the earlier immigrants. Over time, this

historical effect has waned as the number of pre–World War II immigrants declined. By 1990, 84 percent of the Asian immigrants in this country for more than a quarter century were citizens.

The influence of time on the naturalization rate can also be seen in data that track comparable groups over time. As stated earlier, census data are cross-sectional; consequently, we are inferring a dynamic process from observed differences among groups at the same point in time. For example, because the naturalization rate in 1990 for those in the country for eleven to fifteen years was higher than the rate for those in the country for six to ten years, we infer that the increase was due to being in the country an additional five years.[15] This is a reasonable assumption given the relative stability of the pattern of naturalization rates observed in figure 3.2a.

It is possible to go one step further with the analysis of how naturalization rates change with time. While the census data are not longitudinal data, the samples can be used to estimate changes for a given cohort over time. For example, the group whose members were between eighteen to forty years old in 1970 would be roughly the same group with members between twenty-eight and fifty in 1980, and thirty-eight to sixty in 1990.[16] While the census sample does not include the same individuals in all three

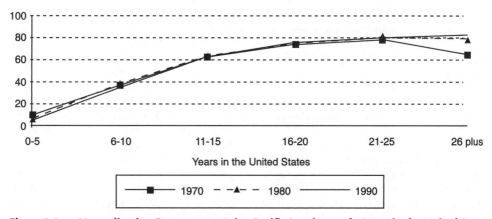

Figure 3.2a    Naturalization Rates among Asian Pacific Immigrants by Years in the United States

Table 3.2d    Estimated Naturalization Rates of Asian Immigrants (percent)

| Years in U.S. | Cross-section average (70–90) | Pseudo panel estimates |
|---|---|---|
| 0–5 | 7% | 8% |
| 6–10 | 36 | 33 |
| 11–15 | 63 | 64 |
| 16–20 | 74 | 77 |
| 21–25 | 81 | 81 |

Note: Estimates from Public Use Micro Samples.

decades, the law of large numbers enables us to use the data to develop representative profiles as this cohort aged over time. This method can be further refined by dividing the cohort by period of entry into the United States and tracking each group over time. Using this approach, we can estimate longitudinal changes in naturalization for each cohort. Table 3.2d compares the results of this exercise with the rates observed in cross-sectional analysis. Although there are differences, they are minor. In fact, the patterns are remarkably similar.

While time in the U.S. is perhaps the single most important factor in determining the naturalization rate, it is important to note that what is observed is not a simple process. Changes in the rate are based on a more fundamental phenomenon: acculturation that unfolds over time, such as learning English language, acquiring a knowledge of U.S. institutions, and strengthening one's sense of identity as an American. These changes are often slowed by everyday demands. Most immigrants must work to earn a living and cope with family responsibilities, all of which consume considerable time and energy.

Despite the observed robustness of the relationship between time in this country and the naturalization rates, it is also clear that larger societal forces influence this process. This is evident in the persistent dampening effect of historical discrimination. More recently, the growth of anti-immigrant sentiments, particularly in California, has also affected the behavior of immigrants. The fear created by efforts such as Proposition 187 has led to a notice-able increase in the numbers seeking citizenship.

## Intra-Cohort Varations

Time and the underlying acculturation process are not the only factors affecting naturalization. There are significant variations in the rates after controlling for years in the United States. Table 3.2e reports statistics based on the 1990 Census for three groups defined by years in the United States. The analysis focuses on the six-to twenty-year range when the changes in the rates are most dramatic. The data reveal that ethnicity, age, English language ability, and education influence the level of naturalization.

Among the major ethnic groups, the difference between the highest and lowest naturalization rates is about 50 percentage points. Japanese immigrants exhibited the lowest rates. For those in the country from six to ten years, only one in fourteen was a citizen. Although the rate increased with longer residency in the United States, only one in three of those in the country sixteen to twenty years was a citizen. This extraordinary low level of naturalization may be tied to Japanese transnational corporations. With increased trade with the United States, many of these companies establish operations in this country and bring with them a significant number of nationals. These employees and their families have established sizable visible communities in places like New York City and parts of Southern California. This international movement has set up a migration of other

Table 3.2e    Detailed Naturalization Rates of Asian Immigrants

| | Years in the United States | | |
|---|---|---|---|
| | 6–10 | 11–15 | 16–20 |
| By ethnicity | | | |
| Japanese | 7% | 18% | 35% |
| Chinese | 34 | 67 | 80 |
| Filipinos | 45 | 73 | 83 |
| Koreans | 27 | 62 | 82 |
| SE Asians | 32 | 62 | N.A. |
| Asian Indians | 26 | 53 | 68 |
| By age | | | |
| 18–29 | 34% | 67% | 80% |
| 30–39 | 35 | 65 | 76 |
| 40–49 | 33 | 64 | 77 |
| 50–59 | 29 | 59 | 75 |
| 60 plus | 23 | 44 | 60 |
| By education level | | | |
| 0–8 years | 17% | 36% | 56% |
| 9–11 years | 29 | 54 | 69 |
| High school | 34 | 61 | 71 |
| Some college | 43 | 70 | 77 |
| Bachelor's | 39 | 73 | 83 |
| Master's | 25 | 67 | 79 |
| Doctorate | 15 | 49 | 75 |
| By English language ability | | | |
| None | 6% | 12% | 26% |
| Poor | 22 | 47 | 66 |
| Good | 39 | 69 | 76 |
| Very good | 38 | 68 | 79 |
| Only English | 33 | 62 | 77 |

Note: Estimates from Public Use Micro Samples

Japanese who work in the restaurants, clubs, and other businesses serving the corporate-based Japanese communities. Many of these Japanese do not see themselves as immigrants, even after being in the country for a number of years.

Filipinos are at the other end of the spectrum with the highest naturalization rates. They are the most "Americanized" group of Asian immigrants. A history of being an U.S. colony (1898 to 1946) has left a legacy in the Philippines where English, once the official language, remains the language of choice for many Filipinos. Moreover, many aspects of U.S. culture have become deeply embedded in Filipino society and identity.

This pre-migration acculturation has facilitated the naturalization process among Filipino immigrants in the United States. This "advantage" is particularly noticeable among the 1990 Census respondents who had been here for six to ten years, nearly half of whom were citizens.

The other four Asian immigrant groups in table 3.2e exhibited naturalization rates between those for the Japanese and Filipinos. With longer residency, however, the level for the four groups approached that for Filipinos. In other words, the early advantage enjoyed by Filipinos in terms of "Americanization" disappeared as the other groups acculturated. Interestingly, Southeast Asians were similar to Chinese and Koreans. One might expect a difference because Southeast Asians are predominantly refugees, while the others are predominantly non-refugee immigrants. Refugees are less likely to have migrated by choice but rather as a consequence of massive political turmoil. Non-refugee immigrants, on the other hand, made a conscious decision to come to the United States. This difference means that refugees are less likely to have formed a pre-migration sense of attachment to the United States; thus, they are less likely to naturalize during their earlier years in this country. On the other hand, Southeast Asian refugees are more likely to be forced to cut ties with the home country because of a revolutionary change in government, thus pushing them to form a new allegiance to the United States. These offsetting effects may account for the similarity in the naturalization rates of Southeast Asians and those for Chinese and Koreans.

The rates in table 3.2e also reveal that citizenship is more likely for younger immigrants and those with a better command of the English language. The effect of age is probably due to the fact that older immigrants have greater difficulties acculturating. They have spent most of their lives in another society and culture, and breaking their attachment is not easy. Middle-age immigrants are also burdened by the daily demands of working and raising a family. Younger immigrants, on the other hand, have the advantage of being raised and educated in the United States.

Differences in English-language ability also generate variations in the naturalization rates. Among those who do not speak English, only one in ten was a citizen in 1990. Even among those who had lived in the country for sixteen to twenty years, only one in four was naturalized. The rates generally improved with English language ability. Those in the "very good" category, for example, were three to six times more likely to be naturalized than those who did not speak English.

Educational attainment also influenced the odds of being a citizen, but not in a linear fashion. Among the 1990 sample, the naturalization rate increased with years of schooling in the range up to an undergraduate education. For example, among immigrants in the country for six to ten years, those with some college education were more than twice as likely to be naturalized than those with no more than an elementary school education. The educational effect, however, was smaller among those in the country for sixteen to twenty years. This pattern suggests that more formal education enabled an immigrant to more quickly acquire the knowledge required to pass the naturalization exam.

For those with graduate training, education played a different role. Those with a doctorate degree had lower naturalization rates than those with a master's degree[17], who in turn had lower rates than those with a bachelor's degree. This adverse effect of additional schooling was particularly noticeable among those in the country for six to ten years. This is not surprising since many of those with more than an undergraduate education were in the country on temporary visas to pursue additional graduate and post-doctorate training, and thus were not eligible for citizenship (Ong et al. 1992). Over time, the relative numbers with temporary visas declined either because they returned to their home countries or because they became permanent residents. Nonetheless, the naturalization rates of those with doctorate degrees were lower than those with bachelor's degrees even among those with over eleven years of residency in the United States.

The data support the thesis that age, English language ability, and education influence the naturalization rate, but it is important to recognize that these causal factors are related to each other. The elderly, for example, are more likely to have a poor command of English and to have less education. On the other hand, those with advanced degrees are more likely to have a better command of English. We used multivariate analysis (logit regressions) to determine if these factors have an independent effect on odds of an immigrant becoming a citizen.[18] The results are consistent with the patterns discussed above: the odds decrease with age but increase with English language ability, and the effect of education is nonlinear, with the odds increasing up to an undergraduate education and then decreasing with additional graduate training. Moreover, the ethnic variations discussed earlier also hold, with Filipinos having the highest odds and the Japanese the lowest odds.

## BECOMING VOTERS: THE ELECTORAL PARTICIPATION OF ASIAN IMMIGRANTS

In recent years, a number of political commentators and scholars have speculated about whether Asian Americans will become a major new force in American electoral politics, perhaps akin to American Jews, because of their dramatic demographic growth and concentration in certain key electoral states like California, New York, and Texas (Tachibana 1986; Cain 1988; Stokes 1988; Nakanishi 1991; Karnow 1992; Miller 1995). Many believe that if Asian Americans, like American Jewish voters, come to represent a proportion of the electorate that is comparable to, if not greater than, their share of the total population then they could become a highly influential "swing vote" in critical local, state, and presidential elections. In California, for example, if Asian Americans, who are one-in-ten residents of the state also became one-in-ten voters—who will continue to control the nation's largest number of Congressional seats and presidential electoral college votes—then they could play a strategically important role in national and local elections. Indeed, their voting potential coupled with their proven record of campaign funding could elevate Asian Americans to the status of leading actors in the grand theater of American politics (*Asianweek* 1984).

During the past decade, there has been an unmistakable increase in the political participation and presence of Asian Americans in electoral politics. The 1995 edition of the "Asian Pacific American Political Roster and Resource Guide" (Nakanishi and Lai 1995) listed over 1,200 Asian American elected and major appointed officials for thirty-one different states, as well as the federal government. In comparison, the first edition of this political directory, published in 1978, listed several hundred politicians, primarily holding offices in the states of Hawaii and California (Nakanishi 1978). The vast majority of those officials were second and third generation Asian Americans, primarily Japanese Americans. In contrast, a growing number of recently elected office-holders have been immigrants such as Jay Kim of Walnut, California, the first Korean American elected to Congress; David Valderrama, the first Filipino American elected as a Delegate to the Assembly of Maryland; and City Councilman Tony Lam of Westminster, California, the first Vietnamese American elected to public office. In the past few years, Asian American candidates also have run well-financed, professional campaigns for mayor of some of the nation's largest cities, including Los Angeles, San Francisco, and Oakland.

However, beyond this seemingly optimistic and glowing assessment of Asian American electoral achievements among the most actively involved leaders is the reality of an immigrant-dominant population which has yet to reach its full political potential, especially in transforming its extraordinary population growth into comparable proportions of individuals who register to vote, and actually vote during elections. In California, for example, Asian Americans may represent one-in-ten residents, but it is estimated that they are no more than one-in-twenty of the state's registered voters and three-of-a-hundred of those who actually vote (The Field Institute 1992).

In many respects, the present and future size, characteristics, and impact of the Asian American electorate at both the grassroots and leadership levels is dynamically evolving in relation to historical and contemporary conditions, as well as structural and individual-level factors. For example, early Chinese and Japanese immigrants were disenfranchised and excluded from fully participating in American life because of a plethora of discriminatory laws and policies, perhaps the most crucial being *Ozawa v. United States* (1922), which forbade Asian immigrants from becoming naturalized citizens. This legal barrier prevented early Asian immigrants from being involved in electoral politics of any form—be it the type of ward politics practiced by European immigrants in cities in the Atlantic and Midwestern states or to simply vote for their preference in a presidential election—and substantially delayed the development of electoral participation and representation by Asian Americans until the second and subsequent generations; decades after their initial period of immigration. Early Asian immigrants and their descendants also were scapegoated for political gain by opportunistic politicians and anti-Asian social movements and political parties, the most disastrous episode being the incarceration of 120,000 Japanese Americans during World War II. This legacy of political exclusion and isolation has many contemporary manifestations. Asian American civil rights groups remain vigilant in seeking the elimination of a number of "political structural barriers," as Kwoh and Hui (1993) have written, such as the unfair redistricting of Asian American communities and the lack of bilingual ballots and voting materials which prevent Asian Americans from exercising their full voting rights (Bai 1991). Likewise, grassroots voter registration campaigns in Asian American communities have had to confront and overcome deep-seated views of political inefficacy, political alienation, and mistrust of government held by large sectors of the Asian American population, as well as the lack of genuine attention and interest by elected officials and the major political parties towards the unique public policy and quality-of-life needs and issues of Asian Americans (Nakanishi 1992).

This section of the report analyzes the levels and determinants of voter registration and voting for naturalized Asian immigrants over the age of 18 in comparison with native-born Asian Americans and other racial and ethnic populations. The analysis is based on the 1990, 1992, and 1994 Current Population Surveys (CPS) conducted by the Census Bureau, which included information on voter registration and voting for Asian Americans. The 1994 CPS data, which will be the primary focus of analysis, was particularly useful because it provided detailed information on the citizenship status of individuals similar to the decennial census, as mentioned in the previous section on naturalization. It was therefore possible to differentiate between Asian Americans not only who were foreign-born and native-born, but also immigrants and refugees who were naturalized and those who were not.

However, this data source unfortunately does not allow us to analyze differences in electoral participation among the array of Asian ethnic communities. Previous studies have found that rates of voter registration vary markedly, with Japanese Americans having the highest proportion of registered voters and Southeast Asians having the lowest percentage (Nakanishi 1991). Although CPS data have limitations, the advantages are that they allow us to examine both national and regional trends with a sufficiently large sample of Asian Americans,[19] and to analyze potential differences in registration and voting rates in relation to native-born and naturalized citizens, which has rarely been examined rigorously (Din 1984; Nakanishi 1991; Horton 1995; Shinagawa 1995; Tam 1995).

The major findings are that Asian immigrants and refugees have lower rates of voter registration than native-born citizens. However, Asian naturalized citizens who have been in this country for over twenty years have rates of registration that are comparable to or exceed those of native-borns, while those who arrived over thirty years ago have higher rates of both registration and voting. As in the case of naturalization rates, multiple regression analysis found that year of entry was the single most important factor in determining voter registration rates. In terms of actual voting, two other factors along with year of entry—educational attainment and age—were found to be the best predictors. And finally, the characteristics of Asian American voters as a whole, as well as between native-born and foreign-born, are reflective of an ethnic electorate that is far from being monolithic with respect to political party affiliations, ideological preferences, and voting preferences. Rather, it has many dimensions of diversity, which are influencing its continued development.

## Rates of Voter Registration

The Asian population in the United States is characterized by the largest proportion of individuals over the age of eighteen (hereafter, adult) who cannot take the first step towards participating in American electoral politics because they are not citizens. In 1994, 55 percent of adult Asians were not citizens in contrast to 44 percent of the Latinos, 5 percent African Americans, and 2 percent non-Hispanic whites. The proportion of non-citizens varied by geographic region, with Honolulu having the lowest percentage of non-citizens among its adult Asian population (21 percent), and New York (73 percent) having the highest. 63 percent of the adult Asians in Los Angeles County and 52 percent in the Oakland-San Francisco region also were not citizens.

Nationwide, in 1994, there were approximately 1,166,450 Asian American registered voters, of whom 58 percent (680,750) were U.S.-born and 42 percent (485,700) were foreign-born (table 3.2f). California's Asian American electorate, which accounted for 40 percent of the country's

Asian American registered voters, mirrored the nation's composition of U.S.-born (58 percent) to foreign-born (42 percent) voters. Hawaii, on the other hand, which has witnessed far less immigration than many mainland states, had an overwhelmingly U.S.-born Asian American electorate (88 percent). Hawaii's Asian American voter profile was similar to that of other racial and ethnic populations, which had substantially higher proportions of U.S.-born voters: 87 percent of all Latino voters, 99 percent of African Americans, and 98 percent non-Hispanic Whites.

Asian American citizens (by birth or naturalization) exhibited very low overall rates of voter registration. Nationally, 1994 CPS census data estimated that 53 percent of all Asian American citizens were registered, in contrast to 61 percent of African Americans and 69 percent of non-Hispanic whites. Latino citizens had identical rates of voter registration as Asian Americans (53 percent). In 1992 similar patterns were observed for these population groups in Los Angeles, Oakland-San Francisco, New York, and Honolulu. Indeed, in some regions, the differences in voter registration rates between Asian Americans and non-Hispanic whites, who usually have the highest rates of registration, were quite substantial. In 1992, for example, in the Oakland-San Francisco region, 56 percent of all adult Asian American citizens were registered to vote in comparison with 86 percent of non-Hispanic whites, 73 percent African Americans, and 63 percent Latino American citizens. At the same time, there were differences in voter registration rates for different Asian American communities, with Los Angeles having

**Table 3.2f   Distribution of Naturalized and U.S.-Born Asian American Registered Voters (1994)**

|  | California | Hawaii | Rest of nation | National total |
|---|---|---|---|---|
| U.S.-born | 271,820 (58%) | 218,580 (88%) | 189,790 (42%) | 680,190 (58%) |
| Naturalized | 194,840 (42%) | 29,170 (12%) | 261,680 (58%) | 485,710 (42%) |
| Total | 466,660 | 247,770 | 451,470 | 1,165,990 |
| % of national total | 40% | 21% | 39% | 100% |

*Source:* Current Population Survey 1994.

the highest (64 percent) and New York (54 percent) having the lowest. Many previous studies have found that Asian Americans have lower rates of voter registration than African Americans and non-Hispanic whites, and usually the same or somewhat lower rates than that of Latinos. Although this is a consistent finding, it is nonetheless an extremely puzzling one because of the relatively high, group-level attainment levels of Asian Americans in education and other socioeconomic variables, which have been long associated with active electoral participation in political science research (Nakanishi 1986a, 1991; Cain 1988; Field Institute 1992; Erie and Brackman 1993; Lien 1994).

Among Asian American citizens, those who were born in the United States have a higher *overall* rate of voter registration than those who were born abroad and have become naturalized. In 1994, as table 3.2g illustrates, 56 percent of all U.S.-born Asian Americans were registered compared to 49 percent of those who were naturalized. Indeed, foreign-born Asian American citizens had among the lowest rates of any group, including Latino naturalized citizens

(53 percent). However, in terms of electoral participation beyond registration, both Asian American naturalized and native-born voters had among the highest rates of voting during the 1994 elections. Therefore, Asian immigrants appear to reflect a provocative series of discrete, non-linear trends from becoming citizens to becoming registered voters and then to becoming actual voters: they have one of the highest rates of naturalization after immigrating, but one of the lowest rates of voter registration after becoming citizens. However, once they are registered, Asian American naturalized citizens have among the highest rates of voting of any group.

A closer and more detailed examination of Asian naturalized citizens indicates that those who immigrated over twenty years ago, prior to 1975, have rates of voter registration comparable to, if not greater than, those who were born in this country (tables 3.2h and 3.2i). Indeed, this was the case for practically all age groups, educational attainment levels, and for women. On the other hand, Asian naturalized citizens who immigrated within the past twenty years have rates of registration that are substan-

**Table 3.2g    Voter Registration and Turnout Rates (1994)**

|  | % registered to vote | % voted in 1994 elections |
|---|---|---|
| Asian Americans |  |  |
| U.S.-born | 56% | 78% |
| Foreign born | 49 | 74 |
| Overall | 53 | 76 |
| Latinos |  |  |
| U.S.-born | 53% | 62% |
| Foreign born | 53 | 74 |
| Overall | 53 | 64 |
| African Americans |  |  |
| U.S.-born | 61% | 63% |
| Foreign born | 58 | 78 |
| Overall | 61 | 63 |
| Non-Hispanic whites |  |  |
| U.S.-born | 69% | 73% |
| Foreign born | 68 | 78 |
| Overall | 69 | 73 |

*Source:* Current Population Survey 1994.

Table 3.2h    Registration and Voting by Year of Immigration
for Naturalized and U.S.-Born Citizens (1994)

|  | % Registered to vote year of immigration for naturalized citizens | % actually voted |
|---|---|---|
| Pre–1965 | 77% | 92% |
| 1965–1974 | 57 | 66 |
| 1975–1985 | 43 | 71 |
| 1986–1994 | 26 | 81 |
| Overall | 49 | 74 |
| U.S.-born | 56 | 78 |

Source: Current Population Survey 1994

tially lower than native-born citizens and naturalized citizens who arrived before 1975. This was consistent for practically all age and educational attainment levels, as well as for men and women. Like naturalization, multiple regression analysis revealed that year of entry was the best predictor of voter registration for Asian naturalized citizens. For voting, in contrast, year of entry, educational attainment, and age were the strongest explanatory variables for Asian naturalized registered voters.

Like the process of naturalization, the importance of time-dependent variables for electoral participation is consistent with the view that immigrants and refugees must oftentimes undergo a prolonged and multifaceted process of social adaptation

Table 3.2i    Detailed Rates of Voter Registration of Asian American
Naturalized and U.S.-Born Citizens, Eighteen Years and Older

|  | Number of years in the U.S. (naturalized citizens) | | | | |
|---|---|---|---|---|---|
|  | 6–10 | 11–14 | 15–19 | 20+ | U.S.-born |
| By Age |  |  |  |  |  |
| 18–24 | 0 | 20% | 15% | 10% | 26% |
| 25–29 | 13 | 16 | 0 | 31 | 25 |
| 30–39 | 3 | 15 | 4 | 40 | 31 |
| 40–49 | 8 | 37 | 42 | 20 | 24 |
| 50–59 | 0 | 19 | 20 | 51 | 22 |
| 60 plus | 0 | 0 | 12 | 41 | 40 |
| By education level |  |  |  |  |  |
| 0–8 years | 0 | 11% | 26% | 33% | 24% |
| 9–12 years | 0 | 0 | 13 | 45 | 16 |
| High school | 16 | 20 | 33 | 28 | 16 |
| Some college | 1 | 18 | 23 | 28 | 32 |
| Bachelor's | 5 | 12 | 27 | 45 | 43 |
| Graduate degree | 0 | 66 | 18 | 41 | 35 |
| By gender |  |  |  |  |  |
| Males | 6% | 20% | 23% | 29% | 32% |
| Females | 6 | 21 | 27 | 39 | 29 |

Source: Current Population Survey 1994

and learning before fully participating in their newly adopted country. To become actively involved in American electoral politics, and to become politically acculturated, may be one of the most complex, lengthy, and least understood learning experiences. Adult Asian immigrants and refugees, like other groups of migrants (Gittleman 1982), largely acquired their core political values, attitudes, and behavioral orientations in sociopolitical systems that were different in a variety of ways from that of the United States. Some of their countries of origin did not have universal suffrage, others were dominated by a single political party (which made voting nearly inconsequential), and still others were in extreme political upheaval as a result of civil war or international conflict. Indeed, one of the major reasons why many Asian refugees left their homelands was to escape some of the most horrendous political situations ever, like the killing fields in Cambodia.

As a result, previously learned lessons and orientations towards government and political activities may not be easily supplanted nor supplemented. For example, adult education classes in American civics and government, which immigrants usually take to prepare for their naturalization examinations, expose them to the most rudimentary facts about American government, but probably have little or no impact on their preexisting political belief systems, their general sense of political efficacy and trust towards government, or their knowledge of the traditions, current policy debates, and political party agendas of American politics. Learning about, and more importantly becoming actively involved in politics "American style" through registering to vote and voting in elections, probably takes place through a range of personal and group experiences that go beyond citizenship classes, and evolves over time and in conjunction with other aspects of acculturating to American life and society.

The Asian American electorate is clearly in the process of transformation and change. Its future characteristics and impact will be largely determined by the extent to which newly naturalized Asian immigrants and refugees are incorporated into the political system, and are encouraged to register to vote and to cast their ballots. An electorate that "looks like Asian America," in all of its dimensions of diversity, especially in becoming predominantly foreign-born rather than reflecting its current native-born majority profile, may have far different partisan preferences and public policy priorities. For example, the Asian Pacific American voters in the City of Monterey Park in Los Angeles County may be illustrative (table 3.2j). In 1984, there was a plurality of Democrats (43 percent) over Republicans (31 percent) among Chinese American voters, but also an extremely high proportion of individuals (25 percent) who specified no party affiliations, and considered themselves to be independents. [20] By 1989, Chinese American voters, who accounted for the vast majority of new registered voters in Monterey Park since 1984, were nearly evenly divided among Democrats (35 percent), Republicans (37 percent), and no party independents (26 percent) (Nakanishi 1986a, 1991). Moreover, the Asian American electorate in the city changed its overall partisan orientation through the addition of these new, largely Chinese American registered voters. In 1984, Asian Pacific American voters as a whole in Monterey Park showed a slight majority for the Democrats. By 1989, with an increase of over 2,500 new registered voters, it was no longer possible to characterize the Asian American electorate in the city in this manner. In an analogous fashion, on a larger national scale, the Asian American electorate at both the grassroots and leadership levels have been and will continue to undergo significant changes with the increased political participation of Asian immigrants and refugees in the future.

## CONCLUSION AND RECOMMENDATIONS

Large-scale immigration from Asia since the enactment of the Immigration Act of 1965 has had a dramatic impact on many

**Table 3.2j    Asian Pacific American Registered Voters, Monterey Park, California (1984 and 1989)**

|  | Number registered | Democrats | Republicans | Other parties | No party |
|---|---|---|---|---|---|
| 1984 Citywide | 22,021 | 13,657 | 5,564 | 368 | 2,290 |
|  | (100%) | (62%) | (25%) | (2%) | (10%) |
| 1989 Citywide | 23,184 | 13,243 | 6,684 | 369 | 2,888 |
|  | (100%) | (57%) | (29%) | (2%) | (13%) |
| 1984–1989 Net gain/loss | +1,163 | −414 | +1,120 | +1 | +598 |
| 1984 Asian Pacific total | 6,441 | 3,265 | 1,944 | 54 | 1,178 |
|  | (100%) | (51%) | (30%) | (1%) | (18%) |
| 1984 Asian Pacific total | 8,988 | 3,754 | 3,198 | 168 | 1,868 |
|  | (100%) | (42%) | (36%) | (2%) | (21%) |
| 1984–1989 Net gain/loss | +2547 | +489 | +1254 | +114 | +690 |
| 1984 Non-Asian Pacific total | 15,438 | 10,392 | 3,620 | 314 | 1,112 |
|  | (100%) | (67%) | (23%) | (2%) | (7%) |
| 1989 Non-Asian Pacific total | 14,196 | 9,489 | 3,486 | 201 | 1,020 |
|  | (100%) | (67%) | (25%) | (1%) | (7%) |
| 1984–1989 Net gain/loss | −1,242 | −903 | −134 | −113 | −92 |
| 1984 Chinese Americans | 3,152 | 1,360 | 972 | 23 | 797 |
|  | (100%) | (43%) | (31%) | (1%) | (25%) |
| 1989 Chinese Americans | 5,356 | 1,868 | 1,989 | 100 | 1,399 |
|  | (100%) | (35%) | (37%) | (2%) | (26%) |
| 1984–1989 Net gain/loss | +2,204 | +508 | +1,017 | +77 | +602 |
| 1984 Japanese Americans | 2,586 | 1,429 | 838 | 21 | 298 |
|  | (100%) | (55%) | (32%) | (1%) | (12%) |
| 1989 Japanese Americans | 2,919 | 1,516 | 991 | 42 | 370 |
|  | (100%) | (52%) | (34%) | (1%) | (13%) |
| 1984–1989 Net gain/loss | +343 | +87 | +153 | +21 | +72 |

*Source:* UCLA Asian Pacific American Voter Registration Project.

states and regions across the nation, as well as on the Asian American population. From a largely native-born group of 1.5 million in 1970, Asian Pacific Americans[21] became a predominantly immigrant population of 3.5 million in 1980. By 1990, the population had doubled again to 7.2 million nationwide, of which 66 percent were foreign-born. Recent projections estimate that

Asian Pacific Americans will continue to increase to nearly 12 million by 2000, and nearly 20 million by 2020. The foreign-born sector is expected to remain in the majority until 2020, and probably beyond (Ong and Hee 1993).

The issues of naturalization and electoral participation, which were examined in this report, are therefore expected to remain compelling and critical for both the Asian American population and for American society generally for many years to come. Our analysis indicates that Asian immigrants have the highest rates of naturalization of any group, including those who came from Europe, and do not remain permanent aliens in this country. They "Americanize," become full citizens, participate actively in all sectors of American life, and should be entitled to all their citizenship rights and privileges. At the same time, we found that Asian immigrants, like their native-born counterparts, have extremely low overall rates of voter registration in comparison with other groups. However, Asian immigrants appear to attain levels of political involvement that are the same, if not better, than those of native-born Asian citizens with the passage of a substantial period of time—over two decades—and with increased acculturation.

The political incorporation of Asian naturalized (*and* native-born citizens) into the American electoral system needs to be accelerated. The contemporary remnants of the political exclusion and isolation that Asian Americans experienced in the past must be fully confronted and eliminated not only by Asian American groups, but also by the two major political parties and others who believe that citizens should be able to fully exercise their right of franchise. Unfair redistricting of Asian American communities, lack of bilingual voter registration application forms and ballots, and opposition to the implementation of legislation like the National Voter Registration Act of 1993 (aka Motor Voter Act) perpetuate "political structural barriers," which must be challenged and replaced by fair and inclusive political practices and policies. Asian immigrants have much to contribute to all aspects of American political life—as voters, campaign workers, financial donors, policy experts, and elected officials—and must be allowed to and encouraged to participate fully. By doing so, we will continue a political tradition as old as the nation itself of benefiting from the special leadership talents and contributions

of individuals who came to the United States from all corners of the world, and shaped its domestic and international programs and policies.

In recent years, the incentive and necessity for Asian immigrants and their native-born counterparts to naturalize and become more involved in electoral politics have been greatly enhanced in both obvious and unexpected ways. Politicians and the major political parties, which had long neglected to address the unique public policy interests and quality-of-life concerns of Asian Americans, have become increasing responsive and attentive, especially to the growing sector of the Asian American population that contributes sizable amounts to political campaign coffers. Less interest, however, has been shown towards augmenting the long-term voting potential of Asian Americans, and few attempts have been made by the Democratic or Republican parties to finance voter registration and education campaigns in Asian American communities. However, the increasing number of Asian Americans, especially those of immigrant background, who are seeking public office appears to be stimulating greater electoral participation among Asian Americans at the grassroots level. For example, it is becoming a common practice for Asian American candidates to make special efforts in seeking monetary donations and in registering new voters among Asian Americans in the jurisdictions in which they are running for office.

These activities provide Asian immigrants with important and direct vantage points from which to understand the workings of the American political system, thereby facilitating their political acculturation. At the same time, a wide array of advocacy and social services groups have formed in Asian American communities across the nation, and a number of different outreach campaigns have been launched to promote citizenship and to register individuals, particularly those who have just become citizens at naturalization ceremonies. And finally, disastrous events like the civil unrest in Los Angeles in 1992, in which over 2,000 Korean American and Asian-owned businesses were destroyed, have underscored the need for immigrant-dominant communities to place greater organizational and leadership activities towards augmenting their access to and influence in local government and other policy arenas, as well as to increase their representation in voter registration rolls.

The decade of the 1990s and the start of the new century, which are widely viewed in glowing and optimistic terms because of seemingly positive demographic trends, will be a significant period to witness and analyze because of the extraordinary challenges and opportunities that it will undoubtedly present for Asian Americans in realizing their full potential as citizens and electoral participants. However, the level of success that they will achieve in the future will not be solely determined by the Asian American population, or its leaders and organizations. It will undoubtedly require the assistance and intervention of a wide array of groups and leaders in both the private and public sectors. Whether or not Asian Americans become a major new political force in the American electoral system is nearly impossible to predict with any precision. However, our ability to raise and seriously entertain such a question in the context of the historical conditions of disenfranchisement and exclusion that Asian Americans faced in the past is quite revealing in itself.

## NOTES

1. Albert Gore, "Keynote Address," July 14, 1995, Pasadena Hilton, Pasadena, California.

2. The 1995 Personal Responsibility Act.

3. Citizenship criteria are: (1) immigrants who are at least eighteen years of age, (2) have been lawfully admitted to the United States for permanent residence, (3) have lived in the United States continuously for five consecutive years, (4) are able to speak, read and write English, (5) pass an exam on United States government and history, (6) be of good moral character, and (7) are able to show loyalty to the U.S. by taking an oath of allegiance. There are exceptions to these rules: (1) the spouse or

child of a United States citizen becomes eligible in three years, (2) a child who immigrates with his or her parent may become a citizen when the parent naturalizes, (3) an adopted children is eligible for administrative naturalization, (4) an alien who served in World War I, World War II, Korean War, Vietnam, or Grenada may naturalize without permanent residence requirements in some situations, (5) an alien who has served in the Armed Forces for three years may be able to naturalize without meeting certain requirements, (6) former U.S. citizens may waive some requirements, and (7) employees of organizations that promote the United States interests in foreign countries may naturalize without meeting these requirements.

4. The number of adult Asian immigrants in the samples are over 10,000 for 1970, 87,000 for 1980, and 182,000 for 1990.

5. The 1970 Census used only four categories: naturalized U.S. citizen, alien, born abroad of American parents, and native-born.

6. The number of years in this country is estimated based on time of entry into the United States. The census does not report whether a respondent has been in the country continuously.

7. The observed change can be decomposed into three components: (1) the difference due to a change in the composition of the population holding the rates for each subgroup constant, (2) the difference due to a change in the rates holding the composition constant, and (3) the difference due to the interaction of the changes in rates and composition.

8. The contribution of lower rates with each cohort can be estimated through decomposition with one component being the change in within group rates between 1970 and 1990, holding the composition by years in the United States to that observed for 1970. The calculations indicate that the within-group drop in naturalization rates accounts for 53 percent of the overall decline for all immigrants—that is, 12.5 of the 23.5 percentage points difference in the naturalization rates for 1970 and 1990.

9. For the purpose of this chapter, the four major racial groups are defined as Asians, African Americans, non-Hispanic whites, and Hispanics. The Hispanic classification is nominally an ethnic classification, but being Hispanic

in U.S. society is often ascriptive in a manner similar to membership in a racial group.

10. The rates are based on administrative records on the total number of legal immigrants admitted and the total number of persons who naturalized. The rates reported in the text are for the cohort of immigrants who entered between 1970 and 1979. The number of persons from this cohort who naturalized is based on INS records from 1970 to 1990.

11. The two other nations are Mexico and the Dominican Republic, with rates of 14 and 22 percent, respectively.

12. The categories beyond twenty years for the 1980 differ from those for the other two censuses. For the 1980 Census, the categories are twenty-one to twenty-nine years and thirty-plus years.

13. The low rate is also due to the inclusion of foreign-born persons in the United States on temporary visas. As stated earlier, the census does not differentiate between permanent immigrants and those on temporary visas. The latter are likely to be here for a short time, thus are concentrated among newly arrived aliens.

14. The estimate depends on assumptions regarding the naturalization rate in the fifth year and the fifteenth year and the relative number who would never naturalize. One difficulty making an estimate is the nonlinear nature of the naturalization rates, with a noticeable decrease in the change with more years in the United States. If we assume that the rates were 10 percent in the fifth year and 70 percent in the fifteenth year, and that 10 percent would never naturalize, then two-thirds of all naturalization would have occurred in the five- to fifteen-year range.

15. An alternative explanation is that the difference was due to historical circumstances unique to each group. In other words, the experiences of the eleven- to fifteen-year group would not be repeated for the six- to ten-year group over the next five years; consequently, the difference in the naturalization rates between the two groups observed in the cross-sectional data would not be an accurate predictor of the increase in rate experienced by the six- to ten-year group over the subsequent five years.

16. There are changes in the cohort from one census to another due to death, emigration, and changes in how respondents report their time of entry into the United States. It is, however, beyond the scope of this study to examine how these factors may affect our estimates.

17. This includes those with a nondoctorate professional degree.

18. The results are available from the author.

19. The 1994 CPS included 3,317 Asians out of a total sample of 102,197. The 1990 survey included 2,914 Asians among 105,875, and the 1992 had 3,443 Asians among 102,901. Both weighted and unweighted data were analyzed for this report.

20. Other studies have also found that some groups of Asian American voters register in higher than expected proportions as "no party" or independents. See Din 1984 and Chen et al. 1989.

21. These population figures include both Asian Americans and Pacific Islanders (e.g., Hawaiians, Samoans, Guamanians, Tongans, Fijians, Palauans, Northern Mariana Islanders, and Tahitians). From 1980 to 1990, Pacific Islanders increased by 41 percent from 259,566 to 365,024.

## REFERENCES

Asianweek. 1984. "Asians Called a 'Major National Force' in Political. Fund-raising," Asianweek (June 1): 5.

Bai, Su Sun. 1991. "Affirmative Pursuit of Political Equality for Asian Pacific Americans: Reclaiming the Voting Rights Act," University of Pennsylvania Law Review 139(3): 731–67.

Borjas, G. 1990. Friends or Strangers: The Impact of Immigrants on the U.S. Economy. New York: Basic Books, Inc.

Cain, Bruce E. 1988. "Asian-American electoral power: imminent or illusory?" Election Politics 5: 27–30.

Chen, Marion, Woei-Ming New, and John Tsutakawa. 1989. "Empowerment in New York Chinatown: Our Work as Student Interns," Amerasia Journal 15: 199–206.

Din, Grant. 1984. "An Analysis of Asian/Pacific American Registration and Voting Patterns in San Francisco," M.A. Thesis, Claremont Graduate School.

Erie, Steven P. and Harold Brackman. 1993. Paths to Political Incorporation for Latinos and Asian Pacifics in California._Berkeley: The California Policy Seminar.

The Field Institute. 1992. "A Digest on Califor-nia's Political Demography," November, 6.

Gittleman, Zvi. 1982. *Becoming Israelis: Polit-ical Resocialization of Soviet and American Immigrants.* New York: Praeger.

Gurwitt, Rob. 1990. "Have Asian Americans Arrived Politically? Not Quite," *Governing* (November): 32–38.

Hammer, Tomas. 1978. "Migration and Poli-tics: Delimitation and Organization of a Research Field," paper presented to the Workshop on International Migration and Politics, European Consortium on Political Research, Grenoble, France.

Hing, Bill. 1993. *The Making and Remaking of Asian America through Immigration.* Stan-ford: Stanford University Press.

Isaacs, Stephen D. 1974. *Jews and American Politics.* Garden City: Doubleday and Com-pany.

Jasso, Guillermina and Mark R. Rosenzweig. 1990. *The New Chosen People: Immigrants in the United States* (The Population of the U.S. in the 1980s Census Monograph Series). For the National Committee for Research on the 1980 Census. New York: Russel Sage Foundation.

Karnow, Stanley. 1992. "Apathetic Asian Amer-icans? Why Their Success Hasn't Spilled Over into Politics," *Washington Post,* November 29: C1, C2.

Kwoh, Stewart and Mindy Hui. 1993. "Empow-ering Our Communities: Political Policy," in LEAP Asian Pacific American Public Policy Institute and the UCLA Asian American Stud-ies Center, *The State of Asian Pacific Amer-ica: Policy Issues to the Year 2020.* Los Ange-les: LEAP Asian Pacific American Public Policy Institute and the UCLA Asian Ameri-can Studies Center, 189–97.

Liang, Zai. 1994. "On the Measurement of Naturalization," *Demography* 2(3): 525–48.

Lien, Pei-te. 1994. "Ethnicity and Political Par-ticipation: A Comparison Between Asian and Mexican Americans," *Political Behavior* 16(2): 237–64.

Miller, John. 1995. "Asian Americans Head For Politics," *The American Enterprise* 6: 56–58.

Nakanishi, Don T. 1986a. "Asian American Politics: An Agenda for Research," *Amerasia Journal* 12: 1–27.

———. 1986b. *The UCLA Asian Pacific Ameri-can Voter Registration Study.* Los Angeles: Asian Pacific American Legal Center.

———. 1989. "A Quota on Excellence? The Debate on Asian American Admissions," *Change,* (November/December): 38–47.

———. 1991. "The Next Swing Vote? Asian Pacific Americans and California Politics." In Byran Jackson and Michael Preston, eds., *Racial and Ethnic Politics in California.* Berkeley Institute for Governmental Studies, 25–54.

———. 1993. "Surviving Democracy's 'Mis-take': Japanese Americans and Executive Order 9066," *Amerasia Journal* 19: 7–35

Ong, Paul, Lucie Cheng, and Leslie Evans. 1992. "Migration of Highly-Educated Asians and Global Dynamics," *Asian and Pacific Migration Journal* 1(3–4): 543–84.

Ong, Paul and Suzanne Hee. 1993. "The Growth of the Asian Pacific American Popu-lation: 20 million in 2020." In LEAP Asian Pacific American Public Policy Institute and the UCLA Asian American Studies Center, *The State of Asian Pacific America: Policy Issues to the Year 2020.* Los Angeles: LEAP Asian Pacific American Public Policy Insti-tute and the UCLA Asian American Studies Center, 11–24.

Skerry, Peter. 1993. *Mexican Americans: The Ambivalent Minority.* New York: The Free Press.

Stokes, Bruce. 1988. "Learning the Game," *National Journal* 43 (October 22): 2649–54.

Tachibana, Judy. 1986. "California's Asians: Power from a Growing Population," *Califor-nia Journal* 17: 534–43.

Tam, Wendy. 1995. "Asians—A Monolithic Voting Bloc?" *Political Behavior* 17(2): 223–49.

Tomas Rivera Center. 1994. *Mexican Ameri-cans: Are They an Ambivalent Minority.* Claremont, Calif.: The Tomas Rivera Center.

U.S. Immigration and Naturalization Service. 1991. *Statistical Yearbook of the Immigration and Naturalization Service, 1990.* Washing-ton D.C: U.S. Government Printing Office.

Yang, Philip Q. 1994a. "Explaining Immigrant Naturalization," *International Migration Review* 28(3): 449–77.

———. 1994b. "Ethnicity and Naturalization," *Ethnic & Racial Studies* 17(4): 593–618.

# The 'Four Prisons' and
# the Movements of Liberation

## Asian American Activism
## from the 1960s to the 1990s

*Glenn Omatsu*

~~~~~~~~~~~~~~~~~~~~~~~~~~~~~~~~~~~~~~~~~~~~~~~~~~~~~~~~~~~~~~~~~~~~~~~~

According to Ali Shariati, an Iranian philosopher, each of us exists within four prisons.[1] First is the prison imposed on us by history and geography; from this confinement, we can escape only by gaining a knowledge of science and technology. Second is the prison of history; our freedom comes when we understand how historical forces operate. The third prison is our society's social and class structure; from this prison, only a revolutionary ideology can provide the way to liberation. The final prison is the self. Each of us is composed of good and evil elements, and we must each choose between them.

The analysis of our four prisons provides a way of understanding the movements that swept across America in the 1960s and molded the consciousness of one generation of Asian Americans. The movements were struggles for liberation from many prisons. They were struggles that confronted the historical forces of racism,

poverty, war, and exploitation. They were struggles that generated new ideologies, based mainly on the teachings and actions of Third World leaders. And they were struggles that redefined human values—the values that shape how people live their daily lives and interact with each other. Above all, they were struggles that transformed the lives of "ordinary" people as they confronted the prisons around them.

For Asian Americans, these struggles profoundly changed our communities. They spawned numerous grassroots organizations. They created an extensive network of student organizations and Asian American Studies classes. They recovered buried cultural traditions as well as produced a new generation of writers, poets, and artists. But most importantly, the struggles deeply affected Asian American consciousness. They redefined racial and ethnic identity, promoted new ways of thinking about communities, and challenged prevailing notions of power and authority.

Yet, in the two decades that have followed, scholars have reinterpreted the movements in narrower ways. I learned about this reinterpretation when I attended a class recently in Asian American Studies at UCLA. The professor described the

Omatsu, Glenn. "The 'Four Prisons' and the Movements of Liberation: Asia American Activism from the 1960s to the 1990s." In *The State of Asian Pacific America: Activism and Resistance in the 1990s* (Boston: South End Press, 1994), 19–69. Reprinted with permission.

period from the late 1950s to the early 1970s as a single epoch involving the persistent efforts of racial minorities and their white supporters to secure civil rights. Young Asian Americans, the professor stated, were swept into this campaign and by later anti-war protests to assert their own racial identity. The most important influence on Asian Americans during this period was Dr. Martin Luther King Jr., who inspired them to demand access to policymakers and initiate advocacy programs for their own communities. Meanwhile, students and professors fought to legitimize Asian American Studies in college curricula and for representation of Asians in American society. The lecture was cogent, tightly organized, and well-received by the audience of students—many of them new immigrants or the children of new immigrants. There was only one problem: the reinterpretation was wrong on every aspect.

Those who took part in the mass struggles of the 1960s and early 1970s will know that the birth of the Asian American movement coincided not with the initial campaign for civil rights but with the later demand for black liberation; that the leading influence was not Martin Luther King Jr., but Malcolm X; that the focus of a generation of Asian American activists was not on asserting racial pride but reclaiming a tradition of militant struggle by earlier generations; that the movement was not centered on the aura of racial identity but embraced fundamental questions of oppression and power; that the movement consisted of not only college students but large numbers of community forces, including the elderly, workers, and high school youth; and that the main thrust was not one of seeking legitimacy and representation within American society but the larger goal of liberation.

It may be difficult for a new generation—raised on the Asian American code words of the 1980s stressing "advocacy," "access," "legitimacy," "empowerment," and "assertiveness"—to understand the urgency of Malcolm X's demand for freedom "by any means necessary," Mao's

challenge to "serve the people," the slogans of "power to the people" and "self-determination," the principles of "mass line" organizing and "united front" work, or the conviction that people—not elites—make history. But these ideas galvanized thousands of Asian Americans and reshaped our communities. And it is these concepts that we must grasp to understand the scope and intensity of our movement and what it created.

But are these concepts relevant to Asian Americans today? In our community—where new immigrants and refugees constitute the majority of Asian Americans—can we find a legacy from the struggles of two decades ago? Are the ideas of the movement alive today, or have they atrophied into relics—the curiosities of a bygone era of youthful and excessive idealism?

By asking these questions, we, as Asian Americans, participate in a larger national debate: the reevaluation of the impact of the 1960s on American society today. This debate is occurring all around us: in sharp exchanges over "family values" and the status of women and gays in American society; in clashes in schools over curricular reform and multiculturalism; in differences among policymakers over the urban crisis and approaches to rebuilding Los Angeles and other inner cities after the 1992 uprisings; and continuing reexaminations of U.S. involvement in Indochina more than two decades ago and the relevance of that war to U.S. military intervention in Iraq, Somalia, and Bosnia.

What happened in the 1960s that made such an impact on America? Why do discussions about that decade provoke so much emotion today? And do the movements of the 1960s serve as the same controversial reference point for Asian Americans?

## THE UNITED STATES DURING THE 1960S

In recent years, the movements of the 1960s have come under intense attack. One national bestseller, Allan Bloom's *Closing of the American Mind*, criticizes the movements for undermining the bedrock of Western thought.[2] According to Bloom, nothing positive resulted from the mass upheavals of the 1960s. He singles out black studies and affirmative-action programs and calls for eliminating them from universities.

Activists who have continued political work provide contrasting assessments. Their books include Todd Gitlin's *The Sixties: Years of Hope, Days of Rage*; James Miller's *"Democracy Is in the Streets": From Port Huron to the Siege of Chicago*; Ronald Fraser's *1968: A Student Generation in Revolt*; Tom Hayden's *Reunion: A Memoir*; Tariqa Ali's *Street Fighting Years*; George Katsiaficas' *The Imagination of the New Left: A Global Analysis of 1968* and special issues of various journals, including *Witness*, *Socialist Review*, and *Radical America*.

However, as Winifred Breines states in an interesting review essay titled "Whose New Left?" most of the retrospects have been written by white male activists from elite backgrounds and reproduce their relationship to these movements.[3] Their accounts tend to divide the period into two phases: the "good" phase of the early 1960s, characterized by participatory democracy; followed by the post-1968 phase, when movement politics "degenerated" into violence and sectarianism.

"Almost all books about the New Left note a turning point or an ending in 1968 when the leadership of the movement turned toward militancy and violence and SDS [Students for a Democratic Society] as an organization was collapsing," Breines observes. The retrospects commonly identify the key weaknesses of the movements as the absence of effective organization, the lack of discipline, and utopian thinking. Breines disagrees with these interpretations:

The movement was not simply unruly and undisciplined; it was experimenting with antihierarchical organizational forms . . . There were many centers of

action in the movement, many actions, many interpretations, many visions, many experiences. There was no [organizational] unity because each group, region, campus, commune, collective, and demonstration developed differently, but all shared in a spontaneous opposition to racism and inequality, the war in Vietnam, and the repressiveness of American social norms and culture, including centralization and hierarchy.[4]

Breines believes that the most important contributions of activists were their moral urgency, their emphasis on direct action, their focus on community building, and their commitment to mass democracy.

Similarly, Sheila Collins in *The Rainbow Challenge*, a book focusing on the Jesse Jackson presidential campaign of 1984 and the formation of the National Rainbow Coalition, assesses the movements of the 1960s very positively.[5] She contents that the Jackson campaign was built on the grassroots organizing experience of activists who emerged from the struggles for civil rights, women's liberation, peace and social justice, and community building during the 1960s. Moreover, activists' participation in these movements shaped their vision of America, which, in turn, became the basis for the platform of the Rainbow Coalition twenty years later.

According to Collins, the movements that occurred in the United States in the sixties were also part of a worldwide trend, a trend Latin American theologians call the era of the "eruption of the poor" into history. In America, the revolt of the "politically submerged" and "economically marginalized" posed a major ideological challenge to ruling elites:

The civil rights and black power movement exploded several dominant assumptions about the nature of American society, thus challenging the cultural hegemony of the white ruling elite and causing everyone else in the society to redefine their relationship to centers of power, creating a groundswell of support for radical democratic participation in every aspect of institutional life.[6]

Collins contends that the mass movements created a "crisis of legitimation" for ruling circles. This crisis, she believes, was "far more serious than most historians—even those of the left—have credited it with being."

Ronald Fraser also emphasizes the ideological challenge raised by the movements due to their mass, democratic character, and their "disrespect for arbitrary and exploitative authority." In *1968: A Student Generation in Revolt*, Fraser explains how these concepts influenced one generation of activists:

[T]he anti-authoritarianism challenged almost every shibboleth of Western society. Parliamentary democracy, the authority of presidents . . . and [the policies of] governments to further racism, conduct imperialist wars or oppress sectors of the population at home, the rule of capital and the fiats of factory bosses, the dictates of university administrators, the sacredness of the family, sexuality, bourgeois culture—nothing was in principle sacrosanct . . . Overall . . . [there was] a lack of deference towards institutions and values that demean[ed] people and a concomitant awareness of people's rights.[7]

## THE SAN FRANCISCO STATE STRIKE'S LEGACY

The retrospects about the 1960s produced so far have ignored Asian Americans. Yet, the books cited above—plus the review essay by Winifred Breines—provide us with some interesting points to compare and contrast. For example, 1968 represented a turning point for Asian Americans and other sectors of American society. But while white male leaders saw the year as marking the decline of the movement, 1968

for Asian Americans was a year of birth. It marked the beginning of the San Francisco State strike and all that followed

The strike, the longest student strike in U.S. history, was the first campus uprising involving Asian Americans as a collective force.[8] Under the Third World Liberation Front—a coalition of African American, Latino, American Indian, and Asian American campus groups—students "seized the time" to demand ethnic studies, open admissions, and a redefinition of the education system. Although their five-month strike was brutally repressed and resulted in only partial victories, students won the nation's first School of Ethnic Studies.

Yet, we cannot measure the legacy of the strike for Asian Americans only in the tangible items it achieved, such as new classes and new faculty; the strike also critically transformed the consciousness of its participants who, in turn, profoundly altered their communities' political landscape. Through their participation, a generation of Asian American student activists reclaimed a heritage of struggle—linking their lives to the tradition of militancy garment and restaurant workers, and Japanese American concentration camp resisters. Moreover, these Asian American students—and their community supporters—liberated themselves from the prisons surrounding their lives and forged a new vision for their communities, creating numerous grassroots projects and empowering previously ignored and disenfranchised sectors of society. The statement of goals and principles of one campus organization. Philippine-American Collegiate Endeavor (PACE), during the strike captures this new vision:

We seek . . . simply to function as human beings, to control our own lives. Initially, following the myth of the American Dream, we worked to attend predominantly white colleges, but we have learned through direct analysis that it is impossible for our people, so-called minorities, to function as human beings, in a racist society in which white always comes first .

. . So we have decided to fuse ourselves with the masses of Third World people, to create, through struggle, a new humanity, a new humanism, a New World Consciousness, and within that context collectively control our own destinies.[9]

The San Francisco State strike is important not only as a beginning point for the Asian American movement, but also because it crystallizes several themes that would characterize Asian American struggles in the following decade. First, the strike occurred at a working-class campus and involved a coalition of Third World students linked to their communities. Second, students rooted their strike in the tradition of resistance by past generations of minority peoples in America. Third, strike leaders drew inspiration—as well as new ideology—from international Third World leaders and revolutions occurring in Asia, Africa, Latin America, and the Middle East. Fourth, the strike in its demands for open admissions, community control of education, ethnic studies, and self-determination confronted basic questions of power and oppression in America. Finally, strike participants raised their demands through a strategy of mass mobilizations and militant, direct action.

In the decade following the strike, several themes would reverberate in the struggles in Asian American communities across the nation. These included housing and anti-eviction campaigns, efforts to defend education rights, union organizing drives, campaigns for jobs and social services, and demands for democratic rights, equality, and justice. Mo Nishida, an organizer in Los Angeles, recalls the broad scope of movement activities in his city:

Our movement flowered. At one time, we had active student organizations on every campus around Los Angeles, fought for ethnic studies, equal opportunity programs, high potential programs at UCLA, and for students doing community work in "Serve the Peo-

ple" programs. In the community, we had, besides [Asian American] Hard Core, four area youth-oriented groups working against drugs (on the Westside, Eastside, Gardena, and the Virgil district). There were also parents' groups, which worked with parents of the youth and more.[10]

In Asian American communities in Los Angeles, San Francisco, Sacramento, Stockton, San Jose, Seattle, New York, and Honolulu, activists created "serve the people" organizations—mass networks built on the principles of "mass line" organizing. Youth initiated many of these organizations—some from college campuses and others from high schools and the streets—but other members of the community, including small-business people, workers, senior citizens, and new immigrants soon joined.

The *mass* character of community struggles is the least appreciated aspect of our movement today. It is commonly believed that the movement involved only college students. In fact, a range of people, including high-school youth, tenants, small-business people, former prison inmates, former addicts, the elderly, and workers embraced the struggles. But exactly who were these people, and what did their participation mean to the movement?

Historian George Lipsitz has studied similar, largely "anonymous" participants in civil rights campaigns in African American communities. He describes one such man, Ivory Perry of St. Louis:

Ivory Perry led no important organizations, delivered no important speeches, and received no significant recognition or reward for his social activism. But for more than 30 years he had passed out leaflets, carried the picket signs, and planned the flamboyant confrontations that made the Civil Rights Movements effective in St. Louis and across the nation. His continuous commitment at the local level had goaded others into action, kept alive hopes of eventual victory in the face of short-term defeats, and provided a relatively powerless community with an effective lever for social change. The anonymity of his activism suggests layers of social protest activity missing from most scholarly accounts, while the persistence of his involvement undermines prevailing academic judgments about mass protests as outbursts of immediate anger and spasmodic manifestations of hysteria.[11]

Those active in Asian American communities during the late 1960s and early 1970s know there were many Ivory Perrys. They were the people who demonstrated at eviction sites, packed City Hall hearing rooms, volunteered to staff health fairs, and helped with day-to-day operations of the first community drop-in centers, legal defense offices, and senior citizen projects. They were the women and men who took the concept of "serve the people" and turned it into a material force, transforming the political face of our communities.

## THE 'CULTURAL REVOLUTION' IN ASIAN AMERICAN COMMUNITIES

But we would be wrong to describe this transformation of our communities as solely "political"—at least as our society narrowly defines the term today. The transformation also involved a cultural vitality that opened new ways of viewing the world. Unlike today—where Asian American communities categorize "culture" and "politics" into different spheres of professional activity—in the late 1960s they did not divide them so rigidly or hierarachically. Writers, artists, and musicians were "cultural workers," usually closely associated with communities, and saw their work as "serving the people." Like other community activists, cultural workers defined the period as a "decisive moment" for Asian Americans—a time for reclaiming the past and changing the future.

The "decisive moment" was also a time for questioning and transforming moral values. Through their political and cultural work, activists challenged systems of rank and privilege, structures of hierarchy and bureaucracy, forms of exploitation and inequality, and notions of selfishness and individualism. Through their activism in mass organizations, they promoted a new moral vision centered on democratic participation, cooperative work styles, and collective decision-making. Pioneer poet Russell C. Leong describes the affinity between this new generation of cultural workers and their communities, focusing on the work of the Asian American Writers' Workshop, located in the basement of the International Hotel in San Francisco Chinatown/Manilatown:

We were a post-World War II generation mostly in our twenties and thirties; in or out of local schools and colleges . . . [We] gravitated toward cities—San Francisco, Los Angles, New York—where movements for ethnic studies and inner city blocks of Asian communities coincided . . . We read as we wrote—not in isolation—but in the company of our neighbors in Manilatown pool halls, barrio parks, Chinatown basements . . . Above all, we poets were a tribe of storytellers . . . Storytellers live in communities where they write for family and friends. The relationship between the teller and listener is neighborly, because the teller of stories must also listen.[12]

But as storytellers, cultural workers did more than simply describe events around them. By witnessing and participating in the movement, they helped to shape community consciousness. San Francisco poet Al Robles focuses on this process of vision making:

While living and working in our little, tiny communities, in the midst of towering highrises, we fought the oppressor, the landlord, the developer, the banks, City Hall. But most of all, we celebrated through our culture; music, dance, song and poetry—not only the best we knew but the best we had. The poets were and always have been an integral part of the community. It was through poetry—through a poetical vision to live out the ritual in dignity as human beings.[13]

The transformation of poets, writers, and artists into cultural workers and vision makers reflected larger changes occurring in every sector of the Asian American community. In education, teachers, and students redefined the learning process, discovering new ways of sharing knowledge different from traditional, authoritarian, top-down approaches. In the social-service sector, social workers and other professionals became "community workers" and under the slogan of "serve the people" redefined the traditional counselor/client relationship by stressing interaction, dialogue, and community building. Within community organizations, members experimented with new organizational structures and collective leadership styles, discarding hierarchical and bureaucratic forms where a handful of commanders made all the decisions. Everywhere, activists and ordinary people grappled with change.

Overall, this "cultural revolution" in the Asian American community echoes themes we have encountered earlier: Third World consciousness, participatory democracy, community building, historical rooting, liberation, and transformation. Why were these concepts so important to a generation of activists? What did they mean? And do they still have relevance for Asian American communities today?

Political analyst Raymond Williams and historian Warren Susman have suggested the use of "keywords" to study historical periods, especially times of great social change.[14] Keywords are terms, concepts, and ideas that emerge as themes of a period, reflecting vital concerns and changing values. For Asian Americans in the 1980s and 1990s, the keywords are "advocacy," "access," "legitimacy," "empowerment," and "assertiveness." These keywords tell us much about the shape of our community today, especially the growing role of young professionals and their aspirations in U.S. society. In contrast, the keywords of the late 1960s and early 1970s—"consciousness," "theory," "ideology," "participatory democracy," "community," and "liberation"—point to different concerns and values.

The keywords of two decades ago point to an approach to political work that activists widely shared, especially those working in grassroots struggles in Asian American neighborhoods, such as the Chinatowns, Little Tokyos, Manilatowns, and International Districts around the nation. This political approach focused on the relationship between political consciousness and social change, and can be best summarized in a popular slogan of the period: "Theory becomes a material force when it is grasped by the masses." Asian American activists believed that they could promote political change through direct action and mass education that raised political consciousness in the community, especially among the unorganized—low-income workers, tenants, small-business people, high school youth, etc. Thus, activists saw political consciousness as rising not from study groups, but from involving people in the process of social change—through their confronting the institutions of power around them and creating new visions of community life based on these struggles.

Generally, academics studying the movements of the 1960s—including academics in Asian American Studies—have dismissed the political theory of that time as murky and eclectic, and simplistic notions of Marxism and capitalism.[15] To a large extent, the thinking was eclectic; Asian American activists drew from Marx, Lenin, Stalin, and Mao—and also from Frantz Fanon, Malcolm X, Che Guevara, Kim Il-sung, and Amilcar Cabral, as well as Korean revolutionary Kim San, W. E. B. DuBois, Frederick Douglass, Paulo Freire, the Black Panther Party, the Young Lords, the women's liberation movement, and many other resistance struggles. But in their obsessive search for theoretical clarity and consistency, these academics miss the bigger picture. What is significant is not the content of ideas activists adopted, but what activists did with the ideas. What Asian American activists did was to use the ideas drawn from many different movements to redefine the Asian American experience.

Central to this redefinition was a slogan that appeared at nearly every Asian American rally during that period: "The people, and the people alone, are the motive force in the making of world history." Originating in the Chinese revolution, Asian American activists adapted the slogan to the tasks of community building, historical rooting, and creating new values. Thus, the slogan came to capture six new ways of thinking about Asian Americans.

1. Asian Americans became active participants in the making of history, reversing standard accounts that had treated Asian Americans as marginal objects.
2. Activists saw history as created by large numbers of people acting together, not by elites.
3. This view of history provided a new way of looking at our communities. Activists believed that ordinary people could make their own history by learning how historical forces operated and by transforming this knowledge into a material force to change their lives.
4. This realization defined a political strategy: Political power came from grassroots organizing, from the bottom up.
5. This strategy required activists to develop a broad analysis of the Asian American condition—to uncover the interconnections in seemingly separate events, such as the war in Indochina, corporate redevelopment of Asian American communities, and the exploitation of Asian immigrants in garment shops. In their political analyses, activists linked the day-to-day struggles of Asian Americans to larger events and issues. The anti-eviction campaign of tenants in Chi-

natown and the International District against powerful corporations became one with the resistance movements of peasants in Vietnam, the Philippines, and Latin America—or, as summarized in a popular slogan of the period, there was "one struggle, [but] many fronts."
6. This new understanding challenged activists to build mass, democratic organizations, especially within unorganized sectors of the community. Through these new organizations, Asian Americans expanded democracy for all sectors of the community and gained the power to participate in the broader movement for political change taking place throughout the world.

The redefinition of the Asian American experience stands as the most important legacy from this period. As described above, this legacy represents far more than an ethnic awakening. The redefinition began with an analysis of power and domination in American society. It provided a way for understanding the historical forces surrounding us. And most importantly, it presented a strategy and challenge for changing our future. This challenge, I believe, still confronts us today.

## THE LATE 1970S: REVERSING DIRECTION

As we continue to delve into the vitality of the movements of the 1960s, one question becomes more and more persistent: Why did these movements, possessing so much vigor and urgency, seem to disintegrate in the late 1970s and the early 1980s? Why did a society in motion toward progressive change seem to suddenly reverse direction?

As in the larger Left movement, Asian American activists heatedly debate this question.[16] Some mention the strategy of repression—including assassinations—U.S. ruling circles launched in response to the mass rebellions. Others cite the accompanying programs of co-optation that elites designed to channel mass discontent into traditional political arenas. Some focus on the New Right's rise, culminating in the Reagan presidency. Still others emphasize the sectarianism among political forces within the movement, or target the inability of the movement as a whole to base itself more broadly within communities.

Each of these analyses provides a partial answer. But missing in most analyses by Asian American activists is the most critical factor: the devastating corporate offensive of the mid-1970s. We will remember the 1970s as a time of economic crisis and staggering inflation. Eventually, historians may more accurately describe it as the years of "one-sided class war." Transnational corporations based in the United States launched a broad attack on the American people, especially African American communities. Several books provide an excellent analysis of the corporate offensive. One of the best, most accessible accounts is *What's Wrong with the U.S. Economy?* written in 1982 by the Institute for Labor Education and Research.[17] My analysis draws from that.

Corporate executives based their offensive on two conclusions: First, the economic crisis in the early 1970s—marked by declining corporate profits—occurred because American working people were earning too much; and second, the mass struggles of the previous decades had created "too much democracy" in America. The Trilateral Commission—headed by David Rockefeller and composed of corporate executives and politicians from the United States, Europe, and Japan—posed the problem starkly: Either people would have to accept less, or corporations would have to accept less. An article in *Business Week* identified the solution: "Some people will obviously have to do with less . . . Yet it will be a hard pill for many Americans to swallow—the idea of doing with less so that big business can have more."

But in order for corporations to "have more," U.S. ruling circles had to deal with the widespread discontent that had erupted throughout America. We sometimes forget today that in the mid-1970s a large number of Americans had grown cynical about U.S. business and political leaders. People routinely called politicians—including President Nixon and Vice President Agnew—crooks, liars, and criminals. Increasingly, they began to blame the largest corporations for their economic problems. One poll showed that half the population believed that "big business is the source of most of what's wrong in this country today." A series of Harris polls found that those expressing "a great deal of confidence" in the heads of corporations had fallen from 55 percent in 1966 to only 15 percent in 1975. By the fall of 1975, public-opinion analysts testifying before a congressional committee reported, according to the *New York Times*, "that public confidence in the government and in the country's economic future is probably lower than it has ever been since they began to measure such things scientifically." These developments stunned many corporate leaders. "How did we let the educational system fail the free-enterprise system?" one executive asked.

U.S. ruling elites realized that restoring faith in free enterprise could only be achieved through an intensive ideological assault on those challenging the system. The ideological campaign was combined with a political offensive, aimed at the broad gains in democratic rights that Americans, especially African Americans, had achieved through the mass struggles of previous decades. According to corporate leaders, there was "too much democracy" in America, which meant too little "governability." In a 1975 Trilateral Commission report, Harvard political scientist Samuel Huntington analyzed the problem caused by "previously passive or unorganized groups in the population [which were] now engaged in concerted efforts to establish their claims to opportunities, positions, rewards, and privileges which they had not considered themselves entitled to before." According to Huntington, this upsurge in "democratic fervor" coincided with "markedly higher levels of self-consciousness on the part of blacks, Indians, Chicanos, white ethnic groups, students and women, all of whom became mobilized and organized in new ways." Huntington saw these developments as creating a crisis for those in power:

> The essence of the democratic surge of the 1960s was a general challenge to existing systems of authority, public and private. In one form or another, the challenge manifested itself in the family, the university, business, public and private associations, politics, the government bureaucracy, and the military service. People no longer felt the same obligation to obey those whom they had previously considered superior to themselves in age, rank, status, expertise, character, or talents.[18]

The mass pressures, Huntington contended, had "produced problems for the governability of democracy in the 1970s." The government, he concluded, must find a way to exercise more control. And that meant curtailing the rights of "major economic groups."

The ensuing corporate campaign was a "one-sided class war": plant closures in U.S. industries and transfer of production overseas, massive layoffs in remaining industries, shifts of capital investment from one region of the country to other regions and other parts of the globe, and demands by corporations for concessions in wages and benefits from workers in nearly every sector of the economy.

The Reagan presidency culminated and institutionalized this offensive. The Reagan platform called for restoring "traditional" American values, especially faith in the system of free enterprise. Reaganomics promoted economic recovery by getting government "off the backs" of businesspeople, reducing taxation of the rich, and cutting social programs for the poor. Meanwhile, racism and exploitation became respectable under the new mantle of patriotism and economic recovery.

## THE WINTER OF CIVIL RIGHTS

The corporate assault ravaged many American neighborhoods, but African American communities absorbed its harshest impact. A study by the Center on Budget and Policy Priorities measures the national impact:

- Between 1970 and 1980, the number of poor African Americans rose by 24 percent from 1.4 million to 1.8 million.
- In the 1980s, the overall African American median incomes was 57 percent that of whites, a decline of nearly four percentage points from the early 1970s.
- In 1986, females headed 42 percent of all African American families, the majority of which lived below the poverty line.
- In 1978, 8.4 percent of African American families had incomes under $5,000 a year. By 1987, that figure had grown to 13.5 percent. In that year, a third of all African Americans were poor.[19]
- By 1990, nearly half of all African American children grew up in provety.[20]

Manning Marable provides a stark assessment of this devastation in *How Capitalism Underdeveloped Black America*:

> What is qualitatively *new* about the current period is that the racist/capitalist state under Reagan has proceeded down a public policy road which could inevitably involve the complete obliteration of the entire Black reserve army of labor and sections of the Black working class. The decision to save capitalism at all costs, to provide adequate capital for restructuring of the private sector, fundamentally conflicts with the survival of millions of people who are now permanently outside the workplace. Reaganomics must, if it intends to succeed, place the onerous burden of unemployment on the shoulders of the poor (Blacks, Latinos, and even whites) so securely that middle to upper income

Americans will not protest in the vicious suppression of this stratum.[21]

The corporate offensive, combined with widespread government repression, brutally destroyed grassroots groups in the African American community. This war against the poor ripped apart the social fabric of neighborhoods across America, leaving them vulnerable to drugs and gang violence. The inner cities became the home of the "underclass" and a new politics of inner-directed violence and despair.

Historian Vincent Harding, in *The Other American Revolutions*, summarizes the 1970s as the "winter" of civil rights, a period in which there was "a dangerous loss of hope among black people, hope in ourselves, hope in the possibility of any real change, hope in any moral, creative force beyond the flatness of our lives."[22]

In summary, the corporate offensive—especially its devastation of the African American community—provides the necessary backdrop for understanding why the mass movements of the 1960s seemed to disintegrate. Liberation movements, especially in the African American community, did not disappear, but a major focus of their activity shifted to issues of day-to-day survival.

## THE 1980S: AN AMBIGUOUS PERIOD FOR ASIAN AMERICAN EMPOWERMENT

For African Americans and many other people of color, the period from the mid-1970s through the Reagan and Bush presidencies became a winter of civil rights, a time of corporate assault on their livelihoods and an erosion of hard-won rights. But for Asian Americans, the meaning of this period is much more ambiguous. On the one hand, great suffering marked the period: growing poverty for increasing numbers of Asian Americans—especially refugees from Southeast Asia; a rising trend of racist hate crimes directed toward Asian Americans of all ethnicities and income levels; and sharpening class polarization within our communities—with a widening gap between the very rich and the very poor. But advances also characterized the period. With the reform of U.S. immigration laws in 1965, the Asian American population grew dramatically, creating new enclaves—including suburban settlements—and revitalizing more established communities, such as Chinatowns, around the nation. Some recent immigrant businesspeople, with small capital holdings, found economic opportunities in inner city neighborhoods. Meanwhile, Asian American youth enrolled in record numbers in colleges and universities across the United States. Asian American families moved into suburbs, crashing previously lily-white neighborhoods. And a small but significant group of Asian American politicians, such as Mike Woo and Warren Furutani, scored important electoral victories in the mainstream political arena, taking the concept of political empowerment to a new level of achievement.

During the winter of civil rights, Asian American activists also launched several impressive political campaigns at the grassroots level. Japanese Americans joined together to win redress and reparations. Filipino Americans rallied in solidarity with the "People Power" movement in the Philippines to topple the powerful Marcos dictatorship. Chinese Americans created new political alignments and mobilized community support for the pro-democracy struggle in China. Korean Americans responded to the massacre of civilians by the South Korean dictatorship in Kwangjuu with massive demonstrations and relief efforts, and established an important network of organizations in America, including Young Koreans United. Samoan Americans rose up against police abuse in Los Angeles; Pacific Islanders demanded removal of nuclear weapons and wastes from their homelands; and Hawaiians fought for the right of self-determination and recovery of their lands. And large numbers of Asian

Americans and Pacific Islanders worked actively in the 1984 and 1988 presidential campaigns of Jesse Jackson, helping to build the Rainbow Coalition.

Significantly, these accomplishments occurred in the midst of the Reagan presidency and U.S. politics' turn to the Right. How did certain sectors of the Asian American community achieve these gains amidst conservatism?

There is no simple answer. Mainstream analysts and some Asian Americans have stressed the "model minority" concept. According to this analysis, Asian Americans—in contrast to other people of color in America—have survived adversity and advanced because of their emphasis on education and family values, their community cohesion, and other aspects of their cultural heritage. Other scholars have severely criticized this viewpoint, stressing instead structural changes in the global economy and shifts in U.S. government policy since the 1960s. According to their analysis, the reform of U.S. immigration laws and sweeping economic changes in advanced capitalist nations, such as deindustrialization and the development of new technologies, brought an influx of highly educated new Asian immigrants to America. The characteristics of these new immigrants stand in sharp contrast to those of past generations, and provide a broader social and economic base for developing our communities. Still other political thinkers have emphasized the key role played by political expatriates—both right-wing and left-wing—in various communities, but most especially in the Vietnamese, Filipino, and Korean communities. These expatriates brought political resources from their homelands—e.g., political networks, organizing experience, and, in a few cases, access to large amounts of funds—and have used these resources to change the political landscape of ethnic enclaves. Still other analysts have examined the growing economic and political power of nations of the Asia Pacific and its impact on Asians in America. According to these analysts, we can link the advances of Asian Americans dur-

ing this period to the rising influence of their former homelands and the dawning of what some call "the Pacific Century." Finally, some academics have focused on the significance of small-business activities of new Asian immigrants, arguing that this sector is most responsible for the changing status of Asian Americans in the 1980s. According to their analysis, Asian immigrant entrepreneurs secured an economic niche in inner city neighborhoods because they had access to start-up capital (through rotating credit associations or from family members) and they filled a vacuum created when white businesses fled.[23]

Thus, we have multiple interpretations for why some sectors of the Asian American community advanced economically and politically during the winter of civil rights. But two critical factors are missing from the analyses that can help us better understand the peculiar shape of our community in the 1980s and its ambiguous character when compared to other communities of color. First is the legacy of grassroots organizing from the Asian American movement, and second is the dramatic rise of young professionals as a significant force in the community.

A stereotype about the movements of the 1960s is that they produced nothing enduring—they flared brightly for an instant and then quickly died. However, evidence from the Asian American movement contradicts this commonly held belief. Through meticulous organizing campaigns, Asian American activists created an extensive network of grassroots formations. Unlike similar groups in African American communities—which government repression targeted and brutally destroyed—a significant number of Asian American groups survived the 1980s. Thus far, no researcher has analyzed the impact of the corporate offensive and government repression on grassroots organizations in different communities of color during the late 1970s. When this research is done, I think it will show that U.S. ruling elites viewed the movement in the African American community as a major threat due to its power and influence over other communities. In contrast, the movement in the Asian American community received much less attention due to its much smaller size and influence. As a result, Asian American grassroots formations during the 1970s escaped decimation and gained the time and space to survive, grow, and adapt to changing politics.

The survival of grassroots organizations is significant because it helped to cushion the impact of the war against the poor in Asian American communities. More important, the grassroots formations provided the foundation for many of the successful empowerment campaigns occurring in the 1980s. For example, Japanese Americans built their national effort to win reparations for their internment during World War II on the experiences of grassroots neighborhood organizations' housing and anti-eviction struggles of the early 1970s. Movement activists learned from their confrontations with systems of power and applied these lessons to the more difficult political fights of the 1980s. Thus, a direct link exists between the mass struggles of activists in the late 1960s and the "empowerment" approach of Asian Americans in the 1980s and 1990s.

But while similarities exist in political organizing of the late 1960s and the 1980s, there is one crucial difference: Who is being empowered? In the late 1960s and 1970s, activists focused on bringing "power to the people"—the most disenfranchised of the community, such low-income workers, youth, former prisoners and addicts, senior citizens, tenants, and small-business people. In contrast, the "empowerment" of young professionals in Asian American communities marks the decade of the 1980s. The professionals—children of the civil rights' struggles of the 1950s and 1960s—directly benefited from the campaigns for desegregation, especially in the suburbs; the removal of quotas in colleges and professional schools; and the expansion of job opportunities for middle-class people of color in fields such as law, medicine, and education.

During the 1980s, young professionals altered the political terrain in our commu-

nities.[24] They created countless new groups in nearly every profession: law, medicine, social work, psychology, education, journalism, business, and arts and culture. They initiated new political advocacy groups, leadership training projects, and various national coalitions and consortiums. They organized political caucuses in the Democratic and Republican parties. And they joined the governing boards of many community agencies. Thus, young professionals—through their sheer numbers, their penchant for self-organization, and their high level of activity—defined the Asian American community of the 1980s, shaping it in ways very different from other communities of color.

The emergence of young professionals as community leaders also aided mass political mobilizations. By combining with grassroots forces from the Asian American movement, young professionals advanced struggles against racism and discrimination. In fact, many of the successful Asian American battles of the past decade resulted from this strategic alignment.

The growing power of young professionals has also brought a diversification of political viewpoints to our communities. While many professionals embrace concerns originally raised by movement activists, a surprisingly large number have moved toward neo-conservatism. The emergence of neo-conservatism in our community is a fascinating phenomenon, one we should analyze and appreciate. Perhaps more than any other phenomenon, it helps to explain the political ambiguity of Asian American empowerment in the decade of the 1980s.

## STRANGE AND NEW POLITICAL ANIMALS: ASIAN AMERICAN NEO-CONSERVATIVES

Item: At many universities in recent years some of the harshest opponents of affirmative action have been Chinese Americans and Korean Americans who define themselves as political conservatives. This, in and of itself, is not new or significant. We have always had Asian American conservatives who have spoken out against affirmative action. But what is new is their affiliation. Many participate actively in Asian American student organizations traditionally associated with campus activism.

Item: In the San Francisco newspaper *Asian Week*, one of the most interesting columnists is Arthur Hu, who writes about anti-Asian quotas in universities, political empowerment, and other issues relating to our communities. He also regularly chastises those in terms "liberals, progressives, Marxists, and activists." In a recent column, he wrote: "The Left today has the nerve to blame AIDS, drugs, the dissolution of the family, welfare dependency, gang violence, and educational failure on Ronald Reagan's conservatism" Hu, in turn, criticizes the Left for "tearing down religion, family, structure, and authority; promoting drugs, promiscuity, and abdication of personal responsibility."[25]

Item: During the militant, three-year campaign to win tenure for UCLA Professor Don Nakanishi, one of the key student leaders was a Japanese American Republican, Matthew J. Endo. Aside from joining the campus-community steering committee, he also mobilized support from fraternities, something that progressive activists could not do. Matt prides himself on being a Republican and a life member of the National Rifle Association. He aspires to become a CEO in a corporation but worries about the upsurge in racism against Asian Pacific peoples and the failure of both Republicans and Democrats to address this issue.

The Asian American neo-conservatives are a new and interesting political phenomenon. They are new because they are creatures born from the Reagan-Bush era of supply-side economics, class and racial polarization, and the emphasis on elitism and individual advancement. And they are interesting because they also represent a legacy from the civil rights struggles, especially the Asian American movement. The neo-conservatives embody these seemingly contradictory origins.

- They are proud to be Asian American. But they denounce the Asian American movement of the late 1960s and early 1970s as destructive.
- They speak out against racism against Asian Americans. But they believe that only by ending affirmative action programs and breaking with prevailing civil rights thinking of the past four decades can we end racism.
- They express concern for Asian American community issues. But they contend that the agenda set by the "liberal Asian American establishment" ignores community needs.
- They vehemently oppose quotas blocking admissions of Asian Americans at colleges and universities. But they link anti-Asian quotas to affirmative-actions programs for "less qualified" African American, Latinos, and American Indians.
- They acknowledge the continuing discrimination against African Americans, Latinos, and American Indians in U.S. society. But they believe that the main barrier blocking advancement for other people of color is "cultural"— that unlike Asians, these groups supposedly come from cultures that do not sufficiently emphasize education, family cohesion, and traditional values.

Where did these neo-conservatives come from? What do they represent? And why is it important for progressive peoples to understand their presence?

Progressives cannot dismiss Asian American neo-conservatives as simple-minded Republicans. Although they hold views similar at times to Patrick Buchanan and William Buckley, they are not clones of white conservatives. Nor are they racists, fellow travelers of the Ku Klux Klan, or ideologues attached to Reagan and Bush. Perhaps the group they most resemble is the African American neo-conservatives: the Shelby Steeles, Clarence Thomases, and Tony Browns of this period. Like these men, they are professionals and feel little kinship for people of lower classes. Like these men, they oppose prevailing civil rights thinking, emphasizing reliance on government intervention and social programs. And like these men, they have gained from affirmative action, but they now believe that America has somehow become a society where other people of color can advance through their own "qualifications."

Neo-conservative people of color have embraced thinkers such as the late Martin Luther King Jr. but have appropriated his message to fit their own ideology. In his speeches and writings, King dreamed of the day when racism would be eliminated—when African Americans would be recognized in U.S. society for the "content of our character, not the color of our skin." He called upon all in America to wage militant struggle to achieve this dream. Today, neo-conservatives have subverted his message. They believe that racism in U.S. society has declined in significance, and that people of color can now abandon mass militancy and advance individually by cultivating the content of their character through self-help programs and educational attainment, and retrieving traditional family values. They criticize prevailing "civil rights thinking" as overemphasizing the barriers of racism and relying on "external forces" (i.e., government intervention through social programs) to address the problem.

Asian American neo-conservative closely resemble their African American counterparts in their criticism of government "entitlement" programs and their defense of traditional culture and family values. But Asian American neo-conservatives are not exactly the same as their African American counterparts. The growth of neo-conservative thinking among Asian Americans during the past twenty-five years reflects the peculiar conditions in our community, notably the emerging power of young professionals. Thus to truly understand Asian American neo-conservatives, we need to look at their evolution through the prism of Asian American politics from the late 1960s to the early 1990s.

Twenty-five years ago, Asian American neo-conservatives did not exist. Our community then had only traditional conservatives—those who opposed ethnic studies, the antiwar movement, and other militant grassroots struggles. The traditional conservatives denounced Asian American concerns as "special interest politics" and labeled the assertion of Asian American ethnic identity as "separatist" thinking. For the traditional conservative, a basic contradiction existed in identifying oneself as Asian American and conservative.

Ironically, the liberation struggles of the 1960s—and the accompanying Asian American movement—spawned a new conservative thinker. The movement partially transformed the educational curriculum through ethnic studies, enabling all Asian Americans to assert pride in their ethnic heritage. The movement accelerated the desegregation of suburbs, enabling middle-class Asian Americans to move into all-white neighborhoods. Today, the neo-conservatives are mostly young, middle-class professionals who grew up in white suburbs apart from the poor and people of color. As students, they attended the elite universities. Their only experience with racism is name-calling or "glass ceilings" blocking personal career advancement—and not poverty and violence.

It is due to their professional status and their roots in the Asian American movement that the neo-conservatives exist in uneasy alliance with traditional conservatives in our community. Neo-conservatives are appalled by the violence and rabid anti-communism of reactionary sectors of the Vietnamese community, Chinese from Taiwan tied to the oppressive ruling Kuomintang party, and Korean expatriates attached to the Korean Central Intelligence Agency. They are also uncomfortable with older conservatives, those coming from small-business backgrounds who warily eye the neo-conservatives, considering them as political opportunists.

Neo-conservatives differ from traditional conservatives not only because of their youth and their professional status but most important of all, their political coming of age in the Reagan era. Like their African American counterparts, they are children of the corporate offensive against workers, the massive transfer of resources from the poor to the rich, and the rebirth of so-called "traditional values."

It is their schooling in Reaganomics and their willingness to defend the current structure of power and privilege in America that gives neo-conservative people of color value in today's political landscape. Thus, Manning Marable describes the key role played by African American neo-conservatives:

> The singular service that [they] . . . provide is a new and more accurate understanding of what exactly constitutes conservatism within the Black experience . . . Black conservatives are traditionally hostile to Black participation in trade unions, and urge a close cooperation with white business leaders. Hostile to the welfare state, they call for increased "self-help" programs run by Blacks at local and community levels. Conservatives often accept the institutionalized forms of patriarchy, acknowledging a secondary role for Black women within economics, political life and intellectual work. They usually have a pronounced bias towards organizational authoritarianism and theoretical rigidity.[26]

Marable's analysis points to the basic contradiction for African American neo-conservatives. They are unable to address fundamental problems facing their community: racist violence, grinding poverty, and the unwillingness of corporate and government policymakers to deal with these issues.

Asian American neo-conservatives face similar difficulties when confronted by the stark realities of the post-Reagan period:

- The neo-conservatives acknowledge continuing discrimination in U.S. society but deny the existence of institutional racism and structural inequality. For them, racism lies in the realm of attitudes and "culture" and not institutions of power. Thus, they emphasize individual advancement as the way to overcome racism. They believe that people of color can rise through merit, which they contend can be measured objectively through tests, grades, and educational attainment.

- The neo-conservatives ignore questions of wealth and privilege in American society. In their obsession with "merit," "qualifications," and "objective" criteria, their focus is on dismantling affirmative-action programs and "government entitlements" from the civil rights era. But poverty and racism existed long before the Civil Rights Movement. They are embedded in the system of inequality that has long characterized U.S. society.

- The neo-conservatives are essentially elitist who fear expansion of democracy at the grassroots level. They speak a language of individual advancement, not mass empowerment. They propose a strategy of alignment with existing centers of power and not the creation of new power bases among the disenfranchised sectors of society. Their message is directed to professionals, much like themselves. They have nothing to offer to immigrant workers in sweatshops, the homeless, Cambodian youth in street gangs, or community college youth.

- As relative newcomers to Asian American issues, the neo-conservatives lack understanding of history, especially how concerns in the community have developed over time. Although they aggressively speak out about issues, they lack experience in organizing around these issues. The neo-conservatives function best in the realm of ideas; they have difficulty dealing with concrete situations.

However, by stimulating discussion over how Asian American define community problems, the neo-conservatives bring a vibrancy to community issues by contributing a different viewpoint. Thus, the debate between Asian American neo-conservatives and progressives is positive because it clarifies issues and enables both groups to reach constituencies that each could not otherwise reach.

Unfortunately, this debate is also occurring in a larger and more dangerous context: the campaign by mainstream conservatives to redefine civil rights in America. As part of their strategy, conservatives in the national political arena have targeted our communities. There are high stakes here, and conservatives regard the Asian American neo-conservatives as small players to be sacrificed.

The high stakes are evident in an article by William McGurn entitled "The Silent Minority" appearing in the conservative digest *National Review*.[27] In his essay, he urges Republicans to actively recruit and incorporate Asian Americans into party activities. According to McGurn, a basic affinity exists between Republican values and Asian American values: Many Asian immigrants own small businesses; they oppose communism; they are fiercely pro-defense; they boast strong families; they value freedom; and in their approach to civil rights, they stress opportunities not government "set-asides." McGurn then chastises fellow Republicans for their "crushing indifference" to Asian American issues. He laments how Republicans have lost opportunities by not speaking out on key issues such as the conflict between Korean immigrant merchants and African Americans, the controversy over anti-Asian quotas in universities, and the upsurge in anti-Asian violence.

McGurn sees Republican intervention on these issues strategically—as a way of redefining the race question in American society and shifting the debate on civil rights away from reliance on "an increasingly narrow band of black and liberal interest groups." According to McGurn:

Precisely because Asian Americans are making it in their adoptive land, they hold the potential not only to add to Republican rolls but to define a bona-

fide American language of civil rights. Today we have only one language of civil rights, and it is inextricably linked to government intervention, from racial quotas to set-aside government contracts. It is also an exclusively black-establishment language, where America's myriad other minorities are relegated to second-class citizenship.[28]

McGurn's article presages a period of intense and unprecedented conservative interest in Asian American issues. We can expect conservative commentaries to intensify black-Asian conflicts in inner cities, the controversy over affirmative action, and the internal community debate over designating Asian Americans as a "model minority."

Thus, in the coming period, Asian American communities are likely to become crowded places. Unlike the late 1960s, issues affecting our communities will no longer be the domain of progressive forces only. Increasingly, we will hear viewpoints from Asian American neo-conservatives as well as mainstream conservatives. How well will activists meet this new challenge?

## GRASSROOTS ORGANIZING IN THE 1990s: THE CHALLENGE OF EXPANDING DEMOCRACY

Time would pass, old empires would fall and new ones take their place, the relations of countries and the relations of classes had to change, before I discovered that it is not quality of goods and utility which matter, but movement; not where you are or what you have, but where you have come from, where you are going, and the rate at which you are getting there.[29]

—C. L. R. James

On the eve of the twenty-first century, the Asian American community is vastly different from that of the late 1960s. The community has grown dramatically. In 1970, there were only 1.5 million Asian Americans, almost entirely concentrated in

Hawaii and California. By 1980, there were 3.7 million, and in 1990, 7.9 million—with major Asian communities in New York, Minnesota, Pennsylvania, and Texas. According to census projections, the Asian American population should exceed 10 million by the year 2000, and will reach 20 million by the year 2020.[30]

Moreover, in contrast to the late 1960s—when Chinese and Japanese Americans comprised the majority of Asian Americans, today's community is ethnically diverse—consisting of nearly thirty major ethnic groups, each with a distinct culture. Today's community is also economically different from the 1960s. Compared to other sectors of the U.S. population, there are higher proportions of Asian Americans who are very rich and very poor. This gap between wealth and poverty has created a sharp class polarization in our community, a phenomenon yet to be studied.

But the changes for Asian Americans during the past twenty-five years have not been simply demographic. This political landscape has also changed due to new immigrants and refugees, the polarization between rich and poor, and the emergence of young professionals as a vital new force. Following the approach of C. L. R. James, we have traced the origins of these changes. We now need to analyze where these changes will take us in the decade ahead.

Ideologically and politically, activists confront a new and interesting paradox in the Asian American community of the 1990s. On the one hand, there is a great upsurge of interest in the community and all things Asian American. Almost daily, we hear about new groups forming across the country. In contrast to twenty-five years ago, when interest in the community was minimal and when only progressive activists joined Asian American organizations, we now find a situation where many different groups—including conservatives and neo-conservatives, bankers and business executives, and young professionals in all fields—have taken up the banner of Asian American identity.

On the other hand, we have not seen a corresponding growth in consciousness—of what it means to be Asian American—as we approach the twenty-first century. Unlike African Americans, most Asian Americans today have yet to articulate the "particularities" of issues affecting our community, whether these be the debate over affirmative action, the controversy regarding multiculturalism, or the very definition of empowerment. We have an ideological vacuum, and activists will compete with neo-conservatives, mainstream conservatives, and others to fill it.

We have a political vacuum as well. In recent years, growing numbers of Asian Americans have become involved in community issues. But almost all have come from middle-class and professional backgrounds. Meanwhile, vast segments of our community are not coming forward. In fact, during the past decade the fundamental weakness for activists has been the lack of grassroots organizing among the disenfranchised sectors of our community: youth outside of colleges and universities, the poor, and new immigrant workers. Twenty-five years ago, the greatest strength of the Asian American movement was the ability of activists to organize the unorganized and to bring new political players into community politics. Activists targeted high-school youth, tenants, small-business people, former prison inmates, gang members, the elderly, and workers. Activists helped them build new grassroots organizations, expanding power and democracy in our communities. Can a new generation of activists do the same?

To respond to this challenge, activists will need both a political strategy and a new ideological vision. Politically, activists must find ways to expand democracy by creating new grassroots formations, activating new political players, and building new coalitions. Ideologically, activists must forge a new moral vision, reclaiming the militancy and moral urgency of past generations and reaffirming the commitment to participatory democracy, community building, and collective styles of leadership.

Where will this political strategy and new consciousness come from? More than fifty years ago, revolutionary leader Mao Zedong asked a similar question:

Where do correct ideas come from? Do they drop from the skies? No. Are they innate in the mind? No. They come from social practice, and from it alone . . . In their social practice, people engage in various kinds of struggle and gain rich experience, both from their successes and their failures.[31]

In the current "social practice" of Asian American activists across the nation, several grassroots organizing projects can serve as the basis for a political strategy and a new moral vision for the 1990s. I will focus on three projects that are concentrating on the growing numbers of poor and working poor in our community. Through their grassroots efforts, these three groups are demonstrating how collective power can expand democracy, and how, in the process, activists can forge a new moral vision.

The three groups—the Chinese Progressive Association (CPA) Workers Center in Boston, Asian Immigrant Women Advocates (AIWA) in Oakland, and Korean Immigrant Worker Advocates (KIWA) in Los Angeles—address local needs. Although each organization works with different ethnic groups, their history of organizing has remarkable similarities. Each organization is composed of low-income immigrant workers. Each has taken up more than "labor" issues. And each group has fashioned very effective "united front" campaigns involving other sectors of the community. Thus, although each project is relatively small, collectively their accomplishments illustrate the power of grassroots organizing, the creativity and talents of "ordinary" people in taking up difficult issues, and the ability of grassroots forces to alter the political landscape of their community. Significantly, the focus of each group is working people in the Asian American community—a sector that is numerically large and growing larger. However,

despite their numbers, workers in the Asian American community during the past decade have become voiceless and silent. Today, in discussions about community issues, no one places garment workers, nurses' aides, waiters, and secretaries at the forefront of the debate to define priorities. And no one thinks about the working class as the cutting edge of the Asian American experience. Yet, if we begin to list the basic questions now confronting Asian Americans—racism and sexism, economic justice and human rights, coalition building, and community empowerment—we would find that it is the working class, of all sectors in our community, that is making the most interesting breakthroughs on these questions. They are doing this through groups such as KIWA, AIWA, and the CPA Workers Center. Why, then, are the voices of workers submerged in our community? Why has the working class become silent?

Three trends have pushed labor issues in our community into the background during the past two decades: the rising power of young professionals in our community; the influx of new immigrants and refugees, and the fascination of social scientists and policy institutes with the phenomenon of immigrant entrepreneurship; and the lack of grassroots organizing by activists among new immigrant workers.

Thus, although the majority of Asian Americans work for a living, we have relatively little understanding about the central place of work in the lives of Asian Americans, especially in low-income industries such as garment work, restaurant work, clerical and office work, and other service occupations. Moreover, we are ignorant about the role that labor struggles have played in shaping our history.[32] This labor history is part of the legacy that activists must reclaim.

In contrast to the lack of knowledge about Asian American workers, we have a much greater understanding about the role of young professionals, students, and, most of all, small-business people. In fact, immigrant entrepreneurs, especially Korean immigrants, are perhaps the most studied people of our community. However, as sociologist Edna Bonacich notes, the profile of most Asian immigrant entrepreneurs closely resembles that of workers, due to their low earning power, their long work hours, and their lack of job-related benefits. Thus, Bonacich suggests that while the world outlook of Asian immigrant entrepreneurs may be petit bourgeoisie, their life conditions are those of the working class and might better be studied as a "labor" question. Asian immigrant small business, she contends, play the role of "cheap labor in American capitalism."[33]

Other researchers have only begun to investigate the extent of poverty among Asian Americans and the meaning of poverty for our community. In California, the rate of poverty for Asian Americans rose from about 10 percent in 1980 to 18 percent in 1990. But more important, researchers found that there are higher numbers of "working poor" (as opposed to "jobless poor") in the Asian American community than for other ethnic groups. Thus, in contrast to other Americans, Asian Americans are poor not because they lack jobs but because the jobs they have pay very low wages. According to researchers Dean Toji and James Johnson Jr., "Perhaps contrary to common belief, about half of the poor work—including about a quarter of poor adults who work full-time and year-round. Poverty, then, is a labor question."[34]

Activists in groups such as KIWA, AIWA, and the CPA Workers Center are strategically focusing on the "working poor" in the Asian American community. KIWA—which was founded in 1992—is working with low-income Korean immigrants in Los Angeles Koreatown, including garment workers and employees in small businesses. AIWA—founded in 1983—organizes Chinese garment workers, Vietnamese garment and electronics workers, and Korean hotel maids and electronics assemblers. And the CPA Workers Center—which traces its roots to the landmark struggle of Chinese garment workers in Boston in 1985—is composed primarily of Chinese

immigrant women. Although their main focus is on workers, each group has also mobilized students and social service providers to support their campaigns. Through these alliances, each group has carried out successful community organizing strategies.

The focus of the three groups on community-based organizing distinguishes them from traditional unions. Miriam Ching Louie of AIWA explains this distinction:

AIWA's base is simultaneously worker, female, Asian, and immigrant, and the organization has developed by blending together several different organizing techniques. As compared to the traditional union organizing strategy, AIWA's approach focuses on the needs of its constituency. Popular literacy/conscientization /transformation [based on the teachings of Paulo Freire] is a learning and teaching method which taps into people's life experiences as part of a broader reality, source of knowledge, and guide to action. Community-based organizing takes a holistic view of racial/ethnic people and organizes for social change, not only so that the people can win immediate improvement in their lives, but so that they can also develop their own power in the course of waging the fight.[35]

Aiwa's focus on grassroots organizing is illustrated by its "Garment Workers' Justice Campaign," launched in late 1992 to assist Chinese immigrant women who were denied pay by a garment contractor. AIWA organizers shaped the campaign to respond to the peculiar features of the garment industry. The industry in the San Francisco Bay Area is the nation's third largest—following New York and Los Angeles—and employs some 20,000 seamstresses, 85 percent of them Asian immigrant women. The structure of the industry is a pyramid with retailers and manufacturers at the top, contractors in the middle, and immigrant women working at the bottom. Manufacturers make the main share of profits in the industry; they set the price for contractors. Meanwhile, immigrant women work under sweatshop conditions.

In their campaign, AIWA and the workers initially confronted the contractor for the workers' back pay. When they discovered that the contractor owed a number of creditors, they took the unusual step of holding the garment manufacturer, Jessica McClintock, accountable for the unpaid wages. McClintock operates ten boutiques and sells dresses through department stores. The dresses—which garment workers are paid $5 to make—retail in stores for $175. AIWA and the workers conducted their campaign through a series of high-profile demonstrations at McClintock boutiques, including picketlines and rallies in ten cities by supporters. AIWA designed these demonstrations not only to put pressure on McClintock and educate others in the community about inequities in the structure of the garment industry, but also to serve as vehicles for empowerment for the immigrant women participating the campaign. Through this campaign, the women workers learned how to confront institutional power, how to forge alliances with other groups in the community, and how to carry out effective tactics based on their collective power.[36]

Thus, through its activities promoting immigrant women's rights, AIWA is expanding democracy in the community. It is bringing labor issues to the forefront of community discussions. It is creating new grassroots caucuses among previously unorganized sectors of the community, and forming new political alignments with supporters, such as students, young professionals, labor unions, and social service providers. Finally, AIWA is developing a cadre of politically sophisticated immigrant women and promoting a new leadership style based on popular literacy, community building, and collective power.

Similarly, in Boston, the CPA Workers Center is expanding democracy through its grassroots efforts around worker rights. The Center emerged out of the Chinese immigrant women's campaign to deal with the closing of a large garment factory in Boston in 1985.[37] The shutdown displaced 350 workers and severely impacted the local Chinese community due to the community's high concentration of jobs in the garment industry. However, with the assistance of the Chinese Progressive Alliance, the workers formed a labor-community-student coalition and waged an eighteen-month campaign to win job retraining and job replacement. Lydia Lowe, director of the CPA Workers Center, describes how the victory of Chinese immigrant women led to creation of the Workers Center, which, in turn, has helped other workplace campaigns in the Chinese community:

This core of women activated through the campaign joined with community supporters from the CPA to found a community-based workers' mutual aid and resource center, based at CPA . . . Through the Workers Center, immigrant share their experience, collectively sum up lessons learned, find out about their rights, and develop mutual support and organizing strategies. Today, the Workers Center involves immigrant workers from each of its successive organizing efforts, and is a unique place in the community where ordinary workers can walk in and participate as activists and decision-makers.[38]

Moreover, forming the Workers Center reshaped politics in the local Chinese community, turning garment workers and other immigrant laborers into active political players. "Previously the silent majority, immigrant workers are gaining increasing respect as a force to be reckoned within the local Chinese community," states Lowe.

In Los Angeles, the formation of KIWA in March 1992—only a month before the uprisings—has had a similar impact. Through its programs, KIWA is bringing labor issues to the forefront of the Asian American community, educating labor unions about the needs of Asian American workers, and forming coalitions with other grassroots forces in the city to deal with inter-ethnic tensions. KIWA is uniquely positioned to take up these tasks. Out of the multitude of Asian American organizations in Los Angeles, KIWA distinguishes itself as the only organization governed by a board of directors of mainly workers.

KIWA's key role in the labor movement and community politics is evident in the recent controversy involving the Koreana Wilshire Hotel.[39] The controversy began in late 1991 when Koreana Hotel Co. Ltd., a South Korean corporation, bought the Wilshire Hyatt in Los Angeles. The change in ownership meant that 175 unionized members, predominantly Latino immigrants, were out of jobs. Meanwhile, the new hotel management hired a new work force, paying them an average of $1.50 per hour less than the former unionized work force. The former workers, represented by Hotel Employees and Restaurant Employees (HERE) Local 11, called upon labor unions and groups from the Asian American, African American, and Latino communities to protest Koreana's union-busting efforts. Local 11 defined the dispute as not only a labor issue, but a civil rights issue. With the help of groups such as KIWA and the Asian Pacific American Labor Alliance, Local 11 initiated a letter-writing campaign against Koreana, began a community boycott of the hotel, and organized militant actions outside the hotel, including rallies, marches, and a picket line, as well as civil disobedience at the nearby Korean consulate. In each of these actions, Local 11 worked closely with KIWA and members of the Asian American community. Due to the mass pressure, in late 1992 the Koreana management agreed to negotiate with Local 11 to end the controversy and rehire the union members.

Throughout the campaign, KIWA played a pivotal role by assisting Local 11 to build alliances with the Asian American community. In addition, KIWA members promoted labor consciousness in the Korean community by urging the community to boycott the hotel. KIWA members also spoke at Local 11 rallies, mobilized for picket lines, and worked with the union in its efforts to

put pressure on the South Korean government. By taking these steps, KIWA prevented the controversy from pitting the Korean community against Latinos and further enflaming inter-ethnic tensions in Los Angeles.

Also, through campaigns such as this one, KIWA is educating Asian immigrants about unions; training workers around the tasks of political leadership; and creating new centers of power in the community by combining the resources of workers, young professionals, and social service providers.

Thus, through grassroots organizing, KIWA—like AIWA and the CPA Workers Center—is expanding democracy in the Asian American community. Moreover, the three groups collectively are reshaping community consciousness. They are sharpening debate and dialogue around issues and redefining such important concepts as empowerment. What is their vision of empowerment, and how does it differ from prevailing definitions?

## THE TWENTY-FIRST CENTURY: BUILDING AN ASIAN AMERICAN MOVEMENT

[A] movement is an idea, a philosophy . . . Leadership, I feel, is only incidental to the movement. The movement should be the most important thing. The movement must go beyond its leaders. It must be something that is continuous, with goals and ideas that the leadership can then build on.[40]

—Philip Vera Cruz

In the late 1960s, Asian American activists sought to forge a new approach to leadership that would not replicate traditional Eurocentric models (i.e., rigid hierarchies with a single executive at the top, invariably a white male, who commanded an endless chain of assistants). In their search for alternatives, activists experimented with various ideas borrowed from other movements, but most of all, activists benefited from the advice and guidance of "elders" within the Asian American community—women and men with years of grassroots organizing experience in the community, the workplace, and the progressive political movement. One such "elder" was Filipino immigrant labor leader Philip Vera Cruz, then in his sixties. Vera Cruz represented the *manong* generation—the first wave of Filipinos who came to the United States in the early twentieth century and worked in agricultural fields, canneries, hotels, and restaurants.

Now eighty-eight years old, Vera Cruz continues to educate a new generation of activists. His lifetime of experience in grassroots organizing embodies the historic themes of Asian American activism: devotion to the rights of working people, commitment to democracy and liberation, steadfast solidarity with all who face oppression throughout the world, and the courage to challenge existing institutions of power and to create new institutions as the need arises. These themes have defined his life and shaped his approach to the question of empowerment—an approach that is different from standard definitions in our community today.

Vera Cruz is best known for his role in building the United Farm Workers (UFW), a culmination of his many years of organizing in agricultural fields. In 1965, he was working with the Agricultural Workers Organizing Committee, AFL–CIO, when Filipino farmworkers sat down in the Coachella vineyards of central California. This sit-down launched the famous grape strike and boycott, eventually leading to the formation of the UFW. Many books and articles have told the story of the UFW and its leader Cesar Chavez. But until recently, no one has focused on the historic role of Filipinos in building this movement. Craig Scharlin and Lilia Villanueva have filled that vacuum with their new publication about Vera Cruz's life.

Following the successful grape boycott, Vera Cruz became a UFW vice president and remained with the union until 1977, when he left due to political differences with the leadership. He was critical of the lack of rank-and-file democracy in the union, and the leadership's embrace of the Marcos dictatorship in the Philippines. Since 1979, Vera Cruz has lived in Bakersfield, California, and has continued to devote his life to unionism and social justice, and to the education of a new generation of Asian American youth.

Vera Cruz's life experiences have shaped a broad view of empowerment. For Vera Cruz, empowerment is grassroots power: the expansion of democracy for the many. Becoming empowered means gaining the capacity to advocate not for one's own concerns but for the liberation of all oppressed peoples. Becoming empowered means being able to fundamentally change the relationship of power and oppression in society. Thus, Vera Cruz's vision is very different from that of today's young professionals. For them, empowerment is leadership development for an elite. Becoming empowered means gaining the skills to advocate for the community by gaining access to decision makers. Thus, for young professionals, the key leadership quality to develop is assertiveness. Through assertiveness, leaders gain access to policymakers as well as the power to mobilize their followers. In contrast, Vera Cruz stresses the leadership trait of humility. For him, leaders are "only incidental to the movement"—the movement is "the most important thing." For Vera Cruz, empowerment is a process where people join to develop goals and ideas to create a larger movement—a movement "that the leadership can then build on."

Vera Cruz's understanding of empowerment has evolved from his own social practice. Through his experiences in the UFW and the AFL-CIO, Vera Cruz learned about the empty democracy of bureaucratic unions and the limitations of the charismatic leadership style of Cesar Chavez. Through his years of toil as a farmworker, he recognized the importance of worker solidarity and militancy and the capacity of common people to create alternative institutions of grassroots power. Through his work with Filipino and Mexican immigrants, he saw the necessity of coalition-building and worker unity that crossed ethnic and racial boundaries. He has shared these lessons with several generations of Asian American activists.

But aside from sharing a concept of empowerment, Vera Cruz has also promoted a larger moral vision, placing his lifetime of political struggle in the framework of the movement for liberation. Three keywords distinguish his moral vision: "compassion," "solidarity," and "commitment." Vera Cruz's lifetime of action represents compassion for all victims of oppression, solidarity with all fighting for liberation, and commitment to the ideals of democracy and social justice.

Activists today need to learn from Vera Cruz's compassion, solidarity, commitment, and humility to create a new moral vision for our community. In our grassroots organizing, we need a vision that can redefine empowerment—that can bring questions of power, domination, and liberation to the forefront of our work. We need a vision that can help us respond to the challenge of conservatives and neo-conservatives, and sharpen dialogue with young professionals. We need a new moral vision that can help fill the ideological vacuum in today's community.

Nowhere is the ideological challenge greater than in the current debate over the model minority stereotype. The stereotype has become the dominant image of Asian Americans for mainstream society, and has generated intense debate among all sectors of our community. This debate provides an opportunity for activists to expand political awareness and, in the process, redefine the Asian American experience for the 1990s.

In the current controversy, however, activists criticize the model minority stereotype politically but not ideologically. Activists correctly target how the concept fails to deal with Asian American realities: the growing population of poor and working poor, the large numbers of youth who are not excelling in school, and the hardships and family problems of small-business people who are not "making it" in U.S. society. Activists also correctly point out the political ramifications of the model minority stereotype: the pitting of minority groups

against each other, and growing inter-ethnic tensions in U.S. society. In contrast, conservative and neo-conservative proponents of the model minority concept argue from the standpoint of both political realities and a larger moral vision. They highlight Asian American accomplishments: "whiz kids" in elementary schools; growing numbers of Asian Americans in business, politics, and the professions; and the record enrollment of youth in colleges and universities. Conservatives and neo-conservatives attribute these accomplishments to Asian culture and tradition, respect for authority, family cohesion, sacrifice and toil, rugged individualism, and self-reliance—moral values that they root in conservative thinking. Conservatives and neo-conservatives recognize that "facts" gain power from attachment to ideologies. As a result, they appropriate Asian culture and values to promote their arguments.

But is Asian culture inherently conservative—or does it also have a tradition of militancy and liberation? Do sacrifice, toil, and family values comprise a conservative moral vision only—or do these qualities also constitute the core of radical and revolutionary thinking? By asking these questions, activists can push the debate over the model minority concept to a new, ideological level. Moreover, by focusing on ideology, activists can delve into the stereotype's deeper meaning. They can help others understand the stereotype's origins and why it has become the dominant image for Asian Americans today.

Historically, the model minority stereotype first arose in the late 1950s—the creation of sociologists attempting to explain low levels of juvenile delinquency among Chinese and Japanese Americans.[41] The stereotype remained a social-science construct until the 1960s when a few conservative political commentators began to use it to contrast Asian Americans' "respect for law and order" to African Americans' involvement in civil rights marches, rallies, and sit-ins. By the late 1970s, the stereotype moved into the political mainstream, coinciding with the influx of new Asian immigrants into all part of the United States. But the widespread acceptance of the stereotype was not simply due to the increase in the Asian American population or the new attention focused on our community from mainstream institutions. More importantly, it coincided with the rise of the New Right and the corporate offensive against the poor. As discussed earlier, this offensive economically devastated poor communities and stripped away hard-won political gains. This offensive also included an ideological campaign designed to restore trust in capitalism and values associated with free enterprise. Meanwhile, conservatives and neo-conservatives fought to redefine the language of civil rights by attacking federal government "entitlement" programs while criticizing the African American "liberal establishment."

In this political climate, the model minority stereotype flourished. It symbolized the moral vision of capitalism in the 1980s: a celebration of traditional values, an emphasis on hard work and self-reliance, a respect for authority, and an attack on prevailing civil rights thinking associated with the African American community. Thus, the stereotype took on an ideological importance above and beyond the Asian American community. The hard-working immigrant merchant and the refugee student winning the local spelling bee have become the symbols for the resurrection of capitalist values in the last part of the twentieth century.

Yet, we know a gap exists between symbol and reality. Today, capitalism in America is not about small-business activities; it is about powerful transnational corporations and their intricate links to nation-states and the world capitalist system. Capitalist values no longer revolve around hard work and self-reliance; they deal with wealth and assets, and the capacity of the rich to invest, speculate, and obtain government contracts. And the fruits of capitalism in the last part of the twentieth century are not immigrant entrepreneurship and the revival of urban areas; they are more likely to be low-paying jobs, unemployment, bankruptcies, and homelessness.

However, as corporations, banks, and other institutions abandon the inner city, the immigrant merchant—especially the Korean small business—emerges as the main symbol of capitalism in these neighborhoods. For inner city residents, the Asian immigrant becomes the target for their wrath against corporate devastation of their neighborhoods. Moreover, as this symbol merges with other historical stereotypes of Asians, the result is highly charged imagery, which perhaps underlies the ferocity of anti-Asian violence in this period, such as the destruction of Korean small business during the Los Angeles uprisings. The Asian immigrant becomes a symbol of wealth—and also greed; a symbol of hard work—and also materialism; a symbol of intelligence—and also arrogance; a symbol of self-reliance—and also selfishness and lack of community concern. Thus, today the model minority stereotype has become a complex symbol through the confluence of many images imposed on us by social scientists, the New Right, and the urban policies of corporate and political elites.

Pioneer Korean immigrant journalist K. W. Lee—another of our Asian American "elders"—worries about how the melding of symbols, images, and stereotypes is shaping the perception of our community, especially among other people of color. "We are not seen as a compassionate people," states Lee. "Others see us as smart, hard-working, and good at making money—but not as sharing with others. We are not seen as a people who march at the forefront of the struggle for civil rights or the campaign to end poverty."[42] Like Philip Vera Cruz, Lee believes that Asian Americans must retrieve a heritage of compassion and solidarity from our past and use these values to construct a new moral vision for our future. Asian Americans must cast off the images imposed on us by others.

Thus, as we approach the end of the twentieth century, activists are confronted with a task similar to confronting activists in the late 1960s: the need to redefine the Asian American experience. And as an earlier generation discovered, redefining means more than ethnic awakening. It means confronting the fundamental questions of power and domination in U.S. society. It means expanding democracy and community consciousness. It means liberating ourselves from the prisons still surrounding our lives.

In our efforts to redefine the Asian American experience, activists will have the guidance and help of elders like K. W. Lee and Philip Vera Cruz. And we can also draw from the rich legacy of struggle of other liberation movements.

Thus, in closing this chapter, I want to quote from two great teachers from the 1960s: Malcolm X and Martin Luther King Jr. Their words and actions galvanized the consciousness of one generation of youth, and their message of compassion continues to speak to a new generations in the 1990s.

Since their assassinations in the mid-1960s, however, mainstream commentators have stereotyped the two men and often pitted one against the other. They portray Malcolm X as the angry black separatist who advocated violence and hatred against white people. Meanwhile, they make Martin Luther King Jr., the messenger of love and nonviolence. In the minds of most Americans, both men—in the words of historian Manning Marable—are "frozen in time."[43]

But as Marable and other African American historians note, both King and Malcolm X evolved, and became very different men in the years before their assassinations. Both men came to see the African American struggle in the United States in a worldwide context, as part of the revolutionary stirrings and mass uprisings happening across the globe. Both men became internationalists, strongly condemning U.S. exploitation of Third World nations and urging solidarity among all oppressed peoples. Finally, both men called for a redefinition of human values; they believed that people in the United States, especially, needed to move away from materialism and embrace a more compassionate worldview.

If we, too, as Asian Americans, are to evolve in our political and ideological understanding, we need to learn from the wisdom of both men. As we work for our own empowerment, we must ask ourselves a series of questions. Will we fight only for ourselves, or will we embrace the concerns of all oppressed peoples? Will we overcome our own oppression and help to create a new society, or will we become a new exploiter group in the present American hierarchy of inequality? Will we define our goal of empowerment solely in terms of individual advancement for a few, or as the collective liberation for all peoples?

These are revolutionary times. All over the globe men are revolting against old systems of exploitation and oppression, and out of the wombs of a frail world, new systems of justice and equality are being born. The shirtless and barefoot people of the land are rising up as never before. "The people who sat in the darkness have seen a great light." We in the West must support these revolutions. It is a sad fact that, because of comfort, complacency, a morbid fear of communism, and our proneness to adjust to injustice, the Western nations that initiated so much of the revolutionary spirit of the modern world have now become the arch antirevolutionaries . . . Our only hope today lies in our ability to recapture the revolutionary spirit and to go out into a sometimes hostile world declaring eternal hostility to poverty, racism, and militarism.[44]

—Martin Luther King, Jr.

I believe that there will ultimately be a clash between the oppressed and those who do the oppressing. I believe that there will be a clash between those who want freedom, justice, and equality for everyone and those who want to continue the system of exploitation. I believe that there will be that kind of clash, but I don't think it will be based on the color of the skin.[45]

—Malcolm X

## NOTES

1. Iranian philosopher Ali Shariati's four prisons analysis was shared with me by a member of the Iranian Students Union, Confederation of Iranian Students, San Francisco, 1977.

2. Allan Bloom, *The Closing of the American Mind* (New York: Simon & Schuster, 1987).

3. Winifred Brfeines, "Whose New Left?" *Journal of American History* 75(2) (September 1988).

4. Brfeines, "Whose New Left?" 543.

5. Sheila D. Collins, *The Rainbow Challenge: The Jackson Campaign and the Future of U.S. Politics* (New York: Monthly Review Press, 1986).

6. Collins, *The Rainbow Challenge,* 16.

7. Ronald Fraser, *1968: A Student Generation in Revolt* (New York: Pantheon Books), 354–55.

8. Karen Umemoto, "'On Strike!' San Francisco State College Strike, 1968–69: The Role of Asian American Students," *Amerasia Journal* 15(1) (1989).

9. "Statement of the Philippine-American Collegiate Endeavor (PACE) Philosophy and Goals," mimeograph: quoted in *Umemoto,* 15.

10. Mo Nishida, "A Revolutionary Nationalist Perspective of the San Francisco State Strike," *Amerasia Journal* 15(1) (1989): 166–67.

11. George Lipsitz, "Grassroots Activists and Social Change: The Story of Ivory Perry," *CAAS Newsletter* (UCLA Center for Afro-American Studies, 1986). See also, George Lipsitz, *A Life in the Struggle: Ivory Perry and the Culture of Opposition* (Philadelphia: Temple University Press, 1988).

12. Russell C. Leong, "Poetry within Earshot: Notes of an Asian American Generation, 1968–1978," *Amerasia Journal* 15(1) (1989): 166–67.

13. Al Robles, "Hanging on to the Carabao's Tail," *Amerasia Journal* 15(1) (1989): 205.

14. Warren J. Susman, *Culture as History: The Transformation of American Society in the Twentieth Century* (New York: Pantheon Books, 1973); Raymond Williams, *Keywords: A Vocabulary of Culture and Society,* rev. ed. (New York: Oxford University Press, 1976).

15. John M. Liu and Lucie Cheng, "A Dialogue on Race and Class: Asian American Studies and Marxism," *The Left Academy,* vol. 3, eds. Bertell Ollman and Edward Vernoff (Westport, Conn.: Praeger, 1986).

16. See Mary Kao, compiler, "Public Record, 1989: What Have We Learned from the 60s and 70s?" *Amerasia Journal* 15(1) (1989): 95–158.

17. Institute for Labor Education and Research, *What's Wrong with the U.S. Economy? A Popular Guide for the Rest of Us* (Boston: South End Press, 1982). See especially chapters 1 and 19.

18. Samuel Huntington, "The United States," in *The Crisis of Democracy: Report on the Governability of Democracies to the Trilateral Commission,* Michel Crozier, ed. (New York: New York University Press, 1975).

19. Center on Budget and Policy Priorities, *Still Far from the Dream: Recent Developments in Black Income, Employment and Poverty* (Washington, D.C., 1988).

20. Center for the Study of Social Policy, *Kids Count: State Profiles of Child Well-Being* (Washington, D.C., 1992).

21. Manning Marable, *How Capitalism Underdeveloped Black America* (Boston: South End Press, 1983), 252–53.

22. Vincent Harding, *The Other American Revolution* (Los Angeles: UCLA Center for Afro-American Studies, and Atlanta: Institute of the Black World, 1980), 224.

23. For analyses of the changing status of Asian Americans, see Lucie Cheng and Edna Bonacich, eds., *Labor Immigration Under Capitalism: Asian Workers in the United States before World War II* (Berkeley: University of California Press, 1984); Paul Ong, Edna Bonacich, and Lucie Cheng, eds., *Struggles for a Place: The New Asian Immigrants in the Restructuring Political Economy* (Philadelphia: Temple University Press, 1993); and Sucheng Chang, *Asian Americans: An Interpretive History* (Boston: Twayne Publishers, 1991).

24. For an analysis of the growing power of Asian American young professionals, see Yen Espiritu and Paul Ong, "Class Constraints on Racial Solidarity among Asian Americans," *Struggles for a Place* (Philadelphia: Temple University Press, 1993).

25. Arthur Hu, "AIDS and Race," *Asian Week,* December 13, 1991.

26. Marable, *How Capitalism Underdeveloped Black America,* 182.

27. William McGurn, "The Silent Minority," *National Review,* June 24, 1991.

28. McGurn, "The Silent Minority," 19.

29. C.L.R. James, *Beyond a Boundary* (New York: Pantheon Books, 1983), 116–17.

30. LEAP Asian Pacific American Public Policy Institute and UCLA Asian American Studies Center, *The State of Asian Pacific America: Policy Issues to the Year 2020* (Los Angeles: LEAP and UCLEA Asian American Studies Center, 1993).

31. Mao Zedong, "Where Do Correct Ideas Come From?" *Four Essays on Philosophy* (Beijing: Foreign Languages Press, 1996), 134.

32. See "Asian Pacific American Workers: Contemporary Issues in the Labor Movement," Glenn Omatsu and Edna Bonacich, eds., *Amerasia Journal* 18(1) (1992).

33. Edna Bonacich, "The Social Costs of Immigrant Entrepreneurship," *Amerasia Journal* 14(1) (1988).

34. Dean S. Toji and James H. Johnson Jr., "Asian and Pacific Islander American Poverty: The Working Poor and the Jobless Poor," *Amerasia Journal* 18(1) (1992): 85.

35. Miriam Ching Louie, "Immigrant Asian Women in Bay Area Garment Sweatshops: 'After Sewing, Laundry, Cleaning and Cooking, I Have No Breath Left to Sing,'" *Amerasia Journal* 18(1) (1992): 12.

36. Miriam Ching Louie, "Asian and Latina Women Take on the Garment Giants," *Cross-Roads*, March 1993.

37. Peter N. Kiang and Man Chak Ng, "Through Strength and Struggle: Boston's Asian American Student/Community/Labor Solidarity," *Amerasia Journal* 15(1) (1989).

38. Lydia Lowe, "Paving the Way: Chinese Immigrant Workers and Community-based Labor Organizing in Boston," *Amerasia Journal* 18(1) (1992): 41.

39. Namju Cho, "Check Out, Not In: Koreana Wilshire/Hyatt Take-over and the Los Angeles Korean Community," *Amerasia Journal* 18(1) (1992).

40. Craig Scharlin and Lilia V. Villanueva, *Philip Vera Cruz: A Personal History of Filipino Immigrants and the Farmworkers Movement* (Los Angeles: UCLA Labor Center and UCLA Asian American Studies Center, 1992), 104.

41. For an overview of the evolution of the "model minority" stereotype in the social sciences, see Shirley Hune, *Pacific Migration to the United States: Trends and Themes in Historical and Sociological Literature* (New York: Research Institute on Immigration and Ethnic Studies of the Smithsonian Institution, 1977), reprinted in *Asian American Studies: An Annotated Bibliography and Research Guide*, Hyung-chan Kim, ed. (Westport, Conn: Greenwood Press, 1989). For comparisons of the "model minority" stereotype in two different decades, see "Success Story of One Minority Group in U.S.," *U.S. News and World Report*, December 26, 1966, reprinted in Amy Tachiki et al., eds., *Roots: An Asian American Reader*, (Los Angeles: UCLA Asian American Studies Center, 1971); and the essay by William McGurn, "The Silent Minority," *National Review*, June 24, 1991.

42. Author's interview with K.W. Lee, Los Angeles, California, October 1991.

43. Manning Marable, *On Malcolm X: His Message & Meaning* (Westfield, N.J.: Open Magazine Pamphlet Series, 1992).

44. Martin Luther King Jr., "Beyond Vietnam" speech, Riverside Church, New York, April 1967.

45. Malcolm X, interview on Pierre Breton Show, January 19, 1965, in George Breitman, ed., *Malcolm X Speaks*, (New York: Grove Press, 1966), 216.

# 3.4

# Serve the People
## An Exploration of the
## Asian American Movement

*Kim Geron*

〰〰〰〰〰〰〰〰〰〰〰〰〰〰〰〰〰〰〰〰〰〰〰〰

In the late 1960s, efforts by Asian American students to build ethnic studies programs that included the study of Asian Americans were the start of what would become a new pan-ethnic social movement—the Asian American movement (AAM). In addition to the formation of a pan-ethnic collective identity, these efforts ushered in a significant change in the image and visibility of Asian Americans in the social and political life of the United States. The post–1965 Immigration Act enabled millions of immigrants from Asia, including large numbers of political refugees, to enter the United States. The emergence of a high percentage of foreign-born Asian Americans on the mainland may appear to make the discussion of the AAM seem no longer relevant to the discussion of the contemporary Asian American political experience. I argue in this chapter that the approach to political organizing and the methods employed by the AAM are still vitally important and instructive for the pan-Asian community, which continues to confront problems of racial profiling, stereotypical media images,

institutional discrimination, and the challenge of coalescing disparate immigrant and American-born Asian ethnic and religious communities.

In order to understand the continuing significance of the AAM in the twenty-first century, I address two research issues. First, I explore the concept of a social movement and analyze whether it is useful to describe the collective experiences of Asian Americans that began in the late 1960s. Is this just a convenient label that mirrors other social movements of the era, or is there evidence of sustained identifiable collective actions that successfully challenged existing institutions of power in this country? Second, I examine what happened to the AAM after the Vietnam War ended in 1975. Did the initial efforts of young activists to organize the Asian American community become institutionalized into professional and nonprofit agencies or did these efforts spawn continued efforts at grassroots mobilization? To answer these questions, it is necessary to analyze group experiences using theory as a guide to explain group behavior. The format of this chapter is as follows: first, I use social movement theory to examine what motivated Asian Americans and Pacific Islanders to collectively organize and what organizational

Geron, Kim. "Serve the People: An Exploration of the Asian American Movement using Social Movement Theory." Unpublished article.

forms the movement created to transform society and themselves; second, I describe the three streams of political actors that founded the AAM; third, I use four case studies of organizing efforts by Asian Americans to illustrate the grassroots character of the AAM in California; and, fourth, I explore what happened to the AAM after the end of the Vietnam War in 1975.

## PERSPECTIVES ON THE ASIAN AMERICAN MOVEMENT

Most scholars who study the 1960s do not mention the development of the AAM; however, in the 1980s and 1990s, Asian American scholars and activists began to address this hole in the literature. They used a variety of approaches to explore the Asian American movement experience. Most scholars view the AAM as a quest for identity as Asian Americans. Wei (1992) conducted an extensive study of the AAM, which he views as a social movement. The emphasis of this work is on the social history of the movement and "the evaluation of the Movement's effort to develop a unique but cohesive ethnic identity" (Wei 1992, 9). The application of social movement theory is not explored.

Similarly, Espiritu (1992) discusses how diverse national origin groups came together to create a new, and enlarged, pan-ethnic group. The formation of a pan-Asian ethnicity, by the children of immigrants, was a strategy to unite Asians. As Espiritu notes, "Although broader social struggles and internal demographic changes provided the impetus of the Asian American movement, it was the group's politics—confrontational and explicitly pan-Asian—that shaped the movement's content" (p. 31). Espiritu's thesis is that the main thrust of the AAM was identity formation, and she views the AAM as a concept that was transformed at a later date. "Although originally conceived by young Asian American activists, the pan-Asian concept was subsequently institutionalized by professionals and community groups" (Espiritu 1992, 52).

The construction of pan-Asian ethnicity is based on the theory of racial formation by Omi and Winant (1986, 1994), who argue that race is socially constructed and can be transformed into different racial meanings based on government actions and social consciousness. While Omi and Winant do not specifically analyze the AAM, they do address the racial minority movements of the 1960s. The focus of their research does not fully address the details of the movement construction that was integral to the establishment and maintenance of the Asian American movement. Instead, they focus on the construction of racial identity. Chan (1991) briefly explores the AAM in the broad context of an interpretive history of Asian Americans. In general, the efforts of young Asian American activists are viewed as a group of people disconnected from their ethnic communities. In an assessment that is similar to Wei's (1993) dichotomization of the movement into revolutionaries and reformers, Chan views the AAM as divided into two kinds of political activists—radicals and reformers. The radicals' efforts had little effect, according to Chan; however, the reformers created community agencies that continue to exist (Chan 1991, 175).

Activist scholar Glenn Omatsu (1994) moves beyond ethnic awakening and identity formation and argues that participants in the AAM saw themselves as participants in the making of history. Omatsu states that "activists saw history as created by large numbers of people, not by elites," and that political power grows from grassroots organizing, from the bottom up, not top down. He also argues, "This new understanding challenged activist to build mass, democratic organizations, especially within unorganized sectors of the community. Through these new organizations, Asian Americans expanded democracy for all sectors of the community" (Omatsu 1994, 32). This perspective captures the visionary ideals expressed by the AAM, but more importantly it captures the motivation of the AAM participants "to serve the people" and to expand democracy and community consciousness. Omatsu's article demonstrates that the AAM was not solely about identity politics, but also about how activists sought to build a movement among the least well-off segments of the pan-Asian community, in solidarity with other oppressed peoples internationally, and to do so by creating new leadership and organization.

These perspectives, while providing valuable insights, do not provide a complete answer to the questions of who were the participants of the AAM, how they constructed the movement, and what were the ideas they used to frame the struggles they were engaged in. The next section will explore the application of social movement theory to explain the rise of Asian American pan-ethnic consciousness and solidarity, the growth of new organizational forms, and the activation of poor, working class, elderly, youth, and women activists.

## SOCIAL MOVEMENT THEORY AND THE ASIAN AMERICAN MOVEMENT

To begin our discussion of the Asian American movement, we must define what is a social movement. Darnovsky, Epstein, and Flacks (1995) state that "social movements are collective efforts by socially and politically subordinated people to challenge the conditions and assumptions of their lives. These efforts are a distinctive sort of social activity: collective action becomes a movement when participants refuse to accept the boundaries of established institutional rules and routinized roles. Single instances of such popular defiance don't make a movement; the term refers to persistent, patterned, and widely distributed collective challenges to the status quo." This definition is useful as it can be applied to a wide range of group experiences including Asian Americans.

To comparatively study the emergence and development of social movements, some scholars have focused on three key factors: (1) the structure or context of *political opportunities* available to the move-

ment; (2) the forms of organization, or *mobilizing structures*, recruitment, and indigenous forms of organizing/organization; (3) shared meanings that people bring into the movement, or the *framing processes* (McAdam, McCarthy, and Zaid 1996). The first factor to consider in understanding the development of a social movement is the importance of the broader political system in structuring the opportunities for collective action. Movement scholars aim to explain the emergence of a particular social movement on the basis of changes in the institutional structure of a given national system. Social movements are shaped by the broader set of political constraints and opportunities unique to the national context in which they are embedded.

The 1960s era of mass upheavals and new social movements took place as part of what Tarrow (1998) calls the *political opportunities*—the consistent but not necessarily formal, permanent, or national dimensions of the political struggle that encourage people to engage in contentious politics. During such periods, there are cycles of contention, and if many of the early actions are successful, these types of activities spread to ordinary people; as Tarrow explains, "during such a period, the opportunities created by early risers provide incentives for new movement organizations" (1998, 24).

There are four dimensions of political opportunities: (1) the degree of openness of the political system to influence and participation by insurgent groups; (2) the stability or instability of political alignments, with instabilities being associated with increased opportunities for insurgent groups; (3) the presence or absence of influential allies available to support policy demands of insurgents; (4) the presence or absence of political splits or conflicts within the political and economic elites (Tarrow 1998). During the late 1960s, political elites were sharply divided on most social issues confronting the country, and the political system was undergoing major instability. For example, the liberal wing of the Democratic Party was pressured by mass upheavals during this period to support many of the movements of the period. This wing of the Democratic Party, led by presidential candidate Robert Kennedy in 1968, openly supported the United Farm Workers America union (UFWA) grape boycott and the Chicano high school blowouts in East Los Angeles, and opposed continued U.S. involvement in the Vietnam War.

All four of these elements were present during this period of the late 1960s. The external dynamics of the opportunities available in the political system coupled with the long pent up frustration and underground organizing networks that already existed enabled numerous new social movements to emerge including the environmental, women's, gay and lesbian, and people of color movements. Unfortunately, most scholars of the 1960s have ignored the significant organizing efforts of the Chicano, Native American, and Asian American movements (Munoz 1989).

The formation of the AAM began in 1968. The AAM started after the height of the Civil Rights Movement and during the height of the black power movement (Hsaio 1998). The politics of the black liberation movement were more explicitly antigovernment, with strong sentiments for self-determination and radical transformation of society, alongside of demands for civil rights and equality. The strongest external influences on the AAM during the 1968–1970 period were the black liberation movement and national liberation struggles in the developing world, rather than the traditional civil rights organizations. The tenor and tempo of the period, and the external influence of the black liberation movement, meant that racial minorities adopted the use of militant confrontational tactics and were heavily influenced by the U.S. government's violent attacks on suspected antigovernment change agents. The timing of the entrance of the AAM, the political opportunities available during this period, and the influence of external factors had a profound influence on questions of how to achieve goals and who to build alliances with in the Asian American communities.[1]

If the political system shapes the prospects for collective action and the forms movements take, their influence is not independent of the various kinds of mobilizing structures groups seek to organize. Mobilizing structures are the collective vehicles, informal as well as formal, through which people mobilize and engage in collective action. The theory of mobilizing processes and structures is known as resource mobilization theory, which seeks to break with the grievance-based conceptions of social movements and to focus on mobilizing processes and the formal organizational manifestations of these processes—the social movement organizations.[2]

In resource mobilization theory, ideological orientation and motivations were taken for granted; instead, the variability of resources, both internal and external to the movement, becomes the most important factor in explaining the emergence and development of insurgency. Resource mobilization theory examines the variety of both tangible and intangible resources available to facilitate the success of social movements. However, judging movement success or failure based on external support resources limits crucial exploration of the emergence of ideas, identities, and values that motivate many movement participants. The young AAM had virtually no outside economic or political support, unlike the more mature African American Civil Rights Movement that received large amounts of material resources from liberal whites. The AAM also differed in other respects from the Civil Rights Movement because the AAM lacked strong community institutional support, which, for example, the black churches and black colleges provided to the Civil Rights Movement. In many cases, in the Asian American communities, the established ethnic community leaders and organizations opposed the AAM activists, viewing them as a direct challenge to their leadership and authority. External resources available to the AAM were limited to a few churches, social service organizations, and public universities (Wong 1972).

The second trend in the mobilizing structures literature revolves around those who focus on the critical role of various grassroots settings—work and neighborhood. Morris (1981, 1984) and McAdam (1982) both analyzed the critical role played by local black institutions in the emergence of the Civil Rights Movement. In the AAM, initially, the crucial role was played by college campus environments, specifically, student organizations and the resources that were achieved as Asian American studies programs were established that created physical locations for meetings, educational events, and communications nationally (Umemoto 1989). In the community, preexisting organizations and new organizational forms were created that provided centers for resistance and opposition to the status quo. The common characteristics of these organizations included efforts at democratic functioning that were inclusive of both sexes in leadership, membership of immigrants and American born, and the encouragement of grassroots participation. These organized forms stood in stark contrast to the closed academic environment on campuses, and the traditional organizations in the ethnic communities based around business interests. The institutionalization of new movement organizations combined to facilitate and structure oppositional meanings and cultural expression.

At the beginning phases of a movement, indigenous resources are important, as external support is sporadic. The presence of indigenous resources within a dominated community does not ensure that a movement will emerge. Rather, movements are deliberately organized and developed by activists who seize and create opportunities for protest. Social activists play creative roles in organizing and developing movements; they must skillfully direct and transform indigenous resources in a manner that can be used to develop and sustain social protest, such as the role black activists played in historically black college campuses and within the black church during the Civil Rights Movement (Morris 1984).

Even the availability of resources and strategically placed activists will not crystallize into a protest movement if a dominated group has not developed tactics and strategies that can be effectively used in confrontations with a system of domination. When these three elements are present, then a movement center can be established. "A local movement center is a distinctive form of social organization specifically developed by members of a dominated group to produce, organize, coordinate, finance and sustain social protest"(Morris 1984, 284). The International Hotel, as well as the surrounding community storefronts in San Francisco, was an example of a local movement center for the progressive elements of the Asian American movement in the 1960s and 1970s.

While the combination of political opportunities and mobilizing structures affords groups a certain structural potential for action, they still are insufficient to account for collective action. Mediating between opportunity, organization and action are the shared meanings and definitions that people bring to their situation. At a minimum level, people need to feel aggrieved about some basic aspect of their lives and optimistic that by acting collectively they can redress the problem. Conditioning the presence or absence of these perspectives is social psychological dynamics—collective attribution and social construction known as the framing process. Buechler (2000) states that "framing means focusing attention on some bounded phenomenon by imparting meaning and significance to elements within the frame and setting them apart from what is outside the frame. In the context of social movements, framing refers to the interactive, collective ways that movement actors assign meanings to their activities in the conduct of social movement activism."

While activating mobilizing framing is important, movements must also engage in additional frame alignments to increase their recruitment efforts. This frame alignment is the linking of individual level and social movement organizations in order to draw deeply held beliefs and link those values and beliefs to movement issues. In this process, someone's preexisting values provide the fuel that can be used to recruit them into the movement. The significance of this third factor is to address the relationship of ideas and sentiments with frame transformation into collective action. Movement entrepreneurs orient their movements' frames toward action in particular contexts. They must compete with mainstream media, and the dominant culture's manipulation of framing for cultural supremacy. The ability of movement leadership to frame an issue into an injustice against a whole group of people, in such a way as to be oppositional, and strikes an emotional chord that will spur individuals into action is crucial (McAdam 1982).

The AAM grew rapidly because its message that Asian Americans were victims of institutional racism challenged the media-hyped "model minority" myth that pitted Asian Americans against other people of color. This blatant attempt to sow divisions among America's minority groups was opposed by Asian Americans, particularly young people, who identified strongly with other oppressed groups. For example, in New York City, women community activists: Yuri Kochiyama, Kazu Iijima, and Minn Matsuda, were able to draw attention to the racist nature of the U.S.-Vietnamese conflict and the manner that the Vietnamese people were portrayed by the media, which aroused strong emotions among many Asian Americans (Hsaio 1998). Asian American women activists were also conscious of highlighting the leading roles played by Vietnamese women revolutionaries that inspired many young Asian American women to become involved in activism in this country (Yoshimura 1989).

## ROOTS OF THE ASIAN AMERICAN MOVEMENT

In their timing and form, social movements reflect the specific opportunities that give

them life. In addition to the importance of collective identity formation, a movement is composed of large numbers of people in motion collectively to achieve radical or systemic change in the current order. Why was the AAM able to develop and grow during the late 1960s and early 1970s? What was the composition of the people and their motivation to build the Asian movement?

One could argue that the origins of the AAM lay in the collective struggles of countless numbers of Asian Pacific Americans for equal treatment under the law and in opposition to racial discrimination and racial violence. Asian Americans waged campaigns against acts of discrimination that were directed toward them. However, due to uneven political, social, and economic development, Asian American ethnic communities generally carried out their resistance, isolated from one another, within the context and limitations imposed on them by the dominant political and social structures of that era.

The forced removal of Japanese Americans during World War II, during the same period of time as the Japanese military government invaded the Philippines, Korea, China, and eleven other nations did not create a sense of solidarity among Asian Americans against anti-Japanese Americans actions by the U.S. government. Rather, Chinese, Koreans, and Filipinos in the United States all adopted similar actions that distinguished themselves in various ways (wearing buttons, putting signs in their storefronts, etc.) from Japanese who were being rounded up and placed in internment camps (Takaki 1989). Historically, external homeland politics and narrow nationalism have played a critical role in mitigating efforts at unity. This was not a new phenomenon, as early Japanese immigrant leaders attempted to distinguish themselves from Chinese laborers using ethnic disidentification (Daniels 1988).

In the post–World War II era, Asian Americans grew to outnumber immigrants due to immigration restrictions before 1965 and the growth of U.S.-born second and third generations (Espiritu 1992, 26). As the

Asian population became a native-born community, linguistic and cultural differences began to decrease. Also, assimilation to America and its cultural values increased among the American-born generations. English-speaking Asian Americans began to work, socialize, and interact on a more routine basis. The insular communities were beginning to dissolve, except in historic ethnic enclaves. New housing patterns also drew more Asian Americans together in urban and suburban social settings. Old-world antagonisms also declined because American-born Asian Americans did not maintain the historical hostilities that influenced their parents' generation. These intercommunity factors played an important role in socializing young Asian Americans together. Combined with the external factors of the influence of the oppositional culture of the late 1960s, a foundation was laid to construct the AAM.

## THREE STREAMS OF ASIAN MOVEMENT ACTIVISTS

The crucial element in any movement construction is its participants. Who were the participants in the formation of the AAM? There were three streams of activists that collectively constructed the AAM. What all three had in common was similar experiences being portrayed as *the other*, the unknown, the outsiders, whether it was in the pre–World War II era, 1940s, 1950s, or 1960s. In the 1960s, increasing numbers of American-born as well as recent immigrants from Asia were attending college. In addition, Asian students attending college on student visas also became politicized and joined in campus activities. On several college campuses, these three types of Asian American students, both women and men, participated in antiwar and people of color events, as individuals and as members of specific ethnic clubs or organizations. The demand for relevant course materials including the study of Asian American history was a common demand

raised by Asian American student activists. The killing of Vietnamese peasants by the U.S. military caused Asian American student activists to question their own loyalties. Did they have more in common with the Vietnamese guerrillas fighting the U.S. government, or with the regime in South Vietnam that was being supported financially and militarily by their own government? They also began to recognize that they had more in common with fellow Asian Americans of different ethnicities than with others on campus. Soon, pan-Asian cooperation and new organizations emerged in 1968–1970 (Wong 1972). Asian women led some of the new organizational formations, such as the Asian American Political Alliance chapter at San Francisco State (Umemoto 1989). Not only were Asians demanding Asian Studies programs, they were challenging traditional stereotypes of Asian women as quiet and submissive. Asian American women continued to play leadership roles as the AAM moved off campuses to involvement in community issues ("Asian Women as Leaders" 1971; Yoshimura 1989).

The widespread poverty and social problems in urban centers also spawned a second group of AAM activists who lived and worked in traditional ethnic enclaves. Asian community youth were a combination of immigrants and American born (Hing 2000). Their involvement came through community-based institutions including social service centers, churches, and informal familial networks. However, unlike the African American struggle, the role of the church in the Asian American community was substantially different. In Asian American communities, for example, Buddhist churches were extremely conservative and generally not willing to become involved in social activism. Further, other community institutions that were tied to business interests were not receptive to the ideas and beliefs being espoused by Asian American activists such as support for the People's Republic of China, and the Vietnamese and other national liberation struggles in the developing world. This meant that community youth had to build political support and funding sources without mainstream institutional support. There were, however, a small minority of churches, such as the Methodist Church in the Japanese American community, and Cameron House in San Francisco Chinatown, where social and recreation programs existed, that spawned Asian American youth becoming active in the AAM.

Many Asian community youth also became involved in community service programs and through these activities were drawn into the AAM. In San Francisco, the Japanese Community Youth Council was a center for Asian American youth in Nihonmachi (Japantown). In Los Angeles, the formation of the Japanese American Community Services of Southern California by second-generation Japanese Americans in the early 1960s spawned numerous organizations and activists in the late 1960s and early 1970s (Chin 1973). Asian community youth, many of them involved with petty crimes, were caught up in the criminal justice system, and also faced the harassment and brutality of local law enforcement agencies. Some of the young people became politicized and joined the movement in different communities as the AAM offered a positive alternative vision to drugs and crime (Hing 2000, Tasaki 2000).

The third stream was veteran labor and community activists, some of whom had ties with the Communist Party. Others were fiercely independent, and still others were strong Democrats; they provided a bridge from the previous generation of activists to a new generation of young activists, offering organizing experience and working-class militance. They interjected a strong class-based character to the AAM. These individuals were involved in community networks of small businesses, associations of overseas Asians, tenants, church groups, medical care, youth service, and elderly service providers.

In the Japanese American community, for example, a group of Nisei, or second generation Japanese Americans, were civil rights activists active in and around the Japanese American Civil Liberties (JACL), one of the oldest Asian American civil rights organization. These activists, following World War II, and the repressive Cold War politics, combined with a strong anti-Japanese climate, carried out quiet organizing. However, events of the 1960s brought them into action on numerous fronts. A long-time labor and community organizer describes the activities of one JACL chapter in the 1970s, "Dissatisfied with the conservatism of the existing chapters . . . they organized this new chapter as a vehicle through which to broadly share social and political philosophies. . . . The JACL Bay Area Community Chapter supported the Asian Anti-War Coalition, United Farm Workers Union, Coalition to Cut Military Spending, and Greater Chinese American Sewing company strikers" (Yoneda 1983, 197).

These Nisei activists had strong ties to the community. Many of these community activists became involved not only in antiwar activities but also antiredevelopment campaigns, and later participated in building the redress and reparations movement of Japanese Americans in the late 1970s and 1980s. In the Chinese community, there were radical and progressive elements that were forced underground in the repressive 1950s who became energized with the emergence of the AAM in the 1960s (Hing 2000). Also, the Manongs (first-generation Filipino sojourners) had a long history of labor organizing and played an important role in educating students about labor organizing. Other veteran activists and progressive minded community members became active in some aspect of the AAM through community, labor, and anti-Vietnam War actions. These three streams of activists: students with institution resources from college campuses, community youth, and progressive community and labor activists were all instrumental in the construction of the AAM and institutional building on the campuses, communities, and workplaces.

## NEW ORGANIZATIONAL FORMATIONS

In addition to the opportunities that are created during certain periods for movement creation and the recruitment of movement participants, there is a need to develop new indigenous organizations to build organizational structures for movement growth and stabilization. This was critical because in the late 1960s, Asian Americans had limited ability to lobby the U.S. government directly for claims except for civil rights organizations, such as the Japanese American Citizens League (JACL). Other Asian community organizations including local chamber of commerce and family associations were ethnic-specific and kept ties with homeland governments and capital.

In the AAM, the initial pan-Asian student organizations led to the creation of numerous community-based Asian American organizations. Most of these new groups consciously identified with the AAM. One example was the Asian Law Caucus (ALC), which was founded by progressive attorneys in the San Francisco Bay Area in 1972. One of the founding members, Dale Minami, stated, "Above all we expected to exercise law with a political emphasis-defending 'political' cases, attacking racism in institutions, highlighting society's neglect of Asian American concerns, and supporting the work of progressive community organizations" (Minami 1975).

The ALC is an example of an organization that formed and was conscious of its role as a part of the AAM.[3] Other civil rights organizations that formed during this period were also conscious of being both ethnic specific and inclusive of the broader Asian American community including Chinese for Affirmative Action that was formed in 1969 in San Francisco, and the Organization of Chinese Americans—a nationwide advocacy organization for Chinese and Asian Americans, which was founded in 1973. Other pan-Asian organiza-

tions formed to meet specific needs, for example, Asian Neighborhood Design, a San Francisco Bay Area community-based nonprofit development corporation grew out of the need for development projects in low-income Asian communities.

These organizations were typical of the new organizations that sprung up during this period of rapid movement development and institutionalization of the AAM. They reflected varying political levels from liberal to radical. While all of them viewed themselves as part of the AAM, they did not all have the same goals and philosophies. For example, there were a number of Asian American organizations, such as East Wind, I Wor Kuen (IWK), Katipunan ng mga Demokratikong Pilipino (KDP), Wei Min She, and Workers Viewpoint Organization, that affiliated with, or were self-defined, as revolutionary organizations, and recruited AAM activists into their organizational structures. Many of their members played active and leading roles in major issues and campaigns. This wide spectrum of organizations involved in the AAM enabled different levels of participation and political ideologies and helped to propel the continued growth of the AAM. While differences emerged in the course of the formation and growth of the AAM over strategy and tactics, priorities, and ideologies, these distinctions should not overshadow the important step forward represented by the emergence of the AAM.

The new social protests of the AAM depended on "communal resources and relied on substantial personal commitments for a specific conflict. . . . Challengers need a different type of resource—highly committed activists" (Lo 1992, 236). The recruitment of Asian American activists was a critical component of the AAM. Activists in the Asian American community were unable to tap into mass markets for contributions, and they were forced to rely on localized constituencies for support. By and large, the AAM was built on community-based movements that organized networks of supporters and built connections within their ethnic communities and the broader pan-Asian movement.

The use of indigenous forms of organizing that were able to reflect the spirit of resistance in each ethnic community was a popular method to inspire new activism. In the next section we will examine four challenger organizing efforts. They represent the types of grassroots organizing that occurred during the mid- to late 1970s when the AAM organized collective actions among broader segments of the Asian community. This period from 1972 to 1978 represents a more sophisticated form of community-based organizing than during the initial founding of the AAM from 1968 to 1971.

## A BRIEF EXPLORATION OF ASIAN AMERICAN MOVEMENT CAMPAIGNS

Numerous grassroots campaigns were waged throughout the 1970s in the Asian American community following the end of the war in Vietnam. Some of the issues that sparked community organizing efforts included bilingual education, unionization and labor rights on the job, land struggles in Hawaii, and defense of historic ethnic enclaves. We will next explore both pan-Asian and ethnic-specific challenger organizing efforts: Bay Area Asian Coalition Against the War (BAACAW), International Hotel, Committee Against Nihonmachi Eviction (CANE), and Little Tokyo People's Rights Organization (LTPRO). These brief case studies highlight the specific characteristics in collective identity, mobilizing structures, and the framing process that reflect the unique development of the AAM. These California-based campaigns were similar to efforts by Asian Americans in other parts of the country. They offer lessons that transcend specific geographic locations to reflect commonalities of interest articulation.

### "The Vietnam War Is a Racist War"

The first case study is the Bay Area Asian Coalition Against the War (BAACAW). This organization formed in 1972 to build an Asian presence in the large anti-war movement in the San Francisco Bay Area. After repeated efforts failed to transform the politics of a large antiwar group, from what was perceived as a narrow focus on American youth involved in the war through their slogan of "bring the boys home," to a broader, anti-imperialist perspective that called for solidarity with the Vietnamese people in their struggle for self-determination from U.S. domination, BAACAW was formed in May 1972 (Kalayaan 1972). Hundreds and hundreds of Asian Americans, primarily students, young people, and community activists mobilized as part of larger anti-war rallies; they also participated in teach-ins on college campuses and in ethnic communities. BAACAW was organized into several regions, with each region serving as a mini-movement center. For example, in the East Bay area, the center was the Asian Student Union on the University of California Berkeley campus; in San Francisco, there were several centers including San Francisco State College, Japantown, and Chinatown/Manilatown. The coalition's orientation was pan-Asian, the focus of activity was on organizing and mobilizing the entire Asian community to oppose the war and support the efforts of Southeast Asians opposed to U.S. aggression. BAACAW's membership was broad based and typical of most AAM activities of the period. The coalition included wide participation from ethnic-specific groups, Asian student organizations, religious figures, church organizations, civil rights groups, and leftist organizations. BAACAW carried out organizing, agitating, and educational activities until the war ended in 1975. The coalition was able to take the broad issues involved in the war and link them to community issues and problems. This proved to be moderately effective in reaching Asian community members in low-income communities, many of whom were recent immigrants, who were faced with immediate issues of affordable housing, jobs, and equality of education.[4] The coalition was more successful in reaching young Asian Americans, many of whom became active in the AAM through their outreach efforts.

In addition to the Asian American anti-war movement, the declaration of martial law on September 21, 1972, in the Philippines by Ferdinand Marcos, and backed by the United States, polarized the Filipino community in this country (Bello and Reyes 1987). Many Filipino Americans became active in politics in opposition to the dictatorship of Marcos. Filipino American anti-Marcos forces and Asian American anti-Vietnam War activists worked together to coordinate their activities and were well known for their colorful and creative contingents in anti-war demonstrations and the use of art and culture to capture the fighting spirit of, and solidarity with, Asian and Pacific Island peoples.

## Save the International Hotel!

The second case study is the International Hotel Campaign. In the late 1960s, Milton Meyers, a powerful landowner in San Francisco, attempted to evict elderly tenants, predominantly Filipino Manongs, out of the International Hotel. This decaying single residence hotel occupied the last block of a once thriving Manilatown community that was destroyed in the 1950s and 1960s as part of urban renewal efforts to expand the downtown business district. After tenants successfully stalled the initial efforts to evict them, the building was transformed into a thriving movement community center as grassroots community organizations, arts and cultural groups, and a bookstore moved into the street-level storefront of the hotel. Together, the tenants and community organizations waged a nine-year campaign to preserve the hotel for low-cost housing and affordable storefronts for small business and community organizations.

From 1968 to 1977, thousands of people waged a militant protest against the eviction from the hotel. It became one of the longest-running urban campaigns in the post–1960s era. The campaign to preserve low-cost housing for Filipino and other tenants at the International Hotel was waged by a broad coalition of forces including most segments of the local AAM, as well as affordable housing advocates, gay and lesbian activists, trade unions, women, and other progressive groups. Some of the Manongs who lived in the International Hotel were veterans of labor strife in the fields and they waged a courageous battle to remain in their residence.

In particular, 1975 to 1977 was an intense period of mass street protests and pitched battles with the local state apparatus to halt the evictions at the I-Hotel. Hundreds of students, community members, and supporters from many Asian American communities, as well as other supporters in the San Francisco area were tied together by an intricate phone tree system that mobilized hundreds of people, at a moment's notice, to block attempts to evict the tenants from the hotel. While affordable housing attorneys delayed evictions in the courts, the International Hotel Tenants Association and their support committee carried out grassroots organizing in the Filipino community and the broader Asian American community to raise funds and conduct educational outreach.

Beyond street protests, the hotel became a symbol, a rallying cry, for many Asian Americans of the destruction of their historic communities to make way for the expansion of international capital in ethnic enclaves, due to the land values of the property located strategically adjacent to downtown business districts. This campaign is an example of how a struggle to preserve low-cost housing grew into a focal point of the AAM through the adept use of the framing process. The tenants and the community organizations were able to frame the campaign as more than just the tearing down of a residence hotel; the International Hotel was transformed into the key battleground for affordable housing in San Francisco, and an attack on elderly Asian immigrant workers.

The International Hotel struggle was catapulted into the cause célèbre in the city's activist circles. Posters that announced "Fight for the International Hotel: decent low-income housing is everybody's right" were widely distributed; the campaign skillfully utilized Asian American cultural workers to dramatize the issue. The hotel campaign raised awareness of the need for APAs to fight together to defeat evictions from their historical communities, and, in the process, the campaign sustained and helped contribute to building a more complex AAM that included alliances and internal conflicts, and added to the preexisting social networks that generated activists into movements (Toribio 2000).

Although the tenants were forcibly evicted in a night of terror shown on newscasts internationally in 1977, and the I-Hotel was eventually torn down, the legacy of the campaign continues to live on. The I-Hotel is an example of the many community struggles up and down the West Coast in Delano, Seattle, Stockton, Sacramento, San Jose, Los Angeles, San Diego, and other locations that inspired young Asian Americans and veteran community activists to organize to defend their communities from hegemonic forces that sought to dominate local ethnic economies with global capital using the power of the state.

## The Defense of Historic Nihonmachis in California

The next two case studies explore the efforts of community activists in San Francisco's Nihonmachi (Japantown) and Los Angeles's Little Tokyo to preserve these historic communities from the negative consequences of global capital and urban redevelopment. In San Francisco, thousands of community residents were forced out of their long time residences, block by block, by the San Francisco Redevelopment Agency beginning in the late 1950s as part of a larger master plan to "revitalize" the African American community in the neighboring Fillmore District. The shining example of redevelopment was the Japan Trade Center, whose construction forced the removal of hundreds of residents and small businesses for the construction of a monu-

ment to Japanese corporate businesses (CANE 1973).

Student and community activists began to question what was happening in the historic Japanese American community, and began to challenge government sponsored global capital investment over the rights of elderly and working poor tenants. While some local business leaders were supporters of redevelopment, community residents, who wanted to remain in Nihonmachi for cultural, social, and financial reasons did not want to be forced out.

Together, community residents, small businesses, community activists, and students from local college campuses formed the Committee Against Nihonmachi Eviction (CANE) in 1973. The main activities of this organization initially were to provide information to tenants regarding their rights, and to organize broad support for tenants and businesses that decided to resist being evicted by the San Francisco Redevelopment Agency. Some of the organizing methods included mobilizing residents and their supporters to attend hearings at city hall to demand the halt to further evictions from the community and to demand replacement housing that was affordable. At times, CANE members employed civil disobedience tactics, such as they occupied buildings in the community, and sat-in at the redevelopment agency, and refused to leave until they were forcibly evicted by the Sheriff's Department to dramatize the need for low-cost housing. The CANE organization lasted well into the 1980s, and grew from a small organization of tenants into the Japanese Community Progressive Association (JCPA). The leadership of CANE and its later incarnation was conscious of the need to build ethnic awareness and pride as Japanese Americans and for others affected by redevelopment. Through the formation of an all volunteer community organization, and the construction of a network of supporters and resources, CANE was able to sustain the movement and transform it from an antiredevelopment organization into a Japanese civil rights organization that later became involved in the redress and reparations movement in the Japanese community. CANE's literature captures their perspective:

> In the two-year history of CANE, we have fought long and hard to preserve our community from the wrecker's ball of RDA. . . . We gain strength from the understanding that ours is not an isolated struggle, but is in fact linked with other movements. . . . The CANE struggle is a historic confrontation of the rich and the poor and is part of the ongoing struggle Japanese Americans for justice and dignity as a people (CANE Newsletter April 1975).

During the 1970s, a major effort to redevelop the historic Japanese community, known as Little Tokyo, located in downtown Los Angeles, was also under way. The Los Angeles Community Redevelopment Agency, as part of efforts to revitalize the downtown area beginning in the late 1940s, sought to turn the historic Little Tokyo area into a tourism venue. The redevelopment agency allied itself with the Japanese Chamber of Commerce, an organization of Japanese businesses, and created the Little Tokyo Community Development Advisory Committee (LTCDAC) to give credibility to their redevelopment efforts (LTPRO August 1977). While promises were made to tear down old structures and replace them with low and moderate income housing, by the early 1970s, these promises had fallen short. Low-rent hotels were being demolished and long-time residents of all nationalities were forced to leave Little Tokyo.

In 1973, these actions prompted the formation of a community-based Little Tokyo Redevelopment Task Force (LTRTF) which questioned the misinformation that was spread by the redevelopment agency and its community spokespersons (Little Tokyo Redevelopment Task Force 1973). In 1976, the ongoing battle to preserve Little Tokyo led to the formation of the Little Tokyo People's Rights Organization (LTPRO). This multinational organization included workers, residents, and supporters from the greater Los Angeles area. LTPRO challenged the actions of the L.A. Community Redevelopment Agency and Japan-based East West Development Corporation that wished to build a luxury hotel and parking garage where community service organizations, small businesses, and residents had lived and worked together for many years (LTPRO 1976). What began as a grassroots struggle against redevelopment and tourism grew into a broad social movement within the Japanese American community and also received broad support from the larger Asian American community.

LTPRO continued to function for many years opposing the effects of redevelopment and fighting to preserve the destruction of the historic Japanese American community center. Eventually, its efforts evolved into other important issues such as redress and reparations for Japanese Americans. Today, the fight to retain a historic community is being waged by community activists, some of whom were former members of LTPRO, who are active in economic development and the construction of affordable housing and social and recreational facilities to rebuild a center for the Japanese American community in Southern California (Toji 2000).

## WHAT HAPPENED TO THE ASIAN AMERICAN MOVEMENT?

The second research question that this chapter set out to answer is what happened to the AAM; did it fade away after the turmoil of the 1960s? While most accounts of the AAM describe a high point in the late 1960s and early 1970s, during the height of the anti–Vietnam War movement, there is no consensus of what became of the AAM. Did it decline and if so, why? If it did not decline, what did occur? Did it transition into something else? Some scholars describe the movement's inception around issues of pan-ethnic identity politics, ethnic studies, and antiwar activities and transition into topical issues or events that dramatize the current plight of Asian Americans including Asian American political empowerment, anti-Asian violence, redress and reparations for Japanese Americans, and the impact of new immigration on the Asian American community (Chan 1991; Fong 1998). Another scholar views the AAM as being divided into two camps, with reformers constructing viable alternative community institutions and "learning to function effectively in the American political system," while revolutionaries "established Maoist sects. But by the middle of the 1970s, lapsed into sectarianism . . . vying for power in the radical community" (Wei 1993, 10). Another scholar discusses the limitations of pan-Asianism and problems of ethnic chauvinism within the Asian American community (Espiritu 1992). Omatsu (1994) attributes the decline of the AAM to the corporate offensive launched in the 1970s against working people and people of color.

I argue the AAM developed sophisticated campaigns that were sustained over time and grew more effective in challenging power holders and building broad grassroots movements *after* the end of the U.S–Vietnamese conflict. As the case studies of the International Hotel and the Japanese American antiredevelopment struggles demonstrate, the AAM did not end with the conclusion of the Vietnam War. Drawing on the charisma of movement organizers, the tactical experiences gained in numerous campaigns on campuses, workplaces, and communities, and the energy of a new post–1960s generation of movement activists, the AAM continued to flourish and grow after 1975. The upward trajectory in the number of large-scale, mass-based pan-Asian organizing projects increased substantially in the mid to late 1970s, including the culmination of a nine-year campaign waged by tenants at the International Hotel in San Francisco, the formation of two regional Asian Pacific Student networks, a nationwide campaign against the Bakke decision in 1978 by Asian Americans and other people of color, and the growth of the anti-Marcos movement were among the many campaigns spearheaded by Asian American activists.

The activities of Asian Americans in these campaigns, and others including electoral and antinuclear weapons campaigns, the successful redress and reparations campaign in the Japanese American community, and the anti-Asian violence organizing efforts around the murder of Vincent Chin in Detroit in 1982 have spawned ongoing organizing projects that continue to this day. These pan-Asian organizing projects were carried out in the context of developing intra-ethnic solidarity. They are examples of a few of the notable accomplishments of the AAM that flourished well into the 1980s and 1990s.

These organizing efforts were led by community activists, some of whom were influenced by revolutionary ideas and viewed these immediate struggles as part of an overall organizing project for fundamental change in this country. Many individuals joined in specific issue campaigns, became committed community activists, and continued to remain active, as other issues arose, in new organizing efforts. Most individuals, however, would become active in one issue and participate in a more limited fashion. The core membership of many of these movements that flourished in the Asian community in the 1970s and into the 1980s were veterans of the AAM. Precisely because these more mature organizing efforts had experienced leadership that understood the importance of strategy and tactics, attempted to apply political theory to practical issues, understood the importance of building a "united front" of various class forces against a specific target, and built grassroots organization with community support, they were very effective and grew into national in scope organizing efforts.

## CONCLUSION

It has become convenient to situate the AAM as a phenomenon of a particular era of rebelliousness by young Americans. This is unfortunate and fails to capture what was new, inventive, and creative in the social construction of the AAM. This chapter is the beginning effort of a larger research project that aims to capture the collective experiences of a social movement that constructed new identities, new institutions, and new leadership, as well as new forms of cultural expression in ethnic communities and pan-Asian community organizing efforts. This chapter only scratches the surface of a generally neglected aspect of Asian Americans: the grassroots organizing efforts of community activists, students, and workers to build a sense of community, of solidarity, with others seemingly different in class status, ethnicity, and gender, yet, still sharing "a bright spirit of intercultural experience, of resistance, and of proud survival" (Matsuda 2000).

In spite of the dissimilarities in languages, cultures, and orientation to U.S. politics, there are growing efforts by segments of the Asian American community to cooperate and build pan-ethnic coalitions and pan-Asian organizations. Witness the creation of new nationwide organizations in the 1990s including challenger and mainstream interest groups. In the 1990s, several new Asian American radical organizations formed in different parts of the country (Fujino and Leung 2000). Also, a group of young people started republishing *Gidra* magazine, an Asian American newspaper that published for five years between 1969 and 1974 (Gidra Spring 1999). In the year 2000, an organization formed that is called 80-20, a pan-Asian effort initiated by prominent Chinese Americans to build a unified voting bloc in this country to increase the leverage of Asian Americans in the mainstream political arena.

Within the Asian American community, some politically connected and economically powerful elements have ties to influential elites, economic wealth, and the media. However, the not so subtle racialized attacks on Asian Americans for fundraising violations, the discriminatory incarceration of Wen Ho Lee by the U.S. government, and the ongoing anti-Asian violence around the country all illustrate the need for continued efforts for challenger

groups at the grassroots level, along with traditional forms of interest group lobbying, to articulate the concerns of the Asian Pacific American community. The need to organize across ethnic, class, and gender lines to build a movement of Asian Americans is still a powerful unifying message for the rapidly growing Asian American community that now numbers more than 10 million people.

An important lesson to be drawn from the actions of the AAM is the need to combine consistent and sustained organizing with ongoing political education about globalization and the important role Asian Americans have played, and will continue to play, in the construction of a multiethnic America. This will require ongoing education in ethnic studies programs by community activists and scholars, to immigrant and American-born Asian American students. This means placing questions about identity into a larger discussion of the global forces operating today, as well as the structural, political, and cultural dynamics that surround the Asian American experience.

## NOTES

1. Beyond national specific opportunity structures, an additional factor that has had a major impact on Asian Americans is the impact of global economic restructuring. Following the economic crisis that emerged, following the post–World War II boom, the need for large numbers of professional, service, and business entrepreneurs drew large numbers of Asian immigrants (Bonacich, Cheng, Chinchilla, Hamilton, and Ong 1994). This was combined with the entrance of large numbers of political refuges from Southeast Asia. Together, the effects of U.S. foreign policy and the rapid globalization of production have structured how Asia is viewed as a market internationally, and how Asian Americans are viewed domestically. While limited space does not allow for further exploration of this topic, globalization is the international context in which the AAM developed and the change in composition of Asian Americans occurred within.

2. Until the early 1970s, the dominant approach to the study of collective behavior

and social movements explored a wide range of sources for rapid social and economic change, including fads, large crowds, panic, riots, and sects. These societal strains were viewed as creating structural changes (Smelser 1962), or frustration and anger (Gurr 1969). These theories share the same assumption that individual deprivations, breakdowns of the social order, and individualized psychological reactions to these breakdowns are important preconditions for the emergence of social movements. Noninstitutional collective behavior is formed to meet the unstructured situations of a breakdown of social control.

Some of the limitations of the earlier collective behavior models became obvious in the 1960s when large mobilizations were created by the Civil Rights Movement and other movements. These grassroots social movements caused a shift in theoretical assumptions. The mass character of these newly emerging movements contradicted the previous interpretation of deprivation and fear guiding irrational and deviant behavior. This observation is evident in the formation of the AAM. The beginnings of the AAM were on college campuses among middle-class and working-class students who were not the most deprived economically or emotionally as discussed by collective behavior scholars.

3. Piven and Cloward (1977) also pursed the relationship between social movements and the political system; they noted that as electoral coalitions were transformed in the 1930s and 1960s, protest movements arose. Piven and Cloward also advanced the notion that the 1960s groups dissolved in the 1970s because they were coopted by the social system. They view the professional organizers, the movement leaders, as inducing failure, since they tend to direct a group's effort toward institutionalization rather than toward radical change. The formation of institutions such as the Asian Law Caucus and other legal and professional organizations in Asian communities was a direct result of the AAM. Their presence did not dilute insurgent organizations but rather supplemented them by pursuing legal avenues of protest.

4. San Francisco's Chinese community sued the San Francisco school district over the lack of bilingual educational services, which was upheld in the landmark *Lau v. Nichols* suit.

## REFERENCES

"Asian Women as Leaders." 1971. *Rodan* 1(9).

Bello, Madge, and Vincent Reyes. 1987. "Filipino Americans and the Marcos Overthrow: The Transformation of Political Consciousness." *Amerasia Journal*.

Bonacich, Edna, Lucie Cheng, Norma Chinchilla, Nora Hamilton, and Paul Ong, eds. 1994. Introduction to *Global Production: The Apparel Industry in the Pacific Rim*. Philadelphia: Temple University Press.

Buechler, Steven M. 2000. *Social Movements in Advanced Capitalism: The Political Economy and Cultural Construction of Social Activism*. Oxford: Oxford University Press.

Chan, Sucheng. 1991. *Asian Americans: An Interpretive History*. Boston: Twayne.

Chin, Rocky. 1973. "The House That JACS Built." *Bridge* 2(6).

Committee Against Nihonmachi Eviction. 1975. "CANE Opposes Tourism." April newsletter.

———. 1973. "CANE: Fight for Housing." Position paper.

Darnovksy, Marcy, Barbara Epstein, and Richard Flacks, eds. 1995. *Cultural Politics and Social Movements*. Philadelphia: Temple University Press.

Espiritu, Yen Le. 1992. *Asian American Panethnicity: Bridging Institutions and Identities*. Philadelphia: Temple University Press.

Fujino, Diane C., and Kye Leung. 2000. "Radical Resistance in Conservative Times: New Asian American Organizations in the 1990s." In *Legacy to Liberation: Politics and Culture of Revolutionary Asian Pacific America*. San Francisco: Big Red Media/AK Press.

Gidra. 1987. At www.gidra.net/Spring_99/bring_it_back.html.

Gurr, Ted. 1969. *Why Men Rebel*. Princeton: Princeton University Press.

Hing, Alex. 2000. Interview by Fred Ho and Steve Yip. In *Legacy to Liberation: Politics and Culture of Revolutionary Asian Pacific America*. San Francisco: Big Red Media/AK Press.

Hsiao, Andrew. 1998. "The Hidden History of Asian American Activism in New York City." *Social Policy* (Summer): 23–31.

*Kalayaan* (newspaper). 1972. 2(1) (May–June).

———. 1972. 1(6) (February–March).

———. 1972. 2(2) (August–September).

*Little Tokyo People's Rights Organization Newsletter.* 1977. August newsletter.

Little Tokyo Redevelopment Task Force publication. 1973.

Lo, Clarence Y. H. 1992. "Communities of Challengers in Social Movement Theory." In Aldon D. Morris and Carol M. Mueller, eds., *Frontiers in Social Movement Theory.* New Haven: Yale University Press.

Matsuda, Mari J. 2000. "Here on Planet Asian America." Speech delivered at the Asian Law Caucus twenty-eighth anniversary celebration on March 31, 2000, San Francisco. Speech reprinted in *The Reporter* 22(1).

McAdam, Douglas. 1982. *The Political Process and the Development of Black Insurgency.* Chicago: University of Chicago Press.

McAdam, Douglas, J. D. McCarthy, and M. N. Zald. 1996. "Introduction: Opportunities, Mobilizing Structures, and Framing Process: Toward a Synthetic, Comparative Perspective on Social Movements." In *Comparative Perspectives on Social Movements: Political Opportunities, Mobilizing Structures, and Cultural Framings.* Cambridge: Cambridge University Press.

Minami, Dale. 1975. "Asian Law Caucus: Experiment in an Alternative." *Amerasia Journal.*

Morris, Aldon D. 1981. "Black Southern Student Sit-In Movement: An Analysis of Internal organization." *American Sociological Review* (December): 755–67.

———. 1984. *The Origins of the Civil Rights Movement: Black Communities Organizing for Change.* New York: Free Press.

———. 1992. "Political Consciousness and Collective Action." In Aldon D. Morris and Carol McClurg Mueller, eds., *Frontiers in Social Movement Theory.* New Haven: Yale University Press.

Munoz, Carlos, Jr. 1989. *Youth, Identity, Power: The Chicano Movement.* New York: Verso.

Omatsu, Glenn. 1994. "The Four Prisons and the Movements of Liberation: Asian American Activism from the 1960s to the 1990s." In Karin Aguilar-San Juan, ed., *The State of Asian America: Activism and Resistance in the 1990s.* Boston: South End.

Omi, Michael, and Howard Winant. 1994. *Racial Formation in the United States: From the 1960s to the 1990s.* 2d ed. New York: Routledge.

Piven, Frances Fox, and Richard Cloward. 1977. *Poor People's Movements.* New York: Vintage.

Smelser, Neil J. 1962. *Theory of Collective Behavior.* New York: Free Press.

Tasaki, Ray. 2000. "New Dawn Rising: History and Summation of the Japan Town Collective." In Fred Ho, ed., *Legacy to Liberation: Politics and Culture of Revolutionary Asian Pacific America.* San Francisco: Big Red Media/AK Press.

Takaki, Ronald. 1989. *Strangers from a Different Shore: A History of Asian Americans.* New York: Penguin.

Tarrow, Sidney. 1998. *The Power in Movement: Social Movements and Contentious Politics.* 2nd ed. Cambridge: Cambridge University Press.

Toji, Dean. 2000. Personal interview, June 20. Former editor of the *LTPRO Newsletter* who is currently active in the campaign to build a community gym and more affordable housing in Little Tokyo, Los Angeles. He is assistant professor of Asian American Studies at California State University, Long Beach.

Toribio, Helen C. 2000. "Dare to Struggle: The KDP and Filipino American Politics." *Legacy to Liberation: Politics and Culture of Revolutionary Asian Pacific America.* San Francisco: Big Red Media/AK Press.

Umemoto, Karen. 1989. "On Strike! San Francisco State College Strike, 1968–1969: The Role of Asian American Studies." *Amerasia Journal* 15(1).

Wang, L. Ling-Chi. 1991. "The Politics of Ethnic Identity and Empowerment: The Asian American Community since the 1960s." *Asian American Policy Review* 2 (Spring).

Wei, William. 1993. *The Asian American Movement.* Philadelphia: Temple University Press.

Wong, Paul. 1972. "The Emergence of the Asian-American Movement." *Bridge* 2(1).

Yoneda, Karl. 1983. *Ganbatte: Sixty-Year Struggle of a Kibei Worker.* Los Angeles: Asian American Studies Center, UCLA.

Yoshimura, Evelyn. 1989. "How I Became an Activist and What It All Means to Me." *Amerasia Journal* 15(1): 106–9.

## 3.5

# New Immigrants, New Forms of Transnational Community

## Post–1965 Indian Migrations

*Sandhya Shukla*

In April of 1999, for the negligible sum of $1,000, India began to issue the "Persons of Indian Origin Card" to enable Indians in the diaspora to visit India sans visa, own property, buy government bonds and apply to universities in India, for a period of twenty years.[1] A link between the more cultural yearnings for homeland and the economic agenda of the state might be seen in public officials' divergent justifications for the program: Home Minister L. K. Advani, from the Bharatiya Janata Party, noted: "I have seen the hunger of Indians abroad to have their children linked to their country of origin," while chief commissioner for Investments and Non-Resident Indians at the Indian Investment Center of the government, A.R. Nanda, pronounced: "I hope the new card will encourage more investment."[2] Such statements and the very initiation of a program to give "national" rights to "non-nationals" offer a crystallization of academic arguments about the changing nature of the nation-state, the mutability and mobility of cul-

ture, and most of all, the transformed circumstances of migrants in the world, in what some have called the era of "globalization."[3] Group longings for a place and a culture far away give rise to a collective imaginary that is "India," and the flexible accumulation of late capitalism produces both an international economic class of Indians and also a particular trajectory of externally directed development for the emergent nation-state of India.

In such a moment, it is difficult to clearly delineate what is "local" and what is "global." Contemporary proclamations about the demise of the nation-state seem premature at best in the context of countries all over the world, and in Asia most dramatically, increasing their participation in the world economy not only through a relationship with the West, but also through the marshalling of new internal consumer markets and workforces, and enhanced, locally developed systems of technology for export. The rise of nationalist sentiments conditions, rather, contradicts such formations and thus the local-political sphere comes into a sustained dialogue with the international-economic space. The structures and cultures of migrant communities hardly undermine

Skukla, Sandhya. "New Immigrants, New Forms of Transnational Community: Post–1965 Indian Migrations." *Amerasian Journal* 25(3): 19–38. Reprinted with permission.

national identifications; in their "transnational"[4] activities that extend across a variety of borders they animate intense attachments to nation-states. And postwar Indian
diasporas, in the United States and elsewhere, provide rich analytical terrain for
the complex question of where the nation
begins and ends.

Conceptualizing cultural moments of
the Indian diaspora, however, requires
some shift in the consideration of the very
idea of "community."[5] Scholars and popular observers alike are accustomed to think
of community as comprising a set of peoples with shared interests around work,
residence, culture, or generation; indeed a
group of such factors is commonly cited as
integral to "community formation." Geography often plays a central role in how
community is understood; many studies of
ethnic communities, in particular, have
been shaped by an attention to specific
parts of urban spaces in which immigrants
have located themselves and eventually,
become American, through negotiations
between nostalgia for homeland cultures
and the demands of work and urban life in
the United States.[6] Ideas of ethnic community formation, in their emphasis on U.S.-
based localities, have thus been associated
with the eventual process of national
assimilation that immigrants from northern, southern, and eastern Europe were
able to accomplish, if not be completely
defined by.[7]

But the experiences of many groups of
post–1965 immigrants actively militate
against classic narratives of national citizenship. Often such contestations take shape
through new class identities. Largely middle-
class groups of immigrants from the Third
World, of successful Caribbean Americans,
Latin Americans, and Asian Americans, for
example, have affirmed multiple connections to place, to the nation of origin as well
as to the United States. Related to their dispersal through broad swaths of urban America and through a variety of professional
occupational spaces, these migrants' group
identities have extended far beyond the
neighborhood or workplace; it is not possible

to locate the meanings of community life
within the borders of a few city blocks, or any
other urban location. Such new spatial organizations of ethnicity—not only in the context
of the United States, but in other parts of the
world as well—structurally undermine the
premises of assimilation, of absorption into a
main body.

Indian migrant subjects' recasting of
ideas of community on the levels of ethnicity and nationality—in a form of transnationalism—represents how the discourse of
mobility, and of Indianness in its many
forms, can be at once a language of locality,
of serving to articulate migrants' place in
American society, and of (inter-)nationality,
to shore up their position in a particular
notion (and materiality) of India. This stage
of building and defining community across
time and space accommodates the specific
business and residential concentrations of
Indian immigrants in the United States that
establish geography as a primary referent
for "community," as well as the more generalized constellations of "Indian-ness,"
both imaginative and institutionalized,
that make for a diasporic social formation,
of what might also be called a set of communities. Stories of the past, of colonialism, of independence, of difficulties in
immigrating, and of limited economic
opportunity all sustain relationships
between the different modes of people coming together and self-identifying as a
group—claiming an ethnic identity (of
being "Indian") within the rubric of multicultural societies like the United States—
and of developing a sense of shared political
and economic interests—the stuff of "community." Perhaps most of all, there is the
nation-state of India, independent for less
than twenty years when immigration began
to proceed to the United States in full force,
developing in the cognizance of many of its
peoples desiring a connection to the homeland.

This essay is an attempt to map some of
these complexities and contradictions. It
moves, like Indian ethnicity itself, between
diasporic (and transnational) formations
and local renderings of "Indianness," to

reveal a multiplicity of meanings for the concepts of community and national citizenship in post–1965 United States. It operates on the assumption that ideas of community, ethnicity, and nationality contain complex relationships that beg unraveling. Through unconventional renderings of community in domestic and international frameworks, we might contemplate how the particularities of Indian migration, as well as the specificities of its historical period, finesse the transition between the local and the global.

The historical trajectory of Indian diasporic formations begins well before Indian independence and extends from the early 1800s, as agricultural laborers went to the Caribbean and Africa and formed communities in outposts of the British empire that continued to imaginatively engage "India" as a source and site of identification. In the United States, as well, workers from Punjab in the early 1900s participated in a range of political and cultural activities premised on an Indian subjectivity, despite being, in a literal sense, colonial subjects of Great Britain. Political struggles for Indian independence, and against British colonialism, proved tremendously important in creating a sense of shared identity among Indians traveling the world, within and through local communities formed by work and cultural affairs. One might even make the argument that it was outside of India that migrants seized the very freedom to become Indian.

While Indian independence in 1947 signified a profound historical shift in the consciousness of migrants, making them citizens of a nation-state in new ways, the elaborate project of making India independent, expressed in a variety of forms, continues to shape how Indians have thought of themselves in the world during the postwar period. Composing sources for Indian capital formation, identifying audiences for Indian nationalist addresses, as well as creating a public based on consumption might all be seen as operations of the broader project that must link together broad notions of Indianness and local (and material) realities

of settlement. The effort to create the category of the Non-Resident Indian, or NRI, illustrates some of the successes of this bridging of the local interests of Indian migrants in the diaspora and broader needs of the nation-state, what in effect is an instance of "Indian community."

The impetus for the Indian migrant community formation of NRIs emerged, interestingly enough, not from the diaspora, but from India itself. In the middle to late 1970s, the nation-state of India, like most in the "Third World," faced the increasing concentration of growth in narrow segments of the economy, and the approach of stagnation in its broader industrial sectors, all in the context of a balance of payments crisis. All internal and external counsel at the time, from a variety of political perspectives, pointed toward the inevitability of attracting investors from outside India (as other ascendant Asian countries had done), yet history's admonitions about autonomy (and the language of postwar, Third Worldist nationalism) also wielded persuasive power. What Partha Chatterjee has described as a "developmental ideology," in which the postcolonial state "acquired its representativeness by directing a program of economic development on behalf of the nation"[8] faced the challenges of a global economy, not only in India, but also in Latin America and the Caribbean. But complex negotiations on the nature of the Indian economy coincided with the increasing economic success and population concentrations of Indian immigrants all over the world, in Hong Kong and southeast Asia, and in Western countries like the United States.

While Indians had begun migrating en masse to the United States since the late 1960s, it was during the 1970s that Indians began to develop organizations and newspapers to define themselves self-consciously as a community. Perhaps even more importantly, the United States Indian population was one in which the immigrants had by this time become primarily economically prosperous and well placed in a variety of technical and scientific fields. This was in marked contrast to the British Indian population, which had had a very different history of integration into the labor market, and which was not nearly as financially successful as its American counterpart.

Anchored on one end by Indian professionals in the diaspora, and on the other end by a "developmental" nation-state, a new international Indian community was formed in the 1970s through, most literally, the processing of financial remittances to the homeland nation-state and more symbolically, the careful nursing among immigrants of an investment very far away. In 1973, the Indian Foreign Exchange Regulation Act discussed the "person not resident in India," and by 1975, members of the Indian Investment Center had begun to approach and hold seminars for immigrant associations in the United States, with the purpose of soliciting monies for new Indian industries.[9]

In these efforts, the Indian state, by defining its national interest in a particular way, and with relation to a specific group of Indians abroad, was in essence creating the material basis for what we might understand as a new kind of migrant community in the 1970s: NRIs. It is significant here that the Indian government (and economy) had a stake and role in how this community formed itself and located its own objectives alongside the physical and psychic dislocations that were producing a desire for a relationship with the homeland among Indian immigrants. The transnational force of the community worked in two directions, both back to India and out to its migrants, who might also be thought of as nationals. The terms of diaspora itself, then, need some reworking, for the homeland in this case is more than a distant imaginary, it is an important global player in its own right that claims and acts upon its migrants' cultural citizenship in material ways. Yet this is not to discount its symbolic importance; the concept of India as a national-utopia was also extremely powerful and functioned in concert with the actual nation-state.

Embedded in the articulations of Indian Americans within this international forma-

tion were also the demands and possibilities of settlement in the United States. Relatively new Indian immigrants of this period were located in ambiguous racial contexts, in which they did not easily fit into the established categories of "white," "black," or even "Asian," and partly in response to that, actively sought out "Indianness" as a site for identity formation. Recent memories of a powerful anti-colonial struggle created a conceptual landscape in which Indian national identity made a great deal of sense, unlike the case of other immigrants. For example, "being Italian" for Italian Americans who had not recently experienced intense forms of nationalism, required larger scale ideological efforts. Indian immigrants had already begun to build cultural and political associations like the Association of Indians in America and the Federation of Indian Associations and create newspapers, among others, *India Abroad*, to address (and possibly, construct) a diasporic community. And, beginning in the 1970s, investment in India, in manufacturing concerns and technological ventures, had become a major interest for middle-class Indians in the United States.

A number of important cultural productions linked together local social life (and its attendant push for ethnic identity) and new transnational economic practices. The development of the newspaper *India Abroad* reveals the multiple cultural and economic considerations at work in the formation of an NRI community. It was in the late 1960s, at the early stage of the influx of immigrants into the United States, that Gopal Raju, an immigrant from south India living in New York, looked around him and saw the development of significant populations of Indians. He sensed the need for a publication to provide news to these diverse peoples and started *India Abroad* in 1970, first as a monthly, then as a fortnightly and finally as a weekly paper. Addressing the inception of a coherent and self-conscious Indian immigrant community, Raju's choice of a name for the paper reflected the broadly diasporic address necessary to travel through all types of difference: religious, regional and linguistic. The discursive gesture of a nation being constructed outside of its state ("India, abroad") also lent the community formation it mirrored a degree of domestic and international mobility; it created and supported the transnational in ways that are central to how "ethnicity" would be developed.

It was also around this time that Indian immigrants began mobilizing around an effort to introduce "Asian Indian" as a category into the national census questionnaire. The varied classificatory possibilities for Indians in the United States had always been a matter of some debate,[10] even for earlier Indian populations in California and the Pacific Northwest. In the post–1965 period, the ambiguities did not pertain to qualifications for naturalization and citizenship, but instead, more to issues of ethnic identity. Finding a place for themselves in the evolving multicultural landscape of the United States involved for Indians a self- and group-naming within perhaps the most public and authoritative language of all: the government census. While they had previously been able to include themselves under the category of "Asian," which described different countries of descent, or, presumably "white" as well, Indian Americans articulated the need for a term that would singularly express subcontinental Indian origin. This movement must be read against the availability of other choices, like "Asian," that might have produced alternative political (and perhaps, racial) alliances. But even more profoundly, this moment constituted an expression of and investment in Indianness (and, by extension, India) as basic to the production of ethnic identity. Designation of Indian origin in the locality of the United States reveals the symbolic and material reproduction of Indian identity by the nation-state of India, on a more global plane, precisely because of the simultaneity of the movements for ethnic recognition and transnational community. The 1980 census, with its new box marked "Asian Indian," marked a stage in the production of Indians through a range of different spatial locations.

The "Asian Indian" in the United States developed alongside the "NRI." *India Abroad* initially sought a broader audience; editor Gopal Raju noted his original intention to "cover all Indians outside India, including the United States, Canada, and Britain."[11] But the explosion of populations of Indians all over North America and Britain (not to mention other places) made such an endeavor too difficult to organize, and the U.S. edition of the newspaper, with its local reading population, became central to the production of "India, abroad." The discursive imagining of a diasporic community, through this instance of print culture, occurred not through a proposed connection between Indians in the United States and Indians in Britain, say, but instead through the continued production of the NRI and this figure's relationship to India. NRI was becoming a more general, catch-all category for Indian middle classes in the diaspora, and *India Abroad*'s embrace of and, perhaps, hand in, that development might be partly seen through Benedict Anderson's discussions of "print capitalism" participating in the production of "imagined communities." He has noted: "If we turn to the newspaper as cultural product, we will be struck by its profound fictiveness."[12] The paper reflected and created community in a construction of India, in symbolic form, but also through material relationships—not easily subsumed under the rubric of "fictions"—that made the very category of NRI so meaningful to a range of subjects.

Political and cultural orientations to India were reflected in the subject matter of *India Abroad*. Early editions of the paper read very much like newspapers from India, with the special inclusion of columns that described cultural events of immigrants residing in the New York area, for dance and music programs especially. The material interests of Indian capitalism were well represented; in article after article of early editions of *India Abroad*, one can see alongside the economic stirrings of immigrants for individual betterment, the clearly articulated needs of the Indian nation-state.

Investment in India was the raison d'etre for many *India Abroad*-sponsored activities.

Throughout the 1970s, articles touted the stability of developing Indian enterprises, with advice about how to invest in India. In 1974, the Indian embassy and the Council of Scientific and Industrial Research of India sponsored a series of seminars in the United States that were devoted, as *India Abroad* opined, to "help India meet her needs."[13] Not only did the newspaper report these activities, it actively participated in their production through a set of relationships with Indian government officials, business groups, and immigrants in the United States. Making such links clear, one article reads: "Last year, *India Abroad* had publicized the CSIR (Council of Scientific and Industrial Research of India) director-general's visit to this country with a view to introducing him to Indian scientists who would be interested in returning to India. . ."[14] But the director-general himself had a different idea of how those in the diaspora could help India by remaining in the diaspora. The article reports him saying:

> The response has been more than I could possibly handle. . .[but] since it was not possible to provide suitable jobs at that time . . .it was contended that it would be best to work out ways how they might still help India while continuing to live in the United States.

The producers of *India Abroad*, too, soon realized that both the needs of India and the practical goals of the developing immigrant community converged not in realizing the fantasy of return but in the fostering of links between Indian business enterprise and United States capital, as it had begun to reside in the Indian immigrant community. Articles over the next year, 1974, specifically underscored the favorable climate for investment,[15] and at year's end, the chairman of the Federation of Indian Export Organizations visited the offices of the paper in New York.

This close relationship, between a business organization in India and a major organ for immigrant news, is one representation among many of the nurturing of Indian American (NRI) interests around material objectives in India. It also reflects a primary mode of affiliation for a developing Indian diasporic community: economic and political transnationalism. Even at an early stage of development of immigrant populations, an intense concern with the state of the Indian economy and politics back home accompanied the more widely observed cultural connection to things Indian. It is possible to see this tendency not only in the pages of *India Abroad*, but also in other immigrant newspapers that developed in the 1980s, such as *News-India* and *India Monitor*, in the work of political and cultural associations, and, as we shall see below, in the development of entrepreneurial communities. Indeed immigrants' sense of otherness developed simultaneously with the progression of Indian nationalism (both political and economic), along the trajectory from a form of Third-Worldism (and its counterpart in the non-aligned movement) toward national-global capitalist development.

That the reference point for being Indian in the United States, from the 1970s until the present, has been a sustained interest in India shows how ethnic identity (here), the process of becoming Indian American has been shaped by that intense national(ist) focus on another place. It is distinct from the homeland nostalgia of earlier immigrant groups precisely because of the specific historical and political conditions of post–1965 immigrant experience, in which the nation-state of India embarks on a number of new international projects.[16] This form of diasporic community, with political, financial, and cultural interests that traverse not only local geographic lines (like the neighborhood) but also national boundaries, is also grounded in the process of class formation. The members of the first large-scale Indian migration to the United States came in the 1960s to greet an economy that was in a period of expansion. The occupational experiences of mostly middle-class and credentialed Indians during this period seemed to match the ideals and actu-

alities of growth and opportunity. Technological transformations meant new jobs in
medicine, the sciences (natural and
applied), business, and education, for which
this group of Indians was exceptionally
qualified. It was this early group of economically successful migrants that economic
(and cultural) appeals from India spoke to.
And it was this developing Indian American middle-class that assumed a central
role in producing a sense of community in
the diaspora: through financial remittances,
through the leadership of groups like the
Association of Indians in America, and
through the production of cultural perform-
ances.[17]

While the diasporic Indianness of the
community I am describing had a specific
class component, it also produced a field of
meaning for a whole range of Indians to utilize in building a sense of identity. More
material relationships between business
enterprises in India and Indian Americans,
and between members of Indian political
parties and immigrant associations
acquired a symbolic importance beyond the
literal participation of immigrants in those
activities. They had ideological effects, by
creating a sense of shared interest and identity outside of the country for those with
very different social and economic characteristics. What was in effect a diasporic
imaginary, of the nation of India, captured
different groups of people, sub-communi-
ties even, but in its totality, also produced a
community itself. That invocation of
"Indian community," however fictive it
might seem for such a diverse group of elements, nonetheless remained present in the
lives of many middle-class Indian immigrants.

While the NRI as a diasporic formation
embodies some of the shifts in what it
means to think of community outside the
neighborhood, with Indianness in the
transnational, not the local site, more territorial renderings of "Indian community"
also yield similar insights. Since the 1970s,
with the increasing growth and concentration of Indian populations in a number of
U.S. cities, particularly the New York met-

ropolitan area, Chicago, and Los Angeles,
new centers of Indian American business
arose to serve the needs and desires of
immigrant consumers. Colloquially and in
some cases, formally, known as "Little
Indias," these geographical spaces represent possibilities for Indian community
formation of a different kind from the NRI-
diaspora, but remain in some important
ways linked to it.

Jackson Heights, New York, is perhaps the
most prominent signifier for an Indian space
in the diaspora. Its concentration of electronics stores, sari shops, and eateries, in the city
of New York where Indian immigrants are
most populous, constitute for many an
important site for consuming and realizing a
sense of being Indian. That process is centered on consumption, so not surprisingly,
the beginnings of a "Little India" in Jackson
Heights can be indexed to the story of an
electronic goods store. In 1973, Subhas Ghai
and Raj Gandhi anticipated a market for specific kinds of consumer products when they
started "Sam and Raj" on the corner of 74th
Street and Broadway in Jackson Heights.
These engineer-founders had deliberated for
a long time over where to undertake their
business venture and finally decided that
this location, close to a stop for the number
7 subway train—that cuts a major artery
through the heart of Queens—would draw in
the increasing Indian populations from all
over the borough. Mr. Ghai says that the
movement of other Indian stores that
quickly followed to the area—like India Sari
Palace and Sinha Appliance—was also envi-
sioned, and to some degree, planned. He has
noted: "It was our dream."[18]

Sam and Raj were wildly successful, marketing and selling highly desirable 220-volt
electronic goods that could be taken to
India and Europe. The store achieved leg-
endary name-recognition throughout the
diaspora by serving a variety of Indians:
American citizens, resident "aliens," and
tourists alike. Not only did locals stop in to
pick up televisions, radios, and video
recorders on their way home to India for a
visit, but Indian businessmen and others
also made it a point to seek out low prices

for goods that were very expensive and/or unavailable in the subcontinent.

By 1980, the majority of the 74th Street block between Roosevelt Avenue and 37th Avenue housed South Asian shops. Because the goods—food, clothing, and electronics—had relevance for the cultures more widely of people from Pakistan and Bangladesh as well as from India, non-Indian South Asian merchants also occupied stores in Jackson Heights, and almost all of the businesses began to market themselves to "Indo-Pak-Bangla" constituencies. The area eventually comprised over a hundred stores in the area (on the block itself and a few surrounding blocks) that were South Asian-owned, and/or had almost exclusively South Asian clientele.[19]

While some Indians have lived in the immediate Jackson Heights area, they did not make up a residential majority or even a significant minority in the extremely diverse area, which to this day continues to have significant numbers of Jewish, Greek, Italian, Columbian, Korean, and Japanese peoples. Most of the shop owners live on Long Island or in more well-to-do areas of Queens, and the workers in the stores, when not related to the owners, come from various parts of Queens. Though the resident Indian population in the area certainly frequents the shops, it is hardly central to the production of 74th Street as an ethnic space; merchants rely on a broader, dispersed constituency for their goods.

The crowds of South Asians in the 74th Street area, that succeed in making this place appear to others to be an "Indian space,"[20] exist on shopping days. The "Indian community" represented here is both transitional and transient, and defined not by residence but by consumption. While territory does play a role in defining this community—it is in and through Jackson Heights that consumption is realized—it is articulated to an audience beyond whom it literally contains. Shared interests here include the distribution and sale of consumer goods like saris and appliances and services, like those in an Indian beauty salon. The ethnic consumer market, almost completely South Asian and in large part Indian, is not specific to the Queens Indian population that can most readily access the area, but more dispersed, extending outward to reach Indian populations throughout New York, New Jersey, and Connecticut.

"Sam & Raj" gained international fame as the immigrant population increased and as India began to develop important sectors of its economy, in electronics, in particular. And Jackson Heights has become a famously "Indian" area. This ethnic place has stood in for a whole set of historic experiences that span the globe. The representation of 74th Street, even to the locals, vacillates between a broad, diasporic meaning and more localized understandings of community. Popular renderings of such an "Indian community" occurred with reference to both the shopping area and to the shoppers who existed there every day and most especially on weekends, but also assume a xenophobic or exoticist cast, with an air of being foreign—the very term "Little India" can certainly be read in a variety of ways. Many Indian and American shoppers alike are surprised to hear that Indians do not make up the residential majority in the area.[21]

The production and consumption of ethnic goods in Jackson Heights shuts off at six or seven o'clock. The "community" there is akin to a kind of performance, with a beginning and an end, and regulated by the customs of United States consumer capitalism. Ethnic production and consumption are based only secondarily in local investments, in the city blocks and the residential neighborhood, and assume more meaning in symbolic and material renderings of India, for the most part, and of Pakistan and Bangladesh additionally. International references shape the consumer experiences in Jackson Heights and construct ethnicity for all parties involved. The temporary, almost fleeting nature of that consumption and production of Indianness in Jackson Heights has made for a very different type of ethnic community than those in Italian or Irish neighborhoods in Brooklyn and Queens, for example.

Jackson Heights is but one example of an entrepreneurial concentration that has responded to the consumer needs of an increasing population of immigrants, and that has produced a relationship between the more materially observable place and the imaginative (re)creation of Indianness. Similar processes can be seen in the development of Artesia, California, on the outskirts of the city of Los Angeles. Though the formal designation of this as a "Little India" has been a matter of some debate,[22] Angelenos and others commonly refer to a three-block area, centered around the main thoroughfare of Pioneer Boulevard, just outside the Los Angeles city limits, as such. Using strikingly similar language to Subhas Ghai in Jackson Heights, Ramesh Mahajan, the president of the Little India Chamber of Commerce in Artesia, said the idea for the expansion of a small concentration of Indian shops into its present form of 120 stores presented itself in a dream.[23] The area's merchants cater to Indian immigrants who live in nearby Cerritos, as well as to large Indian populations all over Orange County andsouthern California. Artesia itself only has an Asian population of 15 percent [24]—a number that includes Chinese, Korean, Japanese, Filipino, and Indian immigrants—yet it, like Jackson Heights, has become a famously "Indian" area. Consumption-oriented Artesia also serves as a cultural and political focal point for the broader nonresident Indian community; it was there that the fiftieth anniversary independence day parade took place, it houses the largest Indian immigrant newspaper in southern California, and in some sense it has become representative of Indian culture to outsiders. More than Jackson Heights, Artesia has absorbed and accommodated the recent fashion craze over things Indian; stories abound in the area of local shops being frequented by famous Hollywood actresses and designers. In this way, the area performs as an Indian community for both the "inside" and "outside."

Even in the tri-state (New York, New Jersey, and Connecticut) region, Indian business areas are multiplying, as the popula-

tions that they serve, reproduce, and embody have become more diversified and complex. Edison, New Jersey, and Philadelphia also boast of spaces where Indian food can be consumed and saris and jewelry can be purchased; Edison, particularly, serves a more suburban and affluent population that has moved away from and no longer wants to travel to multiethnic and multiclass Queens. While all these areas become represented as "Little Indias," then, they construct different kinds of "Indian community." Jackson Heights now produces Indianness to signify broader South Asian needs and desires, Artesia represents southern California middle-class Indian community, and Edison embodies Indian immigrant community constructed out of occupational specification and, to some extent, white flight.

Interestingly, these ethnic places do similarly illuminate the dynamics of change in metropolitan areas, where "the city" has expanded to include areas previously thought of as suburban, to appeal to middle-class people who put at a premium in their lives access to certain cultural needs. This is also to note that increasing populations of immigrants who have attained some measure of financial security in the United States and yet continue to think of themselves as Indian, Chinese, or Korean, for example, are coincident with and contribute to this reorganization of urban space.

New ethnic communities represented by Jackson Heights, Artesia, and Edison are formed by a wide range of shared national interests, articulated on one level to economic success in the United States (to the ability to buy and sell) and to cultural and financial attachments to India. Merchants and, to some extent, consumers, actualize a production of "India" through consolations and investments in a local space that, in strategic fashion, can absorb the breadth of a variety of other Indian communities, regional/ethnic, religious, class-specific, and social. Emerging from a certain success of middle-class Indian Americans, "Little Indias" have effects that radiate outward to encompass working-class south Asians who desire products, like foodstuffs and clothing, to recreate their cultures in a foreign place.

The NRI and the "Little India" illustrate new types of diasporic community formation. Shared interests exist in renderings of the nation, of India, in material, cultural, and political terms, for immigrants all over the United States (and the world). In these communities, transnationality, an ability to economically, physically, and imaginatively cross borders, shapes the lived experience of their members and participants. In establishing a sense of what Indianness is, on a large scale, these communities may be seen to play down the process of Americanization; this occurs in spite of the fact that evocations of the American dream operate in and through immigrants' ideas about themselves.[25] Aihwa Ong's notion of flexible citizenship, "the cultural logics of capitalist accumulation, travel, and displacement that induce subjects to respond fluidly and opportunistically to changing political-economic conditions,"[26] seems relevant here. In the cases I have described, the middle classes authorize Indianness, and seem to draw the parameters of particular forms of "community." But I would argue as well that their products, of an NRI-identity in the pages of *India Abroad*, and of a consumer market in Queens, elicit participation by other class segments of the immigrant population, and thus establish broader meanings for that transnational identity beyond its entrepreneurs.

This is not, however, to say that other communities do not present challenges to this formation of Indian identity, and in the process construct new sites for the construction of ethnicity outside of what are, in effect, mainstream authorities.[27] New generations in particular experience and construct affiliations in altogether different and in some cases more progressive forms. Changes in Indian, Pakistani, and Bangladeshi migrant populations have also produced shifts in the types of community formed in the United States, most notably around work identities: South Asian cab drivers all over New York and Guyanese Indian factory and airport workers in Queens desire different alliances with each other and with other Indians.

Transnational relationships redefine nations as well as peoples. From the late 1970s to the present, and with the rise of an Indian neoliberalism that can proceed alongside and within discourses of national development, regulations on NRIs have continued to decrease and state appeals to them have multiplied exponentially. The "Persons of Indian Origin Card" program that opened this essay is only the latest chapter in a broader set of developments. One can hardly help but notice the ironies of the nation of India in this contemporary moment claiming as a type of citizen the Indian migrant abroad who has benefitted from the developmentalist policies of the Indian state, such as scientific and technical education, but who nonetheless acts as a "foreign" investor. How we understand this scenario of nationality and migration has a great deal to do with the degree of flexibility we can accord to ideas of community, nation, and culture.

## NOTES

This essay took shape from talks I gave in early 1999 at Wesleyan University and the University of California, Irvine. Many thanks to the various interlocutors in those venues whose questions or comments greatly improved the argumentation herein.

1. Celia W. Dugger, "India Offers Rights to Attract Its Offspring's Cash," *The New York Times*, April 4, 1999, 12; P. Jayaram, "Government Launches PIO Card to Attract Diaspora," *India Abroad*, April 9, 1999, 4.

2. P. Jayaram, "Government Launches PIO Card to Attract Diaspora," 4.

3. And here I do not mean to suggest that the "global economy" is a new phenomenon; as many have elaborated, the very history of capitalism is international from its outset. But it does make some sense to see recent developments, of investment and "flexibility" as distinctive, much as David Harvey has outlined for the period he calls "late capitalism" in *The Condition of Post-*

*modernity* (Oxford: Basil Blackwell, 1989). Essays in Anthony D. King, ed., *Culture, Globalization and the World-System: Contemporary Conditions for the Representation of Identity*, (London: The Macmillan Press, Ltd., 1991) also engage this issue in ways that I have found useful.

4. Nina Glick Schiller, Linda Basch and Cristina Szanton Blanc, *Towards a Transnational Perspective on Migration: Race, Ethnicity and Nationalism Reconsidered* (New York: New York Academy, 1992). I use the term "transnationalism" with obvious reference to the wonderful work of these authors, but extend it to cover imaginaries that lie beyond more material social practices.

5. Sherry Ortner has observed that understanding second-generation middle-class (this is media-influenced) cultures requires similar reorderings of what we take to be "the field," in "Generation X: Anthropology in a Media-Saturated World," *Cultural Anthropology* 13(3) (1998): 414–40.

6. The point of reference for such historiographical and social scientific trends is European immigration. David Emmons, *The Butte Irish: Class and Ethnicity in an American Mining Town, 1875–1925* (Urbana and Chicago: University of Illinois Press, 1989) and Robert Anthony Orsi, *The Madonna of 115th Street: Faith and Community in Italian Harlem, 1880–1950* (New Haven and London: Yale University Press, 1985) are two fine examples of this scholarship.

7. Though this may in fact have been overstated by meta-histories of these histories; there may be a way in which more social scientific analyses of assimilation (for example, in the Chicago School's work of the 1940s), or public policy accounts, have foregrounded assimilation and the loss of homeland cultures in ways that have not been borne out, even by the experiences of white ethnic Americans. Robert Orsi's book, for example, never uses terms such as "transnational" or "diaspora," but nonetheless provides more nuanced readings of Italian American culture than any assimilationist explanation could offer.

8. Partha Chatterjee, *The Nation and Its Fragments: Colonial and Postcolonial Histories*

(Princeton: Princeton University Press, 1993), 203.

9. Maxine Fisher discusses this in her *The Indians of New York City* (Columbia, Mo.: South Asia Books, 1980).

10. The Bhagat Singh Thind Case in 1923, cited by a number of historians, including Joan Jensen, *Passage from India* (New Haven: Yale University Press, 1988), 256–59 and Sucheng Chan, *Asian Americans: An Interpretive History* (Boston: Twayne Publishers, 1990), 94, exemplifies the many debates surrounding the racial identity of Indians before United States laws of naturalization and citizenship in the pre–1965 period.

11. Interview with Gopal Raju, New York, February 13, 1995.

12. Benedict Anderson, *Imagined Communities: Reflections on the Origin and Spread of Nationalism* (London and New York: Verso, 1983), 37.

13. "Indian Scientists in U.S. Discuss Ways to Help India Meet Her Needs," *India Abroad*, November 15, 1974, 5.

14. "Indian Scientists Discuss Ways to Help India," 5.

15. See Pavan Sahgal, "India Gives Foreign Investors High Returns: Conditions are Misrepresented by Press Here," *India Abroad*, December 6, 1974, 5.

16. A second part of this argument is the political transnationalism in which Indian political parties maintain strong financial links to NRIs; the Bharatiya Janata Party (BJP), for example, has developed a group called the Overseas Friends of the BJP, which has financed and publicized the rightist party in India and can even be seen to have contributed to its rise in India.

17. Arthur W. Helweg and Usha M. Helweg, *An Immigrant Success Story: East Indians in America* (London: Hurst & Company, 1990) details some of these developments.

18. Interview with Subhas Ghai, New York, July 14, 1995.

19. Yet, interestingly enough, merchants from a wide variety of national backgrounds, have supported the formal designation of this area as a "Little India" for commercial purposes. For more on this debate, and its repercussions, see Sandhya Shukla, "India

Abroad: Transnational Ethnic Cultures in the United States and Britain, 1947–1997," Ph.D. dissertation, chapter two, 1998.

20. "Bazaar with the Feel of Bombay, Right in Queens," *New York Times*, January 4, 1993, B1; "India Casts its Subtle Spell in Queens," *New York Times*, August 19, 1994, C1.

21. This insight is based on a number of informal interviews that I have conducted with neighborhood residents.

22. Scott Harris, "Little India," *Los Angeles Times*, September 1, 1992, B1; and "Little India in Artesia—Why Not?," *Los Angeles Times*, September 6, 1992, M4.

23. Harris, "Little India," D12.

24. Harris, "Little India," D12.

25. Almost all respondents in the research on Indian Americans that I have conducted cite the American Dream in their stories about themselves. This forms another argument about the simultaneous belief in America and attachment to India that I do not have space to engage here.

26. Aihwa Ong, *Flexible Citizenship: The Cultural Logics of Transnationality* (Durham, N.C., and London: Duke University Press, 1999), 6.

27. Indeed, the other pieces in this volume on progressive South Asian cultures wonderfully illustrate how those interventions take place.

## 3.6

# Ethnicity and Political Adaptation
## Comparing Filipinos, Koreans, and the Vietnamese in Southern California

### Pei-te Lien

~~~~~~~~~~~~~~~~~~~~~~~~~~~~~~~~~~~~~~~~~~~~~~~~~~~~~~~~~~~~~~~~~~~

A much-neglected topic in Asian American Studies is the microlevel processes of political adaptation of immigrants from different Asian origins. Part of the reasons for the lack of research deals with the preoccupation of the extant literature with economic and sociocultural adaptation processes of Asian immigrants. Another reason has to do with the absence of publicly accessible data—particularly large-scale, systematically collected social science data. How has ethnicity influenced the extent of political adaptation of Korean, Filipino, and Vietnamese Americans in the 1990s? What are the similarities and differences in the correlates of citizenship intent, naturalization, and voter registration across the three Asian American ethnic groups? This study addresses these questions by empirically analyzing the 1990 census data and three survey datasets collected in recent years by a *Los Angeles Times* poll in Southern California.

Lien, Pei-te. "Ethnicity and Political Adaptation: Comparing Filipinos, Koreans, and the Vietnamese in Southern California." Unpublished article.

### MODELING IMMIGRANT ADAPTATION: THEORETICAL CONSIDERATIONS

The adaptation of immigrants to the United States has been a subject of sustained interest to scholars of various social science disciplines. Throughout the years, numerous models estimating the degree of possible assimilation and differentiation of immigrant groups from various parts of the world to America have been proposed, empirically challenged, revised, and revisited (e.g., Gordon 1964; Portes and Bach 1985; Jiobu 1988; Feagin and Feagin 1993; Portes and Zhou 1993; DeWind and Kasinitz 1997). Today, although few would question the assimilationist stance that the American nation should be the focus of analysis, many also maintain that immigrant adaptation is a pluralistic and multistage process that may involve sociopolitical factors across national borders (Hein 1995; Rumbaut 1997). Immigrants may be assimilated culturally by adopting mainstream customs, dress, food, and language and socially by joining mainstream clubs and organizations as well as developing friendship and family networks over time.

But many may also seek to maintain close contacts with their original ethnic culture, organizations, and friends. Whereas some groups and individuals may adapt to mainstream economic practices and values with little difficulty, they may encounter obstacles when trying to move up the social and/or political ladders because of past political socialization and the limited opportunity structure afforded them by the host society and politics.

Today, for immigrants from Asia in the post–1965 era, the U.S. door of immigration is relatively open and minorities can enjoy basic protection in terms of equal employment opportunity, naturalization, and voting rights; they may engage themselves simultaneously in different facets and stages of adaptation. This in itself is an indication of progress, compared to the categorical denial of entry and mobility to early immigrant groups. However, this also presents a tremendous challenge to those who try to assess, in the aggregate, the social and political status of the contemporary Asian American community. Although recent census data indicate that Asian Americans outperform other racial/ethnic groups in terms of educational achievement and income, a significant chasm exists among major Asian ethnic groups. To what extent do groups of Asian origin differ from each other in terms of social and political adaptation? How well does socioeconomic background, compared to other sets of factors, explain differences in the rates of political adaptation for each ethnic group? This study examines survey data collected from three Asian groups in Southern California to answer these questions.

In an election-centered democracy, a prerequisite of political empowerment for any immigrant group is to increase the number of citizens and registered voters. The term "political adaptation" is used interchangeably with political integration in this study to refer to this process when one prepares to participate in mainstream electoral politics. For newcomers to the U.S. system, their degree of adaptation or integration into the U.S. political system may be indi-cated in an ascending order by the possession of citizenship intent, naturalized citizenship, and voter registration, with each succeeding act demanding more resources and commitment from the immigrants.

For American-born Asians, U.S. citizenship is a birthright affirmed by *Won Kim Ark* (1898). For foreign-born Asians, U.S. citizenship was not accessible to all until after 1952. Cleared of this and other legal barriers, it still is a personal decision that depends on the joint operation of at least three sets of factors: individual characteristics, conditions of the homeland country, and the perceived benefits of U.S. citizenship (Jasso and Rosenzweig 1990). Immigrants may not intend to pursue U.S. citizenship if they do not value the ability to sponsor the immigration of relatives, to have greater job opportunity, to register and vote, and, after 1996, to receive social welfare benefits.[1] To acquire U.S. citizenship, foreign-born adults who maintain a legal residence in the United States often need to go through a lengthy and complicated process of naturalization. Basically, it requires continuous U.S. residency for at least five years and physical presence in the United States for at least half of the five years immediately prior to filing the petition for naturalization.[2] Even after meeting the time requirement, some may still not be able to acquire citizenship because of the failure to complete citizenship tests or a reluctance to explicitly repudiate allegiance to their countries of origin.

Once naturalized, immigrants need to face another hurdle before they are able to vote in elections. Today, voter registration may be considered a relatively simple procedure of filling out a brief form that is now widely available in many public places such as motor vehicle registration offices, libraries, and social service agencies, thanks to the Motor Voter Act of 1992. Even so, registration can be discouraged by the thirty-day residency requirement and the need to reregister after each change of primary residence in most localities of the nation. For naturalized citizens, particularly those with a non-English language background and/or those who did not immigrate until adulthood, the likelihood of registering to vote can be further hindered by the lack of foreign-language forms and other election materials,[3] ignorance about the proper procedures, fear of election officials, and a general lack of desire or efficacy in the abilities of government to solve problems.

In all, immigrant political integration may be influenced most by the length of time spent in the United States; but it may also be predicted by an array of other factors. Past scholars studying Asian immigrants and refugees have identified a number of personal and societal factors that may determine the extent of initial adaptation: prior socioeconomic background (education, job skills), demographic characteristics (age, sex), life experience in the country of origin, motivation/expectation of life in the United States, modes of exit and transit, availability of family and kinship support, compatibility of ethnic culture with host society norms and values, cohesion of local ethnic community, and time of entry/place of resettlement, which may entail differences immigrants or refugees received in terms of economic assistance and public acceptance or resistance (Haines 1989, 1996; Jasso and Rosenzweig 1990; Kitano and Daniels 1995).

Depending on their communication skills, family and social network, residential segregation, home country situations, and attitudes and behaviors extended by the host society, immigrants may also develop various patterns of adaptation over time that can be used to predict political integration. A useful typology to describe this process would include acculturation, structural (familial, residential, and marital) integration, group consciousness (personal discrimination, group deprivation), and attachment to homeland. These are the major components of ethnicity initially suggested by Gordon (1964) but revised by observing behaviors of non-European immigrants (Padilla 1985; Williams and Ortega 1990; Lien 1994, 1997). The emergence of these dimensions may not follow a linear pattern; they may be interactive (Kim 1989) and adhesive or sycretic in nature (Hurh 1980; Hurh and Kim 1984a, 1984b; Rutledge 1992; Kim and Hurh 1993). Because of the changing character of the U.S. economy over the past two decades and the deteriorating social environment in inner-city areas where new immigrants tend to congregate, doubts have also been raised if contemporary assimilation should be considered as a subtractive or an additive process for immigrant children (Daniels 1990; Reimers 1992; Portes and Zhou 1993; Rumbaut 1996). Still, this typology remains a useful tool to characterize the pluralistic nature of today's adaptation and will be used in competition with socioeconomic and demographic factors to identity important variables shaping political adaptation among the three groups of survey respondents specified below.

Filipinos, Koreans, and Vietnamese represent three main groups of new Asian immigration to the United States. They differ more or less from each other in terms of the time and mode of entry, extent of prior exposure to U.S. culture and capitalist economy, and the contexts of exit and reception. However, their home countries all have significant U.S. military and political involvement in the past, and they all came in droves in the past few decades and chose Southern California as their major destination of international or internal migration. Thus, although different group immigration history and its involvement with the United States may dictate different rates of integration, common experience of immigration and exposure to stimuli in the shared geopolitical environment may generate similar behavioral response patterns among members of each immigrant group. Following previous findings or observations on immigrant/refugee adaptation, it is hypothesized that, regardless of ethnic group origin, greater political adaptation within each immigrant group will be associated with longer time spent in the United States, male sex, higher socioeconomic status, greater acculturation, and greater success at social structural integration. This may not be affected by the degree of ethnic group consciousness, but it may be negatively associated with residual attachment to the homeland in Asia.

## COMING TO SOUTHERN CALIFORNIA

### Filipinos

This is an Asian group that had a significant population in the United States prior to the "liberalization" of U.S. immigration policy in 1965 (Hing 1993). Because of past colonization, Filipinos have maintained significant cultural, political, economic, and military ties with the United States since 1898. After the Spanish-American War, Filipinos became U.S. nationals through the Treaty of Paris. This unique political status obligated them to show allegiance to Old Glory, to be assimilated into the U.S. culture through the implementation of a public educational system modeled after that on the U.S. mainland, and to remain a supplier of raw materials in exchange for manufactured goods made in the U.S. market economy (Min 1987; Liu and Cheng 1994; Espiritu 1995). It also enabled them to escape immigration restrictions applied to other Asians and enter the U.S. to seek education, employment, and a better quality of life until 1934, when the colony was turned into a Commonwealth and an annual immigration quota of fifty was instituted. Except for those who had served three or more years in the U.S. Navy, Marine Corps, or the Naval Auxiliary Service and received an honorable discharge, Filipino immigrants were not permitted to petition for citizenship until 1946, when the annual quota increased to one hundred (Melendy 1977). Ironically, in the same year Filipinos were rewarded the right to naturalization because of their wartime contributions, a Rescission Act exempted more than 100,000 Filipino veterans from equal benefits. They were prevented from seeking citizenship until 1990 (Eljera 1997).

In spite of continued immigration restriction between 1952 and 1965, more than 32,000 Filipinos arrived outside of the quota system as family members of U.S citizens, about half of them war brides of World War II veterans (Kitano and Daniels 1995). The scrapping of the quota system in 1965 in association with developments in Asia brought in large numbers of professionals as well as family members of U.S. citizens and permanent residents (Liu and Cheng 1994). This not only makes the Philippines the largest sending nation in terms of recent Asian immigration, but increased the diversity in the American community in terms of immigration generation, job skills, income, and attachment to host and homeland cultures and politics.

### Koreans

Although the presence of Koreans in Los Angeles can be dated to as far back as 1904, the development of the Korean community was again severely hampered by U.S. immigration policies. No immigration was allowed between 1924 and 1952. Even though racist criteria against Korean naturalization were removed in the McCarran-Walter Act, only a nominal number of Koreans were able to immigrate under the quota system before 1965. Like the Filipinos, most of the 15,000 Koreans who immigrated during this period entered as war brides. When the U.S. Bureau of Census first counted Koreans as a distinct ethnic group in 1970, fewer than 9,000 were enumerated in Los Angeles County.[4] By 1990, the Korean population in the county was sixteen times larger. As is the case with the Filipino community, this remarkable rate of population growth within a relatively brief time span can be attributed to strong U.S. military, political, cultural, and business ties with the peninsula (Kim 1981; Light and Bonacich 1988; Reimers 1992; Ong, Bonacich, and Cheng 1994). Because of U.S. indoctrination and connections, many well-educated middle-class South Koreans left behind their urban enclaves for economic improvement, a better educational environment, and political freedom in the "land of opportunity." They, in turn, brought in members with more diverse class background through family reunions.

Unlike the Filipinos, all Koreans share a native language that is used in their public schools. This absence of an Anglophone element is one of the reasons for the relative lack of English proficiency and the concentration of Korean immigrants in small businesses. Their Confucian and Protestant religious backgrounds may provide additional incentives. However, the availability of start-up cash, family labor, an existing support network, and close U.S.-South Korean trade relations were more important factors (Min 1987, 1996). Significantly, these Koreans also tend to operate their businesses in minority neighborhoods and experienced hostility and rejection from some of their black and Latino customers. These interracial conflicts were epitomized in the 1992 L.A. riots, as Koreans suffered the majority of the losses. The positive side of this Korean immigrant experience is that it has served to heighten group consciousness and foster a higher level of solidarity than that present in other Asian ethnic communities (Min 1996).

## Vietnamese

This group differs significantly from the two other groups in that emigration was mostly involuntary and Vietnamese nationals entered outside of regular immigration channels. However, like Koreans, the Vietnamese community grew recently and quickly. In April 1975, as Saigon fell, about 132,000 refugees from South Vietnam resettled in all fifty states. Between 1979 and 1982, about 270,000 "boat people" arrived. In each subsequent year up to 1992, an average of 24,000 Vietnamese entered, mostly as refugees; more entered as nonrefugee immigrants after 1990. Unlike those who entered in 1975, the post–1975 refugees and immigrants came mostly from rural backgrounds, with little education, knowledge of English, or transferable occupational skills. They also suffered the disorientation of prolonged stays in refugee camps, often after surviving traumatic experiences at sea

or on land involving death of relatives, rapes, beatings, and robberies (Routledge 1992; Rumbaut 1996).

As political refugees, many face a triply disadvantaged situation of adaptation by having a tumultuous war experience in their country of origin, the rupture of cultural and social relations in transit, and lack of preparation and—particularly for the first wave of refugees—preexisting community structure in the host country (Haines 1996). Although they were able to receive federal government assistance in food, housing, jobs, and medical care for various lengths of time, they were not able to resettle as a group in one locality. Further, the peak year of their arrival (1980) coincided with both the influx of Cuban and Haitian refugees in South Florida and the most severe economic recession since the Great Depression (Rumbaut 1996). This, coupled with the image of a failed war, contributed to rising hostility in the public mind and reduced benefits for the new arrivals. Thus the policy of forced dispersal failed to prevent a secondary migration of the Vietnamese and other Southeast Asian groups from all over the United States to Southern California in the 1980s.

## CENSUS FINDINGS

In 1990, close to half (47 percent) of the Vietnamese nationwide resided in California and 59 percent of them lived in the six Southern California counties where samples of opinion surveys used in this study were drawn. About half (52 percent) of Filipinos nationwide can be found in the state and 53 percent of them in the six-county region. For Koreans, their concentration in the Los Angeles County represents 57 percent of the statewide and 18 percent of the ethnic population nationwide.

In Southern California, the majority of Filipinos and Koreans resided in Los Angeles County in 1990; one-fourth of the Filipinos resided in San Diego County. The largest concentration of the Vietnamese was in Orange County; however more than one-third also lived in Los Angeles County. The socioeconomic characteristics of each group generally reflect the immigration history discussed above. As a group, Filipinos appear to be most acculturated and economically incorporated. They have the smallest percentage of individuals reported having problems in English, highest percentage of college education, highest rate of labor force participation, highest amount of family and per capita income, lowest foreign-born rate, and highest citizenship and naturalization rates.[5] However, the community is still predominantly foreign-born and contains as high a percentage of recent arrivals as that of the two other ethnic groups. Filipinos' desire to sponsor relatives may not only boost naturalization rate but explain the effect of having the largest share of families with three or more workers.

Both Koreans and the Vietnamese are alike in the percentages of individuals who are foreign-born, bilingual, don't speak English "very well," and participate in the labor force. However, the Vietnamese have higher rates of naturalization and citizenship—perhaps reflecting their special refugee status, which enables them to receive reduced residency requirements for naturalization as well as their greater need to sponsor relatives. Symbolic of their triply disadvantaged status as refugees, the Vietnamese have the lowest rates of college education, per capita income, and the highest rate of unemployment. Koreans, on the other hand, have a much higher rate of college education and amount of per capita income, but they also have the highest rates of recent arrivals, self-employed or unpaid family workers, and lowest rate of families with three or more workers among the three groups.

Although census data provide important indicators of social and political adaptation, the usefulness of the data in answering the research questions is limited by the small number of questions asked and the decennial timeframe of ethnic data. More recent survey data are used next to show the commonalities and differences in the correlates of political adaptation across the three Asian ethnic groups.

## SURVEY DATA AND MEASURES

The datasets used in this study were collected by the *Los Angeles Times* between 1992 and 1995 polling adults with Korean, Vietnamese, or Filipino surnames who resided in Southern California at the time of the interviews. Telephone surveys were conducted with 750 Korean residents in Los Angeles County as well as with 861 Vietnamese and 750 Filipino residents of five additional counties: Orange, San Diego, San Bernadino, Riverside, and Ventura. Random-digit dialing techniques were used to produce about one-third of the Korean sample; the rest were drawn from lists of Korean-surnamed households countywide. Separate lists of ethnic surnames were used to draw the Vietnamese and Filipino samples from phone directories in the six counties. Vietnamese residents of Orange County were oversampled to produce 58 percent of the Vietnamese sample. The margin of sampling error is plus or minus 5 percent for the Korean sample and plus or minus 4 percent for the other two. Information about interview dates and languages used is reported in table 3.6a.

These surveys are unique not only in their pioneering nature of collecting large-scale Asian community opinion in a systematic manner, but that they were conducted by interviewers who spoke both English and the home language of the specific group of respondents. These two features increase the reliability of results and permit findings to be generalized to the Southern California region when weighed data adjusted to conform with census figures on population characteristics such as sex, age, and region are used. However, they are also limited by common drawbacks from using phone surveys and surname samples. The former prohibits the interviewing of those who have unlisted phone numbers or who did not have access to phones. The latter restricts sampling to those individuals who bear the

**Table 3.6a  Percentage Distribution of Political Adaptation and Its Correlates among Korean, Vietnamese, and Filipino Americans**

|  | Vietnamese | Koreans | Filipinos |
|---|---|---|---|
| Base N | 861 | 749 | 750 |
| % Ethnic language interview | 89 | 91 | 46 |
| *Interview dates* | *3/28–4/19/94* | *2/26–3/27/92* | *12/4–22/95* |
| *Political adaptation* |  |  |  |
| Citizens | 49% | 36% | 73% |
|     Naturalized (foreign-borns) | 48 | 34 | 68 |
| Expected citizenship | 81 | 42 | 67 |
|   (among noncitizens) |  |  |  |
| Voter registration | 29 | 18 | 50 |
|   (among citizens) | 59 | 51 | 69 |
| Party registration (among registered) |  |  |  |
|     Democrats | 24 | 44 | 40 |
|     Republicans | 61 | 47 | 38 |
|     Other party | 1 | * | 5 |
|     No party/independent | 13 | 9 | 17 |
| *Socioeconomic background* |  |  |  |
| Education |  |  |  |
|     High school | 51% | 34% | 13% |
|     College graduate | 20 | 49 | 60 |
| Income |  |  |  |
|     20K | 51 | 24 | 9 |
|     50K | 14 | 31 | 43 |
| Unemployed | 10 | 3 | 3 |
| In labor force | 53 | 63 | 75 |
| Occupational types (among employed) |  |  |  |
|     Professional | 26 | 15 | 29 |
|     Technician | 18 | 14 | 11 |
|     White collar, clerical | 7 | 13 | 14 |
|     Administrative | 6 | 8 | 13 |
|     Executive | 4 | 3 | 8 |
|     Owner | 5 | 19 | 4 |
|     Unskilled labor | 14 | 4 | 2 |
| *Demographic background* |  |  |  |
| Foreign-born | 98% | 98% | 84% |
| Age in years |  |  |  |
|     (18–27) | 30 | 22 | 23 |
|     (28–37) | 34 | 29 | 27 |
|     (38–49) | 22 | 22 | 26 |
|     (50–64) | 12 | 16 | 16 |
|     (65+) | 3 | 11 | 8 |
| Years of stay in the U.S. |  |  |  |
|     (0–5) | 31 | 29 | 17 |
|     (6–10) | 17 | 31 | 19 |
|     (11–15) | 33 | 19 | 17 |
|     (16–20) | 18 | 15 | 17 |

*(continued)*

**Table 3.6a** *(continued)*

|  | Vietnamese | Koreans | Filipinos |
|---|---|---|---|
| (21+) | 1 | 5 | 30 |
| Female | 48 | 51 | 55 |
| *Acculturation* | | | |
| Speak English very/just well | 68% | 53% | 95% |
| Speak English mostly or exclusively in everyday life | 12 | 14 | 39 |
| Use English media mostly or exclusively in everyday life | 37 | 24 | 77 |
| *Structural Integration* | | | |
| Friendship racial/ethnic makeup | | | |
|     White | 19% | 50% | 55% |
|     Black | 9 | 23 | 46 |
|     Latino | 10 | 35 | 47 |
|     Co-ethnic | 46 | n/a | 75 |
|     Other Asian | 15 | 33 | 43 |
|     Cross-racial/ethnic | 32 | 63 | 75 |
| Neighborhood racial/ethnic makeup | | | |
|     Mostly white | 36 | 39 | 22 |
|     Mostly black | 3 | 3 | 3 |
|     Mostly Latino | 12 | 9 | 13 |
|     Mostly co-ethnic | 11 | 13 | 14 |
|     Mostly other Asian | 9 | 8 | 5 |
|     Pretty evenly mixed | 24 | 25 | 41 |
| *Marital assimilation* | | | |
| Approve intermarriage | 51% | 58% | 75% |
| Disapprove intermarriage | 15 | 36 | 7 |
| *Personal experience of discrimination* | | | |
| A great deal/fair amount | 9% | 12% | 10% |
| Some amount, not much | 32 | 35 | 37 |
|   —Sites of discrimination— | | | |
|     Jobs/promotion | 39 | 23 | 56 |
|     Education | 17 | 14 | 12 |
|     Business | 12 | 17 | 18 |
|     Government | 7 | 14 | 8 |
|     Strangers | 26 | 30 | 36 |
|     Cultural differences | 19 | 5 | 13 |
|     Neighborhood | 17 | n/a | 16 |
| *Group deprivation* | | | |
| Worse group condition | 12% | 8% | 4% |
| Expect/prefer to move back to homeland | 21% | 20% | 38% |

*Notes:* Original data were collected in Southern California and released to the author through the Roper Center for Public Opinion Research. The author appreciates financial support from a Faculty Research Grant at the University of Utah to purchase the datasets.
*Source: Los Angeles Times* Polls #267, #331, and #370.

Asian surnames identified in a prepared surname list. This is biased against those who have unusual surnames or carry a non-Asian surname through adoption or marriage. Additionally, the three-year span in the time frame of interviews between the Korean and the Filipino sample may threaten the comparability of results. However, these concerns should not invalidate the potential contribution of findings reported here. At a minimum, findings reported may serve as a base of information to compare with findings from future research.

Summary results of respondents' political adaptation and socioeconomic background are reported in table 3.6a. Compared to the 1990 census, survey respondents are over-represented by foreign-borns in each of the groups—reflecting the dominance of first-generation immigrants among adults in each surveyed group. This boosts the percentages of those who do not have a very good command of English, and it lowers the rates of citizenship among Koreans and the Vietnamese. However, perhaps because of the high naturalization rate of Filipinos, their citizenship rate is higher than what was reported in the census. For both the Korean and the Filipino samples, the percentage of college education is higher, but the percentages of household income over $50,000 and of various employment indicators are about the same as reported in the census. For the Vietnamese sample, the percentages of college education and unemployment are the same as in the census, but a much higher percentage of survey respondents are recent arrivals, and the percentages of labor force participants and high income earners are much lower than found in the census. However, the general trend of political and economic adaptation across groups illustrated by census data is consistent with these survey results. Among the three Asian ethnic groups, Filipinos are the most politically and socioeconomically adapted, the Koreans are the least politically adapted, and the Vietnamese are the least economically adapted. An important caveat needs to be made here: after the LA riots that took place one month

after the completion of the Korean survey, Korean community organizations and leaders pushed hard to mobilize the community by conducting citizenship and voter registration drives. Numbers reported here are likely to have underestimated the comparative political adaptation of Korean Americans, whereas the campaign and passage of the anti-immigrant initiative (Proposition 187) in November 1994 may have boosted Filipino naturalization and registration rates.

Among Korean respondents, about one-third were naturalized citizens, about two-fifth of the noncitizens expected to become so in the next few years, and about one-half of citizens have registered to vote. Among the Vietnamese, close to one-half of them were naturalized, about every eight out of ten noncitizens expected to become citizens, and about 60 percent of citizens have registered to vote. Among Filipinos, close to 70 percent were naturalized citizens or anticipated becoming citizens, and a similar percentage of citizens have registered to vote. Because political integration depends on a series of interconnected decisions or conditions, a four-point scale of political integration is created to index the level of commitments and efforts involved in each succeeding act. A value of 3 is assigned to those who registered to vote, a value of 2 to those who were naturalized but not registered, a value of 1 to those who were not naturalized but expected to become one in the next few years, and a value of 0 to those who had done nothing.

To identify important factors associated with political integration, a number of sociopsychological variables are used to gauge the various dimensions in the adaptation typology mentioned earlier. Acculturation is estimated by proficiency with the English language and the extent of using English relative to non-English home language in both oral and written forms. An acculturation index is created by taking the average of the summed scores of the three variables.[6] Structural integration is measured by racial/ethnic makeup of friends, neighbors, and spouse.[7] A respondent is considered more structurally integrated if he or she is able to develop friendships and holds a supportive attitude toward marriage[8] across racial and ethnic lines. An individual is considered residing in a segregated environment when neighbors are reported as mostly coethnics. Group consciousness attributable to behavior reception is measured by one's having personal experiences of discrimination; that associated with attitudinal reception is indicated by perceptions that their own group condition is worse off than other minorities.[9] Lastly, the strength of attachment to one's homeland is gauged by the expectation or preference of settling back there sometime in the future.[10]

These sociopsychological variables relating to the formation of ethnicity are used along with indicators of socioeconomic status (education, family income, employment status) and demographic background (age, gender, length of stay, percentage of life spent in the United States) to estimate the extent of political adaptation.[11] Both zero-order correlation coefficients and ordinary least squares-based regression coefficients are reported in tables 3.6b to 3.6d. Their efficacy in predicting immigrant political integration for each of the three groups of Asians is assessed by comparing the significance of the unstandardized coefficients (b) and the sizes of the standardized coefficients (B, assuming equal unit of measurement) in each group among the three sets of variables identified above.

## SURVEY RESULTS AND DISCUSSION

Consistent with census findings, the socioeconomic and sociopsychological variables in table 3.6a show that Filipinos have the highest levels of college education and upper-income families as well as the highest degree of acculturation in terms of English proficiency and reliance on English in direct and mediated communication. They also show that Filipinos have the greatest degree of structural integration in terms of having nonethnic friends, living in integrated neighborhood, and support for interracial marriage. By contrast, both Koreans and the Vietnamese are low in the percentage of English use. Compared with Koreans, the Vietnamese have a higher proportion of individuals who use English media mostly or exclusively on a daily basis; they have lower degrees of cross-racial friendships but also lower disapproval rates of interracial marriage.

Yet Filipinos share with the two other groups in experiences of residential segregation and discrimination. Between 11 percent and 14 percent of respondents in each group report residing almost exclusively among members of their own ethnic group. A small but similar percentage of individuals in each group also report having experienced a great deal or a fair amount of personal discrimination. For each group, discrimination occurs most frequently in the workplace, followed by discrimination from strangers. Except for the Vietnamese, only a negligible percentage of respondents perceive their group as being less able to receive social acceptance and adequate opportunities. Yet, when asked to choose between their host and home countries, a surprisingly high percentage of Filipinos (38 percent) than Koreans (20 percent) or Vietnamese (21 percent) prefer to spend the rest of their lives back in their home country.

The zero-order bivariate relationships between political integration and the three sets of predictors are reported as r (Pearson correlation coefficients) in the last column of tables 3.6b to 3.6d. In all three groups, the strongest correlation coefficients are length of time and percent of life spent in the United States, followed by acculturation for Koreans and Filipinos, and income for the Vietnamese. For all three groups, sense of group deprivation and age are among the smallest of all coefficients. Based on bivariate observations, socioeconomic factors correlate most strongly with the Vietnamese and most weakly with Filipino respondents. The sizes of coefficients for demographic variables are almost identical across the three groups, whereas the sizes of sociopsychological variables are far

**Table 3.6b  Multiple Regression Estimations of the Political Adaptation of Koreans in Los Angeles (1992) (N=549)**

| Models | I | II | III | B | r |
|---|---|---|---|---|---|
| (1) Socioeconomic education | .06* | .05* | .04% | .07 | .23*** |
| | (.03) | (.03) | (.02) | | |
| Income | .10*** | .04 | .03 | .06 | .28*** |
| | (.03) | (.02) | (.02) | | |
| Employed | .16 | .18* | .07 | .03 | .16*** |
| | (.10) | (.09) | (.09) | | |
| U.S. education | .57*** | .06 | −.07 | −.03 | .29*** |
| | (.10) | (.10) | (.10) | | |
| (2) Demographic Length of stay | | .26*** | .23*** | .25 | .59*** |
| | | (.06) | (.06) | | |
| Age | | .06 | .08* | .09 | .02 |
| | | (.04) | (.04) | | |
| % Political life in U.S. | | 1.88*** | 1.75*** | .32 | .59*** |
| | | (.36) | (.36) | | |
| Male | | .09 | .18* | .08 | .12*** |
| | | (.08) | (.08) | | |
| (3) Socio-psychological Acculturation | | | .14* | .11 | .41*** |
| | | | (.06) | | |
| Crossracial friendship | | | −.02 | −.01 | .21*** |
| | | | (.09) | | |
| Support intermarriage | | | .25*** | .17 | .18*** |
| | | | (.05) | | |
| Personal discrimination | | | −.02 | −.01 | .07* |
| | | | (.05) | | |
| Group deprivation | | | −.06 | −.01 | .06 |
| | | | (.14) | | |
| Ethnic neighborhood | | | .06 | .01 | −.17*** |
| | | | (.11) | | |
| Attachment to homeland | | | −.27** | −.10 | −.26*** |
| | | | (.09) | | |
| Constant | .07 | −1.01 | −1.33 | | |
| | (.17) | (.19) | (.26) | | |
| Adjusted R2 | .15 | .42 | .46 | | |
| F | 24.46 | 51.21 | 32.64 | | |

*Note:* The dependent variable is scored 3 if respondent is registered to vote. It is scored 2 if respondent is naturalized but not registered. It is scored 1 if respondent is not naturalized but expects to become one in the next few years.

Numerical entries are unstandardized regression coefficients except where noted. Standard errors are in parentheses. B=standardized regression coefficient. r = Pearson correlation coefficient. .+p. 10 * p. 05 ** p. 01 *** p. 001.

*Source: Los Angeles Times* Polls #267, #331, and #370.

**Table 3.6c    Multiple Regression Estimations of the Political Adaptation of Vietnamese in Southern California (1994) (N=645)**

| Models | I | II | III | B | r |
|---|---|---|---|---|---|
| **(1) Socioeconomic** | | | | | |
| Education | .08*** | .07*** | .05** | .11 | .39*** |
| | (.02) | (.02) | (.02) | | |
| Income | .19*** | .09*** | .09*** | .17 | .48*** |
| | (.02) | (.02) | (.02) | | |
| Employed | .12+ | .05 | .02 | .01 | .29*** |
| | (.07) | (.07) | (.07) | | |
| **(2) Demographic** | | | | | |
| Length of stay | | .43*** | .44*** | .57 | .60*** |
| | | (.06) | (.06) | | |
| Age | | −.02 | −.00 | −.01 | .02 |
| | | (.04) | (.04) | | |
| % Political life in U.S. | | −.31 | −.49 | −.11 | .51*** |
| | | (.34) | (.35) | | |
| Male | | −.03 | −.04 | −.02 | .14*** |
| | | (.06) | (.06) | | |
| **(3) Socio-psychological** | | | | | |
| Acculturation | | | .13* | .10 | .39*** |
| | | | (.06) | | |
| Crossracial friendship | | | −.02 | −.01 | .19*** |
| | | | (.07) | | |
| Support intermarriage | | | .08* | .05 | .14*** |
| | | | (.03) | | |
| Personal discrimination | | | .02 | .02 | .19*** |
| | | | (.04) | | |
| Group deprivation | | | −.10 | −.04 | .05 |
| | | | (.08) | | |
| Ethnic neighborhood | | | −.04 | −.01 | −.08* |
| | | | (.08) | | |
| Attachment to homeland | | | −.05 | −.02 | −.05 |
| | | | (.07) | | |
| Constant | .73 | −.20 | −.48 | | |
| | (.08) | (.11) | (.17) | | |
| Adjusted R2 | .24 | .44 | .45 | | |
| F | 70.49 | 74.51 | 38.97 | | |

*Note:* The dependent variable is scored 3 if respondent is registered to vote. It is scored 2 if respondent is naturalized but not registered. It is scored 1 if respondent is not naturalized but expects to become one in the next few years.

Numerical entries are unstandardized regression coefficients except where noted. Standard errors are in parentheses. B=standardized regression coefficient. r = Pearson correlation coefficient.

.+p. 10 * p. 05 ** p. 01 *** p. 001.

*Source: Los Angeles Times* Polls #267, #331, and #370.

**Table 3.6d  Multiple Regression Estimations of the Political Adaptation of Filipinos in Southern California, (1995) (N=594)**

| Models | I | II | III | B | r |
|---|---|---|---|---|---|
| (1) Socioeconomic | | | | | |
| Education | .00 | .03 | .02 | .03 | .07* |
| | (.03) | (.03) | (.03) | | |
| Income | .10*** | .00 | .00 | .00 | .20*** |
| | (.02) | (.02) | (.02) | | |
| Employed | .05 | .18* | .18* | .07 | .05 |
| | (.10) | (.08) | (.08) | | |
| (2) Demographic | | | | | |
| Length of stay | | .31*** | .30*** | .46 | .62*** |
| | | (.05) | (.06) | | |
| Age | | .04 | .05 | .05 | .06 |
| | | (.04) | (.04) | | |
| % Political life in U.S. | | .81* | .81* | .25 | .50*** |
| | | (.35) | (.37) | | |
| Foreign-born | | .40** | .40** | .16 | −.23*** |
| | | (.15) | (.15) | | |
| Male | | .10 | .10% | .05 | .13*** |
| | | (.06) | (.06) | | |
| 3) Socio-psychological | | | | | |
| Acculturation | | | −.03 | −.02 | .28*** |
| | | | (.08) | | |
| Crossracial friendship | | | .15* | .06 | .19*** |
| | | | (.08) | | |
| Support intermarriage | | | .01 | .03 | .07* |
| | | | (.04) | | |
| Personal discrimination | | | .06 | .05 | .15*** |
| | | | (.04) | | |
| Group deprivation | | | .21% | .05 | .06 |
| | | | (.13) | | |
| Ethnic neighborhood | | | −.01 | −.00 | −.06 |
| | | | (.10) | | |
| Attachment to homeland | | | −.08 | −.03 | −.26*** |
| | | | (.08) | | |
| Constant | 1.63 | −.32 | −.38 | | |
| | (.21) | (.25) | (.35) | | |
| Adjusted R2 | .03 | .40 | .40 | | |
| F | 6.47 | 49.76 | 27.43 | | |

Note: The dependent variable is scored 3 if respondent is registered to vote. It is scored 2 if respondent is naturalized but not registered. It is scored 1 if respondent is not naturalized but expects to become one in the next few years.

Numerical entries are unstandardized regression coefficients except where noted. Standard errors are in parentheses. B=standardized regression coefficient. r = Pearson correlation coefficient.
.+ρ. 10 * ρ. 05 ** ρ. 01 *** ρ. 001.

Source: *Los Angeles Times* Polls #267, #331, and #370.

from unanimous. For instance, for the Vietnamese, the anticipation to return to their homeland in the near future has little to do with the extent of integration; it correlates negatively with integration in the two other groups. For Koreans, residing in an ethnic neighborhood is associated with less integration; it has little do with integration for respondents in the two other groups. In contrast, the experience of personal discrimination correlates fairly strongly with integration, except for Koreans. The direct relationship between support of outmarriage and political integration is also fairly strong, except for Filipinos.

The independent contribution of each of the three sets of predictors is tested in multivariate models. As shown in column Is of tables 3.6b to 3.6d, socioeconomic factors are able to explain 24 percent of all the variations in political adaptation among the Vietnamese, but only 3 percent among Filipinos. When demographic variables are added (columns IIs of tables 3.6b to 3.6d), the explanatory power of the Filipino model jumps to 40 percent. The explanatory power of the Korean and Vietnamese models also increases significantly, but in smaller steps. In the Korean model, percentage of political life replaces U.S. education as the most important predictors. In the Filipino model, employment status replaces income as the only socioeconomic indictor to impact integration. Among the Vietnamese, the importance of education and income is reduced but not replaced by demographic variables.

When sociopsychological variables are taken into consideration, results in all the column IIIs of tables 3.6b to 3.6d seem to indicate that they add little to the explanatory power of the models. Length of stay remains robust and is the most important variable to predict political integration for the Vietnamese and Filipinos. For Koreans, this variable is not as important as having spent a greater share of one's life in the United States and holding supportive attitude toward intermarriage. For them, the yearning to return to Korea may interfere with the integration process; whereas

being male, more acculturated in English language, and older may be associated with greater adaptation. For the Vietnamese, neither percentage of life nor age is useful to predict integration; but having more income and education are. Yet, like Koreans, their integration can also be increased by more acculturation and support for intermarriage. For Filipinos, all the time-related demographic indicators except age tend to affect the propensity of political integration. Namely, other conditions being equal, a Filipino is more likely to become a registered voter if he or she is foreign-born and stayed longer years in the United States and spent a greater share of his or her life in the United States. However, among the socioeconomic and sociopsychological variables, only being employed and having close friends who are of other races can be associated with greater adaptation.

Several patterns seem to emerge from the preceding discussion. Filipino political integration is best predicted by demographic variables. Vietnamese integration is mostly influenced by length of stay but also by socioeconomic status. Demographic variables are strong predictors, too, of Korean integration, but indicators of sociopsychological attitudes shaping ethnic group identity play a more important role for Koreans than for other groups studied here. Because of intergroup differences in immigration history, group resources, and societal contexts, the only common variable to predict political adaptation for all three groups is length of time, even though it is second to percentage of lifetime in the Korean sample. However, equally important are the null findings of variables that are to index the not-so-positive side of the adaptation experience such as group deprivation, personal discrimination, and residential segregation. None of these variables appear to hamper integration in any of the groups. For both the Vietnamese and Filipinos, attachment to homeland does not interfere with integration when other variables are controlled. Yet, other factors being equal, those Filipinos who feel their group benefits have been unfairly deprived are marginally more likely to have greater integration scores.

## CONCLUSION

Taken as a whole, each group provides some support for the hypothesis derived from past findings that greater political integration is associated with longer time spent in the United States, male sex, higher socioeconomic status, greater acculturation, and greater social structural integration; that it may not be affected by the sense of group consciousness; and that it may be negatively associated with residual attachment to the homeland. However, there are many between-group differences. For instance, both education and income are important predictors only among the Vietnamese, whereas being employed is significant only among Filipinos. Longer years of stay is vital to predict integration for all, but it is second in importance to the percentage of lifetime spent in the United States among Koreans. Age and gender are not significant variables except among Koreans. Acculturation and support for interracial marriage are significant predictors, but not among Filipinos. Lastly, attachment to homeland may discourage integration, but this does not apply to Filipinos and the Vietnamese.

These results indicate that adaptation models developed from observing behaviors of either one Asian ethnic group or the pan-Asian group may be limited in its generalizability to a multiple number of Asian ethnic groups in the 1990s. This finding should come as no surprise given the divergent forces originated either in or outside of the United States that have mitigated the opportunities and development of Asian immigration and adaptation for each of the groups examined. However, they also indicate that certain variables such as length of stay, percentage of life spent in the United States, and indicators of group consciousness have more universal implications than other variables, which have greater usefulness in making biethnic rather than multiethnic predictions.

Combining both multivariate findings with bivariate observations reported earlier, it appears that the greater integration of the Filipino community is advantaged by demographic variables; the integration of the Vietnamese is disadvantaged by their lower socioeconomic status; and the low political integration scores among Koreans prior to the L.A. riots can be attributed to both demographic and sociopsychological factors. Given the volatile nature of the racial and ethnic politics in Southern California in the 1990s, future studies need to collect multigroup data within a single time frame and amended with other elements of a sound research design to facilitate comparison of the effect of ethnicity on political adaptation.

## NOTES

1. Provisions in the welfare reform laws passed by the 104th Congress in 1996 were to strip legal permanent residents of Medicaid and other social security benefits unless they are refugees, asylum seekers, parolees, veterans, and members of the armed services and their families, persons for whom deportation is being withheld, or permanent residents with forty quarters of covered work under the Social Security Act.

2. Important exceptions to this set of rules, such as reducing or waiving residency requirements to spouses of U.S. citizens, spouses of certain U.S. citizens stationed abroad, children adopted by U.S. citizens, or military personnel serving in the U.S. armed forces, may be particularly beneficial to expedite the naturalization process for certain groups of immigrants.

3. Although Asians are a designated minority that is protected by the foreign-language provision of the 1975 Voting Rights Amendment, which requires the printing of foreign language ballots and related materials if 5 percent of the population uses the language, the law is more discriminatory to Asians because of the multilingual and residentially dispersed characteristics of the population. A recent change of criterion to 10,000 people in a jurisdiction is expected to alleviate some of the problems.

4. This figure might reflect a gross undercount due to sampling bias, misclassification,

and the systematic omission of certain persons of Korean origin (Yu 1977).

5. The exceptions are the college education rate and per capita income in San Diego County. The concentration of low-ranking navy families in the area may provide some explanations (Espiritu 1995).

6. The three variables for *acculturation* are: "How well do you speak English: very well, or just well, or not well, or not at all?"; "In your everyday life, do you speak (Korean, Vietnamese, Tagalog) exclusively, mostly, (Korean, Vietnamese, Tagalog) and English equally, mostly English or do you speak English exclusively?"; "Are the periodicals you read and the broadcasts you listen to exclusively (Korean, Vietnamese, Tagalog), mostly, about half- (Korean, Vietnamese, Tagalog) and half English, or mostly English or English exclusively?" The interitem alpha for Koreans is .83, for Vietnamese .77, and for Filipinos .61.

7. Exact question wording and coding schemes are: *Cross-racial friendship* "Are any of your friends white, or black, or Latino or non- (Korean, Vietnamese, Filipino) Asian or what?" 1 = have nonethnic friends, 0 = otherwise; *Ethnic Neighborhood* "How would you describe the racial and ethnic makeup of the neighborhood where you live? Would you say it is mostly white, or mostly black, or mostly Latino, or mostly (Korean, Vietnamese, Filipino), or is it mostly non-(Korean, Vietnamese, Filipino) Asian, or is it mostly some other ethnic/racial group, or would you say the racial and/or ethnic makeup is pretty evenly mixed?" 1 = neighbors are mostly coethnics, 0 = otherwise; *Support Intermarriage* "Would you approve or disapprove if someone in your family married a person of a different racial or ethnic background than yours?" 2 = approve strongly, 1 = approve somewhat.

8. This is a surrogate measure of marriage assimilation for recent immigrants, for almost all of the respondents reported marrying a coethnic, probably before they departed their homeland.

9. Exact question wording and coding schemes are: *Personal Discrimination* "Because you are (Korean, Vietnamese, Filipino), have you personally been discriminated against a great deal, a fair amount, some but not much, or practically not at all during the time you've lived in Southern California?" 4 = a great deal, 3 = a fair amount, 2 = some, 1 = not at all; *Group Deprivation* (for Koreans) "How would you rate the situation for Koreans relative to other minorities in Southern California such as blacks and Latinos: do you think Koreans are generally better off, or are they worse off or are they in just about the same situation as other minorities?" 1 = group condition worse off, 0 = otherwise; (for the Vietnamese and Filipinos) "Thinking of the (Vietnamese, Filipinos) who live in Southern California and their ability to get adequate housing, and education, and job opportunities and social acceptance by whites, and things like that, generally speaking, do you think conditions for (the Vietnamese, Filipinos) in Southern California are very good, or good, or bad, or very bad?" 2 = group condition very bad, 1 = group condition bad.

10. Exact question wording and coding schemes for *Attachment to Homeland* is: (for Koreans) "Generally speaking, where do you expect you and your children will end up living in the years to come: in Korea, in California, somewhere in the United States other than California or elsewhere?" 1 = Korea, 0 = otherwise; (for the Vietnamese) "Now that the trade embargo is lifted, what are the chances that you will move to Vietnam to live permanently in the next few years? Is that very likely, somewhat likely, somewhat unlikely or very unlikely? 1 = very or somewhat likely, 0 = otherwise; (for Filipinos) "All things considered, if you had to choose, where would you prefer to live for the rest of your life—in the United States, or in the Philippines?" 1 = prefer Philippines, 0 = otherwise.

11. Three measures of the effects of time—age, length of stay, and percentage of life in the United States (length/age)—are proposed here to take into consideration the complex situation of foreign-borns whose life experiences transgress national borders (space). An additional variable—nativity—is included in the Filipino models where a significant number of respondents were not foreign-born.

## REFERENCES

Daniels, Roger. 1990. *Coming to America.* New York: HarperCollins.

DeWind, Josh, and Philip Kasinitz.1997. "Everything Old Is New Again? Processes and Theories of Immigrant Incorporation." *International Migration Review* 31: 1096–1111.

Eljera, Bert. "Battling the Bureaucracy." 1997. *Asianweek*, February 28.

Espiritu, Yen L. 1992. *Asian American Panethnicity*. Philadelphia: Temple University Press.

———. ed. 1995. *Filipino American Lives*. Philadelphia: Temple University Press, 1995.

Feagin, Joe, and Clairece Feagin. 1993. *Racial and Ethnic Relations*. 4th ed. Englewood Cliffs, N.J.: Prentice-Hall.

Gordon, Milton M. 1964. *Assimilation in America Life*. New York: Oxford University Press,.

Haines, David. 1989. *Refugees as Immigrants: Cambodians, Laotians, and Vietnamese in America*. Totowa, N.J.: Rowman & Littlefield.

———. 1996. "Patterns in Refugee Resettlement and Adaptation." In *Refugees in America in the 1990s*, 28–59. Westport, Conn.: Greenwood.

Hein, Jeremy. 1995. *From Vietnam, Laos, and Cambodia: A Refugee Experience in the United States*. New York: Twayne.

Hing, Bill Ong. 1993. *Making and Remaking Asian America through Immigration Policy, 1850–1990*. Stanford, Calif.: Stanford University Press.

Hurh, Won M. 1980. "Towards a Korean-American Ethnicity: Some Theoretical Models." *Ethnic and Racial Studies* 3: 444–64.

Hurh, Won M., and Kwang C. Kim. 1984a. *Korean Immigrants in America: A Structural Analysis of Ethnic Confinement and Adhesive Adaptation*. Madison, N.J.: Farleigh Dickinson University Press.

——— 1984b. "Adhesive Sociocultural Adaptation of Korean Immigrants in the U.S.: An Alternative Strategy of Minority Adaptation." *International Migration Review* 18: 188–217.

Jasso, Guillermina, and Mark R. Rosenzweig. 1990. *The New Chosen People: Immigrants in the United States*. New York: Russell Sage Foundation.

Jiobu, Robert M. *Ethnicity and Assimilation*. 1988. New York: State University of New York Press.

Kim, Illsoo. 1981. *New Urban Immigrants: The Korean Community in New York*. Princeton: Princeton University Press.

Kim, Kwang Chung, and Won Moo Hurh. 1993. "Beyond Assimilation and Pluralism: Syncretic Sociocultural Adaptation of Korean Immigrants in the U.S." *Ethnic and Racial Studies* 16: 696–713.

Kim, Young Y. 1989. "Personal, Social, and Economic Adaptation: 1975–1979 Arrivals in Illinois." In David Haines, ed., *Refugees as Immigrants*, 86–104. Totowa, N.J.: Rowman & Littlefield.

Kitano, Harry L., and Roger Daniels. 1995. *Asian-Americans: Emerging Minorities*. 2d ed. Englewood Cliffs, N.J.: Prentice-Hall.

Lien, Pei-te. 1994. "Ethnicity and Political Participation: A Comparison between Asian and Mexican Americans." *Political Behavior* 16: 237–64.

———. 1997. *The Political Participation of Asian Americans: Voting Behavior in Southern California*. New York: Garland.

Light, Ivan, and Edna Bonacich. 1988. *Immigrant Entrepreneurs: Koreans in Los Angeles, 1965–1982*. Berkeley: University of California Press.

Liu, John, and Lucie Cheng. 1994. "Pacific Rim Development and the Duality of Post-1965 Asian Immigration to the United States." In Paul Ong, Edna Bonacich, and Lucie Cheng, eds., *The New Asian Immigration in Los Angeles and Global Restructuring*, 74–99. Philadelphia: Temple University Press.

Melendy, H. Brett. 1977. *Asians in America: Filipinos, Koreans, and East Indians*. New York: Twayne.

Min, Pyong Gap. 1987. "Filipino and Korean Immigrants in Small Business: A Comparative Analysis." *Amerasia* 13(1): 53–71.

———. 1996. "The Entrepreneurial Adaptation of Korean Immigrants." In Silvia Pedraza and Ruben Rumbaut, eds., *Origins and Destinies: Immigration, Race, and Ethnicity in America*, 302–14. Belmont, Calif.: Wadsworth.

Ong, Paul, Edna Bonacich, and Lucie Cheng, eds. 1994. *The New Asian Immigration in Los Angeles and Global Restructuring*. Philadelphia: Temple University Press.

Padilla, Felix M. 1985. "On the Nature of Latino Ethnicity." In Rodolfo de la Garza et al., eds., *The Mexican-American Experience*, 332–45. Austin: University of Texas Press.

Portes, Alejandro, and Robert Bach. 1985. *Latin Journey: Cuban and Mexican Immigrants in* the United States. Berkeley: University of California Press.

Portes, Alejandro, and Min Zhou. 1993. "The New Second Generation: Segmented Assimilation and Its Variants." *Annals of the American Academy of Political and Social Sciences* 530: 74–96.

Reimers, David M. 1992. *Still the Golden Door: The Third World Comes to America.* 2d ed. New York: Columbia University Press.

Routledge, Paul James. 1992. *The Vietnamese Experience in America.* Bloomington: Indiana University Press.

Rumbaut, Ruben. 1996. "A Legacy of War: Refugees from Vietnam, Laos, and Cambodia." In Silvia Pedraza and Ruben Rumbaut, eds., *Origins and Destinies: Immigration, Race, and Ethnicity in America*, 319–33. Belmont, Calif.: Wadsworth.

———. 1997. "Assimilation and Its Discontents: Between Rhetoric and Reality." *International Migration Review* 31: 923–60.

Williams, J. Allen, Jr., and Suzanne Ortega. 1990. "Dimensions of Ethnic Assimilation: An Empirical Appraisal of Gordon's Typology." *Social Science Quarterly* 71: 697–710.

# 3.7

# Gender and Political Involvement among Chinese Americans in Southern California

*Janelle S. Wong*

〰〰〰〰〰〰〰〰〰〰〰〰〰〰〰〰〰〰〰〰〰〰〰〰

Traditional research on the relationship between gender and involvement in the political system has focused almost exclusively on Anglo whites. However, researchers have recently begun to examine the ways in which gender affects the political participation of non-Anglo white groups (Welch and Sigelman 1989, 1991; Montoya 1996; Hardy Fanta 1993; Jones-Correa 1998; Jennings 1993; Montoya, Hardy-Fanta, Garcia 2000), including Asian Americans (Lien 1998a; Shah 1997; Chow 1989; Chu 1989; Junn 1997; Lien 2001). This quantitative case study of the predictors of political participation among Chinese Americans in Southern California attempts to build on this growing body of research.[1]

This analysis has two goals. The first is to compare rates of participation *between* Chinese American women and men. The second is to explore the predictors of participation *among* Chinese American women and *among* Chinese American men. I examine three important aspects of involvement in the political system among Chinese American women and men, including gen-

eral activity in American politics, involvement in ethnic community organizations, and participation through campaign contributions.

## GENDER AND POLITICAL INVOLVEMENT AMONG ASIAN AMERICANS: IS THERE A GENDER GAP?

Until recently, the general literature on gender and political involvement focused, explicitly or implicitly, on Anglo whites. Most early studies of gender and active political participation suggested that women were less politically active than men (Anderson 1975; Welch 1977; Clark and Clark 1986). Today, differences in participation between women and men depend on type of political activity. Since 1980, the proportion of eligible female adults who have turned out to vote has surpassed the proportion of eligible men who have turned out to vote (Center for American Women and Politics 2000). In terms of other types of activities, such as making a campaign contribution, contacting an elected official, or affiliating with a political organization, women tend to be slightly less participatory

Wong, Janelle S. "Gender and Political Involvement among Chinese Americans in Southern California." Unpublished article.

than men (Verba, Schlozman, and Brady 1995, 254). It is important to recognize that many studies focus on involvement in the formal political system and thus define "political activity" in a way that excludes consideration of women's long history of organizational and grassroots participation in public, and especially local community, life (Randall 1987; Cott 1990). However, Verba et al. find that, contrary to what might be expected, women tend to participate less than men in "more informal, ad hoc activities such as working with others in the community or getting involved in a political organization" (p. 256).

In the last few years, researchers have made a meaningful effort to explore the relationship between gender, political attitudes, and participation among minority groups, including Asian Americans. Pei-te Lien (2001; 1998a, 1998b, 1997, 1994), for example, is the author of several pioneering studies that consider the role of gender in shaping Asian American political participation. Her analysis of data from the Current Population Survey, for instance, suggests that among adult citizens, Asian American women tend to be as likely to register and vote as Asian men (Lien 2001). She finds that gender is not a significant predictor of registration or voting rates (Lien 1998a).[2] Similarly, Lien (1997) finds little relationship between gender and likelihood of participation in an analysis of a 1993 *Los Angeles Times* poll that focused on Asian Americans in Southern California. These findings are also consistent with her analysis of political participation (including voting and nonvoting activities, such as working in a community organization or attending a rally, meeting, or fundraising event) among Asian Americans who took part in a 1984 survey conducted in California (Lien 1994). In sum, the available data suggests that while Asian Americans, as a group, tend to lag behind whites and blacks in terms of political participation (Lien 1997, Ong and Nakanishi 1996; Junn 1997; Nakanishi 1991), Asian American women and men become involved in politics in the United States (electoral and

nonelectoral, formal and informal community politics) at similar rates.

## PREDICTORS OF POLITICAL PARTICIPATION

Recent research, cited above, finds little evidence of a "participation gender gap" between Asian American women and men. However, lack of a gender gap in participation does not necessarily mean that Asian American women and men participate in American politics for the same reasons. The primary purpose of this chapter is to explore whether the predictors of political participation are the same for women and men. Do the same hypotheses explain participation among women and men? I concentrate on the case of Chinese Americans in Southern California to begin this line of research. The main hypotheses I explore have to do with the gendered nature of migration, labor participation, and race relations. What is the connection between these gendered processes and political involvement?

### Gender and Migration among Chinese Americans

Historical research shows that migration patterns have been quite gendered among Chinese Americans. Many scholars have noted that most of the first century of Chinese migration to the United States was marked by the dominance of male migrants (Chan 1991; Takaki 1989; Yung 1986). Espiritu (1997) argues that the major reasons for this gendered migration flow were labor-recruiting patterns and legal restrictions that limited the migration of Chinese women. She and others (Takaki 1989, 39) point out that employers in the United States avoided the costs of providing housing and basic needs to the families of workers by excluding women from the recruitment process. Employers also excluded women because they believed that men were better able to endure harsh labor conditions and would constitute a more mobile workforce. In addition, Espiritu (1997) notes that American immigration laws were directed at discouraging Chinese women from migrating to the United States. For instance, in 1875 Congress passed a law that banned "prostitutes" from China and other Asian countries from entering the country. Because U.S. immigration officials suspected the majority of Chinese women of being prostitutes, this law sharply limited the number of Chinese women who were able to enter the county. As a result, in 1890, Chinese women were just 3.6 percent of the total number of Chinese immigrants in the United States (Espiritu 1997, 18).

During and after World War II, the number of Chinese immigrant women in the United States began to increase after exclusionary laws were overturned and new economic opportunities became available. Chan (1991) maintains that in the postwar years, an increasing percentage of Chinese immigrants to the United States were female. The trend continues in the contemporary period. In the 1990s, about 70 percent of the Chinese American population in the United States consisted of immigrants and 51 percent of immigrants from China were female, compared to 49 percent of the U.S.-born Chinese American population (Jiobu 1996, 55).[3] Thus, Chinese women represent the majority of the current immigration flow. Most Chinese immigrant women in the United States were granted visas aimed at family reunification.

Because immigrants make up a large proportion of the Chinese American population in the United States, in this chapter I explore immigrant status and factors related to immigrant adaptation to the United States as possible predictors of political participation among Chinese American women and men. For example, I examine whether immigrant status, English language skills, and length of residence affect the participation of Chinese American women and Chinese American men.

Although U.S. laws and other factors have shaped Chinese women's and men's immigration experiences in different ways, my first hypothesis is that because they are likely to be less familiar with the American political system, both Chinese American immigrant women and immigrant men will tend to participate less in American politics than those who are U.S.-born. Similarly, I suspect that because the majority of information about U.S. politics is channeled through the English media, those who are not comfortable speaking English will be less involved in the political system. It is likely, for instance, that those who do not feel comfortable speaking English may also feel less informed about U.S. politics. Therefore, they may be reluctant to participate in a system they do not feel they understand well. Finally, based on previous research (Wong 1998; Ong and Nakanishi 1996), I believe there will be a strong relationship between length of residence and political participation. Over time, immigrants are likely to gain experience with the political system. As a result of this exposure and adaptation to U.S. life, I hypothesize that they will feel more comfortable participating in American politics.

## Labor and Gender Relations

Many Chinese immigrant women come to the United States as family members of permanent residents or American citizens. They also arrive as workers. Fifty-nine percent of Chinese American women were in the labor force in 1990, compared to just 44 percent in 1960 (Amott and Matthaei 1996, 214). In terms of occupational stratification, Amott and Matthaei's (1996) data show that nearly one-third of Chinese American women held a managerial, administrative, or professional position in 1990. About 20 percent of Chinese American women were employed in clerical positions in 1990. It is important to recognize, though, that Chinese American women continue to face gender inequalities in earnings from employment. For example, in 1990 the median earnings for full-time Chinese American women workers was $23,277 compared to $31,746 for Chinese

American men (Amott and Matthaei 1996).[4]

Despite the relatively high concentration of Chinese American women in professional occupations, over one-third of Chinese American women, especially immigrant women who possess few marketable skills, remain trapped in labor-intensive industries at the bottom of the labor market hierarchy. For example, Kwong (1997) claims that Chinese women who have poor language or other marketable skills are likely to find work in the garment industry. He also claims that in New York's Chinatown there were approximately 500 garment factories employing 20,000 Chinese women in 1996 (p. 26). Low wages and harsh working conditions characterize employment in the factories. However, Kwong (1997) identifies the garment factory as a potential site of political resistance and activism. For example, Chinese American women working in the garment factories have organized for fair labor contracts through demonstration and mobilization of workers. Others make similar observations. For example, Louie (1997) notes recent efforts by Asian Immigrant Women Advocates (AIWA), a community based group in California, to organize "immigrant women working in the garment, electronics, hotel, restaurant, nursing home, janitorial, and other low-wage industries in the San Francisco Bay Area and Santa Clara County's 'Silicon Valley'" (p. 128).

Amott and Matthaei (1996) report that 64 percent of married Chinese American women participate in the labor force (p. 214). Some researchers suggest that wage work may allow women more economic independence and increase their status within the family (Kibria 1993; Hondagneu-Sotelo 1994; Grasmuck and Pessar 1991). It is likely that Chinese American women may be experiencing increasing economic independence. Despite their economic independence, however, Chinese American women may still find themselves limited by a patriarchal structure within the home (Espiritu 1997; Amott and Matthaei 1996; Chen 1992). In a study of 100 Chinese households in Queens, New York, Chen (1992) suggests that in working-class and self-employed households, women perform the great majority of household work. Among those in the professional class, "women still do most of the housework but men help slightly more than do the men in the other two classes" (p. 77). Thus, though employment outside the home may allow Chinese American women to challenge traditional patriarchal hierarchies because the family relies on their wage earnings, the division of labor between men and women within the household is likely to remain unequal and privilege Chinese American men.

This chapter focuses on the ways in which employment outside of the home affects political participation in the United States among Chinese Americans. In particular, the literature suggests two competing hypotheses about the effects of employment outside of the home on Chinese American women's involvement in the political system. The first, based on studies that find that the workplace can be a site of resistance and activism (Kwong 1997), is that those women employed outside of the home will be more politicized than those who are not wage workers. That is, women who are employed outside of the home will be more involved in the political system. The second hypothesis suggests that because Chinese American women who are employed outside of the home continue to carry the burden of household work, they will have less time to devote to political activities than those who are not employed outside of the home. In this case, one would expect Chinese American women employed outside of the home to be less involved in the political system than those who do not perform employed work outside of the home.

In addition to employment, I examine the ways in which being married and having children under seventeen affect the political participation of Chinese American women and men. Being married or having children living at home may depress political participation among Chinese American women because unequal household responsibilities may leave Chinese American women with less time to participate. On the other hand, some researchers have hypothesized that when people have children, they become more involved in politics. For example, those with children may become more involved with school board politics than those who do not have children (Niemi et al. 1985, 301). Some existing data on Asian Americans who seek elected office seem to contradict this hypothesis. For instance, Judy Chu (1989) reports that in 1985 less than 1 percent (p. 48) of the approximately 7,000 school board seats in California were occupied by Asian American women (p. 409). She also finds that in areas that were "heavily impacted by Asian American students," like the Alhambra School District, which included a student population that was over 45 percent Asian American, no school board members were Asian American. In addition, Chu (1989) suggests that Asian American women who become involved in the U.S. political system by seeking office often face major demands on their time with family. One former school board member she interviewed claimed that she would not run for office for a third term because "her sons were entering their adolescence, a period she feels requires more attention" (p. 419). Again, the gendered nature of reproductive work within the home is likely to have a great impact on both women's labor outside of the home and their ability to participate in U.S. politics.

## Gender and Race

Scholars have made important theoretical contributions to the ways in which race and gender (and class and heterosexism) operate simultaneously to structure social, economic, and racial systems in the United States (Crenshaw 1989; Collins 1990; Leong 1996; Aguilar-San Juan 1997; Espiritu 1997). Aguilar-San Juan (1997), for example, contends that "although in theory we can isolate one dimension of social life (the experience of being female) from another

(the experience of being Asian American), in fact such a one-dimensional moment never exists" (p. xi). Espiritu (1997) advances the idea that "as categories of difference, race and gender relations do not parallel but intersect and confirm each other" (p. 12).

Chinese American women and men are likely to experience race in the United States in qualitatively different ways. For example, racial stereotypes of Asian Americans, including Chinese Americans, are gendered in the U.S. Espiritu (1997) posits that "the contemporary model-minority stereotype further emasculates Asian American men as passive and malleable" (p. 91). This stereotype, she claims, is often used to justify the social and economic discrimination Asian American men contend with in their everyday lives. In contrast to the asexual stereotypes of Asian American men, Asian American women are often stereotyped as hypersexual exotics (the aggressive prostitute) and/or submissive and obedient. Lu (1997) writes that "in media-driven U.S. culture, representations of Asian women play a significant role in both reflecting and shaping our status, our self-image, and our potential" (p. 18). Furthermore, Espiritu (1997) argues that stereotypes of Asian American women hinder their economic mobility and may lead to sexual exploitation and abuse.

In this chapter I examine how the convergence of race and gender may affect political participation among Chinese Americans. How do the ways that Chinese American women and men experience race affect their political involvement? In particular, I investigate whether personal experience with discrimination helps explain the political participation of Chinese American women and Chinese American men. Two hypotheses are tested. The first is that experiences with discrimination will lead to more participation because individuals will seek to challenge racial inequality through political activism. This hypothesis suggests that racial discrimination is interpreted as a "political problem" among Chinese Americans. The second hypothesis is that those who experience discrimination will feel alienated from American life, including American politics. In this case, we might expect those who experience discrimination to participate less in the political process because they do not feel like they are an important part of the political system.

I also examine whether men and women who are part of racially integrated social networks tend to become more involved in American politics than those whose social networks consist only of coethnics. Whites and blacks are more likely to participate in U.S. politics than Asian Americans (Lien 1997). In some cases Asian Americans' participation also lags behind that of Latinos (Junn 1997). Because non-Asians tend to be more involved in the political system than Asians, non-Asians may represent important sources of information about opportunities for Chinese Americans to become more involved in politics. I hypothesize that those Chinese Americans who have more contact with members of ethnic or racial groups that tend to be more involved in American politics will be more likely to participate than those who do but are not part of racially integrated social networks.

## DATA AND METHODS

The data for this study come from a 1997 *Los Angeles Times* (LAT) poll. Telephone interviews were conducted with 773 adult Chinese residents of six counties in Southern California (Los Angeles, Ventura, San Bernadino, Orange, Riverside, and San Diego). The languages used were Mandarin, Cantonese, and English. Telephone numbers were generated from a list of Chinese surnames from telephone directories in the Southern California counties. These data are limited in some critical respects. First, the pool of potential respondents included only those who could be identified as Chinese by surname and listed their numbers in the directories. Second, as with all telephone surveys, only those households with telephones could be contacted. For these reasons, the LAT survey is not necessarily representative of Chinese Americans in Southern California and certainly not representative of Chinese Americans in the United States as a whole. Despite these critical limitations, the LAT survey represents one of the only attempts to interview a large sample of Asian Americans on their political attitudes and participation. It is also one of the few surveys that is available to the public for secondary analysis. Descriptive statistics of the sample are shown in table 3.7a. Weighted and unweighted frequencies are included.

## Model Specification

Three measures of political participation are used in this study (see box 3.7a for exact question wording). They include self-reported activity in American politics (general involvement in the American political system), activity in Chinese cultural or community organizations (local or ethnic political involvement), and campaign contributions (nonvoting participation).[5] Though the survey included measures of vote registration and party identification, the number of respondents who answered these questions was too small to permit in-depth analysis.

Based on the literature reviewed above, I include immigration-related factors, indicators of employment status and family structure, and measures of experiences with racial discrimination and interracial social relationships as independent variables. Socioeconomic status was also taken into consideration.

The first step in this analysis was to compare rates of participation among Asian American women and men. The next step was to perform separate analyses of the male and female samples in order to assess the predictors of political participation among each of the two groups. Multivariate regression was used to conduct the analysis. The basic model used in the analysis was:

**Table 3.7a    Chinese American Men and Women in Southern California**

| | Descriptive Statistics | | | |
|---|---|---|---|---|
| | Men 371 | | Women 402 | |
| N | | | | |
| | *weighted* | *unweighted* | *weighted* | *unweighted* |
| Median income | $40–49,900 | $40–49,900 | $30–39,000 | $40–49,900 |
| Median education | College graduate | College graduate | Some college | College graduate |
| Mean age (standard deviation) | 41.3 (16.3) | 41.2 (16.4) | 39.8 (15.7) | 40.8 (15.9) |
| Mean length of residence (standard deviation) | 18.5 (13.5) | 18.0 (12.92) | 16.64 (11.8) | 17.4 (12.1) |
| Immigrant | 83.4% | 82.2% | 90.3% | 89.8% |
| Citizen | 74.6 | 76.7 | 70.5 | 71.8 |
| Prefer to speak English | 52.5 | 56.1 | 38.4 | 2.5 |
| Racially integrated social network | 37.9 | 39.9 | 29.0 | 31.2 |
| Employed full-time, part-time, or self-employed | 69.1 | 68.2 | 53.4 | 54.2 |
| Married | 59.4 | 58.6 | 68.9 | 70.3 |
| Children under seventeen years old | 30.5 | 30.4 | 39.3 | 38.7 |

*Source:* 1997 *Los Angeles Times* Survey #396.

$$PP = a + b_1 \text{(income)} + b_2 \text{(education)} + b_3 \text{(age)} + b_4 \text{(immigrant)} + b_5 \text{(English)} + b_6 \text{(length of residence)} + b_7 \text{(employed)} + b_8 \text{(married)} + b_9 \text{(children)} + b_{10} \text{(discrimination)} + b_{11} \text{(social)}$$

Where

PP = R's political participation. Measures of activity in American politics and activity in Chinese cultural or community organizations are continuous. Measure of campaign donation activity is dichotomous (0–1) (see box 3.7a for question wording and coding).

Income = R's family income

Education = R's educational attainment

Age = R's age in years

Immigrant = Immigrant Status (0–1)

English = R prefers to use English rather than Cantonese or Mandarin (0–1)

Length of Residence = Years that R has lived in the United States

Employed = R is employed outside of the home full-time, part-time or self-employed (0–1)

Married = R is married (0–1)

Children = R has children under age 17 (0–1)

Discrimination = R has experienced racial or ethnic discrimination personally

---

**Box 3.7a** *Los Angeles Times* **Survey #396. Political Participation Question Wording**

*Los Angeles Times. Active Political Participation.* "How active are you in American Politics: are you very active, or somewhat active, or not too active, or not active at all in American politics?"

    1    Not active at all
    2    Not that active
    3    Somewhat active
    4    Very Active

*Los Angeles Times. Active in Chinese Cultural or Community Organizations.* "On another subject, how active are you in local Chinese community or cultural organizations: are you very active, or somewhat active, or not too active, or not active at all in American politics?"

    1    Not active at all
    2    Not that active
    3    Somewhat active
    4    Very Active

*Los Angeles Times. Campaign Contributions.* "Have you ever given money to a political candidate's campaign, or not?"

    0    Never Given Money
    1    Given money

---

Social = R is part of a racially integrated social network (non-Asian friends) (0–1)

Because women and men were analyzed separately, the findings presented below do not tell us which variables account for any differences in participation *between* the two groups. Instead, this model is designed to identify differences *among* each group. What are the predictors of participation among Chinese American women? What are the predictors of participation among Chinese American men?

## FINDINGS AND DISCUSSION

### Is There a Gender Gap in Chinese American Participation?

The results of this study (table 3.7b) offer little evidence of a gender gap in terms of the political participation of Chinese Americans in the LAT sample. For instance, as illustrated in the first row of table 3.7b, in terms of activity in American politics, about 25 percent of men and 20 percent of women indicate that they are "somewhat" or "very" active. This difference is not large. Turning to the second row of table 3.7b, one observes that an equal percentage (about 20 percent) of men and women are "somewhat active" or "very active" in Chinese cultural or community organizations. Finally, the last row of table 3.7b suggests that women contribute to campaigns at the same rate as men. To save space I do not include results from a multiple regression analysis I performed to examine whether being female was a useful predictor of participation. However, even when socioeconomic status, length of residence, English preference, and immigrant status are held constant using regression techniques, Chinese American men and women appear to participate in all activities at similar rates. In other words, I did not find that gender was a useful predictor of political participation among Chinese Americans living in Southern California.

**Table 3.7b    Political Participation among Chinese American Women and Men**

|  | Men | Women |
|---|---|---|
| **Active in U.S. politics** | | |
| Not at all | 50.9% | 64.6% |
| Not that active | 24.1 | 15.7 |
| Somewhat active | 23.4 | 18.0 |
| Very active | 1.7 | 1.7 |
| **Active in Chinese cultural or community organizations** | | |
| Not at all | 49.2% | 53.2% |
| Not that active | 31.9 | 27.7 |
| Somewhat active | 14.8 | 16.7 |
| Very active | 4.1 | 2.4 |
| **Ever given money to a political campaign** | | |
| Given money | 18.2% | 12.8% |
| Never given money | 81.8 | 87.2 |

*Notes:* Entries are weighted frequencies. Total percents may not add up to 100 due to rounding.
*Source: Los Angeles Times* Survey #396.

These results are consistent with past research on Asian American political participation. Lien (1998a), for example, finds that compared to other groups, neither gender nor the interaction between gender and race has an independent impact on rates of voting, registration, and turnout compared to other racial groups. Lien's research suggests that among Asian Americans, racial group differences have a greater influence than gender differences on Asian Americans' political participation. That is, the rate of participation among Asian Americans as a group is depressed (compared to non-Latino whites), but Asian American men and women do not differ in terms of rates of political activity.

What accounts for the absence of a gender gap among Chinese Americans in the LAT sample? Perhaps, as Lien (1998a) proposes, being Asian American in the United States has such a strong negative effect on political participation that the effects of other factors, like gender, no longer appear important. As with other communities of color, community leaders and norms may emphasize issues of race or ethnicity at the

expense of gender related concerns. That is, the acknowledgment of gender inequality may be seen as a threat to the appearance of a united (racial) front. Thus, members of the Asian American or Chinese American community may be socialized in ways that promote racial group solidarity or identification while discouraging critiques of gender inequality within the group. For example, Helen Zia (Chiang et al. 1997) describes the marginalization of feminist issues within Asian American communities. She claims "something that I've heard many times over is that when sexual harassment occurs to Asian women by Asian men, Asian women feel they cannot come forward. The community pressure is so great—it would look like they were trying to betray the community" (p. 66).[6]

## The Predictors of Political Participation among Chinese American Women and Men

Research, including that presented above, has established that Asian Americans and

Chinese Americans tend to exhibit similar rates of political participation. However, these findings do not reveal whether the same hypotheses explain participation among Chinese American women and men. Do Chinese American women and men become politically active for the same reasons? To answer this question, I disaggregated the LAT sample by gender and analyzed the two groups (Chinese American men and Chinese American women) separately. Again, it is important to remember that the findings that follow do not account for differences or similarities in participation *between* the two groups. I first discuss the findings of this research by focusing on the female sample. Then I examine the results of this study with attention to the male sample.

## Political Participation among Chinese American Women

### Self-Reported "Activity in American Politics" among Chinese American Women

The first column of data presented in table 3.7c under the column heading "Political Activity" examines the relationship between the independent variables of interest (immigration related factors, employment and family structure, personal discrimination, and social network composition) and "activity in American politics" among Chinese American women, controlling for socioeconomic status. In terms of predictors of participation, one key finding has to do with labor force participation. There is a strong negative relationship between employment outside of the home and involvement in the political system among Chinese American women, other conditions being equal. On the other hand, once employment outside of the home is accounted for, being married or having children under eighteen appears to have little effect on women's general participation in American politics.

Higher levels of education, preferring to speak English, and personal experience with discrimination also contribute to political participation among Chinese American women. Note that even after controlling for English preference and length of residence, being an immigrant still has a negative effect on women's participation. In a separate analysis (not reported here due to space constraints), a variable that indicated whether the respondent was a citizen of the United States or not was included in the model. Inclusion of this variable did not change the results presented here. In fact, citizenship did not appear to have a significant effect on the participation of either Chinese American women or Chinese American men.

How can these findings be explained? First, the findings seem to suggest that Chinese American women who are employed outside of the home are not politicized in the workplace. In fact, they appear to participate less than those women who are not employed. I would argue that the results of this study are more consistent with the view that Chinese American women who are employed outside of the home have less time to devote to political activities than those who are not employed outside of the home because they continue to carry the burden of household work in addition to their work outside of the home.

In contrast to employment outside of the home, experience with discrimination appears to be relevant to Chinese American women's activity in American politics. One explanation for the fact that discrimination has a large, positive effect on women's political participation is that Chinese American women who are most concerned with their racial status are likely to be those who are most involved in politics. Perhaps experience with discrimination makes women more aware of racial oppression and leads them to engage in the political system in order to challenge racial hierarchies. Experience with personal discrimination may have a politicizing effect among Chinese American women.

In addition, the findings indicate that female immigrants are less active in American politics than those who were born in the United States, but that length

**Table 3.7c    Determinants of Political Participation among Chinese American Women**

| Independent variables | Self-reported Political Activity in American Politics N=134 | | Active in Chinese Cultural or Community Organizations N=133 | | Active through Campaign Contributions N=134 | |
|---|---|---|---|---|---|---|
| | **B** | **Standard error** | **B** | **Standard error** | **B** | **Standard error** |
| Income | −0.01 | 0.04 | 0.02 | 0.05 | **0.34** | 0.10 |
| Education | **0.07** | 0.03 | **0.12** | 0.04 | 0.32 | 0.18 |
| Age | 0.00 | 0.01 | 0.00 | 0.01 | −0.02 | 0.04 |
| Immigrant status | **−0.77** | 0.25 | *0.53* | 0.30 | **−2.31** | 1.20 |
| English language preference | **0.34** | 0.14 | 0.03 | 0.18 | 0.36 | 0.61 |
| Length of residence among immigrants | **0.03** | 0.01 | 0.00 | 0.01 | **0.09** | 0.05 |
| Employed full time, part time, self-employed | **−0.28** | 0.14 | **−0.34** | 0.17 | 0.85 | 0.75 |
| Married | 0.02 | 0.20 | *−0.44* | 0.24 | 1.40 | 1.15 |
| Children under seventeen | −0.08 | 0.14 | 0.19 | 0.17 | −0.01 | 0.63 |
| Racially integrated social network | 0.20 | 0.14 | **−0.43** | 0.17 | −0.89 | 0.62 |
| Experience with personal discrimination | **0.54** | 0.23 | 0.40 | 0.28 | −0.68 | 1.21 |
| Constant | 1.64 | 0.38 | 1.05 | 0.47 | 25.59 | 2.19 |
| | R-Square= .37 | | R-Square=.17 | | −2 Log-Likelihood at Convergence= .96.512 Prob< Chi-Square=.000 | |

*Note:* Controlling for citizenship did not change basic results above, coefficient for citizenship was positive, but not statistically significant. Entries typed in bold are significant at p< .05. Entries typed in italics are significant at p <. 10.

*Source: Los Angeles Times* Survey #396.

of residence and English language preference are associated with increased involvement in the U.S. political system. This finding supports the idea that because immigrants are less familiar with the political system than their U.S.-born counterparts, they will participate less, other conditions being equal. The fact that length of residence and English preference are positively related to Chinese American women's participation is consistent with

the hypothesis that as immigrants gain familiarity with the political system over time they become more involved in American politics (see also Converse 1969; Ong and Nakanishi 1996). This finding is consistent with previous studies (Wong 2000) in which I suggest that although immigrants tend to be less involved than the U.S.-born in American politics when they first arrive in the United States, their likelihood of participating increases with each year of residence and cumulative exposure to the political system.

Finally, education is strongly related to increased political participation among Chinese American women. That is, women who are educated are more likely to participate than women who are uneducated. Traditional theories of political participation have long posited a strong link between education and political participation, claiming that "education enhances participation more or less directly by developing skills that are relevant to politics— the ability to speak and write. . . imparting information about government and politics, and by encouraging attitudes such as a sense of civic responsibility" (Verba, Schlozman, and Brady 1995, 305). While this is likely to be the case among all individuals, including Chinese American women, it is important to note that though Asian American women tend to be slightly more educated than white women, "white women are on average far more [politically] active than Asian women, despite an educational disadvantage" (Junn 1997, 393).

### Involvement in Chinese Cultural or Community Politics among Chinese American Women

Education appears to be the primary determinant of participation in Chinese cultural or community organizations among Chinese American women (table 3.7c, under column heading "Active in Chinese Cultural or Community Organizations"). Though the results are not statistically significant, experience with personal discrimination is also associated positively with more participation in Chinese cultural or community organizations among Chinese American women. Thus, there is some limited evidence that experience with racial discrimination may lead women to participate in ethnic politics. It is possible, for instance, that those who experience discrimination are motivated to challenge the American racial hierarchy through participation in ethnic organizations that focus on civil rights issues.

Being part of a racially integrated social network is negatively related to activity in Chinese cultural or community organizations among Chinese American women. This relationship is statistically significant. Chinese American women who are part of a racially integrated social network are much less likely than those who only have Asian American friends to become involved in Chinese cultural or community organizations. It may be that Chinese American women whose friendships are based in the Asian American community are more likely to take part in politics related to the Asian American and, in particular, the Chinese American, community.

Finally, it is interesting to note that Chinese American women who are employed outside of the home do not participate in Chinese cultural or community organizations at the same rate as those women who are not employed. Similarly, those Chinese American women who are married tend to participate at lower rates than those who are not married. Again, it seems quite plausible that Chinese American women who are working outside the home are also likely to bear the primary responsibility for household work and have little extra time to devote to politics.

### Campaign Contributions among Chinese American women

The hypothesis above (having to do with constraints on women's time and their political participation) appears to be confirmed to some extent by the results in the last column of data in table 3.7c. Donating money to a campaign requires a minimal amount of time compared to other types of political activity, such as registering to vote, attending a meeting, or writing a letter to an editor or elected official. The "double" burden of maintaining the household and labor force participation outside of the home probably has a less negative impact on women's participation in this area of participation. Therefore, it is interesting to observe that Chinese American women who are employed outside of the home are no less likely than those who are not employed outside of the home to make a campaign contribution. In fact, among Chinese American women, work outside of the home is positively related to campaign finance activity. However, the results are not statistically significant. It is likely that those who are working outside of the home have more financial resources to donate to a political campaign.

In the realm of campaign finance, the main predictor of participation among Chinese American women is length of residence. Those women who have lived in the United States for a long period of time are more likely to contribute money to a campaign than those women who have lived in the United States for a short length of time, all other conditions being equal. Again, I would argue that length of residence may be related to increased familiarity with U.S. politics and that those who are most familiar with the political system will also be the most involved in the political process.

## Summary of Chinese American Women's Participation

To summarize, several of the hypotheses described earlier seem to apply to Chinese American women's involvement in American politics. First, this research supports the hypothesis that lack of exposure to the political system may depress political participation among immigrants initially. However, as they gain experience and familiarity with American politics, Chinese American immigrant women are likely to participate more. Second, employment outside of the home is negatively related to self-reported activity in American politics and involvement in Chinese cultural or community politics. This finding is consistent with the hypothesis that because Chinese American women who work outside of the home are also likely to be responsible for the majority of unpaid work *within* the home, they will have little extra time to devote to active political participation. Once employment outside of the home is accounted for, though, Chinese American women who are

married or who have children are no less likely to participate than those who are not married or who do not have children. Finally, women who experience personal discrimination are more likely to be active in U.S. politics generally or to participate in Chinese cultural or community activities than those who have not experienced discrimination. Among Chinese American women, the hypothesis that experiences with discrimination might influence some individuals to get more involved in the political system is supported to some extent. It may be that Chinese Americans who experience discrimination view political activism as a means of challenging racial hierarchies.

## Political Participation among Chinese American Men

Participation in American politics among Chinese American men is predicted primarily by whether individuals are part of a racially integrated social network (table 3.7d). Men who have non-Asian American friends are more likely to participate than those who have only Asian American friends. This relationship is statistically significant. In contrast, age and being an immigrant are both negatively related to political participation among Chinese American men, other conditions being equal. These relationships are also statistically significant.

How can general participation in American politics among Chinese American men be explained? The only hypothesis that is confirmed is that the development of a racially integrated social network increases the participation of Chinese American men. Perhaps those men who have non-Asian American friends are likely to participate more than those who do not have non-Asian American friends because they are exposed to more opportunities for participation. Since non-Asian American individuals, especially blacks and whites, are likely to be more involved with politics in the U.S. than Chinese Americans, members of these groups may be more likely than

**Table 3.7d    Determinants of Political Participation among Chinese American Men: Self-Reported Political Activity in American Politics**

| Independent variables | B | Standard error |
|---|---|---|
| Income | −.02 | .04 |
| Education | .06 | .04 |
| Age | **−.02** | .01 |
| Immigrant status | **−.48** | .22 |
| English language preference | .12 | .15 |
| Length of residence among immigrants | *.02* | .01 |
| Employed full time, part time, self-employed | .44 | .50 |
| Married | .07 | .19 |
| Children under seventeen | .00 | .15 |
| Racially integrated social network | **.29** | .13 |
| Experience with personal discrimination | .13 | .17 |
| Constant | 1.79 | .62 |
| **R-Square** | **.15** | |
| N | 202 | |

Note: Controlling for citizenship did not change basic results above, coefficient for citizenship was positive, but not statistically significant. Entries typed in bold are significant at $p < .05$. Entries typed in italics are significant at $p < .10$.

Source: Los Angeles Times Survey #396.

other Asian Americans to share information about opportunities to get involved in the U.S. political system.

Although the results are not shown in the tables to save space, one observes that education is the only variable that is a useful predictor of involvement in Chinese cultural or community organizations among Chinese American men. Why is education so important in terms of men's participation in ethnic organizations? Perhaps Chinese American men are exposed to issues related to race, identity, and community through education. Increased exposure might lead to more activism related to these issues. For example, Chinese American men may be introduced to Chinese American history in Asian American studies courses offered at institutions of higher education. A greater knowledge and understanding of their history and identity may

then influence Chinese American men to become involved in political institutions that are aimed at improving conditions for the Chinese American community.

Similar to Chinese American women, the main predictors of Chinese American men's likelihood of contributing money to a political campaign are immigrant status and length of residence (again these results are not shown in the tables for space considerations). Chinese American male immigrants are not as likely as those born in the United States to be familiar with political candidates and are, therefore, probably less likely to contribute to any candidate's campaign. As their time in the United States lengthens, immigrants, including Chinese American men, are likely to become more informed about the political process and particular political candidates. Increased knowledge of U.S. politics may then lead to more involvement, such as donating money to a political campaign. In addition, because candidates also more likely to become familiar with immigrant communities and potential constituents as time passes, they are more likely to contact longtime residents of an immigrant community. It is interesting that income, or having more monetary resources to donate, is not a strong predictor of campaign donation activity among Chinese American men.

## Summary of Chinese American Men's Participation

Several hypotheses seem to explain political participation among Chinese American men. First, the development of a racially integrated social network increases Chinese American men's general activity in American politics. This suggests that contact with members of groups that tend to participate more than Asian Americans in the political system is likely to have a positive effect on the political involvement of Chinese American men. Perhaps their non-Asian American friends are mobilizing Chinese American men. Second, Chinese American men who are immigrants are less likely to participate in political activities than those who are not immigrants. A participation gap between immigrants and the U.S.-born might be explained by the fact that immigrants are less familiar with politics than their U.S.-born counterparts. Lack of familiarity with the political system may translate into lack of participation. In some cases, such as campaign finance activity, political participation is likely to increase with length of residence in the country. I contend that the positive relationship between length of residence and political participation has to do with Chinese immigrant men becoming more familiar with the American political system over time.

## CONCLUSION

This study found no difference in rates of political participation among Chinese American men and women. However, it did identify some important predictors of participation among Chinese American women and among Chinese American men.[7]

One of the primary findings presented in this chapter is that Chinese American women who are employed outside of the home are much less likely than those who are not employed outside of the home to indicate that they are "active in American politics" or active in Chinese cultural or community activities. One explanation for this discrepancy in participation is that it results from an unequal distribution of household work within Chinese American women's homes (Chen 1992). It is probable that Chinese American women who work in the labor force outside of the home continue to bear responsibility for household work and that the "double day" created by unpaid domestic work leaves them with little time to participate actively in politics. Because most Chinese American men may not necessarily take responsibility for household work *in addition* to their paid labor outside of the home, employment appears to have little negative effect on those men who work outside the home compared to those men who do not.

This study also highlights the role of experience with discrimination in determining whether Chinese American women participate in the American political system. Among Chinese American women there is a statistically significant relationship between self-reported participation in American politics and personal experience with racial discrimination. Further analysis reveals that this relationship is likely to depend on type of political activity, since the relationship between experience with discrimination and involvement through campaign donations is actually negative (though not statistically significant) among Asian American women. Perhaps, as I suggested earlier, women who become involved in the political system do so because they are motivated by a desire to challenge the American racial hierarchy. Experience with discrimination was not a "strong" predictor of participation among Chinese American men but was positively related to each type of participation considered in this study.

Finally, adaptation to American social and political life appears to be a key determinant of Chinese American women's participation. For instance, length of residence and preferring to speak English are positively related to Chinese women's general activity in American politics and likelihood of donating to a political campaign. These variables also appear to have a positive effect on men's participation, though the standard errors associated with these variables are relatively larger for the male sample. These findings suggest that exposure to the American political system and a sense of familiarity with American politics is key to the participation of both Chinese American women and men.

Because this study suggests that activity in American politics may be predicted by different factors, depending on an individual's gender, political mobilization strategies that do not pay attention to gender may be less than effective. Given the findings presented in this chapter, it would appear that maximizing the political participation of Chinese American women and men may require gender-specific strategies. For example, organizers should consider that increasing the involvement of Chinese American women is likely to require addressing inequalities in household work responsibility. Since this study identified constraints that may prevent Chinese American women who work both inside and outside the home from participating, mobilization aimed at challenging patriarchal structures within the home may be especially important to increasing Chinese American women's involvement in U.S. politics.

In addition, because there is a strong relationship between experience with discrimination and Chinese American women's self-reported activity in American politics, a mobilization strategy that focuses on challenging racial inequalities is likely to increase the political participation of Chinese American women. Similarly, a mobilization strategy aimed at improving Chinese American women's English-language skills would probably increase their involvement in the political system.

Because the development of a racially integrated social network is likely to have a strongly positive effect on the participation of Chinese American men, mobilization efforts might focus on increasing men's involvement in multiracial coalitions to improve their political participation.

The study discussed in this chapter focused on the predictors of political participation among Chinese American men and women in Southern California. In fact, I found that while Chinese American men and women tend to become involved in the American political system at similar rates, their involvement may be predicted by different factors. The most useful predictors of involvement in the political system among Chinese American are not always the most useful for predicting involvement among Chinese American men. This finding has implications for the political mobilization of Chinese American women and men. One of the major implications of the study is that mobilization efforts aimed at increasing the participation of Chinese American women and men should employ strategies which recognize that Chinese American women and men may become involved, or be discouraged from participating, in politics for different reasons. Lack of attention to these gender-specific motivations for political involvement may result in less political participation among both Chinese American women and men.

## NOTES

1. Throughout the chapter I use the terms "Asian American" and "Chinese American" to refer to individuals of Asian or Chinese origin who are living in America. The term does not imply citizenship or that individuals were born in the United States.

2. Lien (1998a) reports that Asian American women differ in partisanship and some policy preferences from Asian American men. For example, she finds that Asian American women are less likely to identify as Democrats and less likely to support affirmative action compared to Asian American men.

3. Chinese were the largest Asian ethnic group in the United States in 2000 (Barnes and Bennett 2002).

4. This trend is similar among the Asian American population as a whole; Asian American women's median earning in 1997 was $29,120 compared to $35,528 for Asian American men. However, Asian American women earned more than their white female counterparts ($26,732). By comparison, the median earnings of white men in 1997 was $37,893 (Lien 2001, 208).

5. This last measure deserves comment. Lien (1997) notes that beginning in the mid-1980s media attention began to focus on campaign donations by Asian Americans in the United States (p. 4). While it is true that Asian Americans tend to donate money disproportionately to their numbers in the general population, Lien (1997) cautions that "the higher amount of money donated by Asians as a whole does not necessarily indicate that more Asians are involved in the political process" (p. 9). Furthermore, Uhlaner, Cain and Kiewiet (1989) do not find that Asian Americans included in a multiethnic sample of Californians contributed money to campaigns at higher rates than non-Latino whites.

6. For a discussion of ethnic community leaders silencing feminist issues or the issues of other marginalized members of the ethnic community, see also (Shah 1997; Maira 2000).

7. Although this study identified some important predictors of political participation, the results (R-Square statistics) also indicate that the factors examined here do not explain fully the participation of Chinese American women or men. Clearly, more research is needed on the political participation of this understudied community.

## REFERENCES

Aguilar-San Juan, Karin. 1997. "Foreword: Breathing Fire, Confronting Power, and Other Necessary Acts of Resistance." In Sonia Shah, ed., *Dragon Ladies: Asian American Feminists Breathe Fire*, ix–xi. Boston: South End.

Amott, Teresa, and Julie Matthaei. 1996. *Race, Gender, and Work*. Rev. ed. Boston: South End.

Anderson, Kristi. 1975. "Working Women and Political Participation, 1952–1972." *American Journal of Political Science* 19: 439–55.

Barnes, Jessica, and Claudette Bennett. 2002. *The Asian Population: 2000*. Census 2000 Brief. U.S. Census Bureau. At www.census.gov/prod/2002pubs/c2kbr01-16.pdf.

Chan, Sucheng. 1991. "The Exclusion of Chinese Women." In Sucheng Chan, ed., *Entry Denied: Exclusion and the Chinese Community in America, 1882–1943*, 94–146. Philadelphia: Temple University Press.

Chen, Hsiang-Shui. 1992. *Chinatown No More: Taiwan Immigrants in Contemporary New York*. Ithaca: Cornell University Press.

Chiang, Pamela, Milyoung Cho, Elaine H. Kim, Meizhu Lui, and Helen Zia. 1997. "On Asian America, Feminism, and Agenda-Making: A Roundtable Discussion. In Sonia Shah, ed., *Dragon Ladies: Asian American Feminists Breathe Fire*, 57–72. Boston: South End.

Cho, Wendy K Tam. 1998. "Naturalization, Socialization, Participation: Immigrants and (Non-) Voting." *Journal of Politics*.

Chow, Ester Ngan-Ling. 1989. "The Feminist Movement: Where Are All the Asian American Women?" In Asian Women United, ed., *Making Waves: An Anthology of Writing by and about Asian American Women*, 362–77. Boston: Beacon.

Chu, Judy. 1989. "Asian Pacific American Women in Mainstream Politics." In Asian Women United, ed., *Making Waves: An Anthology of Writing by and about Asian American Women*, 405–22. Boston: Beacon.

Clark, Cal, and Janet Clark. 1986. "Models of Gender and Political Participation in the United States." *Women and Politics* 6: 5–25.

Converse, Philip E. 1969. "Of Time and Partisan Stability." *Comparative Political Studies* 2: 139–71.

Collins, Patricia Hill. 1990. *Black Feminist Thought: Knowledge, Consciousness, and the Politics of Empowerment*. New York: Routledge.

Cott, Nancy. 1990. "Across the Great Divide: Women and Politics before and after 1920." In Louise A. Tilly and Patricia Gurin, eds., *Women, Politics, and Change*. New York: Russell Sage.

Crenshaw, Kimberle. 1989. "Demarginalizing the Intersection of Race and Sex: A Black Feminist Critique of Antidiscrimination Doctrine, Feminist Theory, and Antiracist Politics." In *University of Chicago Legal Forum: Feminism in the Law: Theory, Practice, and Criticism,* 129–67. Chicago: University of Chicago Press.

Donato, K. M. 1992. "Understanding U.S. Immigration: Why Some Countries Send Women and Others Send Men." In D. Gabaccia, ed., *Seeking Common Ground: Multidisciplinary Studies of Immigrant Women in the United States,* 159–84. Westport, Conn.: Greenwood.

Espiritu, Yen Le. 1997. *Asian American Women and Men: Labor, Laws, and Love.* Thousand Oaks, Calif.: Sage.

Hardy-Fanta, Carol. 1993. *Latina Politics, Latino Politics: Gender, Culture, and Political Participation in Boston.* Philadelphia: Temple University Press.

Hing, Bill Ong. 1996. "Reframing the Immigration Debate: An Overview." In Bill Ong Hing and Ronald Lee, ed., *Reframing the Immigration Debate,* 1–34. Los Angeles: LEAP Asian Pacific American Public Policy Institute/UCLA Asian American Studies Center.

Hondagneu-Sotelo, Pierrette. 1994. *Gendered Transitions: Mexican Experiences of Immigration.* Berkeley: University of California Press.

Jennings, Jerry. 1993. *Voting and Registration in the Election of November 1992.* Washington, D.C.: U.S. Government Printing Office.

Jiobu, Robert M. 1996. "Recent Asian Pacific Immigrants: The Demographic Background." In Bill Ong Hing and Ronald Lee, ed., *Reframing the Immigration Debate,* 35–58. Los Angeles: LEAP Asian Pacific American Public Policy Institute and UCLA Asian American Studies Center.

Jones-Correa, Michael. 1998. "Different Paths: Gender, Immigration, and Political Participation." *International Migration Review* (Summer): 326–49.

Junn, Jane. 1997. "Assimilating or Coloring Participation? Gender, Race, and Democratic Political Participation." In Cathy J. Cohen, Kathleen B. Jones, and Joan Tronto, eds., *Women Transforming Politics,* 387–97. New York: New York University Press.

Kwong, Peter. 1996. *The New Chinatown.* (Rev. ed.) New York: Hill & Wang.

——. 1997. "American Sweatshops 1980s Style: Chinese Women Garment Workers." In Cathy J. Cohen, Kathleen B. Jones, and Joan Tronto, eds., *Women Transforming Politics,* 84–93. New York: New York University Press.

Leong, Russell, ed. 1996. *Asian American Sexualities: Dimensions of the Gay and Lesbian Experience.* New York: Routledge.

Lien, Pei-te. 1994. "Ethnicity and Political Participation: A Comparison between Asian and Mexican Americans." *Political Behavior* 16: 237–64.

——. 1997. *The Political Participation of Asian Americans: Voting Behavior in Southern California.* New York: Garland.

——. 1998a. "Does the Gender Gap in Political Attitudes and Behavior Vary across Racial Groups? Comparing Asians to Whites, Blacks, and Latinos." *Political Research Quarterly* 51: 869–94.

——. 1998b. "Who Votes in Multiracial America? An Analysis of Voting Registration and Turnout by Race and Ethnicity, 1990–1996." Paper presented at the 1998 annual meeting of the American Political Science Association, Boston.

——. 2001. *The Making of Asian America through Political Participation.* Philadelphia: Temple University Press.

Louie, Miriam Ching. 1997. "Breaking the Cycle: Women Workers Confront Corporate Greed Globally." In Sonia Shah, ed., *Dragon Ladies: Asian American Feminists Breathe Fire,* 121–31. Boston: South End, 1997.

Lu, Lynn. 1997. "Critical Visions: The Representation and Resistance of Asian Women." In Sonia Shah, ed., *Dragon Ladies: Asian American Feminists Breathe Fire,* 17–28. Boston: South End.

Maira, Sunaina. 2000. "Ideologies of Authenticity: Youth, Politics, and Diaspora." *Amerasia Journal* 25(3): 139–49.

Montoya, Lisa J. 1996. "Latino Gender Differences in Public Opinion: Results from the Latino National Political Survey." *Hispanic Journal of Behavioral Sciences* 18: 255–76.

Montoya, Lisa J., Carol Hardy-Fanta, and Sonia Garcia. 2000. "Latina Politics: Gender, Participation, and Leadership." *PS: Political Science and Politics* 33: 555–62.

Nakanishi, Don T. 1991. "The Next Swing Vote? Asian Pacific Americans and California Politics." In Byron O. Jackson and Michael B. Preston, eds. *Racial and Ethnic Politics in California*, 25–54. Berkeley: IGS Press.

Niemi, Richard G., G. Bingham Powell Jr., Harold W. Stanley, and C. Lawrence Evans. 1985. "Testing the Converse Partisanship Model with New Electorates." *Comparative Political Studies* 18: 300–322.

Ong, Paul, and Don T. Nakanishi. 1996. "Becoming Citizens, Becoming Voters: The Naturalization and Political Participation of Asian Pacific Immigrants." In Bill Ong Hing and Ronald Lee. ed., *Reframing the Immigration Debate.* Los Angeles: LEAP Asian Pacific American Public Policy Institute/UCLA Asian American Studies Center.

Randall, Vicky. 1987. *Women and Politics: An International Perspective.* 2d ed. Chicago: University of Chicago Press.

Shah, Purvi. 1997. "Redefining the Home: How Community Elites Silence Feminist Activism." In Sonia Shah, ed., *Dragon Ladies: Asian American Feminists Breathe Fire,* 46–56. Boston: South End.

Shah, Sonia, ed. 1997. *Dragon Ladies: Asian American Feminists Breathe Fire.* Boston: South End.

Takaki, Ronald. 1989. *Strangers from a Different Shore: A History of Asian Americans.* Boston: Little, Brown.

Uhlaner, Carole, J. 1991. "Perceived Discrimination and Prejudice and the Coalition Prospects of Blacks, Latinos, and Asian Americans." In Byran O. Jackson and Michael B. Preston, eds., *Racial and Ethnic Politics in California,* 339–96. Berkeley: IGS Press.

Uhlaner, Carole J., Bruce E. Cain, and D. Roderick Kiewiet. 1989. "Political Participation of Ethnic Minorities in the 1980s." *Political Behavior* 11: 195–231.

Verba, Sidney, Kay Lehman Schlozman, and Henry E. Brady. 1995. *Voice and Equality: Civic Voluntarism and American Politics.* Cambridge: Harvard University Press.

Welch, Susan. 1977. "Women as Political Animals? A Test of Some Explanations for Male-Female Political Participation Differences." *American Journal of Political Science* 21: 711–30.

Welch, Susan, and Lee Sigelman. 1989. "A Black Gender Gap?" *Social Science Quarterly* 70: 120–33.

———. 1991. "A Gender Gap among Hispanics? A Comparison with Blacks and Anglos." *Western Political Quarterly* 45: 181–99.

Wong, Janelle S. 2000. "The Effects of Age and Political Exposure on the Development of Party Identification among Asian American and Latino Immigrants in the United States." *Political Behavior* 22(4): 341–71.

Yung, Judy. 1990. *Chinese Women of America: A Pictorial Essay.* Seattle: University of Washington Press.

# 3.8

# Beyond "Politics by Other Means"?

## Empowerment Strategies for
## Los Angeles' Asian Pacific Community

*Harold Brackman and Steven P. Erie*

〰〰〰〰〰〰〰〰〰〰〰〰〰〰〰〰〰〰〰〰〰〰〰〰〰〰〰〰

Asian Pacific politics has been character-ized as "politics by other means," for exam-ple, indirect influence through interest group lobbying, targeted campaign contri-butions, litigation, and protest rather than through the traditional direct electoral routes of voting and officeholding. This model of indirect group influence puts the best face possible on the fact that, histori-cally, Asian Pacific Americans have been highly underrepresented among voters and elected officeholders.[1]

In the 1990s, are Asian Pacific Ameri-cans successfully making the transition to electorally based empowerment, as the nation's other ethnic groups have done? In this chapter we examine the electoral empowerment prospects of Asian Pacific Americans in seemingly the best case for a breakthrough outside of Hawaii: the Los

Brackman, Harold, and Steven P. Erie. "Beyond 'Politics by Other Means'? Empowerment Strate-gies for Los Angeles' Asian Pacific Community." In Michael Peter Smith and Joe R. Feagin, eds., *The Bubbling Cauldron: Race, Ethnicity, and the Urban Crisis*, (Minneapolis: University of Min-nesota Press, 1995), 282–303. Reprinted with per-mission.

Angeles metropolitan area. Measured by officeholding, minority political influence is more advanced in the Los Angeles met-ropolitan area than elsewhere in Califor-nia. In 1991 over 40 percent of the state's forty-eight Asian Pacific elected officials came from the Los Angeles area. In Los Angeles County, California's demo-graphic future already has arrived. By 1990 the metropolitan area contained over one-third of the state's Asian Pacific residents.

Analyzing both obstacles to minority electoral empowerment and strategies to overcome them in an important metropoli-tan test case, we will also argue that, nor-matively, "politics by other means" cannot substitute for full democratic participation by Asian Pacific Americans.

Unlike the Bay Area, where Chinese Americans make up over one-half of the Asian community, in southern California no nationality group constitutes over 30 percent of the overall Asian Pacific population. The Chinese, Filipino, Korean, and Japanese com-munities each have 125,000 to 250,000 mem-bers, followed by smaller numbers of Viet-namese, Asian Indians, Cambodians, Thais, Laotians, and Pacific Islanders. This diversity offers unique challenges for pan-Asian coalition building.

## ASIAN PACIFIC ELECTORAL BEHAVIOR

### The Pyramid
### of Voter Participation

Electoral power can be conceived of as the peak of a pyramid that is very difficult for Asian Pacific Americans to climb because of distinctive patterns of age, citizenship, voter registration, and turnout. Asian Pacific Americans—deriving either by birth or ancestry from East and Southeast Asia, the Indian subcontinent, and the Pacific Basin archipelagos—made up 10 percent of California's 1990 population. Yet they represented only 7 percent of the state's vote-eligible adult citizens and 3 percent of its actual voters. Partly as a consequence of limited group electoral power, there were no Asian Pacific state legislators between 1980 and 1992.

The dynamics of Asian Pacific voter underrepresentation in California are both similar to and different from those of Latinos, the state's other highly underrepresented ethnic group. Both Asian Pacifics and Latinos are proportionately—and substantially—handicapped by young populations. In 1990 adults made up only 61 percent of the Asian Pacific and Latino communities compared with 74 percent of the black and 85 percent of the Anglo populations. Among adults, Asian Pacifics had higher citizenship rates than Latinos—73 percent versus 62 percent. Among adult citizens, however, Asian Pacifics had lower voter registration rates than Latino voters, but had similar depressed turnout rates—33 percent. The cumulative effects of the barriers of age, citizenship, voter registration, and turnout on minority empowerment are staggering. The number of Asian Pacific voters would increase by nearly fivefold if the community's age, citizenship, registration, and voter profiles matched those of the Anglo population.[2]

Asian Pacific Americans have greater need for voter registration campaigns, while Latinos are more in need of citizenship drives. This differential mobilization logic is underscored when we analyze the changes over time in Asian and Latino citizenship and registration rates. Citizenship rates for adult Asians have increased significantly—both absolutely and relative to Latinos—since 1986. In that year the adult Asian citizenship rate closely mirrored that for Latinos—60 percent versus 57 percent. By 1990, however, the Asian citizenship rate jumped to 73 percent while the Latino rate had barely increased to 62 percent. Conversely, the Asian voter registration rate for adult citizens plummeted from 45 to 35 percent between 1986 and 1990 while the Latino registration rate remained relatively constant at slightly over 40 percent.

The UCLA Asian Pacific American Voter Registration Study estimated that in 1984 Japanese Americans, with the highest citizenship rate, had the highest voter registration rate—43 percent—among adult Asians in Los Angeles County. In contrast, only an estimated 35 percent of the region's adult Chinese, 29 percent of Samoans, 27 percent of Filipinos, 17 percent of Asian Indians, 13 percent of Koreans, and 4 percent of Vietnamese were registered voters. There are also significant group differences among Asian Pacific Americans in party allegiance as well as turnout rates. Compared with Anglos, however, Asian Pacifics are both less partisan and less likely to vote.[3]

### A Political Balance Sheet

The still prevalent image of Asians as a model minority is actually a double exposure. It pictures them as both economic overachievers and political underachievers. Observers offer a wide variety of explanations—and even differ over whether political quiescence really is a cause for concern—but virtually none challenges the view that Asian Pacifics remain politically a population of silent Americans.

As the 1990s opened, there was some evidence to support a more positive assessment. Despite limited Asian Pacific voting strength, Asians were beginning to be elected to local office. In 1980 Filipino Tony Trias, appointed to fill a vacancy on the Los Angeles Unified school board, was the sole Asian American to hold a major city or county elected office. Ten years later, Warren Furutani had won a seat on the school board and Julia Wu on the Community College Board. Elected in 1985 in a 10 percent Asian Pacific district, Michael Woo became Los Angeles' first Asian Pacific councilman. In 1993, however, Woo failed in his bid to become the city's first Asian American mayor.

Building on earlier officeholding gains in the incorporated suburbs of the San Gabriel Valley, Monterey Park in 1990 became the first mainland U.S. city to have two Chinese Americans serving on its city council. Unfortunately, local Asian officeholding gains did not extend to state and federal offices. Between 1962 and 1992, no Asian Pacific from southern California served in the House of Representatives. Given these still limited realities of minority voting and officeholding, Asian Pacific politics, even in the supposedly breakthrough Los Angeles region, has primarily remained "politics by other means," namely, indirect group influence rather than electoral representation. For example, Asian Pacifics nationwide contributed $10 million to the 1988 presidential candidates and in California gave $1.5 million to the 1990 gubernatorial candidates.

## EXPLAINING THE ASIAN PACIFIC PARTICIPATION DEFICIT

We will consider the most often identified barriers to the electoral empowerment of Asian Pacifics under two explanatory heading: "Old World" imports or attitudes and experiences brought here by the immigrant generation and "New World" impediments, including internal disunity as well as the impact of discrimination. Three "Old World" factors limiting Asian Pacific political participation stand out in the literature: antidemocratic civic traditions, excessive preoccupation with home-country politics, and non-English monolingualism.

### Antidemocratic Norms

Low participation rates ostensibly reflect the enduring imprint of the Buddhist-Confucianist culture emphasizing hierarchy, subordination to authority, passivity, and resignation. Stanley Sue and Devald Sue observe a "traditionalist" Chinese-American personality type—deferential, reserved, inhibited, and passive—that shapes political behavior as well as social interaction. Among Japanese American, Harry Kitano finds an apolitical orientation rooted in such Japanese values as *enyro* (nonagressiveness) and *gaman* (uncomplaining acceptance). Regarding Korean immigrants in Los Angeles, Yung-Hwan Jo traces their "unassertive, indifferent, and even fatalistic posture" back to the neo-Confucian ethic. Similar cultural-religious interpretations have been applied to Filipinos, Laotians, and Samoans.[4]

In a pioneering study of the political participation of California's minorities, Carole Uhlaner, Bruce Cain, and Roderick Kiewiet have attempted to isolate the influence of imported cultural norms on group political behavior. Controlling for citizenship, age, and socioeconomic status, they found that the participation gap between Latinos and Anglos virtually disappeared. Among Asian Pacific Americans, however, there remained a small but significant residue that might possibly be due to cultural factors. It remains a daunting task, however, to operationalize and test the influence of such amorphous cultural factors.[5]

### Home-Country Politics

Homeland ties have an effect that is easier to document although complicated to interpret. From earlier studies describing Chiang Kai-shek's Kuomintang—the Chinese nationalist party—as "the real power" in Los Angeles' Chinatown to more recent studies assessing homeland politics as "the most vital force shaping Koreatown," this explanation figures prominently in accounts of the political dynamics of various Asian Pacific communities. In the early twentieth century, Asian

Pacific communities in West Coast cities became incubators of overseas nationalist movements. Their purpose was to reform or revolutionize China and Japan, as well as to liberate Korea from Japan and India from the British. Gradually, the initiative passed from activist exiles to repressive home-country governments intent upon politically containing their overseas populations.

During the Vietnam War, these containment tactics were copied by military regimes in Seoul and the Marcos martial law government in the Philippines. In conjunction with intelligence agents, consular bureaucrats penetrated the politics of Asian Pacific American communities. They typically were abetted by the ethnic media (subsidized by or even headquartered in the home country) and by local ethnic business elites dependent upon foreign bank loans and government subsidies. The resulting pattern of blocked political autonomy—what has been termed "sponsored immigrant politics"—forced ethnic concerns about the welfare of the ancestral homeland into narrow and rigid pro-government channels. Authoritarian governments in Taiwan, Korea, and the Philippines promoted reflex loyalty to anticommunist orthodoxy.

In the 1970s Asian Pacific Americans belatedly began an internal debate about whether inordinate preoccupation with home-country affairs served as a distraction from the challenges of participating in U.S. politics. Recoiling from foreign governmental domination of their communities, Asian Americans embraced an assimilationist strategy of group empowerment through greater electoral participation and office-holding. The 1980s challenged two major assumptions of the assimilationist model: first, that home-country political preoccupations would entirely wither away in the second and subsequent generations, and, second, that there was a zero-sum relationship between Asian Pacific involvement in foreign versus domestic issues. Beginning with the 1979 Koreagate scandal and the 1980 Kwangju Uprising, the Korean communities of Los Angeles and New York

each threw off consular domination in favor of community activism. They became simultaneously involved in both local political issues and overseas human rights concerns. The Koreans set the precedent for parallel home/abroad hybrid activism in the 1980s among other Asian Pacific groups. This suggests an additive rather than a zero-sum model of domestic/foreign political concerns.

## Language Difficulties

Virtually all observers consider lack of English proficiency a significant empowerment problem for Asian Americans. According to the 1980 census, one-half of Los Angeles County's Asian Americans listed a language other than English as primary. There are enormous differences in the English language capabilities of different Asian Pacific groups. Of predominantly native-born Japanese Americans, 32 percent classified themselves as "not speaking English very well," compared with 69 percent of the predominantly foreign-born Koreans and 82 percent of the Vietnamese. Filipinos and Asian Indians were as proficient in English as the Japanese because they came from countries with strong bilingual traditions.

The Immigration Reform and Control Act (IRCA) of 1986 imposed English literacy as a requirement for amnestied aliens seeking permanent residence and, ultimately, citizenship. These literacy barriers contradict the spirit of the 1975 Amendments to the Voting Rights Act mandating bilingual ballots for each language spoken by 5 percent or more of the local voting population.

Government policy, however, is not solely responsible for the divisive political consequences of language patterns among Asian Pacific Americans. Language diversity is both cause and correlate of political factionalism within and between Asian Pacific communities. The question of who speaks for Chinatown or Monterey Park is a matter not just of political opinion but of language. Mandarin speakers from Taiwan,

Cantonese speakers from Hong Kong, and "ABC" (American-born Chinese) English speakers have problems communicating, politically and otherwise. In addition to this factionalizing Tower of Babel effect non-English monolingualism constricts the flow of political information to Asian Pacifics. Almost one-half of Los Angeles Koreans have never read an English-language newspaper. Even more politically disadvantaged are the one-third of Laotians and Cambodians illiterate in their own language.

Language barriers to Asian Pacific empowerment are real, but their impact should not be exaggerated. Among Asian Americans, a consensus seems to be emerging around support for the "English Plus." This calls for concerted efforts to acquire English while retaining and transmitting the home-country language. Grassroots implementation of the English Plus philosophy is dramatically increasing the English proficiency of Asian Pacifics both absolutely and relative to Latinos.

The following explanations of the Asian Pacific electoral participation deficit emphasize New World impediments rather than foreign causes.

## Discriminatory Burdens

Virtually every chapter in national and state history until after World War II was a lesson in political exclusion for Asian Pacifics—from the Gold Rush Foreign Miners Tax and the 1879 state constitution's anti-Chinese provisions, to the anti-Japanese Alien Land Law of the Progressive Era, to the Immigration Restriction Acts and the U.S. Supreme Court's Ozawa and Thind decisions of the 1920s denying Asian Pacifics the rights of immigration and naturalization, to the Tydings-McDuffie Act of the New Deal effectively extending the immigration ban to Filipino nationals, to the culminating tragedy of the World War II internment.

Racial prohibitions on the acquisition of citizenship were not removed until 1943 in the case of foreign-born Chinese, 1946 in the case of Asian Indians and Filipinos born

abroad, and 1952 in the case of Japanese immigrants and other Asian Pacifics. It is important to remember that today's native-born, middle-aged Asian Pacifics were born into a society that granted them citizenship but that had denied their immigrant parents the rights to naturalize, to vote, to hold public office, to qualify for civil service jobs, and even to receive federal welfare relief during the Depression.

The conventional wisdom is that the "enforced passivity" characteristic of the immigrant generation begins to give way in the second generation to a politics of "reactive ethnicity" or collective self-assertion. However, this occurred only to a limited degree among Asian Pacific Americans. The formation of the Chinese American Citizens Alliance in 1904 and the Japanese American Citizens League in 1930 reflected organized attempts to implement this second generation logic. However, the power structure outside and inside the Asian Pacific community stunted these early political efforts. Beginning in the 1950s, there were individual political success stories among the Asian Pacific—particularly among the Japanese Americans. But not until the third and fourth generations emerged during the 1960s and 1970s did the politics of Asian Pacific self-assertion enjoy a real upswing.

Despite political gains culminating in the passage of the Redress and Reparation Act of 1988, discrimination continues to have a chilling effect both on native-born Asian Pacifics and on newer immigrants who manifest the political insecurities typical of the first generation. The perceived anti-Asian backlash of the 1980s—for example, the dramatic rise in anti-Asian hate crimes and the unfriendly English Only movement—and more subtle forms of discrimination—for example, the glass ceiling effect—keep alive even among third- and fourth-generation Asian Pacifics a sense of political alienation.

## Demographic and Socioeconomic Depressants

Underlying demographic and class patterns create significant political differences between and within Asian Pacific groups, further depressing participation rates. The 1980 foreign-born proportion among Los Angeles County's Asian Pacific Americans ranged from a high of 93 percent among the Vietnamese to a low of 29 percent among the Japanese. The median age of the region's Asian Pacific population was twenty-eight compared with thirty-six among Anglos. Noncitizenship and nonvoting-age status dramatically reduce the proportion of eligible voters in various Asian Pacific communities, particularly those from Southeast Asia.

Leaving aside the Pacific Islanders, the native-born proportion among Asian Pacifics correlates fairly closely with median family income—with Japanese at the top and immigrants from Southeast Asia on the bottom. Within Asian communities, the proportion of foreign-born can also mark a significant economic-political demarcation. Native-born Chinese and Koreans are still better off overall than newcomers, despite the high profile of the so-called Cadillac immigrants from Korea, Taiwan, and Hong Kong. In contrast, the most disadvantaged groups among Filipinos are drawn disproportionately from native-born cohorts with roots in the migratory farm labor experience. These complex internal group differences sometimes obscure the existence of what has been called "an invisible poor" Asian Pacific population, which includes unemployed Hmong, downtown Chinese, and the elderly Japanese, and aging Filipino farm laborers.

The popular image of Asian Pacifics as a superachieving minority is contradicted by the economic experiences of Pacific Islanders and Southeast Asians. In 1980, Samoans, for example, had a 30 percent poverty rate and a 33 percent dependency rate on welfare, social security, or disability pensions. Overall, Pacific Islanders and Southeast Asians were more dependent upon public assistance than were African Americans and Latinos. Throughout the 1980s, the Asian American poverty rate remained one and a half to two times the rate for non-Hispanic whites, hinting at the existence of an underclass. High levels of

poverty and welfare dependency among some Asian Pacific groups serve as barriers to political mobilization.

## ELECTORAL EMPOWERMENT STRATEGIES

Asian Pacific activists are increasingly preoccupied with reapportionment and leadership development as strategies to achieve political incorporation. This reflects the recognition that mass empowerment is stillborn without elite facilitation.

### Reapportionment and Redistricting

Asian Pacifics lagged in connection with boundary redrawing following the 1980 census. They concentrated instead on lobbying for the adoption of the new "Asian and Pacific Islander" umbrella classification that gave their nine major nationality groups stronger government affirmative action claims. Relative inattention to city, county, state, and federal electoral boundaries carried a price tag reflected, for example, in the gerrymandering of Los Angeles' Koreatown into three city council, two state senate, and three U.S. House districts.

In the early 1990s, the Coalition of Asian Pacific Americans for Fair Representation (CAPAFR) joined the NAACP Legal Defense Fund and the Mexican American Legal Defense and Education Fund (MALDEF) as a player in the state and federal reapportionment-redistricting games. At the local level, one key question involves at-large versus district elections. The conventional wisdom holds that the lack of geographic concentration makes ethnic politics more expensive and less valuable for Asian Pacific Americans. This is certainly true for some Asian Pacific groups like Asian Indians, who are not numerous enough to overcome their substantial residential dispersion. But it does not necessarily hold true when a diffusely settled Asian Pacific population grows large enough to become a plurality within community boundaries.

In fact, there is a consensus in suburban Monterey Park and Gardena that at-large elections enabling Asian Pacific Americans to marshal their broad-based strength have served them well. For example, Monterey Park City Councilwoman Judy Chu opposed district elections both on the philosophical ground that is racially polarizes and on the pragmatic ground that at-large Monterey Park had two Asian Pacific councilpersons while district-based Alhambra had none. In the city of Los Angeles, however, a concentration strategy exploiting the logic of district representation might make more political sense. In the case of Greater Chinatown, for example, relatively small boundary modifications—together with a major voter registration effort—might give a future Chinese American candidate the inside track in the first councilman district race.

But the concentration strategy is not without problems. First, should it aim at single or a multiple Asian Pacific groups, for example, Chinese Americans or a pan-Asian coalition? Second, is this strategy really superior to a more inclusive rainbow strategy that creates districts where cross-ethnic, cross-class coalitions can win? Bruce Cain and Roderick Kiewiets' 1984 study shows that two-thirds of winning Asian Pacific candidates in California came from districts less than 10 percent Asian Pacific, yet these same winning candidates represented districts with at least a 40 percent minority population. An Asian Pacific candidate like Michael Woo wanting to be elected mayor of Los Angeles has to be a crossover politican.[6]

## Leadership Development

The paucity of political leaders is a key barrier to Asian Pacific empowerment. Career politicians represent the most obvious source of community political leadership. The Asian Pacific community has produced a sizeable business and professional class but—perhaps as a consequence—few political leaders. Moreover, the few Asian Pacific career politicians have exercised what Kurt Lewin had called "leadership from the periphery." That is, the most successful politicians of Asian Pacific background are crossover leaders who identify least with the Asian Pacific community. Examples from the recent California past include former U.S. senator S. I. Hayakawa and former Democratic state senator Alfred Song—both of whom had quite chilly relations with the organized Japanese and Korean communities, respectively.

A potential source of future political leadership is the growing pool of Asian Pacific political aides, especially the sixty-four serving in the state legislature. The southern California Asian Pacific Legislative Staff Caucus—comprising federal, state, county, and municipal aides—alone has some fifty members. As Fernando Guerra has shown, over one-third of minority officeholders statewide—and all six of Los Angeles' urban and suburban Asian Pacific councilpersons in 1990—began their careers as political aides. Because of the scarcity of Asian Pacific officeholders, however, their mentors generally have not been Asian Pacific. All too frequently Asian Pacific aides have not been groomed as protégés or successors.[7]

Despite Republican-sponsored "how-to" campaign seminars designed to overcome middle-class Asian Pacific resistance to more active participation in politics, the Asian Pacific business class still is not generally receptive to career opportunities in politics. There is more receptivity on the part of Asian Pacific professionals; indeed, even Asia Pacific office seekers who come from the "for-profit" sector are more likely to be self-employed engineers or accountants than entrepreneurs. Well-worn professional routes into a political career include human services and teaching. High poverty rates among Pacific Islanders and Southeast Asians provide an opening for Asian Pacific social service providers to act as gatekeepers between the community and government.

Whatever the source, empowerment will remain an uncompleted process until Asian

Pacific Americans produce a generation of leaders capable of putting to rest the community's reputation as a politically passive population. The theory that such leaders are not born but can be made inspires the strong commitment to leadership development by such organizations as Leadership Education for Asian Pacifics (LEAP). Paralleling Latino leadership development programs are the Chinese American Policy Internship Program and the structured internship program of the Korean American Coalition

## Community Organizing

A new wave of electorally oriented Asian Pacific community organizations has been created since 1970 in response to demands for group self-assertion. Founded in 1983, the Korean American Coalition combines an explicit function as a recruiting channel for political aides and potential candidates. Other examples of new-wave community organizations include the Chinese American Association of Southern California, the Taiwanese American Citizens League, the Indo-American Political Association of Southern California, and the Union of Democratic Filipinos. Also included are ethnic political action committees (PACs) like CAPAC among the Chinese, FAPAC among the Filipinos, KAPAC among the Koreans, and the pan-Asian APAC. In addition to targeted campaign contributing, the Asian Pacific PACs may help produce new political leaders. Particularly influential among local Asian Pacific community organizations is the Asian Pacific American Legal Center (APALC), which lobbies and litigates on immigration, civil rights, and empowerment issues.

Asian Pacific Americans would especially benefit from registration-and-turnout campaigns to help them enter the house of full democratic participation. For example, modeled on the Latino Southwest Voter Registration Education Project, the UCLA Asian Pacific Voter Project has mounted nonpartisan voter registration drives in Monterey Park but with only limited suc-

cess. A real breakthrough will probably require partisan campaigns mounted by the Democrats and the Republicans; both parties could gain by greater targeting of Asian Pacifics, but neither has yet shown much interest.

## INTERGROUP COALITION BUILDING

In their influential study *Protest Is Not Enough*, Rufus Browning, Dale Rogers Marshall, and David Tabb have portrayed coalition building across ethnic, racial, and class lines as the best vehicle for a minority group to move from political exclusion to inclusion and empowerment.[8] The challenge of intergroup outreach is both unique and compelling for Asian Pacific Americans.

### Pan-Asian Coalitions

A pan-Asian coalition faces the formidable task of melding together a dozen larger and three dozen smaller nationalities from East Asia, Southeast Asia, the Indian subcontinent, and the Pacific Islands. This formulation, however, begs the anterior question of how disparate Asian Pacific groups can overcome internal divisions before they can unite with one another. The severity of the problem of internal unification around a national self-identity is partly a function of the homogeneity—or lack thereof—prevailing in the country of origin. At one end of the spectrum are Japanese and Koreans, who come from strong like-minded national cultures. At the other end are Filipinos, Asian Indians, and Southeast Asian groups who have to overcome the pluralist mosaic of regional, religious, and linguistic differences they bring from the old country. Even the Chinese community—which often looks monolithic to outside observers, including other Asian Pacifics—is viewed quite differently by insiders.

There are, however, strong countervailing pan-Asian tendencies. These coalitional tendencies date back to the 1960s, when the "Asian Power" battle cry was raised in emulation of the Black Panthers. Pan-Asianism was institutionalized in the 1970s by Asian Pacific groups lobbying for government affirmative action and group entitlement programs. Both nationality group loyalties and transnational commitments are likely to continue to coexist in uneasy tension among Asian Pacifics. The office of Los Angeles Mayor Tom Bradley, for example, recognized the pervasive influence of nationality by maintaining four group liaisons—Chinese, Japanese, Korean, and Filipino—with the Filipino given the additional responsibility for representing the smaller Vietnamese and Thai communities.

Ivan Light and Edna Bonacich's path-breaking study of the Los Angeles Korean community highlights the multiple—and instrumental—layers of group identification that shape political behavior. To protect their major group interest in the garment industry, Korean manufacturers have organized on an ethnic-specific basis by forming the Korean Sewing Contractors Association. Because a more inclusive pan-Asian strategy was needed to compete for federal set-asides for minority contractors, Korean entrepreneurs jointed wider Asian Pacific groups lobbying before Congress and the Small Business Administration. Finally, in the retail liquor industry, the Korean presence was not large enough for an ethnic-specific organization and group preference was not a policy objective. Hence Korean-American liquor store owners chose as their preferred lobbying vehicle the Southern California Retail Liquor Dealers Association—a rainbow trade association.[9]

## Asian Pacifics and Other Minorities

The downtown Anglo business community remains an important part of the city's governing or policymaking coalition, but electoral power within the Anglo community has shifted away from WASP suburbanites toward Jewish voters on the West Side and in Fairfax and the San Fernando Valley. The black-Jewish coalition that dominated Los Angeles politics during the five terms of Mayor Tom Bradley has developed severe strains, This unraveling process has fueled hopes for the emergence of a new rainbow alignment in which Asian Pacifics would subordinate both nationality and pan-Asian concerns to the imperatives of a black-brown-yellow coalition.

The rainbow model, however, is an ideological gloss that obscures as much as it illuminates the realities of ethnic power in Los Angeles. In terms of their relations with African Americans, Asian Pacific Americans have long-standing roles as junior partners in the Bradley coalition. Mayor Bradley's cultivation of Asian Pacific businessmen began when he served on the city council in the 1960s. Asian Pacifics contributed 10 percent of the campaign funding for the Bradley gubernatorial attempts of 1982 and 1986. Also, by the 1980s Asian Pacifics had become major contributors to Bradley's mayoral reelection campaigns.

The tragic intergroup tensions that caused a near meltdown of black-Asian Pacific relations during the 1992 Los Angeles riots can best be understood in terms of an ethnic succession model involving conflicts over neighborhood turf, business opportunities, and political preferment. During the 1970s and 1980s, Koreans, Pacific Islanders, and Indochinese joined Latinos in moving into once solidly black South Central Los Angeles. Merchant-customer frictions became the flash point for violence that overwhelmed the conciliatory efforts of organizations like the Black Korean Alliance (BKA).

Even before the 1992 riots, affluent Asian Pacific Americans in the multiethnic South Bay showed minimal interest in politically coalescing with African Americans. City Councilman Michael Woo did better among black voters in his 1993 run for mayor because of his high-profile role in the ouster of Police Chief Daryl Gates following the Rodney King beating. However, a broad-based Asian Pacific rainbow alliance with African Americans seems less plausible than ad hoc, piecemeal coalitions limited to certain areas such as the inner city, where economically depressed Filipinos, Pacific Islanders, and Indochinese may make common cause with blacks around a social services agenda.

Parallel hopes for a durable political marriage between Asian Pacific money and Latino votes also may be difficult to fulfill. The more likely outcome is a multiplication of covert liaisons, such as that between pro-growth councilman Richard Alatorre and Chinese American developers, and single-issue alliances, such as the countervailing slow-growth Latino and Asian Coalition to Improve Our Neighborhoods (LACTION).

## PUBLIC POLICY AND ASIAN PACIFIC EMPOWERMENT

Given the limited success to date of Asian Pacific electoral empowerment, "politics by other means" continues to be the primary strategy of group influence. Asian Pacific political organizations—whether utilizing lobbying, litigation, or protest tactics—have been active in shaping civil rights, economic, and foreign policy issues of particular concern to their communities.[10]

### Civil Rights

Civil rights issues are a major preoccupation of the Asian Pacific community. Memories of past mistreatment are given new resonance for Asian Pacifics by discrimination currently suffered by both immigrant newcomers and the upwardly mobile native-born. For the Japanese Americans community, past injustices were the central contemporary civil rights issues until amends were made for World War II internment with the passage of the reparations bill. Under Sansei, or third-generation, leadership, the National Coalition for Redress/Reparations (NCRR) became the model for new-style civil rights advocacy organizations among Asian Pacific Americans, such as the National Network for

Immigration and Refugee Rights (NNIRR), the Alliance of Asian Pacific Americans, and the National Civil Rights Legal Consortium. These groups are involved in efforts to forge a common Asian Pacific agenda around an umbrella package of civil rights issues, including immigration reform, bilingualism, educational and employment discrimination, and the battle against antiminority hate crimes.

Asian Pacific lobbying groups moved from a secondary and uncertain role in connection with the Immigration Reform and Control Act (IRCA) of 1986 to a primary and dynamic role in connection with the Immigration Act of 1990. Asian American organizations—notably the Pacific Leadership Council of Los Angeles—helped shape key compromises embodied in the 1990 act.

For the predominantly newcomer Asian Pacific communities like the Koreans and Vietnamese, civil rights tends to be synonymous with the twin issues of immigration reform and language rights, defined as opposition to English Only but support for English Plus. But for native-born, more established Asian Pacific communities such as third- and fourth-generation Japanese and Chinese, affirmative action is the pivot of the Asian Pacific civil rights agenda. There is widespread agreement that minority preferences remain a necessary tool for advancing Asian pacific economic interests.

In the educational area, Asian Pacific support for affirmative action is qualified by fears of de facto admissions quotas or ceilings. The crux of the matter in California has involved the University of California admissions process—especially at Berkeley and UCLA—where the Asian Pacific proportion of the student body rose to more than 20 percent in the early 1980s while the Anglo proportion dropped below 50 percent. In response, the two campuses reclassified and altered their admissions policies and practices accordingly. Asian Pacific enrollment at both campuses declined in the mid-1980s as token preferences given Filipinos, Southeast Asians, and Pacific Islanders masked the sharp cutbacks in slots allocated to Chinese and Japanese Americans. In 1987 Asian Pacifics began a political long march that has reversed what has been called "the unwritten law by the admissions offices" against Asian Pacific applicants to the University of California.

## Economic Development

Growth and ethnic succession long have been intertwined in California. As California enters the Pacific Rim era, an ethnic dialectic between established Anglos and emerging Asian Pacifics has become a central issue of metropolitan growth in the Los Angeles area.

### Downtown Redevelopment

While Asian Pacifics heretofore have taken a back seat to African Americans and even to Latinos in the electoral arena, their visibility as interest groups is much higher in the politics of downtown redevelopment. The reason is the centrality of Little Tokyo and Chinatown to Los Angeles' audacious effort since the 1960s to "invent a modern downtown" for itself. Created in 1948, Los Angeles' powerful Community Redevelopment Agency (CRA) has concentrated its renovation efforts on the North Central—Civic Center area, which is the historic core of Japanese and Chinese Los Angeles. The 1965 Los Angeles Master Plan and the 1972 Central City Plan both envisaged coordinated development of an "International Zone" in which Little Tokyo, Chinatown, and Olvera Street would serve a tourist-and-amenities function in relation to the central business district.

Little Tokyo was promised affordable housing, small business assistance, affirmative action preferences in construction hiring, and the establishment of a new community center. Federal urban redevelopment funding cutbacks, however, defeated or delayed these priorities, despite the lobbying efforts of the Little Tokyo People's Rights Organization, the Little Tokyo Development Corporation, the Affirmative Action Task Force, and the Japanese American Cultural and Community Center (JACCC).

To expand the community's economic base, the CRA in the early 1970s proposed a high-rise hotel. The New Otani Hotel was built by Kajima International and financed by the East-West Development Corporation—a consortium of thirty of Japan's largest financial institutions. Opened in 1978, the Japanese Village Plaza rehoused some of the displaced businesses. The Plaza, however, was quickly overshadowed by the new Weller Court shops "Little Tokyo's Rodeo Drive"—which were largely owned by Japanese nationals. A more positive development from the standpoint of community activists in the 1970s was the building of 300 units of senior citizen housing in the Little Tokyo Towers and the completion of the JACCC building. By 1981 the parameters of Little Tokyo redevelopment were set, with three-quarters of the forty-seven-acre "action area" either redeveloped or planned for redevelopment.

Little Tokyo redevelopment provides a window into the complex political dynamics and conflicts within the Japanese American community, as well as within broader Asian Pacific communities. First, there was considerable tension between commercial and community-oriented definitions of "redevelopment." the Sansei—many of them gentrifying "yappies" (young Asian Pacific professionals)—sought expanded neighborhood social services and cultural institutions rather than new business opportunities. Local neighborhood revitalization campaigns during the 1970s served as a training ground for young Japanese American activists who, during the 1980s, spearheaded the national campaign for redress and reparations.

Second, Little Tokyo experienced the increasing influence of Japanese multinationals and their overseas representatives. Anchored by Little Tokyo, Japanese investment in downtown Los Angeles has been massive. According to one 1989 estimate, the Japanese owned 30 percent of prime downtown office space. Little Tokyo community activists and small business owners have enjoyed only modest successes fighting "Big Tokyo" business interests and city hall.

Unlike Little Tokyo, Chinatown has a long-standing indigenous tradition of redevelopment dating back to the establishment of "New Chinatown" in 1938. In parallel with Little Tokyo, Chinatown revived these traditions during the 1970s with the Mandarin Plaza, the first of many shopping-and-office complexes. During the 1980s Chinese investors from East and Southeast Asia purchased banks, trading companies, and media outlets in the community. Whereas in San Francisco the major overseas Chinese investment influx has been from Hong Kong, in Los Angeles it has come from Taiwan.

As with Little Tokyo, Chinatown developers and community activists have had different definitions of desirable redevelopment. CRA generosity to Chinatown developers has made the community the major arena for redevelopment for inner-city Asian Pacific Americans. Chinatown community activists have fought the CRA, city hall, and state government over a range of projects, including plans to double the size of the county men's jail—already "the largest standing prison in the free world"—on the southern fringes of Chinatown.

## Suburban Development

In recent decades the San Gabriel Valley has emerged as the new Asian Pacific suburban frontier. The Valley's Asian Pacific population mushroomed from 114,000 in 1980 to an estimated 273,000 in 1990. Monterey Park has become the model in miniature and in extremis for the overlapping ethnic succession and economic development battles being fought throughout southern California's suburbs. In 1982 an Asian Pacific-Latino alliance that promised moderate growth and increased crime control defeated an antidevelopment slate of Anglo city council candidates put forward by the Residents' Association of Monterey Park (RAMP). Later that year RAMP forced a special election on two antigrowth proposi-

tions requiring voter approval for major zoning changes. The propositions passed over the opposition of the city council majority. However, under the leadership of Mayor Lily Chen—America's first Chinese woman mayor—the city council in 1983 began granting wholesale zoning variances for the construction of mini-malls and condominiums.

RAMP made the 1986 council election a referendum on "throwing the big buck developers out of City Hall." Mayor Chen and two Latinos were swept from office. In power, however, RAMP proved to be an unstable coalition of Anglo populists primarily concerned with controlling land use and nativists intent on imposing language uniformity.

The resultant ethnic polarization sparked the counterorganization of a multiracial alliance called the Coalition for Harmony in Monterey Park (CHAMP). CHAMP lobbying pressure blocked a two-thirds English sign ordinance and forced the city council to rescind an English Only resolution. The Chinese community—backed by developer money—then launched a voter registration campaign spearheaded by the Asian Pacific Voter Registration Project (APVRP), modeled after the Southwest Voter Registration Education Project (SVREP). In 1988 the Asian Pacific community produced a strong candidate for the city council, clinical psychologist Judy Chu. Campaigning as a moderate on the growth issue, Chu finished first in a field of eight candidates. The 1990 municipal elections, with two more minority councilpersons victorious, represented another resounding victory for racial pluralism.

Asian Pacific voters in both the inner city and the suburbs prefer to steer clear of the extremes in the growth politics debate. In the inner city, they gravitate toward multiracial moderate-growth coalitions that support limited commercial development provided it generates minority jobs and underwrites affordable housing. Asian Pacific Americans who have moved to the suburbs also seem to be more tolerant of new development than are established Anglo residents. They are attracted to a moderate growth platform that promises quality development to help pay for city services and to keep the tax rate down. However, they are unwilling to sacrifice residential livability for development. Obviously, the reconciliation of these diverse priorities becomes a difficult task when a politician turns from making campaign promises to trying to deliver on them in office.

## Foreign Policy Issues

We look here at the efforts by current generations of Asian Pacifics to build transpacific political and economic connections and thereby to help create a new Pacific Rim-based future for California.

### Political Linkages

Rather than a politically random movement between countries equilibrated only by supply-and-demand pressures, Asian Pacific immigration is very much directed along political, military, and economic salients connecting the United States to specific countries. For example, it is impossible to imagine that the Philippines, Korea, and Taiwan would be such major immigration sources except for the defense and trading partnerships forged between these countries and the United States after World War II. These partnerships put into a different perspective the home-country political preoccupations of Asian Pacific Americans.

The policy issues involved range from basing rights in the Philippines, to arms aid for Pakistan, to troop deployments in Korea, to defense commitments in Taiwan, to U.S. control of Guam and Samoa, to the reestablishment of diplomatic relations with Vietnam. These home-country issues—which also are U.S. foreign policy issues—are of lively concern to L.A.'s Asian Pacific communities.

Democratically involved, highly educated Asian Pacific Americans have also moved the human rights agenda to the center of Pacific Rim concerns. They have pressured

not only the U.S. government but repressive regimes in the Philippines under Marcos, South Korea under Chung Hee Park and his successors, India under Indira Gandhi, Pakistan under General Zia-ul-Haq, Taiwan under the KMT, and mainland China after Tiananmen Square. Although the effectiveness of Asian Pacific human rights pressures has been highly uneven, Asians are likely to continue to be an important two-way communication channel promoting democratic dialogue throughout the Pacific Rim.

### Foreign Investment

As the 1980s ended, Japanese banks controlled 25 percent of California's banking assets and 30 percent of outstanding loans. Japanese corporations employed 70,000 Californians, and Japanese investors were investing $6 billion a year in the state's burgeoning real estate market. The acquisition of a significant share of California's assets by Japanese as well as Chinese and Korean interests has revived a controversy over foreign ownership that had been dormant in California since the era of the alien land law.

The "middleman minority" theory that has been widely applied to Asian Pacific entrepreneurs has both a domestic and a foreign component. On the one hand, such entrepreneurs are portrayed as merchant intermediaries between the Anglo majority and nonwhite minorities, particularly African American ghetto dwellers. On the other hand, they occupy an intermediate position between Asian capital and the American market.

U.S. immigration law, in fact, codifies the international version of the middleman theory by converting the economic capital and overseas connections of Asian Pacific immigrants into a national asset. Economically based "priority worker" quota preferences are available to certain multinational business executives and to aliens with special business expertise. The economic logic of the immigration law is most direct in the case of the "immigrant investor preference." This preference has recently been liberalized to create 7.000 openings a year for immigrants prepared to invest at lest $1 million in business employing ten or more workers.

Joel Kotkin argues that while the 1980s represented the decade of Japanese investment in California, the 1990s promises to be the decade of the overseas Chinese. He adds, however, that "even defining the nationality of these Chinese—Americans, Taiwanese, Hong Kong—is virtually impossible. . . . These transpacific nomads, known in Taiwan as *tai kun fai jen*, or 'spacemen,' represented a new breed—Chinese entrepreneurs shuttling between Taipei or Hong Kong and such California cities as Torrance, Monterey Park, and Mountain View."[11]

Political movements embracing economic populism or nationalism can fuel nativist hostility to the indigenous Asian Pacific community. In 1989, before the speculative California real estate bubble burst, Congressman Mel Levine argued, "I can easily imagine Asian investors being pointed out as scapegoats for rising prices in the residential real estate market." Ironically, in the early 1990s these same Asian Pacific investors may be blamed for withdrawing capital from the declining California market.

## International Trade

Nearly one half of California's $63 billion in exports in 1989 went to Asia, making the Golden State second only to the United States itself as a trading partner of Japan. Estimates are that by 1995 one in six jobs in Greater Los Angeles will depend upon foreign trade, up from one in ten in 1990. Willingly or not, Asian Pacifics have been injected even more centrally into the debate over foreign trade than over foreign investment. One the negative side, they have been pictured as a weapon in the arsenal of overseas producers who, for example, give wholesale preferences to Korean import-export businesses in Los Angeles in order to flood the American market.

On the positive side, Asian Pacific Americans are being given a starring role in combating the trade deficit by the California Commission for Economic Development's Advisory Council on Asia. According to Lieutenant Governor Leo McCarthy, "The Asian American population in this state is our greatest asset; [they know the] environment and know the language, culture, and all the nuances of doing business [and] are very anxious to help California compete."

As the 1990s unfolded, California's world position owed much more to Asian Pacifics than merely the capital brought by immigrant investors. Relocating Hong Kong Chinese, for example, utilizes their wide-ranging connections to open up vast reaches of Southeast Asia to California economic penetration. Looking even further ahead, young Vietnamese may help the United States to peacefully return to Indochina through trade in the early twenty-first century.

But prosperity without empowerment is a precarious basis for social peace, as Asians on the other side of the Pacific Rim—particularly Chinese throughout Southeast Asia—have sadly learned. Despite the policy successes of a strategy of "politics by other means," California's Asian Pacific community remains politically vulnerable to backlash. The social compact appropriate for California's multiethnic future can only be built on the secure foundation of full democratic participation.

### NOTES

1. We wish to acknowledge the financial support of the California Policy Seminar for our research. For fuller documentation of our research, see Steven P. Erie, Harold Brackman, and James Warren Ingram III, *Paths to Political Incorporation for Latinos and Asian Pacifics in California* (Berkeley: California Policy Seminar, 1993).

2. Field Institute, "A Digest of California's Political Demography," *California Opinion Index,* August 1990, 5.

3. Don T. Nakanishi, *The UCLA Asian Pacific American Voter Registration Project* (Los Angeles: Asian Pacific American Legal Center, 1986).

4. Stanley Sue and Devald W. Sue, "Chinese American Personality and Mental Health," *Amerasia Journal* 1(2) (July 1971): 36–49; Harry H. L. Kitano, *Japanese Americans: The Evolution of a Subculture* (Englewood Cliffs, N.J.: Prentice-Hall, 1976): 191–92; Yung-Hwan Jo, "Problems and Strategies of Participation in American Politics," in Eui-Young Yu, Earl H. Phillips, and Eun Sik Yang, eds., *Koreans in Los Angeles: Prospects and Promises,* (Los Angeles: Koryo Research Institute, Center for Korean American and Korean Studies, California State University, 1982), 203, 208.

5. Carole T. Uhlaner, Bruce E. Cain, and D. Roderick Kiewiet, "Political Participation of Ethnic Minorities in the 1980s," *Political Behavior* 11(3) (September 1989): 212, 217–18; Alejandro Portes and Ruben G. Rumbaut, *Immigrant America: A Portrait* (Berkeley: University of California Press, 1990), 11, 114, 125, 134–35.

6. Bruce E. Cain and D. Roderick Kiewiet, "Minorities in California," paper presented at the California Institute of Technology Symposium, Seaver Institute, March 5, 1996, I–28.

7. Fernando J. Guerra "The Emergence of Ethnic Officeholders in California," in Byran O. Jackson and Michael B. Preston, eds., *Racial and Ethnic Politics in California,* (Berkeley: Institute of Governmental Studies Press, University of California, 1991), 126.

8. Rufus Browning, Dale Rogers Marshall, and David Tabb, *Protest Is Not Enough* (Berkeley: University of California Press, 1984).

9. Ivan Light and Edna Bonacich, *Immigrant Entrepreneurs: Koreans in Los Angeles* (Berkeley: University of California Press, 1988), 322–27.

10. See, for example, *The State of Asian Pacific America: Policy Issues to the Year 2020* (Los Angeles: LEAP Asian Pacific American Public Policy Institute and UCLA Asian American Studies Center, 1993).

11. Joel Kotkin, *Tribes: How Race, Religion, and Identity Determine Success in the New Global Economy* (New York: Random House, 1993), 168.

# 3.9

# Asian Pacific Americans and the Pan-Ethnic Question

*James S. Lai*

~~~~~~~~~~~~~~~~~~~~~~~~~~~~~~~~~~~~~~~~~~~~~~~~~~~~~~~~~~~~~~~~~~~~~~~~~~~~~~

Discussion of Asian Pacific Americans in state and local politics has traditionally centered around their aggregate population numbers, and thus their political potential as a "swing vote" (Nakanishi 1991; Ong and Nakanishi 1996; Nakanishi 1998). Despite this potential, Asian Pacific Americans have been hampered by comparatively low voter registration and turnout rates during the 1990s (Field Institute Poll 1994; Asian Pacific American Legal Center of Southern California 1996). Ironically the factors that have inhibited Asian Pacific Americans from higher voter participation rates stem from the very root of their potential—the growing population and demographic diversity among Asian and Pacific Islanders. California is on the nation's cutting edge for these recent changes. According to U.S. Census figures, during the period from 1960 to 1980, the California Asian Pacific American population increased from less than .3 million to 2.8 million. By 1980, Asian Pacific Americans held a 10 percent share of California's population (Nakanishi 1998). In 1990, 40 percent of the nation's Asian Pacific American population (almost 10 million people) resided in California, and in turn, nearly 34 percent of the state's Asian Pacific Americans lived in Los Angeles County (Shinagawa 1996).

Paralleling this overall growth, the Asian Pacific American community has also become more demographically diverse as a result of the 1965 amendments to the Immigration and Naturalization Act. According to the 1994 Current Population Survey, there are over thirty ethnic groups that fall within the category of Asian and Pacific Islanders. In Los Angeles County, nearly 80 percent of those Asian Pacific Americans ten years or older are foreign born (Ong and Azores 1991). One of the characteristics of this ethnically diverse and foreign-born population is their low voter turnout rates.[1] Asian Pacific Americans have the lowest voter registration of all racial groups, with a registration rate of 39 percent, constituting only 4 percent of California's voters, compared to a 65 percent registration rate for Whites (non-Hispanics), 58 percent for African Americans, and 42 percent for Hispanics (Ong, Espiritu, and Azores

Lai, James S. "Asian Pacific Americans and the Pan-Ethnic Question." In Richard A. Keiser and Katherine Underwood, eds., *Minority Politics at the New Millennium* (New York: Garland Publishers, 2000), 203–26. Reprinted with permission.

1991). Ethnic diversity and low voter registration rates complicate any discussion of an Asian Pacific American "swing vote."

Whether Asian and Pacific Islanders can coalesce into a unified political bloc is an important question that will be explored in this chapter.[2] Indeed, in this chapter I argue that the extent of Asian Pacific American political influence in the next millennium will be determined, in part, by their ability to unite their diverse interests in pan-ethnic coalitions. Pan-ethnicity is a social concept that entails a collective vision bridging diverse identities and interests. I explore the potential for a pan-Asian Pacific American coalition in electoral politics by examining two case studies: the 1991 California 46th Assembly District special primary election; and the 1993 Los Angeles mayoral election. These case studies were selected because at least one major Asian American candidate ran in both instances, and because a large and diverse Asian Pacific American constituency was present in both election districts. I contend that the creation of pan-ethnic coalitions depends on the efforts of those who view elections as opportunities for bridge building rather than "go it alone" roads. In Los Angeles, the important players are community-based organizations; individuals who are perceived as "leaders;" the ethnic media; and candidates who strategically seek cross-ethnic support. I examine general patterns of campaign contributions made to the Asian Pacific American candidates to determine whether pan-ethnic coalitions were generated in either of the two cases.[3] The data suggest that a pan-ethnic coalition was not created in the 1991 46th Assembly District special primary election; monetary support for candidates was ethnic-group specific. On the other hand, pan-ethnic support for Michael Woo was evident among his Asian American contributors in the 1993 Los Angeles mayoral election.

## PAN-ETHNICITY AND ITS ORIGINS

The term pan-ethnicity dates from the late 1960s, and was originally used in the context of social movements led by second and third generation Chinese and Japanese American college students. It connotes the ability of diverse ethnic groups to view their interests and identities as a collective racial group (Espiritu 1992; Wei 1993; Espiritu and Ong 1994). For Asian Pacific Americans, this concept has been operationalized by socio-psychological factors such as perceived discrimination due to race; knowledge of their leaders; support for race-based policy issues (e.g., affirmative action and the Redress Movement for Japanese Americans); and intermarriage (Lien 1997). The underlying goal of those who embrace pan-ethnicity is to unify diverse groups based on their common racial categorization rather than their ethnic heritage.

Scholars have argued that the pan-ethnic movement among Asian Pacific Americans symbolizes the movement away from an ethnic-based paradigm to a racial formation paradigm, in which the latter represented a means to make policy demands on the racial state (Omi and Winant 1986). The main purpose of this strategy is simple: there is power in numbers. A collective group identity could transform (under certain circumstances) the separate elements of the Asian Pacific American community into a more cohesive unit, which, in turn, could increase their effectiveness in influencing policy outcomes or political elections.

Early political studies on immigrant racial and ethnic groups argued that race and ethnicity became less important factors over time as the groups became more assimilated (Dahl 1961; Wolfinger 1965; Verba and Nie 1972). Race and ethnicity in today's political environment, however, has taken on a heightened salience. Bruce Cain, for example, has observed a trend in California politics for ethnic groups to "go it alone" (Cain 1991). This is particularly the case among recent immigrant Asian ethnic groups (post-1965) who do not necessarily identify with issues that marked the political struggles of more established Asian American groups during the 1960s.

Factors that diminish the potential for a pan-Asian identity among recent Asian immigrants include differences in socioeconomic background such as education and income, generation issues, and homeland politics (Espiritu 1992; Wei 1993; Espiritu and Ong 1994; Lien 1997). For example, many Vietnamese who came to the U.S. during the 1970s, entered as refugees (those who flee from homeland persecution under life or death circumstances), whereas Koreans who arrived in subsequent decades did so as immigrants under non-life threatening circumstances. Both groups have had different political experiences in their respective homelands and in the United States, therefore they do not share identical perspectives. As a result, cross-ethnic unity in the electoral arena can by no means be taken for granted; pan-Asian Pacific American coalitions do not automatically materialize. They are a constructed phenomenon shaped by the efforts of the following strategic-minded players: community-based organizations; individuals seen as leaders in the Asian Pacific American community; the ethnic press; and candidates running for office. The next section explores how they prevented the development of a pan-ethnic coalition in the 1991 46th Assembly District special primary election.

## THE 1991 CALIFORNIA 46TH ASSEMBLY DISTRICT SPECIAL PRIMARY ELECTION: PAN-ETHNIC POLITICAL COALITION FAILURE

The 1991 46th Assembly District primary election was a "special" election held to fill the mid-term retirement of the incumbent, Mike Roos. The 46th Assembly District was solidly Democratic; approximately 64 percent of its voters were registered Democrats

and 22 percent of its voters were registered Republicans (California Journal 1990). At that time, the population was reported to be 40 percent Latino, 38 percent white, 16 percent Asian and Pacific Islander, and 5 percent African American (Rafu Shimpo 1991). As a result of Roos' sudden retirement announcement, the Democratic characteristics of this assembly district, and the fact that it contained large portions of Koreatown and Filipino Town, three Asian Americans entered the race: T. S. Chung (Korean American), Keith Umemoto (Japanese American), and Joselyn Geaga Yap (Filipino American).[4] Both Chung and Yap were political novices. Chung was an attorney and Yap was a social worker. Umemoto was a consultant to the California Senate Committee on Budget and Fiscal Review. His father, Kaz Umemoto, once ran for the same Assembly District seat in 1977. Barbara Friedman was also one of the fifteen candidates who sought the Democratic nomination. Friedman had a prior history of public service: she served as Chief of Staff for Assemblyman Burt Margolin and Chief Deputy to Los Angeles City Controller Rick Tuttle.

The final result of the June 4th special election, as seen in table 3.9a, was that Barbara Friedman finished in first place. T. S. Chung, Joselyn Geaga Yap, and Keith Umemoto finished, respectively, in second, third, and fifth place.

## The Role of Asian Pacific American Leadership in Community-Based Organizations and the California Democratic Party

Community-based organizations can play a role in the construction of a pan-ethnic

**Table 3.9a    46th Assembly District Primary Election Results**

| Candidates | Barbara Friedman | T. S. Chung | Joselyn Geaga Yap | Keith Umemoto |
|---|---|---|---|---|
| Total votes—at polls | 2,838 | 1,186 | 1,376 | 1,263 |
| Total votes—absentee | 589 | 1,087 | 604 | 428 |
| Finish total | 3,427 | 2,273 | 1,980 | 1,691 |
| Primary finish | First | Second | Third | Fifth |

coalition. In the 1991 46th Assembly District primary, community-based organization leaders, who were worried about Asian voter support splintered between the three Asian candidates, tried to find one consensus candidate. The negotiation effort was led by Asian Pacific American leaders from various Northern and Southern California community-based organizations as well as the Asian Pacific American Caucus of the California Democratic Party. There were two meetings in Los Angeles on the issue, both initiated by leaders from these two groups. The first meeting took place over lunch with several community leaders present. According to Jai Lee Wong, a consultant for the Los Angeles County Human Relations Commission who was involved with planning the Southern California meetings:

> The first meeting was a closed meeting over lunch that did not involve any of the candidates. I called a meeting at Bill Tan's office to strategize how to get the three candidates together, to try to get a different reading on the candidates (J. L. Wong, interview conducted October 24, 1993).

It was decided that a second, mediating meeting, with all three candidates present, should be held. The hope was that in-person pressure and persuasion from California's Asian Pacific American community elite would convince two candidates to withdraw from the race.

The second meeting occurred in the law office of Violet Rabaya (a prominent figure in the Asian Pacific American Caucus) and was attended by approximately fifteen leaders and professionals from various community-based organizations, along with the three candidates. The outcome was a disappointment to those who arranged the mediation session. None of the three candidates would concede, and all affirmed their desire to stay in the race.

Why did Asian Pacific American community leaders fail in their attempt to produce a consensus candidate, which would have facilitated a pan-ethnic electoral coalition? One reason is that post-1965 ethnic groups (e.g., Koreans, Filipinos, Vietnamese) resent the relative power and status held by more established ethnic groups (e.g., Chinese and Japanese). Consequently many of these recent immigrant groups may not view pan-ethnic coalitions as a viable means to pursue their political interests, particularly in winning a "voice of their own." As Joselyn Geaga Yap succinctly put it:

> As a function of having been here longer, the Japanese and Chinese communities are in more places of power and influence. So there is a degree of envy by Filipinos and the Koreans when they see that the mainstream views all of us as the same way: a monolithic, homogenous group . . . Because of a lack of understanding among these coalitions, the fragmentation becomes almost inevitable (J. G. Yap, interview conducted October 24, 1993).

## Ethnic-Specific Media Coverage

The ethnic media did little to promote cross-ethnic support for the three Asian American candidates. Given the large Asian bilingual population in Los Angeles, the ethnic media has the potential to play an important role in educating their respective communities about the political necessity of cross-ethnic coalitions. However, in this election, the three major Los Angeles newspapers that serve the Korean American, Filipino American, and Japanese American communities focused on candidates believed to be of special interest to their readers. This was particularly the case for the Filipino and Korean American newspapers.

The *Los Angeles Filipino Bulletin* gave exclusive coverage to Joselyn Geaga Yap's campaign. It even published an article authored by Yap, which gave her an opportunity to "personally" communicate to readers her qualifications as a potential officeholder. Yap also discussed the relationship of Filipino Americans' socio-economic visibility to their political status:

The Filipino American community's lack of social and economic visibility has, in the past, translated to a lack of political presence and, consequently, to a politically weakened community. As the largest Asian American population group in the country and in California, we are determined to establish a stronger political presence and take a more active role in charting our political future (*Los Angeles Filipino Bulletin* 1991, 1).

Moreover, the May 1991 edition of the *Los Angeles Filipino Bulletin* (a monthly paper) contained three pro-Yap pieces. On the front page were two items urging Filipino Americans to vote for Yap. One was a boxed statement situated at the top right section of the front page that simply stated: "Get the vote out for Joselyn Geaga Yap Assemblywoman 46th District. Vote on June 4." The other front-page item was a short editorial piece entitled "Joselyn Yap's Candidacy is a Victory for Us." The term "us" was a clear reference to Filipino Americans as the editorial argued that the community would greatly benefit from electing Yap to office.

The *Korea Times*'s coverage of the 46th Assembly District primary was designed to mobilize Korean American support for T. S. Chung's campaign. The newspaper simply ignored other candidates, including Umemoto and Yap. One article prominently featured an interview with T. S. Chung, who emphasized the political urgency for the Los Angeles Korean American community:

Everyone in the Korean American community with whom I have spoken feels we have to run in this election. When a vacancy opens in the district with the largest number of Koreans living in, if we don't assert our rights and build our candidates, we are never going to be treated as a serious player (*Korea Times* 1991a, 1).

*Rafu Shimpo*'s coverage of the 1991 46th Assembly District primary election was more equitable. *Rafu Shimpo* ran three election-related articles covering all three Asian candidates. The difficulty in developing a pan-ethnic coalition was suggested in the front-page headline of the May 22 edition: "46th District Tests Ethnic Loyalties: Three Candidates, Representing Different Asian Pacific Ethnic Groups, Test the Community's Ethnic and Personal Alliances." This article analyzed the three Asian Pacific American candidates' campaigns and their political impact on voters. Unlike the *Korea Times* and the *Los Angeles Filipino Bulletin*, the *Rafu Shimpo* article also mentioned non-Asian candidates such as Barbara Friedman (*Rafu Shimpo* 1991).

## Ethnic-Specific Monetary Campaign Contributions

Campaign contribution patterns indicate that a pan-ethnic coalition did not exist in the 1991 46th Assembly District primary election. To assess the extent to which campaign contributions were ethnic-specific, I analyzed data from Chung, Yap, and Umemoto's campaign disclosure forms for the filing period of January 1, 1991 to June 30, 1991. Official monetary contributions were coded into the following categories: race and ethnicity, amount per contribution, individual vs. business, and geographic location. The category of race was divided into three subcategories: Asian, non-Asian, and unknown. The Asian subcategory was further divided into Asian ethnicities. A surname dictionary was used to identify ethnicity.[5] These data indicate that all three candidates received ethnic-specific contributions. However, Chung and Yap received a greater proportion of their money from co-ethnics than did Umemoto.

T. S. Chung received a total of $237,807 from 626 contributors. Over three-quarters (76.7 percent) of these contributors were Korean American individuals or businesses. Their donations comprised 77 percent of the total contributions made to Chung. The second largest category of contributions

(15 percent) was unknown individuals and businesses, whose donations were 17.2 percent of the money received by Chung. Only 5.4 percent of Chung's contributors were non-Asian, and they provided 4 percent of his money.

Joselyn Geaga Yap received a total of $64,146 from 352 contributors. Almost 83 percent of these contributors were Filipino American individuals, businesses, and community-based organizations. Their donations were 88.1 percent of the total contributions made to Yap. Non-Asians constituted the second largest category of contributors (13.1 percent); they gave 10 percent of the money received by Yap. Other Asian(s) were 4.5 percent of Yap's contributors and they provided just 1.8 percent of the money she received during the primary campaign cycle.

Keith Umemoto received a total of $137,983 from 324 contributors. Half of these contributors (50.3 percent) were non-Asian. They donated 72.1 percent of the money received by Umemoto. A plurality (42.3 percent) of Umemoto's contributors were Japanese American individuals, businesses, and community-based organizations, and they provided 25.5 percent of his campaign money. About 7 percent of Umemoto's contributors were other Asians, and they provided just 2.4 percent of his war chest.

The geographic location of contributors further illuminates the pattern of ethnic-specific contributions. The contribution data were coded into six areas: within Los Angeles County, Southern California (outside of Los Angeles County), Northern California (within Sacramento County and vicinity), Northern California (Bay Area and vicinity), outside of California (within the United States), and not available. Most of the campaign contributions given to all three Asian Pacific American candidates came from within Los Angeles County (the location of the 46th Assembly District). Eighty-two percent of Chung's contributors, 59.4 percent of Yap's contributors, and 58.6 percent of Umemoto's contributors were located in Los Angeles County. Northern California was the second largest

source of contributions for both Umemoto and Yap. About 20 percent of Umemoto's contributions came from the greater Sacramento County area, while 24.4 percent of Yap's contributions lived in the Bay Area and vicinity. Five percent of Chung's contributions (his second largest geographic category) lived in Southern California, outside of Los Angeles County.

The ethnic composition of T. S. Chung and Joselyn Geaga Yap's contributors from their primary and secondary geographic sources was predominantly Korean and Filipino, respectively. In contrast, the ethnic composition of Keith Umemoto's secondary geographic source of contributors, Northern California (within Sacramento County and vicinity), was not primarily Japanese Americans but rather non-Asian individuals and professional/labor associations. These findings indicate differences in the three candidates' political connections. Umemoto tapped into his work-related contacts at the state capitol, while Chung and Yap drew upon more local and ethnic-specific resources. Chung, for example, received contributions from international Korean corporations with Los Angeles headquarters.[6]

What might explain ethnic-specific campaign contributions during the 1991 46th Assembly District primary election? First, the political stakes were much greater for the Los Angeles Filipino and Korean American communities than for the Japanese American community. The 46th Assembly District encompassed all or large portions of both Filipino Town and Koreatown, whereas Little Tokyo was situated in the neighboring 47th Assembly District. Filipino and Korean Americans represented over 53 percent of the Asian and Pacific Islander population in over forty-eight census tracts situated in the 46th Assembly District (Lai 1994). Therefore, a critical mass of both Filipino and Korean American constituents existed in the 1991 46th Assembly District that could be tapped for both monetary contributions and votes. Secondly, the district's political landscape thus led candidates to believe that their individual (and their group) interests would be best advanced by pursuing an ethnic-specific campaign strategy. Chung's campaign manager, Charles Kim, indicated their goal was to attract contributions and votes from the Korean American community, which was seen as favorably predisposed towards a Korean American candidate (C. Kim, interview conducted February 8, 1994).

Korean and Filipino Americans were acutely interested in electing a candidate of their "own" to the State Assembly because Chinese and Japanese Americans have historically dominated Asian electoral politics. In fact, one criticism leveled at pan-Asian organizations is that Chinese and Japanese Americans have tended to dominate leadership positions (*Korea Times* 1991b; Espiritu and Ong 1994). There is some evidence, at least in Los Angeles, that post-1965 ethnic groups are aware they need to work together to increase their political clout—both within the Asian Pacific American community and in electoral politics in general. Shortly after the 1991 46th Assembly District primary, the *Korea Times* reported that Chung and Yap had said they would try not to run against each other in the future. Their discussion marked "...the first time that an Asian subgroup has been targeted by Koreans as an ally in pursuing political office" (*Korea Times* 1991b).

The 1991 46th Assembly District primary election illustrates a situation where three Asian candidates rejected the well-coordinated request of community leaders for a consensus candidate, and instead pursued independent, ethnic-specific support. The ethnic press focused coverage on candidates of interest to their readers and largely eschewed the subject of cross-ethnic electoral collaboration. In contrast, Michael Woo's 1993 mayoral campaign provides us with an example of a broadly focused strategy that sought support from all Asian Pacific American groups. Woo's campaign also suggests that, under certain circumstances, symbolic leadership can be used as a way to bridge diverse ethnic interests.

## THE 1993 LOS ANGELES MAYORAL ELECTION: TRANSCENDING ETHNIC DIFFERENCES THROUGH A PAN-ETHNIC CAMPAIGN STRATEGY AND THE SYMBOLIC LEADER

The 1993 Los Angeles mayoral election represented the end of the liberal, bi-racial coalition that had kept Mayor Tom Bradley in office for twenty years, and simultaneously marked the shift to a multiracial electoral paradigm (Sonenshein 1993). This non-partisan election pitted Michael Woo, the first Chinese American to be elected to the Los Angeles City Council in 1985, against the multimillionaire businessman Richard Riordan. Woo decided to participate in the city's public finance and matching funds program while Riordan self-financed his campaign.

The general election exit poll results indicated that Asian Americans supported Woo over Riordan, 69 percent and 31 percent, respectively. Riordan received 54 percent of the overall vote compared to 46 percent for Woo.

As the previous case study suggested, a candidate's campaign strategy can either facilitate or hinder the formation of a pan-ethnic coalition. In nonpartisan elections candidates have complete latitude to decide whether to follow a narrowly or broadly focused campaign strategy. To counter Riordan's deep pockets, Woo pursued a broad-based campaign finance strategy and appealed to Asian Pacific American contributors both in Los Angeles County and nationwide. David Lang, Woo's Campaign Finance Co-Director, contends that there was a deliberate effort to solicit potential Asian Pacific American donors:

We specifically targeted Asian Americans outside of California, particularly Chinese Americans . . . Our strategy was based on cultivating and developing a relationship with Asian Americans, Chinese Americans in particular (D. Lang, interview conducted November 7, 1995).

Clearly the strategy paid off. Woo's selective courting of Chinese Americans, and playing upon an ethnic connection, helps to explain why they gave the most money to his campaign. Woo's appeal was not limited to Chinese Americans, however.

In the eyes of many Asian Pacific Americans, Woo's mayoral candidacy represented a historic opportunity because Los Angeles is home to the mainland's largest Asian and Pacific Islander populations. The symbolic importance of electing an Asian Pacific American to Los Angeles' top office was widely understood. In fact, Asian Pacific Americans held fundraisers for Woo's Los Angeles mayoral campaign in cities as far away as New York City.

To determine whether there was substantive pan-Asian American support for Woo's candidacy, I analyzed campaign contributions he received in the following five months: September 1992, November 1992, January 1993, March 1993, and May 1993. Table 3.9f shows Woo's total contribution amount was $1,989,246. Non-Asians contributed the largest share of Woo's money (39.1 percent). Businesses followed in second place; they gave Woo almost 35 percent of his total contributions. Asians constituted the third largest category of donors and provided Woo with 24.8 percent of his contributions. Within this category, Chinese Americans dominated by giving 19 percent to Woo, while the other Asian ethnic groups (combined) contributed 6 percent.

Over two-thirds of Woo's contributions came from within Los Angeles County. This geographic concentration can be explained in two ways. First, the Los Angeles mayoral race was a local election so Woo focused his media advertisements and direct mailings on voters within the city. Second, a significant number of Asian voters and contributors lived in Los Angeles. According to the 1990 Census, the largest Asian Pacific American population of any mainland U.S. city was that of Los Angeles, where 9.8 percent of the population was Asian Pacific American (Ong and Azores 1991).

Almost 20 percent of Woo's campaign contributions came from Asian Americans living outside California. Woo received 179 contributions (19.6 percent of his total Asian American contributions) from the following seventeen states: Illinois, Ohio, New York, Virginia, Texas, Maryland, Washington, Michigan, New Jersey, Arizona, Wisconsin, Missouri, Pennsylvania, Florida, Minnesota, Louisiana, and Arkansas. According to 1990 U.S. Census figures, none of these states contained an Asian and Pacific Islander population greater than 4 percent of the total population.

## A Pan-Ethnic Pattern among Woo Contributors

The findings suggest a pattern of pan-ethnic support among Woo's Asian American contributors. To reiterate, Asian Americans provided about 25 percent of Woo's campaign contributions. Chinese Americans were the dominant source of this money. They gave Woo $375,423, which was nearly 76 percent of all Asian contributions. However, other Asian ethnic groups made substantial donations. In particular, Japanese Americans and Asian Indians contributed amounts proportionate to their share of Los Angeles' Asian American population. Japanese Americans provided 9.1 percent of the money contributed to Woo by Asian Americans ($44,874), and they represented 13.3 percent the city's Asian and Pacific Islander population. Asian Indians provided 4.5 percent of the money contributed to Woo by Asian Americans ($22,328), and they were approximately 5 percent of the Asian and Pacific Islander population (Ong and Azores 1991).

The Asian American contributions to Woo's mayoral campaign may be viewed as significant in two ways. First, the findings illustrate the salience of campaign contributions among Asian Americans. According to the Los Angeles Times general and primary election exit polls, Asian Americans represented only 4 percent of the total voter turnout, the lowest of all racial groups (Los Angeles Times 1993). At the same time, Asian American were almost one-quarter of Woo's campaign contributors. Secondly, the diversity of Woo's Asian American contributors is an encouraging indication that a pan-Asian American identity may have existed in the context of his campaign. Such diversity has been non-existent in past local elections with an Asian American candidate. For example, in 1988, Judy Chu, a Chinese American, ran for Monterey Park (California) City Council. Chu received $14,698 in campaign contributions. Most of this money (89 percent) was given by Chinese and Japanese Americans. She did not receive contributions from members of other Asian American ethnic groups.

## POLITICAL AGENTS AND PAN-ETHNIC COALITIONS: THEIR ROLE IN BUILDING FUTURE ALLIANCES

The 1991 46th Assembly District primary and the 1993 Los Angeles mayoral election indicate that certain factors—community-based organizations, the ethnic media, candidate strategy, and symbolic leadership—affect the development of pan-ethnic coalitions. In the 46th Assembly District primary election, community-based organizations and their leadership were unable to convince ambitious candidates that a unity campaign was the "best" course of action. While unsuccessful in this instance, leadership rooted in community-based organizations still has tremendous potential to mobilize Asian and Pacific Islander groups around various political issues.

Asian Pacific American community-based organizations represent one of the fastest growing areas in the Southern California public service sector. Asian Pacific American community-based organizations attempt to meet the needs of the diverse ethnic groups; their work ranges from job training and placement to immigrant and refugee assistance. In 1997, there were over 250 such pan-Asian organizations in Los Angeles and Orange counties (*Asian and Pacific Islander Community Directory:*

*Los Angeles and Orange Counties*, 1997). Civil rights and electorally oriented pan-Asian organizations such as the Asian Pacific American Legal Center of Southern California, the Asian Pacific American Labor Alliance, and the Korean American Coalition play integral roles in the political education of Asian Pacific Americans through a broad-range of political activities such as "get out the vote" drives, exit polling of Asian and Pacific Islanders, political education forums, and litigation. Thus these grassroots organizations may play a critical role in the forging of new cross-ethnic alliances.

The ethnic media could also play a vital role in nurturing pan-ethnic coalitions. It certainly did not encourage collaborative or mutually supportive relationships in the 1991 46th Assembly District primary election. The *Korea Times* and the *Los Angeles Filipino Bulletin* both emphasized the importance of getting "one of their own" elected into the State Assembly. In contrast, the *Rafu Shimpo's* coverage of the 1991 46th Assembly District primary election stressed the importance of pan-ethnic coalition building. Los Angeles County has a network of more than 195 Asian and Pacific Islander media outlets that provide news and information to their respective bilingual populations (Asian and Pacific Islander Community Directory: Los Angeles and Orange Counties, 1997). With the cooperation of this extensive media network, community-based organizations could inform the larger Asian Pacific American community about pertinent issues and the benefits of pan-ethnic coalitions. Furthermore, community-based organizations and the ethnic media could work together to gather information on the needs and concerns of post–1965 ethnic groups in order to foster cohesiveness.

Another political agent that can either inhibit or facilitate the development and maintenance of inter-ethnic/racial coalitions is an effective leader or leadership (Stone 1989; Browning, Marshall, and Tabb 1990; Sonenshein 1993). The symbolic leader may promote a collective Asian

American identity, as demonstrated by Michael Woo's 1993 Los Angeles mayoral campaign. For many Asian Pacific Americans, Woo's campaign represented a galvanizing political force, which allowed him to transcend ethnic divisions. The lack of a well known and trusted symbolic leader in the 1991 46th Assembly District primary election would partially explain the failure of a consensus candidate strategy. Stewart Kwoh, the Executive Director of the Asian Pacific American Legal Center of Southern California, supports this position and argues that:

> [A] candidate that is going to receive the backing of a cross-section of Asian Pacific Americans has to represent the aspirations and the hopes of those people. Much of the time that will mean that the person has to have some track record in the other Asian and Pacific Islander communities, fighting for certain interests, being visible in the community, having some sort of track record on issues or services, representing certain existing politicians, and providing certain constituent services (S. Kwoh, interview conducted January 25, 1994).

The three Asian Pacific American candidates who ran in the 1991 46th Assembly District primary were political novices and did not have the experience, proven track record or visibility that would be required for a unity campaign.

Asian Pacific American political leaders must possess cross-over appeal to other groups besides Asian Pacific Americans (Brackman and Erie 1995). Michael Woo was such a candidate as he received nearly 86 percent, 54 percent, and 43 percent of the African American, Latino, and white liberal votes, respectively (Sonenshein 1993). Perhaps the future's most prominent political leaders will come from the large pool of Asian Pacific American political aides (Brackman and Erie 1995). However, many of these aides often do not choose to run for office, and must be encouraged by the state parties and Asian Pacific American community leadership to do so. Another source of future political leadership is community-based organizations. As the number of Asian Pacific American electorally oriented community-based organizations increase, these groups will incubate Asian Pacific American political leaders with experience in coalition politics (Park 1998).

Given California's weak political party system, a candidate's campaign strategy in mobilizing voters and contributors helps to determine whether or not a pan-ethnic coalition will develop. In the 1991 46th Assembly District primary election, candidates mobilized voters and contributors from their respective ethnic groups, and ignored the warning of Democratic Party and community leaders that to do so would split the Asian American vote. In contrast, Woo's campaign strategy during the 1993 Los Angeles mayoral election was to target a broad spectrum of Asian ethnic contributors from Los Angeles County and outside of California. This, along with the symbolic nature of his candidacy, would explain why a pan-ethnic trend emerged from Woo's Asian American campaign contributors.

Other political factors with potential to impact the formation of future pan-ethnic coalitions include race-based policy issues such as hate crimes against Asian Pacific Americans, affirmative action, and anti-immigration policies. According to a 1996 national survey of Asian Pacific American voters, ethnic unity exists on race-based policies (*Asian Week* 1996). Pan-Asian coalitions have been successfully created around such issues. An example is the pan-Asian organization American Citizens for Justice that was formed in 1984 to monitor hate crimes against Asian Pacific Americans across the country. This organization consisted of liberal and conservative American-born and immigrant Chinese, Japanese, Filipinos, and Koreans (Zia 1984). Since then, other pan-Asian organizations such as the National Asian Pacific American Legal Consortium in Washington, D.C., continue to monitor hate crimes. Race-based public policies may also provide a stimulus for Asian Pacific Americans to develop coalitions with other groups and to seek greater elected representation (Preston and Lai 1998).

If pan-ethnic coalitions can be developed and maintained around key issues at the local and state levels, the political implications for Asian Pacific Americans are significant. For example, the development of a pan-Asian identity has been found to facilitate voter turnout. During the 1990s, Southern California Asian Pacific American voters who personally experienced discrimination because of their race/ethnicity were more likely to vote than Asian Pacific Americans with higher education or socioeconomic attainment (Lien 1997).

Efforts to build pan-ethnic coalitions may also be bolstered by increases in Asian Pacific American elected representation. There are more candidates of various Asian ethnicities running for office and winning federal, state, and local positions than ever before. During the June 1998 primary elections in California, a record twenty-four candidates ran for such positions with fourteen winning nominations. There are currently over 2,000 Asian and Pacific Islander elected and appointed officials from over thirty-one states compared to less than 500 in 1978 (*National Asian Pacific American Political Almanac* 1998–1999). As the numbers of elected Asian Pacific American candidates grow, the urgency of post-1965 Asian Pacific American groups to work only on behalf of "one of their own" will diminish. In turn, this should enhance the likelihood that ethnic groups would support each other's candidates at the ballot box.

The future of Asian Pacific American electoral politics—and gains in empowerment via pan-ethnic identity and collaboration—will most likely be shaped and influenced by community-based organizations, the ethnic media, symbolic leadership, and candidate campaign strategy. Scholars of Asian Pacific American politics argue that it is necessary to extend traditional approaches towards political behavior (e.g., voting) to include nontraditional actors and their influences on Asian Pacific American behavior and attitudes (Nakanishi 1986;

Lien 1997; Nakanishi 1998; Saito 1998). Growth in the size and ethnic diversity of the Asian Pacific American population presents special challenges to scholars and activists alike. Building pan-Asian coalitions designed to increase Asian Pacific American political influence is a difficult task, but one with potentially high rewards. For that reason, it is well worth our attention in the next millennium.

## NOTES

1. Asian Pacific Americans, and other minorities, have usually been undersampled in most statewide and local election exit polls (Lien 1997; Cain and MacDonald 1998). As a result, estimates of Asian Pacific American voter turnout have been subject to criticism by scholars of Asian Pacific American politics (Ong and Nakanishi 1996).

2. This is not to downplay the significance of the need for Asian Pacific Americans to coalesce with other racial groups in California and elsewhere. The ability of Asian Pacific Americans to develop and maintain advantageous coalitions with other racial and ethnic groups will be central to their future political incorporation (Erie and Brackman 1993; Jennings 1994).

3. Asian Pacific Americans have a history of being large campaign contributors to federal, state, and local campaigns (Tachibana 1986; Nakanishi 1991; Lai 1994; Lien 1997). This is primarily because one does not have to be a citizen or a registered voter to give a campaign contribution. One only needs to be a legal permanent resident in the United States at the time the contribution was given (Alexander 1991). Given their proclivity toward campaign contributions combined with the limitations of exit poll data (i.e., the absence of exit poll data at the voter level that operationalizes for Asian ethnicity; the undersampling of Asian and Pacific Islander respondents; and their low voter turnout rate), analyzing campaign contribution data allows one to address pan-Asian Pacific American coalitions more effectively.

4. The author wishes to clarify the spellings of the ethnic enclaves and groups that will be discussed throughout this chapter. The spellings of "Koreatown" and "Filipino Town" are adopted from the respective ethnic communities. The

term "Filipino American" will be used as opposed to "Pilipino American," as it is more commonly used.

5. Several limitations are associated with the surname identification method. One limitation of surname identification was that some surnames could be either Asian or Non-Asian (e.g., Lee). These contributions were placed in the Unknown category. Another limitation in surname identification involved interracial marriage, whereby surnames of contributors could have been changed.

6. Official campaign contribution reports for T. S. Chung indicate he received monetary contributions from the following international Korean corporations with headquarters in the United States: Hyundai Corporation USA (5/20/91); Sangyong International, Inc. (5/20/91); and Dongkuk International, Inc. (5/20/91).

## REFERENCES

Alexander, H. E. 1991. *Reform and Reality: The Financing of State and Local Campaigns.* New York: Twentieth-Century Fund Press.

*Asian and Pacific Islander Community Directory for Los Angeles and Orange Counties.* 1997. (7th ed.). Los Angeles: UCLA Asian American Studies Center.

Asian Pacific American Legal Center of Southern California. 1996. *1996 Southern California Asian Pacific American Exit Poll Report: An Analysis of APA Voter Behavior and Opinions.*

*Asian Week.* 1996. "Asian Americans on the Issues: The Results of a National Survey of Asian American Voters." (August 23): 14–17.

Brackman, H., and S. P, Erie. 1995. "Beyond 'Politics by Other Means': Empowerment Strategies for Los Angeles' Asian Pacific Community." In M. P. Smith and J. R. Feagin, eds. *The Bubbling Cauldron: Race, Ethnicity, and the Urban Crisis,* 282–303. Minneapolis: University of Minnesota Press.

Browning, R. P., D. R. Marshall, and D. H. Tabb. 1990. "Minority Mobilization in Ten Cities: Failures and Successes." In R. P. Browning, D. R. Marshall, and D. H. Tabb, eds. *Racial Politics in American Cities,* 8–32. New York: Longman.

Cain, B. E. 1991. "The Contemporary Context of Ethnic and Racial Politics in Californian." In B. O. Jackson and M. B. Preston, eds. *Racial and Ethnic Politics in California,* Vol. I, 9–24. Berkeley: Institute of Governmental Studies Press.

Cain, B. E., and K. MacDonald. 1998. "Race and Party Politics in the 1996 U.S. Presidential Election." In B. O. Jackson and M. B. Preston, eds. *Racial and Ethnic Politics in California,* Vol. II, 199–232. Berkeley: Institute of Governmental Studies Press.

*California Journal.* 1990. "Legislative District Maps of California Supplement."

Dahl, R. 1961. *Who Governs?* New Haven, Conn.: Yale University Press.

Erie, S. P., and H. Brackman. 1993. *Paths to Political Incorporation for Latinos and Asian Pacifics in California.* University of California, The California Policy Seminar.

Espiritu, Y. L. 1992. *Asian American Panethnicity: Bridging Institutions and Identities.* Philadelphia: Temple University Press.

Espiritu, Y. L., and P. M. Ong. 1994. "Class Constaints on Racial Solidarity among Asian Americans." In P. M. Ong, E. Bonacich, and L. Cheng, eds. *The New Asian Immigration in Los Angeles and Global Restructuring,* 295–322. Philadelphia: Temple University Press.

"Field Institute Poll." 1994. In J. S. Lai, ed. *1996 National Asian Pacific American Political Almanac,* 7th ed. Los Angeles: UCLA Asian American Studies Center.

Horton, J. 1989. "The Politics of Ethnic Change: Grass-Roots Responses to Economic and Demographic Restructuring in Monterey Park, California." *Urban Geography* 10: 578–92.

Jennings, J. 1994. "Changing Urban Policy Paradigms: Impact of Black and Latino Coalitions." In J. Jennings, ed. *Blacks, Latinos, and Asians in Urban America,* 3–16. Westport, Conn.: Praeger.

*Korea Times.* 1991a. "Son of Koreatown: T. S. Chung Seeks Seat in Sacramento." March 20: 1.

———. 1991b. "Coalition in the Making: Koreans and Filipinos Close Ranks for Future Elections." July 21: 1.

Lai, J. S. 1994. At the Threshold of the Golden Door—Ethnic Politics and Pan-Asian Pacific American Coalition Building. Unpublished master's thesis. University of California, Los Angeles.

Lien, P. 1997. *The Political Participation of Asian Americans: Voting Behavior in Southern California.* New York: Garland Publishing.

Los Angeles City Ethics Commission. 1993. Michael Woo for Los Angeles Mayor. California Long Form 490, Schedule A.

Los Angeles County Registrar Recorder's Office, Office of Campaign Reporting. 1991a. Tong Soo Chung for 46th Assembly. California Long Form 490, Schedule A.

———. 1991b. Keith Umemoto for 46th Assembly. California Long Form 490, Schedule A.

———. 1991c. Joselyn Geag Yap for 46th Assembly. California Long Form 490, Schedule A.

*Los Angeles Times.* 1993. 1993 Los Angeles Mayoral Election General and Primary Exit Poll Results. June 10: A25.

Nakanishi, D. T. 1991. "The Next Swing Vote? Asian Pacific Americans and California Politics." In B. O. Jackson and M. B. Preston, eds. *Racial and Ethnic Politics in California*, Vol. I, 25–54. Berkeley: Institute of Governmental Studies Press.

———. 1998. "When Numbers Do Not Add Up: Asian Pacific Americans and California Politics." In B. O. Jackson and M. B. Preston, eds. *Racial and Ethnic Politics in California*, Vol. II, 3–43. Berkeley: Institute of Governmental Studies Press.

*National Asian Pacific Political Almanac.* 1998–1999. (8th ed.). Los Angeles: UCLA Asian American Studies Center.

Omi, M., and H. Winant. 1986. *Racial Formation in the United States: From the 1960s to the 1980s.* New York: Routledge.

Ong, P. M., and T. Azores. 1991. *Asian Pacific Americans in Los Angeles: A Demographic Profile.* Los Angeles: LEAP Public Policy Institute and UCLA Asian American Studies Center.

Ong, P. M., and D. T. Nakanishi. 1996. "Becoming Citizens, Becoming Voters: The Naturalization and Poltical Participation of Asian Pacific Immigrants." In B. O. Hing and R. Lee, eds. *Reframing the Immigration Debate*, 275–305. Los Angeles: LEAP Public Policy Institute and UCLA Asian American Studies Center.

Ong, P. M., Y. L. Espiritu, and T. Azores. 1991. *Redistricting and Political Empowerment of*

*Asian Pacific Americans in Los Angeles: A Position Paper.* Los Angeles: LEAP Public Policy Institute and UCLA Asian American Studies Center.

Park, E. 1998. "Competing Visions: Political Formation of Korean Americans in Los Angeles, 1992–1997." *Amerasian Journal* 24: 1, 41–58.

Preston, M. B., and J. S. Lai. 1998. "The Symbolic Politics of Affirmative Action." In B. O. Jackson and M. B. Preston, eds. *Racial and Ethnic Politics in California*, Vol. II, 161–198. Berkeley: Institute of Governmental Studies Press.

*Rafu Shrimpo.* 1991. "46th District Tests Ethnic Loyalties: Three Candidates, Representing Different Asian Pacific Ethnic Groups, Test the Community's Ethnic and Personal Alliances." May 22: 3.

Saito, L. T. 1998. "Beyond Numbers: Asian American and Latino Politics in Los Angeles' San Gabriel Valley." In B. O. Jackson and M. B. Preston, eds. *Racial and Ethnic Politics in California*, Vol. II, 45–72. Berkeley: Institute of Governmental Studies Press.

Shinagawa, L. H. 1996. "The Impact of Immigration on the Demography of Asian Pacific Americans." In B. O. Hing and R. Lee, eds. *Reframing the Immigration Debate*, 59–130. Los Angeles: LEAP Public Policy Institute and UCLA Asian American Studies Center.

Sonenshein, R. J. 1993. *Politics in Black and White: Race and Power in Los Angeles.* Princeton, N.J.: Princeton University Press.

Stone, C. N. 1989. *Regime Politics: Governing Atlanta: 1946–1988.* Lawrence, Kan.: University of Kansas Press.

Tachibana, J. 1986. "California's Asians: Power from a Growing Population. *California Journal* 17: 534–43.

Verba, S., and N. Nie. 1972. *Participation in America.* New York: Harper & Row.

Wei, W. 1993. Philadelphia: Temple University Press. *The Asian American Movement.*

Wolfinger, R. E. 1965. "The Development and Persistence of Ethnic Voting. *American Political Science Review* 59: 898–908.

Yap, J. G. 1991. "Lack of Visibility Spells a Weakened Voice in Politics." Los *Angeles Filipino Bulletin* (April): 1.

Zia, H. 1984. "The New Violence." Bridge 9(2): 18–23.

# 3.10

# The Backdoor and the Backlash
## Campaign Finance and the
## Politicization of Chinese Americans

*Taeku Lee*

~~~~~~~~~~~~~~~~~~~~~~~~~~~~~~~~~~~~~~~~~~~~~~~~~~~~~~~~~~~~~~~~~~~~~~~

Since the fall of 1996 the political activities of Asian Pacific Americans have been pulled unexpectedly and unceremoniously into the swirl of controversy encircling the Clinton presidency.[1] In the brief history of this issue, a cast of obscure characters notable hitherto only as behind-the-scenes fund raisers—John Huang, Charlie Yah-lin Trie, Johnny Chung, Marie Hsia, Yogesh Gandhi, Eugene and Nora Lum, among others—have been thrown onto the center stage of contemporary Asian American politics. In some respects, such limelight is relatively uncharted territory for Asian Americans, who have more often been distinguished for their relative political invisibility and their inclination for political influence through backchannels like campaign contributions. In other respects, such limelight is more familiar terrain for Asian Americans—yet another strain of the racial resentment and nativism that has marked the history of Asians in America and, more generally, the politics and policies affecting predominantly immi-

grant ethnic communities at the end of the twentieth century.

As Don Nakanishi (1998) points out, the spin on the political status of Asian Americans has been almost wholly beyond the control of Asian Americans themselves as a result of the campaign finance controversy. The issue of allegedly illegal fundraising and improper influence-peddling by select Asian and Asian American donors quickly overshadowed the significant inroads that Asian American elected and appointed officials forged in the 1996 elections. The critical response from leaders within the Asian Pacific American community has been swift, but often neither unequivocal nor univocal. While some decry the anti-Asian rhetoric and practices, others decry the moral bankruptcy of our nation's electoral system, and still other decry the personal avarice of individuals like Charlie Yah Lin Trie and Johnny Chung.[2]

In each case, however, the Asian American leadership have noted the searing political backlash that has resulted from the campaign finance controversy. Prominently, a coalition of Asian American leaders and organizations filed a formal complaint with the U.S. Commission on Civil Rights in September 1997 in response to the

Lee, Taeku. "The Backdoor and the Backlash: Campaign Finance and the Politicization of Chinese Americans." *Asian American Policy Review* IX: 30–55. Reprinted with permission.

media's coverage on this issue, the Democratic National Committee's (DNC) in-house investigations, and the Republican-led congressional investigations. Among other things, this formal complaint condemns the dubious manner of the DNC's in-house investigation and the revivification of some of the worst stereotypes about Asian Americans by the mass media and members of the House of Representatives on this issue. Importantly, while the Asian American leadership has spoken, the voices of ordinary Asian Americans are largely unheard and unknown.

The impetus behind this paper in the first instance is to "move beyond a cataloging of the slights and insults" (Watanabe 1998, 2) and to discipline the welter of public speculation and media coverage on this issue with some hard-nosed analysis. The paper is comprised of two parts. First, I review existing studies of media coverage on this issue and consider the extent to which the media is implicated in perpetuating negative representations of Asians in America. I then focus on the ethnic group that has been most visibly implicated in this controversy—U.S. residents of Chinese descent—and examine what data from a 1997 *Los Angeles Times* poll tells us about the perspectives of rank-and-file Chinese Americans on this matter. Specifically, I examine the conditions under which Chinese Americans: (1) make an explicitly negative, racialized assessment of ongoing congressional investigations, and (2) view the media's coverage on this issue to be unfair.[3]

## MEDIA COVERAGE ON THE CAMPAIGN FINANCE ISSUE

The first observation about media coverage on the allegedly illegal Asian campaign finance activities is its sheer volume and questionable content. As Ling-chi Wang, one of the most outspoken critics of John Huang and other Asian Pacific Americans implicated in the controversy writes. "[n]ot since the protracted national debate over whether the Chinese should be excluded

from the United States in the 1870s and early 1880s have we seen more sustained media coverage and acrimonious debate on the so-called 'Asian connection'" (1998b, 1). At least for the moment, stories about the heroic struggles of hard-working, "model minority" immigrants have receded in media representations of Asian Pacific Americans, only to be replaced by unsubtle allusions to a "Yellow Peril" and "Red Peril" who are "perpetual foreigners" within U.S. borders. In an especially malignant instance of this, *The National Review* in March 1997 published a cover depicting president and Mrs. Clinton as "the Manchurian Candidates," garbed in Chinese silk, coolie hat, and Mao cap and grinning ear-to-ear with buck teeth, slanted eyes, and other "Orientalized" characterizations.

As Helen Zia put it in *The Nation*, "[t]he images of yellow spooks at the White House, with ties to Indonesia and the post-glasnost Evil Empire, China, was too tempting for pundits and politicians not to exploit" (1997, 10). In a petition submitted to the U.S. Commission on Civil Rights, a coalition of Asian American leaders and organizations pointed an inculpatory finger at the mass media for their negative coverage on this issue. For those who have closely followed the history of Asian immigrants in the United States, media coverage on the campaign finance issue is a stark reminder of "the peculiarly American way in which the media portray [Asian Americans] as eternal foreigners, regardless of our pedigrees" (Zia 1997, 10).[4]

Perhaps the most systematic critique of media coverage on this matter to date has been Frank Wu and May Nicholson's "Racial Aspects of Media Coverage on the John Huang Matter" (1997). Wu and Nicholson look at media coverage surrounding John Huang's fund-raising activities between October 7, 1996 (the date the story broke) and January 20, 1997 (President Clinton's inauguration) in six media outlets: the *Wall Street Journal*, the *New York Times*, the *Boston Globe*, the *Washington Post*, the *Los Angeles Times*, and *Newsweek*. Wu and Nicholson note the

**Box 3.10a    Event History of the Campaign Finance Issue**

| | |
|---|---|
| July 1994 | John Huang enters Clinton administration as Deputy Assistant Secretary of Commerce Department. |
| December 1995 | Huang leaves the commerce Department to become a fund-raiser for Democratic National Committee (DNC). |
| June 1996 | FBI agents warn six members of Congress that they may be targeted for illegal contributions from China. |
| October 1996 | Final month of 1996 Presidential campaign. Bob Dole alleges campaign improprieties, especially with regard to foreign money infiltration into Democratic coffers, a central theme in his campaign. |
| October 3, 1996 | John Huang is "suspended" by DNC. |
| October 15, 1996 | Newt Gingrich makes statement about John Huang and the Lippo Group suggesting campaign improprieties. |
| October 19, 1996 | Huang fined by DNC. |
| November 1996 | Commerce Department's inspector general opens investigation into Huang. |
| December 5, 1996 | Commerce officials discover John Huang had top-secret security clearance even after he left Commerce Department post. |
| January 1997 | FBI director Louis Frech assigns 25 agents to investigate Huang and the Lippo Group after a request by Congressman Gerald Solomon (R-NY). |
| January 27, 1997 | Yah Lin "Charlie" Trie indicted as a result of Justice Department investigation on illegal foreign contributions. |
| February 1997 | *Washington Post* reports that special Justice Department task force is investigating possible Chinese influence in U.S. elections. |
| February 1997 | Senate committee votes to issue subpoenas for Lippo Group records. |
| March 11, 1997 | Senate votes to expand investigation probe on improper/illegal activities in campaign fund-raising. |
| April 1997 | Documents relating to Huang's tenure at the DNC released to public. |
| July 8, 1997 | Public hearings on campaign finance improprieties of 1996 open in the Senate, led by Chair Sen. Fred D. Thompson (R-TN) |
| February 1998 | Maria Hsia, DNC fundraiser, indicted on charges of using false cover to funnel illegal funds into election campaign. |
| February 1998 | Democrats and Republicans from the Senate committee investigating allegations against Chinese government present drafts. Drafts are contradictory. Republicans are more accusatory. |
| July 13, 1998 | Thai businesswoman, Pauline Kanchanalak, charged with conspiring to funnel illegal foreign money into President Clinton" 1996 reelection campaign. |

following themes in the newspapers they examine:

1. The media assumes that John Huang represents all Asian Pacific Americans, Huang, Riady, Trie, and others never acquired an identity in news reports *as individuals*, but rather as the Chinese, the Indonesian, or the Asian American.[5]
2. The media consistently regards race as relevant to the issue. Where sources are identified by race, it is almost always Asian Pacific Americans, and the interests and motives of Asian Pacific Americans are always presumed to be *as Asian Pacific Americans.*[6]
3. The media applies double (and changing) standards to Asian Pacific Americans because Asian Pacific Americans are scrutinized for activities that other special interests have long been complicit to.
4. The media pursues this issue with an ease and swiftness that reflects overreaction and evokes a long history of marking Asian Pacific Americans as perpetual foreigners and a "Yellow Peril."[7]
5. The media fails to distinguish between Asians and Asian Pacific Americans.
6. The media assumes guilt by association. Notably, by linking John Huang to Jay Kim and Charlie Trie and Michael Kojima, they assume a linkage between each of these individual cases, given by their race.
7. The media uses racial/cultural explanations to interpret wrongful and illegal actions. John Huang's identity is not only racialized and presumed to be Chinese rather than Chinese-American, but his actions are culturally essentialized to Chinese practices and a pan-Asian predisposition to use special favors, bribery, and political corruption as a means to political power.
8. The media links the issue of campaign finance to Asian immigration. The insinuation here is that the allegedly illegal fund-raising activities were preconditioned on expectations of extra-legal influence on immigration policies.[8]
9. The media, despite placing Asian Pacific Americans as the ostensible subject of the congressional hearings, confers little voice or agency to Asian Pacific Americans on the issue.
10. The media's editorials suggest that any critical mention of race was a misappropriation of "the race card."[9]

Following the observations of Wu and Nicholson and others, Lee and Hahn (1998) conducted content analysis of print media coverage to systematically assess how prevalent negative representations of Asian Americans have been. Specifically, Lee and Hahn examine the content of print media coverage from seven newspapers: the *New York Times*, the *Washington Post*, *USA Today*, the *Los Angeles Times*, the *San Francisco Chronicle*, the *San Diego Union-Tribune*, and the *Sacramento Bee*. The content analysis codes for six dimensions of media coverage on Asians/Asian Americans concerning the campaign finance issue: (1) "invisibility" (whether or not Asian Americans are given "voice" in articles); (2) "homogeneity" (whether or not articles distinguish between constituent Asian American ethnic groups; (3) "perpetual foreigner" (whether or not articles distinguish between Asians and Asian Americans); (4) "Yellow Peril" (whether or not articles treat the allegedly illegal activities of Asians/Asian Americans as an invasive threat to U.S. democracy and the U.S. political system; (5) "cultural essentialism" (whether or not articles attribute the campaign finance activities in question to Asian "culture"); and (6) "issue synecdoche" (whether or not media coverage fails to distinguish an isolated dimension of the issue of campaign finance reform (i.e., alleged Asian/Asian American improprieties) from the more systemic issue at hand.

The results from Lee and Hahn's analysis clearly show that critics of media coverage like Wu and Nicholson are close to the

mark. In more than 60 percent of the articles, no Asian Americans are quoted; in
more than three-quarters of the articles, no
distinctions between Asian American sub-
groups are visible; in almost 60 percent of
the articles, there is some insinuation of an
Asian American "Yellow Peril"; and in
more than two-thirds of the items. Asian
Pacific American campaign contribution
activities are equated with the issue of campaign finance reform in toto. Lee and Hahn
also find that the tenor of media coverage
becomes more heated and more editorial-
ized as the Senate begins their hearings on
campaign finance reform, that negative
stereotyping is evident in both news articles and op-eds, and that media coverage
differs (usually less negative) when newspapers that have a sizeable Asian American
readership (i.e., the California papers in
their dataset) and when news items are
written by Asian Americans.[10]

At the same time, media coverage is not
uniformly and unambiguously consistent
with critics' assessments. For one thing,
some negative representations are significantly less prevalent than others: references
to Asian Pacific Americans as "perpetual
foreigners" is found in less than 40 percent
of the news items, and the use of totalizing
cultural explanations is evident in only
about 10 percent of the news items. For
another, although there is much historical
and contemporaneous evidence that the
media representations that Lee and Hahn
examine *are* negative, such valenced readings of media coverage are difficult and contentious. This is especially so when imput-
ing motive, either to individual journalists
and commentators or to a singular, monolithic, hegemonic "mass media."[11] What's
more, the consequences of such coverage
depend crucially on the author and the
audience.[12]

Even taking these necessary caveats
about the reliability of content analysis
into account, the account of how Asian
Americans have been depicted in the mass
media on the campaign finance issue is
sobering indeed. This is especially so
because such media coverage often presents
a misleading (if not outright wrong) view of

Asian Americans. For example, Lee (2000c)
shows that Chinese American Republicans
are much more likely to engage in campaign contributions and that these contributors fundamentally view themselves as
political and economic stakeholders within
the United States (and not their countries of
origin). Importantly, Lee (2000a) also shows
that exposure to mass media, beliefs about
the fairness of media coverage, and factual
knowledge about Asian Americans play a
critical role in the anti-Asian American
sentiments and stereotypes that blacks,
whites, and Latinos express on policy matters that impact the Asian Pacific American
community.

## ASSESSING THE
## CONGRESSIONAL INVESTIGATIONS

In what remains, our analytic gaze is
inverted from media representations of
Asian Pacific Americans to the actual experiences and beliefs of Asian Americans
themselves. That is, we examine how Chinese Americans assess the nation's primary
social and political institutions vis-à-vis the
campaign finance controversy. If media coverage on this issue is inaccurate and evokes
historically negative stereotypes about
Asian Americans, do Chinese Americans
take umbrage? Do they view the ongoings as
discriminatory and offensive? Do they
assess the nation's principal social (i.e.,
mass media) and political (i.e., Congress)
institutions through a racialized lens?

The data come from a 1977 *Los Angeles
Times* poll of Chinese Americans in Southern California.[13] There are nuances to
polling predominantly immigrant ethnic
communities that limit what we can infer
from these data. To mention just two, the
sampling of Chinese Americans in the 1997
*Los Angeles Times* may not be fully representative and survey data on Asian Americans are susceptible to subtleties in the text
and language of the interviews.

Such caveats warn us against accepting
the results of poll data on Asian Americans
too enthusiastically or uncritically (see Lee
1998 and Lee 2000a).

These caveats notwithstanding, survey data on Asian Americans remain singularly rare and the *Los Angeles Times* survey is the *only* poll in the two-year history of the campaign finance issue in which Asian Americans themselves have been interviewed.[14] As Asian Americans rapidly emerge into the political limelight and as that limelight suspectingly glares back at Asian Americans, a clearer understanding of how the Asian American mass public negotiates such precarious racial currents is increasingly urgent. What's more, the *Los Angeles Times* has a proven commitment to understanding Asian American mass opinion, having conducted surveys of other Asian American ethnic groups—Filipino, Korean, and Vietnamese Americans—as well as a multiracial survey of attitudes about Asian Americans in Southern California.[15]

The 1997 *Los Angeles Times* survey findings indicate that Chinese Americans take a somewhat negative, but divided, view of the congressional proceedings. About 57 percent of respondents who are not undecided find the investigations offensive and 52 percent of respondents find the hearings discriminatory. This skepticism extends in respondents' evaluations of the institutions involved in this affair as well. Fully 75 percent of respondents view the investigations as insincere and purely partisan, while 52 percent of respondents decry the unfairness of media coverage on this issue.

Taken at face value, these marginal frequencies suggest a discernibly racialized response. Sociologists like Portes and Bach (1985) and Portes and Rumbaut (1996) have carefully detailed the multiple pathways toward the "reactive formation" of ethnic identity and solidarity. Such studies, notably suggest that a politicized ethnic identity often follows a generational changes as predominantly immigrant ethnic groups face everyday insults and more coordinated nativist campaigns in a society that remains deeply divided by social markers like race, gender, class, and citizenship status. Portes and Rumbaut thus argue that such "ethnic resilience is a uniquely American product because it has seldom reflected linear continuity with the immigrants' culture, but rather has emerged in reaction to the situation, views, and discrimination they faced on arrival" (1996, 95). A focal public event like the campaign finance controversy that places a predominantly immigrant ethnic group under attack, then, might plausibly evoke a racialized response among in-group members.[16]

What we make of the campaign finance controversy and its long-term impact on racial politics in the United States, however, depends on what form this racialized response takes. On this point, more recent works by Lopez and Espiritu (1992) and Kibria (1997) suggest that ethnic resilience and assimilationism present a false choice, and that "pan-ethnic" racial formations, like the category of "Asian American," are increasingly a third option. That is, even if Asians in America do pull together in response to events like the campaign finance controversy, it matters whether they do so as Asian Americans or as members of particularistic ethnic sub-groups. Generally, evidence for an overarching Asian American "pan-ethnicity" is modest and isolated. But as Espiritu 91992) shows, where pan-Asian formations do occur, they often do so as a manifestation of "reactive solidarity" in response to anti-Asian incidents.[17]

In contemporary politics, evidence that link such a pan-ethnic formulation to political opinions and policy preferences is unremarkable (Conway and Lien 1997; Lien 1997a). In addition, unlike African Americans (or, to a lesser extent, Latinos), Asian Americans split their loyalties fairly evenly between the Democratic and Republican parties and between political liberalism and conservatism (Cain, Kiewiet, and Uhlaner 1991; Ong and Nakanishi 1996). And on issues directly affecting the Asian American as a group, such as affirmative action, welfare reform, immigration policy, and California's referendum initiatives, there is often no distinguishable bloc voting among Asian Americans (Lee 2000a). Thus Asian American appear to many to be better situated to play a strategic role as a "swing vote" rather than an active role in a progressive, multiracial Democratic coalition (Nakanishi 1991).

A key insight to note in considering this welter of evidence is that most Asian ethnic sub-groups in the United States are predominantly immigrant. Fully 85 percent of respondents to the 1997 *Los Angeles Times* poll are foreign-born. The strength of Asian ethnic or pan-Asian ties, the degree of Asian American political mobilization, and the contours of Asian American political preferences are thus transient and rapidly evolving matters. As Lin and Jamal (1997) note, predominantly immigrant groups present an almost ideal "natural experiment" for the study of political socialization. We should not, then, either wishfully accept the idea of a fixed, unitary, homogeneous "Asian American" political identity or presume that the absence of such an identity at present implies the impossibility of such a conception in the future.[18] Accordingly, research on Asian American mass opinion would do well to examine the conditions under which Asian Americans do view an issue or event through a racial/immigrant lens.

In this chapter, then, I examine whether or not the campaign finance controversy is just such an instance for Chinese Americans in Southern California.[19] The 1997 *Los Angeles Times* allows us to test the impact of factors such as one's immigrant status, one's evaluations of political institutions, the mass media, and indigenous community institutions, one's level of political awareness, one's personal experience with racism, and one's personal views about immigrating to the United States on assessments of the congressional investigations. The dependent variable is whether or not respondents, as Chinese Americans, view the congressional investigations as discriminatory. This measure simultaneously captures respondents' views on campaign finance, the nation's political institutions, and anti-Asian discrimination.

The explanatory variables begin with age, educational level, family income, and gender. Again these measures examine if sociodemographic and economic cleavages

shape assessments of the congressional hearings. With a predominantly immigrant population such as Chinese Americans, however, there are more explicit generational and time-dependent sociodemographics differences to consider. As with the model of political contributions, second and third generation respondents are distinguished from immigrant Chinese, and I include a measure of the number of years lived in the United States as a permanent resident. As noted earlier, a plausible expectation from sociological accounts is that second and third generation Chinese Americans will exhibit a stronger sense of "ethnic resilience" and thus voice opposition to the congressional hearings (Portes and Rumbaut 1996).

The expectation that generation per se predicts one's attitudes leaves open the question of how it does so. As Wong (1999) compellingly demonstrates, properly understanding the effect of generational change on the political attitudes of Asian Americans is crucial. In this paper, I compare the effect of generation per se against several measures that might describe what happens over the course of generations. Specifically, I consider the immigrant experiences, racial predispositions, and institutional attachments that might capture the political socialization that Chinese Americans undergo across generations in the United States.

I first consider the respondents' political status and institutional ties. Citizenship and partisanship, again, measure one's chosen political identity. How citizenship is likely to affect one's view of congressional investigations is uncertain, but if that citizen ship has an ethnic component (i.e., as a Chinese American, or Asian American), then it may predict a negative view. Given the ostensibly partisan nature of this issue (i.e., the Republican leadership has largely initiated aggressive investigations and pushed for the appointment of an independent counsel). Chinese Americans' views on the discriminatory nature of the investigations may split down party lines as well. Additionally, partisanship also gauges the extent to which attachments to mainstream political institutions in themselves yield distinct viewpoints on this issue (i.e., by comparing respondents who register with either party against respondents who do not register with a political party).[20]

Along these lines, I also consider the impact of another mainstream institution, the mass media. Respondents are asked whether or not they follow the allegations of illegal Asian American fundraising in the media closely or not. At first blush, media attention ought to indicate the influence of the media's information or interpretations on respondents' opinions. Close attention to media coverage on this issue might simply reflect differences in respondent political awareness, however. Such respondents may be more generally knowledgeable about politics or be more invested in the outcome of political matters. Thus media attention may not reflect anything about media exposure per se, but rather, it may reflect respondent characteristics.[21] A second media variable is the respondent's assessments of the media as an institution itself. Specifically, respondents are asked whether or not they consider the mass media's coverage of the Asian American campaign contributions issue as fair or unfair.[22] The expectations here are fairly clear: if respondents view media coverage as unfair, they are more likely to take a dim view of ongoing investigations; if they view the coverage as essentially fair, then they might be more tolerant of ongoing investigations. [23]

In addition to these measure of mainstream institutions, I consider the influence of indigenous institutions and social ties.[24] The particular measure here is whether or not respondents value ethnic centers like Chinatown or San Gabriel Valley (home to Monterey Park).[25] The importance of an ethnic center not only captures the influence of institutional and social ties to a physical Chinese American community, but also indirectly estimates the impact of ethnic group consciousness.[26]

Thus far, our explanatory variables assess respondents' immigrant and racialized

experiences only obliquely. The last set of variables take a more direct look at the immigrant-based and racialized worldviews of respondents. First, I consider whether personal experience with discrimination makes one more likely to view the congressional investigations as discriminatory. Here two distinct contexts of experience with discrimination are examined: discrimination in institutional settings and discrimination in informal, social interactions. Discrimination in institutional settings pools together respondents who report discriminatory experiences in employment decisions (getting a job or being promoted in existing jobs), in education, in housing, in interactions with government agencies, and in business or retail transactions. Discrimination in informal settings is comprised of respondents who report discrimination in their interactions with neighbors, strangers, or as a result of linguistic and cultural misunderstandings. Because these measures are self-reported, the actual circumstances of a given incident might be reported by one individual as institutionalized racism and another as informal discrimination. This aside, what clearly differs across these individuals is the *ex post* interpretation.[27]

Keeping this in mind, I expect respondents who report racism in institutional settings to perceive the ongoing investigations as discriminatory. There ought to be a connection between having personally experienced discrimination in events where civil rights protections are expected and one's interpretation of the congressional hearings. What about discrimination in informal settings? One possibility is that, even in these settings, there will be a positive relationship. Another is that there might be no relationship at all, since it is a much more situational, individualized, apolitical view about the context of ethnic discrimination. Perhaps the most intriguing possibility, however, is that there will be a negative, opposite relationship. If respondents willfully (perhaps even ideologically) choose to interpret discriminatory incidents as situational, individual, and apolitical, then they might more willingly view the congressional investigations as nondiscriminatory and inoffensive.

In addition to experience with anti-Asian discrimination, I also test the effects of whether or not respondents view racism as a barrier to the well-being of Chinese Americans. In this question, racism is compared to language, culture, integration into mainstream society, and adequate job training as possible impediments to the success of Chinese Americans. Regardless of one's personal experience with discrimination, I expect that respondents who view discrimination as a general problem for Chinese Americans will be more likely to view the congressional hearings as discriminatory.

More generally, I include an attitudinal measure of one's immigrant experience. How a respondent evaluates her personal decision to immigrate may shape how she evaluates political events like the campaign finance controversy. The key hypothesis here is that respondents who report that "life here in the United States [has] turned out better than you expected" might interpret even contradictory events in the best possible light, and therefore take a more conciliatory, positive view of the ongoing investigations.

Lastly, two language-related measures are included to assess the role that language plays in shaping one's immigrant experience and political socialization. As I estimated earlier, the language in which interviews are conducted may significantly and systematically influence the answers that respondents give to questions. Here, we directly test whether a non-English interview makes a difference in one's assessments of the congressional hearings. To the extent that comfort with a Chinese dialect may imply a greater sense of ethnic resilience, we may expect respondents interviewed in Mandarin or Cantonese to be more likely to see the investigations as discriminatory. To rule out the possibility that respondents may choose to be interviewed in a Chinese dialect simply because of greater proficiency in a non-English language or greater everyday use of Chinese dialects, I control for respondents' degree of "language segregation"—an addictive index of respondents' use of a Chinese dialect in everyday encounters (at home, at work, and in commercial transactions).[28]

## RESULTS AND DISCUSSION

The results are shown in table 3.10a. For the most part, sociodemographic and socioeconomic factors appear not to influence whether Chinese Americans view the congressional hearings as discriminatory. The two salient exceptions are respondent age and length of permanent residence in the United States (among immigrant respondents). The fact that older Chinese Americans are less likely to see discrimination is generally consistent with Schuman, Stech, Bobo, and Krysan's (1998) findings on age and racial attitudes. Among Chinese immigrants to the United States, however, this effect is offset by the number of years of permanent residence.

Table 3.10b shows predicted probabilities calculated relative to a hypothetical "mean" respondent. By this calculus, table 3.10b shows that immigrant Chinese who have lived in the United States for twenty-four years are about 22 percent more likely to view the congressional investigations as discriminatory than newly arrived Chinese immigrants to the United States.

Importantly, generation per se appears to bear no effect on whether Chinese Americans view the congressional hearings as discriminatory. If anything, the effect is likely to be opposite, where second and third generation Chinese Americans are actually more likely to view the issue as not discriminatory. As the results in the model suggest, it is immigrant-specific, racialized experiences and beliefs that occur across generations and over one's tenure in the United States that most forcefully condition how Chinese Americans assess this issue.

While attachment to dominant political institutions in itself may not predict

**Table 3.10a    Are Congressional Investigations Discriminatory?**

*Dependent variable*: "As you may know, Congress is investigating alleged illegal campaign contributions by Asian nationals to President Clinton's reelection campaign in 1996, as well as some congressional election campaigns. The congressional committees are looking primarily at contributions made by donors who have Asian sounding names for any illegal donations. . . . Do you think this is a form of discrimination against Asians in this country?"

| Variable | Coefficients | (Standard errors) | Mean of $\chi^1$ |
|---|---|---|---|
| Age | −.017 | (.005)** | 40.34 |
| Educational level | 0.092 | (.064) | 3.47 |
| Family income | −.016 | (.042) | 5.02 |
| Female | 0.119 | (.143) | 0.34 |
| U.S. citizen | 0.111 | (.201) | 0.77 |
| Democrat | 0.063 | (.195) | 0.19 |
| Republican | −.112 | (.1888)** | 0.22 |
| Ideology | 0.065 | (.067) | 2.99 |
| Second generation | −.379 | (.258) | 0.24 |
| Years in U.S. as permanent resident | 0.022 | (.009)* | 10.32 |
| Issue-specific media attention | 0.075 | (.073) | 2.49 |
| Fairness of media coverage | 0.268 | (.065)** | 3.07 |
| Importance of ethnic center | 0.083 | (.048)^ | 3.96 |
| Experience institutional discrimination | 0.325 | (.098)** | 0.56 |
| Experience situational discrimination | −.130 | (.131) | 0.36 |
| Racism as barrier to Chinese Americans | 0.550 | (.222)** | 0.12 |
| Satisfied with life in U.S. \| Immigrant | −.264 | (.092)** | 1.61 |
| Language of interviewer effect | 0.425 | (.189)* | 0.38 |
| Language segregation | 0.051 | (.103) | 1.16 |
| Constant | −1.24 | (.523) | |

| | | |
|---|---|---|
| Number of observations | 417 | |
| Restricted log-likelihood | −289.01 | |
| Goodness of fit $\chi^2$) | 87.05 | |
| McFadden's pseudo-$R^2$ | .151 | |
| Percent correctly predicted | 68.1 | ($H_o$549.4) |

*Notes:* Cell entries are maximum likelihood probit parameter estimates and their corresponding standard errors in parenthesis. **=$p<.01$; *=$p<.05$; ^=$p<.10$.

*Source:* 1997 *Los Angeles Times* Survey #396.

assessments on the campaign finance controversy, this by no means implies that institutions play no role in shaping respondents' opinions. Respondents' who judge the media coverage on the campaign contributions issue as unfair are much more likely to view the congressional hearings as discriminatory. Table 3.10c shows this as the strongest effect on respondents' assessments. Chinese Americans who perceive the media coverage to be fundamentally unfair are fully 40 percent more likely to view the congressional hearings as discriminatory than their counterparts who see the media's coverage as very fair.[29]

Furthermore, respondents who value ethnic centers like Chinatown and San Gabriel Valley are somewhat more likely to see the investigations as offensive and discriminatory. As suggested earlier, this result tips off the impact of indigenous institutions and social ties on the assessments of Chinese Americans. It also weakly and indirectly supports the general link between ethnic

**Table 3.10b    Predicted Probabilities: Congress Discriminatory?**

| Variables of Interest | Probability Estimate | Probability Ratio | Probability Difference |
|---|---|---|---|
| *Years in U.S. as permanent resident†* | | | |
| μ σ (0 years) | .422 | | |
| μ (−10 years) | .512 | 1.21 | .090 |
| μ† σ (−24 years) | .637 | 1.51 | .215 |
| *Fairness of media coverage* | | | |
| Very fair | .299 | | |
| Somewhat fair | .398 | 1.33 | .099 |
| Not sure | .504 | 1.69 | .205 |
| Somewhat unfair | .610 | 2.04 | .311 |
| Very unfair | .708 | 2.37 | .409 |
| *Experiences w/institutional discrimination* | | | |
| None | .439 | | |
| One context | .568 | 1.29 | .129 |
| Two contexts | .690 | 1.57 | .251 |
| Three or more contexts | .794 | 1.81 | .355 |
| *Racism as barrier to Chinese Americans* | | | |
| Disagree | .485 | | |
| Agree | .696 | 1.44 | .211 |
| *Satisfied with Life in U.S. as Immigrant* | | | |
| Better than expected | .368 | | |
| As expected | .471 | 1.28 | .103 |
| Worse than expected | .576 | 1.57 | .208 |
| Not immigrant | .676 | 1.84 | .308 |
| *Language of interview* | | | |
| English | .447 | | |
| Cantonese or Mandarin | .618 | 1.38 | .171 |

*Notes:* †Partial effects of number of years in the U.S. as a permanent resident are calculated as standard deviations from the mean number of years (approximately fourteen years in the U.S.). Since the distribution is skewed to the right, the lower bound is taken at zero.

*Source:* 1997 *Los Angeles Times* Survey #396. Predicted probabilities are calculated for each measure of interest by holding all other explanatory variables at their mean values. See Greene 1997.

group consciousness and one's views on the campaign contributions issue.

The remaining measures of Chinese Americans' immigrant-based, racialized opinions all show striking results. To begin, experience with discrimination plays a significant role in shaping assessments of the congressional hearings, but not uniformly so. Rather, the context and personal interpretation of that experience may actually lead to opposite effects. Respondents who report personal experiences with discrimination in at least one institutional context are 13 percent more likely than those who report no such experiences to view the congressional investiga-

tions as discriminatory. Respondents who report such experiences in three or more institutional contexts are more than 35 percent more likely to view the congressional investigations as discriminatory. By contrast, reporting personal experiences with discrimination in informal settings may have no effect on their views about the campaign contributions issue. If anything, such experiences in informal settings appear to make respondents less likely to see any discrimination in this issue.[30]

Moving from personal experience to attitudes, respondents' views about barriers facing Chinese Americans and their narratives

**Table 3.10c   Are the Congressional Investigations Offensive?**

*Dependable Variable*: "As you may know, Congress is investigating alleged illegal campaign contributions by Asian nationals to President Clinton's reelection campaign in 1996, as well as some congressional election campaigns. The congressional committees are looking primarily at contributions made by donors who have Asian sounding names for any illegal donations. . . . Are you offended or not offended by these congressional committees investigating campaign contributions primarily from donors with Asian sounding names, even if that investigation might get at contributions made illegally?"

| Variable | Coefficients | (Standard errors) | Mean of $\chi_I$ |
|---|---|---|---|
| Age | −.005 | (.004) | 41.52 |
| Educational level | 0.046 | (.048) | 3.42 |
| Family income | .006 | (.032) | 4.87 |
| Female | 0.21 | (106)^ | 0.36 |
| U.S. citizen | 0.189 | (.140) | 0.76 |
| Democrat | 0.022 | (139) | 0.19 |
| Republican | −.184 | (.139) | 0.22 |
| Ideology | 0.051 | (.052) | 3.01 |
| Second generation | −.366 | (.199)^ | 0.21 |
| Years in U.S. as permanent resident | 0.001 | (.004) | 10.97 |
| Issue-specific media attention | 0.245 | (.057)** | 2.42 |
| Fairness of media coverage | 0.189 | (.049)** | 3.07 |
| Importance of ethnic center | 0.90 | (0.37)* | 3.98 |
| Experience institutional discrimination | 0.253 | (0.75)** | 0.57 |
| Experience situational discrimination | −.140 | (.098) | 0.34 |
| Racism as barrier to Chinese Americans | −.117 | (.171) | 0.12 |
| Satisfied with life in U.S. \| Immigrant | −.110 | (.070) | 1.67 |
| Language of interviewer effect | 0.179 | (.143) | 0.42 |
| Language of segregation | −.099 | (0.78) | 1.20 |
| μ(0) | −.544 | (.384) | |
| μ(1) | 0.596 | (.061) | |
| μ(2) | 1.263 | (.078) | |
| μ(3) | 2.383 | (.109) | |
| | | | |
| Number of observations | .476 | | |
| Restricted log-likelihood | −742.322 | | |
| McFadden's pseudo-$R^2$ | .058 | | |
| Goodness of fit ($\chi^2$) | 85.95 | | |

*Notes:* Cell entries are maximum likelihood ordered probit parameter estimates with corresponding standard errors in paentheses. **5$p<$.01; *=$p<$.05; ^=$p<$.10.
   *Source:* 1997 *Los Angeles Times Survey* #396.

about immigrating to the United States significantly shape their views on the congressional hearings. Respondents who view structurally racism against Chinese Americans are about 21 percent more likely to find the hearings discriminatory than those who see no such structural barriers. Respondents who find life as an immigrant in the United States worse than expected are also about 21 percent more likely to see discrimination than those who find life in the United States better than expected.

Lastly, the results in tables 3.10a and 3.10b bolster the potential import of the language in which surveys of predominantly immigrant ethnic communities are conducted. Respondents who are interviewed in Mandarin or Cantonese are fully 17 percent more likely to find the congressional hearing discriminatory than respondents interviewed in English. This finding intimates that language-of-interview is not simply a question of measurement error or a matter of language proficiency (note that everyday language use is controlled for). Rather, language-of-interview may alter responses significantly and in a politically meaningful way.[31] That is, interviews conducted in a Chinese dialect appear to result in different conversations than interviews conducted in English. Thus prior studies based on data from surveys that interview exclusively in English may miss important dimensions of Asian American opinion.[32]

Taken together, the above results make a powerful case that one's particular immigrant experience—specifically, the racial/ethnic content of that experience—plays a vital role in how Chinese Americans evaluate Congress on the issue of Asian American campaign finance improprieties. The racial, immigrant cast on this issue is evident even when respondents are asked whether the congressional investigations are offensive (that is, absent the explicit mention of racial discrimination). Table 3.10c shows this question modeled with the same set of explanatory measures as in table 3.10b. Respondents' views on racism as a barrier to opportunity loses its statistical significance, and the effects of respondents' satisfaction with life in the U.S. and the language-of-interview fades to a faint suggestion. That said, personal experience with discrimination and the perceived importance of ethnic centers retain a significant, strong sway.

This net can be cast even wider to consider whether a racial, immigrant account holds with assessments of a nongovernmental institution on this issue. Specifically, I examine whether or not respondents view the media coverage (defined as "television and the press and magazine and radio")

on the campaign finance issue as fair or unfair. Table 3.10d specifies a model that basically replicates the explanatory variables in tables 3.10b and 3.10c, but differs in two important respects.

First, I examine whether respondents who take a cynical view toward the nation's political institutions—measured by whether or not Congress on this issue has been insincere and purely partisan—also view the mass media as unfair. Second, I look at whether respondents who affirm the basic fairness of the opportunity structure in the United Stated towards Chinese Americans also affirm the basic fairness of the mass media on the campaign contributions issue. The rationale in the first instance is that respondents' views about one kind of institution may extend to the mass media. The rationale in the second instance is that respondents' views about fairness in one context may extend to their views about the fairness of the mass media.

The results, shown in table 3.10d, are mostly consistent with the story on respondent assessments of Congress. Respondents who follow the story more closely are also more likely to view the media coverage as unfair. Respondents who view the opportunity structure in the United States as unfair towards Chinese Americans are more likely to view the media coverage as unfair. Respondents who experience racism in institutional settings are more likely to view the media coverage as unfair. Finally, respondents interviewed in a non-English language are more likely to view the media coverage as unfair.

## SUMMARY AND DISCUSSION

This paper has discussed the campaign finance controversy involving Asian/Asian American donors and the response of Chinese Americans to this issue. The findings support the critical denoucements of Asian American commentators against the media and Congress for racializing the issue of campaign contributions and diverting the public's attention from more systemic

**Table 3.10d   Is Media Coverage on This Issue Unfair?**

*Dependent variable*: "Do you think television and the press and magazine and radio are covering the news of alleged illegal contributions made by Asian nationals to the president's reelection campaign fairly or unfairly? (If fairly or unfairly) Do you think it is very (fairly/unfairly) or only somewhat (fairly/unfairly)?"

| Variable | Coefficients | (Standard errors) | Mean of $\chi_I$ |
|---|---|---|---|
| Age | 0.008 | (.003)* | 42.13 |
| Educational level | 0.007 | (.047) | 3.42 |
| Family income | 0.018 | (.031) | 4.83 |
| Female | −.559 | (.107) | 0.38 |
| Democrat | 0.064 | (.145) | 0.18 |
| Republican | −.527 | (.133) | 0.21 |
| U.S. citizen | 0.130 | (.145) | 0.76 |
| Issue-specific media attention | 0.126 | (.056)* | 2.43 |
| Cynicism about sincerity of Congress | 0.237 | (.069)** | 1.48 |
| Second generation | 0.127 | (.148) | 0.20 |
| Years in U.S. as permanent resident | 0.004 | (.004) | 11.16 |
| Racism as barrier to Chinese Americans | −.113 | (.142) | 0.12 |
| Experience Institutional Discrimination | 0.158 | (.067)** | 0.53 |
| Experience Situational Discrimination | 0.102 | (.093) | 0.32 |
| Opportunity structure facing Chinese Americans | −.167 | (.101)^ | 3.01 |
| Language of interviewer effect | 0.393 | (.122)** | 0.45 |
| $\mu(0)$ | 0.749 | (.434) | |
| $\mu(1)$ | 1.347 | (.101) | |
| $\mu(2)$ | 2.112 | (.109) | |
| $\mu(3)$ | 3.220 | (.124) | |
| Number of observations | 508 | | |
| Restricted log-likelihood | −730.07 | | |
| Goodness of fit ($\chi^2$) | 66.77 | | |
| McFadden's pseudo-$R^2$ | .046 | | |

*Notes:* Cell entries are maximum likelihood ordered probit parameter estimates with corresponding errors in parenthesis. **=p<01; *=p<.05; ^=p<.10.
*Source:* 1997 *Los Angeles Times* Survey #396.

problems with how elections are financed in the United States. Among other things, media coverage on this issue appears to routinely represent Asian Americans as homogeneous, voiceless, perpetual foreigners, and as a "Yellow Peril." Such media coverage surely feeds into the widespread myth and misconception about the political legitimacy and activism of Asian Americans. It is no surprise, then, that the swirl of suspicion surrounding the campaign finance issue is reflected in the expressly racialized assessments of Congress and the mass media by ordinary Chinese Americans.

For understandable reasons many leaders within the Asian American community have attempted to recast this issue in a more positive, empowering light. To wit, it would indeed be just irony if the campaign finance imbroglio served as a clarion call for Asian Americans to mobilize en masse, rather than as a dirge for what little political influence Asian Americans have wielded to date. The anticipation that this might be so is especially keen given the persistence of negative representations of Asian Americans by political elites and the mass media in more recent spectacles like the alleged espionage of nuclear physicist Wen Ho Lee.

The results of this paper offer some mixed insights on this matter. The fact that the mass media and Congress have implicitly and explicitly evoked a racialized response among the Chinese Americans in the 1997 *Los Angeles Times* lends enticing support for the prospects of an activated Asian American political voice. Clearly, perceiving the political world from a discernibly racialized standpoint is a precondition to finding and expressing an empowered collective voice. Vitally, the findings in this paper describe the keys to developing such a voice: the opinions of Chinese Americans on the campaign finance issue stem from their immigrant experiences, their institutional ties, and their views about discrimination, immigration, and the opportunity structure in the United States. That said, expressing a shared political perspective on a survey is several steps removed from expectations of developing into a mature, organized, and panethnic political voice. Bridging these steps, as with any other social change movement, will require creative leadership, material and organizational resources, and enduring alliances.

As a parting comment, using data from Chinese Americans in Southern California on a single issue to make broadly generalizeable claims about the politics of Asian Americans or predominantly immigrant ethnic communities writ large is admittedly perilous. Yet even from so narrow a thread, we have seen a richly textured account. In fact, the beliefs and sentiments of Chinese Americans in this paper vividly makes the case for specifically and detail in examining Asian American politics. Put succinctly but broadly, researchers must take the heterogeneity, contingency, and fluidity of Asian American politics as a starting point. Each ethnic sub-group falling within the panethnic penumbra of "Asian American" is char-

acterized by a distinct and evolving history of immigration, a distinct and evolving economic and political resource base, and a distinct and evolving set of ideological beliefs, cultural practices, social ties, and community institutions.

## NOTES

1. I use "Asian Pacific American" interchangeably with "Asian American," making no privileged claims for these designations over alternatives like "Asian Pacific Islanders" or "Asian Pacific American Islanders."

2. See, for example, within the same volume of the *National Asian Pacific American Almanac*, commentaries by Akaka (1998), Nakanishi (1998), and Wang (1998a).

3. For expository case, I use the term "Chinese American" to refer to U.S. residents of Chinese descent—citizen and non-citizen immigrants alike—holding in abeyance the necessary precautions about the social/political construction of ethnic/racial/national identity markers and the legal construction of citizenship and immigrant status.

4. This is a history that dates, in legal/political terms, at least as far back as the Chinese Exclusion Act of 1882, the Gentleman's Agreement of 1908, and the National Origins Act of 1924. Journalists like William Randolph Hearst and V. S. McClatchy in the 1920s took an active part in this history by stirring social hysteria around a "Yellow Peril" of Asian immigrants that threatened the integrity of the "American way of life." For general histories of Asian immigrants to the United States, see Chan (1991) and Takaki (1989).

5. Stewart Kwoh and Frank Wu write that "the Huang matter, however, has become much more than an issue of partisan politics. It has turned from a question of one person's dealings into scapegoating of a racial minority group" (1996).

6. Senator Daniel Akaka (D-HI) writes that "hints of the kinds of anti-Asian treatment that have been practiced in the past" are found in "the inappropriate and misguided attention paid by the media, commentators, and public figures to the ethnic heritage of those involved in the fundraising controversy. . . . Clearly, in some quarters, 'Asian' and 'Asian Americans'

are synonymous, unlike the case with Europeans and European Americans. In fact the term, "European Americans' is rarely heard in public discourse, because the ethnic origin of European Americans is not presumed to have a bearing on their patriotism (1998, 25)."

7. The most notorious example of both the dimension of homogeneity and perpetual foreigner status is Ross Perot, who, while visiting the University of Pennsylvania not only mistakenly referred to John Huang as an "Indonesian businessman," but also asked his audience "Wouldn't you like to have someone out there named O'Reilly? Out there hard at work. You know, so far we haven't found an American name."

8. Specifically, John Huang organized a $25,000 per couple fundraising Lunar New Year's event February 19, 1996. The alleged link here is that Asian Pacific Americans at the time were concerned with the slashing of benefits to legal and illegal immigrants and tighter restrictions around immigration, and that Huang happened to have written President Clinton a memo urging the maintenance of "fourth preference" or family preference immigration.

9. Along these lines, Zia (1997) also suggests that certain media outlets considered the protests of leaders within the Asian American community to be illegitimate, and points to the *Boston Globe*'s editorial that such complaints of stereotyping were "a shabby maneuver to avoid scrutiny."

10. On regional effects, Lee and Hahn find that California papers are less likely to negatively stereotype Asian Pacific Americans along every one of the six potentially negative dimension examined. Moreover, Asian Americans are represented as agents of their own destiny on the campaign finance issue in 78 percent of news items in California papers, but only 28 percent of news items in national papers. This finding is consistent with Wu and Nicholson's observation that the *Los Angeles Times* is generally an exception to their findings.

11. Certainly, there is no such monolithic mass media that can be shown using content analysis. In fact an author would have to exercise verbal contortionism to simultaneously represent all six dimensions Lee and Hahn examine, or worse yet, all ten themes that Wu

and Nicholson discuss. That said, there is a now robust social scientific literature on the subtle and not-too-subtle ways in which race is represented in the media. For example, see Entman (1992), Gilens (1999), Gilliam et al. (1996), and Iyengar (1991).

12. Resort to "cultural" explanations of Asian Americans" campaign finance activities, for example, might read differently if inked by William Safire in the *New York Times* than if inked by Connie Kang in the *Los Angeles Times*.

13. Between May 9 and May 27, 1997, the *Los Angeles Times* conducted a poll of 773 telephone interviews of adult Chinese residents of six counties in Southern California—Ventura, Los Angeles, San Bernadino, Orange, Riverside, and San Diego counties. Surveys were conducted by Interviewing Services of America, Inc., in Mandarin, Cantonese, and English. The sampling frame for this survey was individuals with Chinese surnames in telephone directories in the six counties examined.

14. Most of what we know in published academic research on Asian American mass opinion come from four surveys, the 1984 Institute of Governmental Studies poll, the 1992 Los Angeles County Social Survey, the 1993/94 Los Angeles Study of Urban Inequality, and the 1993 *Los Angeles Times* survey used in the paper.

15. As with each of these polls, the *Los Angeles Times* takes pains to consult with several key leaders and academics within the Chinese American community in Southern California. The roster here includes Stewart Kwoh (of the Asian Pacific American Legal Center of Southern California), Peter Woo (of the Chinese Chamber of Commerce), and Michael Woo (former LA City Council member). These ethnic-specific *Los Angeles Times* polls also avoid an important potential pitfall that mars most existing survey data on Asian Americans: allowing respondents the option to be interviewed in a non-English language. Given Census Bureau data that 73 percent of Asian Americans speak a language other than English at home, the language-of-interview when polling predominantly immigrant ethnic groups is potentially crucial. As Lee (2000b) shows, the language in which respondents are interviewed can signifi-

cantly and systematically influence data on their political opinions.

16. Among other things, national origin thus presents itself as the primary basis for group identification to the exclusion of alternative bases such as class.

17. The two other kinds of conditions in which Espiritu finds pan-Asian formations are in top-down political constructions of government agencies and in pragmatic, situational, and ultimately transitory electoral and campaign coalitions.

18. Rather, we recognize and take advantage of the fluid and shifting nature of Asian American political identity. An especially illuminating discussion of the ways in which Asian American identity is characterized by "heterogeneity, hybridity, and multiplicity" and crosses legal political, economic, social, and cultural boundaries can be found in Lowe (1996).

19. One important caveat is that the survey does not permit a test of a perhaps more interesting question, namely, whether or not this political spectacle will leave a lasting racial imprint on the minds of the *Los Angeles Times* respondents. That is, the details of how our elected officials, political institutions, and media actors respond to the campaign finance issue may serve as a focal, mobilizing event that contributes to the formation of a politicized ethnic identity. As Omi and Winant suggest along these lines, "far from intervening in racial conflicts, the state is itself increasingly the pre-eminent site of racial conflict" (1994, 82). Testing for the campaign finance controversy as an instance of racial formation requires longitudinal data, and the only available data are cross-sectional.

20. There are, unfortunately, no measures of intensity of partisanship in this survey.

21. The expectations that ensue from these two possibilities diverge somewhat. As Zaller (1992) shows, receptivity to novel political messages is nonlinear with respect to political awareness. Respondents who are most aware are not the most likely to absorb a stream of political information as new (because, put simply, they already know better); rather, respondents who are moderately aware are the most likely to take in new information.

22. Because we are controlling for the perceived fairness of the media coverage, I would argue that media exposure is a more direct measure of political awareness, rather than the substantive content transmitted through the media.

23. Lee (2000a) shows that perceived bias in media coverage plays a significant part in shaping anti-Asian stereotypes, sentiments, and policy preferences.

24. See Cohen (1999), Dawson (2000) and Lee (forthcoming) on the influence of indigenous institutions and social ties on the political attitudes of racial minorities.

25. For research on the political significance of San Gabriel Valley, see Saito and Horton (1994) and Horton (1995).

26. Given, that is, the relatively innocuous assumption that respondents with the strongest sense of Chinese American identity are more likely to value centers like Chinatown and San Gabriel Valley. It is, obviously, not a measure that can distinguish between an ethnic conception (i.e., as Chinese American) from a pan-ethnic conception (as Asian Americans).

27. This also begs the question of why identical incidents are not perceived by respondents as discrimination of any form.

28. This language segregation index also allows us to test, albeit obliquely, Cho's (1999) contention that respondents' English proficiency tells us something important about their political socialization and, by implication, their political attitudes as well.

29. The question wording does not specify or imply the object of the unfairness—i.e., unfair toward Asian Americans or President Clinton.

30. In a modified specification, discrimination in informal settings achieves weakly significant effects (p. 10).

31. The allusion here is to the well-studied phenomenon of "race-of-interviewer effects" (see Schuman and Converse 1971; Sanders 1995; Hurtado 1994).

32. See Uhlaner, Cain, and Kiewiet (1989), Bobo and Suh (1995), Bobo and Hutchings (1996), Conway and Lien (1997).

## REFERENCES

Akaka, Daniel. 1998. From the Senate Floor: Asian Americans and the Political Fundraising

Investigation. In James S. Lai, ed., *1998–99 National Asian Pacific American Political Almanac*. Los Angeles: UCLA Asian American Studies Center.

Bobo, Lawrence and Vincent Hutchings. 1996. "Perceptions of Racial Group Competition." *American Sociological Review* 61(6): 951–71.

Bobo, Lawrence and Susan Suh. 1995. Surveying Racial Discrimination: Analyses from a Multiethnic Labor Market. Russell Sage Foundation Working Paper #75.

Cain, Bruce, Roderick Kiewiet, Carole Uhlaner. 1991. The Acquisition of Partisanship by Latinos and Asian Americans. *American Journal of Political Science* 35: 390–422.

Chan, Sucheng. 1991. *Asian Americans: An Interpretive History*. Boston: Twayne.

Chen, Lucie and Philip Q. Yang. 1996. "Asians: the 'Model Minority' Deconstructed." In Roger Waldinger and Mehdi Bozorgmeht, eds., *Ethnic Los Angeles*. New York: Russell Sage Foundation.

Cho, Wendy K. Tam. 1999. "Naturalization, Socialization, Participation: Immigrants and (Non)Voting." *Journal of Politics* 16(4).

Chopra, Aneesh, Ajay Kuntamukkala, and Keith Reeves. 1997. 1996 Survey on the Public Policy Concerns of the Indian-American Community. *Asian American Policy Review* VII (Spring): 115–31.

Cohen, Cathy. 1999. *Boundaries of Blackness: AIDS and the Breakdown of Black Politics*. Chicago: The University of Chicago Press.

Conway, M. Margaret and Pei-te Lien. 1997. "Predicting Support for Affirmative Action among Four Racial/Ethnic Groups." Presented at the 1997 Annual Meeting of the American Political Science Association, Washington D.C.

Dawson, Michael C. 2000. *Black Visions: The Roots of Contemporary African-American Political Ideologies*. Chicago: The University of Chicago Press.

Davis, Darren W. 1997. The Direction of Race of Interviewer Effects among African-Americans: Donning the Black Mark. *American Journal of Political Science* 41(1): 309–322.

Din, Grant. 1984. "An Analysis of Asian/Pacific Registration and Voting Patterns in San Fran-cisco." Master's Thesis, Claremont Graduate School.

Entman, Robert. 1992. "Blacks in the News." *Journalism Quarterly* 69: 341–61.

Espiritu, Yen Le and Paul Ong. 1994. "Class Constraints on Racial Solidarity Among Asian Americans." In Paul Ong, Edna Bonacich, and Lucie Cheng, eds. *The New Asian Immigration in Los Angeles and Global Restructuring*. Philadelphia: Temple University Press, 295–321.

Espiritu, Yen Le. *Asian American Panethnicity*. 1992. Philadelphia: Temple University Press.

Gilens, Martin. *Why Americans Hate Welfare*. 1999. Chicago: The University of Chicago.

Gilliam, Franklin Jr., Shanto Iyengar, Adam Simon, and Oliver Wright. 1999. "Crime in Black and White." *Harvard International Journal of Press/Politics* 1(3).

Horton, John. 1995. *The Politics of Diversity: Immigrants, Resistance, and Change in Monterey Park, CA*. Philadelphia: Temple University Press.

Hurtado, Aida. 1994. "Does Similarity Breed Respect? Interviewer Evaluations of Mexican-Descent Respondents in a Bilingual Survey." *Public Opinion Quarterly* 58: 77–95.

Iyengar, Shanto. 1991. *Is Anyone Responsible?* Chicago: University of Chicago Press.

Jiobu, Robert M. 1996. "Recent Asian Pacific Immigrants: The Demographic Background." In Bill Ong Hing and Ronald Lee, eds., *The State of Asian Pacific America: Reframing the Immigration Debate*. Los Angeles: LEAP Asian Pacific American Public Policy Institute and UCLA Asian American Studies Center.

Junn, Jane. 1997. "Assimilating or Coloring Participation? Gender, Race, and Democratic Political Participation." In Cathy Cohen, Kathleen Jones, and Joan Tronto, eds. *Women Transforming Politics*. New York: New York University Press.

Kibria, Nazli. 1997. "The Construction of 'Asian American': Reflections on Intermarriage and Ethnic Identity among Second Generation Chinese and Korean Americans." *Ethnic and Racial Studies* 20(3): 523–44.

Kwoh, Steward, and Frank Wu. 1996. "Don't Build Reform on a Scapegoat." *Los Angeles Times*, October 24, op-ed.

Lee, Tacku. Forthcoming. *Two Nations, Separate Grooves: Black Insurgency and the Activation of Mass Opinion in the United States from 1948 to the mid-1960s.* Chicago: University of Chicago Press.

———. 2000a. "Racial Attitudes and the Color Line(s) at the Close of the Twentieth Century." In Paul Ong, ed., *The State of Asian Pacific Americans: Transforming Race Relations.* Los Angeles: LEAP/UCLA Asian Pacific American Public Policy Institute.

———. 2000b. "Language-of-Interview Effects and Polling the Opinions of Asian Americans." Unpublished manuscript. The Kennedy School of Government, Harvard University.

———. 2000c. "The Social Bases of Political Participation among Predominantly Immigrant Racial Minorities." Unpublished manuscript. The Kennedy School of Government, Harvard University.

———. 1998. "Survey or Surveillance? Campaign Finance and Polling the Political Opinions of Chinese Americans." Presented at the 1998 Annual Meeting of the Association of Asian American Studies, Honolulu, Hawaii.

Lee, Tacku and Albert Hahn. 1998. "Campaign Finance, the Mass Media, and the Racial Formation of Asian Americans." Unpublished manuscript. The Kennedy School of Government, Harvard University.

Lien, Pei-te. 1997a. *The Political Participation of Asian Americans.* New York: Garland.

———. 1997b. "Does Under-Participation Matter? An Examination of Policy Opinions among Asian Americans." *Asian American Policy Review* VII (Spring): 38–54.

———. 1994. "Ethnicity and Political Participation: A Comparison between Asians and Mexican Americans." *Political Behavior* 16.

Lin, Ann Chih and Amaney Jamal. 1997. "Navigating a New World: The Political Association of Arab Immigrants." Presented at the 1997 Annual Meeting of the American Political Science Association, Washington, D.C.

Lopez, David E. 1996. "Language: Diversity and Assimilation." In Roger Waldinger and Mehdi Bozorgmehr, eds., *Ethnic Los Angeles.* New York: Russell Sage Foundation.

Lopez, David E., and Yen Le Espiritu. 1990. "Panethnicity in the United States: A Theoretical Framework." *Ethnic and Racial Studies* 13(2): 198–224.

Lowe, Lisa. *Immigrant Acts.* 1996. Durham, N.C.: Duke University Press.

Nakanishi, Don T. 1998. "Drive-by Victims of DNC Greed." In James S. Lai, ed., *1998–99 National Asian Pacific American Political Almanac.* Los Angeles: UCLA Asian American Studies Center.

———. 1991. "The Next Swing Vote? Asian Pacific Americans and California Politics." In Bryan O. Jackson and Michael Preston, eds., *Racial and Ethnic Politics in California,* 25–54, Berkeley: Institute of Governmental Studies Press.

Omi, Michael and Howard Winant. 1994. *Racial Formation in the United States* (2nd ed.). New York: Routledge.

Ong, Paul, ed. 1994. *The State of Asian Pacific America: Economic Diversity, Issues, and Policies.* Los Angeles: LEAP Asian Pacific American Public Policy Institute and UCLA Asian American Studies Center.

Ong, Paul, and Don T. Nakanishi. 1996. "Becoming Citizens, Becoming Votes: The Naturalization and Political Participation of Asian Pacific Immigrants." In Bill Ong Hing and Ronald Lee, eds., *The State of Asian Pacific America: Reframing the Immigration Debate.* Los Angeles: LEAP/UCLA.

Portes, Alejandro, and Robert L. Bach. 1985. *Latin Journey: Cuban and Mexican Immigrants in the United States.* Berkeley: University of California Press.

Portes, Alejandro and Ruben G. Rumbaut. 1996. *Immigrant America* (2nd ed.). Berkeley: University of California Press.

Saito, Leland and John Horton. 1994. "The New Chinese Immigration and the Rise of Asian American Politics in Monterey Park, Calif." In Paul Ong, Edna Bonacich, and Lucie Cheng, eds., *The New Asian Immigration in Los Angeles and Global Restructuring.*

Sanders, Lynn M. 1995. "What Is Whiteness? Race-of-Interviewer Effects When All the Interviews are Black." Unpublished manuscript. Chicago: The University of Chicago.

Schuman, Howard and Jean M. Converse. 1971. "The Effects of Black and White Interviewers on Black Response." *Public Opinion Quarterly* 35(1).

Schuman, Howard, Charlotte Stech, Lawrence Bobo, and Maria Krysan. 1998. *Racial Attitudes in America* (rev. ed). Cambridge, Mass.: Harvard University Press.

Shinagawa, Larry Hajime. 1996. "The Impact of Immigration on the Demography of Asian Pacific Americans." In Bill Ong Hing and Ronald Lee, eds., *The State of Asian Pacific America: Reframing the Immigration Debate.* Los Angeles: LEAP/UCLA.

Takaki, Ronald. 1989. *Strangers from a Different Shore*. New York: Penguin.

Tam, Wendy K. 1995. Asians—A Monolithic Voting Bloc? *Political Behavior* 17(2): 223–49.

Uhlaner, Carole Jean, Bruce F. Cain, and D. Roderick Kiewiet. 1989."Political Participation of Ethnic Minorities in the 1980s." *Political Behavior* 11: 195–221.

U.S. Commission on Civil Rights. 1998. *Briefing on Civil Rights Implications in the Treatment of Asian Pacific Americans during the Campaign Finance Controversy.* Washington, D.C.: U.S. Commission on Civil Rights.

Wang, I. Ling-chi. 1998a. "Asian Americans for Campaign Finance Reform." In James S. Lai, ed., *1998–99 National Asian Pacific American Political Almanac.* Los Angeles: UCLA Asian American Studies Center.

———. 1998b. "Race, Class, Citizenship, and Extraterritoriality: Asian Americans and the 1996 Campaign Finance Scandal." *Amerasia Journal* 24(1) (Spring): 1–21.

Wang, Theodore Hsien and Frank H. Wu. 1996. "Beyond the Model Minority Myth." In George E. Curry, ed., *The Affirmative Action Debate.* Reading, Mass.: Addison-Wesley.

Watanabe, Paul. 1998. "What Is to Be Done? The Political Meeting of the Asian American Campaign Finance Controversy." Prepared for the Asian Americans and Politics Conference at the Woodrow Wilson Center, Washington, D.C., March 12–14.

Wong, Janelle. 1999. "Political Attitude Formation among Latinos and Asian Americans." Presented at the Annual Meeting of the Midwest Political Science Association, Chicago.

Wu, Frank and May Nicholson. 1997. "Have You No Decency? Racial Aspects of Media Coverage on the John Huang Matter." *Asian American Policy Review* VII (Spring): 1–37.

Zaller, John. 1992. *The Nature and Origins of Mass Opinion.* Cambridge, UK: Cambridge University Press.

Zia, Helen. 1997. "Can Asian Americans Turn the Media Tide?" *The Nation* 265(21) (December 22): 10.

# 3.11

# Race, Class, Citizenship, and Extraterritoriality
## Asian Americans and the 1996 Campaign Finance Scandal

*L. Ling-chi Wang*

〰〰〰〰〰〰〰〰〰〰〰〰〰〰〰〰〰〰〰〰〰〰〰〰〰〰〰〰〰

Not since the protracted national debate over whether the Chinese should be excluded from the U.S. in the 1870s and early 1880s have we seen more sustained media coverage and acrimonious debate on the "Asian connection" than in the campaign finance scandal of 1996. Based on my own collection and estimate, no less than 4,000 articles have been published on the subject (newspapers and magazines) between September 1996 and February 1998. As of this writing, no end is in sight for this long-running media obsession and partisan brawl among the political elite.

At the eye of the storm are two key figures, John Huang and Charlie Yah-lin Trie, two Asian American donors/fundraisers for Clinton's reelection and the Democratic National Committee (DNC). They are joined by "a supporting cast," which includes Johnny Chung, Maria Hsia, Eugene and Nora Lum, Yogesh Gandhi, Congressman Jay Kim, and Chong Lo, and a cast of "extras," made up of business executives from Asian countries, like James

Riady of Indonesia, Pauline Kanchanalak of Thailand, Liu Tai-ying of Taiwan, Wang Jun of China, Johnny Lee of South Korea, among others. The two central figures have become household names, as well known as world-class Asian American figure skaters, Kristi Yamaguchi and Michelle Kwan, even if notoriety is achieved through adverse publicity.

What's more, not since the advent of the Asian American movement in the late 1960s have Asian Americans experienced a more significant civil rights setback than the one resulting from the deluge of negative, and at times, racist coverage of the scandal, as outlined in the Asian American petition to the U.S. Commission on Civil Rights.[1] Not surprisingly, Asian Americans across the nation were stunned by the unwanted national attention and many felt outraged, betrayed, ashamed, violated, discouraged, injured, or insulted, depending on their perspectives on the scandal and their class positions within the Asian American communities and in society at large.

How do we sort through and interpret the daily barrage of sensational disclosures, media spins, and counter-spins? How do we begin to analyze and understand what has been happening to Asian

Wang, L. Ling-chi. "Race, Class, Citizenship, and Extraterritoriality: Asian Americans and the 1996 Campaign Finance Scandal." *Amerasia Journal* 24(1): 1–21. Reprinted with permission.

Americans in general and to the leaders and organizations implicated—directly and indirectly—in the scandal in particular? Are they representative of what Asian America has become in an age dominated by transnational capital? Are Asian Americans simply innocent victims of political drive-by shooting, as some have alleged? Or, are they being singled out by the media, Republican leaders, and the law-enforcement agencies in the U.S. Department of Justice because they are Asians? Are they an integral part of what has seriously gone wrong with the post-Watergate campaign finance reform law? Exactly whose interests do these Asian Americans represent? What are the implications for Asian American community development and political empowerment in the long run?

These are some of the complex questions that must be addressed by scholars in Asian American studies and community activists concerned about the political development of Asian American communities, if we are to learn anything from the scandal and the racially charged political discourse surrounding the scandal. Even more important is what appropriate trajectory Asian Americans must pursue to achieve political empowerment if they possess neither the numerical strength of Euro-Americans, African Americans, and Latino Americans, nor the solidarity and financial clout of Jewish Americans.

## RACIALIZATION OF THE SCANDAL

First, there is obviously a racial dimension to the entire scandal, as documented in the Asian American petition filed before the U.S. Commission on Civil Rights. Indeed, the media and partisan power struggle played a decisive role in racializing the scandal and political corruption. For example, two months before the 1996 presidential election, Bill Clinton's two challengers—Republican Bob Dole and Independent Ross Perot—had already tried every conceivable political strategy and

arsenal at their disposal to try to seize political power from the Democratic incumbent. But they failed to make a dent into Clinton's commanding lead at the poll. Perhaps out of desperation, and with the help of columnists like William Safire of the *New York Times* and the editorial writers of the *Wall Street Journal*, they decided to dip into the well-entrenched, rich national reservoir of anti-Asian sentiment: they launched an all-out attack on Clinton and the DNC for using John Huang to raise money from illegal foreign Asian sources, most notably James Riady, owner of the Indonesia-based, multinational Lippo Group.[2] Their intention was to incite voter anger against an alleged foreign Asian plot to buy influence in Washington, D.C. and to undermine voters' trust in Clinton. Before long, the foreign "Asian connection" and "Asian Americans" became synonymous with political corruption and foreign subversion, even though Huang and Trie raised about $4.5 million out of the total of $2.2 billion raised and spent in the 1996 federal elections.[3] In fact, Dole, Perot, and the national media went out of their way to "Asianize" or "Orientalize" the political corruption and to lay the problem of corruption squarely on several Asian Americans and their "foreign connections" in several Asian countries, not the least of which was "communist" China.[4] (The China connection was established initially by the fact that the Lippo Group had investments in China, just as it had investments in the United States and several countries throughout the world). Instantly, James Riady, John Huang, Charlie Yah-lin Trie, and others became household names and the mysteries around them deepened with each new disclosure or leak.

In essence, Asian Americans became the menacing "new yellow peril," and worse yet, the "new yellow peril" also happened to be the "red peril." Clinton, Gore, and the DNC were indirectly accused of selling out the presidency and national interests and of compromising even our national security by accepting money from foreigners and by having "foreign Asian guests" in several events in the White House. This line of nationalist thinking and argument persisted throughout 1997 with Safire insinuating regularly in his *New York Times* columns that several Asian Americans, including John Huang and Charlie Trie, were "Red Chinese" spies. The China conspiracy took on a life of its own in the media and a favorite pastime among the China-bashers from the Left and the Right when Bob Woodward of the Watergate-fame reported similar allegations in a sensational "exclusive" in February 1996 in the *Washington Post*.[5] The Woodward article was based on leaks supposedly from counterintelligence sources in the FBI. Since there has been no independent confirmation of the allegation, the leaks could have been politically calculated disinformation campaign, either to discredit Clinton or to make him look like an innocent victim of some vicious "communist plot." Led by Sen. Fred Thompson, Republican chairman of the Senate Governmental Affairs Committee, several committees of both houses also pursued the same line of investigation, aimed at times to discredit Clinton and the DNC and, at other times, to incite fear of and hostility toward "Red" China. The Thompson Committee conducted four months of highly publicized public hearings, from July to October 1997, aimed at proving two theses: (1) "Red China" laundered money to influence Clinton and subvert American democracy and (2) John Huang and Charlie Trie were Red China's spies.[6]

However, the Senate hearings ended abruptly in disarray in November 1997, failing to incite public outrage against Clinton and produce any credible evidence in support of its two theses.[7] The hearings also raised disturbing questions about the GOP strategy of concentrating primarily on alleged Asian American wrong-doings and demonizing China on the one hand and ignoring the central issue of campaign finance reform on the other hand. The Thompson Committee succeeded in using the media to discredit Clinton, the DNC, and China and to divert public attention

from the need for campaign finance reform. It also succeeded in racializing the political scandal and demonizing China in the service of American xenophobic nationalism or nativism. The 1977 Congress recessed in December with no findings on the scandal and no legislative measures to reform the campaign finance system. As soon as the Monica Lewinsky scandal erupted, both politicians and the media found a new distraction.

## PLAYING THE RACE CARD

But to stop at the superficial level of the partisan power struggle and media sensationalism is to overlook the cynical playing of the race card by the leaders of both political parties and the media. From the start, both Democrats and Republicans played it. The latest round had its origin in the Clinton presidential campaign. Under chairman Ron Brown, the DNC quietly reinstated what his predecessor, Paul Kirk, had eliminated in 1985, the constituent and ethnic caucuses, and developed a racial strategy in an attempt to expand the party's political mobilization and fundraising capability in various constituencies including minority communities across the nation. John Huang, a former executive of the Indonesian Lippo Group, was recruited to work under then Secretary Ron Brown in the U.S. Commerce Department after the Clinton victory in 1992. He was brought into the DNC in December 1995 specifically to raise "soft money," $7 million to be exact, from Asian American communities to help jump-start Clinton's 1996 re-election campaign.[8] Since Asian American communities had neither the deep-pockets nor the tradition of big-time political giving, Huang, Trie, and others turned to transnational Asian sources in Indonesia, Thailand, Taiwan, Hong Kong, South Korea, Japan, etc. (It is unclear if Huang, Trie, and the DNC knowingly conflated Asian Americans and foreign Asians when they decided to solicit political donations from these transnational sources). The rapid integration of the global economy after the Cold War, especially in the growing ties between the United States and dynamic East and Southeast Asian economies and in increasing Asian investment in the Asian American communities, made their fundraising strategy easy. Besides, Huang had the necessary credentials and connections to accept the DNC assignment and to exploit the transnational connections.

However, Dole, Perot, and anti-Clinton forces in the media saw the role of John Huang quite differently: They detected his vulnerability and decided to exploit the racist sentiment against Asians and Asian Americans, as has been done repeatedly throughout the history of the United States. They accused Clinton and the DNC of selling the presidency to foreign Asians and Asian Americans, deliberately conflating the two and treating both as foreigners. Overnight, the scandal was racialized and Asian Americans were collectively and effectively *de-naturalized* in the eyes of the public. In addition to putting Clinton and Democrats on the defensive, the perception that all Asians were foreigners or noncitizens had the immediate effect of rendering them convenient targets for public suspicion, resentment, and outrage.

Sensing their vulnerability, Clinton and the DNC decided to play the same race card, but to turn it on the Republicans. At the suggestion of Sen. Christopher Dodd, the general chair of the DNC, several Asian American national leaders and organizations called a series of coordinated pre-election national press conferences before the November presidential election, in which they angrily accused Dole, Perot, and the media of being racist toward Asian Americans, for depicting Asian Americans indiscriminately as foreigners and characterizing Asian contributions as "foreigners buying up America."[9]

Suddenly, Huang became a victim of Republican and media racism and a symbol of oppressed Asian America. "The Huang matter has become much more than an issue of partisan politics. It has turned from a question of one person's dealings into scapegoating of a racial minority group,"

wrote press conference participants, Stewart Kwoh of Los Angeles and Frank Wu of Washington, D.C., in an op-ed column in the *Los Angeles Times* October 24, 1996. The strategy would have been effective if many of the big donations had not come from questionable, if not illegal foreign sources, as post-election investigations soon uncovered. The DNC was forced to return several million dollars to the original donors. It also made several national Asian American organizations vulnerable to editorial ridicule (e.g., the *Boston Globe*, January 21, 1997 and the *Washington Post* on July 10, 1997) and attacks by Asian American Republicans, most notably Susan Au Allen of the U.S. Pan Asian American Chamber of Commerce. She openly accused Asian American leaders and organizations of defending inappropriate fundraising or wrong-doings by John Huang and others at a public briefing at the U.S. Commission on Civil Rights in December 1997.

Unfortunately for Asian Americans, the Clinton victory did not bring an end to the playing of the race card. Immediately after the election, as Republican leaders and national media pressed U.S. Attorney General Janet Reno for the appointment of an Independent Counsel to investigate Clinton, Gore, and the DNC in the scandal, the Democrats quickly dumped Huang on November 17 and began to treat Asian Americans, including some big donors, as if they were strangers or worse—lepers, foreigners, criminals, and subversives. Under mounting pressure, the Democrats played the race card in two different ways. First, the DNC decided after the November election to conduct its own in-house investigation. The primary political objectives were to do some internal housecleaning and above all, to demonstrate its commitment to "clean money, including an announcement that it would, hence forth," accept money from *citizens only*, not permanent residents and American subsidiaries of foreign corporations. It hired an army of private auditors and investigators to look for donors of "dirty money," which turned out to mean mostly

Asian and Asian American donations. Suddenly, all major Asian donors became targets of overzealous investigation, harassment, and intimidation. The tactic backfired: many Asian Americans felt harassed, criminalized, or insulted and they protested loudly and rightly accused the DNC of trying to sanitize its image at the expense of Asian Americans.[10]

Secondly, the Clinton administration decided to also distance itself from Asian Americans in the appointment of high-ranking officials, reneging, thus, on a Clinton promise to have his cabinet reflect the diversity of America. In spite of intense lobbying under the leadership of the Asian Pacific American Coalition for Presidential Appointments, Clinton failed to name any Asian American to both cabinet-level and sub-cabinet positions. (A belated attempt to appoint Bill Lann Lee to the position of the U.S. assistant attorney general for civil rights toward the end of 1997 ended in failure). Asian Americans became the "collateral casualties," to borrow military jargon, in the racialized scandal and partisan power struggle. Former chancellor of University of California, Berkeley, Chang-lin Tien, was among the first casualties and even invited Asian American guests of the White House were subjected to humiliation and harassment.[11] In short, both Democrats and Republicans treated Asian Americans as pawns!

## CLASS AND MONEY POLITICS IN THE COMMUNITIES

The most direct benefit from racializing political corruption by both political parties is the diversion of public attention from the crisis facing American democracy. Instead of addressing the systemic problem of money corruption in politics, politicians discovered the perfect distraction: blame the problem on Asian Americans and the unscrupulous "spies" or "agents" of "communist" China. Since the money raised by John Huang, Charlie Trie, and other Asian Americans represents only a tiny fraction of what both parties raised and spent in 1996

and since no evidence has been uncovered on the alleged role of China in trying to subvert American democracy, we must conclude that the racialization of corruption and the sub-plot of "communist subversion" are calculated attempts by both parties to divert public attention from the real issue, campaign finance reform. Little wonder, both parties have expressed no interest in passing even the toothless McCain-Feingold campaign finance reform bill.[12] Money has effectively become the lifeline of, and prerequisite for, participating in American democracy. Americans have become increasingly alienated from the electoral process. No wonder the fastest growing and by far the largest political party in the United States today is neither Republican nor Democrat, but the party of nonvoters. Money has made a mockery of American democracy! The United States may be the oldest democracy on earth, in terms of voter participation and access to government, but it has become the most undemocratic country in substance among all the democracies in the world today.

Missing also in this highly racialized political discourse over the role of John Huang, Charlie Trie, and other Asian Americans in the campaign finance scandal is what or whose interests these Asian American leaders really represent. John Huang himself has steadfastly insisted that his sole motive in going into the DNC to do fundraising is to help empower and to represent the interests of Asian Americans across the nation.[13] To him, the only way for the Asian American minority to gain political power and to make its voice heard in the United States is to make significant contributions to politicians. Many Asian American political leaders shared this view. In a comprehensive defense of John Huang, for example, Keith Umemoto wrote,

The relatively low numbers of Asian Pacific American voters compared with other groups and our scarcity of Asian Pacific American representatives holding elected offices accounted for our lack of political influence. One of the ways we have begun to generate success in gaining access and recognition has been through financial contributions. . . . John left the private sector to devote his energy to public service and to help elevate the power of our community by serving as *a bridge* between the influential Asian donors he had access to and the Asian Pacific American community in general.[14]

Yet, when we examine the various fundraising schemes Huang and others had devised and examine the class background of the big Asian donors, it becomes very clear that they represent the interests of a very small class of people within the Asian American communities: a handful of the rich business entrepreneurs and professionals and above all, persons with extensive connections to transnational Asian capital and multinational corporations based in places like Indonesia, Thailand, Hong Kong, Taiwan, South Korea, and Japan.[15] This is hardly surprising: the overwhelming majority of Asian Americans do not have available cash to make the kind of political donations John Huang and others demanded and brought in. In fact, the majority of Asian Americans fall within the lower and middle classes, desiring only to work hard to make ends meet and above all, to put their children through schools. Their idea of making it, in other words, is not making huge donations to politicians of either party.

The class-based donations generated by Huang, Trie, and others have their roots in the transformation of Asian economies and the expansion of transnationalism since early 1970s. The geopolitical realignment in Asia following the U.S.-China detente in 1972 and the ensuing influx of Asian immigrants, refugees, and capital to the United States inaugurated several new trends in the development of the Asian American communities, not the least of which was increasing demographic, linguistic, and cultural diversity among Asian Americans and growing division and conflict along class and national origin lines within each of the Asian American communities.

An example of this conflict is the struggle since 1968 over the International Hotel. The conflict became a housing struggle between a Chinese Thai tycoon, Supasit Mahaguna, and the poor Chinese and Filipino elderly at the International Hotel in San Francisco Chinatown.[16] Owned by San Francisco real estate magnate, Walter Schorenstein of Milton Meyer Co., the hotel was sold to Mahaguna in the midst of a political upheaval in Thailand in 1973. The real Asian American victims of transnational capital, as Peter Kwong's study on New York City's Chinatown since the 1970s demonstrates, are the poor and disadvantaged working class. The Riady's investment in the United States through the Lippo Group likewise reflects the pattern of capital flight since the early 1970s. John Huang and Charlie Trie, in fact, represent a similar convergence of newly emergent class interests, transnational capital, and not infrequently, foreign political interests in the Asian American communities, hitherto ignored by the mainstream media and perhaps forgotten by many Asian Americans as well.[17]

From the perspective of Asian American history, persons like John Huang, Johnny Chung, and Charlie Trie are not totally unknown or without their predecessors. Among the earlier big donors, fundraisers, power-brokers, or influence-peddlers are figures including Eddie Chin of New York and Pius Lee of San Francisco of the 1980s; Tongsun Park and Susie Park Thompson of Washington, D.C., in the so-called Koreagate in 1970s; Anna Chennault of Washington, D.C., of the 1960s, a key figure on the Finance Committee of the National Republican Committee; and H.H. Kung of New York and Albert Chow and Doon Yen Wong of San Francisco in the 1950s.[18] Instead of representing the interests and rights of lower- and middle-class Asian Americans in the communities, they represented primarily the interests of transnational political and economic elite in their insatiable pursuit of profit, market penetration, and political influence. In this sense, what these prominent figures have done, does not differ much from what all foreign CEOs, corporations, and governments do routinely in the United States to protect their interests by buying political access and influence and extracting economic favors for themselves, whether they are the Riadys of Indonesia, the Bronfmans of Canada, the Rothchilds of France, the Murdochs of Australia, or the Bill Gates of the United States. They represent class and transnational capital interests, competing for resource, market share, profit, and ultimately, access to political power.

## CITIZENSHIP AND EXTRATERRITORIALITY

Two other neglected issues of importance in the scandal are citizenship and extraterritoriality, both of which have been largely overlooked by both scholars and the media. Citizenship is the creation and legacy of the modern European nation-state and nationalism and by definition, a legal and political device designed to convey privileges to some and to exclude others. Thus, Asian immigrants were denied citizenship before World War II and since then, Asian Americans have continued to be seen and treated as if they were foreigners, even though, since the late 1960s, the Asian American movement has been doing its utmost to debunk the stereotype and to assert Asian American citizenship. It is this racist legacy or nativism that the Republicans and media sought to reignite and incite and to broadly represent Asian Americans as untrustworthy and unscrupulous aliens eager to buy influence into the Clinton administration and to subvert American democracy and national security. The strategy succeeded in "denaturalizing" Asian Americans and in compelling the Clinton administration to treat Asian Americans as political untouchable, as we saw above. In the context of a partisan political power struggle, Asian Americans were considered weak and expendable, whether they were citizens or not and whether their rights as citizens had been compromised or not. The inevitable outcome was political exclusion.

However, traditional nationalist notions of citizenship, nation-state, sovereignty, national borders, and political loyalty have been called into question and have been undergoing rapid transformation in the age of transnationalism, aided in no small measure by the United States, and its multinational and transnational corporations. American transnational corporations and their subsidiaries of foreign-owned corporations in the United States are treated as U.S. corporations and, under the laws of the United States, as persons with the same rights and privileges protected by the Constitution, including the right to contribute huge amounts of money, though not the right to vote. The Lippo Group of Indonesia, along with thousands of foreign corporations with registered branch offices and subsidiaries in the United States, are entitled to make legitimate political contributions with virtually no legal restriction and to use their contributions to help elect politicians and influence legislation. Many of the executives of these foreign subsidiaries are permanent residents who can also make generous political contributions, even if they have no right to vote. This, of course, is how wealthy business executives routinely gain more effective access to elected officials than American citizens in the United States. In this regard, the campaign finance scandal has raised important questions about citizenship and the role of transnational corporations and permanent residents in U.S. politics. This issue should have placed the status of foreign subsidiaries, permanent residents, and persons with dual citizenship at the center of campaign finance reform. Incredibly, none of these have been given public attention, not even in the Senate hearings.

Lastly, an integral component of transnationalism is extraterritoriality, an idea deeply embedded in the history of Western colonialism and imperialism in Asia, in particular, in the infamous unequal treaties imposed by Western imperialist powers on China, between 1842, at the end of the Opium War, and 1949. Under the unequal treaty system, China was forced to surrender significant sectors of its sovereign power to the Western imperialists, including customs duties in treaty ports, immunity from Chinese legal jurisdiction, foreign concessions or privileged zones, special treatment of foreign business and Christian missions, and free military access to Chinese ports. This type of extraterritorial power undermined the Chinese sovereign state and inspired Chinese nationalism at home and abroad. Not quite as harsh as what the United States and other countries had imposed on China under the unequal treaties, the U.S. government, businesses, and the so-called nongovernmental organizations (NGOs), have, since the Cold War began, routinely carried out this tradition by interfering both covertly and overtly with other countries' political and economic affairs, including massive use of public money to influence elections in well over 100 countries, the most recent of which was in the Boris Yeltsin's presidential campaign.[19] In fact, our long-standing practice of intervening in the political affairs of other countries has severely undermined the credibility of our claim of Chinese or Indonesian interference with the 1996 presidential election. Worse yet, even as politicians and newspapers conducted their investigation into and denounced claims of Chinese interference in the electoral process, at no time did they mention, much less show any interest in, investigating what the U.S. government, transnational corporations, and NGOs have been doing in influencing and manipulating the internal affairs of countries worldwide.

Within the Asian American communities, there is also a perverse reciprocity in the exercise of extraterritorial domination. Historically, due to racist and exclusionary policies toward Asian immigrants, Asian American ghettoes were established and community affairs were left largely to the control of the business elite and above all, to agents of foreign Asian governments. Throughout their histories, Asian Americans were discriminated against by the mainstream, and their community affairs were dominated and manipulated by the business and political interests of their homeland countries, giving rise to the highly institutionalized extraterritorial domination of Asian governments. For example, the Chinese American and Korean American communities were used by Taiwan and South Korea to support their respective military dictatorships throughout the Cold War and to lobby the interests of the two governments.[20] Community dissidents or critics were invariably intimidated, harassed, and sometimes, subjected to physical violence, including murder. Since the early 1970s, foreign Asian businesses have frequently used Asian American communities for their investment and as their covers or beachheads for launching their penetration into the American market.[21] These investments have had a profound impact on the lives and businesses in the Asian American communities, especially in terms of class relations and political development. The influx of transnational capital in the past twenty-five years has brought mixed blessings into the communities and has effectively marginalized the original vision and mission of the Asian American movement, replacing grassroots political mobilization for community improvement and empowerment with money-influence politics. Some of the most important fundraising activities of John Huang, in fact, fit into this historical pattern.[22] If Asian Americans are to achieve full freedom and citizenship in the United States, they must be liberated from the new forms of racial oppression and extraterritorial domination as manifested through the campaign finance scandal.

## CONCLUSION

One of the most remarkable things about the so-called "Asian connection" in the 1996 campaign finance scandal was how a molehill was transformed into a mountain by the media; the Republican leaders, a few right-wing columnists, and the Thompson Committee succeeded in portraying China as the No. 1 villain without a shred of evidence. John Huang was personally responsible for raising about $3.5 million out of a total of $2.2 billion raised and spent in just the 1996 federal elections, excluding money raised and spent in state and local elections. Yet, he and other Asian American fund-raisers received at least 90 percent of media coverage. In the process, they became the obsession of Republican-controlled congressional hearings and the targets of endless investigation by the operatives of both parties and by the U.S. Department of Justice. (The obsession was finally eclipsed by the Monica Lewinsky/Paula Jones story in late 1997.) By indiscriminately mingling reporting with opinion and speculation, the media and Republicans deliberately conflated Asian Americans with foreign Asians and fabricated an imagined connection and conspiracy between Asian contributors with "Red" China, already being vilified and demonized by both the Right (anti-abortion, Christian Right, pro-Taiwan, isolationists, Patrick Buchanan, Jesse Helm, etc.) and the Left (human rights groups, AFL-CIO, pro-Tibet, environmentalists, Richard Gephardt, Nancy Pelosi, etc.) in the post–Cold War era.

Both Democrats and Republicans in the political elite generously exploited the race card for their respective advantages and against each other as they had done routinely. Since the arrival of the Chinese, during the Gold Rush and succeeding Asian immigrants were repeatedly used by political parties to incite nativism and racism and to garner populist votes. In the 1996 election, the Democrats targeted Asian Americans and foreign Asians to raise some "soft money" to jump-start the Clinton re-election campaign while the Republicans seized upon the vulnerability of the Democrats by exploiting the anti-Asian and anti-foreign sentiment with the so-called foreign "Asian connection" to discredit Clinton and the Democrats. Sensing their vulnerability, the Democrats advanced the anti-Asian thesis before the November election, only to distance and abandon Asian Americans after the election in order to protect the Clinton presidency and to demonstrate their commitment to the so-called "clean money" and politics. In short, both parties unscrupulously used Asian Americans to racialize the issue of political corruption and in the process, to divert public demand for campaign finance reform.

Racialization of the campaign finance scandal seriously challenged Asian Americans across the nation, especially the political and intellectual leadership of the communities. The major questions were how Asian Americans should correctly analyze and understand the issue and how best to respond to the issue. Certainly, it was important for Asian American community leaders and activists to meet the challenge head-on. Before the November 1996 election, one strategy was to view it solely as an issue of identity politics and incorporation within the existing campaign finance political patronage system and to mobilize the communities accordingly to fight media and Republican racism where community leaders being victimized by racism. This analysis and strategy assumed innocence and above all, homogeneity within the Asian American communities. The same perspective saw no flaw in the campaign finance system and the political institution. If everyone was doing it, why couldn't the Asians do it as well! This, in fact, was the dominant perspective. It is, in my opinion, short-sighted and wrong. As more and more disclosures of wrong-doing came to light after the election, the position rapidly lost its credibility.

Another scenario was to view John Huang and his collaborators as representatives of an increasingly fragmented Asian American community, separated by national origin, generation, linguistic, and cultural differences—and, above all, class distinctions—and to see Huang as a representative of a growing transnational business and professional elite in the Asian American communities. This elite, according to this analysis, is fully integrated with transnational, and at times, Asian flight capital which needs to establish a beachhead in the United States Asian American communities come in handy and they become the vehicle used to penetrate the U.S. market and politics for its own interests. Accordingly, the Asian

American communities become a convenient shelter for investment and extraterritorial economic and political domination and penetration. The interests of transnational capital is incompatible with the interests of the communities. Contradiction between these interests in the Asian American communities becomes inevitable and, as a consequence, community development and welfare are rendered secondary or subordinate to the interests of transnational capital. From the vantage of transnational capital, conflation of Asian Americans and foreign Asians or obfuscation of citizens and aliens is strategically necessary and expedient if the elite were to dominate the communities and move smoothly and swiftly into the world of corporate America and be competitive in both politics and economics. From the point of view of the American corporate elite, Asian Americans provided also an effective bridge for American penetration into the emerging Asian economies.

Still another perspective on the Asian entanglement in the campaign finance scandal is to see John Huang and other Asian Americans as symptomatic of a larger problem in American democracy. From this point of view, Asian Americans embroiled in the scandal represent the tip of an iceberg called political corruption. Money, according this view, has become the prerequisite for democratic participation and the only means toward gaining both access and influence in politics. This is the cancer in American democracy. From this perspective, Asian Americans have been dealt a severe blow and setback because of the racialization of the scandal. They have become "denaturalized" and effectively linked to an alleged Chinese conspiracy. By viewing the John Huang case as a symptom of a larger problem and racialization as a pretext to divert public attention from the need for campaign finance reform, Asian Americans can treat the setback as a rare opportunity to clarify many key issues in both the communities and the nation, to deal effectively and unapologetically against racism. Asian Americans can join forces with other public interest and community groups in a nation-wide movement to achieve substantive, not superficial or procedural, campaign finance reform. Such efforts would help revive and restore democracy in the United States. As long as money is inextricably tied to the electoral process, more and more Americans, including Asian Americans, will be alienated from and drop out of the political process. Public financing of elections appears to be the only viable remedy to remove the cancer and to restore faith in democracy.

## NOTES

1. "In the U.S. Commission on Civil Rights: Petition for Hearing," a twenty-three-page petition submitted by attorneys Edward M. Chen and Dale Minami on behalf of several Asian American individuals and organizations, September 10, 1997. K. Connie Kang and Robert L. Jackson, "Asian Americans Charge Fund-Raising Scandal Bias," Los Angeles Times, September 12, 1997; Steven A. Holmes, "Asian American Groups File a Complaint of Bias in Inquiries and Coverage," New York Times, September 12, 1997. In response to the petition, the U.S. Commission on Civil Rights prepared a forty-three-page briefing paper, "Asian Pacific American Petition: Brief Paper," and conducted a public briefing session on December 5, 1997 in which several witnesses, including this writer, presented evidence of civil rights violations to the commission. See, Wendy Koch, "Asian Groups Protest Probe," San Francisco Examiner, December 6, 1997; Helen Zia, "Can Asian Americans Turn the Media Tide?" The Nation 265 (21) (December 22, 1997): 10.

2. In rapid succession, William Safire wrote several columns on the so-called "Asian connection": "The Asian Connection," "Get Riady, Get Set," "Absence of Outrage," "Lippo Suction," "Huang Huang Blues," and "Helping Janet Reno," in New York Times, October 7, 10, 21, 28, November 4, and December 5, 1996; "Wealthy Indonesian Businessman Has Strong Ties to Clinton" and "Family Tied to Democratic Party Gifts Built an Indonesian Empire," New York Times, October 11 and 20, 1996; "Soft Money, Easy Access," Newsweek, October 13, 1997; Peter Waldman, "East Meets West: By Courting Clinton, Lippo Gains

Stature," *Wall Street Journal*, October 16, 1996; "Candidates for Sale: Clinton's Asia Connection," a cover-story of *Newsweek*, October 28, 1996; Kevin Merida and Serge F. Kovaleski, "Mysteries Arise All Along the Asian Money Trail," *Washington Post*, November 1, 1996; John Greenwald, "The Cash Machine: Was Huang a Maverick or Part of a Scheme to Shake down Foreign Tycoons?" *Time*, November 11, 1996; Sara Fritz, "Huang, Riady Paths Crossed at Commerce," *Los Angeles Times*, December 4, 1996. For a summary of the unfolding scandal at the end of 1996, see, "Column One: How DNC Got Caught in a Donor Dilemma," *Los Angeles Times*, December 23, 1996; David E. Rosenbaum, "In Political Money Game, The Year of Big Loopholes," *New York Times*, December 26, 1996; Ruth Marcus and Charles R. Babcock, "The System Cracks under the Weight of Cash," *Washington Post*, February 9, 1997.

3. The $2.2 billion-figure comes from a report published by the Center for Responsive Politics, a public interest research organization based in Washington, D.C. The report entitled The *Big Picture: Money Follows Power Shift on Capital Hill*, was released on November 25, 1997. ('Cost of '96 Campaigns Sets Record at $2.2 Billion," *New York Times*, November 25, 1997. The complete report can be read on the internet at the Center's webpage at www.crp.org.) See also, Ellen Miller and Randy Kehlen, "Mischievous Myths about Money in Politics," *Dollars and Sense*, July/August 1996, 22–27 and Anthony Corrado, "Campaign '96: Money Talks," *In These Times* 20(26) (November 11, 1996): 18–21.

4. The so-called China connection of money raised by Huang, Trie and others did not surface until *New York Times* columnist, William Safire first constructed the link in his article, "I Remember Larry," *New York Times*, January 2, 1997; "Beware the Princelings (of China)," *New York Times*, February 13, 1997. Before that January 2 date, most of the allegations of wrongdoing were based on money raised from the Riadys and the Lippo Group of Indonesia. A possible source of this thesis may be found in a right-wing publication, *The American Spectator*, which published two articles by James Ring Adams, "What's Up in Jakarta?" and "John Huang's Bamboo Network," respectively, in September 1995 and December 1996. The China connection was given a new boost when the press reported that Wang Jun, Chairman of the Poly Technologies group, the Chinese army's arms exporting company, was among the guests in one of the many coffee gatherings at the White House on February 6, 1996. See Michael Weisskopf and Lena H. Sun, "Trie Gained Entree for Chinese Official," *Washington Post*, December 20, 1996; David E. Sanger, "Businessman at White House Social Has Close Ties to China's Military Power," *New York Times*, December 21, 1996; Steven Mufson, "Chinese Denies Seeking White House Visit," *The Washington Post*, March 16, 1997.

5. Bob Woodward and Brian Duffy, "Chinese Embassy Role in Fund-Raising Probed," *Washington Post*, February 13, 1997. See also Mark Hosenball and Evan Thomas, "White House: A China Connection?" and "A Break in the Case," *Newsweek*, February 24 and May 19, 1997; Keen Silverstein, "The New China Hands: How the Fortune 500 Is China's Strongest Lobby," *The Nation*, February 17, 1997, 11–16; Nigel Holloway, "The China Connection," *The Far Eastern Economic Review* (Hong Kong), February 27, 1997, 16; David Johnston, "U.S. Agency Secretly Monitored Chinese in '96 on Political Gifts," *New York Times*, March 13, 1997; "The China Connection," *Economist* (London), March 15, 1997; Kenneth R. Timmerman, "All Roads Lead to China" and "China's 22nd Province (California)," *The American Spectator*, March 1997, 30–38 and October 1997; Marcus W. Brauchli, Phil Kuntz, and Leslie Chang, "Vying for Influence: Fund-Raising Flap Has Roots in Bitter Rivalry between China, Taiwan," *Wall Street Journal*, April 4, 1997. Among the most sensational reports is the cover story, "Selling Out? China Syndrome" by Rich Lowry, in *The National Review* 49(5), March 24, 1997, 38–40; Phil Kuntz, "Asian Tycoon with Ties to China Visited White House," *Wall Street Journal*, July 31, 1997; Christopher Matthews, "Clinton's Open-door Policy with China," *San Francisco Examiner*, July 13, 1997. Even after the failure of the Senate committee to substantiate the original points raised by his article,

Woodward continued to press his points based on leaks, "FBI Had Overlooked Key Files in Probe Chinese Influence," *Washington Post,* November 14, 1997. For a different take on this point, see David Sanger, "Asian Money, American Fears," *The New York Times,* January 5, 1997; Joel Kotkin, "Asian Americans Left Holding the Bay," *Wall Street Journal,* January 23, 1997; Franklin Foer, "The Chinese Connection," *The Slate,* March 15, 1997; "America's Dose of Sinophobia," *The Economist,* March 29, 1997, 35–36.

6. David E. Rosenbaum, "Huang May Yet Testify to Senate Panel: As Hearings Open, Chairman Alleges a Chinese Plot," *New York Times,* July 9, 1997. Sen. Thompson's opening statement can be found in the *New York Times,* July 9, 1997, A-11; Lance Gay, "Foreign Influence—Lifting the Veil," *San Francisco Examiner,* July 6, 1997. Even as the Republicans on the Thompson Committee were publicly advancing the Chinese conspiracy theory, Sheila Kaplan of the MS-NBC reported July 21, 1997 that no one on the committee subscribed to the theory. Sheila Kaplan, "GOP Backpedals on Huang Accusation So Far; Hearings Are Leaving Republicans Dissatisfied."

7. Francis X. Clines, "Campaign Panel to End Hearings on Fund-Raising" and David E. Rosenbaum "News Analysis: Senate Committee Failed to Zero in on the Verities of Campaign Finance" in *New York Times,* November 1, 1997. In its 1,500-page draft final report, the Thompson Committee blamed Clinton, Gore, and the DNC for widespread improper fundraising, but it failed to substantiate the two primary theses of the Republicans. See Jill Abramson and Don Van Natta Jr., "Draft of Report for G.O.P. Attacks Clinton Campaign" and David E. Sanger and Don Van Natta Jr., "'China Area' Tied to 'Illegal' Gifts: Senate Republicans Can't Link the Contributions to Beijing," *New York Times,* February 8 and 11, 1998. The draft report is so vague that the editorials of *New York Times* and *Washington Post* could not agree on its findings of the China connection. The *New York Times* saw credibility in the China thesis, but not *The Washington Post.* "The Prince of Scandal Fatigue," *The New York Times,* February 12, 1998 and "The China Con-

nection," *The Washington Post,* February 12, 1998.

8. The DNC Plan for the Asian American fundraising drive is entitled, "National Asian Pacific American Campaign Plan," code name "Constituency Outreach Plan." The plan was drawn up in April 1996 by the Asian Pacific American Working Group, formed in February 1996, which included several prominent Asian American political insiders in the Beltway. Tim Weiner and David E. Sanger, "Democrats Hoped to Raise $7 Million from Asians in the U.S.," *The New York Times,* December 28, 1996; Ruth Marcus, "Oval Office Meeting Set DNC Asian Funds Network in Motion," *The Washington Post,* December 29, 1996.

9. The role of Sen. Dodd in instigating the strategy and press conferences was not known until after the election. His role was discovered among the DNC documents subpoenaed by the Justice Department. See Jill Zuckman, "DNC Stumbles on Asian Issue," *Boston Globe,* January 19, 1997. The four press conferences were held in New York, Los Angeles, Chicago, and Washington, D.C. The press conference in Washington, D.C., included representatives from the Congressional Asian Pacific American Caucus Institute (CAPACI), the Organization of Chinese Americans (OCA), the Japanese American Citizens League (JACL), Filipino American Civil Rights Advocates (FACRA), National Conference of Korean American Leaders (NCKAL), India Abroad Center for Political Awareness and the American Association for Physicians from India. See Michael Fletcher, "Coalition Says DNC Fundraising Flap Generating 'Asian-Bashing,'" *The Washington Post,* October 23, 1996; Connie K. Kang, "Asian Gifts Coverage Called Stereotyping,' *Los Angeles Times,* October 23, 1996; Frank H. Wu, "The John Huang Affair: The Controversy Involves Much More than Dollars for the DNC," *Asianweek,* November 1, 1997. Two of the participants at the press conferences, Stewart Kwoh and Frank Wu, also co-authored an op-ed piece, "Don't Build Reform on a Scapegoat," *Los Angeles Times,* October 24, 1996.

10. On February 28, 1997, the DNC announced the results of its audit and its decision not to accept "any contribution from any individual who is not a U.S. citizen," meaning,

"contributions from legal permanent residents" and "contribution from a U.S. subsidiary of a foreign company or any other corporation which is majority-owned by non-U.S. citizens" are no longer lawful and acceptable. Alison Mitchell, "Democrats Say They Will Return More Money with Murky Sources," New York Times, February 22, 1997; K. Connie Kang, "Asian Americans Bristle at Democrats 'Interrogation,'" Los Angeles Times, February 27, 1997; "Thanked with an Insult: Asian Americans Are Right to Be Offended by Democrats' Inquiries—An Editorial," Los Angeles Times, March 3, 1997.

11. Seth Rosenfeld, "Tien Ties to Asia Money May Have Cost Him Job: Source Says Clinton Leery of Hearings for a Cabinet Post," The San Francisco Examiner, December 22, 1996; Lena Sun, "Asian Names Scrutinized at White House; Guards Stopped Citizens Who Looked 'Foreign,'" Washington Post, September 11, 1997.

12. The McCain-Feingold bill (S. 25, 105th Congress, 1st Session, January 21, 1997) is designed to ban the "soft money" contributions and to advance several incremental reforms, among which are more stringent disclosure requirements, strong regulatory power for the Federal Election Commission, and restrictions on the so-called "issue advertisements." Examples of bipartisan opposition to the McCain-Feingold bill and any kind of campaign finance reform can be seen from the following sample headlines from the New York Times in 1997: "GOP Panel See No Major Flaw in Fund-Raising Rules," July 19, 1997; "Despite Controversy, Money Continues to Pour into Party Coffers," August 6, 1997; "The Talk in Washington: With Eyes on 2000, the Big Issue Is Money," September 3, 1997; "Campaign Finance Measure Blocked in Senate Votes," October 8, 1997; and "After 1996, Campaign Finance Laws in Shreds," November 2, 1997; Doug Ireland, "Thompson's Supporting Role: The Senator Follows the Script to Preserve Corrupt Campaign Financing," The Nation, July 21, 1997, 21–24. For a debate on campaign finance reform issues, see the special issue of the American Prospect: A Journal for the Liberal Imagination 36, January/February, 1998; "Money and Politics: Politicians for Rent," The Economist, February 8, 1997, 23–25.

13. Ying Chan, "Assailed Dem; Cash Man Talks," The New York Daily News, June 16, 1997 and "Huang: Fund-Raising Charges Biased," an exclusive interview of John Huang with the Zhongguo Shibao (The China Times of Taiwan), translated by the Associated Press, December 3, 1997. "I only hoped to try my utmost to help Asian Americans exercise some strength," he said in the interview. He also blamed "muckraking by the media" for what he called "unfair allegations against Asian Americans." See also, "From Hero to Political Hot Potato: John Huang Brought in Millions for Democrats while Working to Give Asian Americans Clout" and "John Huang: Man in Middle of Political Storm," Los Angeles Times, October 19 and 23, 1996; K. Connie Kang, David Rosenzweig, and Alan Miller, "John Huang, A Changed Lifestyle, Friends Say," Los Angeles Times, August 3, 1997; Michael Isikoff and Mark Hosenball, "Scandal: Calling All Lawyers," Newsweek, November 11, 1996; Stephen Labaton, "Democrats Urged Huang to Raise More Money," New York Times, December 22, 1996; Leslie Wayne, "Huang Donated Thousands to Congressional Contests," New York Times, March 2, 1997; Brian Duffy, "A Fund-Raiser's Rise and Fall," Washington Post, May 13, 1997.

14. Umemoto, Keith, "In Defense of John Huang," Asian Week, November 29, 1996, 7. This article is representative of the view of most of the Asian American political insiders.

15. For a highly Orientalized depiction of the major Asian figures involved in the scandal, see Lena Sun and J. Pomfret, "The Curious Cast of Asian Donors; Some Sought Access to Clinton, Others' Motives Remain Murky," Washington Post, January 27, 1997. For the various schemes used to raise political donations from Asian and Asian American sources, see "South Korean's Firms (Cheong Am America Inc.); Democrats Reimburse Temple for Fund-Raiser" and "Principals Say (Hsi Lai) Temple Event Was Explicit Fund-Raiser," Los Angeles Times, October 19 and November 3, 1996; "Vanish After Gift to Democrats," The Los Angeles Times, October 17, 1996; 'Controversy Swirling around (Yogesh) Gandhi Donation Grows," Los Angeles Times, October 24, 1996; "Democrats Return $324,000 Gift from Gandhi Relative,"

*The Los Angeles Times*, November 7, 1996; Glenn F. Bunting, "Democrats Return $253,,500 to Thai Businesswoman (Pauline Kanchanalak)," *The Los Angeles Times*, November 21, 1997; Alan C. Miller, "Democrats Give Back More Disputed Money (from Indonesian Couple)," *Los Angeles Times*, November 23, 1996; Jonathan Peterson and Sara Fritz, "Clinton Legal Team Returns $600,000 in Contributions," *Los Angeles Times*, December 17, 1996; Christopher Drew, "Asian Links of a Donor Put Gifts to Democrats in Doubt," *The New York Times*, February 22, 1997; Judy Keen, Judi Hasson and Tom Squitieri, "Dinner Raised $488,000—And Questions," *USA Today*, February 7, 1997; Nancy Gibbs, "Cash-and-Carry Diplomacy," *Time*, February 24, 1997, 22–25; Michael Duffy and Michael Weisskopf, "Johnny Come Often," *Newsweek*, March 3, 1997, 24–28; *Eyal Press*, "The Suharto Lobby," *The Progressive* 61:5, May 1997, 19–31; D. Van Natta, "Donations to Democrats Traced to Phony Firms and Dead Person," *The New York Times*, July 6, 1997. Thus far, three Asian Americans have been convicted of illegal activities in connection with campaign fund-raising. Nora T. and Gene K.J. Lum, wife and husband, were convicted and sentenced to 10-month imprisonment for funneling illegal contributions to several politicians. See George Lardner Jr., "Two Donors Agree to Plead Guilty" and "Judge Sets 10-Month Term in Political Donations Case," *The Washington Post*, May 22 and September 10, 1997. The couple was also the focus of a special *Frontline* report, "The Fixers," produced by Michael Kirk and Kenneth Levis, aired April 14, 1997, and a long article, "American Guanxi" by Peter J. Boyer in *The New Yorker* 72:8, April 14, 1997, 48–61. Republican Congressman Jay Kim pleaded guilty to illegal fund-raising and misuse of campaign money. See, David Rosensweig, "Rep. Kim, Wife to Plead Guilty to Misdemeanors," *The Los Angeles Times*, August 1, 1997; Walter Pincus, "Kim Probe Found Wide Variety of Campaign Violations," *The Washington Post*, August 19, 1997. Charlie Yah-lin Trie, a key figure in the scandal, surrendered himself to law enforcement authorities on February 3, 1998. See David Johnston, "Key Figure in Campaign Fundraising Inquiry Surrenders to Federal Authorities," *The New York Times*, February 4, 1998. For a case study on how the Chinese American community in San Francisco became fragmented by class and politics, see L. Ling-chi Wang, "Exclusion and Fragmentation in Ethnic Politics: Chinese Americans in Urban Politics," in *The Politics of Minority Coalitions: Race, Ethnicity, and Shared Uncertainties*, edited by Wilbur C. Rich, 129–42 (Westport, Conn.: Praeger, 1996).

16. Beatrice Dong, "An Analysis of the International Hotel Struggle," a Senior Honors Thesis, Department of Ethnic Studies, University of California, Berkeley, November 22, 1994.

17. Peter Kwong, *The New Chinatown*. New York: Wang and Hill, 1987. For articles on foreign government interests in U.S. politics and government, see, Jill Abramson, "Taiwan Won Platform Terms with Democrats," *The Wall Street Journal*, October 25, 1996; "Taiwan Political Donations Implicated in the U.S. Presidential Election (in Chinese)," in the *Yazhou Zhoukan* (Hong Kong), October 15, 1996; Paul Jacob, "In Jakarta: Riady's Actions Benefited Indonesia, Says Suharto's Son," *The Strait Times* (Singapore), October 20, 1996; Sara Fritz and Rone Tempest, "Ex-Clinton Aide Arranged for Taiwan Connection," *The Los Angeles Times*, October 30, 1996; Keith Richburg and Dan Morgan, "Taiwanese: Ex-Clinton Aide Said He Was Raising Money," *The Washington Post*, October 30, 1996; John M. Broder, "Taiwan Lobbying in U.S. Gets Results," *The Los Angeles Times*, November 4, 1996; Michael Isidoff and Melinda Liu, "Scandal: Now, The Taiwan Axis," *The Newsweek*, November 4, 1996; Maggie Farley, "Claim of Campaign Offer Clouds Taiwan Diplomacy" and "Clinton Met Foreign Donor to Discuss U.S.-China Trade," *The Los Angeles Times*, November 9 and 16, 1996; "Indonesian Fulfills Aim for Firm, Nation," *The Los Angeles Times*, October 16, 1996; Stephen Labaton, "Indonesian Magnate and Clinton Talked Policy, White House Says," *The New York Times*, November 5, 1996; Sharon LaFraniere and Susan Schmidt, "NSC Gave Warnings about Asian Donors," *The Washington Post*, February 15, 1997.

18. No systematic study has been done of the ways foreign Asian governments have tried

to buy political and foreign policy influence in the U.S. through the various Asian American communities. The following articles provide a glimpse into how Asian governments extended their extraterritorial domination in the Asian American communities to interfere with American politics: Alejandro A. Esclamado, "The Story of the Marcos Coercion;" Woon-Ha Kim, "The Activities of the South Korean Central Intelligence Agency in the U.S.;" Brett de Bary and Victor Nee, "The Kuomintang in Chinatown;" H. Mark Lai, "China Politics and the U.S. Chinese Communities." All these studies are found in *Counterpoint: Perspectives on Asian America*, edited by Emma Gee and published by the Asian American Studies Center of the University of California, Los Angeles, 1976. For more general studies see, Ross Y. Koen, *The China Lobby in American Politics* (New York: Harper, 1974); Stanley D. Bachrack, *The Committee of One Million: 'China Lobby' Politics, 1953–1971* (New York: Columbia University Press, 1976); and Robert Boettcher, *Gifts of Deceit: Sun Myung Moon, Tongsun Park and the Korean Scandal* (New York: Holt, Rinehart and Winston, 1980). For a recent example, see Laurence Zuckerman, "Taiwan Keeps a Step Ahead of China in U.S. Lobbying," *The New York Times*, March 14, 1997. For a more theoretical treatment of the subject of extraterritoriality in the Chinese American experience, see L. Ling-chi Wang, "The Structure of Dual Domination: Toward a Paradigm for the Study of the Chinese Diaspora in the United States," in *Amerasia Journal*, 21(1–2) (1995): 149–170.

19. Norman Solomon, "Money Scandals: 'Mr. Smith' Goes to Washington," The *Minneapolis Star-Tribune*, March 16, 1997; Wendy Koch, "U.S. Helps Sway Vote in Foreign Countries; Taxpayers Bankroll Overseas Programs," *The San Francisco Examiner*, October 24, 1997; John Broder, "Foreign Taint on National Election? A Boomerang for U.S.," *The New York Times*, March 31, 1997; James Risen, Alan Miller, "DNC Donor's Offer of Funds to Yeltsin Told," *The Los Angeles Times*, September 10, 1997.

20. Illsoo Kim, *New Urban Immigrants: The Korean Community in New York*, 225–241. Princeton University Press, 1981; L. Ling-chi Wang, *Politics of Assimilation and Repression: A History of the Chinese in the U.S. since World War II*, 1981, Chapter 8, an unpublished manuscript, Ethnic Studies Library, University of California, Berkeley. See also, L. Ling-chi Wang, "The Structure of Dual Domination: Toward a Paradigm for the Study of the Chinese Diaspora in the United States," in *Amerasia Journal* 21(1–2) (1995), 149–170.

21. For a general discussion on the transformation of the Asian American communities since the 1970s, see L. Ling-chi Wang, "The Politics of Ethnic Identity and Empowerment: The Asian American Community since the 1960s," in *Asian American Policy Review*, Vol. II (Spring 1991), 51–55. The most famous example of extraterritorial domination and repression by a foreign Asian government is the political assassination of Chinese American journalist, Henry Liu, by hired agents of the Taiwan government on October 15, 1994 in his home in Daly City, California, because he had written articles and books critical of Taiwan's president Chiang Ching-kuo. For a detailed account of this case, see David Kaplan, *Fire of the Dragon: Politics, Murder, and the Kuomintang* (New York: Athenium, 1992). See also, "Henry Liu: Justice Is Stonewalled," by L. Ling-chi Wang, in *Silenced: The Unsolved Murders of Immigrant Journalists in the United State*, edited by Juan Gonzalez (New York: Committee to Protect Journalists, 47–56. Only very preliminary studies have been made on the foreign Asian investments in the Asian American communities. Among them are: Peter Kwong, *The New Chinatown* (New York: Hill and Wang, 1987); Paul Ong, Edna Bonacich, and Lucie Cheng, *The New Asian Immigration in Los Angeles and Global Restructuring* (Philadelphia: Temple University Press, 1994);Timothy Fong, *The First Suburban Chinatown: The Remaking of Monterey Park, California* (Philadelphia: Temple University Press, 1994).

22. This conclusion is based on my own review of Asian American contributions through John Huang in the 1996–96 cycle. The big contributors, those contributing more than $5,000, made up a lion's share of the $3.5 million he raised for the DNC and the Clinton re-election campaign. Most of the biggest donors have extensive foreign connections.

# 3.12

# Profiling Principle

## The Prosecution of Wen Ho Lee
## and the Defense of Asian Americans

*Frank H. Wu*

~~~~~~~~~~~~~~~~~~~~~~~~~~~~~~~~~~~~~~~~~~~~~~~~~~~~~~~~~~~~~~~~~~~~~~~~~~~~~~~~~~~~~~~~

We should avoid the common question of whether wrongful racial profiling occurred in the Wen Ho Lee case, because the simplicity of the inquiry conceals the subtle error of its implication. Like the designation of "Chinese spy," which can refer to either a spy for China or a spy who is of Chinese descent, the question of whether wrongful racial profiling occurred in the Wen Ho Lee case confuses two distinct questions. There is the question of whether racial profiling occurred, and then there is the question of whether any such racial profiling was wrongful. One is a descriptive question, and the other is a normative question.

The confusion of the factual inquiry with the moral judgment, however, is hidden in the heart of the controversy over racial profiling. As a consequence of this confusion, the debate over the Lee case has the two sides arguing different issues. When the prosecution states, "there was no wrongful racial profiling," they have in mind the crucial word "wrongful." When the defense

Wu, Frank. "Profiling Principle: the Prosecution of Wen Ho Lee and the Defense of Asian Americans." *UCLA Asian American Law Journal* 7: 52. Reprinted with permission.

states, "there was wrongful racial profiling," they take for granted that any racial profiling must be deemed wrongful.

The proponents of the prosecution have had little choice but to concede that the investigation of Lee in some manner may have relied on race—there has been too much testimony from insiders to deny at least the strong possibility—and they have presented a sophisticated version of the argument for rational discrimination. They have insisted that because mainland China targets potential sources of secret information from individuals of Chinese ancestry, it makes sense for the counterintelligence operation, as a defensive measure, to do so as well. The opponents of the prosecution have concentrated their efforts on arguing that Lee was a victim of a selective inquiry and double standards. They have had greater difficulty not in showing that race may have been involved in focusing on Lee, but instead, in explaining why the use of that factor would be wrong if it is logical. (One side is concerned about issues of national security, and the other side is concerned about due process; that is another debate altogether, albeit related to racial profiling.)

The prosecution has the easier case than the defense in this respect: the prosecution can prevail if it either demonstrates that Lee was not treated any differently than a white counterpart would have been, or that any such difference in treatment was appropriate. After all, not even the greatest idealists have ever argued that every individual must be accorded identical treatment by a democratic government under any conceivable circumstance; distinctions can and must be made. The defense faces a significant burden: It must not only establish that there was some use of race, but it must also then plead that even a use of race under circumstances that seem as compelling as any government would ever be able to demonstrate nonetheless remains improper.

In the actual debate, each side has made an unwarranted assumption. The prosecution advocates have assumed that a utilitarian calculus should be used to achieve justice: They appear content to show the rationality of the use of race, under the assumption that what is rational is by definition right. The defense advocates have assumed that absolute civil rights are necessary to ensure justice: They seem willing to show that the use of race by itself is enough to warrant condemnation of the practice.

The persecution argument can be refuted by several means. Most obviously, its cost-benefit methodology can be accepted but its particular analysis rejected. It is especially utilitarians who would be appalled at the poor use of their technique. The Lee investigation failed to achieve its own stated objectives. While Lee may have been guilty of minor offenses, the government itself was forced to concede that he was not the so-called "Chinese spy" and never transferred secrets to any foreign power. As is typical of instances of racial profiling and abuse of prosecutorial power. Lee, was investigated for something altogether different from that which he was indicted; it was not simply a lesser charge but an unrelated one. The charges had nothing to do with an intentional transfer of information to China. The Lee investigation also produced unanticipated externalities: Potential Asian immigrant and Asian American employees avoided the labs, and current employees reconsidered whether they wished to stay there, both of which are detrimental to the government in recruiting talented employees.

In addition, utilitarianism is subject to all the usual attacks. In this particular context, utilitarianism is vulnerable to the familiar argument that civil rights by their nature, and any rights, cannot be trumped by the results of mere accounting. Rights are incommensurable in the marketplace. They cannot be readily quantified, and they defy comparison. If an anti-discrimination principle has any meaning at all, it must be at its most effective when it is least attractive. Otherwise, the right is not even a privilege.

There also is a peculiar problem in the Lee case. The perpetual foreigner syndrome that afflicts Asian Americans in general affects Lee in particular. The perpetual foreigner assumption—that Asians are sojourners, visitors, and/or guest who cannot overcome an inherent alien status— makes it easy to deprive Asian Americans of civil rights. Asian Americans are not integrated into a paradigm of civil rights because the poor treatment accorded Asian Americans is based not on their race but on their alienage, and therefore is acceptable.

A consensus has developed that discrimination on the basis of race is improper. A consensus remains, however, that discrimination on the basis of citizenship is proper. Citizens may enter the country; foreigners must seek permission. Indeed, serious theorists contend that the sovereignty of the nation and the meaning of citizenship status—ideas that undoubtedly have real consequence as matters of law and culture— cannot exist without a distinction between citizens and aliens that favors the former and literally disenfranchises the latter. Of course, the crux of the perpetual foreigner syndrome is race and not alienage. Race has been equated with alienage either by definition or as a proxy. Asian racial background is correlated to foreign status—the Chinese Exclusion Act, the Asiatic Barred Zone, and the racial prerequisite to naturalization enforced in the Ozawa[1] and Thind[2] cases were versions of this phenomenon. "Where are you really from?", "How do you like it in our country?", and "If you don't like it here, you can go back to where you came from," are the de facto version of it.

Here, the perpetual foreigner syndrome expresses itself in an especially acute manner. Structurally, the "Chinese look for spies among Chinese Americans" argument as a justification for selecting Lee is identical to that presented for the Japanese American internment. It is the proposition that the United States government can deprive its citizens of their civil rights because a hostile power has taken certain actions. It also can be interpreted as allowing a foreign government such as China or Japan to divest United States citizens of their rights. Described from this perspective, it appears more absurd, especially because it is unlikely that most Americans would accept a similar forfeiture of their own rights based on the activities of another country. Yet the Lee case was rarely viewed from this angle, perhaps because Lee himself was treated rhetorically as if he were a foreigner rather than a citizen.

However, the defense argument suffers because Lee's supporters responded in turn with their own utilitarian arguments and, in some instances, were offended by the more robust case they could have presented. The conventional argument for Lee was premised on the irrationality of pursuing him. The reasoning proceeded along the following lines: There is no reason to suppose that Lee would be a spy for China because of his race.

This approach suffers from major flaws. Inevitably, if the approach is to be more than an assertion taken on faith, it degenerates into an empirical debate, namely whether it is rational or irrational to believe that there is some slightly higher likelihood that a person is basically the same, save for his or her heritage. Because a significant amount of the information used to consider the question is classified and because of the usual problems of imperfect knowledge, this contest turns out to proceed in the abstract and with assumptions.

Moreover, to argue that it is irrational to single out Lee suggests that if it is rational, it is permissible.

In other words, the defense advances an argument only for instrumental behavior. It is a plea that the government remain rational about conduct, not a demand that the government respect civil rights. An argument for rationality is ineffective if there is a fundamental disagreement about what is rational, which is bound to occur if there is even modest pluralism. People can and are likely to agree to behave rationally, but even a sincerely shared preference for rationality does not necessarily produce that same sense for rationality and, to some extent, excludes the possibility of multiple options within a reasonable range.

The better approach is more critical of the government, not less critical. The better approach, however, requires a concession for the sake of argument. Although some are not willing to make this concession, such an inability to make concessions reflects a commitment to ideology that is not strategic. The concession is that it is reasonable (or, to present it in a milder form, it is not absurd) to believe that there is some slightly higher likelihood that a person of Chinese heritage would betray the United States to China, rather than a person who is basically the same save for his or her heritage. Or consider the mildest means of expressing a similar line of reasoning. It is not absurd to believe that there is some slightly higher likelihood that a person of Chinese heritage can speak a Chinese dialect than a person who is basically the same save for his or her heritage. Or to use an example with statistical support beyond doubt, a majority of Asians in the United States are foreign-born, not merely that a higher percentage of Asians than whites are foreign-born—no effort by the government to sort out who is foreign-born based on Asian background could be better than 50 percent accurate.

The case that incorporates any of these concessions is stronger than the case that does not. It is stronger because it makes significant the notion of rights.

Once this concession has been made, the genuine issues have been joined. The real debate can be conducted. That debate is whether in those rare instances where racial discrimination is, in fact, rational discrimination—there are examples form which we can infer probabilities with a degree of certainty as Bayesian statistical analysis would suggest—it is a course of action we as a society wish to sanction. There are other interesting questions, but they are empirical questions: Do the premises obtain? Do people engage in preference falsification? Do they behave in bad faith? Are there countervailing costs? Are there opportunity costs in the failure to act? Even after irrational discrimination has been defeated, the possibility of rational discrimination can be threatening.

In legal terms, this debate concerns the difference between "rationality" review and "strict scrutiny" review. The levels of judicial intervention in majoritarian processes may differ only as procedural devices, allocating the burden of proof to the citizen in "rationality" review and the government in "strict scrutiny" review, recognizing in each instance certain presumptions and fictions. Or they may differ as substantive standards, so that the evidence that would satisfy the less demanding "rationality" review would not pass the more rigorous "strict scrutiny" review. In such a regime, an application of a Bayesian formula would be sufficient for "rationality" review. By itself, it would fail "strict scrutiny" review because of the requirements of "compelling state interest" and "least restrictive means" ("narrow tailoring"). If "rationality" review and "strict scrutiny" review are to be distinguished, with the latter made more than a burden-shifting procedure, racial profiling cannot pass muster solely by its rationality (the naming of "rationality" review as such is not accidental').

The Lee case also should prompt Asian Americans to realize a number of features of contemporary racial dynamics. These may be new to Asian Americans (and, for that matter, nonacademics), but they are established insights applied to new contexts.

The inquiry as to whether Lee had committed a crime on the one hand, and the inquiry as to whether he was able to assert his civil rights and whether he was given due process on the other hand are different inquiries, but the former must be considered subordinate to the latter. The guilt-innocence inquiry cannot be pursued with justice unless and until the civil rights-due process inquiry has been resolved A reversal of priorities, with the civil rights-due process matter deferred, ensures that a guilty judgment will dominate the discourse even if it is likely to be faulty. It sets the inordinately high threshold for requiring an absolutely pure party as the challenger to systemic problems.

The persecution of Lee can occur without any intentional wrong doers but can become racial, thanks to a volatile combination of factors ranging from partisan politics and the institutional goals of media outlets, to official indifference and the stereotypical images of popular culture. The U.S. Attorney ultimately responsible for the Lee case was Chinese American. The Secretary of Energy who initially approved the choices in the Lee case was the highest-ranking Latino in the federal government. The Clinton administration was liberal, and it had even promoted progressive rules against racial profiling. It boasted more Asian Americans among its ranks than any other executive branch, by a high order of magnitude. Other than perhaps one individual, Notra Trulock, as to whom press reports suggested a pattern of previous bias, none of the persons involved could be accused with much foundation of being a "racist."

The Lee case also requires Asian Americans to consider again the value of multiracial coalitions and to redouble their efforts toward such coalitions. Asian Americans were moderately successful in maintaining pan-Asian coalitions, even though Japanese Americans with memories of the interment identified with Chinese Americans much more visibly than with other Asian ethnicities. Asian Americans were largely unsuccessful in connecting Wen Ho Lee to "driving while black." Some actively tried to distinguish Lee, as an unassuming scientist, from drug dealers, preferring an image of middle-class conformity while avoiding association with stereotypes of people of color. Some Asian American commentary implied that racial profiling of Asian Americans was altogether different from that applied to African Americans. Ironically, Asian Americans appeared largely unaware of the possibility that their selective concern would confirm the accusation that Asian American were acting out of ethnic solidarity.

The lawyers who represented Lee, however, deserve the utmost respect. They won for a client and a cause when virtually all observers, however sympathetic, would have dismissed their prospects while wishing them well. They vindicated Lee,

charged with theft of the nation's nuclear "crown jewel," and equated him to the Rosenbergs, who were sentenced to death during the Cold War era—making him a martyr and shaming his tormentors. The greatest testament to their practical victory would be principled policies.

If legal academics have any practical contribution to make to public discourse, it is in pointing out the hard questions. This Foreword has highlighted the hard questions. The attempts to answer follow.

## NOTES

1. *Ozawa v. United States,* 260 U.S. 178 (1922) (holding that a Japanese immigrant was not a "free white person" eligible to naturalize as a citizen).

2. *United States v. Thind,* 261 U.S. 204 (1923) (holding that an Indian immigrant was not a "free white person" eligible to naturalize as a citizen)'.

# 3.13

# Wen Ho Lee and the Consequences of Enduring Asian American Stereotypes

*Spencer K. Turnbull*

~~~~~~~~~~~~~~~~~~~~~~~~~~~~~~~~~~~~~~~~~~~~~~~~~~~~~~~~~~~~~~~~~~~~~~~~~~

It was business as usual for neighboring downtown office workers last spring, but the work had been anything but ordinary for carpenters constructing an impregnable room deep within the federal courthouse in Albuquerque, New Mexico. The carpenters completed a secured compartmented information facility (SCIF), a chamber specially designed for secrecy, and which could not even be penetrated by electronic signals. The SCIF was constructed in anticipation of the trial of Wen Ho Lee, a government nuclear scientist accused of mishandling top-secret U.S. weapons information, and would have been used to review the enormous amount of classified materials implicated by the trial. Little about the trial would be ordinary: not the SCIF, not the top-secret clearance each person involved in the case would have to pass, not the apocalyptic charges that America's nuclear "crown jewels" had been jeopardized. The most serious irregularities, however, are those which appeared to have their roots in Lee's ethnicity. These irregularities warn

that when latent racial stereotypes resurface, even presumptively invulnerable job positions are jeopardized.

After summarizing the events leading up to Lee's arrest, in part I, by emphasizing Lee's Chinese ethnicity, the government and the media argue through invoked stereotypes that Asian Americans retain a maleficent foreignness that renders them suspect. Part II asserts that the federal government's aggressive treatment of Lee was unusual, suggesting that the Clinton administration used Lee as a scapegoat. Finally, part III concludes that the Wen Ho Lee case resulted in a cloud of suspicion cast over Asian Americans. Specifically, this has a negative impact on their employment opportunities in nuclear scientific research—one of the few fields where they have achieved mobility.

## WEN HO LEE
## AND THE INVESTIGATION
## INTO CHINESE ESPIONAGE

Wen Ho Lee had come a long way, both literally and figuratively, to work at the top-secret "X" Division of Los Alamos National Laboratories (LANL). LANL is a major research facility operated by the Department

Turnbull, Spencer K. "Wen Ho Lee and the Consequences of Enduring Asian American Stereotypes." *UCLA Asian American Law Journal* 7: 72. Reprinted with permission.

of Energy (DOE), where America's nuclear warheads and bombs are designed. Lee was born in 1939 in Nantou, Taiwan, to parents who were poor farmers. He developed a talent for mathematics at Chen Kung University before coming to America in September 1964 to attend Texas A&M University in College Station, Texas. There, Lee earned a master's degree in 1966, followed by a doctorate degree in mechanical engineering in 1969. In 1974, Lee became a naturalized U.S. citizen. Lee began working at LANL in 1980, and shortly thereafter, was assigned to the X Division. An expert in fluid dynamics, he wrote computer "source codes" that simulate how high-explosives can create shock waves to compress a sphere of plutonium, which forms the trigger for hydrogen bombs. These codes were used to help develop and test the weapons for readiness.

On March 6, 1999, Lee's employer appeared in the headlines of the *New York Times*, which broke the story that China had wrongfully obtained nuclear secrets from LANL.[1] The *New York Times* reported that the FBI had a suspect in an espionage case who allegedly had transferred to the Chinese government information on America's most advanced nuclear weapon, the miniaturize W-88 thermonuclear warhead.

The espionage investigation began in 1995, when Central Intelligence Agency (CIA) analysts came into possession of a Chinese government document, which specifically mentioned the W-88 and described its features. The document all but proved that top-secret American nuclear technology had been passed to the Chinese. The CIA decided to focus its search for a leak on LANL, where the W-88 had been designed. Believing that the secrets had been leaked in the mid-1980s, the CIA quickly narrowed in on Lee, who had traveled to Beijing in 1986 and 1988.

In 1999, three years after the FBI began watching Lee's work, it still had not been able to link Lee to any acts of espionage. Nevertheless, just two days after the *New York Times'* report on the W-88 investigation broke, Secretary of Energy Bill Richardson personally fired Lee. At the time of Lee's dismissal, Richardson cited Lee's "failure to properly notify the energy Department and lab officials about contacts with people from a sensitive country, specific instances of failing to properly safeguard classified material and apparently attempting to deceive lab officials about security matters"[2] as grounds for his dismissal. In an interview five months later, Richardson said that investigators' suspicions about Lee were aroused by two trips that Lee made to China in the 1980s. On those occasions, Lee allegedly had unauthorized contact with Chinese officials, which he failed to report—an omission that violates DOE regulations. Both trips, however, had been pre-approved by LANL and the FBI.

After Richardson fired Lee, it was discovered that Lee had improperly downloaded nuclear weapons information from the secure classified "red" partition computers at LANL to unclassified open "green" partition computers, thereby increasing the information's accessibility to unauthorized individuals. In addition, Lee copied these downloaded files onto ten portable data tapes. Seven of the tapes are missing to this day. Lee's attorneys say Lee destroyed them when he was fired, but the FBI fears they still exist and may fall into the wrong hands.[3] In a 1999 interview with *60 Minutes*, Lee maintained that the file transfer was part of his job and that even the unclassified computers he used were protected by three passwords and were within his secure office at LANL. Lee characterized the movement of classified information to unclassified computers as "very common."[4] Regarding the data tapes Lee contends they were simply to protect his time-consuming research from computer crashes. His detractors question why that would be necessary given the sophisticated back-up systems built into LANL computers.

On December 10, 1999, a grand jury returned a fifty-nine count indictment against Lee. Specifically, Lee was charged with violations of the Atomic Energy Act, 42 U.S.C. 2275, pub. L. No. 106-65, 3148(b), 113 Stat. 938 (1999) (Receipt of Restricted Data) and 42 U.S.C. 2276 (Tampering with

Restricted Data), and the Espionage Act, 18 U.S.C. 793 (Gathering, Transmitting, or Losing Defense Information).[5] The indictment alleged that Lee "acted with the intent to injure the United Sates and with the intent to secure an advantage to a foreign nation."[6] Lee was not charged with espionage per se; indeed, the government conceded that Lee did not play a role in the loss of the W-88 technology. Nonetheless, Lee would have faced life imprisonment if convicted.

## RATIFYING STEREOTYPES OF ASIAN AMERICANS AS PERPETUAL FOREIGNERS

The government and media emphasis on Lee's Chinese ethnicity promotes societal perceptions that Asian Americans not only posses divided loyalties, which prevent them from being "real" Americans, but also possess a malignant streak of foreignness, which inevitably renders them suspect.

In *Asian Americans: The "Reticent" Minority and Their Paradoxes,* Pat K. Chew contends that white Americans heartily embrace the notion that Asian Americans are a model minority[7] but have yet to accept them as model Americans. Among the ways in which this belief manifests itself, Chew identifies Americans' tendency to reflexively cast Asian Americans as foreigners. These themes prominently figure in the manner in which Wen Ho Lee's identity has been popularly constructed.

Press reports highlighting Lee's Asian heritage and ignoring his long-time U.S. citizenship reinforce societal perceptions that Asian Americans have divided loyalties. One of the first media outlets to identify Lee by name and link him to the W-88 investigation—the venerable *New York Times*—set the tone for the press coverage that followed when, in its article's lead sentence, it introduced Lee as "[a] Taiwan-born scientist."[8] The *New York Times*, along with countless other media outlets, did not initially report that Lee had been an Amer-

ican citizen for twenty-five years.[9] Thus, the *New York Times* helped ensure that its readers would form their impressions of Lee along ethnic lines that would reinforce latent suspicions about Asian Americans' divided loyalty. One might imagine that such minor editorial moves are insignificant in the construction of Asian American identity, but by subtly tapping into extant, negative perceptions, the media helped revive those stereotypes. Subsequent media coverage that identified Lee as an American citizen probably did little to undo the racial construction that occurred immediately after first sensational reports.

A recent *Washington Times* column exemplifies the extent to which stereotypes of Asian American foreignness are ingrained in U.S. culture. Mocking those who believe Lee has been targeted because of his race, the columnist laments that the focus of their ire has not been on Lee's guilt or innocence. She writes that Lee's supporters are "in high dudgeon not because Mr. Lee may actually be guilty, thus potentially tarnishing the reputations of loyal Americans of Asian origin, but because he was charged in the first places."[10] Implicit in this reasoning is the assumption that some portion of the Asian American population is disloyal. The column, intending to show solicitude for certain "loyal" Asian Americans, instead reveals the stereotypical foundations on which it is based, by defining Asian Americans in terms of their loyalty.

As a result, Americans are likely to use the image of Lee, quasi-American, as the prototype for their images of additional spies who, they are told, are probably still inside their nation's laboratories. The press's exclusive focus on Lee—a Lee largely defined by his foreignness—leads Americans to associate an Asian-looking man with a "spy," even though some say Lee was no more suspicious than the white men at LANL. Robert Vrooman, former head of counterintelligence at LANL and estwhile head of the investigation of Lee, charged that the investigation into the alleged theft by China of American nuclear secrets targeted Chinese Americans, disregarding significant leads on possible non-Chinese suspects. According to Vrooman, a list of seventy possible suspects was compiled based on certain criteria: whether they had access to weapons design information, whether they had traveled to China, and whether they had close relationships with Chinese weapons scientists.[11] This list was reduced to twelve suspects. Vrooman contends that "[t]he short list missed people on the long list who were almost exact clones of Lee," including an individual who worked with Lee, was entitled to the same access as Lee, and had even traveled to China with Lee. "The only difference was ethnicity," Vrooman concluded.[12] Furthermore, Vrooman alleges that investigators ignored evidence that Chinese intelligence attempted to work with scientists who were not Chinese Americans. In light of these questionable investigation practices, one ought to ask why precisely was it that Lee "stuck out like a sore thumb," as one unnamed official put it. It seems to have had more to do with a comfortable fit with stereotypes of Asian Americans as disloyal foreigners than with probability of guilt.

Inflammatory editorials helped keep America's focus squarely on Asians. "China's W-88 Fortune Cookie," read the headline of an editorial in Durham, North Carolina's *Herald Sun*. Its parting words were: "Sleep well tonight. The Chinese haven't mated their W-88 to ICNMs [Intercontinental Nuclear Missiles] aimed at U.S. cities—yet."

The experience of Asian American scientists in the wake of Lee's dismissal from LANL bears out Chew's contention that the treatment of Asian Americans as perpetual foreigners prevents them from becoming full-fledged Americans. According to a Taiwan-born scientist, "[t]hey want us to be American and work in their defense labs, . . . [b]ut they never treat us as Americans. They always treat us like foreigners, like Chinese."[14] Such comments are rich with insight. Beside demonstrating that Chew's thesis is not idle law review theory, this quote suggests that the Asian American identity is constructed along assumptions about proficiency and belonging in the sci-

ences. Asian Americans feel their citizenship remains second-class, and to the extent that the United States does regard them as citizens, they feel that they are more instrumentalities than equals.

Shortly after the circumstantial nature of the accusations against Lee became known, Chinese American intellectuals voiced concerns that the same innocuous behavior for which Lee apparently had been singled out might be used to bring them under suspicion. The theory that Lee used travel to scientific conferences in China as a way of passing American secrets is illustrative. Some Chinese Americans fear that trips to China, common among Chinese Americans maintaining family and professional ties overseas, will now raise suspicion. Changlin Tien, the former chancellor of the University of California, Berkeley, put it succinctly: "In this climate, many Chinese feel they are being watched all the time, as if they are not full citizens."[15] The consequences of constructing Lee along negative, stereotypical lines is inequitable treatment—perceived, as well as actual—of Asian Americans.

The unfolding Lee story appears to be the latest example of the particularly maleficent foreignness that has been ascribed to Asian Americans throughout American history. In *"Foreign-ness & Asian American Identities: Yellowface, World War II Propaganda and Bifurcated Racial Stereotypes*, Keith Aoki traces the deeply ingrained sense of Asian foreignness in American culture to nineteenth-century vaudeville acts, which relied on crude caricatures of Asian cultures. Aoki observes that these acts portrayed the Chinese as an agglomeration of "effeminate, waif-like traits, deferentially bowing and scraping, but secretly scheming the white race's downfall."[16] More than 100 years later, journalists covering the Lee case invoked similar characterizations of the Chinese: "It is difficult to think that the thoroughly pleasant, skilled, and hospitable colleagues [Americans] have come to know would pour extra drinks just to discover new facets of weapons miniaturization."[17] The author suggested that while it may be difficult to think, it should be believed. The deceptive deference and the pernicious intention of the "yellowface" routines described by Aoki are still there: the only change is that the comedic inarticulateness trait has been replaced by a clever model minority scientist.

In addition to their insurmountable foreignness, Asian immigrants have historically been depicted as unfair competitors by the U.S. media. In the nineteenth century, Chinese immigrants trying to enter U.S. labor markets were called unfair competitors on theories ranging from the biological (that they could endure harder work than whites), to the cultural (that Chinese workmen shunned families so that they could horde more money). In the 1980s, the American media ascribed Japan's ascendancy in international business to unfair trade practices, among other things. As the Chinese espionage scandal unfolded, Americans dusted off their theories of unfair Asian competition and refashioned them for the realm of spying.

Media outlets reported that the "unusual" manner in which China gathers intelligence has confounded the standard counterintelligence efforts the United States uses against other countries.[18] The Beijing regime, one is told, does not just use spies to gather specific information. Instead, it recruits many experts in numerous and diverse fields to serve as part-time agents to, as one article puts it, "mov[e] about American society." The article goes on to warn, "[t]he scale of the Chinese effort requires a countervailing willingness on the part of American citizens to be vigilant about Chinese visitors, something many—given our freedoms—are unwilling to do."[19] "Those sneaky Orientals have foiled America again," the author seems to say, "If only they had the decency not to take advantage of America's freedom-loving values, we would have a fighting chance."

FBI officials have characterized Chinese spying as far more difficult to detect than "the more traditional espionage" of U.S. Cold War adversaries. "The Chinese often take advantage of scientific exchanges and other forms of informal contacts, gathering sensitive information from such a wide range of sources that it is often difficult to pinpoint exactly how American secrets leak out."[20] The language suggests that the Chinese are somehow playing outside of the rules, flaunting norms to achieve arbitrage. This theme is reflected in Congress' 1999 Cox Report[21] on Chinese weapons programs, which alleges that open scientific exchanges between the United States and China are responsible for the illegal transfer of U.S. intelligence and that essentially all Chinese visitors to the United States are potential spies. This conclusion was vehemently contested by W. K. H. Panofsky, a highly accomplished physicist who is currently the chairman of the Committee on International Security and Arms Control of the National Academy of Sciences. Panofsky wrote "there is no evidence presented in any of the reports that Chinese scientific visitors have abused their status beyond commonly accepted international norms."[22]

Lee's prosecutors linked him to "cloak and dagger" spy-craft, notwithstanding the fact that Lee had not been charged with any type of espionage. For instance, one of the prosecutors arguing against Lee's pre-trial release warned that Lee must be kept in total seclusion because there was no way to tell whether an apparently innocuous wink or casual comment might be a coded message for an enemy agent.[23]

This acute anxiety over the Chinese may account for the troubling manner in which the government interpreted Lee's behavior, which in any other context would not have aroused suspicion. Richardson suspected Lee might have been involved in espionage based in part on two trips Lee made to China in the 1980s. On those occasions, Lee allegedly had unauthorized contact with Chinese officials, which he failed to report—an omission that violated DOE regulations. Yet the trips themselves were approved in advance by LANL and the FBI.[24] Similarly, the FBI found three letters in Lee's garage from senior scientists at China's Institute of Applied Physics and

Computational Mathematics. The letters asked Lee to send unclassified LANL codes to them or to another institute member studying at Princeton. This strengthened the FBI's belief that Lee was engaged in suspicious activities.[25] it is surprising that the FBI was suspicious given the fact that the DOE was actively encouraging its scientists to foster a spirit of cooperation by sharing such unclassified codes. Both of these examples seem like catch-22s. On the one hand, the government offered its blessing on the actions Lee was about to take. Yet on the other, it ultimately used those acts against him. To make sense of this, one must inevitably confront the premise that Asian Americans are singled out for exacting scrutiny when it comes to questions of loyalty.

These accounts reflect a belief that the involvement of Chinese Americans in espionage is inevitable, and the press often legitimizes this pernicious stereotype with uncritical reporting. Sadly, the assignment of racial guilt is not unprecedented in the United States; the illogic that characterized the "necessity" of interning Japanese Americans serves as an example: "The very fact that no sabotage has taken place to date is a disturbing and confirming indication that such action will be taken [by Japanese Americans]."[26] Despite the ostensibly widespread recognition of the error of internment, such statements share chilling parallels with today's assertions that all Chinese Americans are plausible targets of Beijing's espionage efforts. That America would revert to the mindset that led to internment testifies to the potency of Asian American stereotypes and the work that remains to be done to eradicate them.

## INDICTING THE STEREOTYPICAL FOREIGNER

Shortly after Lee was indicted, the *Washington Post* ran a front page article detailing the inconsistent treatment of U.S. government employees who have mishandled classified information. Whereas the article

documents that government responses to such behavior run a wide gamut from firing to no action at all, it also makes evident that the decision to prosecute Lee was an outlier—even by such elastic standards.[27] The unusually aggressive treatment of Lee by the federal government illuminates a pattern of disparate treatment that suggests that Lee was being used as a scapegoat by the Clinton administration.

Richardson helped set the tone for the unusual treatment of Lee. Just two days after the *New York Times* ran a story saying that the FBI had a suspect in a case of Chinese espionage, Richardson personally fired Lee in an internationally broadcast press conference.[28] The rare, personal involvement of a promotion cabinet member did not end there, however, as Richardson continued to publicly speak out about Lee. After the *60 Minutes* interview in which Lee opined that he may have been singled out because he was the only Asian American working in the weapons design group at LANL, Richardson accused Lee of trying to "use the race card," and complained that "[he] tried to portray himself as a victim after he massively violated our security system."[29] It took several months and sustained outcry from Asian American DOE employees before Richardson toned down his rhetoric against Lee.

Lee's treatment by the judicial branch was equally remarkable. Judge James A. Parker of the U.S. District Court of New Mexico decided to keep Lee in solitary confinement while awaiting trial despite a statutory presumption in favor of the pretrial release of defendants and the congressional intent that very few defendants should be subjected to pretrial detention.[30] Judge Parker weighed the factors outlined in 18 U.S.C.S. §3142(g), to assess whether Lee should be granted pretrial release: the circumstances under which the accused allegedly committed the events; the weight of the evidence against the accused; the accused's character, physical and mental condition, family ties, employment, community ties, criminal history, and the like; and the nature and seriousness of the danger to any person or community that would be posed by the accused's release. Although the court found that a number of factors leaned toward pretrial release, the last factor seemed to guide the court: "[T]he Government has shown by clear and convincing evidence that there is no combination of conditions of release that would reasonably assure the safety of any other person and the community or the nation."[31] Judge Parker did not believe there was any way, short of "heroic" efforts, that Lee could be prevented from somehow passing information to enemy agents if he were anywhere but in prison.[32]

Lee was held in solitary confinement in a Santa Fe, New Mexico, jail, under restrictions tighter than those for any other prisoner in the United States, according to one of his defense attorneys. Lee was allowed out for one hour of exercise each weekday. He could not make or receive phone calls. His visitors were limited to his attorneys, his wife, and his two adult children. His family could visit for only one hour a week, during which time Lee was required to wear wrist and leg shackles while remaining behind a glass partition. Two FBI agents listened in on the visits. After months of negotiations, Lee was allowed to listen to classical music on a portable radio of the type that other prisoners could readily purchase for twenty dollars inside the jail.

While Lee was confined to a cell, his supporters brought attention to a number of irregularities in his case, not the least of which was the decision to prosecute Lee itself. Government reaction to employee security breaches is far from consistent; however, prosecution of civilian security violations is all but unheard of, as long as strong administrative action is taken. According to officials, the Justice Department generally does not prosecute civilians at federal agencies who mishandle secret documents if: (1) there is no evidence of criminal intent; (2) the employee is disciplined administratively by his or her agency; and (3) the information is not passed to a third party.[33] Lee met all three conditions.

As his supporters became convinced that the government was selectively prosecuting Lee, commentators were quick to point out the discrepancies between the treatment of Lee and former CIA director John M. Deutch, who committed serious security violations.[34] Like Lee, Deutch had been accused of mishandling top-secret files, which included memos to the president concerning sensitive covert operations and spy codes. Unlike Lee, Deutch kept these secret files on his nonsecure home computer, which employed no password blocks or encryption and was hooked up to an ordinary, unsecured phone line vulnerable to hackers. Three days after investigation discovered the misplaced classified material, Deutch deleted over a thousand files from his home computers. Prosecutors made much of the fact that Lee deleted files after being told he failed a lie detector test—but prosecutors did not say a word about Deutch. Their silence was all the more shocking since Deutch performed his erasure from his home computer, which was linked to the Internet, whereas Lee deleted the files from his secure LANL office. Deutch apologized and lost his security clearance, but has not been prosecuted. However, the protracted public comparisons of the two cases has caused Attorney General Janet Reno to become "deeply concerned about the appearance of inequity,"[35] and at the time this Comment was written, a new review of the Deutch matter was underway.[36]

Aside from the issue of selective prosecution, facts came to light that suggested the government had manipulated evidence to bolster its case against Lee. CBS News reported in February 2000 that weeks after three experienced DOE polygraphers gave Lee passing scores on a lie detector test, the FBI stepped in and reversed the findings. Lee took the test in December 1998, and did well enough on it that LANL management apologized to him and sent him back to his job at the top-secret X Division. Subsequently the FBI head office sent a memo to headquarters, saying Lee did not appear to be their spy. CBS News speculated that it was the extraordinary pressure on the DOE and FBI to produce a spy that led to the decision to reexamine Lee's polygraph. Richard Keller, former director of the FBI's polygraph program and current chairman of the American Polygraph Association said, "Scores are almost never read differently by trained examiners. It is extremely rare to have scores that are evaluated as nondeceptive by one set of examiners, evaluated as deceptive by another."[37]

The government's case against Lee was further weakened by a revelation in the April 10, 2000, edition of the *Albuquerque Journal*. The *Journal* ran a front-page story, which reported that the files Lee was accused of downloading were not in fact designated secret or confidential, as the indictment against him claimed. That designation came after Lee had been fired from his job at LANL. At the time Lee downloaded the files they bore the security designation PARD, an acronym for "protect as restricted data." PARD data is not subject to the same rigorous precautions applied to material designated secret or confidential, although it is still illegal to transfer it to unsecured computers, as the government had charged Lee with doing. Unlike restricted data, "you could have PARD lying around in your office overnight and there was no problem," said Bob Clark, a scientist who worked on weapons codes at LANL until 1995.[38] Whereas the PARD files on Lee's tapes did contain nuclear secrets that technically fit the legal definition of restricted data, they had never been subject to a formal sensitivity review to determine what category and level of classification applied to them. The DOE has defended the belated reclassification, explaining that it was made after investigators evaluating the material downloaded by Lee discovered that it contained highly sensitive material.[39]

## Washington's Need to Indict Lee

While the impact of these new pieces of information on Lee's case would not have been determined until trial, one could reason that the case against Lee was being reverse-engineered. First, the defendant was chosen, then the case against him was built. The disturbing corollary to that theory is that investigators may have endeavored to find an Asian defendant. Though this is a bold theory, it is not implausible. This comment earlier asserted that negative Asian American stereotypes helped guide the search for a spy in the W-88 investigation, which led to the investigation of Lee. Robert Vrooman, the former head of the Lee investigation went so far as to allege that Lee's race was a decisive factor: Lee was the only Asian American working in the LANL weapons design group where the investigators believed the X-88 designs were stolen.[40] Though investigators were hoping that enough evidence would be found to support espionage charges against their defendant, they had to settle for formalistic charges of mishandling data, supported by evidence rendered vulnerable by the irregularities described above. This begs the question: Why did the government pursue what looked like a misguided, selective prosecution?

A likely answer ties back to the administration's irregular treatment of Lee. The Clinton administration was under enormous political pressure not only to catch a spy in the W-88 investigation, but also to diffuse criticism that it was coddling the Chinese government in Beijing. After Richardson dramatically delivered Lee to the public, there was too much at stake to let him go.

In early 1999, as investigators were sharpening their focus on Lee, Congress was examining charges that the Chinese government had surreptitiously and illegally injected Chinese money into the 1996 presidential campaign. In turn, that investigation reactivated the controversy surrounding the Democratic party's fundraising efforts within the Asian American community.[41] On the trade front, the Clinton administration had recently established the controversial policy of facilitating the sale of supercomputers and satellite technology to China, and was pursuing agreements that would ease the way for American companies hoping to sell commercial nuclear reactors to the Chinese.

Perhaps most significant, however, was the release in early 1999 of the Final Report of the Select Committee on U.S. National Security and Military/Commercial Concerns with the People's Republic of China, popularly known as the Cox Report. Employing inflammatory language, the Cox Report accused China of stealing sensitive U.S. nuclear weapons information and drew spectacular conclusions about the implication for U.S. security of such losses. It also made a case for dramatic changes in policy at U.S. weapons laboratories to counteract Chinese efforts to steal U.S. weapons technology.[42] Although the Cox Report has been widely criticized from the political left, right, and center,[43] its dramatic allegations received heavy press coverage and helped fan the flames of a new "yellow peril," setting the stage for the prosecution of Lee.

Given the high level of public attention generated by the events described above, and a Congress bent on depicting the Clinton administration as soft on Beijing, the administration may have felt it needed to quiet its critics by quickly producing a culprit in the W-88 investigation. This theory helps explain Lee's peculiar, public dismissal by Richardson. In fact, Richardson all but admitted he was succumbing to the political pressure when, justifying a new regime of lie-detector tests for DOE employees, he cited the "need to restore the confidence of Congress and the public."[44] Once the dust had settled, law enforcement agencies working on the case admitted that they were too quick to focus on Lee and neglected other leads in the process—and subsequently cast a wider net.

## THE LEE INVESTIGATION THREATENS ASIAN AMERICAN EMPLOYMENT MOBILITY

Many Asian Americans in the DOE felt that the handling of the Lee investigation meant that they were being closely scrutinized because of their race. As a result many people of Asian descent considered leaving their government jobs and many more have avoided taking these jobs in the first place. Because scientific and technical fields have been one of few readily accessible employment options for Asian Americans, the negative repercussions of the Lee case may disproportionately decrease Asian Americans' job opportunities.

At this point, it should be noted that this Comment considers the cloud of suspicion in the wake of the Lee investigation as covering all Asian Americans not just Chinese Americans. This is primarily because numerous organizations representing various Asian ethnicities recognized the situation as such.[45] Furthermore, Americans often have been unable or disinclined to distinguish between different Asian ethnicities. Thus, to suggest that only Chinese Americans will feel that they are under suspicion is to attribute to Americans a nuance that they are unlikely to have exhibited.[46] The Lee case itself illustrates this. Though Lee was being investigated on suspicion of spying for China, he is from Taiwan, which has significant and tense political differences with China. Whereas Lee's Taiwanese ethnicity provided some basis for presuming that Lee would not want to aid China, the fact that he also falls into the broader ethnic category of Chinese seems to have overshadowed the more particular, and perhaps more relevant, nationality.[47]

In June 1999, the DOE announced that it would begin polygraph testing nuclear-weapons scientists and other employees in sensitive positions.[48] Efforts demonstrate that the government was aggressively ferreting out spies within the national laboratories were underway. Some speculated that the changed climate may cause Chinese Americans to hesitate to go to work for federal agencies. The forecast proved to be an underestimate, as Asian Americans of many ethnicities shunned scientific job opportunities in the federal sector. It is now apparent that LANL, in particular, is suffering a brain drain: five prominent scientists have left, and Asian American post-doctoral fellows dropped from seventy to fifty-five in less than three months.[49]

The actions of the DOE helped bring this situation about. The announcement of mandatory polygraph testing came on the heels of Lee's public dismissal by Richardson, and appeared to figure in the paranoia over Chinese aggression. And in its zeal to show that it was addressing security issues, the DOE announced a measure that would require nationals of twenty-five countries on a "sensitive list" working at national labs to wear red badges with their country of origin to distinguish them from Americans. The easy-to-spot badges are supposed to make it easier for security guards to protect classified areas, but critics contend that they just highlight the DOE's blanket distrust of foreigners.[50] Facing strenuous objections from scientists, the DOE scaled back the program to cover only classified labs like LANL.[51]

Regardless of the merits of the DOE's actions, for many, the die had been cast. According to a report by the LANL, fellows, foreign-born scientists, and others felt uncomfortable in defense facilities in the wake of the Lee case.[52] "They can plant something in my briefcase and I can be fired tomorrow. . . . They think anyone that is not a white male is a potential spy. They will not come out and say that, but it is in their behavior and attitude," said a veteran Asian American scientist who works at the Lawrence Livermore National Laboratory.[53] And the impact may extend beyond the federal sector. The Cox Report, while not specifically associating any alleged loss or theft with open scientific exchanges, alleged that essentially all Chinese visitors to the United States are potential spies. This has brought both foreign and Asian-born U.S. staff members of U.S. companies under suspicion.[54]

Though many Asian American scientists felt that they were unfairly and racially profiled in the wake of the Lee investigation, some observers were unmoved. Addressing the Congressional Asian Pacific Caucus in November 1999, former head of the FBI's Chinese counterintelligence efforts, Paul D. Moore, flatly admitted that racial profiling has been used in counterintelligence operations. When asked by Representative Robert T. Masui (D-CA) whether Chinese Americans were being profiled, Moore answered rhetorically, "What's the opinion?"[55] Moore blamed the need for racial profiling on the Chinese, reiterating the increasingly familiar charge that the Chinese intelligence service targets Chinese citizens who work or study in the U.S., as well as Chinese Americans who attend technical conferences abroad. Thus, as long as Chinese intelligence continues to be "interested obsessively in people of Chinese American ancestry to the exclusion of people from other groups," the FBI will inevitably focus disproportionately on Chinese American scientists. Moore's attitude treats profiling as an inevitable, if unfortunate, baggage of being Chinese in America. *The National Review* scoffed at complaints of racism in the investigation, saying Lee's defenders seem to want affirmative action for security risks: "Minorities can meet lower security standards to ensure that no minority pressure groups will ever have reason to cry racism."[57] Completely unpacking the jumble of meanings in such a statement is beyond the scope of this Comment: it is sufficient to say, however, that some Americans do not understand the significance of racial stereotyping in this context.

The racial stereotyping that is occurring could be especially damaging to Asian Americans because if they feel that they are being pushed out of scientific and technical jobs, barriers to employment are created in a field in which Asian Americans have achieved mobility. It is evident that Asian Americans feel their careers are jeopardized. Stewart Kwoh, the executive director of the Asian Pacific American Legal Center of Southern California, said that he has spoken with three or four people who feel their career chances have been damaged because of the Lee case. Echoing a theme noted elsewhere in this Comment, he added. "People are tired of the sense that they are looked at as permanent foreigners."[58] Kwoh's observation were confirmed by a report of the DOE task force that convened in June 1999to counter the backlash from the Lee case, which said, "Asian-American employees . . . speculated that their opportunities for promotions, choice job assignments, and developmental training have been greatly reduced as a result of this atmosphere of distrust and suspicion."[59] These perceptions are not just speculation. Nine Asian American employees of the Lawrence Livermore National Laboratory have brought racial discrimination claims, and according to one of the employees' attorneys, Bra Yamauchi, the Equal Employment Opportunity Commission is investigating "systemic discrimination" there.[60] Such an atmosphere makes scientific and technical jobs with the government look increasingly less viable for Asian Americans.

The damage that the Lee case has done to work opportunities for Asian Americans may be compounded by other factors. There is evidence that more Asian Americans look for jobs that require a strong educational background, like government scientific and technical jobs, because their mobility in most other areas of the economy is limited.[61] An example of this is the fact that Asian Americans have had little presence in unions, attributable to the fact that they were kept out of labor unions in the 1940s. Similarly, Asians Americans' limited access to participation in sports, politics, and entertainment remains as real today as in the past. Among the few open doors left open for Asian Americans are those into sectors which the Lee investigation has blocked. With circumscribed employment choices, the relative impact on Asian Americans is greater than just the sum of jobs lost. Furthermore, popular perceptions that Asian Americans are well-received in scientific jobs and therefore, do not face employment discrimination may continue to remain while in reality the actual viability of working in those jobs is decreasing.

In the wake of the task force report cited above, Richardson presented an eight-point plan to address concerns of racial discrimination at DOE facilities. "Look, we're admitting a problem, a problem caused by this incident," Richardson said, referring to heightened security measures taken after the arrest of Lee.[62] Richardson appointed an ombudsman, Jeremy S. Wu, a deputy director of the Department of Agriculture's

office of Civil Rights, to field the concerns of Asian American DOE employees. He also announced an agency-wide "stand down" to consider diversity issues and explains the task force's findings to DOE employees. Richardson called for contact between the department and the chief executive officers of all DOE contractors to highlight the department's concern about the report's findings, implementation of a system for tracking diversity management programs at each facility, and he authorized a new policy for recruiting foreign scientists to the national labs to ensure they remain at the cutting edge of technology.[63] Richardson's plan was met with skepticism of its potential for positive impact. Henry Tang, chairman of the nonpartisan Chinese American watchdog group "Committee of 100," has warned that a successful review must "examine how this atmosphere of mistrust came about," and not just be a "love fest."[64] If Richardson's efforts to address claims of racism within the DOE fail and the best and brightest Asian Americans choose academia or private industry over his agency, the long-term damage to the United States could be greater than that caused by the alleged espionage that started everything.

## CONCLUSION

During the course of the Lee investigation, both the government and media invoked stereotypes that Asian Americans retain a maleficent foreignness that renders them suspect. It has shown that the force of those stereotypes helped turn Lee into a suitable scapegoat for the Clinton administration's troubles with China. Finally, a cloud of suspicion was cast over Asian Americans, compromising their employment opportunities in one of few fields in which they have attained mobility.

Racism in America is no longer out in the open. Now racism lurks in the stereotypes—easily passed proxies for negative racial meanings that are used as substitutes for understanding and engagement. Stereotypes of Asian Americans have been passed around America since the era of yellowface. They have existed for so long that they have grown deceptively smooth with use, causing many to forget the hate and destructive potential they carry. Therein lies their sinister quality. A stereotype is more comfortable to handle from one invocation to the next, yet it never loses its dangerous payload. Perhaps this is why, despite their much vaunted model minority status, racist stereotypes of Asian Americans were so handily dispatched to construct Wen Ho Lee as a foreign spy. The government's ratification of these stereotypes should shatter any illusions that Asian Americans have achieved full equality.

There is some irony in the fact that Lee was accused of being incautious with nuclear secrets, while the government that prosecuted him was itself careless with racial stereotypes, a source of tremendous power in their own right. Only time will tell whose transgression was the most devastating; however, for the Asian American scientists who saw no alternative but to leave their jobs, the government's carelessness has already reaped a bitter harvest.

## NOTES

1. James Risen and Jeff Gerth, "Breach at Los Alamos: A Special Report," *New York Times*, March 6, 1999, A1.

2. James Risen, "U.S. Fires Scientist Suspected of Giving China Bomb Data," *New York Times*, March 9, 1999, A1.

3. Eileen Welsome, "Spies, Lies & Portable Tapes," *Denver Westword*, April 20, 2000, available at LEXIS, New Library, Dnvwst File.

4. *60 Minutes: Spy?* (CBS television broadcast, August 1, 1999).

5. *United States v. Wen Ho Lee*, 79 F. Supp. 2d 1280, 1282 (D.N.M. 1999).

6. Welsome, "Spies, Lies & Portable Tapes."

7. The term "model minority" refers to a popular understanding of Asian Americans as a minority group that has overcome, by virtue of its hard work, intelligence, and cultural values, the challenges that typically face minority groups in the United States. This appellation has been widely criticized, both substantively

and in terms of its implications. See Pat K. Chew, "Asian Americans: The 'Reticent' Minority and Their Paradoxes." *William & Mary Law Review* 36(1) (1994) (arguing that the term model minority contributes to a false impression that Asian Americans are not discriminated against).

8. Risen, "U.S. Fires Scientist."

9. See also editorial, "Nuclear Espionage," *Herald Sun* (Durham), August 8, 1999, A18. But see *The World Today: Who Is Wen Ho Lee?* (CNN television broadcast, March 10, 1999).

10. Diana West, "20th-Century Baggage," *Washington Times*, December 31, 1999, A19 (emphasis added).

11. See Dan Stober, "Former Counterintelligence Official Alleges Racial Profiling in Lee Case," *San Jose Mercury News*, February 19, 2000, available at LEXIS, New Jersey Library, Sjmerc File.

12. Stober, "Former Counterintelligence Official Alleges Racial Profiling in Lee Case."

13. "Nuclear Espionage."

14. Robin Paul Ajello and Ron Gluckman. "The Spy of the Century?" *Asiaweek*, April 21, 20000, 28.

15. Fox Butterfield and Joseph Kahn, "Chinese Scientists Say Furor Over Spy Charges Clouding Their Career," *Plain Dealer* (Cleveland), May 16, 1999, 24A.

16. Keith Aoki, "'Foreign-ness' and Asian American Identities: Yellowface, World War II Propaganda and Bifurcated Racial Sterotype," *UCLA Asian Pacific American Law Journal* 4(1) (1999): 22.

17. Douglas H. Paal, "China II: Insecurity Complex," *National Review*, May 31, 1999, available at LEXIS News Library, Natrev File.

18. Paal, "China II: Insecurity Complex"; Risen, "U.S. Fires Scientist."

19. Paal, "China II: Insecurity Complex."

20. Risen, "U.S. Fires Scientist."

21. *The Cox Report* is discussed in greater detail in Part II of the original printing of this chapter.

22. W. K. H. Panofsky, "A Critique of the Cox Report Allegations of Theft of Sensitive U.S. Nuclear Weapons Information," in *The Cox Committee Report: An Assessment* 62 (M.M. May, ed., Center for International Security & Cooperation 1999).

23. See George Koo, "Due Process and Right to a Fair Trial have Gone out the Window for Wen Ho Lee," *Star Tribune* (Minneapolis), January 19, 2000, 15A.

24. *60 Minutes, Spy?* The government's treatment of Lee upon his return from travel to China presents an interesting parallel to the Chinese Exclusion case, *Chae Chan Ping v. United States*, 130 U.S. 581 (1889). In the Chinese Exclusion case, the Supreme Court upheld the Scott Act, which denied reentry into the U.S. of any Chinese resident of the U.S. who left the country, including those overseas at the time the act passed. Thousands of Chinese who had reasonably relied on otherwise valid immigration documents, which were voided by the act, were denied reentry into the U.S. Like the nineteenth-century Chinese, shocked to learn that the rules of reentry had changed while they were away. Lee must have been shocked to have his government-appointed travel deemed inappropriate after his return.

25. See Welsome, "Spies, Lies & Portable Tapes.,"

26. Gen. J. L. DeWitt, *Final Report, Japanese Evacuation from the West Coast* 34 (1942), quoted in *Korematsu v. United States*, 323 U.S. 214, 241 n. 15 (1944) (Murphy, J., dissenting).

27. See Walter Pincus and Vernon Loeb, "U.S. Inconsistent When Secrets Are Loose," *Washington Post*, March. 18, 2000, A1.

28. See "National Security: The Spy Mess," *National Review*, September 13, 1999, available at LEXIS, News Library, Natrev File.

29. "Richardson Accuses Lee of Playing 'Race Card,'" *Common Appeal* (Memphis), August 4, 1999, A7.

30. *United States v. Wen Ho Lee*, 79 F. Supp. 2d at 1286-88.

31. *United States v. Wen Ho Lee*, at 1288.

32. Since the time this Comment was written, Lee and federal prosecutors struck a plea bargain agreement in which Lee pled guilty to one felony count of unlawful retention of national defense information, and was sentenced to time served. Lee was released from prison on September 13, 2000—278 days after his confinement commenced. Judge Parker apologized to Lee for being "misled" into jailing him by the actions of the executive branch.

Ian Hoffman, "*Freed Lee Gets Apology*," *Albuquerque Journal*, September 14, 2000, 1.

33. See Pincus and Loch, "U.S. Inconsistent When Secrets Are Loose."

34. See Editorial, "Wen Ho Lee's CIA Defense," *San Francisco Examiner*, February 7, 2000, A18; Pincus and Loch, "U.S. Inconsistent When Secrets Are Loose"; Robert Scheer, editorial, "CIA's Deutch Heedlessly Disregarded Security," *Los Angeles Times*, February 29, 2000, B7.

35. Pincus and Loch, "U.S. Inconsistent When Secrets Are Loose."

36. See Vernon Loeb, "Panel Criticizes CIA's Investigation of Deutch," *Washington Post*, May 6, 2000, A18. James Risen, "U.S., in a Reversal, Begins an Inquiry into Ex-CIA Head," *New York Times*, May 6, 2000, A1.

37. *CBS Evening News* (CBS television broadcast, February 5, 2000).

38. Ian Hoffman, "Lee Data Constraints Unclear," *Albuquerque Journal*, April 10, 2000, 1.

39. See William J. Broad, "Files in Question in Los Alamos Case Were Reclassified," *New York Times*, April 15, 2000, A1.

40. See Robert Pear, "Suspect in Atom Secrets Case Publicly Denies Aiding China," *New York Times*, August 2, 1999, A7.

41. Many Asian Pacific Americans and immigrants felt that media coverage of and political reaction to the so-called Asian Fundraising Scandal focused discriminatorily on their communities. See U.S. Commission on Civil Rights, *Briefing on Asian Pacific American Petition*, at www.usccr.gov/spa/as_main.htm (last visited May 10, 2000) (providing an overview of the scandal and the allegations of scapegoating and stereotyping of Asian Pacific Americans and immigrants).

42. See *The Cox Committee Report: An Assessment.*

43. *The Cox Report* has been criticized by Republicans, see, e.g., Koo, "Due Process and Right to a Fair Trial Have Gone out the Window for Wen Ho Lee," and Democrats, see President's Foreign Intelligence Advisory Board, *A Technical Reassessment of the Conclusions and Implications of the Cox Committee Report*, www.fas.org/sgp.news/1999/07/chinacox/index. html (last visited May 14, 2000) discussed in

Stephen I. Schwartz, "Phantom Menace," *Bangkok Post*, August 15, 1999, available at LEXIS, News Library, Bngpst File.

44. Laurie Wackler, "DOE Scientists Say "Lie Tests" Won't Work," *Knoxville News-Sentinel*, June 1999, A3.

45. See generally *Morning Edition* (NPR radio broadcast, April 20, 2000); James Sterngold, "Coalition Fears an Asian Bias in Nuclear Case," *New York Times*, December 13, 1999, A1.

46. For instance, the autoworkers who committed the infamous murder of Vincent Chin, a Chinese American, yelled epithets at Chin that suggested they thought he was Japanese.

47. Attorney General Janet Reno commented on this point in June 1999 while testifying before closed session of the Senate Judiciary Committee that focused on Lee. Reno testified that it would be a contradiction to use information that Lee was once suspected of improperly working on behalf of the Taiwanese government (the suspicions proved wrong and Lee was cleared) to make the case that he was not spying for China. "[T]o suggest that you are an agent of a foreign power, to wit, the PRC [People's Republic of China], the immediate question is raised, how are you [a Chinese agent] if you are clearly working for the Taiwanese government on matters that apparently involve nonclassified information?" Welsome, "Spies, Lies & Portable Tapes."

48. See *Morning Edition* (April 20, 2000).

49. Such criticisms of the badge program overlook the argument that it is less arbitrary than a policy that would allow security offices to rely on their own, unregulated methods of stopping people in classified areas. The latter regime would invite profiling based on snap judgments of racial mapping. For instance, one could expect guards to stop anyone who "looks foreign," which would be a far more over-inclusive regime than the badge method. There is simple anecdotal evidence that Asian Americans in particular are assumed to be foreign, simply because of their morphology. See Chew, "Asian Americans: The 'Reticent' Minority," 34–35; Jerry Kang, "Racial Violence against Asian Americans," *Harvard Law Review* 106(1926), 1932 n.40 (1993) (relating experiences in which Asian Americans are assumed to be foreigners). The badge program may still be an iteration too coarse, but this author believes it is better than the alternative scenario outlined here.

50. See "Energy Dept. Drops a Plan for Lab Employees to Wear Ids Stating Their Nationalities," *New York Times*, April 3, 2000, A18.

51. See Vernon Loeb, "Espionage Stir Alienating Foreign Scientists in U.S.," *Washington Post*, November 25, 1999, at G1.

52. Jim Cho, "After the Fire," at aonline.com/channels/news/03-31-2000/index.html (last visited April 29, 2000).

53. See *The Cox Committee Report: An Assessment*, 14.

54. Loeb, "Espionage Stir Alienating Foreign Scientists in U.S."

55. Loeb, "Espionage Stir Alienating Foreign Scientists in U.S."

56. "National Security: The Spy Mess."

57. Sterngold, "Coalition Fears an Asian Bias in Nuclear Case."

58. George Lobsenz, "'Distrust and Suspicion' Rife at Energy after Spying Case," *Defense Weekly* January 31, 2000, available at LEXIS News Library, Defwk File.

59. Tarun Reddy, "Ombudsman among Actions Ordered by DOE to Address Racial Concerns," *Inside Energy/with Fed. Lands*, January 24, 2000, 9.

60. See Stanley Sue and Sumie Okazaki, "Asian-American Educational Achievements: A Phenomenon Search of an Explanation," *American Psychology*, August 1990. The article introduces the concept of relative functionalism, which proposes that Asian Americans perceive, and have experienced, restriction in upward mobilization in careers that are unrelated to education. As a result, education has been of particular importance for Asian Americans.

61. Vernon Loeb, "Energy's Point Man against Bias." *Washington Post*, January 20, 2000, A21.

62. Reddy, "Ombudsman among Actions," 9.

63. Reddy, "Ombudsman among Actions," 9.

64. Reddy, "Ombudsman among Actions," 9.

# 3.14

# Campaigns, Elections, and Elected Officials

*James S. Lai, Wendy K. Tam-Cho,*
*Thomas P. Kim, and Okiyoshi Takeda*

## INTRODUCTION: THE EMERGING POLITICAL STATUS OF ASIAN AMERICAN ELECTED OFFICIALS

Research on Asian American elected officials is scarce. One may be tempted to argue that this reflects the paucity of Asian Americans who hold elected office. In reality, this perspective ignores the emerging political status of Asian American elected officials during the past two decades. The *National Asian Pacific American Political Almanac*, edited by Lai and Nakanishi (2000–2001), lists hundreds of Asian Americans who hold elected offices in national, state, and local governments in addition to a number of appointed officials and judges. The popular image that Asian Americans passively stay away from politics should be modified in light of this group's recurrent political movements in the United States (Wei 1993) and the increasing number of Asian American political candidates who run for

Lai, James S., Wendy Tam-Cho, Oki Takeda, and Thomas P. Kim. "Campaigns, Elections, and Elected Officials." *PS: Political Science & Politics* XXXIV(3). Reprinted with permission.

national and state-level offices (Cho 2000a; Lien forthcoming). The lack of research on Asian American politicians may reflect the general tendency in the study of American politics that voting behavior and public opinion tends to attract the attention of scholars with a quantitative bent. As a result, the various trends illustrating the growing political status of Asian American candidates and elected officials, particularly on the U.S. mainland, must be examined in order to understand their contribution to the emerging dimensions of contemporary racial and ethnic politics.

Asian American political leadership and their roles in campaigns have often been overlooked in the discussion of minority politics due to this community's relatively young and large foreign-born population (Brackman and Erie 1995). In the area of national elected officials, the history of Asian American political leadership on the U.S. mainland entails a long history that dates to the 1956 election of Dalip Singh Saund (D-CA), the first Asian American elected to the U.S. Congress from a mainland state (Coleman 2000). Asian American elected leadership has historically emerged from Hawaii and parts of the U.S. mainland in large Asian-populated states such as California, Washington, Oregon, New York, and Texas.

When discussing the Asian American political leadership, it is important to discuss the distinctions between Hawaii and the U.S. mainland. Asians, Pacific Islanders, and native Hawaiians, combined together, constitute a majority in all of Hawaii's local, state, and federal level districts. As a result of their demographic majority, the perception among Asian Americans in Hawaii is that they are the "mainstream" in regard to local and statewide political incorporation. This numerical representation has historically led to Asian American elected leadership in and from Hawaii in American politics. Many of the most influential and experienced federal level Asian American elected leadership has come from Hawaii, such as U.S. Senators Daniel K. Inouye (D-HI) and Daniel Akaka (D-HI), and U.S. Representative Patsy Mink (D-HI). The ability to elect and to re-elect Asian American leadership from Hawaii is in stark contrast to the struggles of Asian American political leaders on the U.S. mainland, who must pursue mainstream and multiethnic or pan-ethnic strategies. A clear example is California, where over 40 percent of the Asian American population reside in the United States. Even combined, the over thirty Asian and Pacific Islander ethnic groups do not constitute greater than 15 percent of the state population in 2000. As a result, competitive and successful Asian American candidates and elected officials on the U.S. mainland must build political coalitions that are either mainstream and/or multiracial.

## THE CROSS-OVER APPEAL AND CAMPAIGN STRATEGIES OF ASIAN AMERICAN CANDIDATES

In contrast to the African American and Latino candidates, Asian American elected officials on the United States mainland primarily emerge from political districts containing constituencies that are either mainstream or multiracial. At the federal

Congressional level, fourteen out of the seventeen African American House Representatives in 1982 represented districts where African Americans represented 40 percent or more of the population. For Latino elected officials in 1982, seven of the ten Latino House Representatives were elected from districts where Latinos represented 50 percent or more of the population (Moore and Pachon 1985; Espiritu 1992). Although African American elected officials and Latinos have begun to emerge from multiracial districts, historically they have relied on large constituencies from their respective racial groups to be elected. In contrast to African American and Latino elected officials, a majority of the state and federal level Asian Pacific American elected officials on the U.S. mainland tend to represent non-Asian districts.[1] For example, during the 105th Congress, only two of the top fifty congressional districts on the U.S. mainland with the largest Asian Pacific American populations were represented by an Asian Pacific American (*National Directory of Asian Pacific American Organizations* 1997–1998).

In many of these non-Asian majority districts, particularly in California and Washington State, Asian Americans may represent a substantial minority group. Subsequently, Asian American candidates on the United States mainland have differed from their Hawaiian cohorts in that they are more likely to run as "mainstream" or "cross-over" candidates.[2] Previous studies have indicated that Asian American candidates on the United States are most likely among all minority groups to be elected by another racial group (Uhlaner, Cain, and Kiewiet 1989;Lai 2000b). The ability of Asian American candidates to appeal to non-Asian constituents in contemporary politics has challenged traditional notions of racial and ethnic cleavages that were part of multiracial coalitions during the late twentieth century (Rodriguez 1998). Matt Fong, the former California State Treasurer and 1998 California U.S. Senate candidate, argues that Asian Americans represent a "neutral minority" candidate who can appeal to both mainstream and minority groups based on their socioeconomic statuses and historic experiences with discrimination (Rodriguez 1998). Given the fact that Asian Americans are one of the most residentially dispersed groups and their large foreign-born population (nearly 70 percent), successful Asian American candidates at all levels must rely on the votes and support of their non-Asian constituents by focusing on broader campaign issues.

During 2000, neither of the U.S. Congressional districts with the ten largest Asian American populations in the mainland nor the ten fastest growing Asian American districts were represented by an Asian American elected official (Office of Asian Pacific American Outreach, Democratic National Committee 1999).

As illustrated in table 3.14a, in 1990, no Asian majority congressional district currently exists on the United States mainland outside of Hawaii. The largest Asian populated congressional district on the United States mainland is California District 8, where Asians accounted for nearly 28 percent of the constituency. In comparison, Asians represented a clear majority in Hawaii Congressional Districts 1 and 2, where they represented 67 and 57 percent of the constituencies, respectively (Office of Asian Pacific American Outreach, Democratic National Committee 1999). Yet, despite the lack of Asian majority districts at the state and federal levels, political districts with substantial Asian American populations have developed. In California, where nearly 40 percent of the nation's Asian American population reside, it is very likely that an Asian majority district will develop in the near future. The findings in table 3.14a also suggest the political potentials for future Asian American candidates in states like California. While it is likely that an Asian majority district on the U.S. mainland will develop in the future, Asian American candidates will continue to run as either mainstream or multiracial candidates in non-Asian majority districts. However, this trend does not imply or suggest that Asian American constituents do not support an Asian American candidate, particu-

larly those who run within or outside of their political districts, in regard to campaign contributions. As will be illustrated later, Asian American contributors have strongly supported Asian American candidates within and outside of their districts.

The impact of Asian American candidates on group political mobilization at all the levels has taken on various forms in the areas of voting and nonvoting participation (Nakanishi 1986; Lai 2000b). In the area of voting, studies have illustrated that Asian American candidates can bring out Asian voters at the local and state level and increase new voter registration (See Asian Pacific American Legal Center of Southern California Exit Poll 1996). In nonvoting areas, as will be illustrated later, Asian Americans have been shown to give campaign contributions to Asian American candidates at all levels, even those running outside of their districts. Given the importance of campaign money in political elections, Asian American candidates, similar to other minority candidates, have relied on support from community-based, grass-roots organizations for such valuable political resources. Such Asian American community-based organizations also provide other invaluable forms of support for Asian American candidates ranging from campaign volunteers to "get-out-the-vote" drives (Saito and Park 2000; Lai 2000b). In many instances, the support of community-based organizations can make the difference in a local or statewide election for Asian American candidates. For example, in 1998, Republican Matt Fong credited grassroots Asian American organizations and individuals in providing the swing votes necessary to win his closely contested primary victory over his Republican challenger Darryl Issa (Lin 1998).

## ASIAN AMERICAN ELECTED REPRESENTATION IN THE U.S. CONGRESS

Five representatives and two senators of Asian decent serve the current, 107th Congress. Table 3.14b lists all the fifteen past and current voting members of Congress who are

**Table 3.14a  Top Ten Congressional Districts with the Largest Percentage of Asian Americans**

| Rank 1990 | House District | Major City | Asian American % in District | White % | African American % | Hispanic (Any Race) % | Member, 107th Congress (Party, Race) |
|---|---|---|---|---|---|---|---|
| 1 | HI-1 | Honolulu | 66.7% | 29% | 2% | 5% | Abercrombie (D, White) |
| 2 | HI-1 | Hilo | 57.1 | 38 | 2 | 9 | Mink (D, Asian) |
| 3 | CA-8 | San Francisco | 27.8 | 52 | 13 | 15 | Pelosi (D, White) |
| 4 | CA-12 | Daly City | 25.7 | 65 | 4 | 14 | Lantos (D, White) |
| 5 | CA-31 | El Monte | 22.9 | 48 | 2 | 58 | Solis (D, Latino) |
| 6 | CA-30 | Los Angeles | 21.4 | 44 | 3 | 60 | Becerra (D, Latino) |
| 7 | CA-16 | San Jose | 21.1 | 55 | 5 | 36 | Lofgren (D, White) |
| 8 | NY-12 | New York | 19.5 | 34 | 14 | 57 | Velazquez (D, Latino) |
| 9 | CA-13 | Fremont | 19.4 | 64 | 7 | 18 | Stark (D, White) |
| 10 | CA-9 | Oakland | 15.8 | 45 | 32 | 11 | Lee (D, African) |

**Table 3.14b     Asian Americans Who Have Served in the United States Congress**

| Years Served | Member | Ethnicity | Party | District |
|---|---|---|---|---|
| **House** | | | | |
| 1957–1963 | Dalip Singh Saund | South Asian American | Democrat | California 29th |
| 1959–1963 | Daniel K. Inouye | Japanese American | Democrat | Hawaii At-Large |
| 1963–1977 | Spark M. Matsunaga | Japanese American | Democrat | Hawaii At-Large, then 1st |
| 1965–1977 | Patsy T. Mink | Japanese American | Democrat | Hawaii At-Large, then 2nd |
| 1975–1995 | Norman Y. Mineta | Japanese American | Democrat | California 13th, then 15th |
| 1977–1990 | Daniel K. Akaka | Chinese & Native Hawaiian | Democrat | Hawaii 2nd |
| 1979–present | Robert T. Matsui | Japanese American | Democrat | California 3rd, then 5th |
| 1987–1991 | Patricia F. Saiki | Japanese American | Republican | Hawaii 1st |
| 1990–present | Patsy T. Mink | Japanese American | Democrat | D-Hawaii 2nd |
| 1993–present | Robert C. Scott | African & Filipino American | Democrat | Virginia 3rd, |
| 1993–1999 | Jay C. Kim | Korean American | Republican | California 41st |
| 1999–present | David Wu | Chinese American | Democrat | Oregon 1st |
| 2001–present | Mike Honda | Japanese American | Democrat | California 15th |
| **Senate** | | | | |
| 1959–1977 | Hiram L. Fong | Chinese American | Republican | Hawaii |
| 1963–present | Daniel K. Inouye | Japanese American | Democrat | Hawaii |
| 1977–1983 | S. I. Hayakawa | Japanese American | Republican | California |
| 1977–1990 | Spark M. Matsunaga | Japanese American | Democrat | Hawaii |
| 1990–present | Daniel K. Akaka | Chinese & Native Hawaiian | Democrat | Hawaii |

Asian Americans.[3] As one can see, the majority of them are from Hawaii, are Democrats, and are Japanese Americans. It is noteworthy, however, that the first Asian American member of Congress came from a South Asian population group, which has not since been represented on the Hill. Moreover, Filipinos, whose current population nearly matches that of Chinese, the largest Asian American ethnic group in number, have scarcely been elected to Congress.[4]

Like other minority racial and ethnic groups, Asian Americans do not have their own representatives in Congress in proportion to their population share in the nation (4 percent, which corresponds to seventeen House members and four Senators). Referring back to table 3.14a, it is evident that except for the districts represented by Patsy

Mink (D-HI), all districts are represented by members of other races. In particular, it is noteworthy that districts, which encompasses regional Chinatowns (Monterey Park in California 31 and New York City Chinatown 12) are both represented by Latino members. Asian Americans and Latinos exhibit a similar, rapid pattern of population growth. As latecomers they tend to reside in the same geographic areas, but the latter tends to outnumber the former. In Southern California, these two racial groups have competed for mayoral, state assembly, and congressional seats, but at the same time, their political leaders have also sought to collaborate in redistricting and civil rights activities (Saito 1998b).

Given the small, but growing numbers of Asian American congressional members, it is natural that the few Asian American members have assumed the role of advocates for Asian Americans as a whole, and not exclusively in their districts or of their own ethnic groups. The most notable example of this activity is the passage of a bill in 1988 to redress the internment of Japanese Americans during the World War II. In 1942, approximately 120,000 people of Japanese decent, two-thirds of whom were native born, were deprived of their constitutional rights by President Roosevelt's Executive Order 9066 and sent to ten relocation camps in deserted areas in western and central states. Senators Matsunaga and Inouye and Representatives Matsui and Mineta[5] explored ways for redress first by establishing a government commission to investigate the issue and later by introducing bills to authorize financial compensation for survivors (Hatamiya 1993).

Another example of Asian American Congressional members working for their constituencies outside their districts can be seen in the legislative efforts concerning benefits for Filipino veterans. During World War II, hundreds of thousands of residents in the Philippines fought for the United States against Japan, but they became ineligible for U.S. veterans' benefits in a legislative change made as the Philippines became an independent country in 1946. As of today, they receive only half of the benefits that other World War II veterans, who were not U.S. nationals, are entitled to receive. As a result of an immigration act in 1990 that expedited naturalization from the Philippines, 25,000 Filipino veterans currently reside in the United States (mostly California), but many of them are old and in poor living condition (Vergara 1997). Representatives Gilman (R-NY) and Filner (D-CA) have repeatedly introduced legislation to bring equity in the benefits for Filipino veterans and on the Senate side, Inouye (D-HI) has assumed the task to promote the cause.[6] Still another example of Asian American Congressional members working for the greater Asian population is Representative David Wu's (D-OR) resolution in the 106th Congress (1999–2000) to condemn stereotypes against Asian Americans. Between February 1999, when the *New York Times* first reported Chinese "espionage" of U.S. nuclear secrets, and September 2000, when Dr. Wen Ho Lee, who was arrested as the main suspect in the case, was released with 58 of his 59 counts of charged dropped, many Asian Americans feared that they might be treated by society as enemy foreigners regardless of how loyal they were to the country. Wu, who was the vice chair of the Asian Pacific American Caucus in Congress, succeeded in having the concurrent resolution approved by the House, although it eventually failed to pass the Senate (Takeda 2001).

## INCREASED ELECTED REPRESENTATION AT THE LOCAL AND STATE LEVELS

Despite their relative success at the federal level, Asian American candidates have had their most success at the state and local levels. A majority of this electoral success at the state level has historically been in Hawaii (Coleman 2000). In 2000, seventy-three Asian Americans served in state legislatures, mostly from Hawaii (*National Asian Pacific American Political Almanac*). However, during the past forty years, since the 1960s, the number of Asian American elected officials from other states, particularly from the continental United States, has slowly increased.

As illustrated in table 3.14c, Asian American elected officials have made their greatest impact at the local and state-levels since 1978. The numbers for the local positions include the following: schoolboards, city councils, and mayors, while the state positions include state senators and assembly members. The geographic diversity of Asian American elected representation has increased, particularly those on the continental United States. For example, in 2000, continental states containing Asian American state-level elected officials include Washington (3), California (3), Arizona (1), Minnesota (1), and New Hampshire (1).

**Table 3.14c   Total Number of Asian Pacific American Elected Officials in Key Local, State, and Federal Positions**

| Year | Local | State | Federal | Total |
|------|-------|-------|---------|-------|
| 1978 | 52 | 63 | 5 | 120 |
| 1979 | 69 | 68 | 6 | 143 |
| 1980 | 98 | 69 | 6 | 173 |
| 1982 | 109 | 59 | 6 | 174 |
| 1984 | 109 | 59 | 5 | 173 |
| 1995 | 157 | 66 | 8 | 231 |
| 1996 | 181 | 66 | 7 | 254 |
| 1998 | 187 | 67 | 7 | 261 |
| 2000 | 248 | 73 | 7 | 328 |

*Source:* Compiled from the *National Asian American Political Almanac,* First to Ninth Editions.

Some notable Asian American state-level elected officials include California State Assembly Representatives Wilma Chan and Carol Liu, who both became the first Asian American women to be elected to the California State Assembly since March Fong Eu in 1966.

Parallel with this steady increase in elected representation on the United States mainland, Asian American elected officials have also become more ethnically diverse, primarily due to the 1965 reforms to the Immigration and Naturalization Act, which have profoundly shaped the contemporary development of Asians in the United States (Hing 1993). Historically, Japanese and Chinese Americans represented a majority of the early Asian American elected officials with some semblance of representation among Filipino and Korean Americans (Espiritu 1992). However, other Asian ethnic groups, particularly those from Southeast Asia, are slowly incorporating themselves into American politics as candidates. As a result, the current group of Asian American elected officials at all three governmental levels represent the most ethnically diverse group at any point thus far (Lai 2000b). Recent examples at the local level include Tony Lam, who was elected to the city council of Westminster, California in 1992, becoming the first Vietnamese American elected official in the United

States. In 1998, Chanrithy Uong, the first Cambodian American elected official in the United States, was elected to the city council of Lowell, Massachusetts, while Joe Bee Xiong became the first Hmong American elected official when he was elected to the city council of Eau Claire, Wisconsin. At the state level, Hawaii Governor Ben Cayetano became the nation's first Filipino American elected governor in 1994, and Washington State Governor Gary Locke became the first Asian American governor on the United States mainland in 1996 (Coleman 2000). Given these recent trends on the United States mainland, a great deal of hope exists for increased elected representation for Asian Americans at the local and state levels.

## ASIAN AMERICAN CAMPAIGN CONTRIBUTIONS IN FEDERAL LEVEL CAMPAIGNS

When the press or the media discuss minority politics, they are usually referring to black politics, or less frequently, Latino politics. Indeed, they rarely spend much energy on Asian American politics.

Instead, Asian Americans are largely ignored on the political front. Their numbers do not yet match those of the Latino group, and their mobilization pales in comparison to the mobilization of blacks. Hence, they are often seen as politically expendable. One arena, however, in which Asians are given perhaps more than their share of attention is campaign finance. The reasoning is twofold. First, Asian Americans are regarded as big league contributors, far exceeding expected levels of contributing given their small share of the electorate. Second, the widely publicized 1996 campaign finance scandal involving John Huang and Charlie Trie thrust the Asian American campaign donor into the limelight.

Despite the interest in this form of political behavior, there is little scholarly research on the Asian American contributor. Instead, our knowledge in this area can be characterized as emerging folklore, driven by journalistic accounts. Ron Unz states that Asians are on the verge of becoming "Republican Jews" since Americans of Asian descent have deep pockets, "without the liberal guilt" (Unz 1994). In 1996, the Democratic National Committee collected a record-breaking $5 million from John Huang's efforts. Though over $1 million was eventually returned to donors in an attempt to correct ethical lapses (Miller 1996), the dollar amounts are noteworthy, nonetheless. The Republicans, as well, have recognized the large potential source of funds. After Matt Fong introduced Bob Dole at a rally of ethnic supporters in California, Roy Wong, the Asian American "get-out-the-vote" director concluded, "This is the first time the Asian community has been reached out to so aggressively" (Lin 1996). Clearly, both parties have come to view Asian ethnic communities as a rich source

of financial support, still largely untapped. Despite the recent immigrant status of Asian Americans, party leaders believe that "the economic success of many Asian immigrants should soon make them a major source of political funding" (Unz 1994). Indeed, the leanings of the press on this issue are clear. What is not clear is the quality of research that underlies these bold claims and predictions of the future.

Perhaps not surprisingly, a full account of campaign donations from every Asian donor in the period 1978–1998 reveals a less dramatic story. Two points, in particular, are worth correcting.

First, Asian Americans are not predominantly Republican-leaning. Figure 3.14a shows that Chinese and Japanese partisan loyalties are split while Koreans are more Republican and the Vietnamese are the most conservative. Second, figure 3.14b

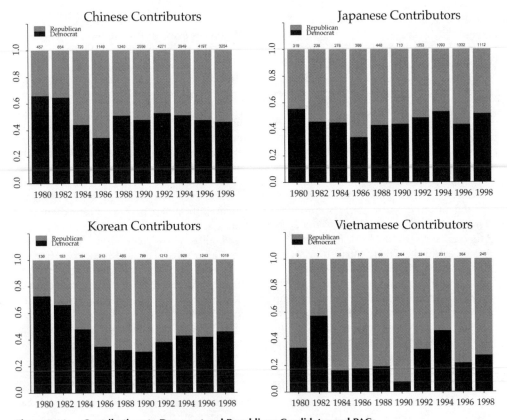

**Figure 3.14a    Contributions to Democrat and Republican Candidates and PACs**
Contributions include all federal campaigns from 1978–1998, except presidential campaigns. Numbers above the bars indicate total number of contributions for that period.

demonstrates that Asian donors respond first and foremost to Asian American candidates, and are not, as journalistic accounts imply, a source of funds for all candidates. The patterns evident in figure 3.14b, while seemingly sporadic, almost perfectly match the campaigns run by the candidates of corresponding ethnicity. In 1988 and 1992, S. B. Woo, a Chinese candidate ran for the Delaware U.S. Senate and the U.S. House, respectively. In 1998, Matt Fong, another Chinese American candidate ran for the U.S. Senate seat in California. Jay Kim, a Korean American candidate ran for the U.S. House in the 1992 through 1998 elections. Robert Matsui and Norman Mineta, Japanese American candidates, were running congressional campaigns throughout the period in question. Apparently, the concept of pan-ethnicity had not yet been entirely embraced by these ethnic contributors. Eth-

nic candidates bring out ethnic contributors but not necessarily the broad class of Asian contributors. In contrast to some earlier work that indicates a rise in pan-ethnicity over time, there does not seem to be a corresponding rise in the realm of campaign finance.

Politically, Asian American contributors do not seem to be behaving in a traditional strategic manner. They are not cohesive as a group, and prefer to fund Asian American candidates outside of their districts rather than specifically those candidates who run in their districts (Cho 2000a). For those who are eagerly awaiting the emergence of the Asian American political giant; however, there are some rays of hope. In particular, if one shifts the focus to Hawaii, where the Asian American culture is more prominent and the mixing of the various ethnicities is more common, one is able to see an Asian

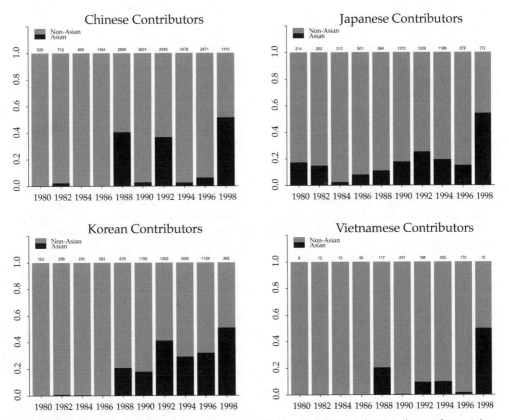

**Figure 3.14b   Contributions from Asian donors (separated by ethnicity) to Asian American and Non-Asian American Candidates**
Contributions include all federal campaigns, including presidential campaigns.

American group that is more strategic. Hence, the continued rapid influx of Asian immigrants into California and other large Asian communities may soon replicate the context and behavior that we observe in Hawaii. The mixing of ethnic groups and the later generations of these early immigrant groups will certainly have some impact. The case in Hawaii is our best guess as to what the effect will be. In Hawaii, although there is still a preference toward Asian candidates, competitive candidates receive more support than less competitive ones, and many contributions are for candidates within the contributor's district or at least within the state. In essence, it seems that this context encourages the group to move beyond ethnic politics, toward a more post-ethnic notion of group identity. At the same time, traditional party politics appear in their expected form (Cho 2000b). All of these observations are bolstered by the patterns that we have seen emerging on the U.S. mainland. In particular, Asian Americans who are younger and live in more multicultural counties seem to conform more to party cues than ethnic cues (Tam 1995).

## ASIAN AMERICAN CAMPAIGN CONTRIBUTIONS AT THE LOCAL AND STATE LEVELS

Similar to those at the federal level, Asian American candidates have relied greatly on Asian American contributors during local and state-level elections (Lai 2000a). In California, Asian Americans have parlayed their contributions to political power in local and statewide elections for both Asian and non-Asian candidates. An example of Asian American contributor support for a local, non-Asian candidate was during Los Angeles mayor Tom Bradley's 1982 and 1986 re-election campaigns. Asian Americans contributed 10 percent of Bradley's statewide donations despite representing only 6 percent of the entire population (Tachibana 1986). Due to their large foreign-born and relatively young population, some

political scholars have viewed campaign contributions as Asian Americans' most viable political strength (Nakanishi 1998; Saito 1998a; Lai 2000a). While no strong pan-ethnic coalition was found to exist among Asian ethnic contributors to federal-level Asian American candidate, local and state-level elections are beginning to reveal a gradual development of a pan-ethnic strategy. A majority of Asian American candidates on the U.S. mainland, as opposed to Hawaii, have emerged from non-Asian majority districts. As a result of their constituencies, Asian American candidates are beginning to realize that those who are most successful have run as mainstream or crossover candidates. Such a crossover candidate strategy does not necessarily preclude Asian American candidates from targeting Asian American contributors. In fact, one recent national survey of current elected officials found that nearly one-third of Asian American local, state, and federal level elected officials relied on Asian American contributions (Lai 2000b).

Perhaps the most vivid example of this cross-over appeal can be seen in 1992 when former Los Angeles city council member Michael Woo ran for mayor of the city of Los Angeles against self-financed, multi-millionaire candidate Richard Riordan. Despite the fact that the Los Angeles mayoral race is a local and nonpartisan election, Woo received contributions from Asian Americans from seventeen different states (Lai 2000a). In total, Woo received approximately a quarter of his total contributions from a national level of Asian American contributors consisting primarily of Chinese Americans. A primary reason was the ethnic pride that many Chinese Americans outside of California felt as Woo, a third generation Chinese American, attempted to become mayor of the nation's second largest city. Although a majority of Woo's Asian contributors were from Chinese Americans, over 10 percent of his Asian contributions came from Japanese, Korean, Filipino, Vietnamese, and Indian Americans. During the 1998 California U.S. Senate primary election, Republican challenger

Matt Fong was able to raise nearly 9 percent of his Asian American contributions from outside of California. Similar to Woo, Chinese Americans consisted of the majority of Asian contributors at nearly 87 percent with 13 percent distributed among Japanese, Korean, Indian, Filipino, and Vietnamese American contributors (Lai 2000b). While the respective Asian American contribution findings of both the Woo and Fong campaigns may be more atypical than the norm, it does indicate a slow but steady progression of the Asian American contributions toward a pan-ethnic identity in California politics. The potentials of constructing such a pan-ethnic identity are increased with the presence of a strong Asian American candidate. However, the challenges of pan-ethnic coalitions, like all political coalitions, is maintaining them along various interests and ideologies (Espiritu 1992; Sonenshein 1993; Espiritu and Ong 1994; Lai 2000a). Given the diverse U.S. immigration patterns and the differing levels of political incorporation among the Asian ethnic groups, perhaps this current developing trend toward pan-ethnicity is more important to consider than an "authentic" pan-ethnic coalition in which all Asian ethnic groups participate equally. There have been numerous local and statewide elections where Asian American contributors have played a significant role in providing key political support to Asian American candidates' campaigns.

## CONCLUSION: TOWARD A RESEARCH AGENDA ON ASIAN AMERICANS AND ELECTED REPRESENTATIVES

We began this chapter with the comment that research on Asian American elected officials and representation issues is scarce. In light of the existing and established trends in Asian American politics that we have outlined above, our introductory statement has turned into a question: why the scarcity of research on the representation of Asian Americans through elected officials?

Paradoxically, part of the answer lies in where scholars of Asian American politics have thus far put forth their greatest efforts. In particular, three significantly more developed literatures in the study of Asian Americans have inadvertently added fuel to the perception of Asian American inactivity in elite electoral politics. First, the literature on the internal heterogeneity of Asian America has led scholars to assume without evidence that the study of mainstream Asian American politics begins and ends with a demonstration of diversity on axes including geography, country of ancestry, partisanship, ideology, levels of political participation, generations, and socioeconomic class. Unable or unwilling to overcome the collective action problems endemic to such diversity, the assumption goes, Asian Americans are not able to manifest themselves into public life.

Second, the literature on state-sponsored discrimination against Asian Americans is quite extensive, and seems to suggest that Asian American political activity has been greatly depressed by racist practices often codified into law, particularly insofar as Asian Americans have been racially stereotyped as the "perpetual foreigner" in the United States. Unable to access the political system or with a stunted political tradition and weak foundation of political experience, the assumption goes, Asian Americans are behind the curve in overcoming the legal-political barriers historically set in front of them.

Synthesizing these two literatures together, we are left with the unproven assumption that research on Asian American political activity within mainstream political institutions is unnecessary given the high degree of internal heterogeneity and the historical legacy of state sponsored discrimination against their participation in mainstream politics. This synthesis leads to the third literature on "politics by other means." This literature suggests that Asian Americans are quite political, but that this political activity is largely manifested in nonelectoral activities, including cultural politics, labor politics, feminist politics, and so forth. Because of the impact of internal heterogeneity and state-sponsored discrimination, the assumption goes, Asian American political energy has been manifested predominantly in these alternative political arenas.

No doubt, a larger, more expansive notion of politics is necessary to capture the full breadth of Asian American political activity. Opting not to privilege national mainstream political activity provides the epistemological space to conduct empirical research showing that Asian Americans are politically minded in a variety of other important areas. But the active participation of Asian Americans in labor politics, feminist politics, and other nonelectoral or "alternative" political arenas does not diminish the importance of politics as it occurs within mainstream national political institutions. When scholars of "politics by other means" insist that we need to look beyond conventionally described mainstream politics, insofar as these scholars broaden their definition of politics in order to accommodate the claim that Asian Americans are not politically passive, they inadvertently suggest that Asian American activity within more narrowly defined mainstream institutional politics does not meaningfully exist. Scholars implicitly assume without evidence that politically organized Asian Americans have no significant relationship with the political institutions that shape the nation's public life, presumably because of the legacy of discrimination and the hurdles to collective action endemic to the political organization of an internally diverse group. Ironically, the push to broaden the understanding of Asian American political activity may lead to the unwarranted conclusion that research on more narrowly defined politics is unnecessary.

Taken together, these literatures tell us that Asian Americans are worthy of study because of what they cannot accomplish, rather than what they can; the research agenda of Asian American politics tends to address its absence rather than its presence in our nation's political institutions. However, the emphasis on internal characteris-

tics obscures the fact that internal heterogeneity does not logically lead to the absence of political activity within mainstream political institutions. After all, every interest group has collective action problems that must be solved if they are to engage in mainstream political activity, and we obviously do not similarly assume that other interest groups are apolitical. And a critique from the opposite perspective (arguing in favor of their apoliticism) might begin by pointing out that state-sponsored discrimination and internal heterogeneity do not demonstrate that Asian Americans would be more politically active in conventional politics if these internally generated centrifugal forces and externally imposed hurdles did not exist. Furthermore, while the state-sanctioned discrimination against Asian Americans likely depressed their political participation in mainstream politics, scholars generally assume that other racial and ethnic groups, which experienced state-sponsored discrimination, have integrated themselves into the nation's political institutions.

In sum, most contemporary scholarship leads more often than not toward the assumption that there is no mainstream Asian American political center to be examined. The actors, goals, strategies, and consequences of Asian Americans organized to influence national political decision-making remain uncertain and under-theorized. Consequently, while scholars of Asian American politics have gone far in identifying the hurdles and prospects of Asian Americans and in clarifying the breadth and depth of Asian American political participation, the literature has had little to say about the relationship between politically organized Asian Americans and external strategic political elites, and it has provided little insight on important political events involving Asian Americans working within mainstream institutions. The writers of this chapter believe the need for an emerging research agenda of Asian American politics; one that will take seriously the relationship between strategic politicians of Asian American descent and the political institutions that define our nation's public life.

## NOTES

1. Asian majority districts on the U.S. mainland exist primarily at the schoolboard district level in California. Interestingly, schoolboard positions have served as a springboard for many Asian American elected officials at all levels. Recent examples include current U.S. Representative Michael Honda, who served as a schoolboard member in San Jose, California, and current Cupertino City Councilmembers Michael Chang and Barry Chang, who both served on the Cupertino Schoolboard prior to their current elected positions.

2. The term "mainstream" is site-specific when comparing Hawaii and the U.S. mainland. In Hawaii, the term "mainstream" equates to Asian, Hawaiian, and Pacific Islander culture given its majority Asian and Pacific Islander population. Therefore, it is important to understand these differences in socio-political contexts when comparing these two geographic areas.

3. Tong's (2000) more inclusive list of thirty-one members includes Resident Commissioners from the Philippines before the World War II and nonvoting members from Guam and American Samoa.

4. Robert Scott's part-Filipino identity came to be known among the Asian American community only recently. In 1994, the first Asian American Filipino governor, Benjamin Cayetano, was elected in Hawaii. Other Asian American governors in U.S. history are George Ariyoshi (D-HI, 1975–1986), John Waihee (D-HI, 1987–1994) and Gary Locke (D-WA, 1997–present).

5. Mineta became the first Asian American cabinet member in 2000 when Richard Daily resigned as the Secretary of Transportation to join the Gore presidential campaign team. President George W. Bush nominated Mineta to be Commerce Secretary (he was the House Commerce committee chair during the 103rd Congress [1993–1994]) and another Asian American, Elaine Chao, to be Labor Secretary. Both nominations were approved by the U.S. Senate.

6. Filipino veterans' demands were partially met during the 106th Congress (1999–2000) when a bill was enacted into law, allowing the veterans to continue to receive 75 percent of Supplementary Security Income (SSI) if they go back to the Philippines. Another bill was enacted into law to appropriate benefits for disabled veterans.

## REFERENCES

Asian Pacific American Legal Center of Southern California. 1996. *1996 Southern California Asian Pacific American Exit Poll Report: An Analysis of APA Voter Behavior and Opinions.*

Brackman, Harold, and Stephen P. Erie. 1995. "Beyond 'Politics by Other Means': Empowerment Strategies for Los Angeles' Asian Pacific Community." In Michael P. Smith and Joe R. Feagin , eds., *The Bubbling Cauldron: Race, Ethnicity, and the Urban Crisis*, 282–303. Minneapolis: University of Minnesota Press.

Cho, Wendy K. Tam. 2000a. "Tapping Motives and Dynamics Behind Campaign Contributions: Insights from the Asian American Case." Working Paper.

———. 2000b. "Foreshadowing Strategic Post-Ethnic Politics: Hawaii as a Natural Experiment." Working Paper.

Coleman, Kevin. 2000. *Asian Pacific American Political Participation and Representation in Elective Office.* CRS Report for Congress. Washington, D.C.: Congressional Research Service.

Downs, Anthony. 1957. *An Economic Theory of Democracy.* New York: Harper and Row.

Espiritu, Yen Le. 1992. *Asian American Panethnicity: Bridging Institutions and Identities.* Philadelphia: Temple University Press.

Espiritu, Yen Le, and Paul Ong. 1994. In Paul Ong, Edna Bonacich, and Lucie Cheng, eds., *The New Asian Immigration in Los Angeles and Global Restructuring*, 295–321. Philadelphia: Temple University Press.

Fong, Timothy P. 1994. *The First Suburban Chinatown: The Remaking of Monterey Park, California.* Philadelphia: Temple University Press.

Hardin, Russell. 1992. *Collective Action.* Baltimore: Johns Hopkins University Press.

Hatamiya, Leslie T. 1993. *Righting a Wrong: Japanese Americans and the Passage of the Civil Liberties Act of 1988.* Stanford, Calif.: Stanford University Press.

Hing, Bill On. 1993. *Making and Remaking Asian America through Immigration Policy,*

*1850–1990*. Stanford, Calif.: Stanford University Press.

Horton, John. 1995. *The Politics of Diversity: Immigration, Resistance, and Change in Monterey Park, California*. Philadelphia: Temple University Press.

Lai, James S. 2000a. "Asian Pacific Americans and the Pan-Ethnic Question." In Richard E. Keiser and Katherine Underwood, eds. *Minority Politics at the Millennium*, 203–226. New York: Garland Publishing.

———. 2000b. "Beyond Voting: The Recruitment of Asian Pacific American and Their Impact on Group Electoral Mobilization." Los Angeles: University of Southern California. Unpublished dissertation.

Lai, James S., and Don T. Nakanishi, eds. 2001. *National Asian Pacific American Political Almanac,* Special Election Edition. Los Angeles: UCLA Asian American Studies Center.

Lien, Pei-te. Forthcoming. *The Making of Asian America through Political Participation*. Philadelphia: Temple University Press.

Lin, Sam Chu. 1998. "Fong Credits Grassroots Campaign as Key Factor in Primary Victory." *Rafu Shimpo*, June 5, 1998, 1, 5.

———. 1996. "Optimism on Both Sides: Campaigns Look to APAs as Swing Votes in 10 States." *AsianWeek*, October 11–17.

Miller, Alan C. 1996. "Democrats Give Back More Disputed Money." *Los Angeles Times*, November 23.

Moore, Joan, and Henry Pachon. 1985. *Hispanics in the United States*. Englewood Cliffs, N.J.: Prentice-Hall.

Nakanishi, Don T. 1986. "Asian American Politics: An Agenda for Research." *Amerasia Journal* 12: 1–27.

———. 1998. "When Numbers Do Not Add Up: Asian Pacific Americans and California Politics." In Michael B. Preston, Bruce E. Cain, and Sandra Bass, eds., *Racial and Ethnic Politics in California*, Volume Two, 3–43. Berkeley: Institute of Governmental Studies.

Office of Asian Pacific American Outreach. 1999. Political Power of Asian Pacific Americans Increases Due to Projected Population Growth. Washington, D.C.: Democratic National Committee.

Olson, Mancur. 1965. *The Logic of Collective Action*. Cambridge, Mass.: Harvard University Press.

Rodriguez, Gregory. 1998. Minority Leader. *The New Republic*. October 19, 1998: 21–24.

Saito, Leland T. 1998a. "Beyond Numbers: Asian American and Latino Politics in Los Angeles' San Gabriel Valley." In Michael B. Preston, Bruce E. Cain, and Sandra Bass, eds, *Racial and Ethnic Politics in California*, Volume Two, 45–72. Berkeley: Institute of Governmental Studies.

———. 1998b. *Race and Politics: Asian Americans, Latinos, and Whites in a Los Angeles Suburb*. Urbana, IL: University of Illinois Press.

Saito, Leland T. and Edward Park. 2000. "Multiracial Collaborations and Coalitions." In Paul M. Ong, ed., *The State of Asian Pacific America: Transforming Race Relations*, 435–74. Los Angeles: LEAP and UCLA Asian American Studies Center.

Sonenshein, Raphael J. 1993. *Politics in Black and White: Race and Power in Los Angeles*. Princeton, N.J.: Princeton University Press.

Tachibana, Judy. 1986. "California's Asians: Power from a Growing Population." *California Journal* 17: 534–43.

Takeda, Okiyoshi. 2001. "The Representation of Asian Americans in the U.S. Political System" in Charles E. Menifield, ed., *Representation of Minorities in the American Political System: Implications for the 21st Century*. Lanham, Md.: University Press of America.

Tam, Wendy K. 1995. "Asians—A Monolithic Voting Bloc?" *Political Behavior* 17: 223–49.

Tong, Lorraine H. 2000. Asian Pacific Americans in the United States Congress. *Congressional Research Service Report for Congress*, 97-398 GOV.

Uhlaner, Carole J., Bruce E. Cain, and D. Roderick Kiewiet. 1989. "Political Participation of Ethnic Minorities in the 1980s." *Political Behavior* 11: 195–232.

Unz, Ron. 1994. "Why National Review is Wrong: Value Added." *National Review* 46(21) (November 7): 56–58.

Vergara, Vanessa B.M. 1997. "Broken Promises and Aging Patriots: An Assessment of U.S. Veteran Benefits for Filipino World War II Veterans." *Asian American Policy Review* 7: 163–82.

Wei, William. 1993. *The Asian American Movement*. Philadelphia: Temple University Press.

# 3.15

# Transcending the
# Bamboo and Glass Ceilings
## Defining the Trajectory to Empower Asian
## Pacific Islander American Women in Politics

*Elena Ong*

〰〰〰〰〰〰〰〰〰〰〰〰〰〰〰〰〰〰〰〰〰〰〰〰〰

## THE STATUS OF WOMEN'S AND ASIAN PACIFIC ISLANDER AMERICAN'S POLITICAL EMPOWERMENT: THE HISTORY OF POLITICAL DISENFRANCHISEMENT AND POLITICAL EMPOWERMENT

The right to citizenship and the right to vote are fundamental rites of passage in our democracy. Unfortunately, when this nation was founded in 1776, Native Americans, African Americans, women, Latinos, and Asian Pacific Islander Americans did not have the same voting rights as white males. Over the course of history, these populations were politically disenfranchised, and it took amending the U.S. Constitution and enacting the Voting Rights Act to rectify these wrongs. As a consequence, these populations, particularly Asian Pacific Islander women and men, have not yet achieved their full promise of political empowerment and political leadership.

### The Political Disenfranchisement of Women and Women of Color

In 1776, our nation's Declaration of Independence proclaimed that "all men" were created equal and that "all men" were endowed with certain inalienable rights—life, liberty, and the pursuit of happiness. To secure these rights, governments were instituted among "men," deriving their just powers from the consent of the governed.[1] In 1787, our nation's U.S. Constitution defined what "all men" referred to, counting "free men" as a whole person, "slaves" as two-thirds a person, and "women" and "Chinese" not at all.[2] In 1870, eighty-three years after the U.S. Constitution was first signed, the Fifteenth Amendment granted suffrage to men of any race, color, or previous condition of servitude.[3] It was not until 1920, fifty years after African American, Native American, and Latino men were granted the right to vote, and 133 years after the U.S. Constitution was first signed, that the Nineteenth Amendment was signed, granting women, regardless of race or ethnic origin, the right to vote. Indeed, women might as well have

Ong, Elena. "Transcending the Bamboo and Glass Ceilings—Defining the Trajectory to Empower Asian Pacific Islander American Women in Politics." In *2001–02 National Asian Pacific American Political Almanac* (Los Angeles: UCLA Asian American Studies Center Press, 2001), 96–129. Reprinted with permission.

been considered "noncitizens" until this time.

## The Political Empowerment of Women and Women of Color

Even before women got the right to vote at the national level, they could run for elected office because they could still be voted into office by white males, who could vote.[4] The very first women to run for, and win, elected office (at the state level and above), got their political start in the Midwest. The first woman to run for the U.S. presidency, Victoria Clafin Woodhull (Equal Rights Party-OH), did so in 1872. While there have been twenty candidates since then, a female has yet to be elected U.S. president.[5] In 1894, twenty-six years before women were granted the right to national suffrage, the first women in the nation to ever be elected to the lower house of a State Legislature were from Colorado: Clara Cressingham (R), Carrie Holly (R), and Frances Klock (R).[6] Two years later, in 1896, Martha Hughes Cannon (D-UT) became the first woman in the nation elected to the upper house of a state legislature. Twenty years later, in 1916, and four years before the passage of Title 19, Jeanette Rankin (MT) became the first woman in the nation to be elected to the U.S. Congress. Then came the Roaring Twenties: three years after the passage of Title 19, in 1923, Soledad Chacon (NM) became the first woman, and the first Latina, in the nation to be elected to a statewide office.[7] Then in 1924, the next woman of color, Cora Belle Reynolds Anderson (MI), was the first Native American woman in the nation to be elected to the lower house of a state Legislature.[8] In 1925, Nellie Tayloe Ross (WY) became the first woman governor. In 1934, Hattie Caraway (AK) became the first woman U.S. senator and Matilda Wilson (MI) became the first woman lieutenant governor in 1940.[9]

But the most important breakthrough to politically empower women of all colors started in 1964 and peaked again in the 1980s. In 1964, the U.S. Congress passed the triple crown of civil rights policies: the 1964 Civil Rights Act, the 1965 Voting Rights Act, and the 1965 Immigration Reform Act. The Civil Rights Movement and the 1964 Civil Rights Act enlightened Americans about the magnitude of discrimination and social injustice in their country. The Civil Rights Act was an effort to provide equal opportunity and rectify the historic discrimination experienced by women, persons of color, immigrants, and persons with limited English-speaking ability.

The legacy of the Civil Rights Movement is that it increased voter participation and turnout rate. Women got politicized, and since 1964 the number of female voters in every presidential election has exceeded the number of male voters.[10] Since 1964, women of color have been empowered to seek higher levels of education and workforce participation, factors that are strongly correlated to increased voter registration and turnout. Since 1984, the rate of voter registration and turnout has increased among women of color.[11] This increase could also be due to the 1965 Voting Rights Act and the 1965 Immigration Reform Act, but it could also be attributed to the fact that beginning in 1966, the nation began to see women of color get elected to higher office. Perhaps it will take another generation before women of color can recognize the power of their vote and demonstrate its strength at the ballot box.

The 1965 Voting Rights Act was an effort to protect the rights of racial and ethnic minorities to participate in the political process by requiring translation of ballot materials, an effort to strengthen minority voter participation and voter turnout, and an effort to strengthen minority representation in government.[12] The 1965 Immigration Reform Act also leveled the playing field for immigrants from Asia by abolishing restrictive national origin quotas and enabling Asian Pacific Islander American families to sponsor the immigration of family members, who, five or ten years later, could potentially be naturalized and become active Asian Pacific Islander American voters. As Asian Pacific Islander American families formed, they gave rise to a new generation of Asian Pacific Islander Americans who registered to vote and turned out to vote, in the 1980s and in decades to follow.[13]

Women have the potential to determine the outcome of any election because they compose at least 51 percent of all votes cast on election day. Moreover, there is a gender gap in politics, and given a choice women tend to vote for Democrats and female candidates. In the decades that followed, the cohesiveness of the women's vote, coupled with the breakthroughs made by women candidates in the dawn of the civil rights era, inspired women throughout the United States to run for political office, to break the glass ceiling at the state and federal levels.

When we look back at "herstory", the glass ceiling in politics prior to the Civil Rights Act was broken by white women (as far back as 1894), by Latina Soledad Chacon in 1923, by Native American Cora Belle Reynolds Anderson in 1924, by Hawaiian Rosalie Keliinoi in 1924, and by Japanese American Patsy Mink in 1956.[14]

But the real breakthroughs for women of color on the mainland did not take place until the 1960s, marked by passage of the Civil Rights Act and Voting Rights Act, and election of women of color to higher office. In 1966, Patsy Mink (HI) became the first Asian Pacific Islander American U.S. congresswoman and that same year, March Fong Eu (CA) became the first Asian Pacific Islander American assemblywoman to serve in the California legislature. In 1967, Ivy Baker Priest (CA) became the first female California constitutional officer, and Yvonne Burke (CA) became the first African American California state assemblywoman. In 1968, Shirley Chisholm (NY) became the first African American woman to serve in the U.S. Congress.[15]

In the 1970s, we witnessed the following breakthroughs. In 1973, Yvonne Burke (CA) became the first African American U.S. congresswoman from California; in 1975, March Fong Eu (CA) became the first Asian Pacific Islander American woman in the nation to serve as secretary of state; in 1975, Polly Baca (CO) became the first

Latina in the nation to serve in the lower house of a state legislature; in 1976, Rose Ann Vuich (CA) became the first California state senator; in 1978, Jean Sadako King (HI) became the first Asian Pacific Islander American woman lieutenant governor; in 1979, Diane Watson (CA) became the first African American woman in the nation to serve in the state senate; in 1979, Polly Baca (CO) became the first Latina in the nation to serve in the state senate.

In the 1980s, we witnessed the following breakthroughs. In 1983, Gloria Molina became the first Latina California assemblywoman; and in 1989, Elena Ros-Lehtinen (FL) became the first Latina U.S. congresswoman.

In the 1990s, and particularly in 1992, "the Year of the Woman," Carol Moseley-Braun (IL) became the first African American woman U.S. Senator and Dianne Feinstein (CA) became the first woman U.S. senator from California. In 1993, Lucille Roybal-Allard (CA) became the first Latina U.S. congresswoman from California; in 1995, Hilda Solis (CA) became the first Latina California state senator; and in 1998, Lynda Lovejoy (NM) became the first Native American woman in America to be elected to a statewide commissionership.[16]

As we embark on the new millennium, we need to credit the 2000 election as a record-breaking election that will fundamentally change the face and complexion of politics and policy decisions in decades to come. In terms of women's gains, 2000 eclipsed 1992, as the "Year of the Woman." In 2001, women will hold a record number of seats in the U.S. Senate (13, or 13 percent of the 100 U.S. Senate seats) and a record number of seats in the U.S. House of Representatives (59, or 13.6 percent of the 435 U.S. House seats). In 2001, women will hold 89, or 27.6 percent, of the 273 statewide elected offices, 394, or 19.9 percent, of the 1,984 state senate seats, and 1,269, or 23.3 percent, of the 5,440 state representative seats.[17]

Women of color also made significant headway because of the highly touted nature of "the ethnic vote" as 2000's "swing vote" and the fact that Americans have expressed greater confidence in electing women of color to higher office. Not only did the 2000 elections usher in the first Latina governor of Puerto Rico, Silda Calderon (PR), we start this millennium knowing that 19, or 26.4 percent, of the 72 women serving in the 107th Congress, will be women of color: 13 African Americans, 1 Caribbean American, 1 Asian Pacific Islander American, and 6 Latinas. We also start this millennium knowing that 5, or 5.6 percent, of the 89 women serving in statewide elective executive office are women of color. We also start this new millennium knowing that 265, or 15.9 percent, of the 1,663 women state legislators are women of color: 46 African American women state senators, 136 African American state representatives, 7 Asian Pacific Islander American women state senators, 12 Asian Pacific Islander American women state representatives, 18 Latina state senators, 36 Latina state representatives, one Native American woman state commissioner, and nine Native American women state representatives.[18]

Clearly, women have been making progress over the years, but even so, women have not yet attained proportional parity in elected office: 50 percent women, 50 percent men. Where women have made the most progress in closing the gap of proportional representation is in statewide elective office—rising from 11 percent women in 1979, to 28 percent women in 2001. Women have also made steady gains in the state legislatures, rising from 10 percent in 1979 to 22 percent in 2001. Women have been making exemplary gains in the U.S. Congress, rising from 3 percent women in 1979 to 14 percent in 2001.[19]

## A Future Trajectory for Women and Women of Color

As one develops the trajectory for women of color in politics, it seems as if a choice has to be made. Will the trajectory for women of color be gender first and race/ethnicity second? Or race/ethnicity first and gender second? Or a simultaneous trajectory of race and gender?

According to the U.S. Census projections for the year 2000, women compose 52 percent of the population at the national level.[20] In recognition of the fact that woman have not yet achieved proportional representation, the National Women's Political Caucus of California established a measurable objective of "50 percent men, 50 percent women in elected office by the year 2020."

According to the 2000 U.S. Census, Asian Pacific Islander Americans constitute the fourth largest minority group in the nation. The United States is now 69.2 percent non-Hispanic white, 12.5 percent African American, 12 percent Latino, 4.2 percent Asian Pacific Islander American, and 2.1 percent other. According to the 2000 U.S. Census, Asian Pacific Islander Americans constitute the third largest minority group in California: 46.7 percent non-Hispanic white, 31.2 percent Latino, 12.2 percent Asian Pacific Islander American, 7 percent African American, and 2.9 percent Other.[21]

While Asian Pacific Islander American political organizations have not yet codified an objective based on proportional representation, proportional representation based on the 2000 U.S. Census statistics would call for 4.2 percent Asian Pacific Islander Americans in federal elected offices in 2001 and 12.2 percent Asian Pacific Islander Americans in California elected offices in 2001. If gender were also taken into account, proportional representation would call for 2.1 percent Asian Pacific Islander American women in federal elected offices in 2001, and 6.1 percent Asian Pacific Islander American in California elected offices in 2001.

## The Political Disenfranchisement of Asian Pacific Islander Americans and Asian Pacific Islander American Women

America was founded as a land of immigrants, but not all immigrants were embraced equally.

The first Asian Pacific Islander American (Chinese) male arrived in the United States in 1785, just nine years after our nation's Declaration of Independence was signed. But it took another 158 years before Chinese men could exercise the right to vote.

The first Asian Pacific Islander American (Chinese) woman to arrive in the United States arrived in 1848, and the first civil marriage between two Asian Pacific Islander Americans (Chinese) in America took place on April 7, 1855. But it took another ninety-five years before Asian Pacific Islander American women could exercise the right to vote.

America has a history of discriminatory laws denying property rights, intermarriage, citizenship, and voting rights to Asian immigrants. As early as 1790, the Naturalization Act stated that only "free white men" could become U.S. citizens. While efforts were made to amend this act to include the Chinese, they were considered "aliens ineligible for citizenship." In 1870, the year the Fifteenth Amendment empowered men of all colors to vote, the Naturalization Act was amended to only extend citizenship to aliens of African ancestry.[22] As early as 1852, the state of Washington banned the Chinese from voting and enacted a Chinese poll tax in 1864.[23] As early as 1858, California law barred the entry of Chinese and Mongolians, and in 1878, *In re Ah Yup* rendered Chinese ineligible for naturalized citizenship[24]. In 1880, California misogyny laws prevented the Chinese from obtaining citizenship through marriage.[25] It was not until 1898, when *Wong Kim Ark v. U.S.* declared that U.S.-born Chinese could not be stripped of their citizenship,[26] and 1918, when World War I Asian servicemen were rewarded with the right to naturalize.

By then, Chinese Americans were already economically and politically disenfranchised. For more than sixty years, the 1882 Chinese Exclusion Act, the 1892 Geary Act, and the 1924 Johnson-Reed Act prevented the immigration of Chinese to America.[27] It was not until 1943, when America needed China's political alliance

during World War II, that U.S. Congress repealed all Chinese exclusion laws and granted the rights of naturalization and a small immigration quota to the Chinese.[28] The first act of political inclusion did not get codified until three years later, in 1946, when Wing F. Ong (AZ) became the first Asian Pacific Islander American in the nation to be elected to office (in the Arizona House of Representatives).[29] Two years later, the War Brides Act was amended to reward Chinese American veterans for defending the nation.[30]

Japanese Americans also experienced discrimination and political disenfranchisement in the U.S. mainland. In 1892, the Japanese in America were denied citizenship because they were neither Chinese nor black. In 1894, the U.S. Circuit Court in Massachusetts declared in *In re Saito* that Japanese were ineligible for naturalization.[31] In 1907, sentiment against Japanese workers heightened, and in 1907, the Gentleman's Agreement barred Japanese men from entry on the mainland, though it did allow Japanese women and their children to reunite with their families.[32] By 1922, *Takoa Ozawa v. U.S.* declared that Japanese were not eligible for naturalized citizenship, and the Cable Act declared that American female citizens would lose their citizenship if they married an alien ineligible for citizenship (a decision that was reversed in 1931).[33]

Fortunately, the politics of the mainland were miles apart from the politics of the territory and later state of Hawaii. In Hawaii, more than half of the population is of Asian Pacific Islander American descent, so as early as 1903, Prince Jonah Kuhio Kalanianaole (HI-territory) became the first Asian Pacific Islander American in the nation appointed to represent the territory of Hawaii in the U.S. House of Representatives.[34] In 1924, Rosalie Keliinoi (HI-territory) became the first Asian Pacific Islander American woman to serve in the lower house of the territory of Hawaii, and in 1943, Alice Kamokilaikaw (HI-territory) became the first Asian Pacific Islander American woman to serve in the upper house of the territory of Hawaii.[35] However, when

Pearl Harbor was attacked in 1941 and World War II was declared, Japanese Americans were perceived with distrust and were deprived of their property rights when they were sent to the concentration camps. In 1950, naturalization laws prohibited the Issei from voting.[36] It was not until 1952 that the McCarran-Walter Act granted the Japanese the right of naturalization and a small immigration quota.[37]

Asian Indian Americans also faced discrimination, and political disenfranchisement. In 1908, when Canada was denying Asian Indians entry, Asian Indians were driven out of Live Oak, California. In 1923, the U.S. denied citizenship to Asian Indians (U.S. vs. Bhagat Singh Thind).[38] It was only after World War II, in 1946, that the Luce-Celler Bill granted naturalization rights and small immigration quotas to Asian Indians.[39] Political empowerment came ten years later, in 1956, when Dalip Singh Saund became the first Asian Indian, and the first Asian Pacific Islander American on the mainland, to be elected to the U.S. House of Representatives.[40]

Filipino Americans experienced a more positive welcome, but that is not to say they avoided discrimination. In 1924, the National Origins Act, which excluded all Asian immigrants from entering the United States, had a special exemption for U.S. nationals from the Philippines.[41] Despite this open door, there was anti-Filipino sentiment. In 1928, Filipino farm workers were driven out of Yakima Valley, and in 1930, there was an anti-Filipino riot in Watsonville, California. In 1934, when the Tydings-McDuffie Act was implemented, Filipino immigration was reduced to fifty persons a year. In 1946, the Luce-Celler Bill granted naturalization rights and small immigration quotas to Filipinos.[42]

### The Political Empowerment of Asian Pacific Islander Americans and Asian Pacific Islander American Women

Given this backdrop of anti-Asian sentiment, denial of citizenship, and hence voting rights, it is understandable why Asian Pacific Islander American women were not as successful as white women and other women of color in running for public office. Many Asian Pacific Islander American men ran for office and were elected before the advent of the Civil Rights Act. Their platform issues had more to do with governance than civil rights. In contrast, Asian Pacific Islander American women, starting with Assemblymember Patsy Mink (HI), who experienced the discrimination of the concentration camps, had a clear civil rights, social, and education agenda.

Asian Pacific Islander American men got their political start in the West, first in the territory of Hawaii and later in Arizona, California, Washington, and Oregon. In 1903, Prince Jonah Kuhio Kalanianole (HI) was the first Asian Pacific Islander American in the nation appointed to the U.S. House of Representatives, representing the territory of Hawaii. In 1946, Wing F. Ong (AZ) became the first Asian Pacific Islander American, and the first Chinese, in the nation to be elected to the state legislature (Arizona House of Representatives). In 1956, Dalip Singh Saund (CA) became the first Asian Pacific Islander American, and the first Asian Indian, elected from the mainland to the U.S. House of Representatives. In 1959, Hiram Leong Fong (HI) became the first Asian Pacific Islander American, and the first Chinese, in the nation to be elected to the U.S. Senate.[43] In 1994, Ben Cateyano (HI) became the first Asian Pacific Islander American, and the first Filipino, to be elected governor.[44] In 1996, Gary Locke (WA) became the first Asian Pacific Islander American on the mainland to be elected governor.

Asian Pacific Islander American women also got their political start in the territory and state of Hawaii, and later California, Washington, and Oregon. In 1924, four years after the passage of Title 19, Rosalie Keliinoi (HI) became the first Asian Pacific Islander American woman in the nation to be elected to "State" Legislature, serving in the lower house of the territory of Hawaii. In 1943, Alice Kamokilaikaw (HI) became the first Asian Pacific Islander American woman in the nation to be elected to the upper house of a "state" legislature, serving as senator of the territory of Hawaii. However, it was not until 1956, thirty-five years after the passage of Title 19, that Patsy Mink (HI) became the first Asian Pacific Islander American woman in the nation to be elected to the lower house of a state legislature. She also became the first Asian Pacific Islander American woman in the nation to be elected to the upper house of the state legislature in 1962, and the first Asian Pacific Islander American woman in the nation to be elected to the U.S. House of Representatives. But the politics of the mainland are miles apart from the politics of Hawaii, and it was not until the Civil Rights Act of 1964 and the Voting Rights Act of 1965 that there was progress for Asian Pacific Islander American women, and other women of color, on the mainland. In 1966, two years after the Civil Rights Act was implemented, March Fong Eu (CA) became the first Asian Pacific Islander American woman in California to be elected to the California Assembly, and in 1974, the first Asian Pacific Islander American woman in the nation, to be elected to the position of secretary of state. In 1979, Jean Sadaka King (HI) became the first Asian Pacific Islander American woman in the nation to be elected lieutenant governor.[45]

*The true empowerment of Asian Pacific Islander American women in elected office should not be measured by political firsts but by a legacy of political succession.*

So far, only two Asian Pacific Islander American women have held the position of U.S. congresswoman, Patsy Mink (HI) (1965–1977; 1989–present) and Patricia Saiki (HI) (1989–1991), whose simultaneous election in 1989 made it a double-win victory for Asian Pacific Islander American women.[46] So far, only two Asian Pacific Islander American women have been elected to the position of lieutenant governor, Jean Sadaka King (HI-1978) and Mazie Hirano (HI-1994), both from Hawaii.[47] In 1966, March Fong Eu (CA) was first elected California assemblywoman, but it was not

until thirty-five years later, in 2000, that two Asian Pacific Islander American women were elected to the California Assembly: Wilma Chan (former Alameda County Board of Supervisors) and Carol Liu (former mayor of La Canada-Flintridge), whose concurrent election made it a double-win victory for Asian Pacific Islander American women in California.[48] When Judy Chu (former mayor and councilwoman of Monterey Park) had the opportunity to win the seat for the Forty-Ninth Assembly District in a special May 15, 2001, election, she became the triple-win victory for Asian Pacific Islander American women in California.[49]

## THE POLITICAL TRAJECTORY

As of April 2001, there were fifty-seven male Asian Pacific Islander American elected officials holding office at the state level and above.[50] That is two, or 2 percent, of all 100 U.S. Senate seats; three (plus two nonvoting delegates), or 0.7 percent, of the 435 U.S. House seats; and only fifty, or 0.6 percent, of 7,747 state-level seats. If the goal is proportional representation, we should be developing the next cohort of elected officials and encouraging exemplary Asian Pacific Islander American men leaders to run for, and win, six seats in the U.S. House of Representatives; and run for, and win, 113 seats in the state legislature/statewide offices. On the upside, there are Asian Pacific Islander American male elected officials developing their political expertise in Hawaii, California, Oregon, Washington, Colorado, Arizona, Minnesota, New Hampshire, New York, and Utah, who are poised to come up the political pipeline. On the downside, there are only eighty-six Asian Pacific Islander American male city mayors and county/city council members,[51] but not a sufficient stream to fill prospective vacancies. Clearly, more Asian Pacific Islander American men need to be encouraged to enter the political arena.

In contrast, there are only a third as many, twenty-one, Asian Pacific American women elected officials holding office at the state level and above. There is no U.S. Senator; only one Asian Pacific American woman in Congress, or 0.2 percent of the 435 U.S. House seats, and only 20, or 0.3 percent, of the 7,747 state-level seats. If the goal is proportional representation, we should be developing the next cohort of elected officials and encouraging exemplary Asian Pacific American women leaders to run for—and win—two U.S. Senate seats; to run for—and win—eight seats in the House of Representatives; and run for—and win— 143 seats in the state legislature and state offices. On the upside, there are many Asian Pacific American women developing their political expertise in Hawaii, California, Washington, Oregon, Maryland, Massachusetts, and New York who are poised to come up the political pipeline. On the downside, there are only twelve Asian Pacific American women city mayors and county and city council members in the local pipelines, not enough to stock the stream of prospective vacancies. Clearly, there needs to be an even greater emphasis on encouraging a larger number of Asian Pacific American women to enter the political arena.

In conclusion, there is a genuine need to politically empower Asian Pacific Islander American women and Asian Pacific Islander American men, but there needs to be an even greater emphasis on empowering Asian Pacific Islander American women.

There are three core components to the trajectory to empower Asian Pacific Islander American women: (1) *Empowering the voter base and delivering the Asian Pacific Islander American women's vote.* The trajectory to empower Asian Pacific Islander American women involves empowering the voter base by increasing literacy/educational attainment, workforce participation, citizenship, and voter registration, for these are the key correlates of increased voter participation/turnout. The trajectory also involves educating voters on the issues and the candidates, and leveraging, and delivering, the Asian Pacific

Islander American women's vote on specific issues and candidates.

(2) *Mentoring and empowering Asian Pacific Islander American women to run for, and win, elected office.* The trajectory to empower Asian Pacific Islander American women involves empowering Asian Pacific Islander American elected officials to transcend the bamboo and glass ceiling and run for, and win, elective offices not yet held by Asian Pacific Islander American woman and in the process become Asian Pacific Islander American female political firsts. It also involves encouraging Asian Pacific Islander American women leaders to get involved in politics, and mentoring new political talent to fill seats that will be vacated by officeholders who seek higher/other political office. It means taking the responsibility to mentor seconds, thirds, and fourths, because it is only in numbers, that Asian Pacific Islander Americans can exercise political clout and political presence.

(3) *Assuring a political infrastructure to support Asian Pacific Islander American women's political empowerment: redistricting/reapportionment, political action committees, and political parties.* The trajectory to empower Asian Pacific Islander American women to seek elected office involves far more than a desire to enter politics. It requires the support of a political party, networks of political support and mentorship, capital, a solid voting base, and the realignment of political infrastructure. The year 2001 is a special one in politics because political districts will be remapped. It will be particularly important to ensure that the lines do not disenfranchise and/or dilute the voice of minority communities and communities that have elected women to public office. It will be critical to take the high road to maximize the opportunity for social justice and draw the lines in a way that empowers one group without disempowering another group. The year 2001 means getting ready for the 2002 and 2004 elections and ensuring that there are political action committees in place to develop and support candidates to run for, and win,

elected office (i.e., Asian Pacific Islander American Women Elect 2002 and 2004 projects), and ensuring that there is concurrent support of political parties in partisan races. It also means making sure that women, who get locked out of Senate races, be groomed for alternate or higher office.

## Trajectory 1:
## Empowering the Voter Base

Asian Pacific Islander American women need to maximize political clout, through focused efforts to increase voter registration and turnout, and deliver the vote.

The right to vote is one of the most important rights of citizenship in a democratic country, yet a substantial number of U.S. citizens choose not to exercise this right. It is important to increase voter turnout by compelling people to get out to vote (i.e., their desire to vote against an initiative that is discriminatory; their desire to vote for a candidate who represents the voters' interests), mounting an effective voter registration drive, and mounting an effective GOTV mobilization that is focused on delivering the ethnic vote and the women's vote. When women vote, candidates of color tend to win; and when women vote, female candidates tend to win.

According to the U.S. Census 2000, Asian Pacific Islander Americans are the fastest growing population in America, and without question, issues concerning Asian Pacific Islander Americans, global defense, and the global economy will emerge in mainstream political circles in the coming year. But population growth, without strong political organization, does not necessarily translate into political clout. For example, in California, Asian Pacific Islander Americans compose 12.2 percent of the population, while African Americans compose 7 percent. African Americans have more political clout because they have a long history of discrimination that gave rise to civil rights organizations like the NAACP that have galvanized a strong and viable African American political power base. In addition, the majority of African Americans are citizens (which contrasts to Asian Pacific Islander Americans and Latinos), who are not only eligible to vote but are high propensity voters. More significantly, when African Americans vote, they deliver 90 percent of their vote to Democrats and specific social issues.

We know the power of the women's vote. Women can often determine the outcome of the election because women constitute the majority of voters. In 1998, more than half, 52.2 percent, of all citizens who were eligible to vote were women. Moreover, women have a higher rate of registration (68.4 percent) than men (65.7 percent), and they show up at the polls at a higher rate than men (45.7 percent versus 44.9 percent).[52]

Women of color also wield political power because they have a higher voting rate than their male counterparts. In 1998, the voting rate for non-Hispanic Asian Pacific American women was 33.4 percent (2.3 percentage points higher than APA men), compared to 33.7 percent for Hispanic women (1.8 percentage points higher than Hispanic men), 43.7 percent for non-Hispanic African American women (4.1 percentage points higher than non-Hispanic African American men), and 47.5 percent for non-Hispanic white women (0.2 percentage points higher than for non-Hispanic white men).[53] In other words, 52 percent of all voters are women, with 52 percent of the Latino vote cast by women, 54 percent of the Asian Pacific Islander American vote cast by women, and 58 percent of the African American vote cast by women.

*In contrast, the power of the Asian Pacific Islander American vote and Asian Pacific Islander American Women's vote is somewhat enigmatic.*

Asian Pacific Islander Americans and Asian Pacific Islander American women are valued because they are a rapidly growing, dynamic segment of the American political mainstream. In California, the Asian Pacific Islander American electorate doubled from 3 percent in 1992 to 6 percent in 1996. Part of this is because Asian Pacific

Islander Americans naturalize at a faster rate than Latinos: even though a high percentage of Asian Pacific Islander Americans are foreign-born, 76 percent of Asian Pacific Islander Americans are citizens, compared to 61 percent of Hispanics.[54] Nationwide, the number of Asian Pacific Islander Americans voting in congressional elections increased by 366,000, as the number of voters between 1994 and 1998 dropped by 2.6 million nationwide.[55] Even though Asian Pacific Islander Americans have a relatively lower voter registration rate, their voter turnout rate rivals that of Latinos. In 1998, non-Hispanic Asian Pacific Islander Americans had a voter registration rate of 49 percent, and a voter turnout rate of 33 percent. In contrast, Hispanics of all races had a registration rate of 55 percent but the same voter turnout rate as Asian Pacific Islander Americans, 33 percent. Non-Hispanic African Americans, on the other hand, have a high registration rate of 64 percent and a voter turnout of 42 percent, while non-Hispanic whites had a voter registration rate of 69 percent, and a voter turnout of 47 percent.[56]

Without question, Asian Pacific Islander Americans and Asian Pacific Islander American women are emerging populations, highly respected for their professional and educational credentials, their economic influence and global reach, and their higher per capita income that enables them to make sizable campaign contributions. However, instead of voting as a homogeneous bloc, Asian Pacific Islander Americans are politically heterogeneous, manifesting a disparate range of political loyalties. For example, Japanese Americans and Filipino Americans tend to vote Democratic, Vietnamese Americans lean Republican, and Korean Americans are split down the center. Chinese Americans, on the other hand, are more likely to check the "decline to state" category than align with a single political party.[57] Asian Pacific Islander Americans are also more challenging to court than the Latino vote. While many Asian Pacific Islander Americans have a strong command of the English language, limited English-speaking Asian Pacific Islander Americans need to have information translated in several languages, while Latinos need to have their information translated into one primary language.

In the 1998 and 2000 presidential elections, Asian Pacific Islander Americans and other minorities were being courted for their "ethnic" or "swing" vote. During that time, initiatives such as Vision 21, Chinese Americans United for Self-Empowerment (CAUSE), and Asian Pacific Islander Americans Vote (Asian Pacific Islander American Vote) countered the image that Asian Pacific Islander Americans were an uninfluential, unorganized political machine. These organizations increased the visibility of Asian Pacific Islander Americans as a political voice and an influential swing vote.

*Did Asian Pacific Islander Americans deliver the vote?*

The presidential exit polls of the 2000 election revealed that at the national level, Asian Pacific Islander Americans delivered 55 percent of their vote, women 54 percent, Latinos 62 percent, African Americans 90 percent, and whites 42 percent of their vote to the Democratic presidential candidate, Al Gore. In California, Asian Pacific Islander Americans delivered 48 percent of their vote, women 58 percent, Latinos 68 percent, African Americans 86 percent, and whites 47 percent of their vote to the Democratic candidate.[58]

## Trajectory 2: Transcending the Bamboo and Glass Ceiling

We need to empower Asian Pacific Islander American women to run for, and win, elected office. We need to empower Asian Pacific Islander American women officeholders to break the bamboo and glass ceilings and become political firsts and, at the same time, cultivate new talent to establish a legacy of future wins for Asian Pacific Islander American women.

We need to recognize the women of all colors who have broken the glass ceiling and become political firsts. Their courage, commitment, experience, and legacy lay the foundation for future wins. The following tables chronicle, at the national and California level, elected women firsts, as well as elected offices that have yet to be held by a woman. To transcend the glass and bamboo ceilings, Asian Pacific Islander American women should be collaborating with elected officials and political candidates of all colors to become political firsts and achieve these goals.

The trajectory should encourage women of all colors to ascend the path not yet taken and inspire women to rise to the challenge and become political firsts:

- Asian Pacific Islander American women should run for, and win, seats that no Asian Pacific Islander American woman has ever been elected to. We need to mentor, encourage, and finance Asian Pacific Islander American women to become the first Asian Pacific Islander American woman in the nation to ever be elected to the post of governor, U.S. senator, U.S. vice president, and U.S. president. In California, we need Asian Pacific Islander American women to run for the position of lieutenant governor, governor, U.S. representatives, U.S. senator, U.S. vice president, and U.S. president.
- Latinas should run for, and win, seats that no Latina has ever been elected to. We need to mentor, encourage, and finance Latinas to become the first Latina in the nation to ever be elected to the post of U.S. senator, U.S. vice president, and U.S. president. In California, we need Latinas to run for statewide office, lieutenant governor, governor, U.S. senator, U.S. vice president, and U.S. president.
- African American women should run for, and win, seats that no African American woman has ever been elected to. We need African American women to be elected to the position of U.S. vice president and U.S. president. In California, we need African American women to run for statewide office, lieutenant governor, governor, U.S. senator, U.S. vice

president, and U.S. president.

- Native American women should run for, and win, seats that no Native American woman has ever been elected to. We need Native American women to run for the position of state senator, lieutenant governor, governor, U.S. senator, U.S. vice president, and U.S. president. In California, we need Native American to run for all of the offices: state assembly, state senate, statewide office, lieutenant governor, governor, U.S. Congress, U.S. Senate, U.S. vice president, and U.S. president.

Women should run for, and win, the U.S. vice presidency and U.S. presidency. In the United States, twenty-one women have run for U.S. president and two women have run for U.S. vice president. To date, no woman has ever been elected to these positions. We need to cultivate the political talent, and strategically orchestrate the demand for a woman chief political executive.

At the same time, the trajectory should empower Asian Pacific Islander American women and Asian Pacific Islander American men to be become political firsts.

### 2001 and Beyond: Cultivating New Talent and Creating a Legacy of Future Wins

The November 2000 elections provided opportunity for new Asian Pacific Islander American political aspirants as well as Asian Pacific Islander American politicians seeking reelection or election to higher office.

At the national level, five Asian Pacific Islander American politicians sought reelection, and all won: Governor Gary Locke (D-WA), U.S. Senator Daniel Akaka (D-HI), U.S. Representative Patsy Mink (D-HI), U.S. Representative Robert Matsui (D-CA), and U.S. Representative David Wu (D-OR). On the other hand, five Asian Pacific Islander American men ran for U.S. representative, but only State Assemblymember Mike Honda (D-CA), who ran for a seat once held by former Asian Pacific Islander American

**Table 3.15a   Elected Women Firsts and Glass Ceilings to be Transcended in the United States**

| | First Woman | First African American Woman | First Asian Pacific American Woman | First Latina Woman | First Native American Woman |
|---|---|---|---|---|---|
| **State Legislature Lower House** | 1894 Colorado: Clara Cressingham Carrie Holly Frances Klock | 1967 California: Yvonne Burke | 1956 Hawaii: Patsy Mink | 1975 Colorado: Polly Baca | 1924 Michigan: Cora Belle Reynolds Anderson |
| **State Legislature Upper House** | 1896 Utah: Martha Cannon | 1979 California: Diane Watson | 1962 Hawaii: Patsy Mink | 1979 Colorado: Polly Baca | 0 |
| **Statewide Elected Office** | 1923 New Mexico: Soledad Chacon | 1993 Indiana: Pamela Carter | 1975 California: March Fong Eu | 1923 New Mexico: Soledad Chacon | 1998 New Mexico: Lynda Lovejoy Reg. Comm. |
| **Lt. Governor** | 1940 Michigan Matilda Wilson | 0 | 1978 Hawaii: Jean Sadaka King | 0 | 0 |
| **Governor** | 1925 Wyoming: Nellie Tayloe Ross | 0 | 0 | 2000 Puerto Rico: Silda Calderon | 0 |
| **U.S. Congress** | 1916 Montana: Jeanette Rankin | 1968 New York: Shirley Chisholm | 1966 Hawaii: Patsy Mink | 1989 Florida: Elena Ros-Lehtinen | 0 |
| **U.S. Senate** | 1932 Arkansas: Hattie Caraway | 1992 Illinois: Carol Moseley-Braun | 0 | 0 | 0 |

*Source:* Center for American Women in Politics, Unpublished Data 2001.

**Table 3.15b  Elected Women Firsts and Glass Ceilings to be Transcended in California**

| | First Woman | First African American Woman | First Asian Pacific American Woman | First Latina Woman | First Native American Woman |
|---|---|---|---|---|---|
| **State Legislature Lower House** | 1918: Esto Broughton Grace Dorris Elizabeth Hughes Anna Saylor | 1967: Yvonne Burke | 1966: March Fong Eu | 1982: Gloria Molina | 0 |
| **State Legislature Upper House** | 1976: Rose Ann Vuich | 1979: Diane Watson | 0 | 1995: Hilda Solis | 0 |
| **Statewide Office** | 1967: Ivy Baker Pries | 0 | 1975: March Fong Eu | 0 | 0 |
| **Lt. Governor** | 0 | 0 | 0 | 0 | 0 |
| **Governor** | 0 | 0 | 0 | 0 | 0 |
| **U.S. Congress** | 1922: Mae Ella Nolan | 1973: Yvonne Burke | 0 | 1993: Lucille Roybal | 0 |
| **U.S. Senate** | 1992: Dianne Feinstein | 0 | 0 | 0 | 0 |

*Source*: Center for American Women in Politics, Unpublished Data 2001.

Table 3.15c    Elected Asian Pacific American Firsts and Bamboo Ceilings to be Transcended in the United States

| | First Asian Pacific American Male Elected in the Nation | First Asian Pacific American Woman Elected in the Nation | First Asian Pacific American Male Elected in California | First Asian Pacific American Woman Elected in California |
|---|---|---|---|---|
| **State Legislature Lower House** | 1946 Arizona: Wing F. Ong | 1956 Hawaii: Patsy Mink | 1963 Alfred Song | 1966 March Fong Eu |
| **State Legislature Upper House** | Not Available | 1962 Hawaii: Patsy Mink | 1967: Alfred Song | 0 |
| **Statewide Elected Office** | Not Available | 1975 California: March Fong Eu, Secretary of State | 1991: Matt Fong, Board of Equalization | 1974 March Fong Eu, Secretary of State |
| **Lt. Governor** | Not Available | 1978: HI Jean Sadaka King | 0 | 0 |
| **Governor** | 1994 Hawaii: Ben Cateyano 1996 Washington: Gary Locke | 0 | 0 | 0 |
| **U.S. Congress** | 1968 California: Dalip Singh Saund | 1966 Hawaii: Patsy Mink | 1975: Norman Y. Mineta | 0 |
| **U.S. Senate** | 1959 Hawaii: Hiram Fong | 0 | 1977: S.I. Hayakawa | 0 |

Source:

Congressmember Norm Mineta, won. With this net gain of one House seat, Asian Pacific Islander Americans will hold 2 percent of U.S. Senate seats (2 of 100), 1.4 percent of House seats (6 of 435), and 2 percent of governorships in the 107th Congress. On the other hand, the situation is status quo for Asian Pacific Islander American women, who did not score any national wins. While one Asian Pacific Islander American woman from California ran, she did not win. The disappointing reality is that Asian Pacific Islander American women, who constitute 2.1 percent of the nation's population, will only compose 0.2 percent of House seats, no U.S. Senate seats, and no governorships in the 107th Congress.

At the state level, the November 2000 elections resulted in more opportunities for Asian Pacific Islander American women. There were twenty-five races for state legislature seats, involving ten APA women and fifteen Asian Pacific Islander American men. Among the females, there were five wins and five losses. Among the men, there were three wins and twelve losses. California is a state where there were significant breakthroughs for Asian Pacific Islander American women. Thirty-five years since the first Asian Pacific Islander American woman held the position of state assemblywoman, three Asian Pacific Islander American women ran for California State Assembly (one Republican, two Democrats), and the two Democratic women won.

In order to sustain a political presence of issues important to Asian Pacific Islander Americans and Asian Pacific Islander American women, we need to do more than develop political firsts; we need to establish a legacy of future wins by providing current officeholders with the opportunity to mentor and pass the torch to Asian Pacific Islander American women and men who are committed to social justice, economic equity, political equity, and reproductive rights up the political ladder. We need to encourage and mentor women and men of all colors to embrace the issues that are important to Asian Pacific Islander Americans and Asian Pacific Islander American women, and

empower them to take leadership on these issues while they are serving in elected office. Given the reality of term limits, current officeholders should be looking to groom successors and mentor new leaders who can build on this point of view.

After all, in 2001:

- Women hold only 14 percent of congressional, 28 percent of statewide elective, and 22 percent of state legislative seats. We are not at 50 percent:50 percent yet.
- Asian Pacific Islander American women hold 0 percent of U.S. Senate seats, 0.2 percent of House seats, and 0.3 percent of state legislative/statewide office seats. We are not at 2.1 percent:2.1 percent yet.
- Asian Pacific Islander American men hold 2 percent of U.S. Senate seats, 0.7 percent of U.S. House seats, and 0.6 percent of State legislative/statewide Office seats. We are not at 2.1 percent:2.1percent yet.
- Women hold only 17 percent of California State Constitutional Office seats, 25 percent of California State Senate seats, and 30 percent of California State Assembly seats. We are not at 50 percent:50 percent yet.
- Asian Pacific Islander American women hold 0 percent of California State Constitutional Office seats, 0 percent of California State Senate seats, and 2.5 percent of California State Assembly seats. We are not at 6.1 percent:6.1 percent yet.
- Asian Pacific Islander American men hold 17 percent of California State Constitutional Office seats, 0 percent of California State Senate seats, and 1.25 percent of California State Assembly seats. With the exception of the constitutional officer seats, we are not at 6.1 percent:6.1 percent yet.

## Trajectory 3:
## Ensuring an Infrastructure to Support Future Political Wins

To ensure that there can be a legacy of future political wins, there needs to be an infrastructure in place that will maximize political clout to support political wins.

Three components are critical to success:

1. Redistricting
2. Political action committees
3. Political mentorship/"wo"mentorship

*(1) Leveraging redistricting/reapportionment to maximize the opportunity for social justice and collaboration to prevent the disenfranchisement of minority communities/women's political representation.* In political terms, redistricting and reapportionment will take center stage in 2001. Redistricting will redraw the boundary lines of electoral districts, while reapportionment will allocate seats based on the results of the 2000 U.S. Census. At the national level, the number of congressional seats will remain fixed, but in California, there could be a net gain. Given the current balance of power in the U.S. House of Representatives, the reapportionment/redistricting process will be challenged from all sides because how the lines are drawn and the seats reallocated will ultimately determine which political party will control the U.S. House of Representatives in 2002 and in subsequent Congresses. State legislators will also challenge how congressional seats are redrawn because in this era of term limits, state legislators have a competing self-interest: how congressional boundaries are drawn could ultimately upset how the lines are drawn for the state senate seat they may aspire to.

The Voting Rights Act has been used to challenge redistricting that severely disenfranchised the voting strength of minority communities and prevented these communities from having political representation (e.g., in Los Angeles, a Korean community's stronghold had been divided into three political districts). In 1991, Mexican American Legal Defense and Educational Fund (MALDEF) advanced a redistricting proposal that ultimately provided an opportunity for a Latina and an African American woman to win seats on the Los Angeles County Board of Supervisors, formerly a bastion of political power that was composed only of white male incumbents.[59] Today, the Voting Rights Act no longer wields the same force. According to the National Association for the Advancement of Colored People (NAACP), the fear of a serious legal challenge is gone because in *Shaw v. Reno*, the U.S. Supreme Court ruled that race can be a factor, but not the only factor, in redistricting and reapportionment. Moreover, U.S. Census 2000 has ushered in a new way of defining race and ethnicity, which could have a long-term impact on redistricting and change the face and complexion of those holding or seeking elected office. As a result, the Asian Pacific American Legal Center, MALDEF, and the NAACP have joined forces to figure out how to draw lines that will empower one group without disempowering another group.[60] This form of political collaboration is a significant breakthrough because instead of succumbing to "divide and conquer" politics, it is a fundamental backbone for highly principled and highly valued "identity and unity" politics.

*(2) Ensuring the political infrastructure to maximize political clout and candidate financing through political action committees (PACs) which have bottom-line principles that address Asian Pacific Islander American women's issues.* The women's political movement has EMILY'S List, the National Women's Political Caucus, the National Organization for Women, Planned Parenthood, the Women's Campaign Fund, the Women's Political Committee, Hispanas Organized for Political Equality—PAC, Latina Lawyers PAC, the Los Angeles African American Women's PAC, and a host of other political action committees to raise money for pro-choice women who are running for elected office. While I have sought to find a parallel PAC that specifically develops Asian Pacific Islander American women candidates for political office, and/or supports candidates who champion Asian Pacific Islander American women's issues, I have not yet found a multijurisdictional PAC that is committed to assuring that candidates have a proven track record, and a

desire to champion: (1) issues related to gender, race/ethnicity, and cultural and linguistic competency in formation of public policy; (2) health issues: pro-choice, pro-environment, pro-safety (support freedom from domestic violence, and gun control); (3) educational and economic equity: Title IX, United Nations Convention to Eliminate All Forms of Discrimination Against Women (CEDAW), comparable worth, pay equity, and women entrepreneur's access to capital and contracting; and (4) political equity: a commitment to bring Asian Pacific Islander American women up the political ladder.

Asian Pacific Islander American women who would like to form a political action committee that addresses issues of concern to Asian Pacific Islander American women, have a few options:

- *Form an Asian Pacific Islander American women's PAC fashioned after HOPE—PAC or LA African American Women's PAC*

I would name this PAC "AWE," or Asian American Women for Equality. Such a PAC would actively identify Asian Pacific Islander American women to run for elected office, help them identify a political mentor, and help them identify the resources they need to wage an effective political campaign. The PAC could also engage in focused endorsement efforts, fund-raising efforts, and GOTV efforts to support their candidate's campaign. The advantage to having an ethnic women's PAC is that it will not lose sight of a core objective: the development of Asian Pacific Islander American women political candidates. Another advantage is that this PAC would have the autonomy to develop its own bottom-line principles, for example, (1) willingness to champion public policy issues addressing race/ethnicity, cultural competence, and linguistic sensitivity; (2) a commitment to address health access/equity (reproductive choice, domestic violence, portable and affordable health coverage, quality child care, quality adult day care, environmental

health); (3) a commitment to address educational and economic equity (Title IX, CEDAW, comparable worth, women's access to capital, etc.); and (4) a commitment to political equity (bring Asian Pacific Islander American women up the political ladder). The disadvantage to having an ethnic women's PAC is that without a commitment to "identity and unity" politics, it could inadvertently restrict who would be eligible to become a member, who would be eligible to be endorsed/to receive funds, who would be eligible to make a contribution, and who would be eligible/be available to give political mentorship. There would be less opportunity for ethnic or gender-based crossover appeal.

- *Form an Asian Pacific Islander American women elect program/PAC within an existing Women's PAC*

Such a PAC would fall under a women's PAC umbrella and actively identify Asian Pacific Islander American women who are interested in running for elected office, and help them identify the resources they need to wage an effective political campaign. The Asian Pacific Islander American woman candidate would be nominated for the umbrella organization's consideration and would be subject to any guidelines the umbrella organization would have regarding endorsement and bottom-line issues (reproductive choice, pay equity, domestic violence, etc.). If the Asian Pacific Islander American woman candidate is endorsed, the candidate will be eligible to receive PAC funds depending on the organization's allocation mechanism (executive decision, committee decision, or individual donor's choice). The advantage to this approach is that race/ethnicity and gender are coupled as a goal. Moreover, the candidate would have access to a more extensive network of women of all colors, all income levels, and all levels of political expertise that she could draw on for financial, volunteer, and political support. In addition, if other women candidates are running in the same race, the Asian Pacific Islander American woman candidate will be in a better situation to assess the risk of splitting the gender vote. The disadvantage to this approach is that unless there is a person assigned to actively recruit Asian Pacific Islander American women candidates for consideration, there may be less ability to generate the steady stream of candidates for the Asian Pacific Islander American women's political ladder.

- *Form an Asian Pacific Islander American women elect program within an existing Asian Pacific Islander American PAC*

Such a PAC would actively identify Asian Pacific Islander American women who are interested in running for elected office and help them identify the resources they need to wage an effective political campaign. The candidate would be nominated for the umbrella organization's consideration and would be subject to any guidelines the umbrella organization would have regarding endorsement and bottom-line issues (reproductive choice, pay equity, domestic violence, etc.). If the Asian Pacific Islander American woman candidate is endorsed, the candidate will be eligible to receive PAC funds depending on the organization's allocation mechanism (executive decision, committee decision, or individual donor's choice). The advantage to this approach is that gender and race/ethnicity are coupled as a goal. Moreover, the candidate would have a more extensive network of men and women to draw on for financial, volunteer, and political support. In addition, if other Asian Pacific Islander American candidates are running in the same race, the Asian Pacific Islander American woman candidate can assess the political risk of splitting the ethnic vote. The disadvantage to this approach is that some fundamental women's rights issues could get sublimated (e.g., reproductive choice and domestic violence).

- *Form a PAC that supports political candidates (regardless of race or gender) who champion Asian Pacific Islander American women's issues*

I would name this PAC the A List because it would actively identify candidates (regardless of race, ethnicity, or gender) who have a proven track record of, and are committed to, championing Asian Pacific Islander American women's issues while in elective office. Members, contributors, and endorsees could be of any race or gender. The advantage to this approach is that it places value on the issues and the candidate's integrity to address the issues. Instead of being perceived as a self-interest PAC (i.e., it's not fair that you endorse and/or fund only Asian Pacific Islander American women), the guiding principles would take precedent. The other advantage to this approach is that it does not preclude candidates because of their race/ethnicity/gender. After all, candidates do not have to be Asian Pacific Islander American women to champion issues for Asian Pacific Islander American women; as long as they are committed to the principles of social justice, they can be effective advocates for Asian Pacific Islander American women. The disadvantage to this approach is whether or not the PAC would be able to raise enough funds to support all of the candidates who are worthy of consideration. The other disadvantage is that it doesn't specifically seek to remedy a core problem—the dearth of Asian Pacific Islander American women in elected office.

- *Form a "Women's Caucus" within the state's political party structure or within the state legislature*

I would propose to your state's political party (i.e., state Democratic Party, state Republican Party) the idea of forming a Women's Caucus to cultivate, mentor, and provide financial and political support to women candidates, with a special focus on women of color. To some degree, the infrastructure for this already exists within the Women's Caucus of the Democratic Party, and the Wish List of the

Republican Party. Some of these organizations have also provided incentives to male elected officials who mentor female candidates. Another approach is to get members of the state legislature to form a Women's Legislative Caucus for the purpose of mentoring Asian Pacific American women for leadership roles within the state legislature.

*(3) Assuring political mentorship.* To address the question of political mentorship and inspire Asian Pacific Islander American women and men to enter politics, I interviewed the three Asian Pacific Islander American women who have been elected to the California State Legislature: March Fong Eu, Wilma Chan, and Carol Liu. I asked each of them three questions: (1) Who or what inspired, or compelled, you to run for elective office? What obstacles did you encounter and how did you overcome them? (2) What is your vision for California? For Asian Pacific Islander Americans? For Asian Pacific Islander American women? (3) Who are the Asian Pacific Islander American women coming up the political ladder, and what is your advice for Asian Pacific Islander American women considering a career in politics?

March Fong Eu is the first Asian Pacific Islander American woman in California to serve in the California Assembly, and the first Asian Pacific Islander American woman in the nation to serve as secretary of state. She will be running for secretary of state in 2002.

I was always interested in politics and public affairs, but it was my interest in my children's education that prompted me to run for elective office. Making sure that my children received a quality education was my top priority as a mother, and the best way to ensure that was to serve on the board of education where I lived. I ran and won. As president of the Alameda County Board of Education, I was heavily involved in legislative educa-

tion policy in Sacramento. Realizing the critical role that state government played in shaping education policy, I sought a state assembly seat, and won, and made education my priority. Education has remained at the top of my list for the eight years I served in the state legislature, along with consumer affairs and environmental issues.

My vision, the most important policy issue for my constituents, for Asian Pacific Islander Americans, and for Asian Pacific Islander American women is education, education, and education. For me, quality education is the key to success for every Californian, regardless of ethnicity or gender. It is the underlying priority, despite critical issues involving the state's infrastructure, power generation transmission, and traffic gridlock. As secretary of state, I will continue my fight to ensure that every Californian has the opportunity for the best education possible, regardless of ethnic background or economic status. After all, receiving a quality education is essential to breaking the barriers that I have long fought . . . the glass ceilings that keep women and minorities from achieving their fullest potential. I take great pride in having been a role model, opening the doors of opportunity through which so many women and Asian Americans have walked—and, I'm not done yet! Add older Californians to the list! I am looking to create a California where public officials are selected based on vision, experience, and expertise, and not gender, ethnicity, age, or any other irrelevant characteristic.

I believe that every person who has an interest in public affairs—to make a difference for this generation and the ones to follow—should be involved in politics. Such involvement may not be running for office, but it should involve participating in public dialogue as well as supporting worthy candidates who are running for office, or meritorious ones holding public office. Many people, and perhaps Asian Pacific Islander American women in particular, are handicapped by the limitations they impose on themselves . . . by setting their sights too low. I have always believed that we should reach for the stars . . . and the heavens beyond. Believe in yourself if you expect others to believe in you. That has always worked for me, and I know it will work for others who are considering a role in politics. It won't guarantee that you will win an election, but it will ensure you the satisfaction of living life to the fullest, come what may. After all, it's not how many times you fall down that is important—it is how many times you get up and try again!

State Assemblywoman Wilma Chan, former Oakland school board member and former member of the Alameda County Board of Supervisors:

My children attended public school in Oakland, which is how I first got involved, gaining firsthand knowledge of the issues parents and students were concerned about. I got involved in politics because of the issues. I got involved, not because of my children, but because of everyone's children—I wanted to ensure that every child had access to a quality education, had access to quality childcare, and had access to translated materials, as appropriate. I got involved because the Oakland School District was operating a state-subsidized child care center, which it thought of discontinuing when a violation was discovered. Concerned about the loss of accessible, quality child care for working parents, I worked with parents and the administration to remedy the problem, and work on to the development of a comprehensive and articulated child care program. I organized trips so parents could lobby in Sacramento for quality childcare and bilingual services.

That's when I realized that I should be running for the Oakland School Board. So in 1990, I ran, and won. Running had its challenges. There had never been an Asian Pacific Islander American or Asian Pacific Islander American woman on the school board, and I had to break the race barrier. I also ran against a slate of three candidates who all had the same consultant. As my first race, I was perceived as the underdog, and it was harder to raise money. But my main strength was my field operation—I had dedicated volunteers, people who were eager to phone bank, distribute mailers, and do the door-to-door groundwork. I campaigned, one person at a time, at speaking engagements, debates, and house parties, and I always stayed focused on the issues. I did not spend a lot of money on the media market, on TV, radio or slate cards. When I ran for the Alameda Board of Supervisors, my district was 60 percent white and 20 percent African American, and the Asian Pacific Islander American base was negligible. My strong suit is that I care about the same issues my constituents, women and families, care about. When I ran for school board, my district was 60 percent white, 10 percent African American, and 30 percent other. Women constituted 52 to 54 percent of the vote, and while the ethnic vote is important, only 5 to 6 percent of Asian Pacific Islander Americans are registered to vote in my district. On the other hand, Asian Pacific Islander Americans were a definite asset in terms of statewide fund-raising; and even though I am a Democrat, I got financial support from Asian Pacific Islander American Republicans.

My vision for California is "healthy kids, ready to learn." As a member of the Alameda County Board of Supervisors, I chaired the local Prop 10 Commission. I also chaired the Select Committee on Children's Health. My vision for educational readiness is broader and more comprehensive than the availability of pre-K childcare. I want parents and their children to have access to health coverage that includes prenatal care, mental care, dental care, physical care, hearing, auxiliary services. I want parents and their children to have the time to read and learn together, so that over the course of their developmental years, ages 0 to 7, children go to school ready to learn, and are already reading by third grade. I recognize that our population is aging rapidly, and that our working adults are members of a sandwich generation—so I want to assure that there are social and health programs and coverage for our seniors. I also want to improve economic development, and I want to address the quality of schools, academic performance, housing affordability, job proximity, and a reduction in freeway congestion and the commute to work.

My vision for Asian Pacific Islander Americans is the same as it is for all Californians, but health, elder care, education are at the top of the list. There is a misperception that Asian Pacific Islander Americans don't need anything, but the fact is there are lower-income Asian Pacific Islander Americans and upper-income Asian Pacific Islander Americans, and recent immigrants who need translation and social services, and assimilated citizens who might encounter the glass ceiling. Asian Pacific Islander Americans have unique issues that do not affect other populations in the same way, e.g., language access, immigration issues, and the glass ceiling, which is why it is so important for the API Legislative Caucus to take leadership on these issues, and educate other legislators to sponsor and support bills related to these issues. My vision for Asian Pacific Islander American women is the same as it is for all Californians, but Asian Pacific Islander American women have unique issues. Roughly 65 percent of the Asian Pacific Islander

American population is immigrant, and there is a major adjustment in family life—the Asian Pacific Islander American community often lives in two cultures, while learning to adapt to an American lifestyle and an American system of service access. There is also a predisposition to breast cancer, and a predisposition to domestic violence.

There are many Asian Pacific Islander American women who should run for higher office—rising stars like Monterey Park City Councilwoman Judy Chu, former San Francisco Supervisor Mabel Teng, and Anna Loo of the Fremont School Board. Ironically, today's Asian Pacific Islander American politicians probably had parents who discouraged them from pursuing a career in politics, encouraging them instead to pursue a safer occupation. For that reason, it is important for twenty-year-olds to have an opportunity to intern in a public office and gain exposure to the realities of elected office. My advice to those who may consider a career in politics is, have a reason for running, and don't do it for the glamour. You have to have a passion to change something, because it is tough to run, and your heart has to be in it. In life, you should pursue your passion, for that is your driving force for survival.

State Assemblymember Carol Liu and former mayor of La Canada Flintridge:

My mother inspired me to be actively involved in the community, by her example. Of course, you couldn't avoid politics on the Berkeley campus in the late '60s and early '70s. I have been involved in supporting favorite causes and candidates running for office for most of my adult life. But it wasn't until 1991 that I decided to run for office myself. After serving for several years in volunteer capacities in the public school system, on the PTA, and for the city, I announced my candidacy for La Canada Flintridge City Council. I was victorious in a race that had four candidates running for three seats. As a result, an incumbent was unseated. I served as mayor of the city in 1996, won an uncontested second term in 1997, and served as mayor again in 1999. The experience I gained and the relationships I established as a local elected official have been invaluable in preparing me for higher office.

My vision for California is to restore the public education system to be the model of excellence it was over thirty years ago when I was growing up and pursuing my education. I also see a place where diversity is not just tolerated but celebrated. I see a place where there is equality of access to education, health services, and economic advancement.

I am supporting Asian Pacific Islander American women running for the State Assembly (Judy Chu) and for election within the California Democratic Party (Alicia Wang). My advice to anyone seeking election to office is—assemble the best team you can to develop and carry out your strategy and communicate your message to the voters. Don't be afraid to ask for help. Your friends, your family, and your past supporters will be the foundation of your campaign. After that, make as many new friends as you can, meet your voters and the leaders from all segments of the communities you will represent. Listen well and commit yourself to representing all segments of the population, not just a selected few.

## CONCLUSION

As we embark on the new millennium, we need to consider our past, our present, and our future. In the past, Asian Pacific Islander American women have experienced discrimination and faced obstacles to running for political office. But instead of insurmountable obstacles, they should be viewed as leadership challenges. Past experiences should be used to ground Asian Pacific Islander American women candidates with the reality of the past and provide an opportunity to develop a vision for a different future.

I ran the numbers for you—numbers from the past, the present, and the future: Asian Pacific Islander Americans, and Asian Pacific Islander American women, are not there yet. So let's build and implement the trajectory. I provided a framework for discussion because our future, and our political destiny, is in our hands. So let's make the best of it. Let's continue the dialogue. Let's continue the mentorship. Let's continue to organize and finance our political potential. And let's run some Asian Pacific Islander American women who will win, and lead, while in elected office!

### NOTES

1. Declaration of Independence, July 4, 1776.

2. U.S. Constitution, proposed May 1787 and ratified between December 7, 1787, and May 29, 1790.

3. U.S. Constitution, Fifteenth Amendment, proposed February 27, 1869, by the Fortieth Congress and ratified on February 3, 1870.

4. Center for American Women in Politics, discussion with Gilda Morales, 2001.

5. Center for American Women in Politics, *Women Presidential Candidates and Vice Presidential Candidates Fact Sheet* (New Brunswick, N.J.: Eagleton Institute of Politics, Rutgers University, 1999).

6. Center for American Women in Politics, *Women in Elected Office: 2001 Fact Sheet* (New Brunswick, N.J.: Eagleton Institute of Politics, Rutgers University, 2001).

7. Center for American Women in Politics, Eagleton Institute of Politics, Rutgers University, unpublished data, 2001.

8. Center for American Women in Politics, unpublished data, 2001.

9. Center for American Women in Politics, unpublished data, 2001.

10. Center for American Women in Politics, *Sex Differences in Voter Turnout* (New

Brunswick, N.J.: Eagleton Institute of Politics, Rutgers University, 2000).

11. Jennifer Day and Avalaura Gaither, *Voting and Registration in the Election of November 1998,* U.S. Census Bureau, Current Population Reports, August 2000. P20-S23RV.

12. Levin Sy, Voting Rights Time Line, in the 1996 *National Asian Pacific American Political Almanac* (Los Angeles: UCLA Asian American Studies Center, 1996).

13. Larry Hajime Shinagawa, "The Impact of Immigration on the Demography of Asian Pacific Americans," in *The State of Asian Pacific America: A Public Policy Report, Reframing the Immigration Debate,* ed. Bill Ong Hing and Ronald Lee (Los Angeles: LEAP Asian Pacific American Public Policy Institute/UCLA Asian American Studies Center, 1996).

14. Center for American Women in Politics, unpublished data, 2001.

15. Center for American Women in Politics, unpublished data, 2001.

16. Center for American Women in Politics, unpublished data, 2001.

17. Center for American Women in Politics, unpublished data, 2001.

18. Center for American Women in Politics, *Women of Color in Elective Office: 2001 Fact Sheet* (New Brunswick, N.J.: Eagleton Institute of Politics, Rutgers University, 2001), updated with information from Leigh Ann Miyasoto, male/female tabulations, April 4, 2001, and information from the secretary of state with reference to special election of March 6, 2001.

19. Center for American Women in Politics, *Women in Elective Office: 2001 Fact Sheet.*

20. U.S. Census Bureau, *Mid-level Population Projections for U.S., 2000,* at http://census.us.gov.

21. Paul Ong et al., *Census 2000 Fact Sheet, March 29, 2001* (Los Angeles: UCLA School of Public Policy and Social Research/Ralph and Goldy Lewis Center for Regional Policy Studies, 2001).

22. Bill Ong Hing, *Making and Remaking Asian America through Immigration Policy, 1850–1990* (Stanford, Calif.: Stanford University Press, 1993), 38–44.

23. "Time Line of Asian American History," at www.geocities.com/Hollywood/Palace/2713/Time line-1600.html.

24. "Time Line of Asian American History."
25. "Time Line of Asian American History."
26. "Time Line of Asian American History."
27. "Time Line of Asian American History."
28. "Time Line of Asian American History."
29. "Time Line of Asian American History."
30. "Time Line of Asian American History."
31. "Time Line of Asian American History."
32. "Time Line of Asian American History."
33. "Time Line of Asian American History."
34. "Time Line of Asian American History."

35. Center for American Women in Politics, unpublished data, 2001.

36. Sucheng Chan, *Asian Americans: An Interpretive History* (Boston: Twayne, 1991).

37. "Time Line of Asian American History."
38. "Time Line of Asian American History."
39. "Time Line of Asian American History."
40. "Time Line of Asian American History."
41. "Time Line of Asian American History."
42. "Time Line of Asian American History."

43. Lorraine Tong, *Asian Pacific American Members and Delegates of the 58th–107th Congresses (1903–2003),* Congressional Research Service, 2001.

44. State of Hawaii, Web site for Governor Cateyano.

45. Center for American Women in Politics, *Hawaii Women in Elective Office: Historical Summary* (New Brunswick, N.J.: Eagleton Institute of Politics, Rutgers University, 2001).

46. Tong, *Asian Pacific American Members.*

47. Center for American Women in Politics, *Hawaii Women in Elective Office.*

48. State of California, Secretary of State, November 2000 election returns.

49. State of California, Secretary of State, candidates running for 49th Assembly District, May 15, 2001 special election.

50. Leigh Ann Miyasoto, Male/Female Tabulations, April 4, 2001.

51. Miyasoto, Male/Female Tabulations.

52. "Time Line of Asian American History."
53. "Time Line of Asian American History."

54. Kevin Coleman, Asian Pacific American Political Participation and Representation in Elective Office, April 13, 2000.

55. "Number of Asian and Pacific Islanders Casting Ballots Up Significantly," Census Bureau Study Says," *U.S. Department of Commerce News,* CB00-138, August 29, 2000.

56. "Number of Asian and Pacific Islanders."

57. "Asian American Vote Split among Democrats and Republicans," *Issues of Democracy,* October 2000. Special issue: "Guide to Election 2000," at www.usinfo.state.gov/journals/itdhr/1000/ijde/sc315.16.htm.

58. Voter News Service, presidential exit polls, November 7, 2000, at www.msnbc.com/m/d2k/g/polls.asp

59. E. Page Bucy, "Redistricting by Lawsuit," *California Journal,* January 1991.

60. A. G. Block, "Putting the Puzzle Pieces Together," *California Journal,* March 2001.

# 3.16

# Remarks at the Tenth Annual Conference of the Committee of 100

*Elaine L. Chao*

~~~~~~~~~~~~~~~~~~~~~~~~~~~~~~~~~~~~~~~~~~~~~~~~~~~

It is wonderful to see so many friends here this evening.

I am especially humbled to be invited to address all of you at the Tenth Annual Conference of the Committee of 100.

Ten years ago, who would have imagined that we would eventually see the appointment of not just one Asian-Pacific American to a presidential Cabinet, but two?

Who would have imagined that in ten years, I would have the privilege of recommending for nomination Shinae Chun, the first Asian Pacific American ever to head the Women's Bureau at the Department of Labor?

Throughout government and politics, Asian Pacific Americans are playing a more public and influential role than ever before.

And most of the credit for that goes to individuals and organization—such as this, Committee of 100—that had the courage to get involved.

Where we find ourselves today is the result of individuals and organizations that saw it as their *patriotic duty to the nation they love* to

enter the public arena, to serve, to speak out, to help make a difference for our country.

It didn't happen by chance. Many people, including many in this room, made significant sacrifices. Many took big risks. Some encountered barriers and discouragement. But none of us gave up—and today, our community is seeing the rewards of that perseverance.

It's an exciting time, not just to be an Asian Pacific American, but to be an American. The world is changing before our eyes.

The economy is changing, and despite the recent ups and downs in the market, I think that in the long-term, it's changing for the better.

Washington is changing. We have a new president, a new administration, and with that inevitably come a bracing sense of new possibilities.

Regardless of how you voted in the last election one campaign promise that President George W. Bush made that I think every American greeted with a sense of relief and gratitude was a pledge to change the tone in Washington.

I can say without qualification that President Bush is keeping his end of the bargain, and in so doing, he is encouraging others to do the same.

U.S. Secretary of Labor Elaine L. Chao. "Remarks at the 10th Annual Conference of the Committee of 100," April 26, 2001 (www.dol.gov/_sec/welcome.html). Reprinted with permission.

He has often said that we can disagree without being disagreeable. We can debate issues without attacking each other's motives or ethics. And in doing so, we establish the essential basis of trust upon which to seek common ground.

The president's focus on changing the tone is about a lot more than just restoring civility to public life, as worthy as that is. It is about renewing the effectiveness of our national government—paralyzed for too long by partisan bickering and mistrust.

And it is already starting to bear fruit. For example, we are no longer fighting about *whether* to cut taxes, but rather *how much* to cut taxes—and in fact, we're relatively close to agreement on that question, as well.

The old rhetoric of class warfare about "tax cuts for the rich" is giving way to a more reasonable debate about economic benefits and budget constraints.

People are also recognizing that the president's agenda is about a lot more than cutting taxes for taxes' sake.

He believes we should end the marriage tax penalty, because we ought to be encouraging families, rather then penalizing them.

He believes we should end the estate tax—also known as the "death tax"—because we ought to encourage people to save and build up their small businesses and family farms, instead of confiscating the fruit of their labors when they try to pass it on to the next generation.

And most fundamentally, the president believes the average American taxpayer deserves a break, because—as he has frequently emphasized to all of us who serve in his cabinet—it's their money, it's their paycheck, it's not ours to spend as we please.

The president knows that not everybody agrees with his point of view, but to him, that's all right.

The point of changing the tone is to have an honest discussion about those disagreements, so that we can ultimately find common ground.

As one past president once said, it's not about choosing between "left" and "right," it's about finding the *way up*—the *way forward* for America.

The same can be said about President Bush's bold plan to reform American education.

A lot of people have made the observation that our community, Asian Pacific Americans, cares especially about education.

I disagree—I think *everyone* cares about education, regardless of who they are.

Every child, every parent, every teacher, every employer, every community.

The only difference is that today, who you are can determine what kind of education you can get. And that's wrong.

President Bush wants to make sure that every child has the chance to get a high-quality education, regardless of who they are or where they live.

A week ago, our schools got a report card, called the National Assessment of Educational Progress. The news wasn't good.

We're in a national education recession—a recession that will inevitably spill over from out schoolrooms to the workrooms if we don't stop it.

In the past eight years, fourth grade reading skills have not improved even slightly: Only 32 percent of fourth-graders are currently proficient in reading. That leaves two-thirds of all fourth-graders lacking the most basic job skill there is.

President Bush has challenged America to reverse this deepening educational recession. To end social promotion in schools, to establish yearly testing of math and reading skills for younger students, and to create a system of accountability in public education, where we demand results in return for the funding we provide to schools.

Some will say we can't afford to make such drastic changes.

But I can tell you, from my vantage point as Secretary of Labor, that we can't afford not to make them.

In countless ways, both large and small, the twenty-first century economy is not the same one we grew up with. We are now in what is called an "information" economy, driven more by knowledge than by traditional activities like manufacturing.

This new economy presents extraordinary opportunities for those who are prepared to take advantage of them: thousands of good-paying, stimulating jobs—in relatively safe working conditions—with limitless potential for advancement.

That's the good news. The bad news is that many of these new jobs go begging because employers can't find the skilled workers to fill them. Meanwhile, thousands of workers desperately want to fill those jobs but need training to be able to do so.

Today's elementary school students are tomorrow's workforce—and we will not be able to sustain the economic growth we have seen this country over the last decade if we do not address the educational and workforce development challenges that confront us.

There's another issue I am very concerned about as Secretary of Labor: In the coming years, the "baby boomer" generation will begin to retire, causing our workforce to shrink. At the same time, the number of retirees drawing on entitlement programs like Social Security and Medicare will reach record heights.

If we don't prepare for this impending worker shortage, the economy, the federal budget, and taxpaying families will pay a huge price.

Labor cost will go through the roof, while payroll taxes will skyrocket to keep our federal retirement programs solvent.

The job that President Bush appointed me to do as his Secretary of Labor is to anticipate these changes and plan for them—to start closing the skills gap today, and find ways to alleviate labor shortages in the future.

To help accomplish this, I have created a new Office of the Twenty-First Century Workforce at the Department, to bring focus and drive to the mission.

And on June 20, we will hold a special Summit on the Twenty-First Century Workforce, where leaders from business, labor unions, government, and academia will address the structural changes that are affecting our workforce and our economy.

We want to find out how businesses are closing the skills gap in their own work-

place. We want to see how unions are identifying and training new groups of workers to meet our country's voracious demand for labor.

And we want to highlight the new pressures and expectations that today's workers have—and find ways to address them.

As I said earlier, it's an exciting time to be in Washington. There are great challenges—but with them come great opportunities to make a difference.

And more than ever before, the community that's represented in this room tonight has the chance to make an impact—to help our country at a promising moment in its history.

For that reason, I want to say to all of you that this is not the time to lose faith.

It's not the time to pull back or waver in our courage.

Many of you have shared your concerns with me over the recent international tensions—between our country and China—and how these tensions could create a backlash against Asian Pacific Americans here at home.

And in fact, there have been some recent instances where the loyalty and patriotism of Asian Pacific Americans has been called into question, even ridiculed.

At one time, the media could be counted on as a watchdog against these kinds of unfair characterizations. Yet sadly, the media has recently been equally complicit in promoting a false, harmful view of our community and our values.

But my purpose tonight is not to criticize or complain.

My reason for raising this is just to say: *Don't be afraid.*

It took great courage and commitment and patriotism to get where we are today, and it will take more of those qualities, in greater measure, to stay the course.

We are Americans. We pay our taxes here. We created jobs here. We raise our families here. This is our country. This is our home.

We are here because we know that America is fundamentally the most decent, tolerant, freedom-loving country in the world. It is a country whose best years always lie ahead.

This is our country. Our community, represented by the people in this room tonight, has the opportunity to make a difference, more than ever before, in building American's prosperity, strength, and peace.

Thank you.

# 3.17

# The One-Hundred Year Journey
## From Houseboy to the Governor's Office

*Gary Locke*

〰〰〰〰〰〰〰〰〰〰〰〰〰〰〰〰〰〰〰〰〰〰〰〰〰〰

My topic today is really the one entitled "A One-Hundred Year Journey: From House-boy to the Governor's Mansion." And we want to talk about this one hundred-year period. I think it's appropriate that I talk to you about this journey because a very special element of this year's Organization of Chinese Americans (OCA) Conference has been to recognize our Asian American pioneers—in education, the sciences, the media, and public service. All of us are part of a long journey, each with its own special character, each begun with different pioneers, each following different paths and directions. But as we look ahead to what lies in front of us, we also see different futures and different destinies.

But if we look back on our Asian American heritage, we find that there is continuity, a kind of irony of fates and values, that really bind us all in our journey together. My family's journey actually started more than one hundred years ago with my great-grandfather, who was a trader, a merchant

Washington State Governor Gary Locke. "The One-Hundred Year Journey: From Houseboy to the Governor's Office." National Conference of the Organization of Chinese Americans, June 29, 1996. Reprinted with permission.

trader. My grandfather was born in China and then came to the United States in the late 1800s. And he actually worked in the State Capital as a houseboy, not far from where I served for eleven years as a state legislator.

He worked as a houseboy in the home of a Mrs. Yaeger. Mrs. Yaeger was very interested in Chinese and Japanese and Asian American immigrants and she took in a lot of Chinese immigrants to work as houseboys in her home. In exchange for work, she became my grandfather's English teacher, his mentor, and helped him with his writing skills. Mrs. Yaeger's house is no longer standing, but a couple years ago, while I was in the state legislature, I had an opportunity to drive by it—and I instantly recognized it from all the family photos that have been in our albums. My aunts and uncles say that they used to visit Mrs. Yaeger later on when she became elderly. They remember going up to the top floor of the house where they could see, about a mile away, the state capitol and what is now the governor's mansion. So it's really amazing that a hundred years later—if Mona and I are successful in our race for governor of the state of Washington—that we will live and start our family in that governor's mansion, just a mile away from where my grandfather started his life here in the United States.

One mile, one hundred years later; I guess you could say the Locke family moves a bit slowly! But eventually you get there. My grandfather learned a lot from Mrs. Yaeger and I think he adapted well to the opportunities and the challenges of living in America. He worked in the canneries and also worked in the logging camps, mostly as a laborer and as a cook. He eventually moved to Seattle where he worked in a variety of places, eventually becoming the head chef at one of the major hospitals in Seattle. And he and my grandmother had nine children.

My grandfather was strongly committed to education and believed that education was the foundation to success and the key to future of America.

He also cared a great deal about the people around him and the people of his community and throughout his lifetime. He and my grandmother were always extending a hand to other immigrants, to other Chinese Americans, as they came to the United States. My aunts and uncles remembered times in which they went without because my grandfather thought that others in the community needed more food than they did. And my father continued this tradition of hard work, commitment to community and family, as well as a love of education. I think that's something that all Chinese Americans really share—the values instilled by our parents of work, responsibility, and education.

Even though my grandfather lived in Olympia and then later lived in Seattle, my father was born in China. Like so many Chinese Americans, my grandfather went back and forth from China to the United States to bring his money back home and have a family. My father was born in Canton, China, in the Puisan Villages. He came to the United States when he was a teenager, lived here during the Depression, went to high school and learned English, and served in the U.S. Army as part of the Normandy Bay Invasion in World War II. He, like hundreds of thousands of children and grandchildren of immigrants, answered the call of duty of our great country in its time of world crisis when freedom and democracy were in jeopardy. After the war was over, he met my mother, who was born in Hong Kong, and they married. All five children were born in the state of Washington, in the Seattle area. For the first few years, we lived in the public housing that was available for returning servicemen and low-income individuals. My father, like his father, became a cook and had a restaurant for many years, after which he decided to go into the grocery business, working seven days a week, including Christmas and holidays, twelve to fourteen hours a day. All of us kids worked first in the restaurants and then later in the grocery store where we did our homework in between serving customers or waiting on tables. I remember so much about how our lives were defined by homework, doing the math tables that our mom and dad wrote out for us at the kitchen table, and then helping our parents at work.

Even though I was born in the United States, I didn't learn English until I went to kindergarten, about the same time that my mom was learning English to become a U.S. citizen. Thanks to government loans, government-backed loans, I was able to get scholarships and loans to go to college at Yale University, and then also to get a law degree from Boston University. One of my first jobs out of law school was as a county prosecutor, prosecuting people for murder, rape, robbery, and assault. It was tough and challenging work but something that gave me an opportunity to help those who had been victimized by crime. My father was actually once a victim of crime. He was almost killed in a grocery store robbery and, thanks to the safety net of government programs (because we had no health insurance), he was able to survive both physically and economically.

I believe that each of us is defined by our background and our family experiences. And my background, and my family's experiences, have emphasized the meaning of values like hard work, education, the family, the meaning of personal responsibility, and that government can only provide an opportunity but cannot guarantee us success. It can only give us those opportunities and serve as a safety net.

In many ways, my family drove me to do more for my community. And that's why I ran for the state legislature of Washington in 1982. I ran as a Democrat against the Democrat incumbent and while people said, "There's no way, Gary, that you could win the Democratic nomination because there are three of you challenging this incumbent. And the incumbent is always guaranteed at least 35 percent of the vote, and so the rest of you challengers, the three challengers, are gonna split up the remaining 65 percentage points. And then if you divide it up evenly, you get about 22 to 23 percent of the vote and the incumbent automatically wins." But, thanks to so many people in the community, the Asian community and others, we had a small army of people who helped ring doorbells and put up yard signs and go door-to-door. I won the primary with 53 percent of the vote. Because it was a solidly Democratic district, it was pretty much a shoe-in for the Democrat to win in the general election. I received about 85 percent of the vote in the general election. Starting then, I worked in the state legislature for eleven years. I guess those math tables came in handy because I became chairman of the Budget Committee and was responsible for deciding the state spending on behalf of the House of Representatives and negotiated with the Senate in helping to establish funding for the entire state of Washington.

I'm proud of the fact that as chairman of the Budget Committee, even though we had tough times, had to make cuts, and had to balance our budget, we were able to put more money toward and emphasize education. For me, education is the great equalizer of society. I believe that a quality education, regardless of your income, regardless of your ethic origin, regardless of your gender—and we are all with a quality education on a level plane here in the United States—is truly the key to opportunity here and across the world. And that's

why it is an absolute duty of the state of Washington—and all states across the country—to invest in education, to invest in our government, and to make sure they have the proper tools and the foundation to realize the opportunity that America stands for. And so we were able to put more money into schools with large minority populations and make sure that we funded bilingual education. We also took care of our colleges and universities, adding opportunities for enrollment and expanding financial aid for children of middle-class families.

We also worked very hard to reform welfare, even before it became a popular issue, spent a lot of time working with dysfunctional families, and made sure that we reformed our mental health systems and our programs for the developmentally disabled and for health care programs in the state of Washington.

After serving for eleven years in the state legislature, I ran for King County Executive. King County is on of the largest countries in the United States and contains one-third the population for the State of Washington. Even though we think of King County primarily as Seattle, it has a lot of farmland, timberland and forests, mines, and gravel pits. We have a great diversity of people. It includes the skyscrapers of Seattle and the rich agricultural lands of eastern King County. And I'm proud of the fact that as King County Executive, I've been able to work with corporations to reinvent government by downsizing it and making it more efficient. We've added more police officers, we've focused on technology, and we've consolidated two governments.

I actually inherited a mandate that is supposed to merge our King County government with our metropolitan government that would operate our transit system and sewage treatment plant. We downsized the government as a result of those consolidations, and we have moved King County forward by streamlining regulations and making it easier for people to operate and succeed within King County.

Now, of course, I'm running for governor. And the journey that was begun by my grandfather and all of our ancestors is not over. The advances that our ancestors have struggled to achieve are not over; they have not yet been fully realized. You know, we talked that discrimination had ended and that the battles of the Civil Rights Era had achieved equality, but now we find that there's a growing mood of hostility and resentment against people of color and people from other lands— particularly at Asian Americans. We're finding that educational opportunities are in jeopardy and that affirmative action is under assault—that there are now quotas for the admission of Asian Americans and Chinese Americans at colleges and universities. And, of course, the backlash against immigrants is revealing itself in immigration laws that penalize Asian immigrants or prevent our families from being united.

The gains that we felt have been achieved over the past several decades now are in jeopardy, and it requires vigilance by all Asian Americans and Chinese Americans and organizations such as the OCA to make sure that those hard fought gains have not been in vain.

In the policy-making circles of government, we, as Asian Americans, are clearly underrepresented. We have never made significant gains, and that is something that must be rectified. We deserve to be at the table making the laws that affect us, making the policies that affect us. If not us, who? If we look at the legacy of America, if we look at our history in the states, we are a land of immigrants. Particularly on the West Coast, Chinese and other Asian Americans have been contributing their blood, sweat, and tears in building up this great area, this great region. We worked like my grandfather; worked in the logging camps, worked in the canneries, in the farms and fields, provided the mercantile and the goods for developing settlers and pioneers. We served in world wars on behalf of this country. We are an integral part of the history of the United States and the state of California, the West Coast, and all the states across the country. It is clear that we deserve to be at

the table helping to influence the laws that affect us.

Don't you care about education? Don't you care about crime? Don't you care about immigration? Don't you care about violence against Asian Americans? Don't you care about job opportunities for our young people? And if we do care, we simply must be involved. And we need to have a stronger political force to make sure that things we care about are seen as no different than the issues that all of America care about. But we must make sure that the issues we care about are heard, represented, and addressed. We need to support Asian American candidates regardless of their party, whether they're running for school boards or governor or Congress. We need to be involved, and that's why there are organizations like OCA. We need to be working to encourage a new generation of political leaders to make sure that the issues that we care about are addressed.

As I said, I'm now running for governor of the state of Washington. And what does this mean to be the first Asian American— the first Chinese American—governor in the continental United States? Well, just as I've been inspired by the work of my family and the other political leaders who have preceded me, to be another pioneer in government will ensure that there will be a path for another generation of Asian American politicians. As governor, I will be able to elevate Asian Americans into political discussions on the issues affecting us—not only in America but in our contacts with Pacific Rim countries. I hope as governor to create a conduit where Asian Americans can contribute their multicultural expertise. I hope as governor to promote Asian American leadership as a working tool to form business relationships, not only for Washington but throughout the United States. I hope as governor to be able to promote a national environment for cultural and economic understanding, exchange, and thought. Most importantly, it will mean helping bring more Asian Americans to the table who influence those policies that we care about. If I'm successful in this challenge, it will only be with your help. It will be because of all those who preceded me in this one hundred-year journey. It will be because of all the sacrifices and hard work of those who have been part of that journey and all of you who assured that the achievements of the past one hundred years have not been in vain.

So the title of this conference is really correctly "You are making today's dream tomorrow's reality." All of you here as members of OCA are making today's dreams tomorrow's reality because you're laying the foundations, you're starting a journey for the next one hundred years for the future generation, you are making sure the hard-fought gains achieved in the last one hundred years will not be in vain, but will be continued. And I just want to thank you for your great work. Let us take time to respect our heritage. Let us take time to reflect on those contributions of all of our ancestors, but let us also be vigilant and committed to looking to the future in making sure that Asian Americans and Chinese Americans take their rightful place at the table of this great country of the United States of America.

Thank you very much.

# 3.18

# Remarks at the University of Rochester Annual Meliora Weekend

*Norman Y. Mineta*

〰〰〰〰〰〰〰〰〰〰〰〰〰〰〰〰〰〰〰〰〰〰〰

Thank you very, very much, President Jackson, for that wonderful introduction. It's a great honor for me to be here with all of you at this critical time in our nation's history.

I would like to thank President Jackson, Dean Bartlett, and the entire university staff for opening this weekend's events to the local community in order to foster a dialogue about freedom. And I would like to thank all of you for taking the time from your busy schedules to be here today.

As all of us know, this is a critical time in our nation's history. Just over one month ago, the United States was subjected to one of the most vicious attacks ever suffered in our history.

Thousands of innocent men and women, from across this nation and from around the world, were brutally murdered in New York City, Washington, D.C., and in Shanksville, Pennsylvania.

And in the space of just a few hours, more than 10,000 children lost one or both of their parents. On behalf of President Bush

U.S. Secretary of Transportation Norman Y. Mineta. "Remarks at the University of Rochester Annual Meliora Weekend." October 12, 2001 (www.dot.gov/affairs/mineta.html). Reprinted with permission.

and Vice President Cheney, I wish to express our deepest sympathies and condolences to those innocent victims of these cowardly attacks.

For the past month, our nation has struggled with how to respond to this outrage.

We have come together to support the families of those who were lost.

We have come together across the political spectrum to support the effort to rebuild the communities that were damaged.

And we have come together in determination to seek out those responsible for these attacks and to bring them to justice.

It has been said that times of crisis bring out the very best in any community, and in any nation. And that is certainly true of America today.

Many of my fellow Americans have been astonished to see our nation's political leadership set aside its partisan disputes and rally together to meet the challenge presented to us by the forces of terror.

As someone who has served in national government for most of the past three decades, including some twenty years in the U.S. Congress, I have to tell you that I was not at all surprised.

Our political leadership may have honest differences of opinion on some issues of public policy—but when our fundamental way of life is attacked, and the right of people to live their lives in safety and without fear, there is no disagreement.

Crises such as this boil down political and policy debates to the most fundamental issues—they bring a sharper focus to the question of who we are as a nation and to the core principles we embrace as a people.

In that sense, America is being tested today—as we have been tested every day since September 11. That test will not stop anytime soon, and how we respond will tell us much about ourselves as a country.

We have faced similar tests in our history, and frankly there have been times when we failed those tests. It will be up to all of us in the coming months and years to make sure that this does not happen again.

As you know, more than a few journalists and historians have taken to describing September 11 as the new Pearl Harbor. The analogy is a good one—once again, the United States has been attacked without warning and without mercy. The attack has awakened us to a danger our nation sometimes felt we would not have to face. And it also strengthened our resolve to face that danger—and remove it.

I think that all of you will understand that, as an American of Japanese ancestry, I find the analogy of Pearl Harbor to be particularly important. It highlights one of the greatest dangers that we will face as a country during this crisis—and that is the danger that in looking for the enemy we may strike out against our own friends and neighbors.

On Sunday morning, December 7, 1941, my family and I attended church at the Japanese Methodist Episcopal Church in my home town of San Jose, California. On our return home, we heard the news that our U.S. naval base at Pearl Harbor had been bombed by the military forces of the Empire of Japan.

As Americans, we were outraged by that attack. And we were fearful, as all Americans were fearful, of when the next attack might come and where it might fall.

But we had an additional cause for fear—because we knew that many of our fellow Americans would not distinguish between us and the pilots flying those planes that bombed Pearl Harbor that day.

Sadly, that fear turned out to be very, very real.

That same afternoon, agents of the Federal Bureau of Investigation began rounding up leaders in our community and shipped those people to Immigration and Naturalization Service detention centers. And in the weeks and months that followed, we saw our status as Americans slowly but surely called into question.

After months of racial scapegoating and fear-mongering on the West Coast and across the country, President Franklin Roosevelt signed Executive Order 9066. That Executive Order authorized the U.S. Army to exclude all persons of Japanese ancestry from the West Coast of the United States.

The army orders that followed applied even to infants of one-sixteenth Japanese ancestry.

When the signs were posted by the military announcing the orders that we were to be forced from our homes and relocated to internment camps across the country, they were addressed in a way that would have made George Orwell proud:

ATTENTION: ALIENS AND NON-ALIENS ALL THOSE OF JAPANESE ANCESTRY.

You may be wondering what a "non-alien" is. Well, a non-alien is me: a native born citizen of the United States of America. And when is the last time you proudly beat your chest, shouting "I am proud to be a non-alien of the United States"?

The Fifth Amendment to the Constitution guarantees that no American should be denied liberty or property without due process of law. But we were not acknowledged as "real" Americans—and the effects were tragic.

We had no trials. No charges were ever brought against us. But desite that fact, more than 120,000 Japanese Americans were forced from our homes in Western states and relocated to camps in desolate isolated locations across the country—placed behind barbed wire, with guard towers over thirty feet, under the watchful eyes of army personnel armed with machine guns.

They said we were in these camps for our own protection, but even as an eleven-year old, I wondered if we are here for our protection why are the machine guns pointed in at us and not out?

Some of us remained in those camps for the duration of World War II. And all of us were scarred by the experience of being rejected by our own country—deemed disloyal for no reason other than our race.

The internment of Japanese Americans during World War II has rightly been called the greatest mass abrogation of civil liberties in our nations's history—and I believe that it stands as a warning to all of us of how dangerous misguided fear can be.

As the events of September 11 unfolded just over a month ago, I know that I was far from alone among Japanese Americans in wondering how this nation would respond. And our greatest fear was that the backlash we had experienced would be visited on our Arab American, South Asian American, and Muslim neighbors.

In the years that followed our internment, we fought to build a recognition that what was done to us was wrong—that it was the result of wartime hysteria, and that it resulted from a tragic failure of political leadership.

And we fought to build a national commitment that nothing like the internment situation would ever happen in this country—to anyone—ever again.

It took us almost a half-century to win that commitment with the passage of the Civil Liberties Act of 1988—which formally apologized and offered redress to the victims of the internment.

We knew that the events of September 11 would represent a test of the commitment we had won. And we knew that the actions of our government and of men and women across the country would tell whether that commitment would be kept.

There was good reason to worry. Over the past month, we have heard reports across the country of Arab Americans, Muslim

Americans, and South Asian Americans being subjected to harassment and discrimination. We have heard reports of innocent men being murdered simply because their killers thought they looked like the enemy.

But the response of the overwhelming majority of Americans, and of our political leadership, has been very different.

I have often said that the day the Civil Liberties Act passed the House of Representatives—September 17, the 200th Anniversary of the signing of the Constitution of the United States—was one of the proudest days of my life.

Over the past month, I have added several more such days to my list.

Across the country, Americans from all walks of life have reached out to their Arab American and Muslim neighbors. Christians, Jews, and Buddhists have stepped forward to guard mosques and Muslim congregations, and to let their neighbors know that we value their membership in our American family.

Every act of violence and discrimination has been countered by multiple acts of friendship and respect—and a commitment that these dastardly terrorist acts will not be allowed to tear apart the American community.

That commitment has been echoed almost unanimously throughout the political leadership of this country—embraced by the leadership in the Congress, and in states and in local governments across the nation.

But there is one moment that will always stand out in my mind—and that was when the president of the United States, President George W. Bush, walked through the door of a mosque in Washington, D.C., to meet with Arab American and Muslim American leaders.

He told them that he understood who our enemy truly is—an isolated group of violent and cowardly extremists.

And he told them who our enemy most emphatically is not—the millions of loyal and honorable Arab and Muslim Americans who call this nation home, and the hundreds of millions of true followers of the Islamic faith around the world.

As an American of Japanese ancestry, and as someone who lived through the terrible events of 1941 and 1942, I could not help but wonder whether history might have been different—whether this nation could have avoided the tragedy of the internment if President Roosevelt had taken a similar step.

We can never know the answer to that question.

But we can resolve today, as Americans, that the tremendous progress we have made toward our goal of equal justice and equal opportunity for all Americans will not be sacrificed to fear.

We have built something in this country that has never before existed in the history of the world. We have built a nation on an idea—not on a race or religion or even a language.

We have built a nation on the idea that all men and women are of equal worth—and that each of us—wherever we come from, whatever language we speak, whatever religion we practice, or whatever nation our parents called home—are equally entitled to call ourselves Americans.

That idea is being tested today. Our political leadership has responded in the best way any of us could have hoped—by reaffirming the ideals of equality and respect that are the foundation of this great nation. And President Bush reiterated that commitment in last night's press conference.

Our civil rights laws that ban discrimination on the basis of race and religion are fully in force—and will be fully enforced. And our national policies will not be driven by, or tolerate, racial and religious scapegoating.

But government, and the actions of government in a democratic society ultimately responds to the beliefs and the actions of its citizens. So the story of how this nation responds to the attacks of September 11 will not be written in Washington, D.C. It will be written by you—and by men and women in neighborhoods, towns, and cities across the country.

The rights and the principles enshrined in the Constitution of this country are the most noble in the world. They represent a promise that we, as Americans, have made to each other. And those rights and those principles are only as strong as our commitment to them.

As an American of Japanese ancestry, I know that commitment can be broken. I have seen it happen.

The terrorists who committed the atrocities of September 11 hope they can shake that commitment. They believe they can use the forces of terror and fear to make us fail our most basic principles, and to break our most sacred promises to each other.

It is my greatest hope that, in the months and years ahead, all of us will join together as Americans to make sure they do not succeed.

Thank you very much.

# 3.19

# My Story
## Being American Means Setting Expectations High

### David Wu

~~~~~~~~~~~~~~~~~~~~~~~~~~~~~~~~~~~~~~~~~~~~~~~~~~~~~~~~~~~~~~~~~~~~~~~~~~

Thank you for being here this morning. I am honored to share the podium with our nation's foremost children's advocate—First Lady Hillary Rodham Clinton. Mrs. Clinton has brought children's issues to the forefront of the American consciousness. The Clinton Administration has more than doubled federal support for Head Start, and launched a historic child care initiative that will make childcare more affordable for working families, increased after-school programs, improved the quality and safety of childcare, and promoted early childhood learning.

I am here this morning to give you my personal commitment to ensuring that every child in America, not just the chosen few, has a fighting chance for a bright future.

Everyone in our nation agrees that our children are our most precious resource. In short, they are our future. Yet, why does our society place such a low priority on their education, and on supporting their parents?

U.S. Representative David Wu. "My Story: Being American Means Setting Expectations High." Remarks made on September 25, 1998, with Hillary Rodham Clinton. Reprinted with permission.

If we care so much about children, how can we allow so many to drift through school without acquiring the skills they need to survive in this world? Why do we allow so many bright young men and women to fall short of their promise because they cannot afford to go to college? How do we tolerate even one child dropping into a life of crime and drugs because they have no hope for the future?

Why is it okay that more and more parents stagnate in low-paying jobs with no benefits, no childcare, no training, and no room for advancement? And how is it that we can stand by as working parents are forced to choose between their job or resorting to substandard childcare?

Our society was built upon the idea that everybody—no matter what the circumstances of their birth—deserves a fair chance to do their very best. But we have a long road to travel before we can say that we are giving all of our children that opportunity. I am running for Congress because I believe that we can make the American dream a reality for all Americans.

No one believes in the American dream more than I do. I was born in Taiwan. When I was an infant, my father left for America to pursue an education. But the immigration

369

laws were not on our side. My sisters, my mother, and I had to stay behind. Over the course of almost seven years, our family lived apart while my father went to school, worked, saved, and waited.

Then, an election changed the course of my life and my family's history. When John Kennedy was elected in 1960, he tossed out the outdated immigration quotas that had separated our family. In October of 1961, our family was reunited in America. If anybody tries to tell you that public decisions do not make a difference—do not believe it. Because I had hard-working, loving parents who encouraged me and caring, motivated teachers who believed in me, I was able to learn English, make the most of my public school education, and go on to Stanford, Harvard, and Yale, to become an attorney, and now a Congressional hopeful.

The older I get, the more I understand just how lucky I am. Many of my grade school and high school classmates struggled to put food on the table—or worse. I cannot help but think that had they had the same kind of encouragement, support, and opportunities that I had, they would be closer to reaching their dreams, too. I will say it again: I am running for Congress because I have unshakable confidence in the American dream. I am committed to promoting anything that ensures that those who are willing to work hard, to persevere through adversity, and to play by the rules will be rewarded with the opportunity to succeed.

Opportunity begins at birth: every child deserves to be born wanted and loved. That is why I support policies that help people make good decisions about parenthood, like honest sex education and confidential family planning and full reproductive choice for all women.

I believe we can help all children get a good and fair start in life by increasing the support for Head Start programs. Head Start has a special place in my heart. My wife Michelle has been a Head Start teacher for seven years. Michelle's first-hand experiences have been an inspiration to me. Her stories of little girls and boys who start out

so behind that they cannot even begin to learn would melt any heart. Without Head Start, these children would start school at a grave disadvantage—a disadvantage that would deepen with each school year.

I believe all children deserve access to a good education in schools that have the resources to hire enough qualified teachers, to classes small enough so that they can receive individual attention, to classroom equipped with current technology, to school buildings that are safe and well-maintained, and to school grounds that are free from crime and drugs.

We can help families by making quality child care more available, making a college education more affordable, providing training for parents or adolescents who are unemployed or want to move up, ensuring that all full-time jobs pay a living wage, and making health insurance more available to all.

And I believe we all have the right to live in a safe, clean, healthy community that is free from the treat of unsafe drinking water or polluted air. A community that is free from unnecessary and burdensome government regulations.

My opponent in this race will accuse me of being soft on crime, weak in the war on drugs. Let me say this clearly: I do not just talk the talk on crime and drugs, I have also walked the walk. And, if my opponent is serious about crime and children, she will join me in calling for responsible gun ownership and ending the epidemic of children being killed with guns. I hunt, I fish, but I strongly advocate responsible gun ownership. People need to use trigger locks and gun safes. Those who leave loaded weapons within reach of children should be punished. And those who buy or sell illegal firearms should feel the full force of the law. Let us keep assault weapons out of our woods, off our streets, and away from our schools.

Schools should be safe havens, places full of hope and possibility. Places where children learn not only how to read and write, but to dream. One of the most important lessons I learned in public schools was that, with hard work and perseverance, truly anything is possible in America.

But nothing is possible without hope. If we want our children to succeed in life, avoid drug abuse, violence, crime, and poverty, we have to instill them with hope in the future. We have to build a society where every child has a fighting chance to not only survive but to find happiness, prosperity, and security.

I think about these things as the father of a fourteen-month-old son. I want our son Matthew to come of age in a society where everything is possible for those who are willing to work—and work hard—for their dreams. At his age, Matthew wakes up every morning expecting the best to happen. My most important job is to keep it that way.

I intend to work hard to fulfill those hopes and expectations for Matthew, for you, and for each and every child, parent, and adult—in Oregon and the nation. Because, for me, being American means setting your expectations high, and always aspiring to do better.

# Part IV

# Contemporary Public Policy
# Issues in the New Millennium

Bill Kochiyama at Redress Meeting. *Courtesy of Corky Lee*

## REPRESENTATIVE WU DENIED ENTRY INTO THE DEPARTMENT OF ENERGY

U.S. Representative David Wu (D-OR) was invited to speak at the Department of Energy's (DOE) Asian Pacific American Heritage Month program. When Representative Wu and his Legislative Director, another Chinese American, checked in at security, DOE security guards questioned their citizenship status and questioned the authenticity of the Congressional identification card. Wu is the only current Chinese American member of Congress (Organization of Chinese Americans, press release, May 29, 2001).

## LAOTIAN AMERICAN MAN MURDERED IN HATE CRIME

A Laotian American man was fatally attacked in a hate crime in Newmarket, New Hampshire, when a 35-year old white male attacked him in a parking lot. According to witnesses, the suspect attacked the victim without provocation during an anti-Asian tirade. The victim was mortally wounded when his head struck the pavement (Organization of Chinese Americans, press release, July 19, 2001).

The public policy challenges of the new millennium for Asian Pacific Americans represent some of the most contentious issues in American society. Part 4 examines policy issues ranging from the struggle for economic power (the national labor movement) to gaining greater political power (the 2001 redistricting process). Asian Pacific Americans have been at the center of these politically charged issues. While we realize other important policy issues exist, we choose these policy areas because they encapsulate a wide range of issues within contemporary Asian Pacific American politics.

Affirmative action is an issue on which Asian Pacific Americans have occupied a precarious position in the national debate between conservatives and liberals. In "The Affirmative Action Divide," Professor Paul Ong argues that current affirmative action policy must move away from the duality of the bipolar paradigm to a nuanced paradigm with Asian Pacific Americans occupying middle positions between blacks and whites. Ong addresses these challenges in various areas of affirmative action from admissions to public contracting.

Another national issue involving Asian Pacific Americans that gained national attention was the Japanese American redress and reparations movement. It began as a local movement that eventually culminated in President Ronald Reagan signing the Civil Liberties Act of 1988 on August 10, 1988, which provided an official national apology and reparation of $20,000 to each Japanese American incarcerated in a concentration camp during World War II. The Civil Liberties Act of 1988 represented the culmination of a social movement among Japanese Americans that began in 1970 and symbolized what some scholars have termed as achieving "the impossible dream" (Maki, Kitano, and Berthold 1999). Kitano and Maki provide an analysis of this movement in the chapter "Japanese American Redress: Proper Alignment Model."

February 19, A Day of Remembrance. *Courtesy of Mike Nakayama*

In contrast to the Japanese American redress and reparations movement, another national movement within the broader Asian Pacific American community has centered on group labor power and workers' rights. "Building an Asian Pacific American Labor Alliance," by Kent Wong, explores the 150-year role that Asian Pacific Americans have played in the U.S. labor movement in seeking justice and equality, and empowering workers. Wong traces this racial group's struggles for workers' rights culminating in the historical establishment of the Asian Pacific American Labor Alliance (APALA), which will likely play a key role in shaping future labor policy for Asian Pacific American workers. As Wong notes, the goals of APALA are similar to other racial minority struggles for economic justice and equality for workers, but various challenges remain.

Professor Edward T. Chang's article, "America's First Multiethnic 'Riots,'" addresses the black–Korean conflict within the context of the most destructive and expensive urban riot in U.S. history, the role of class inequality, and its implications for the Asian Pacific American movement. It provides a timely assessment of a potentially volatile issue in not only Los Angeles but also other large urban cities with multiracial populations.

Finally, the process of redistricting and reapportionment of local, state, and federal political district boundaries that occurs each decade is analyzed in Professor Leland T. Saito's article, "Asian Pacific Americans and Redistricting Challenges in 2001," within the context of Asian Pacific American politics. Saito discusses the impact of the 2001 redistricting process on the political empowerment of Asian Pacific Americans in relation to other minority groups. It provides a glimpse into a complicated political process that is likely to be a volatile issue among racial minority groups as they strive for increased representation and influence in various political districts across the nation.

### REFERENCE
Maki, Mitchell T., Harry H.L. Kitano, and S. Megan Berthold. *Achieving the Impossible Dream: How Japanese Americans Obtained Redress.* Urbana: University of Illinois Press, 1999.

Stop Deportations. *Courtesy of Mary Uyematsu Kao*

# 4.1

# The Affirmative Action Divide

*Paul M. Ong*

~~~~~~~~~~~~~~~~~~~~~~~~~~~~~~~~~~~~~~~~~~~~~~~~~~~~~~~~~~

Over the past decade affirmative action has emerged as the defining wedge issue on race,[1] and Asian Pacific Americans occupy a unique position in this heated political debate. Asian Pacific Americans are materially and ideologically on both sides of the political divide, with some adamantly supporting and other vehemently opposing the policy. Understanding the Asian Pacific American position is important for several reasons. The socioeconomic diversity of Asian Pacific Americans poses troubling questions regarding the underlying purpose and coverage of race-based programs. Just as the other chapters in this book demonstrate, Asian Pacific Americans do not fit easily into the prevailing black-white conceptualization of race, specifically in this case into remedial policies predicated largely on the black experience. Asian Pacific Americans remain significantly disadvantaged in some arenas, thus have a plausible claim for inclusion in group-based programs, but they are not disadvantaged in other arenas.

The socioeconomic status of Asian Pacific Americans points to a complex hierarchy rather than a simple dichotomous order. The simplicity of a black-white paradigm lies in the absolute and interlocking of the group ordering across disparate arenas, from education to work to capital accumulation. The inequality is so pervasive, glaring, and systematic that it is self-evident. In a simple bipolar structure, policies to correct racial inequality are simpler to design and implement, although still controversial with the disputes revolving around the specific causes and solutions. The status of Asian Pacific Americans moves us away from this duality to a more nuanced paradigm with Asian Pacific Americans occupying a middle position between blacks and whites. Even this ordinal depiction fails to capture the complexity. The material standing of Asian Pacific Americans varies significantly from one dimension to another so that the juxtaposition is not fixed. This inconsistency undermines the validity of the prevailing notion about racism. Rectifying the logical flaw is a necessary step to reconceptualizing race.

Ong, Paul M. "The Affirmative Action Divide." In *Transforming Race Relations*, Paul M. Ong, ed. (Los Angeles: LEAP Asian Pacific American Public Policy Institute and UCLA Asian American Studies Center, 2000), 313–61. Reprinted with permission.

The presence of Asian Pacific Americans has also complicated the political debate. In a few geographic locations, Asian Pacific Americans are sufficiently large enough to affect ballot outcomes; consequently, they are courted by proponents and opponents for votes. (For examples, see the chapter by Saito and Park in this book.) The importance of Asian Pacific Americans, however, extends well beyond narrow electoral politics. The ideological position held by Asian Pacific Americans is important symbolically. The affirmative action debate is about the extent of society's obligation to address racial inequality and about the mechanisms that ought to be used. As a minority group with a long history of racial victimization, but also one that has overcome many (albeit not all) racial barriers, the position taken by Asian Pacific Americans is powerful fodder for political polemics. Coming to grips with the Asian Pacific American political position, however, is not easy due to the heterogeneity of the population.

This chapter examines the unique position of Asian Pacific Americans, starting with an overview of the evolution of affirmative action, an important and divisive policy emerging from the Civil Rights Movement. Affirmative action is the contested boundary defining how aggressive government ought to be to redress racial inequality. Unlike the strong public and judicial support for anti-discrimination laws, support for race-based strategies to attenuate group disparity is ambiguous and conditional. The heated debate revolves around programs governing the internal operation of the public sector: government hiring and contracting, and admission to state-supported schools. The next section, "The Socioeconomic Status of Asian Pacific Americans," examines the material positions of Asian Pacific Americans in the three major arenas: education, employment, and business. The statistical evidence reveals a mixed picture of high achievement and under-representation. The variation in socioeconomic status translates to differences in the nature of Asian Pacific American participation in the major affirmative action programs, which is discussed in "The Affirmative Action—Asian Pacific American Nexus." The available information shows that Asian Pacific Americans bear the cost and reap the benefits. Because of this spread, Asian Pacific Americans have taken varying political positions within the affirmative action debate in pursuit of both self-interest and broader principles. The chapter concludes with a discussion on the challenges posed by Asian Pacific Americans for affirmative action.

## THE EVOLUTION OF AFFIRMATIVE ACTION

Affirmative action must be understood as a part of a political movement by blacks and their allies to fight racism and promote socioeconomic justice. The decades leading up to this policy were ones of historic changes. Starting with the integration of the military during World War II, the Civil Rights Movement went on to transform other parts of society, with much of the gains coming in the 1960s. State-supported segregation in public schools ended with the 1954 *Brown v. Board of Education* ruling. President Kennedy used executive power in 1961 to require federal contractors to end any discriminatory employment practices and to establish the Equal Employment Opportunity Commission (EEOC). Congress enacted the Civil Rights Act of 1964 to prohibit discrimination by privately owned facilities open to the public, by federally funded programs, and by both private and public employers. The 1965 Voting Rights Act added force behind the drive to protect the rights of minorities to participate in elections.

Presidents played key roles in setting the pace.[2] Despite campaign promises and inspiring public pronouncement, President Kennedy moved slowly and cautiously, shying away from fully utilizing his discretionary powers and delaying politically risky legislation. Lyndon B. Johnson's view evolved over his career, initially siding with segregationists as a congressman, then accepting the necessity of addressing civil rights issues as Senate Majority Leader, and later pressing for legislation as vice president. As president, he pushed his "Great Society" agenda to attack racial inequality. President Nixon proved enigmatic for initially supporting and then opposing key elements in the civil rights agenda, and his contradictory actions may be best understood as calculated political actions to weaken enemies and garner support.

The enactment of these laws was facilitated by a robust and growing economy, which minimized intergroup conflicts over resources. Paying for the cost of social change from an expanding economic pie enabled this nation to avoid the difficulty of reallocating in a zero-sum game. Even with a favorable economy, the Civil Rights Movement faced obstacles. Some white males, who were vested in the old racial order, fought to preserve the status quo, thus preserving their power and privileges. Opposition, however, was not just limited to overt racists. Most Americans found racial discrimination and prejudice objectionable, but were reluctant to accept the demands of the Civil Rights Movement.[3] The majority felt that the Civil Rights Movement was "moving too fast."

Despite only conditional support from whites, or because of it, the demand for change escalated as the social movement behind the Civil Rights Movement evolved. The initial struggles focused on integrating schools and public facilities, and voter registration drives in the South. Later, the efforts moved north. Despite measurable economic gains, particularly by better-educated minorities, black expectations rose faster than actual progress and fueled frustration. A growing impatience over slow progress, persistent and pervasive poverty, and the lack of economic opportunity gave rise to devastating urban unrest between 1964 to 1968.[4] Black protest shifted the demands from political rights and integration to economic rights, and the cutting edge of the movement moved from established nonviolent organizations to more militant ones espousing black nationalism and group rights.

Affirmative action evolved as a pragmatic and politically motivated strategy to combat racial (and later gender) inequality. During the early stage of the Civil Rights Movement, the dominant strategy centered on ending blatant racism. When the term "affirmative action" was introduced into policy in President Kennedy's 1961 Executive Order 10952, the proposed remedy was strictly anti-discrimination in nature, promoting hiring and terms of employment "without regard to race, creed, color, or national origin." President Johnson's 1965 Executive Order 11246 expanded the notion, requiring federal contractors to develop plans to increase the number of underrepresented minority workers. This expansion transformed the goal from equal opportunity to equal results, that is, to ensure "not just equality as a right and a theory, but equality as a fact and as a result."[5] Even after the Democrats lost the White House, affirmative action continued to gain teeth. The 1970 "Philadelphia Plan," devised during the Nixon administration, required federal contractors to establish hiring timetables and goals. Underutilization was defined as a lack of parity, when a firm employed a labor force that did not mirror the racial and gender composition of the larger labor force. Some private firms and universities also adopted this parity approach, but its application was most pronounced in the public sector, in government hiring and procurement, and admission to state colleges and universities.

The adoption of affirmative action, as a policy, pushed the envelope of what the government ought to do to address racial inequality. Anti-discrimination laws were designed to protect people against individual acts of discrimination, and their enforcement was predicated on responding after the fact. Unfortunately, this approach failed to address systemic and institutionalized factors that disadvantaged minorities as a group. In other words, racial inequality was maintained and reproduced through forces and structures beyond individual acts of discrimination. For many blacks and their supporters, attacking this problem required a radically different strategy operating at the group level. Programs, such as those associated with the "War on Poverty," targeted disadvantaged populations by channeling resources to impoverished neighborhoods, which were highly correlated with race. Affirmative action took an explicit approach by embracing race-conscious tactics, including the minority groups protected by voting rights and anti-discrimination laws.

Most affirmative action programs were not strictly a quota system, but the policy had certainly emerged as a race-based program. It required a redistribution of opportunities, although this often occurred at the margin. Such a reallocation was justified because the existing system of racial privileges was inherently unfair to the oppressed. Nonetheless, affirmative action required some segments to forego some opportunities, not a simple process even if the privileges were unwarranted. This shifting of opportunities, with real and perceived winners and losers, proved to be an extremely controversial policy, raising opposition from white males and also from former supporters of the Civil Rights Movement.[6]

Opponents of affirmative action seized on the policy's race-based nature to challenge its constitutionality, arguing that granting special status to any racial group violates the "due process of law" protected by the Fourteenth Amendment, and anti-discrimination clause of Title VII of the Civil Rights Act of 1964. Starting in 1970, affirmative action programs came under attack in the courts.[7] The first major setback came in 1978 in *Regents of the University of California v. Bakke*. In this case, the Supreme Court decided that the medical school at the University of California, Davis, through its affirmative action program, violated Title VI of the 1965 Civil Rights Act and the Fourteenth Amendment when it denied admission to Allan Bakke. The Court, however, left open the door for the use of race as one flexible factor in the

admissions process, with Justice Powell arguing that the state has a legitimate interest in promoting diversity in the student body. In the 1980s, the Court upheld the voluntary use of affirmative action programs, but it also ruled against preferential protection for minorities in layoffs and imposed a greater burden of proof to justify affirmative action.[8] Further restrictions came in the early 1990s in cases involving contract set-aside programs for minorities. Although the Supreme Court earlier had sanctioned the use of race-conscious contracting programs to remedy past societal discrimination, the Court started imposing the burden of "strict scrutiny" first on local and state governments and later on the federal government. By moving from intermediate to strict scrutiny, the Court imposed a higher standard before affirmative action can be justified. The government must demonstrate that past governmental action contributed to the specific inequality in question, that there is a compelling government interest, and that the program is narrowly tailored to solve only the problem in question. In the 1996 *Hopwood v. Texas*, the Court of Appeals for the Fifth Circuit placed similar limits on admissions programs in higher education, restricting the use of race only when it is necessary to remedy past discrimination by the school itself. Moreover, the court stated that promoting diversity is no longer a compelling state interest, thus making it more difficult to correct any racial imbalance in higher education. While the courts have not outlawed all forms of affirmative action, its application has been severely restricted.[9]

Affirmative action also came under attack from the executive branch. Presidential power proved to be a double-edged sword. Its use had been instrumental in establishing several civil rights policies, programs and agencies, but this approach exposed such actions to changing political winds. This was evident when President Reagan ushered in a neo-conservative era based on an ideology of smaller government, devolution, and supply-side economics.[10] Through selective appointments,

Republican administrations placed individuals opposed to affirmative action in the Civil Rights Division in the Department of Justice and the Department of Education, the U.S. Commission on Civil Rights, and the Equal Employment Opportunity Commission. These appointees in turn weakened affirmative action (and the enforcement of anti-discrimination employment and housing laws). A common theme was to move civil rights away from race-conscious policies to "color-blind" ones. The new mantra was that the government should never use race (or gender) for any public programs, even ones to remedy past discrimination. As anti-affirmative action efforts at the federal level waned with the Democrats recapturing the White House in 1992, the debate shifted to other arenas. In California, for example, Republican Governor Pete Wilson and his appointees on the Board of Regents of the University of California pushed through two resolutions in 1995 directing the university to end the use of race, religion, sex, color, ethnicity, or national origins in its admission process, contracting, and employment.

Opponents of affirmative action have made direct appeal to the voting public through referendums, some successful and others not. In 1996, the voters in California passed Proposition 209, the "Civil Rights Initiative," whose practical implication is to prohibit the state and local jurisdictions from using most affirmative action programs.[11] One year later, the voters in the City of Houston defeated Proposition A, which would have ended affirmative action.[12] In 1998, voters in Washington State passed Initiative 200, forcing the state and its local jurisdictions to stop using affirmative action.[13] Similar initiative and legislative efforts are being pursued in other states, including Colorado, Ohio, Michigan, Missouri, New Jersey, and Texas.[14] Some backers, such as those in Florida, have attempted to soften the impact of abandoning affirmative action with class-based programs designed to assist individuals from disadvantaged neighborhoods and schools, but those are not perfect substitutes.[15]

Despite the victories by opponents of race-conscious policies, the public has no decisive position. A reason for the mixed results on initiatives is that voters are neither totally for nor totally against affirmative action. Race-based policies create a conundrum over how far this nation ought to go to address racial inequality. Most people accept the fact that racial discrimination has not been eliminated, and many believe that something should be done.[16] At the same time, a growing number find that affirmative action goes too far by forcing white men to bear a burden to remedy a societal problem not of their making. In other words, there is support for anti-discrimination policies, but resistance to giving unjustified preferential treatment.[17] This does not mean that the government should not take an active role in eliminating racial inequality. A large majority support "increase recruitment" and a "sincere effort to hire" fully qualified blacks.[18] There is then a nuance in the support and opposition to affirmative action, and how people vote depends on how the debate is worded. This can be seen in a survey of Houston voters prior to the 1997 election.[19] A large majority would support a proposition stating "The City of Houston shall not discriminate against, or grant preferential treatment to, any individual or group on the basis of race, sex, ethnicity, or national origin in the operation of public employment and public contracting." On the other hand, less than a majority would support a proposition stating "Shall the Charter of the City of Houston be amended to end the use of affirmative action for women and minorities in the operation of City of Houston employment and contracting, including ending the current program and any similar programs in the future?" In the end, a majority of the voters opposed Proposition A, which stated "Shall the Charter of the City of Houston be amended to end the use of affirmative action?" If Houston's Proposition A had been worded differently, the outcome could have been different.

The debate over affirmative action has cooled, due in part to a robust economy that has eliminated fears of a zero-sum game, but the future of this policy is very much in the air. Race-based programs to correct racial inequality are not illegal, but the courts have severely limited their application. Political support has waned but not vanished. President Clinton has declared that affirmative action should be "mended, not ended," but this task does not appear to be a priority. The discussion on affirmative action in the report from the Advisory Board to the President's Initiative on Race is largely descriptive and noncommittal.[20] What we have currently is not a coherent policy, and perhaps there never was such a creature.

## THE SOCIOECONOMIC STATUS OF ASIAN PACIFIC AMERICANS

To understand how Asian Pacific Americans are situated within affirmative action programs, it is important to first establish the overall material position of Asian Pacific Americans in three arenas: education, the labor market, and business. Material position refers to measurable outcomes that define the relative standing of Asian Pacific Americans in the racial hierarchy

discussed earlier. This section provides a broad assessment, saving the discussion on the status of Asian Pacific Americans within the public sector to the next section, "The Affirmative Action—Asian Pacific American Nexus." The data indicate that Asian Pacific Americans fare better than other minority groups, and in some areas better than whites.[21] This is not the same, however, as an absence of problems. In education, Asian Pacific Americans are above parity relative to whites by traditional measures but suffer from restrictive quotas. In employment, Asian Pacific Americans are near parity but encounter barriers to selected occupations, particularly to management positions. Asian Pacific American businesses are below parity, experiencing difficulties competing in size and return. It is this dramatic variation in relative standing of Asian Pacific Americans across the three arenas that adds to the complexity of the racial hierarchy.

The one area where Asian Pacific Americans have experienced a high level of achievement is in education. This phenomenon starts early, as seen in the top panel of table 4.1a, which reports the racial/ethnic distribution of Californian schools ranked by performance on standardized tests.[22]

**Table 4.1a    Racial/Ethnic Composition of California Schools (1998)**

| Rank | Asian Pacific American | Black | White | Hispanic |
|---|---|---|---|---|
| Elementary schools | | | | |
| Top 10% | 17.0% | 3.1% | 67.8% | 9.0% |
| 75–90% | 11.5 | 5.2 | 60.8 | 17.9 |
| 50–75% | 7.8 | 8.5 | 48.0 | 30.4 |
| 25–50% | 6.4 | 12.0 | 25.7 | 51.2 |
| 10–25% | 4.9 | 11.9 | 8.5 | 72.2 |
| Bottom 10% | 3.7 | 11.1 | 5.2 | 78.4 |
| High schools | 10.4% | 8.3% | 40.1% | 36.6% |
| Top 10% | 17.8 | 2.8 | 67.8 | 9.0 |
| 75–90% | 9.7 | 3.5 | 67.4 | 15.3 |
| 50–75% | 9.0 | 5.4 | 57.4 | 22.6 |
| 25–50% | 8.6 | 9.2 | 40.0 | 36.8 |
| 10–25% | 8.5 | 10.4 | 17.2 | 58.9 |
| Bottom 10% | 3.6 | 14.4 | 20.1 | 57.1 |

*Source:* Compiled by author from data from California Department of Education.

The data clearly show that African Americans and Hispanics are disproportionately overrepresented in poorly performing elementary schools, and disproportionately underrepresented in highly ranked schools. The opposite is true for Asian Pacific Americans. While Asian Pacific Americans comprise 8 percent of all elementary students, they comprise 17 percent of those in schools in the top 10 percent but only 4 percent in schools in the bottom 10 percent. A similar pattern is apparent at the high-school level. African Americans and Hispanics are concentrated in the worst schools, while Asian Pacific Americans and whites are disproportionately enrolled in the best schools.

There are also racial differences in high-school dropout and completion rates as documented in table 4.1b.[23] Dropout rates were estimated from school enrollment status for those without high-school degrees and between the ages sixteen to nineteen. African American and Hispanic youths are disproportionately more likely not to dropout relative to whites, while Asian Pacific Americans are disproportionately more likely to be enrolled, although the white–Asian Pacific American difference is small. A large number of recent immigrants contributes to the high rate for Hispanics. To minimize this bias, a second set of estimates is made by excluding those who immigrated after the age of thirteen. Even among this restricted population, the dropout rate for Hispanics is the highest among the four racial groups. Of course, some of the dropouts may eventually earn a high school degree or GED. An alternative measure of high school dropout is the percent of young adults (twenty to twenty-four) without a high school degree. The statistics for this measure also show a parallel racial hierarchy, with blacks and Hispanics faring far worse than whites and Asian Pacific Americans. The pattern also holds after excluding those who immigrated after the age of thirteen.

Along with a high rate of completing high school, Asian Pacific Americans are better qualified to compete for entry into institutions of higher learning. This can be seen in the SAT scores, which are widely used by colleges and universities to evaluate applicants. Asian Pacific Americans do not perform as well as whites in the verbal section (1998 average score of 498 out of 800 versus 526), but they more than make up the difference on math (562 versus 528).[24] One of the reasons for the lower Asian Pacific American verbal score is that only 28 percent of the Asian Pacific American test-takers speak English as their sole language, compared to 94 percent of white test-takers.[25] In other words, a disproportionate number of Asian Pacific Americans do not have English as a first language. One can argue that SAT scores are not perfect predictors of performance as undergraduates and that the test is culturally biased, but colleges and universities do use the results in admissions. To the extent that these

**Table 4.1b    Drop-Out Statistics by Race /Ethnicity**

|  | Asian Pacific American | Black | White | Hispanic |
|---|---|---|---|---|
| All |  |  |  |  |
| Not in school, 16–19 | 6% | 15% | 10% | 26% |
| W/o high school degree, 20–24 | 7 | 18 | 8 | 37 |
| Excluding teenage immigrants |  |  |  |  |
| Not in School, 16–19 | 5% | 15% | 10% | 21% |
| W/o high school degree, 20–24 | 7 | 18 | 8 | 30 |

*Source:* Compiled by author from 1997, 1998, and 1999 Current Population Survey.

scores are weighted, Asian Pacific Americans are competitive by this criterion. The relative competitiveness of Asian Pacific Americans can also be seen in the 1996 data from the California Postsecondary Education Commission, which calculates the proportion of high school graduates fulfilling the minimum criteria for admission to the University of California.[26] The Asian Pacific American rate for 1996 (30 percent) is several times higher than that for African Americans (3 percent) and Hispanics (4 percent). More surprisingly, the Asian Pacific American rate is more than twice as high as the rate for white students (13 percent).

Several factors account for the educational achievements of Asian Pacific Americans. Culture values and parental beliefs in the centrality of education for success in this country provide a powerful push for children to succeed. Asian Pacific American achievement is also the product of lower residential segregation of Asian Pacific Americans than other minorities, which is discussed in the chapter by Hum and Zonta in this book. The College Board reports that 37 percent of Asian Pacific American students taking the college entrance examination are in suburbs, which is equal to whites and higher than blacks (22 percent) and Hispanics (25 percent).[27] This translates into Asian Pacific Americans being more likely to reside in better school districts and neighborhoods with the better schools. (At the same time, Asian Pacific Americans are more likely to be in large cities than whites, 37 percent versus 14 percent.) This spatial correlation may be influenced by self-selection, where the quality of education becomes relatively more important for Asian Pacific Americans in deciding residential location. This can be seen in the disproportionate number of Asian Pacific Americans moving to two of the best school districts in the Los Angeles metropolitan area, Cerritos and San Marino.

The accomplishments of Asian Pacific Americans at the high school level carry over to the college and university level. The rate of school enrollment for college-age students (between twenty and twenty-four years old) varies considerably by race: 36 percent for whites, 30 percent for blacks, 22 percent for Hispanics, and 55 percent for Asian Pacific Americans. (If the population excludes immigrants who entered the country after the age of 13, then the enrollment rate for Hispanics is slightly higher, 25 percent.) Asian Pacific Americans are not only attending colleges and universities at a disproportionately higher rate, but they also have a strong presence in the elite universities. This can be seen in table 4.1c, which lists the distribution of the undergraduate student body by ethnicity. The reported percentage for each ethnic group is based on "domestic" students, which does not include foreign students of that ethnic-

**Table 4.1c   1998 Fall Enrollment in Elite Universities by Race/Ethnicity**

|  | Asian Pacific American | White | Hispanic | Black |
|---|---|---|---|---|
| Private |  |  |  |  |
| Harvard | 19% | 46% | 8% | 9% |
| MIT | 28 | 46 | 10 | 6 |
| Stanford | 22 | 49 | 11 | 8 |
| Yale | 17 | 57 | 6 | 7 |
| Public |  |  |  |  |
| Berkeley | 39% | 30% | 11% | 5% |
| UCLA | 38 | 34 | 16 | 6 |
| Michigan | 11 | 71 | 4 | 9 |
| Virginia | 10 | 71 | 2 | 10 |

*Source:* Compiled by author from university web pages.

ity.[28] Among the top private universities listed, Asian Pacific Americans comprise 17 percent to 28 percent of the student population. The range for the top public universities is wider, from 10 percent to 39 percent, with the higher percentage in schools located in states with large concentrations of Asian Pacific Americans. By any reasonable measures, Asian Pacific Americans have had remarkable success in accessing higher education.

Despite the educational achievements of Asian Pacific Americans students, there are problems. There are still significant segments of Asian Pacific American youths who are struggling because they have a limited command of the English language.[29] This partly accounts for lower Asian Pacific American scores on the verbal parts of standardized tests relative to whites. The push for academic success comes with an emotional cost. The parental pressure to succeed creates tremendous anxiety among Asian Pacific American youths and contributes to intergenerational conflicts. Moreover, access to the elite institutions of higher education is not an unqualified success. Since the 1980s, many prestigious colleges and universities have been accused of reacting to the "overrepresentation" of Asian Pacific American by establishing ceilings, a maximum quota, on Asian Pacific American admission.[30] Audits of some elite schools discovered that the admissions rate for Asian Pacific American applicants was lower than that for white applicants, and among those admitted, Asian Pacific Americans had stronger academic qualifications than other groups. One statistical study found that with similar qualifications, Asian Pacific American had a lower probability of being admitted.[31] A lower admissions rate, by itself, is not *prima facie* evidence of discrimination. In some cases, admission processes used nonracial criteria beyond those based on standard academic performance, and these had a disproportionate impact on some groups. For example, private universities gave extra preferences to sons and daughters of alumni, who happened to be predominantly white. One

could argue that this policy merely reproduced the racial inequality of previous generations, but the universities countered that they have legitimate and nonracial reasons for these preferences. In other cases, the evidence pointed to a biased admission process and prejudicial admission officers.[32] Many schools that had such a potential problem have corrected both intended and unintended biases, but Asian Pacific America suspicion has not entirely disappeared. We will return to the quota issue in the next section of this chapter when the discussion focuses on public education.

In the labor market, Asian Pacific Americans have an advantage because of high educational attainment, but do not always receive the same remuneration or occupational status as whites. Table 4.1d reports the educational attainment of those in the prime-working age category, twenty-five to sixty-four years old. Among the four reported racial groups, Asian Pacific American have the highest proportion with four or more years of higher education. The relative difference is even greater for the category that includes advanced degrees (master's, professional degrees, and doctorates). The odds of an Asian Pacific American holding an advanced degree are more than one-and-half times greater than for whites, and four to five times greater than for African Americans and Hispanics. These higher Asian Pacific American rates of educational attainment are the product of two factors. The first is the phenomenon discussed above, that Asian Pacific Americans who are educated in the United States (both native-born and immigrants who come here as children or students) tend to complete more years of education. The second factor is that immigration laws since 1965 have favored those with higher education, particularly those in the professional, scientific, medical, and engineering fields. Moreover, the highly educated immigrant who initially entered through occupational preferences became a sponsor for highly-educated relatives for slots reserved for family reunification, thus adding to the supply of highly educated immigrants.[33]

**Table 4.1d   Education Attainment by Race, Ages 25–64**

|  | Non-Hispanic White | Black | Hispanic | Asian Pacific American |
|---|---|---|---|---|
| Less than high school | 9% | 18% | 42% | 13% |
| High school | 34 | 38 | 28 | 22 |
| Some college | 27 | 28 | 19 | 21 |
| Bachelor's | 20 | 11 | 8 | 29 |
| Advanced degree | 10 | 4 | 3 | 16 |

*Source:* Compiled by author from 1997–1999 Current Population Survey.

Despite the high level of education, Asian Pacific Americans have not been fully able to translate their credentials into commensurate earnings and occupational status. Table 4.1e contains basic statistics for full-time (thirty-five or more hours per week) and year-round (fifty or more weeks per year) workers between the ages twenty-five and sixty-four. Roughly three-quarters of the labor force for each racial group work full-time and year-round (77 percent for whites, 76 percent for blacks, 74 percent for Hispanics, and 77 percent for Asian Pacific Americans).[34] Despite the higher education attainment reported earlier, Asian Pacific Americans lag behind whites in remuneration. In terms of annual earnings, the median for Asian Pacific Americans is slightly lower than for white males ($33,200 versus $32,000). Another measure indicates that Asian Pacific Americans are doing marginally better, 23 percent of whites are among the top one-fifth of all earners compared to 24 percent for Asian Pacific Americans. However, this is surprisingly close given the considerable higher levels of education for Asian Pacific Ameri-cans. Another way of viewing the statistics is to consider what is required to win a place in the top tier: 61 percent of whites in this earnings group have at least a bachelor's degree, while 80 percent of Asian Pacific Americans do. Much of the difference is among those with advanced degrees, 26 percent for whites and 40 percent for Asian Pacific Americans.

The disparity in earnings is associated with the problems faced by Asian Pacific American immigrants, and highly-educated male immigrants in particular.[35] Among males with at least a bachelor's degree, recent Asian Pacific American immigrants earn about 22 percent less than U.S.-born whites, after accounting for differences in age and educational credentials. Assimilation as proxied by long-term residency in this country helps, but even established Asian Pacific American immigrants earn 7 percent less than U.S.-born whites. U.S.-born Asian Pacific American males, on the other hand, earn roughly the same amount as U.S.-born white males. Among females (that is, within gender analysis), the earnings show a different inter-group pattern.

**Table 4.1e   Employment Outcomes by Race, Full-Time, Year-Round Workers**

|  | White | Black | Hispanic | Asian Pacific American |
|---|---|---|---|---|
| Median earnings | $33.2k | $25.4k | $22.0k | $32.0k |
| In the top 20% | 23% | 10% | 9% | 24% |
| In management | 19 | 11 | 9 | 15 |
| In professions | 18 | 12 | 7 | 24 |

*Source:* Compiled by author from 1997–1999 Current Population Survey.

Recent Asian Pacific American immigrants earn 10 percent less than U.S.-born whites, and established Asian Pacific American immigrants reach parity with U.S.-born whites. Interestingly, U.S.-born Asian Pacific American females earn 7 percent more than U.S.-born white females. On the other hand, it is important to note that this "advantage" is far from closing the gender gap, for white females earn 27 percent less than white males. U.S.-born Asian Pacific American females close some of that gap, but their earnings are much closer to that of U.S.-born white females than to U.S.-born white males. In other words, the gender gap remains a dominant factor.

Some of the labor-market disadvantages experienced by Asian Pacific American male and female workers can be attributed to a "glass ceiling," a barrier preventing many from moving into higher management positions.[36] Although qualified and competent for higher management positions, many Asian Pacific Americans are stereotyped as nonassertive, inarticulate, and too technical. The glass ceiling is certainly a major concern within the Asian Pacific American community. A majority of the respondents to a survey of Asian Pacific Americans by *Asian Week* agreed with the statement "There exists a 'glass ceiling' such that many Asian Americans are unfairly prevented from reaching upper management positions in many companies."[37]

The lower probability of being a manager is centered around the highly educated immigrant population.[38] Among males with at least a bachelor's degree, recent Asian Pacific American immigrants have only half the odds of being in management compared with U.S.-born whites, after accounting for difference in age and credentials. Assimilation has no effect because established Asian Pacific American immigrants face the same low odds. The analysis shows that U.S.-born Asian Pacific American males have lower odds of moving into management than U.S.-born whites, but the estimate is not statistically significant because of the small sample size. Among highly educated females, recent Asian

Pacific American immigrants have only about half the chance as U.S.-born whites to being in management, controlling for other factors. Assimilation closes much, but not the entire gap. The odds for established Asian Pacific American immigrants approach that of U.S.-born whites, with the remaining difference being statistically insignificant. There is essentially no difference between U.S.-born whites and U.S.-born Asian Pacific American females. While Asian Pacific American females may be able to close the racial gap within their own gender, they still face the glass ceiling encountered by U.S.-born white females.

By limiting access to managerial position, the glass ceiling has a trickle-down effect on other occupations. An analysis of highly educated workers of both genders shows that U.S.-born Asian Pacific Americans, established immigrants, and recent immigrants have the same odds of being a professional as U.S.-born whites. Asian Pacific American males, regardless of subgroup, have higher odds of being in this occupational layer, indicating that overrepresentation in the professions absorbs the underrepresentation in management. In other words, there appears to be a glass ceiling that keeps them from moving from the professions into management. For females, this phenomenon is not present, a finding that points to the additional complexity imposed by a gender-related glass ceiling.

The lack of parity is most apparent for Asian Pacific Americans in the business world. While Asian Pacific Americans, and immigrants in particular, have a reputation of being entrepreneurs, the self-employment rate (including family members working for no pay) for Asian Pacific Americans is no higher than that for whites, and this is true even when comparing Asian Pacific American immigrants with white immigrants. Table 4.1f provides two sets of self-employment rates for the economically active population between the ages of twenty-five and sixty-four. The first estimate is based on whether the person reported his or her main class of employment as self-employed. According

**Table 4.1f    Self-Employment Outcomes by Race/Ethnicity**

|                                    | White   | Black   | Hispanic | Asian Pacific American |
| ---------------------------------- | ------- | ------- | -------- | ---------------------- |
| Median Earnings                    | $32.3k  | $24.9k  | $21.8k   | $30.4k                 |
| Self-employment (1)                | 13%     | 5%      | 7%       | 13%                    |
| Self-employment (2)                | 16      | 6       | 8        | 15                     |
| With at least a bachelor's degree  | 36      | 27      | 14       | 51                     |

*Source:* Compiled by author from 1997–1999 Current Population Survey.

to this measure, Asian Pacific Americans and whites have the same rate. The second set of estimates includes both the self-employed and those working for others, but also receiving some income from self-employment. The latter captures people who operate a business on the side. While the second estimate for whites is slightly higher than for Asian Pacific Americans, for practical purpose, the levels of self-employment are identical. On the other hand, the economic returns to self-employment are not identical. The data for those working year-round indicate that median total earnings for Asian Pacific Americans is lower than that for whites.[39] The economic disparity is even greater since self-employed Asian Pacific Americans have more years of schooling than whites.

Data from the most recent survey of the characteristics of business owners (1992) show a similar picture.[40] By two measures, Asian Pacific Americans are doing well. Among minorities, Asian Pacific Americans accounted for 31 percent of all firms and received 48 percent of all revenues. While Asian Pacific Americans were faring better than blacks and Hispanics, Asian Pacific Americans were not overrepresented among all owners. Asian Pacific Americans owned 3.5 percent of all businesses and received 2.9 percent of all revenues, which is slightly lower than the Asian Pacific Americans share of the total population (4 percent in 1998). The picture is even less rosy when compared with white owners. Average (mean) revenue for Asian Pacific American firms was only 64 percent of that for white firms. The average Asian Pacific Ameri-

can firm had fewer employees and paid lower wages per worker than white firms. Only 14 percent of white owners worked sixty or more hours a week, but 21 percent of Asian Pacific American owners did. Asian Pacific Americans had smaller markets, with 42 percent serving a neighborhood market compared to only 26 percent for whites. Moreover, 31 percent of Asian Pacific American firms serve a minority-dominated clientele, about four times the level for whites. These facts, along with those presented above, show that Asian Pacific Americans in business still lag far behind whites.

The above analysis of the socioeconomic status of Asian Pacific Americans demonstrates the complex position of Asian Pacific Americans in this nation's racial structure (see table 4.1g). The unique material position of Asian Pacific Americans poses three challenges to a bipolar racial model. The first is that the relative standing of Asian Pacific Americans varies across socioeconomic dimensions. The achievements (vis-à-vis whites and other minorities) in one arena are not replicated in other arenas. This can be seen in the extreme variation in the simplistic Asian Pacific American–white parity indices for education, employment, and business. The second challenge is that the nature of the disadvantages faced by Asian Pacific Americans is not absolute (lower achievements than whites), but relative to what they could achieve if given the same opportunities as whites. For example, Asian Pacific Americans are close to parity with whites in the labor market, but would fare even better if they

Table 4.1g  Business Characteristics by Race/Ethnicity (1992)

|  | Revenues per firm | Employees per firm | Payroll per employee |
|---|---|---|---|
| Group |  |  |  |
| All businesses | $192.7k | 1.6 | $19.1k |
| All minorities | $102.8k | 1.0 | $15.2k |
| Hispanic | $94.4k | 0.9 | $15.6k |
| Black | $51.9k | 0.6 | $13.9k |
| Asian Pacific American | $159.1k | 1.4 | $15.5k |
| White females | $114.6k | 1.1 | $17.0k |
| White males | $249.8k | 2.0 | $20.3k |

Source: Compiled by author from Bureau of the Census data on business owners.

could fully translate educational credentials into employment outcomes. The final challenge is that many of the barriers faced by Asian Pacific Americans are not race-based, or at least not in the way racism has been commonly understood. These obstacles are associated with the immigrant experience, where cultural differences and slow acculturation prevent full incorporation. For some, this observation explains away the inequality; however, the explanation does not answer whether the criteria are economically appropriate or based on unwarranted prejudices. Some evidence points to a racializing of the foreign-born, thus blurring the line between racial processes and immigrant processes. Race, after all, is in part a social construction, and this nation has a long history of racializing Asian Pacific American immigrants.

Clearly, Asian Pacific Americans cannot be simply forced into a dichotomous paradigm by defining them as equivalent to other disadvantage minorities or as identical to the advantaged white population. Moreover, the relative standing of Asian Pacific Americans varies across arenas, precluding the possibility of collapsing outcomes into a single, consistent measure of racial inequality. These facts force us to reconsider race relations as a multigroup and multidimensional hierarchy. The complexity introduced by the material position of Asian Pacific Americans presents both a theoretical and a policy challenge.

## THE AFFIRMATIVE ACTION–ASIAN PACIFIC AMERICAN NEXUS

This section examines the link between Asian Pacific Americans and affirmative action programs in three areas at the center of the political debate, public schools, government employment, and government contracting. Unfortunately, there is a paucity of systematic, consistent, and detailed data across all three sectors; nonetheless, the available information provides intriguing insights. The variation in material position discussed in "The Socioeconomic Status of Asian Pacific Americans" maps into a similar variation within race-based programs. The diversity in socioeconomic outcomes discussed above is accompanied by a parallel diversity in the nexus between Asian Pacific Americans and affirmative action. They both benefit from and bear the cost of the policy. In the field of education, where Asian Pacific Americans have been successful, the issue is whether Asian Pacific Americans should forego a disproportionate share of privileges in publicly supported schools. In the labor market, where Asian Pacific Americans have had conditional success, the issue is which occupational niche is appropriate for Asian Pacific American participation. Finally, in the world of business, where Asian Pacific Americans trail whites, Asian Pacific Americans are more likely to be unconditionally included in affirmative action.

Given the high levels of academic achievement, it is not surprising that Asian Pacific Americans have been largely excluded from affirmative action in public education.[41] Of course, there have been exceptions, most notably when the University of California had included Filipinos. It was felt that Filipinos constituted a highly disadvantage population, uniquely different from the other two major Asian Pacific American groups at that time (Japanese and Chinese), but Filipinos were dropped from the program in the mid-1980s. Although there have been other efforts to include high-poverty Asian Pacific American ethnic groups, it is difficult to make a case because a relatively higher number of students from these groups go onto colleges and universities compared to blacks and Hispanics. Not being included as a target population, however, is not the same as having no relationship to affirmative action.

The prevailing relationship between Asian Pacific Americans and race-based admissions programs is both controversial and troubling. A part of that relationship is indirect and equivalent to that for whites. The number of admission slots available to those not included in affirmative action (whites and Asian Pacific Americans) is tied inversely to the degree that special admission procedures are successful in increasing admissions from targeted populations. Clearly, the policy and program alter the racial distribution, but in practice, the changes are at the margin and small in relative size. Moreover, in situations where past discrimination and institutionalized racism unfairly disadvantages the targeted groups, the reallocation achieves a greater social goal of promoting racial equality. Ideally, the opportunities foregone by whites and Asian Pacific Americans are the unearned privileges, that is, the opportunities that would not have been available to these two groups in the absence of systemic and institutional racism. For those opposed to affirmative action, this shifting of admission slots smacks of unconstitutional reverse discrimination. To increase the moral legitimacy of this objection, some

conservatives have argued that racial preferences hurt not only whites but also Asian Pacific Americans. This appeal, however, has not won over the majority of Asian Pacific Americans. According to one survey, a majority of Asian Pacific Americans are willing to accept "giving preferences to underrepresented minorities in college admissions and scholarships."[42]

The situation is more explosive when restrictive quotas enter the picture, that is, when Asian Pacific Americans suffer a double burden, one from any reallocation generated by affirmative action and the other from an enrollment cap to limit "overrepresentation." It is important to note that the latter practice, to the degree it exists, reallocates some admission slots from Asian Pacific Americans to whites. Unlike affirmative action, restrictive quotas do not correct any past discrimination or institutional racism directed at whites. The one plausible argument is promoting diversity that mirrors the population, but it is doubtful that diversity in the abstract and devoid of the other race-related issues is sufficient to impose restrictive quotas.[43]

As discussed earlier, imposing caps on Asian Pacific American admission has been an issue in institutes of higher learning, and much of the controversy of the 1980s centered around the practices at the two flagship campuses of the University of California, Los Angeles and Berkeley. Both campuses had lower admission rates for Asian Pacific American applicants than for other major groups, precipitating protest from Asian Pacific American activists and parents. When asked about access to the University of California, an overwhelming majority believed Asian Pacific American applicants should be admitted at a rate commensurate with their achievements.[44] While private universities used a policy of providing "legacy" preference to children of alumni (who happen to be predominantly white) to explain and justify a lower admission rates for Asian Pacific American applicants relative to white applicants, the public universities had no such rationale. The concerns were sufficiently strong that the federal government launched an investigation, and the conflict was eventually resolved explicitly at Berkeley and tacitly at UCLA. The controversy in the public universities has subsided, but what remains unresolved is the problematic link between restrictive quotas and affirmative action. That issue reemerged in a different arena, in the public schools of San Francisco.

In the City by the Bay, the link between race-based efforts to correct past discrimination and glaring racial inequality was explicitly tied to restrictive quotas.[45] Although the caps did not explicitly single out any one group, Chinese students eventually were affected by its implementation. Like in other urban school districts, blacks were highly segregated into low performing schools within the San Francisco Unified School District. The local NAACP won a lawsuit in 1971 to desegregate the district and a consent decree in 1983 to strengthen the efforts, with the state providing millions of dollars to implement an integration plan.[46] To produce a more balanced enrollment, the decree required each school to have students from at least four of the nine named groups (American Indian, black, Chinese, Filipino, Japanese, Korean, Spanish-surnamed, other white, and other nonwhite). Furthermore, the agreement established caps on the number for any one group, a maximum of 45 percent on most schools and 40 percent on magnet schools, and these restrictions proved to be lightning rods.

At the heart of the eventual controversy is Lowell High School, the oldest high school west of the Mississippi, the most selective school within the district, and one of the most prestigious high schools in the nation.[47] Its alumni include two Nobel Prize winners, a co-founder of Hewlett Packard, a former governor, a U.S. Supreme Court Justice, and a former president of Yale University. Since the 1960s, Lowell operated as a system-wide academic school with competitive admission. Throughout the 1980s and 1990s, Lowell won state and national honors for its academic excellence. Lowell itself was the target of a 1971 dis-

crimination suit against SFUSD for operating a city-wide academic high school that had a disproportionate low number of minorities, but the district won the right to maintain such a program. Lowell, however, was subject to the 1983 consent decree.

Despite the desegregation effort, non-Asian Pacific American minorities continued to be underrepresented. During the mid-1990s, blacks comprised about 18 percent of the students in the district but only 5 percent of Lowell's students, and the comparable statistics for Latinos are 20 percent district wide and only 10 percent for Lowell.[48] Whites were above parity (16 percent of Lowell while only 13 percent of the district) but not affected by the 40-percent ceiling. Only one group was affected by the enrollment limit. In the mid-1990s, Chinese comprised slightly over 40 percent of Lowell's student body. To keep within the maximum, the admission criterion for Chinese was raised above other groups.[49] Both the restriction and the higher admission standards were not well received by many Chinese parents, eventually leading to a lawsuit against the district to end what was termed discriminatory quotas. In 1999, the court ruled in favor of the plaintiffs, forcing the district to abandon the cap for Lowell and to develop "race-neutral" criteria to maintain diversity.[50]

While the immediate outcome of the lawsuit is discernible, the motivation for the actions taken by the complainants and the long-term implications are much more difficult to pinpoint. Conservatives such as Governor Pete Wilson and University of California Regent Ward Connerly, who were major supporters of Proposition 209, seized on the efforts by the Chinese against the restrictive quotas. They used those efforts to attack affirmative action, accusing the policy as the source of the "perverse" cap on Chinese enrollment and on a system of merit. Some supporters of the suit, however, took exception to this interpretation, stating that they are against discrimination against Chinese, but are for affirmative action. On the other hand, other supporters stated that they are against the use of race under any condition. The reaction from the Left was harsh, with some activists chastising the Chinese for allowing themselves to be used by conservatives.

In the end, the Left argued, the ruling would eventually come back to hurt Asian Pacific Americans because it weakens the society's ability to redress racism. These varying interpretations point to a division within the Chinese public itself as evident in a 1998 CAVEC (Chinese American Voter Education Committee) survey of Chinese surname voters in San Francisco. When asked about their opinions on admission quotas for Lowell High School, 45 percent of the immigrant respondents thought it was a "bad idea," 32 percent thought it was a "good idea," while 23 percent expressed no opinion. The opposition is not surprising, but there is a surprising level of support from one-third of those interviewed. The long-term implication of the Lowell case is not known, but this controversy underscores the difficulty in decoupling Asian Pacific American concerns about restrictive quotas from affirmative action.

The issues in the area of employment are far less controversial. Two types of affirmative-action programs are relevant, direct government hiring and indirect hiring by firms with government contracts. The indirect hiring is not the focus of this chapter, but the effects are worth noting. Firms with federal contractors are under an obligation to develop and implement recruitment and hiring plans when minorities are underrepresented in their labor force, and this obligation also applies to many firms with state and local contracts. Existing econometric analysis, which controls for observable firm characteristics, finds that this requirement has a statistically measurable impact. African Americans have benefited, with their share of employment increasing by a tenth more in the federal contracts.[51] Interestingly, the governmental requirement has the same impact on Asian Pacific Americans, with federal contracting increasing their share by a tenth. While the magnitude of the impacts is small, the findings indicate that affirmative action does open up employment opportunities.

An analysis of direct hiring by the public sector reveals several potential problems for Asian Pacific Americans. Table 4.1h reports the number of full-time workers based on EEOC (Equal Employment Opportunity Commission) data for firms with at least 100 employees, and for state and local gov-

**Table 4.1h   Employment by Race/Ethnicity (1997)**

|  | White | Black | Hispanic | Asian Pacific American |
|---|---|---|---|---|
| All occupations | | | | |
| Private sector | 71% | 15% | 10% | 4% |
| Federal executive branch | 71 | 16 | 6 | 4 |
| State | 73 | 18 | 6 | 2 |
| Local government | 68 | 20 | 9 | 2 |
| Officials/management | | | | |
| Private sector | 88% | 6% | 4% | 3% |
| Federal executive branch | 76 | 14 | 6 | 3 |
| State | 87 | 8 | 3 | 1 |
| Local government | 82 | 11 | 5 | 2 |
| Professional | | | | |
| Private sector | 84% | 6% | 3% | 7% |
| Federal executive branch | 79 | 8 | 4 | 8 |
| State | 78 | 14 | 5 | 3 |
| Local government | 73 | 15 | 6 | 6 |

ernments, and based on the data from the U.S. Office of Personnel Management for federal employment.[52] The top panel shows that Asian Pacific Americans are equally represented in both the federal government and the private sector, but are underrepresented in state and local government employment. It is unclear why the latter exists. It may be due to state and local governments being less committed to recruiting and hiring Asian Pacific Americans. Moreover, there could be a spatial mismatch between where public sector jobs are located and where Asian Pacific Americans reside. Many state capitals are in cities with relatively few Asian Pacific Americans.

Another problem is an unequal distribution of Asian Pacific Americans across occupations within the public sector.[53] Particularly troubling is the data indicating a glass ceiling in government employment.[54] The underrepresentation is apparent whether the Asian Pacific American share of all employees or the Asian Pacific American share of employees in professional occupations is used as the benchmark. A parity index using the former provides a conservative estimate, while a parity index using the latter partially accounts for the higher educational level of Asian Pacific Americans.[55] The ratio ranges from about .5 to .3 depending on which benchmark and which level of government. Moreover, state-specific data for combined state and local government employment indicate that the problem is present in regions with a significant presence of Asian Pacific Americans: .4 to .6 for California, .5 to .9 for Florida, .3 to .8 for Illinois, .3 to .6 for Massachusetts, .2 to .6 for

New Jersey, .4 to .8 for New York, .4 to .7 for Texas, and .5 to .6 for Washington. While a low index is not conclusive evidence of a glass ceiling, it does suggest that Asian Pacific Americans are having difficulties moving into management.

Underrepresentation is not limited to management. There are other occupational niches, and one of the most glaring is protective services. The statistics in table 4.1i show that Asian Pacific Americans comprise only 1 percent of state and local employees in protective services, compared to 2.5 percent of the all state and local employees, a ratio of .4. The lower the index, the greater the underrepresentation. The ratio is even lower in the public sector, where Asian Pacific American professionals outnumber the Asian Pacific American managers by three-to-one. The ratio is particularly low for firefighters, but even for police officers, Asian Pacific Americans are below parity. The problem is present in the regions with a significant presence of Asian Pacific Americans, as indicated by the parity ratio: .4 for California, .4 for Florida, .2 for Illinois, .4 for Massachusetts, .2 for New Jersey, .2 for New York, .3 for Texas, and .6 for Washington.

The underrepresentation in occupational niches has been addressed through selective action, often through court-imposed orders. This is illustrated by the effort to address the small number of Chinese in San Francisco's fire department.[56] (In that city, the Chinese have comprised an overwhelming majority of the Asian Pacific American population.) During the mid-1960s when community leaders first raised the issue of

**Table 4.1i   Employment in Protective Services by Ethnicity, Full-Time State and Local Employment (1997)**

|  | White | Black | Hispanic | Asian Pacific American |
|---|---|---|---|---|
| All occupations | 70.6% | 18.7% | 7.5% | 2.5% |
| Protective services | 72.7 | 17.7 | 8.0 | 1.0 |
| Police | 72.7 | 16.1 | 9.0 | 1.7 |
| Firefighters | 73.2 | 11.1 | 6.8 | 0.8 |
| Corrections | 66.5 | 23.9 | 7.7 | 1.2 |

underrepresentation, only six Chinese (and one black) were among approximately 1,600 firefighters, and that number remained essentially same for a decade. Under a 1974 court order to address this problem, the department was expected to increase the number of Asian Pacific American firefighters to nearly 200.

The one area where Asian Pacific Americans have been unambiguously included is in government contracting, particularly when federal funds are involved. This inclusion is based on the fact that Asian Pacific American firms are less likely to receive government contracts. The standard measure is the disparity index, which is a group's relative share of government contracts divided by that group's share of all businesses. For example, if group A has 10 percent of government contracts but comprises 20 percent of all businesses, then the disparity index is .50, indicating that this group is receiving only half of its "fair" share of government business. An analysis of public contracting in California reveals that Asian Pacific American firms are consistently underutilized by local governments.[57] Even in San Francisco, where Asian Pacific Americans are the largest minority group, the disparity index for Asian Pacific American firms is .19. The problem is not unique to California. After reviewing a large number of disparity studies from throughout the nation, the Urban Institute finds that median value for Asian Pacific American-owned businesses is .19, which is lower than that for women-owned businesses (.26), Hispanic-owned businesses (.36), and black-owned businesses (.41).[58] The low disparity index, along with the problems discussed earlier, has been the basis for including Asian Pacific American in government set-aside programs.[59] This inclusion has continued after a review of federal contract set-aside, which is a part of President Clinton's "mend it, not end it" approach to affirmative action.[60] The inclusion of Asian Pacific Americans poses an interesting question of what is the appropriate or desirable goal.

Asian Pacific Americans have taken advantage of this inclusion through partici-pation in programs to promote minority (and women) contracting. At the national level, Asian Pacific American participation can be seen in the federal government's major effort to help minority firms, the 8(a) Program operated by the Small Business Administration.[61] For the decade spanning the late 1980s to the late 1990s, Asian Pacific Americans increased their participation in both absolute and relative terms, as shown in Table 4.1j. By the end of the twentieth century, they made up nearly a quarter of all 8(a) firms. Asian Pacific Americans are also participants at the state and local level. This can be seen in California's certification program for minority (and women) businesses, which is required to qualify for set-aside contracts. Both state and local agencies use the certification to determine eligibility. Asian Pacific American firms accounted for 29 percent of the state's certified minority businesses.[62] Although data are not readily available for other states, a review of the certification programs in the largest states show that Asian Pacific Americans are among the listed groups eligible for enrollment. Inclusion is driven by the fact that states are required to follow federal guidelines on these matters as a condition for receiving federal funds.

Beyond the active participation of Asian Pacific American entrepreneurs in minority set-aside programs, there is strong support within the Asian Pacific American communities for these programs. This can be seen in a survey conducted Houston prior to the Proposition A vote. When asked if city government should set aside contracts for minority businesses, only a small minority of non-Hispanic whites (37 percent) approved, but a large majority of blacks (71 percent) approved. The percentage for Asian Pacific American approval falls between these two extremes, 61 percent, which is similar to that for Hispanics, 63 percent.[63] Not all Asian Pacific Americans, however, support this type of affirmative action. Edward Chen was a plaintiff in a suit to overturn the results of the election, where a majority voted against the anti-affirmative action initiative.[64]

**Table 4.1j  Participants in Small Business Administration's 8(a) Program by Race**

|  | FY 1988–1991 | FY 1992–1995 | FY 1996–1999 |
|---|---|---|---|
| Race |  |  |  |
| Asian Pacific American | 13% | 19% | 23% |
| Black | 46 | 46 | 44 |
| Latino | 25 | 25 | 25 |
| All others | 16 | 10 | 8 |
| N= | 14,234 | 20,756 | 23,461 |

*Source:* Unpublished data provided by Small Business Administration.

Taken together, the information for the three areas shows that Asian Pacific Americans have taken disparate positions on affirmative action. Not surprisingly, there are systematic and predictable differences across the three areas, but even within a given arena, there are conflicting opinions. These cross currents reveal that Asian Pacific Americans are influenced by both self-interest and larger ideological beliefs. Asian Pacific Americans face the same dilemma facing this nation as a whole on what ought to be done to redress racial inequality. As mentioned earlier, there are difficult trade-offs, and most are willing to accept race-based solutions under certain conditions. There are additional complexities in the Asian Pacific American population.

The one event we can gauge where most Asian Pacific Americans stand on affirmative action as an overarching policy is the vote on the single most important initiative so far, California's 1996 Proposition 209, the so-called California Civil Rights Initiative.[65] The result from a statewide exit poll conducted by the *Los Angeles Times* shows considerable racial variation.[66] The strongest support came from whites (63 percent for), and strong opposition came from blacks (74 percent against). What is surprising is that three-quarters of Hispanics (76 percent) also were against the proposition.[67] The poll also found that a majority of Asian Pacific Americans (61 percent) voted against the proposition; however, the estimate is based on a small number of responses. Two more specialized exit polls in neighborhoods with high concentrations of Asian Pacific Americans also found that a majority, and in fact a large majority, of Asian Pacific Americans voted against the proposition. In Southern California, 76 percent of Asian Pacific Americans voted against 209, and this opposition crossed party lines (78 percent of Asian Pacific American Democrats and 73 percent of Asian Pacific American Republicans).[68] In the San Francisco Bay Area, a similar percentage of Asian Pacific Americans voted against 209 (80 percent), and again the opposition crossed party lines (86 percent of Asian Pacific American Democrats and 63 percent of Asian Pacific American Republicans).[69]

Analyzing one election, however, is not sufficient to discern the dominant Asian Pacific American political position. The Asian Pacific American population is very heterogeneous, and competing factors come into play. The extreme economic and ethnic diversity of this population is very well documented.[70] The Asian Pacific American population is also diverse in its politics, as indicated by party registration data.[71] The emergence of naturalized immigrants as a majority of Asian Pacific American voters further complicates the picture.[72] Many of these new voters are still in the process of formulating opinions on domestic issues such as affirmative action. Their attitudes are fluid, as continued exposure to American society shapes and reshapes their opinions.

The Asian Pacific American political position remains elusive and is up for grabs.

## CONCLUSION—WHAT NEXT?

This nation is at a crucial juncture in addressing racial inequality, with affirmative action as the primary battleground. In a larger political and historical context, the heated and nasty debate marks a dramatic reversal in the search for a solution. The Civil Rights Movement of the 1950s and 1960s transformed the state from one either supporting or turning a blind eye to racism to one attacking racial injustice, at least in its most blatant forms. Legislation was passed to protect voting rights, proscribe housing and employment discrimination, integrate schools and other public facilities, and fight inner-city poverty. One can cynically point out that the elected officials had to be pressured into enacting these laws, that programs were efforts to prevent escalating social unrest, and that implementation was half-hearted. Such a dismissive view, however, too easily denies the hard-earned victories, the progressive policies and programs. The accomplishments should not be judged by a failure to achieve utopia, but gains made in the face of resistance. At the close of the twentieth century, racial politics in America has taken a turn against race-based policies. Those opposed to the civil rights agenda have found an effective weapon by hijacking the principle of fairness to attack the most controversial policy, affirmative action. This counter insurgence has mobilized the mainstream by arguing that the policy is contrary to civil rights principles and constitutional protections. Of course, the idea that race-based laws and programs violate the rights of some (particularly white males) by giving "unfair" preferences to others (primarily minorities) is not new. That assertion has been at the heart of numerous court cases. What is different is an acceptance of this argument by many mainstream politicians and a significant share of the voting public. The battle, however, is far from over.

Asian Pacific Americans occupy a unique position in the political debate because they occupy an ambiguous position within the racial structure. Their presence complicates issues regarding the application of and fundamental justification for affirmative action. On the other hand, resolving these complications can help reformulate a sounder policy. Asian Pacific American concerns cannot be easily pushed aside or folded into a simple black and white framework. Their educational and economic successes preclude them from being classified simply as another disadvantaged minority equivalent to blacks. At the same time, the Asian Pacific American population cannot be simply lumped in with the dominant white population. The social construction of this population as a racial minority is rooted in a long history of anti-Asian racism and reproduced by contemporary anti-Asian prejudices. Some may want to ignore Asian Pacific Americans by asserting that they are a small population. This was true for most of the century, but less so today. Asian Pacific Americans now constitute about 4 percent of the population, and will constitute about 6 percent within a generation. While it is important to note that Asian Pacific Americans cannot be dismissed numerically, it is at least as important to note that the impact of Asian Pacific Americans on race-related policies has not rested on population size. Historically, this group profoundly shaped race relations through the laws enacted against them and the legislative and court victories won by them. Within the contemporary battle over affirmative action, Asian Pacific Americans make two important contributions.

The first is in the realm of symbolic politics. There are those who point to Asian Pacific Americans as a minority group that has experienced historic discrimination, but nonetheless have been able to overcome obstacles without governmental intervention. This "model minority myth" is used to shift the responsibility of closing the racial gap from the larger society to minorities. If one group can do it, so can the others. Some want Asian Pacific Americans to go beyond being a passive model to being spokespersons against affirmative action to fight reverse discrimination against Asian Pacific Americans. This political strategy rests too much on appealing to self-interest and fails to recognize that many Asian Pacific Americans accept the necessity to collectively address racial inequality. As the chapter by Taeku Lee shows, the majority of Asian Pacific Americans believe that blacks, and Hispanics to a lesser degree, suffer from discrimination. This translates into support for some race-based policies. In a 1995 national survey, a majority of Asian Pacific American respondents agreed with the following statement: "White Americans have benefited from past and present discrimination against African Americans, so they should be willing to make up for these wrongs." [73] According to a 1996 survey sponsored by *Asian Week*, slightly more than half of the respondents supported affirmative action and a third opposed it.[74] This shows that many Asian Pacific Americans are driven by a broader sense of this country's obligation.

On the other hand, proponents of race-based programs believe that Asian Pacific Americans can take an equally powerful stance. Liberals want Asian Pacific Americans to be a role model in accepting the sacrifices needed to achieve racial justice. An example of this is the statement by several law professors who support affirmative action. They argue that "Asian Pacific Americans can play an extraordinarily powerful role in the debate because they can declare their support for the programs even when they are not directly benefited by them . . . I am willing to share this burden to help us get beyond racism, to reach a fairer society. I am willing to go beyond my self-interest in order to strive for a community of justice."[75] This call for noble and principled action has great moral appeal, but it minimizes Asian Pacific Americans' legitimate self-interest in the affirmative-action debate. Indeed, within our society, where the pursuit of self-interest is the norm, acknowledging the special needs of Asian Pacific Americans can move the

debate forward, if for no other reason than to challenge prevailing ideas.

There are three challenges. The first questions the notions of the primacy of race.

Asian Pacific Americans are a racial minority, but they are not automatically included in affirmative action programs. As we have seen, inclusion into any particular program (covering higher education, public employment, or government contracting) is predicated on whether Asian Pacific Americans are demonstrably disadvantaged. This practice shows that affirmative action as an institution is flexible and reasonable in situating Asian Pacific Americans. The policy is not, as opponents suggest, blindly wedded to a simplistic application of race. Unfortunately, the treatment of Asian Pacific Americans has been ad hoc rather than based on a well-articulated principle. Such a principle does not preclude a single race from being included in all affirmative action programs when the evidence justifies such a decision, but this result is the product of applying the principle rather than an a priori categorization. Even if the final outcome of starting with this principle may not differ much from what currently exists, the exercise is politically important because it provides the justification that many voters want before they support affirmative action.

The second challenge centers on the types of race-related problems that government should correct. Affirmative action was developed to counter the racism experienced by African Americans in the 1960s; however, the problems confronting other minorities are not of the same nature. This chapter has documented that the disadvantages faced by Asian Pacific Americans are different, with many of the problems rooted in the immigrant experience. Hispanics and Native Americans also face hardships that are generated by disparate historic and contemporary forces. While socioeconomic injustice is a necessary common denominator for governmental action, programs should be tailored to address the underlying race-specific causes.

The final challenge is to debate openly the sacrifices that must be made to achieve racial justice. Proponents of affirmative action are uncomfortable with such a discussion because it shifts the discussion away from the disadvantaged and potentially legitimizes the claim that whites must give up some opportunities. Yet, as we have seen, this point has been and will be an unavoidable element in the debate. An enlightened and socially productive debate requires that both sides engage the issues rather than having one side frame the issue through polemics. For better or worse, Asian Pacific Americans are a part of the debate on the cost of affirmative action, as well as the broader debate on race-based policies.

## NOTES

I am grateful for the assistance provided by Issac Elnecave and Elena Sovhos. Taeku Lee graciously provided tabulations from several opinion polls.

1. See for example: Steven M. Cahn, ed., *The Affirmative Action Debate* (New York: Routledge, 1995); George E. Curry, ed., *The Affirmative Action Debate* (Reading, Mass.: Addison Wesley, 1996); Nicolaus Mills, ed., *Debating Affirmative Action: Race, Gender, Ethnicity, and the Politics of Inclusion* (New York: Dell, 1994); Carol M. Swain, *Race Versus Class, The New Affirmative Action Debate* (Lanham, Md.: University Press of America, 1996).

2. Hugh Davis Graham, *The Civil Rights Era: Origins and Development of National Policy 1960–1972.* (New York: Oxford University Press, 1990); James W. Riddlesperger Jr. and Donald W. Jackson, *Presidential Leadership and Civil Rights Policy* (Westport, Conn.: Greenwood Press, 1995); John David Skrentny, *The Ironies of Affirmative Action: Politics, Culture and Justice in America* (Chicago: The University of Chicago Press, 1996); Mark Stern, *Calculating Visions: Kennedy, Johnson, and Civil Rights* (New Brunswick, N.J.: Rutgers University Press, 1992).

3. Tom Smith, "Intergroup Relations in Contemporary America: An Overview of Survey Research," in Wayne Winborne and Renae Cohen, eds., *Intergroup Relations in the United States: Research Perspectives* (Bloomsburg, Pa.: Hadden Craftsmen, Inc. for the National Conference for Community and Justice,1998) 69–155; and Seymour Martin Lipset and William Schneider, "The Bakke Case: How Would It Be Decided at the Bar of Public Opinion?" *Public Opinion* 2 (April 1978): 38–44.

4. United States. Kerner Commission. *Report of the National Advisory Commission on Civil Disorders* (New York: Bantam Books, 1968).

5. This was a part of his famous 1965 speech at Howard University, where he argued for affirmative action: "You do not take a person who had been hobbled by chains, liberate him, bring him up to the starting gate of a race and then say, 'You are free to compete with all the others,' and still justly believe you have been completely fair. . . . It is not enough to open the gates of opportunity. All of our citizens must have the ability to walk through those gates. . . . Men and women of all races are born with the same range of abilities. But ability is not just the product of birth. Ability is stretched or stunted by the family you live with, . . . the neighborhood . . . the school . . . and the poverty or richness of your surroundings. It is the product of a hundred unseen forces playing upon the infant, the child, and the man." (Stephanopoulos and Edley, *Affirmative Action Review*, 115).

6. George Lipsitz, *The Possessive Investment in Whiteness, How White People Profit from Identity Politics* (Philadelphia: Temple University Press, 1998); Murray Friedman and Peter Binzen. *What Went Wrong?: The Creation and Collapse of the Black-Jewish Alliance* (New York: The Free Press, 1995).

7. Most of the early rulings reaffirmed the legality of anti-discriminatory laws in employment. The Supreme Court ruled that firms could not use employment tests that are not job related and have a disparate impact on protected groups, and that employers must have some legitimate nondiscriminatory business reason for rejecting minority applicants. *Griggs v. Duke Power Co.* (1971), *McDonnell Douglas v. Green* (1973), *Albermarle Paper Co. v. Moody* (1975), and *Washington v. Davis* (1976).

8. *United Steelworkers of America, AFL-CIO-CLC v. Weber* (1979), *Firefighters Local Union No. 1794 v. Stotts* (1984), *Wygant v. Jackson Board of Education* (1986), and *Johnson v. Transportation Agency of Santa Clara County* (1987).

9. The progressively greater restrictions are correlated with an ideological realignment of the Court. From 1969 to 1991, the Republican presidents appointed a new Chief Justice as well as nine additions to the Supreme Court.

10. See Norman C. Amaker, "The Reagan Civil Rights Legacy," in Eric J. Schmertz, Natalie Datlof, and Alexej Ugrinsky, eds., *Ronald Reagan's America, Volume I* (Westport, Conn.: Greenwood Press, 1997); Robert R. Detlefsen, "Affirmative Action and Business Deregulation: On the Reagan Administration's Failure to Revise Executive Order No. 11246," and Charles M. Lamb and Jim Twombly, "Decentralizing Fair Housing Enforcement During the Reagan Presidency," in James W. Riddlesperger Jr. and Donald W. Jackson, eds., *Presidential Leadership and Civil Rights Policy* (Westport, Conn.: Greenwood Press, 1995), 39–70 and 127–48; Peter Gottschalk, "Retrenchment in Antipoverty Programs in the United States: Lessons for the Future," and R. Kent Weaver, "Social Policy in the Reagan Era," in B. B. Kymlicka and Jean V. Matthews, eds., *The Reagan Revolutions?* (Chicago: The Dorsey Press, 1988), 131–45 and 146–65; Raymond Wolters, *Right Turn: William Bradford Reynolds, the Reagan Administration, and Black Civil Rights* (New Brunswick, N.J.: Transaction Publishers, 1996).

11. The specific language of Proposition 209 prohibits the state and local government from supporting programs that "discriminate against, or grant preferential treatment to, any individual or group on the basis of race, sex, color, ethnicity, or national origin in the operation of public employment, public education, or public contracting." For a discussion on the development of Proposition 209, see Lydia Chavez, *The Color Bind: California's Battle to End Affirmative Action* (Berkeley: University of California Press, 1998).

12. "Shall the Charter of the City of Houston be amended to end the use of affirmative action?"

13. "The state shall not discriminate against, or grant preferential treatment to, any individual or group on the basis of race, sex, color, ethnicity, or national origin in the operation of public employment, public education, or public contracting." Election result taken from www.metrokc.gov/elections/98nov/respage1.htm

14. American Civil Rights Coalition, "Connerly Welcomes John Carlson to Washington State Civil Rights Initiative," October 9, 1997, www.acrc1.org/pr100997.html.

15. Franklin Foer, "Brother Jeb's Move to End Affirmative Action, Florida's Bush Says Class Rank Works Better," *U.S. News and World Report*, November 22, 1999: 31; William March, "Affirmative Action Battle Roars Back to Life," *The Tampa Tribune*, November 16, 1999: http://tampatrib.com/fr111613.htm. For a discussion on the limits of class-based programs, see Cecilia A. Conrad, "Affirmative Action and Admission to the University of California," in Paul M. Ong, ed., *Impacts of Affirmative Action: Policies and Consequences in California* (Walnut Creek, Calif.: AltaMira Press, 1999) 171–96.

16. Tom Smith, "Intergroup Relations in Contemporary America: An Overview of Survey Research," in Wayne Winborne and Renae Cohen, eds. *Intergroup Relations in the United States: Research Perspectives* (Bloomsburg, Pa.: Hadden Craftsmen, Inc. for the National Conference for Community and Justice, 1998), 151.

17. Lawrence Bobo and Ryan Smith. "Anti-Poverty Policy, Affirmative Action, and Racial Attitudes," in S. Danzinger, G. Sandefur, and D.Weinberg, eds. *Confronting Poverty: Prescriptions for Change* (New York: Russell Sage Foundation, and Cambridge: Harvard University Press, 1994) 365–95; Dan Morain, "The Times Poll: 60% of State's Voters Say They Back Prop. 209." *Los Angeles Times*, September 19, 1996: A1.

18. Tom Smith, "Intergroup Relations in Contemporary America: An Overview of Survey Research," in Wayne Winborne and Renae Cohen, eds. *Intergroup Relations in the United States: Research Perspectives* (Bloomsburg, Pa.: Hadden Craftsmen, Inc. for the National Conference for Community and Justice, 1998) 144.

19. University of Houston Center for Public Policy and Rice University's Baker Institute

for Public Policy, cited in Julie Mason, *Houston Chronicle*, October 2, 1997.

20. The President's Initiative on Race Advisory Board. *One America in the 21st Century: The President's Initiative on Race* (Washington, D.C.: U.S. Government Printing Office, 1998) 99–102.

21. For this chapter, the term whites refers to the non-Hispanic white population. The broader white category includes a significant number of Hispanics who identify themselves as whites on race questions. However, Hispanic whites occupy a socioeconomic position that is very different than that for non-Hispanic whites; consequently, statistics for all whites differ from those for just non-Hispanic whites. For the purpose of this chapter, non-Hispanic whites are used as a benchmark to determine the relative standing of minority groups. For convenience, the chapter uses the terms whites and non-Hispanic whites interchangeably. This chapter does not include Native Americans because the sample size is too small in many of the data sets; nonetheless, it is important to acknowledge that this group is extremely disadvantaged.

22. Data are the 1998 results for the fourth and eleventh grades for the Stanford 9 test as reported by the California Department of Education's STAR data server at http://star.cde .ca.gov/. The test data are merged with data on the racial/ethnic composition for each school from the same source. The ranking of elementary schools is based on a combined score using results reading, math, language, and spelling. The eleventh grade ranking is based on scores for reading, math, science, and social science tests. We use the percent of the student body that scored at or above the 75th percentile. The composite score may not accurately represent the true performance level of California students; California elementary students may truly be performing at less than the national average or perhaps the benchmark level is improperly set. Nevertheless, the data does provide a useful way to rank the relative performance of elementary schools. The original eleventh grade study used results from reading, math, science, and social science tests.

23. The statistics for tables 4.1b, 4.1c, and 4.1d come from a tabulation by the author of the March Current Population Survey (CPS).

The CPS is a national monthly survey of about 60,000 households, and is used to collect information on labor market conditions, particularly the unemployment rate. The March survey, which produces the Annual Demographic Profile, contains extensive information on current (contemporaneous) status along with work experiences and earnings for the previous year. Since 1989, the CPS has included Asian Pacific Americans as a separate racial category. The surveys for 1997, 1998, and 1999 were pooled to derive a reasonable sample of Asian Pacific Americans. The size of the sample varies according to the needs of a particular analysis. For example, the sample used to calculate wages for the foreign-born, prime-working-age population includes about 3,600 Asian Pacific Americans. The actual number of unique individuals is slightly more than two-thirds of the sample size because the CPS retains a proportion of the March sample over a two-year period. Income data are adjusted to 1998 dollars, and the reported statistics on earnings and hourly wages are the weighted average for the three years (1996, 1997, and 1998). Statistics on the labor market status (e.g., labor force participation rates) are for the survey week.

24. Table 3: Ten-year trends in average SAT scores by racial/ethnic groups, www .collegeboard.org/press/senior98/html/satt3.html

25. SAT Chart 13: Within racial/ethnic groups, first language is related to SAT Verbal scores.

26. "What Are the Eligibility Rates of 1996 Public High School Graduates for the University of California?" (http://www.collegeboard .org/press/senior98/html/satt3.html.

27. SAT Chart 9: Percentages of racial/ethnic groups in large cities and suburbs, class of 1998, http://www.collegeboard .org/press/senior98/html/satc9.html.

28. See www.holyoke.harvard.edu/factbook/ 98-99/;web.mit.edu/facts/enrollment.html;www. stanford.edu/home/standord/facts/undergraduate; www.yale.edu/oir/factsheet; osr.berkeley.edu/ public.student.data/publications/ug/ugf98.html; www.apb.ucla.edu/apb.html; www.umich.edu/ -oapainfo/tables/enr_race.html.

29. For a discussion of this issue and a summary of the literature on Asian Pacific

American students, see Paul M. Ong and Linda C. Wong, "The Social Contract to Educate All Children," in Bill O. Hing and Ronald Le, eds., *Reframing the Immigration Debate* (Los Angeles: LEAP Asian Pacific American Public Policy Institute and UCLA Asian American Studies Center, 1996) 223–65.

30. Don T. Nakanishi, "A Quota on Excellence? The Asian American Admissions Debate," *Change Magazine*, November/December 1989: 39–47; Ling-Chi Wang, "Trends in Admissions for Asian Americans in Colleges and Universities: Higher Education Policy," in *The State of Asian Pacific America: Policy Issues to the Year 2020* (Los Angeles: LEAP Asian Pacific American Public Policy Institute and UCLA Asian American Studies Center, 1993) 49–59; Dana Y. Takagi, *The Retreat from Race: Asian-American Admissions and Racial Politics* (New Brunswick, N.J.: Rutgers University Press, 1992).

31. Thomas J. Kane, "Racial and Ethnic Preferences in College Admissions," in C. Jencks and M. Phillips, eds., *The Black-White Test Score Gap* (Washington, D.C.: Brookings, 1998) 431–56.

32. It is difficult to document many acts of prejudices because they are not conducted openly; nonetheless, there is certainly indirect evidence. This includes stories passed along by those privy to these closed discussions where Asian Pacific Americans are not present. The author has received information from white colleagues who were disturbed by discussions among white administrators about their concerns about and desire to minimize the overrepresentation of Asian Pacific Americans.

33. For the new chain migration, see John Liu, Paul M. Ong, and Carolyn Rosenstein, "Dual-Chain Migration: Post-1965 Filipino Immigration to the United States," *International Migration Review* 25(3): 487–513. For discussion on recent immigration policy, see Paul M. Ong and John Liu, "U.S. Immigration Policies and Asian Migration," in Paul M. Ong, Edna Bonacich, and Lucie Cheng, eds., *The New Asian Immigration in Los Angeles and Global Restructuring* (Philadelphia: Temple University Press, 1994) 45–72. This selective migration has not only produced a highly educated Asian Pacific American immigrant population, but also a highly educated non-Hispanic white immigrant population.

34. This does not take into account those outside of the labor market because they have become discouraged workers. This is a particular problem among black males.

35. Multivariate methods are used to estimate the independent sources of the earnings inequality. Linear regressions are used, with the log of total wages and salaries as the dependent variable. The independent (causal) factors include type of credential (bachelor's, master's, professional, and doctoral degrees), nativity (U.S.-born and foreign-born), age, and race (Asian Pacific American and white). The sample is restricted to those between the ages of twenty-four and sixty-four, working full-time (thirty-five or more hours a week) and year-round (fifty or more weeks a year), holding at least a bachelor's degree, and classified as an employee (i.e., not self-employed). Moreover, immigrants are divided into recent and established immigrants (those in the country approximately less than twelve years and those in the country approximately twelve years or more). For the analysis, the earnings of U.S.-born white males is the ultimate benchmark. The impact of the independent variables is calculated using the exponential function on the estimated coefficients.

36. See United States Commission on Civil Rights, *Civil Rights Issues Facing Asian Americans in the 1990s* (Washington, D.C.: Government Printing Office, February 1992) 131–35; Federal Glass Ceiling Commission, *Good For Business: Making Full Use of the Nation's Human Capital* (Washington, D.C.: Government Printing Office, 1995).

37. "APA Agenda: Asian Americans on the Issues," *Asian Week*, 23–29 August 1996: 14–17. The *Asian Week* survey of 807 Asian Pacific American registered voters was conducted by Meta Information Services between June 25 and July 2, 1996. The sample included persons with Asian Pacific American surnames in California, Massachusetts, Ohio, Pennsylvania, and Washington.

38. To estimate the effects of ethnicity and nativity, logit regressions with the same college/university educated sample are used in the

analysis of the probability of being in management for Asian Pacific Americans and whites working full-time and year-round and between the ages of twenty-four and sixty-four.

39. Total earnings include wages and salaries, self-employment income, and farm income. Wages and salaries are included because many of the firms are incorporated, with the owners paid a salary.

40. U.S. Bureau of the Census, *1992 Economic Census, Characteristics of Business Owners* (Washington, D.C., 1997); U.S. Bureau of the Census, *1992 Economic Census, Women-Owned Businesses* (Washington, D.C., 1996); U.S. Bureau of the Census, *1992 Economic Census, Survey of Minority-Owned Enterprises* (Washington, D.C., 1996); and www.census.gov/Press-Release/cb96-127.html. Some of the statistics for Asian Pacific Americans includes a small number of American Indian firms.

41. Even more interesting is the potential impact of alternative schemes to increase disadvantaged groups. For example, giving preference based on class rather than race (that is, giving greater weight to those from low-income families) would increase the admission rate for Asian Pacific Americans but not for other racial minorities. This not only shows the inadequacy of class-based program to replace race-based programs in promoting admissions for underrepresented minorities, but also reveals the unique position of the Asian Pacific American population, which has a disproportionate number of poor families despite a high average income for the total population. Cecilia A. Conrad, "Affirmative Action and Admission to the University of California," in Paul M. Ong, ed., *Impacts of Affirmative Action: Policies and Consequences in California* (Walnut Creak, Calif.: AltaMira Press, 1999) 171–96.

42. "APA Agenda: Asian Americans on the Issues," *Asian Week*, August 23–29, 1996: 14–17. For that specific item, 54 percent of the respondent supported the statement, 34 percent opposed, and 12 percent had no opinion.

43. Jerry Kang, "Negative Action Against Asian Americans: The Internal Instability of Dworkin's Defense of Affirmative Action," *Harvard Civil Rights-Civil Liberties Law Review*, 31(1) (Winter 1996).

44. See the results form the *Los Angeles Times* Poll #318. Respondents were given this question: "As you may know, Asians make up about 10 percent of California's population but they comprise about 28 percent of the students in the University of California system. Which of these statements comes closer to your view about that: 'If Asians are better qualified, more of them should be admitted to college than others.' or 'Despite qualifications, the racial makeup in colleges should generally mirror the population as a whole.'" 65 percent of Asian Pacific Americans selected the first statement, compared to 42 percent of blacks, 37 percent of Latinos, and 58 percent whites.

45. Julian Guthrie, "School Desegregation Teetering in San Francisco," *San Francisco Examiner*, February 16, 1999; Andrew Quinn, "SF Schools Agree to Drop Race-Based Admissions," *Reuters* February 17, 1999; Alethea Yip, "New Support in School Desegregation Case 'We Want To Emphasize That This Case Is about Ending Discrimination and Not at All about Ending Affirmative Action," *Asian Week*, 5–11 September 1997: www.asianweek.com/090597/schoolnews.html; Jeff Chang, "On the Wrong Side: Chinese Americans Win Anti-Diversity Settlement—and Lose in the End," *Color Lines*, Summer 1999: www.arc.org/C_Lines/CLArchive/story2_2_04.html; Bryant Tan, "Battle over district's consent decree goes to court," November 22, 1996: www.thelowell.org/breaking/news/nov22-districtDecree.html.

46. David L. Kirp, "Race, Politics, and the Courts: School Desegregation in San Francisco," *Harvard Education Review*, 46 (November 1997): 572–611; Nanette Asimov, "District's Long Struggle with Desegregation," *San Francisco Chronicle*, June 19, 1995: A9.

47. San Francisco Unified School District, Lowell on Line, "Distinguished Alumni," www.sfusd.k12.ca.us/schwww/sch697/about/alumni/; "Lowell History, The Oldest Public High School West of the Mississippi," www.sfusd.k12.ca.us/schwww/sch697/about/history/page2.html.

48. Enrollment data taken from the DataQuest web site maintained by the California Department of Education, http://data1.cde.ca.gov/dataquest/.

49. Nanette Asimov and Tara Shioya, "A Test for the Best Public School," *San Francisco Chronicle*, June 21, 1995: A1 and A5.

50. In 1996, SFUSD modified the admission process for Lowell: "The new admissions policy prescribes that 80 percent of the freshmen are to be admitted under one cut-off score computed strictly according to their composite score, which is based on their middle school GPA and CTBS percentile ranking. The remaining 20 percent of the freshmen are selected from a pool of 'value-added' applicants who are given extra points if they produce evidence that meets additional criteria, e.g., took honors courses in middle school, lived in public housing, were eligible for the federal lunch program, participated in extra curricular activities, had parents who did not graduate from high school, etc." www.sfusd .k12.ca.us/schwww/sch697/about/policy/ admissions.html. This new process, however, did not directly address the issue of a cap on enrollment. The use of race has remained unresolved. Ryan Kim, "Foe Blasts School's New Admission Plan," *San Francisco Chronicle*, November 25, 1999: A1 and A9.

51. William M. Rodgers. "Federal-Contractor Status and Minority Employment: A Case Study of California, 1979–1994," in Paul M. Ong, ed., *Impacts of Affirmative Action: Policies and Consequences in California* (Walnut Creek, Calif.: AltaMira Press, 1999) 103–120.

52. United States Equal Employment Opportunity Commission, *Job Pattern for Minorities and Women in State and Local Government, 1997* (Washington, D.C.: GPO, 1997); United States Equal Employment Opportunity Commission, *Job Patterns for Minorities and Women in Private Industry, 1997* (Washington, D.C.: GPO, 1997); United States Equal Employment Opportunity Commission, *1997 State and Local Government Information Survey, Aggregate for National Employment Summary* (Washington, D.C.: 1997) Data Compiled by EEOC Staff; United States Office of Personnel Management, *Federal Civilian Workforce Statistics: Race/National Origin: Employment and Average Salary by White-Collar Occupational Category* (Washington, D.C.: GPO, 1998) 44.

53. The literature indicates that Asian Pacific Americans in the public sector earn less and hold lower positions than whites after controlling for personal characteristics. A summary can be found in M. V. Lee Badgett, "The Impact of Affirmative Action on Public-Sector Employment," in Paul M. Ong, ed., *Impacts of Affirmative Action: Policies and Consequences in California* (Walnut Creek, Calif.: AltaMira Press, 1999) 83–102. Her own analysis shows that in 1990 Asian Pacific Americans in government, and male Asian Pacific Americans in particular, are less likely to hold a managerial or professional job than whites; however, the gap is even greater in the private sector.

54. The precise occupational definitions in table 4.1h are not the same as the CPS-based definitions used in the analysis in the previous section of this chapter, which is based on the Current Population Survey. Nonetheless, the relative distributions are similar. For example, both the EEOC and CPS data show that Asian Pacific Americans in the private sector are only half as likely to be in a management position as in a professional occupation.

55. Because Asian Pacific Americans are better educated, one would expect a proportionately higher share of the management position, but the detail data are not available to estimate what the share should be. However, the multivariate analysis in the previous section indicates that Asian Pacific Americans have reached parity with whites in the professional categories, after accounting for age, educational credentials, and nativity. In other words, the observed Asian Pacific American share of professional jobs is in line with what we expect after taking into account background characteristics. Given that management is also a high-status occupation, we would expect Asian Pacific American share of management position to be roughly equal to that in the professions. In other words, if Asian Pacific Americans hold 7 percent of professional jobs, then we would expect Asian Pacific Americans to hold 7 percent of management jobs given their higher education. The lower the index, the greater the underrepresentation.

56. "Proposal to Better Integrate Fire Department," *San Francisco Chronicle*, May 19, 1965: 3; Jerry Kang, "Negative Action Against Asian Americans: The Internal Instability of Dworkin's Defense of Affirmative Action," *Harvard Civil Rights-Civil Liberties Law Review*, 31(1) (Winter 1996): 21.

57. Tom Larson, "Affirmative Action Programs for Minority and Women-Owned Businesses, in Paul M. Ong, ed., *Impacts of Affirmative Action: Policies and Consequences in California* (Walnut Creek, Calif.: AltaMira Press, 1999) 133–69.

58. Maria E. Enchautegui, Michael Fix, Pamela Loprest, Sarah C. von der Lippe, and Douglas Wissoker, *Do Minority-Owned Businesses Get a Fair Share of Government Contracts?* (Washington, D.C.: The Urban Institute, 1997).

59. The extremely low parity index for Asian Pacific Americans is due in part to the higher level of entrepreneurship of Asian Pacific Americans compared to other minority groups. If the population is used as the numerator to construct a parity index, then the results would show that Asian Pacific Americans fare better than other minorities, although still not as well as whites. This change in the rank order reveals the limitations of such simple measures.

60. Federal Register: "Federal Procurement; Proposed Reforms to Affirmative Action," May 23, 1996, 61(101): 26041–26063; "Federal Acquisition Regulation; Reform of Affirmative Action in Federal Procurement," June 30, 1998, 63(125): 35719–35726.

61. The purpose and objective of the 8(a) program is to assist socially and economically disadvantaged individuals to participate fully and successfully in the business mainstream of the American economy. This goal is accomplished through the expansion of businesses owned by program participants, which, in turn, generates societal benefits through the creation of jobs and wealth. Program participants receive multiyear business development assistance. Because of the selection rules and the underlying composition of disadvantaged firms, the participants in the 8(a) program are predominantly minority, and this is particularly true in the early years.

62. Tabulation by author of California Certification Information System (Calcert) 1999 database, California Department of Transportation.

63. Stephen L. Klineberg, *Houston's Ethnic Communities, Third Edition* (Houston, Tex.: Rice University Press, 1996).

64. Ron Nissimov, 28 June 1998: www .civilrights.org/aa/states/tx.html

65. There is no equivalent exit poll on Asian Pacific Americans for Houston's Proposition A or Washington State's Initiative 200, but there is some indirect information. An inspection of the votes by precinct in King County, which includes Seattle, reveals that most of the predominantly Asian Pacific American neighborhoods (by block groups) coincide with precincts where voters overwhelmingly (75 percent or more) voted against the initiative. www.seattletimes.com/news/local/charts/vote d98/I200county.html, and www.seattletimes .com/news/local/charts/voted98/I200race.html.

66. *Los Angeles Times*, November 7, 1996: A29.

67. A part of the explanation might be that this group had been sensitized to the necessity to fight wedge issues sponsored by conservatives. In 1994, the state passed Proposition 187, an initiative designed to prevent undocumented aliens from public services but also had a strong anti-immigrant undercurrent. *Los Angeles Times*, November 10, 1994: B4.

68. Kathy Feng and Bonnie Tang, *1996 Southern California Asian Pacific American Exit Poll Report: An Analysis of APA Voter Behavior and Opinions* (Los Angeles and Washington, D.C.: Asian Pacific American Legal Center and National Asian Pacific American Legal Consortium, 1997).

69. Larry Shinagawa, *1996 San Francisco Bay Area Exit Poll Report: An Analysis of APA Demographics, Behavior and Political Participation* (San Francisco and Washington, D.C.: Asian Law Caucus and National Asian Pacific American Legal Consortium, 1997).

70. Paul M. Ong and Suzanne Hee, "Economic Diversity, An Overview," in Paul M. Ong, ed., *The State of Asian Pacific America: Economic Diversity, Issues and Policies* (Los Angeles: LEAP Asian Pacific American Public Policy Institute and UCLA Asian American Studies Center, 1994), 31–55; Robert M. Jiobu, "Recent Asian Pacific Immigrants: The Demographic Background," in Bill O. Hing and Ronald Lee, eds., *Reframing the Immigration Debate* (Los Angeles: LEAP Asian Pacific American Public Policy Institute and UCLA Asian American Studies Center, 1996), 35–57.

71. Grant Din, "An Analysis of Asian/ Pacific American Registration and Voting Pat-

terns in San Francisco," master's thesis, Claremont Graduate School, 1984; Don T. Nakanishi, *The UCLA Asian Pacific American Voter Registration Study* (Los Angeles: Asian Pacific American Legal Center, 1986); Paul M. Ong and Don T. Nakanishi, "Becoming Citizens, Becoming Voters: The Naturalization and Political Participation of Asian Pacific Immigrants," in Bill O. Hing and Ronald Lee, eds., *Reframing the Immigration Debate* (Los Angeles: LEAP Asian Pacific American Public Policy Institute and UCLA Asian American Studies Center, 1996), 275–305.

72. Paul M. Ong and David Lee, "Changing of the Guard? The Rise of an Immigrant Majority," paper presented at the Conference on Asian Americans and Politics, The Woodrow Wilson Center, Washington, D.C., March 14, 1998.

73. Post/Kaiser/Harvard Race Poll, 1995. Respondents were asked to choose which of the following two statement represents their opinion: "White Americans have benefited from past and present discrimination against African Americans, so they should be willing to make up for these wrongs" or "Most white Americans have not benefited from past and present discrimination against African Americans/Hispanic Americans/Asian Americans, so they have no responsibility to make up for these wrongs." Forty-six percent of Asian Pacific American respondents selected the first statement when applied to Hispanics or Asian Pacific Americans.

74. "APA Agenda: Asian Americans on the Issues," *Asian Week,* August 23–29, 1996: 14–17. For questions on giving preferences to underrepresented minorities in employment and public contracts, 51 percent agree, 33 disagreed, and 16 percent had no opinion.

75. Gabriel Chin, Sumi Cho, Jerry Kang, and Frank Wu, *Beyond Self-Interest: Asian Pacific Americans Toward a Community of Justice, A Policy Analysis of Affirmative Action* (Los Angeles: LEAP Asian Pacific American Public Policy Institute and UCLA Asian American Studies Center, 1996), 25.

# 4.2

# Japanese American Redress
## The Proper Alignment Model

*Harry H. L. Kitano and Mitchell T. Maki*

〰〰〰〰〰〰〰〰〰〰〰〰〰〰〰〰〰〰〰〰〰〰〰〰〰

On August 10, 1988, President Ronald Reagan signed the Civil Liberties Act of 1988, which granted an apology and authorized monetary payments to Americans of Japanese ancestry for their incarceration during World War II. In October 1990, survivors of the concentration camps began receiving $20,000 and the following letter of apology from President George Bush:

A monetary sum and words alone cannot restore lost years or erase painful memories; neither can they fully convey our Nation's resolve to rectify injustice and to uphold rights of individuals. We can never fully right the wrongs of the past. But we can take a clear stand for justice and recognize that serious injustices were done to Japanese American during World War II.

In enacting a law calling for restitution and offering a sincere apology, your fellow Americans have, in a very real sense, renewed their traditional commitment to the ideals of freedom,

equality and justice. You and your family have our best wishes for the future.

In 1988, there were a number of critical issues such the balanced budget, soaring welfare costs, care of the elderly, medical and health coverage, and crime that were at the forefront of the federal government's policy agenda. In this context, a small minority group was able to obtain a presidential apology and monetary redress payments. The passage of federal legislations authorizing redress and the subsequent securing of appropriations are the hallmarks of the Japanese American redress movement. This movement was initiated within the ethnic minority community, fought in both the legislative and judicial arenas, ultimately supported by a president whose administration initially opposed it, and financed as an entitlement program. The legacy of the Japanese American redress movement, however, goes beyond the unprecedented apology and monetary payments. The redress movement involves the lessons and experiences of a small ethnic minority community engaging in the process of federal public policy making.

Several books have focused on specific aspects of the redress movement (Daniels,

Kitano, Harry H. L., and Mitchell T. Maki. "Japanese American Redress: Proper Alignment Model." *Asian American Policy Review* VII: 55–72. Reprinted with permission.

Taylor, and Kitano 1986; Hohri 1988; Irons 1989; Hatamiya 1993; Takezawa 1995). The purpose of this paper is to present the Kitano-Maki Proper Alignment Model as a framework for understanding how the Civil Liberties Act of 1988 was passed. Additionally, this paper addresses the strategies and key elements that were instrumental in aligning the various public policy streams of influence.

## THE KITANO-MAKI PROPER ALIGNMENT MODEL

The initial idea of a "proper alignment" came from an interview with Congressman Norman Y. Mineta. When asked about the passage of redress, he humorously responded that it might have occurred because of the perfect alignment of the stars, moon, and sun. Such an alignment would be extremely rare, and nature would be the primary force, with humans playing an insignificant role. The possibility of a less celestial alignment of more human elements, however, gave birth to the Kitano-Maki model. The important issue was to identify the streams of influence that needed to be properly aligned, the importance of the human factor, and the interaction among them. The following six streams make up the proper alignment model:

1. History: General American Public
2. History: Community
3. Legislative Branch: the Senate
4. Legislative Branch: the House
5. Judicial Branch
6. Executive Branch

"History" involves the events, experiences, and mood of different time periods that create a context that serves to either prevent or facilitate the creation of specific policy. The "General American Pubic" refers to the mood, attitude, and organization of the mainstream toward a proposed policy. The "Community" refers to a particular group's mood, attitude, and organi-

zation toward a proposed policy. These two streams are interdependent. The general public's perspective of the particular group and, in turn, the group's reaction to that perspective, influence the ratings in both streams.

The "Legislative Branch" is divided into the Senate and the House. These streams reflect the mood and general disposition of the U.S. Congress toward a policy issue. Since most public policy is affected by the Congress, this stream is essential. The "Judicial Branch" reflects the judicial decisions that define the legal parameters of policy development. For federal policy, this stream involves the federal courts' and the U.S. Supreme Court's determinations of whether a particular policy is lawful and the degree to which it can be implemented. Finally, the "Executive Branch" reflects the power of the president of the United States in terms of the ability either to initiate and sustain new policy or to block the new policy through a veto.

For each time period in the different streams, a rating reflects the amount of support and advocacy that a particular policy has garnered. These ratings are based upon the historic data (e.g., archival documents reflecting the mood of the mainstream or particular community, congressional actions, judicial decisions, executive orders or statements) for any given time period. A "positive" (+) rating reflects a high degree of support and advocacy for the proposed policy issue. A "neutral/positive" (N+) reflects more support than opposition, or the absence of any significant resistance. A "neutral" (N) reflects either an equal amount of support and opposition, or a general ambivalence. "Neutral/negative" (N-) reflects greater opposition than support. Finally, "negative" (-) reflects a high degree of opposition or general apathy.

The proper alignment of the development of a new public policy occurs when each of the variables has a "positive" or "neutral/ positive" rating. When this occurs, a window of opportunity is created that can facilitate new public policy. When all the variables are "negative" or "neutral/negative," not only is the passage of a particular policy highly unlikely but there is also a likelihood that a converse policy can be enacted. No one stream is inherently more important than the other. Any stream out of alignment reduces the opportunity for policy to be enacted.

After World War II and the release of Japanese Americans from the camps, conditions gradually changed so that by 1988, all six of the variables had changed from an alignment of negative ratings to one of positive ratings (see table 4.2a). The important question of why it took so long—from the closing of the camps in 1945 to the passage of redress in 1988—can be understood by following the slow but positive changes that occurred in each of the variables in the intervening years. The "proper alignment" for redress legislation was not in place until 1988. The model is presented in table 4.2a. The model divides the history into (1) the pre-World War II years, leading up to the wartime period; (2) the wartime years, 1942–1946; (3) the post-war years by decade; (4) 1988, the passage of redress.

In applying the Kitano-Maki Proper Alignment Model, it is crucial to understand the elements, natural forces, and strategies that affect the changes in the ratings of each variable. Movement within each of the streams of influence is determined by a number of elements. Kingdon (1984) indicates that a policy item's emergence onto the political agenda is "due to the joint effect of several factors coming together at a given point in time, not to the effect of one or another of them singly."[1] Campbell (1992) describes how new ideas and energy, information, political power, timing, and rationality can be influencing factors in the development of public policy. Cohen, March, and Olsen (1972) describe the policy-making process as a "garbage can" of competing and possibly unrelated issues. In the Kitano-Maki Proper Alignment Model, each stream resembles a "garbage can" in which new ideas, energy, information, political power, timing, and rationality all affect the outcome.

There were two main arenas for the redress struggle: the federal government and the community. The federal government was the realm through which formal policy was introduced, sanctioned, and implemented. The community, including both the mainstream public and the Japanese Americans, was the source from which both positive and negative ideas and energy emanated, helping to shape the formal policy-making process. Both arenas were equally important in obtaining redress.

The history streams (Community and Mainstream) are especially affected by the dynamics of resource mobilization (Morris, 1984) and collective behavior (Turner and Killian, 1987). The history streams influence the other streams of the federal government by exerting pressure and affecting

**Table 4.2a    Kitano-Maki Proper Alignment Model**

| Years | History | | Legislative | | Judicial branch | Executive branch |
| | General public | Community | Senate | House | | |
| --- | --- | --- | --- | --- | --- | --- |
| 1987–1988 | + | N+ | + | + | N+ | + |
| 1980–86 | N+ | N+ | N | N+ | N+ | N− |
| 1970s | N+ | N | N | N | N | N+ |
| 1960s | N+ | N | N | N | N | N |
| 1945–50s | N− | N− | N− | N− | N− | N− |
| WWII/Excl | − | − | − | − | − | − |
| Pre-WWII | N− | − | − | − | − | − |

Note: Ratings reflect status at the end of the time period.

the context in which the federal government operates. Turner and Killian (1987) indicate that five major elements transform existing communities and their structures into agents for social change: the development of an emergent norm, feasibility, timeliness, the utilization of preexisting groups, and the presence of extraordinary events solidarity. All five elements played a crucial role in the redress movement.

Of particular importance in the Proper Alignment Model is the notion that the reception that a minority community experiences is closely tied to the chances of passage for specific types of legislation. As the Japanese American community grew in resources and became more positively received by the general American public, the federal branches of government became more sympathetic to the issue of redress. The elements and strategies that influenced policy making were the manner in which the issue of redress was framed, the creation and maintenance of a board coalition of supportive groups, the mobilization of the Japanese American community, political access, perseverance, and good fortune. Each of the different streams of influence experienced a positive progression from negative rating to neutral rating to ultimately positive or neutral/positive rating in 1988.

Our forthcoming book, *The Impossible Dream: Japanese Americans and Redress* will go into much greater detail concerning the model. The Kitano-Maki Proper Alignment Model was developed specifically to address the issue of Japanese American redress. It can, however, be applied to the examination of other policy issues.

### The Pre-World War II Era

During this time period, Japanese and other Asian immigrants were unwanted as equal participants in the American dream. They were victims of racism who were legally considered "aliens ineligible to citizenship"[2] and relegated to the lower rungs of the stratification system. Discrimination was codified; for example, in 1913 and 1920, the California legislature passed Alien Land Acts which prohibited Japanese from owning agricultural land. In 1914, state Attorney General Webb candidly stated the motives behind the measure:

> The fundamental basis of all legislation has been, and is, race undesirability. It (the law) seeks to limit [the Japanese] presence by curtailing their privileges which they may enjoy here, for they will not come in large numbers and long abide with us if they may not acquire land.[3]

Japanese immigrants who were legally in the United States could not apply for naturalization and citizenship. The 1924 Immigration Act prohibited any more Japanese, as well as all other Asians, from legally immigrating. For those already here, a series of other actions—such as anti-miscegenation law, housing restrictions, and restricted job opportunities—treated the Issei, first generation Japanese immigrants, as noncitizens without the protection of the Constitution and reinforced the policy of exclusion.

The Nisei, or second generation, was born between the 1910s and the 1940s and were American citizens by birth. They also, however, faced discrimination and the problem of adjusting to the world of their parents and American society. The Nisei faced a two-sided cultural dilemma. No matter how hard they tried to become "American," they faced rejection from the mainstream community and their parents, who believed that they were becoming "too American" too fast. An additional factor, which continues to the present day, was the inability of the American society to differentiate between Japanese Americans and the actions of Japan. This was an important factor in the wartime incarceration, when the prevailing thought was that since they all looked alike, they must all be alike.

The years prior to the wartime evacuation were difficult times for the Japanese. The mainstream community and the three branches of government were anti-Japanese. Not only were Japanese immigrants denied the basic rights and privileges of citizenship but Japan's military exploits in Manchuria and China made the Japanese the number one enemy. The West Coast media, especially the Hearst Press, was virulently anti-Japanese. C. W. Reynolds (1927) surveyed the files of California newspapers in 1927 and found 20,453 inches of newspaper space written about the Japanese Americans. The general attitude reflected in these items was irritation and hostility. Reynolds also found an increased presence of newspaper attacks on Japanese Americans in election years and during economic depressions. The barriers of legalized racism, cultural differences, and social inaccessibility prohibited the Japanese in America from participated fully in the mainstream society. All Japanese in the United States, whether citizens by birth or aliens, were the targets of hostility and disregard.

The one positive element during this time was the ability of the ethnic community to develop their own resources and social structures. The Issei had their own organizations that reflected their own experiences in Japan, while the Nisei developed their own mini-society based on American models. The Japanese American community during this period had their own hospitals, employment agencies, and small businesses, while social and recreational opportunities were also created primarily within their community. Generational tensions, a common occurrence among immigrant groups, were a part of the Japanese American experience. For example, the Japanese American Citizens League (JACL), one of the first organizations developed by the Nisei, excluded the Issei. Therefore while there was an Issei and Nisei community, living and interacting together on many issues, it was structurally pluralistic. The basic weakness of the ethnic community, however, was its lack of access to the mainstream society, which meant that the people were powerless to influence critical issues such as discrimination and denial of citizenship for the Issei. In terms of our model (see table 4.2a), all of the variables show a "negative," except of the ethnic

community which rates a "neutral/negative" because of the lack of power and access to the political system which was slightly offset by the cohesiveness of the community.

## 1942 to 1945: The War Years

Following the Japanese attack on Pearl Harbor in 1941, for most Americans all Japanese—whether citizens or aliens—were regarded as the enemy. There are a large number of publications covering the war years and the ensuing exclusion and incarceration period (Thomas and Nishimoto 1946; Thomas 1952; Hosokawa 1969; Kitano 1969; Daniels 1971; Weglyn 1976; Harrington 1976; Irons 1983; Daniels 1993; Hirabayasi 1995). The momentum provided by a negative history, the hostility in the mainstream community, and the three branches of the government created a "proper alignment" of negative ratings. When President Franklin D. Roosevelt signed Executive Order 9066 in February 1942, the process leading to the subsequent incarceration of Japanese in the United States was well under way. The Japanese community was no longer a cohesive unit; there were divisions by generation and by pro-America and pro-Japanese sentiments. The JACL, the largest Japanese American organization, advocated cooperation; thus, a divided community was unable to mount an organized protest. There was a "proper alignment" of negative ratings on the national front that enabled the decision for incarceration into the wartime concentration camps to be a popular one. In summary, the historical context was clearly against Japanese in America; the ethnic community was divided and powerless, and both the House and the Senate supported President Roosevelt. Additionally, during this time period, the Supreme Court upheld the convictions of three Japanese Americans, Hirabayashi, Korematsu, and Yasui, who had challenged the race-based curfew and exclusion orders.

## 1945 to 1950s:
## The Post War Period

Ironically, while anti-Japanese feelings were reaching their zenith during World War II, there was positive movement in attitudes toward other Asians. There was the repeal of the Chinese Exclusion Act by the Congress in 1943, which established an immigration quota for China and allowed Chinese aliens (but not other Asians) to become naturalized citizens. Within the next decade, all absolute racial and ethnic barriers to immigration and naturalization were eliminated. Discriminatory legislation was slowly replaced by more inclusive policies. Among the positive signs were the following actions:

- The passage of the Japanese Evacuation Claims Act of 1948, which provided limited compensation for property losses incurred during the evacuation.
- The California Supreme Court ruling that held that the Alien Land Laws violated the equal protection clauses of both the U.S. and California Constitutions.
- The McCarran-Walter Act of 1952, which established a token immigration quota to Japan and upheld the right of the Issei to apply for naturalization and citizenship.
- The U.S. Supreme Court ruling in *Brown v. the Board of Education* (1954) that struck down the doctrine of "separate but equal," which had served to underpin legal segregation.

An event that was to play an important role in the redress movement was the admission of the territory of Hawaii as the fiftieth state of the Union in 1959. This event opened the door for the subsequent election of Japanese Americans to the United States Congress. Beginning in 1959, the community began to develop ethnic representation in the Congress. During the 1950s, however, redress was not a major concern in the Japanese American community[4]; recovering from the concentration camps and making a liv-ing were the major priorities. The period was characterized by inertia, both in the ethnic community and in Congress, with regard to redress. Nevertheless, the streams were becoming less antagonistic toward Japanese in America (N-).

## The 1960s

The 1960s saw the beginning of the Civil Rights Era, when minorities began to demonstrate their dissatisfaction with the status quo. There were protest marches, demonstrations, sit-ins, and riots. Race relations and racial discrimination became targets of concern for the country. Most Japanese Americans, however, were not intimately involved in the Civil Rights Movement. Most were trying to forget the camp experience, and their major concern was to gain economic stability. Some Japanese Americans, however, saw the relationship between the concentration camp experience and the oppression as an assault on their civil rights. A few members of the JACL and other Japanese Americans participated in the 1963 March on Washington, reflecting an awareness that civil rights involved more than black-white struggles. By the end of the 1960s, the Japanese American community was better off financially and had made advances in education, occupation, and housing. The Sansei, third generation, as well as the Nisei, developed a strong sense of ethnic pride, and some began to call for a reassessment of the wartime incarceration. In 1969, Japanese American activists from Southern California organized the first Manzanar Pilgrimage. This was the first of many similar pilgrimages to former concentration camp sites. Redress, however, was still not a high priority in the Japanese American community, although there was a growing interest and awareness of the community's wartime experience (N+).

The mainstream society, in reacting to the pressure of the Civil Rights struggles, began to grapple with issues such as inclusion, equal opportunity, and affirmative action. By the mid-1960s, the media began to treat Japanese Americans more favorably and portrayed them as a "model minority"[5] (N). The Legislative and Executive Branches reflected the changing mood by passing legislation favorable to ethnic minorities (N). In 1967, the Supreme Court also rendered a ruling that was favorable to Japanese Americans who had been incarcerated in the camps[6] (N). As a result of their hard work and the changing political climate, the context in which Japanese Americans found themselves was slowly changing.

## The 1970s

During the 1970s, the Japanese American community initiated important actions that were the forerunners of redress. These actions included the repeal of Title II of the Internal Security Act of 1950[7], the revocation of Executive Order 9066, and the pardoning of Iva Ikuko Toguri ("Tokyo Rose"). Japanese Americans began authoring books about their history and treatment during World War II. The Japanese American community was becoming more organized and politically active. With this increase in activism, generational differences in opinions and perspectives began to surface. Sansei and younger Nisei began to question what they perceived to be the acquiescent behavior of the older generations during World War II. A Nisei writer, Yoshiko Uchida, expressed the generational differences:

> . . . Sansei children, who experienced the Vietnam War, its violent confrontations and protest asked, Why did you let it happen? Why didn't you fight for your civil rights? Why did you go without protest to the concentration camps? . . . It is my generation, however, who lived through the evacuation of 1942 . . . As they listen to our voices from the past, however, I ask that they remember they are listening in a totally different time; in a totally different world.[8]

Redress became a formal issue when Edison Uno, a California community activist

and writer, introduced a redress resolution at the biennial JACL convention in 1970. The National Council of the JACL adopted Uno's resolution in principle, but it took no further action. Few in the community took redress seriously and many were reluctant to push the issue. The 1972 convention affirmed the resolution, but at the 1974 convention, no further action was taken. It was clear that some form of education was necessary, both in the ethnic community and in the halls of Congress. In 1974, there were only ten Senators and eleven Representatives who had been in office during World War II.

In the mid-1970s, the debate in the Japanese American community centered around two questions. The first question was whether to pursue any form of redress. If redress was to be pursued, the second question was what form it should take (e.g., an apology only, individual payments, or community block payments). In opposition to those who supported redress, there was some very strong dissent. One respondent from a redress survey remarked that reparations "won't make a wrong a right, nor will it endear the Japanese Americans to the general public in these troubled economic times . . . shaking our fists and demanding cash reparations for a 30-plus year old injustice cheapens the strength of Japanese spirit and pride (Yamato Damashi)."[9]

While the Japanese American community struggled with its own opinion about redress, it was gaining increased access to Congress. Senators Daniel K. Inouye (D) and Masayuki "Spark" Matsunaga (D) represented Hawaii, while representatives Norman Y. Mineta (D), and later Robert T. Matsui (D)—both of whom had been incarcerated in the camps—were elected from California. Representative Mineta, who was the first member of Congress to have experienced the concentration camps of World War II, recalled his memories of the camps:

> We were treated as prisoners of war, really—not Americans. You have to imagine how we felt looking up at the

guard towers, knowing that their guns were pointed not outward but, in, at us. And I think that the stigma of being accused of disloyalty was even worse than being sent to camp.[10]

At the 1978 JACL National Convention, the organization passed its most strongly worded resolution which specifically called for $25,000 in monetary restitution for individuals who were "detained, interned, or forced to move" from the exclusion zones. Seven months later, the JACL leadership met with the four Democratic Nikkei members of Congress. The Nikkei members questioned the strategy of directly pursuing monetary payments. Senator Inouye, in particular, suggested pursuing the creation of a commission that would serve to educate both the American people and the members of Congress. Based on this meeting and a subsequent vote by the JACL National Committee for Redress, the JACL opted to pursue the creation of a Presidential Commission to explore and gather the facts about the exclusion and incarceration. Legislation was introduced in the 96th Congress to create such a commission. The bill was passed by the Congress and signed by President Jimmy Carter on July 31, 1980.

The process of passing the commission bill helped to sensitize the legislative and executive branches to the need for redress legislation. Not everyone in the Japanese American community, however, was pleased with this strategy. Some felt that the JACL had once again given in to the mainstream society by not directly advocating for monetary redress. Members of the Seattle JACL disagreed with the National JACL and encouraged their freshman representative, Mike Lowry (D-WA), to introduce direct redress monetary legislation. While the commission bill passed, Lowry's bill died in committee. The alignment was not yet right for the passage of monetary redress.

Among the leadership of the Japanese American community, there was name-calling, challenges to personal dignity, personality clashes, and ideological differences. Even though some of these differences and conflicts were deeply seated, they did not derail the movement from the ultimate goal of gaining some form of redress. Mass community support to remember and commemorate the camp experience continued throughout the 1970s. The first "Day of Remembrance" was held on Thanksgiving weekend, 1978 at the Puyallup Fairgrounds in Washington. The event was attended by thousands of Japanese Americans, and it was the fist of many Days of Remembrance in the coming years in numerous cities.

The active role of the ethnic community, combined with its access to the Japanese American congressmen, was critical during the initial stages of redress. Without the energy provided by the ethnic community, the chance for any policy change would have been negligible. The energy provided by members of the ethnic group moved their legislators to take a much more active role in redress. Congressmen Mineta and Matsui, who represented districts with extremely small Japanese American populations, ran the risk of possible backlash. Without the support of the Nikkei legislators, the chances for redress would have been greatly decreased.

The end of the 1970s saw the ethnic community taking a much more active role in working toward redress and applying pressure on its ethnic congressmen (N+). The legislative (N), executive (N+), and judicial (N) branches were becoming more sensitized to the redress issue. The American mainstream, as a whole, was becoming more cognizant of racism and inequality, so that although there was still a neutral stance toward redress, there was a growing awareness that civil rights of minorities had to be addressed (N).

## 1980 to 1986

While the JACL initially took the lead in the redress effort, there were individuals and groups in the Japanese American community who questioned the role of the JACL. Many individuals remembered that the JACL advocated cooperation with the government during the wartime incarceration and questioned how effectively it could lead a redress movement. During the late 1970s and early 1980s, a number of individuals, some with JACL ties, formed other groups that developed different strategies in the redress effort. William Hohri, based in Chicago, and individuals from the Seattle, Washington, area formed the National Council for Japanese American Redress (NCJAR). The NCJAR eventually adopted a judicial strategy through the vehicle of a class action lawsuit. In Seattle, the Washington Coalition of Redress was organized. In Los Angeles, the National Coalition for Redress and Reparations (NCRR) was formed in 1980 in response to concerns about the JACL's commitment to monetary redress. The diversity of organizations was a double-edged sword. While on the one hand, it offered new opportunities to join in the movement, it also created the potential for disruptive competition and rivalry between the groups.

In terms of the redress movement, the 1980s began with the establishment and implementation of the commission on Wartime Relocation and Internment of Civilians (CWRIC). Between July and December 1981, this nine-member commission, which was appointed by the president, the Senate, and the House, held ten public hearings in nine cities and involved twenty days of testimony and more than 750 witnesses. The commission hearings were important for two reasons. First, it served as a fact finding body which eventually produced a written report of findings and recommendations that were very supportive of redress. Second, the commission provided a forum through which the members of the Japanese American community could articulate their pain, anger, and demands for justice. The commission hearings served as a vehicle through which discussions of the incarceration and redress issues were brought into the living rooms and dining rooms of many Japanese American families. The commission hearings provided a cathartic experience that produced greater cross-generational understanding of the exclusion and incarceration experience. Such unity in the community was essential to maintaining the support for redress.

Simultaneous to and following the Commission hearings, redress efforts diversified. On the Judicial front, the NCJAR pursued a class action lawsuit to address the constitutional violations of the exclusion and incarceration. Concurrently, a group of volunteer attorneys headed by Dale Minami, Peter Irons, Peggy Nagae, and Kathryn Bannai filed three separate *writ of coram nobis* suits to overturn the trial court convictions of Gordon Hiraayashi, Fred Korematsu, and Min Yasui.

During the 98th and 99th Congresses, redress legislation was introduced and killed in the assigned subcommittees. Redress, however, was gaining more congressional support (as reflected by the increasing number of co-sponsorships). A particularly effective strategy in garnering this support was the manner in which the issue was framed. The issue of redress was framed not as a special interest bill designed solely to address the injustices suffered by a particular group of people. Rather, redress legislation was presented as addressing the much larger issue of Constitutional rights and the Constitution's promise of equal opportunity for all. Such a strategy appealed to both liberals and conservatives. The redress movement also created and utilized a broad coalition of support across various ethnic, gender, religious, professional, and regional lines. Japanese American veterans were instrumental in helping to publicize their demonstration of loyalty and courage during World War II and, in doing so, neutralized any opposition to redress initiated by any American veterans groups. Finally, the Japanese American community became more sophisticated in developing access to their congressional legislators. In the early 1970s, most Japanese Americans were unfamiliar with the political process and even had difficulty contacting their own local elected officials. By the mid-to-late 1980s, many Japanese American redress activists were regularly communicating with their federal legislators, some even on a first name basis (N+).

During this time period, an increasing number of mainstream groups began to support the notion of redress (N+). In the legislative branch, the Senate (N+) was controlled by the Republican Party, while the House (N+) was controlled by the Democrats. During the 1980s, the judicial stream would influence the redress movement with several significant decisions. While the NCJAR lawsuit lost, two of the three *coram nobis* cases resulted in decisions that unequivocally acknowledged the fundamental error in the convictions of Hirabayashi and Korematsu. These judicial efforts highlighted the constitutional violations involved with the wartime incarceration. Although the U.S. Supreme Court refused to rule on the merits of the NCJAR case, the judicial rulings in the *coram nobis* cases served as a judicial foundation for redress (N+). The major obstacle was the Executive branch, which had consistently opposed all redress legislation (N-).

## 1987 to 1988:
## The 100th Congress

The 100th Congress represented a golden window of opportunity for the passage of redress. The Nikkei members of Congress were at the height of their collective political influence. Senator Inouye possessed seniority and a great deal of political clout in the Senate. Senator Matsunaga was in his second term and was very popular among his colleagues. Representatives Mineta and Mastsui were in their seventh and fifth terms, respectively, and were both well-respected by their colleagues in the House. In addition, the Democrats regained control of both the House and Senate, which resulted in key changes in the heads of subcommittees (+).

The time period of 1977 to 1988 also provided a window of opportunity for the Japanese American community's support (+). The elements of an emergent norm, feasibility, timeliness, preexisting groups,

and an extraordinary event (Turner and Killian 1987) were all present. The community was reaching the height of its organizing and mobilizing efforts. Within the community, there was the sense of mission and conviction that the redress movement was just and right. Members of the community not only saw the tangibility and availability of resources and connections but also had the hope, belief, and self-confidence that they could win redress. There was also a sense of urgency in the community. With an estimated 200 Issei dying each month, redress needed to be obtained as soon as possible. The existing groups fighting for redress continued the struggle, and the movement served as an extraordinary event that facilitated solidarity throughout the community.

## President Reagan
## Signs the Redress Legislation

As the redress legislation worked its way through the Senate and the House, efforts were also being made to secure President Reagan's support. Early testimony from the Department of Justice and other informal discussions indicated the Reagan Administration's opposition to the bill. Two factors were instrumental in obtaining the president's support: the manner in which the issue was presented and the willingness of the Congress to compromise on key technical components of the bill. Grant Ujifusa, the JACL Legislative Education Committee Strategy Chair, reasoned that reminding President Reagan of his personal connection to the issue would help to win his support. Ujifusa asked a personal acquaintance, Governor Thomas Kean of New Jersey, to discuss the issue with President Reagan. Subsequently, Ujifusa asked Governor Kean to send two letters to the President reminding him of how he had participated in a medal ceremony for Kazuo Masuda. Masuda, a Nisei member of the 442nd Regimental Combat Team, had been killed in action in World War II, and his family was denied the right to bury him in a local cemetery in Southern California. On the day of the medal ceremony, Ronald Reagan, who was at that time a captain in the army, read the scripted words:

The blood that has soaked into the sand is all one color. America stands unique in the world, the only country not founded on race, but on a way—an ideal. Not in spite of, but because of our polyglot background, we have had all the strength in the world. That is the American way. Mr. and Mrs. Masuda, just as one member of the family of Americans, speaking to another member, I want to say for what you son Kazuo did—Thanks.[11]

An additional incentive for the president to support the redress bill was the growing political power that the Asian American community was beginning to exercise in California. In 1988, the Asian American community actively lobbied the state senate to deny confirmation of Rep. Dan Lungren to State Treasurer. Lungren served on the CWRIC and was the lone vote of dissension against monetary redress payments. Asian American activists did not forget and joined together with other civil rights, environmental, labor, housing, peace and other progressive organizations which were highly effective in persuading state legislators to reject Lungren's nomination. While the state assembly confirmed the nomination, the state senate denied it by a vote 21 to 19. A key vote belonged to Senator Quentin Kopp (I-CA) who initially pledged to vote for the confirmation. Prior to the vote, numerous letters opposing the nomination inundated his office, which led to Senator Kopp's voting against the confirmation.[12] "In the future, I don't think politicians are going to take the Asian-American community as lightly as Lungren did," said Rep. Matsui.[13]

A final factor in obtaining President Reagan's support was the willingness of the House-Senate conference committee to make some compromises with the Reagan Administration. The Reagan Administration's technical concern included extending the payment period from five to ten years, limiting the amount appropriated to no more than $500 million annually, and implementing an extinguishment clause. These concerns were addressed in the House-Senate conference committee, and upon their resolution, President Reagan signaled his support for the redress legislation through a letter to Rep. Jim Wright (D-TX), the Speaker of the House. The strategy of appealing to the President on a personal and anecdotal level coupled with the demonstration of growing political power facilitated the changing of the variable rating in 1988 from a negative (-) to a positive (+).

## Entitlement

The story of redress is incomplete without an appreciation for the process that secured the entitlement status for the redress payments. The major element involved in this process was the presence of influential inside political power. This political power was found with Senator Inouye. He was the one redress supporter who had the necessary congressional seniority, held a position on the Appropriations Committee, and had enough political chits to "call in." Senator Inouye was responsible for introducing the idea, shepherding the amendment through the committee structure, securing the necessary floor vote, and for procuring the agreement by the House-Senate conference committee. The process involved internal maneuvering and negotiations which were greatly insulated form the influence of the general American constituency. The obtaining of the entitlement status is a good example of how the "rightness" of an idea is not sufficient for its adoption. In the House, Rep. Sidney Yates (D-IL) introduced a similar amendment to make redress an entitlement program. Rep. Yates' amendment was rejected.

## Two Final Elements

Along with all the aforementioned elements that affected the streams of influence on policy-making, two final elements, which are often overlooked, greatly facilitated the passage of redress. The first is perseverance. The modern redress movement spanned nearly twenty years from the time of the initial JACL resolution in 1970 until the passage of the entitlement status in 1989.[14] Prior to the 1970 resolution, a great deal of community organizing work was involved to prepare the Japanese American community for the redress movement. The dedication and perseverance of all the players involved in the redress movement was an intangible element that made the movement possible.

The second element is good fortune. The Japanese American redress story is full of moments of good timing, good fortune, and plain good luck. An example would be Rep. Barney Frank (D-MA) assuming the chair of the Subcommittee on Administrative Law and Governmental Relations of the House Judiciary Committee. The previous chairs had also been Democrats but had failed to move the bill out of committee. Rep. Frank's appointment as chair was not planned but was fortuitous for the redress movement as he was an ardent supporter. Other examples of good fortune involved chance meetings between individuals, the locating of key documents, and the assigning of certain judges. The element of good fortune interacts with the element of perseverance and hard work. Many of the "lucky" events in the redress movement would have been useless were it not for the hard work and preparation that allowed redress supporters to capitalize on them. In regards to the redress effort, luck is best understood vis-à-vis the athletic analogy, "The harder we work, the luckier we get."

## CONCLUSION

The Kitano-Maki Proper Alignment Model was developed in order to explain the passage of the Civil Liberties Act of 1988. What was once viewed as impossible became a reality because of the positive alignment of the mainstream society, the ethnic community, and the three branches of government. The Japanese American community began to mobilize for redress in the 1970s and developed increased access to congressional legislators who sponsored and pushed for legislation. The Japanese American community was fortunate to have Senator Inouye and Matsunaga and Representative Mineta and Matsui in office during the late 1970s and throughout the 1980s. Additionally, opportune changes in congressional committees, the support of a broad coalition of groups, changes in the mass media, favorable judicial decisions, and the ability to reach President Reagan led to the "proper alignment" in 1988. This movement occurred in the context of historic changes in America's view of Japan (from World War II enemy to America's most important ally in Asia) and treatment of Japanese Americans (from exclusion toward inclusion).

As opposed to the proper alignment of the stars, the moon, and the sun, the model emphasizes the human factors—hard work, framing of the issue, conflict management, community cohesion, development of political access, perseverance, and timing. In addition, there was good fortune related to hard work, and the ability to act when opportunities became available. It was the alignment of all the streams—the ethnic community, the larger community, and the three branches of government—that facilitated the passage of Japanese American redress.

The wartime incarceration of Japanese Americans and subsequent redress legislation were unique events. For others seeking to promote public policy change, however, the Kitano-Maki model highlights important lessons of how to align the various streams of influence. The historic context is highly influential and is manifested in the mood of the mainstream society as well as that of the particular community. The cohesion of a community and its ability to have access to those in the power structure who can provide key support and sponsorship is crucial. Judicial rulings, congressional actions, and executive decisions indicate whether momentum is moving in a positive or negative direction. These variables and the factors that facilitated their alignment were critical in the passage of Japanese American redress. The application of these lessons to other policy efforts will play an important role in the securing of public policy that addresses the concerns and issues of other groups who have suffered from discriminatory treatment.

## NOTES

1. John W. Kingdon, *Agendas, Alternatives, and Public Policies.* (Glenville, Ill.L: Scott Foresman, 1984), 188.

2. The phase "aliens ineligible to citizenship" comes from the 1913 Alien Land Law (State of California).

3. Sidney L. Gulick, *The American Japanese Problem.* (New York, Charles Scribner's Sons, 1914), 189.

4. By the 1950s, there had been discussions about and demands for redress. Individuals such as James Omura and Joe Kurihara were early proponents of some form of redress. Additionally, in 1945, there was an All Center Conference in Salt Lake City, Utah, which was attended by representatives of seven of the concentration camps. A demand for redress emanated form this conference.

5. William Peterson, "Success Story, Japanese-American Style," The *New York Times,* January 9 1966: 21. Although the term "model minority" is problematic, it reflected a shift in the general public's view of Japanese Americans as "evil" and "the enemy" to a positive stereotypic caricature.

6. *Honda v. Clark* (1967).

7. Title II authorized he emergency detention of those suspected of espionage or sabotage against the United States. Included in this authorization was the maintenance of detention centers, one of which was Tule Lake.

8. Yoshiko Uchida, *Desert exile: The uprooting of a Japanese American family.* (Seattle: University of Washington Press, 1982), 147.

9. "MDC Reparations Survey," *Pacific Citizen* 81(15) (October 10, 1975): 1.

10. Norman Y. Mineta, as told to S. Schindehette, "The Wounds of War: A California

Congressman Recalls the Trauma of World War II Internment." *People Weekly* 28 (December 14, 1987): 175.

11. "General Stilwell Pins Medal on Sister of Nisei Hero in Ceremony at Masuda Ranch." *Pacific Citizen* 21(24) (December 15, 1945): 2.

12. "Senate Narrowly Rejects Lungren: Small Teasurer Nominee Is Backed by Assembly; Court Test a Possibility," *Los Angeles Times,* February 26 1988: 133.

13. "Quiet Minority Shifts Tactics in California." *Washington Post,* February 25, 1988: A3.

14. The modern redress movement did not end in 1989. The movement presently continues in 1997 as the eligibility of certain categories of individuals (i.e., Japanese from South American countries) is still being contested.

## REFERENCES

Campbell, John C. 1992. *How Policies Change: The Japanese Government and the Aging Society.* Princeton, N.J.: Princeton University Press.

Cohen, Michael; March, James; and Joha Olsen. 1972. "A Garbage Can Model of Organizational Choice." *Administrative Science Quarterly* 17 (March): 1-25.

Daniels, Roger. 1993. *Prisoners without Trial: Japanese Americans in World War II.* New York: Hill and Wang.

Daniels, Roger. 1972. *Concentration Camps, U.S.A.: Japanese Americans and World War II.* New York: Holt, Rinehart, & Winston.

Daniels, Roger; Sandra Taylor, and Harry Kitano, eds. 1986. *Japanese Americans: From Relocation to Redress.* Salt Lake City: University of Utah Press.

Gulick, Sidney L. 1914. *The American Japanese Problem,* New York, Charles Scribner's Sons.

Harrington, Joseph D. 1979. *Yankee Samurai.* Detroit: Pettigrew Enterprises.

Hatamiya, Leslie T. 1993. *Righting a Wrong: Japanese Americans and the Passage of the Civil Liberties Act of 1988.* Stanford: Stanford University Press.

Hirabayashi, Lane R., ed. *Inside an American Concentration Camp.* 1995. Tuscon: University of Illinois Press.

Hohri, William M. 1988. *Repairing America: An Account of the Movement for Japanese*

*American Redress.* Pullman, Wa.: Washington State University Press.

Hosokawa, Bill. 1969. *Nisei: The Quiet Americans.* New York: William Morrow.

Irons, Peter, ed. 1989. *Justice Delayed: the Record of the Japanese American Internment Cases.* Middletown, Conn.: Wesleyan Press.

Irons, Peter. 1983. *Justice at War: The Story of the Japanese American Internment Cases.* New York: Oxford Press.

Kingdon, John W. 1984. *Agendas, Alternatives, and Public Policies.* Glenville, Ill.: Scott Foresman.

Kitano, Harry H. L. 1969. *Japanese Americans: The Evolution of a Subculture.* Englewood Cliffs, N.J.: Prentice-Hall, Inc.

*Los Angeles Times.* 1988. "Senate Narrowly Reject Lungren: Small Treasurer Nominee Is Backed by Assembly; Court Test a Possibility," February 26, Part I: 33.

Mineta, Norman, as told to S. Schindehette. 1987. "The Wounds of War: A California Congressman Recalls the Trauma of World War II Internment." *People Weekly,* 28 (December 14): 175.

Morris, Aldon D. 1984. *The Origins of the Civil Rights Movement: Black Communities Organizing for Change.* New York: The Free Press.

*Pacific Citizen.* 1975. "MDC Reparations Survey," 81 (October 10): 1.

*Pacific Citizen.* 1945. "General Stilwell Pins Medal on Sister of Nisei Hero in Ceremony at Masuda Ranch." 21 (December 15): 2.

Petersen, William. 1966. "Success Story, Japanese-American Style." *The New York Times,* January 9: 21.

"Quiet Minority Shifts Tactics in California." 1988. *Washington Post,* February 25: A3.

Reynolds, C. W. 1927. *Oriental—White Relations in Santa Clara County.* Unpublished doctoral thesis, Stanford University, Palo Alto, California.

Takezawa, Yasuko I. 1995. *Breaking the Silence: Redress and Japanese American Ethnicity.* Ithaca: Cornell University Press.

Thomas, Dorothy. 1952. *The Salvage.* Berkeley: University of California Press.

Thomas, Dorothy and Richard S. Nishimoto. 1946. *The Spoilage.* Berkeley: University of California Press.

Turner, Ralph H. and Lewis M. Killian. 1987. *Collective Behavior.* Third Edition. Englewood Cliffs, New Jersey: Prentice-Hall, Inc.

Uchida, Yoshiko. 1982. *Desert Exile: The Uprooting of a Japanese American Family.* Seattle: University of Washington Press.

Weglyn, Michi. 1976. *Years of Infamy: The Untold Story of America's Concentration Camps.* New York: Morrow.

# 4.3

# Building an Asian Pacific Labor Alliance
## A New Chapter in Our History

### Kent Wong

~~~~~~~~~~~~~~~~~~~~~~~~~~~~~~~~~~~~~~~~~~~~~~~~~~~~~~~~~~~~~~~~~~~~~~~~~~~~~~~~~~~~~~

On May 1, 1992, the Asian Pacific American Labor Alliance held its founding convention in Washington, D.C. This historic gathering drew 500 Asian Pacific unionists from around the country, including garment workers from New York, hotel and restaurant workers from Honolulu, longshore workers from Seattle, nurses from San Francisco, and supermarket workers from Los Angeles.

Although Asian Americans have been part of the U.S. work force for nearly 150 years, this was the first time a national Asian Pacific American labor organization was established within the ranks of the AFL-CIO. The establishment of the Asian Pacific American Labor Alliance signals a new era in the movements to organize Asian Pacific workers, promote their participation within the ranks of the labor movement, and forge a new path in the larger fight for equality and justice.

---

Wong, Kent. "Building an Asian Pacific Labor Alliance: A New Chapter in Our History." In *The State of Asian Pacific America: Activism and Resistance in the 1990s*, Karin Aguilar-San Juan, ed. (Boston: South End Press, 1994), 335–50. Reprinted with permission.

## A BRIEF OVERVIEW OF ASIAN AMERICAN LABOR HISTORY

Asian Pacific American history is inseparably woven with U.S. labor history. Asian Americans have contributed an important, though largely ignored, chapter of U.S. labor history. Asian workers built the transcontinental railroad, worked in mines, planted some of the first crops in California's central valley, developed fishing industries and canneries along the West Coast, and labored in sewing factories, laundries, and restaurants in the emerging cities.

Although Asian Pacific workers have toiled for many generations building this country, the U.S. labor movement historically opposed including Asian American workers in union. Union leaders feared that owners would use Asian labor to lower wages and break strikes. Union leaders also believed that Asian workers could neither be assimilated nor organized. During the late 1800s and early 1900s, labor unions helped lead racist anti-Asian movements.

The 1882 Chinese Exclusion Act, supported by labor unions, was the first immigration law in the history of the United

States that explicitly forbade entry of an entire group of people based on their nationality. Samuel Gompers, founder of the American Federation of Labor, was a lifelong opponent of Chinese immigrant labor and upheld absolute union exclusion of Chinese American workers.

Yet, in spite of the hostility from labor leaders, Asian Pacific workers have consistently organized themselves. As early as 1867, thousands of Chinese American railroad workers organized a strike to demand higher wages. In the 1890s groups of Japanese American immigrants in California formed labor organizations and attempted to strengthen relations between the labor movements in Japan and America.

In 1903, Japanese American farm workers in Oxnard, California, participated in one of the first farmworkers' strikes in the country. A group of Japanese and Mexican workers joined to launch a strike and form a multiracial union of farm workers. Yet when they applied for a charter with the American Federation of Labor, they were denied admission because their membership included Japanese Americans.

In the 1930s, Chinese and Japanese Americans helped establish councils of the unemployed, and actively participated in the 1934 general strike on the West Coast. During the same period, Filipino farmworkers established the Filipino Labor Union, and played a key role in organizing agricultural workers throughout California's Central Valley. Some of these veteran organizers went on to lead the historic Delano rape strike in the 1960s. The formation of the United Farm Workers Union in 1965 was the result of a merger between a Filipino American farmworker organization and a Mexican American farmworker organization.

The strong tradition of Asian Pacific labor activism stands in sharp contrast to the widespread myths that Asians are docile, individualistic, and incapable of being organized, or organizing themselves. These myths led to the U.S. labor movement's failure to embrace immigrant workers and other workers of color.

There are notable exceptions to the labor movement's hostile stance toward Asians. The Industrial Workers of the World, also known as the "Wobblies," was committed to organizing workers of all colors, and recruited Japanese American miners in the early part of the century. The Congress of Industrial Organizations (CIO) also allocated extensive resources to organizing Asian and other workers of color in the 1930s.

## THE EMERGING ASIAN PACIFIC AMERICAN WORK FORCE SINCE THE 1960S

The 1960s and 1970s witnessed a significant rise in Asian American activism, encouraged by the Civil Rights, anti-war, and black and Chicano liberation movements. The majority of activists were college students who organized opposition to the Vietnam War from their campuses. They also took up the struggle for ethnic studies, affirmative action, and others changes within universities.

Asian American student activists later began to develop "serve the people" programs to organize within Asian American communities. They developed numerous youth services, tutorial programs, English as a second language classes, tenant support work, drug programs, health care projects, legal services, and senior services. Greater involvement in the community also led to more interest and support for the struggles of workers and unions.

When the U.S. government lifted racially restrictive immigration quotas with the passage of the Immigration Act of 1966, Asian immigration exploded. The Asian Pacific American population has doubled every ten years since 1960, making Asian Americans currently the fastest growing ethnic group in the country. Asian Pacific Americans will number 10 million by the end of this decade, with over two-thirds immigrants.

The first waves of immigrants from Asia came from China, Japan, and the Philippines. Since the 1960s, large numbers of

Korean, Southeast Asians, Indians, and Pacific Islanders have come to the United States. Like their counterparts over the years, Asian immigrants are mainly working people, highly urbanized, and generally live in ethnic enclaves. Asian immigrant workers are also frequently clustered in racially segregated occupations, and concentrated in garment, electronic and other light manufacturing, supermarkets and food production, and in service industries such as restaurants, hotels, health care, and maintenance.

Though the Asian Pacific work force has risen dramatically, comprehensive data on it is limited. Even the recently released 1990 census data lacks specific demographic data on employment trends or occupations of Asian Pacific Americans.

Although the level of unionization among Asian Pacific workers is still low, a few unions have a positive track record of organizing Asian Pacific workers. The International Ladies Garment Workers Union, Local 23-25, has over 20,000 Asian members in New York City, most of whom are Chinese immigrant women. The American Federation of State, County, and Municipal Employees (AFSCME) and the Service Employees International Union (SEIU) each have significant numbers of Asian Pacific workers in government and health care, especially in California, Hawaii, and New York. Filipinos in particular comprise a large and growing percentage of the workers in the health care industry.

In the area retail food and food processing, the United Food and Commercial Workers (UFCW) represents large numbers of Asian Pacific workers, especially in California. The International Longshoremen and Warehousemen's Union (ILWU) has a long tradition of organizing Asian workers in Hawaii, beginning with plantation and dock workers, as well as in the Northwest among Asian cannery workers. The hotel and restaurant industry also employs large numbers of Asian Pacific workers, and although the vast majority are still unorganized, a growing number of Asian members have joined the union of Hotel Employees and Restaurant Employees (HERE). There is also a sizable Asian membership within the American Federation of Teachers (AFT) and other unions representing school employees.

Unfortunately, however, the labor movement as a whole has failed to allocate sufficient resources to organize Asian Pacific workers. To ensure the survival of the labor movement, unions must organize the new emerging work force, the majority of whom are people of color, immigrants, and women. At the same time, the best hope for Asian Pacific workers to fight exploitation and discrimination in the workplace rests in their active participation in unions.

## WHY UNIONS?

Asian Pacific workers need unions, and unions need Asian Pacific workers. Ultimately, Asian Pacific Americans cannot attain full equality until workers of all colors have equality. The conditions faced by many Asian Pacific immigrant workers are similar to those that confronted earlier waves of Asian immigrants. Many work in unskilled or semi-skilled occupations where exploitation and abuse are common, including minimum wage, overtime, child labor, and health and safety violations. Many Asian immigrant workers lack health insurance, vacation or sick pay, or retirement plans.

To ensure their empowerment, workers must organize. The only way to prevent the historic abuse and exploitation at the hands of employers, who are frequently of the same ethnic groups, is through banding together and demanding change. Unions offer an opportunity to bargain collectively for improved wages, benefits, and working conditions. Unions also provide an opportunity for greater participation, decision making, and leadership development. But, when Asian American organizing efforts have remained outside of the national union structure, they have often led to frustration and defeat. Without access to the resources of the labor movement, without a broader knowledge of effective organizing strategies and bargaining campaigns, most independent union efforts are short-lived.

The legacy of racism within the U.S. labor movement is still felt strongly by people of color today. Most labor unions have few people of color in positions of leadership. Change within the labor movement has involved a long, difficult process encouraged by both direct pressure within the unions as well as criticism from outside the labor movement. The future of the labor movement depends on its ability to overcome these past legacies of racism and exclusion and to forge multiracial unity.

And yet, in the broader fight against racism, labor unions are a critical arena of struggle. In some respects, they have a unique advantage. The United States is a highly segregated society. Most churches, social clubs, and community-based groups are segregated organizations. Unions are among the few multiracial institutions. African Americans, Latinos, Native Americans, Asian Pacific Americans, and European Americans work side-by-side within unions. Union members must work together for a common agenda, and fight together for common demands.

Although racism is still pervasive within the labor movement, and within our society as a whole, this potential for advancing genuine multiracial unity exists in few other institutions. With our rapidly changing, multicultural society, the labor movement must aggressively challenge racism and be at the forefront of building multiracial unity to grow. This includes recruiting and hiring union staff that reflect the diversity of the membership, promoting Asian and other people of color to positions of leadership, and opposing all racial barriers and discrimination in the workplace.

## CHANGES IN THE LABOR MOVEMENT

Significant changes within the labor movement allow greater opportunities for Asian Pacific workers. The U.S. labor movement has been in decline for decades. In the 1960s, unions represented about 35 percent of the U.S. work force. By 1992, that percentage had dropped to about 17 percent. The changing nature of work, the globalization of capital and labor, the shift from an industrial economy to a service economy, and hostile government policies and labor laws all contributed to this substantial decline. The labor movement has also been unwilling and unable to allocate resources necessary to organize the unorganized.

The changing demographics of the U.S. work force and the rapid rise in immigration, especially from Latin America and Asia, raise new challenges and new opportunities for labor. Although European immigrant workers were instrumental in establishing many U.S. labor unions, unions have paid little attention to organizing Asian or Latino immigrants until recently. But the emergence of new progressive labor activists and their reversal of prior exclusionary policies are transforming the movement.

In 1985, the AFL-CIO published a paper entitled, "The Changing Situation of Workers and Their Unions," which analyzed current developments in the work force. The report advocated a series of changes in unions, including addressing new workplace issues, experimenting with different types of union membership to allow for a more diverse membership and promoting innovative organizing methods.

In 1986, Congress passed the Immigration Reform and Control Act. This handed unions a unique opportunity as hundreds of thousands of undocumented workers could apply for amnesty, creating a new pool of potential union recruits. Employers have frequently used the undocumented status of workers and the threat of deportation to deter employee organizing.

In Los Angeles, the AFL-CIO established the California Immigrant Workers Association (CIWA) to assist Latino immigrant workers in obtaining legalization, English instruction, and other benefits. CIWA was also an "associate membership" organization allowing immigrant workers to affiliate with the AFL-CIO. Associate members are not part of a bargaining unit nor does a union contract cover them. The organization's goal is to promote goodwill between the labor movement and Latino community, and to build a foundation for future organizing.

In 1989, the AFL-CIO established the AFL-CIO Organizing Institute to recruit a new generation of union organizers. Designed as a center for strategy, recruitment, and training, the Organizing Institute is committed to advancing the cause of organizing. It assimilates rich lessons within the labor movement, and provides a systematic program to train new organizers through direct internships and placements. It pays special attention to reaching out to women and people of color, and has successfully attracted not only rank-and-file union members, but also community and student activists committed to social change who possess a passion to organize.

New, aggressive leadership within the labor movement has also emerged that is committed to organizing the unorganized and making inroads among more workers of color, immigrants, and women. In 1991, the Teamsters elected insurgent candidate Ron Carey president. This election victory sent shock waves throughout the labor movement, and encouraged other insurgent movements within unions. Carey has assembled a new leadership team committed to improving the image of the Teamster and to organizing. One of Carey's first steps was to allocate $35 million to organizing.

## COMMUNITY-BASED ORGANIZING

These changes within the labor movement have encouraged Asian Pacific labor activists to strengthen unionization efforts within their communities. But they will need new strategies. Traditional union practices, such as shop-by-shop organizing and individual union elections, have proven insufficient to organizing Asian immigrant workers. What is needed is a new community-based model to create labor-community alliances and build on the strength of existing organizations within the Asian American community.

Because many Asian immigrants live and work in ethnic enclaves that have never been unionized, some union activists falsely assume that these communities do not have structure and organization. Important organizations do exist, however, including churches, family associations, social service programs, and mutual aid organizations. The Asian community has its own media, including TV, radio, and newspapers. Any labor organizing strategy should include analyzing and using these existing community structures.

Another false assumption inhibiting organizing efforts is the myth of the "model minority." For many years, certain political leaders and media reports have projected an image of Asians as a model of educational and economic success. This stereotype is a dangerous fallacy that pits Asians against other communities of color and obscures the reality of Asian life.

In truth, a bipolar situation exists within our community. A number of Asian Americans have attained educational and economic success. Some Asian Americans have family roots in this country dating many generations and have succeeded over the years in spite of discrimination. Others are more recent immigrants who are merchants or educated professionals, who arrived in this country with economic resources. But, at the other end of the economic spectrum, our community has large numbers of Asian Pacific immigrant workers whose lifestyle is far from glamorous. Long hours, low wages, and no benefits are standard. Language and cultural barriers keep them trapped in ghettoes.

These sharp class divisions with Asian Pacific communities also reflect cultural particularities. Paternalistic attitudes by Asian bosses are often an extension of previous class relationships that existed in the native countries. Asian immigrant workers may feel in debt to their boss for the opportunity to work. Bonuses for hard work or special gifts during holidays are methods Asian bosses use to foster company loyalty and undermine collective action. In addition, the Asian American merchant class has historically dominated other community and social functions, establishing extensive control over many aspects of workers' lives.

Contract labor is also pervasive in Asian Pacific communities. The garment industry, janitorial services and building maintenance, and construction have used contract labor extensively. Through such labor, employers pay by piece work or on a project-by-project basis. This exacerbates the problems of a transitory work force and limits the bosses' accountability.

Community-based organizing requires thoroughly analyzing the class divisions of the Asian Pacific communities, identifying natural allies, and working with existing leaders who support the goals and ideals of unions. These include progressive religious leaders, elected officials, and social service providers. It also requires genuine reciprocity between labor unions and the Asian Pacific community: forging a common agenda, supporting each other's causes and issues, and building genuine solidarity. Unions must support issues of concern within the community, from redress and reparations for Japanese Americans interned during World War II to voting rights and affirmative action.

## THE RISE IN ASIAN PACIFIC LABOR ACTIVISM

For the past fifteen years, Asian American labor activists have been working through meetings and new organizations to strengthen unionization efforts. In San Francisco, the Asian American Federation of Union Members (AAFUM) emerged from this work. AAFUM members helped successfully unionize the *Chinese Times* newspaper workers in the late 1970s. In the mid-1980s, the successful organizing drive of janitors at the San Francisco International Airport resulted in the first group of Korean Americans to be unionized.

In New York, the Asian American Labor Committee organizes annual labor festivals in the Asian community, strengthening the presence of unions in the community and building greater labor-community alliances.

In Los Angeles, the Alliance of Asian Pacific Labor (AAPL), established in 1987, successfully brings together virtually all of the key Asian Union staff and rank-and-file leaders throughout Los Angeles and Orange Counties. Since I have personally been involved in its development, I will describe its work in greater detail.

Although many of the active members had worked for years in the labor movement, few had met to address the specific concerns they shared as Asian Pacific labor activists. Now Japanese, Chinese, Filipinos, Koreans, Vietnamese, and Indians from dozens of unions work to unite immigrant and American-born women and men. They have sought to ensure diversity within the organization, partly by conducting broad outreach to various Asian Pacific communities. Through its efforts, AAPL has become an important support network for Asian American unionists, including actively encouraging unions to recruit and promote new Asian American unionists. For example, AAPL has recruited student interns for numerous unions throughout Southern California. With limited numbers of Asians on union staffs, especially with bilingual abilities, internships have provided an opportunity to tap the skill and enthusiasm of these students as well as to encourage them to consider future career options in labor.

Since its inception, AAPL has held monthly memberships meetings to promote ongoing education for labor activists, build labor solidarity between unions, and encourage labor/community alliances. AAPL has succeeded in establishing a labor movement presence within the Los Angeles Asian American community by sending representatives to conferences, events, and meetings, distributing literature, publicizing labor activities through the Asian American media, and promoting union consciousness. AAPL has involved itself in community issues involving language rights, redistricting, voter registration, and political empowerment.

Within the labor movement, AAPL has also worked to oppose "Japan-bashing" and misdirected anti-Asian sentiment. The heated trade wars between the United States and Japan have resulted in many workers blaming Japanese corporations for the demise of U.S. industry. Not only does this let U.S. corporate and governmental policy off the hook, it results in increased anti-Asian violence at home. AAPL believes Asians in the labor movement need to promote fair trade proposals that promote job creation and economic growth, while countering the ugly consequences of racist rhetoric. Toward this goal, AAPL has also sponsored events with labor representatives from Korea, Japan, the Philippines, Taiwan, and China to foster international labor solidarity.

## RECENT EXPERIENCES
## IN ORGANIZING

During one hotly contested campaign in 1989, the United Auto Workers (UAW) contracted AAPL for assistance in preventing a union decertification drive. The union feared a group of Vietnamese workers would vote against them. With help of a Vietnamese speaking student intern, AAPL contacted the Vietnamese workers. The workers raised valid criticisms that the union was completely inaccessible. To remedy the situation, the union began translating its meetings and union fliers and reaching out to Vietnamese workers. It won over the Vietnamese workers, who played a crucial role in the UAW victory. Since that time, some of the Vietnamese workers have continued to play a leading role in the union and have also taken on an active role within AAPL.

Another significant victory occurred within the Aluminum, Brick, and Glass Workers Union. This union was also facing a decertification vote, and also feared a group of Vietnamese workers would vote

against them. The union contacted AAPL member Ho Lai, a Vietnamese American organizer for the United Food and Commercial Workers Union (UFCW), for assistance. He developed a mobilization plan, and set up house meetings with the workers, many of whom the union had never approached. His work was critical in defeating the decertification drive, for which Ho Lai received special thanks and acknowledgment from the vice-president of the unions. Since the election, union members have elected a Vietnamese shop steward and developed an active Vietnamese participant on the negotiating committee.

During the height of a contract campaign by the Hotel Employees and Restaurant Employees against the Hyatt Hotels in Los Angeles, AAPL again played an important role in reaching to Asian Pacific Hyatt workers and the larger Asian Pacific community. The Hyatt workers include a large number of Filipino and Chinese immigrants. AAPL mobilized support within the Asian Pacific community by encouraging organizations to honor the boycott and held a special press conference for the Asian press. The campaign ultimately ended in victory, the workers won a favorable contract, and the campaign successfully cultivated an expanding group of union allies within the Asian Community.

AAPL was also involved in another, less successful, campaign with workers at Radio Korea, the largest Korean radio station in the country. The radio station required its employees to work seven days a week and holidays for intolerably low wages and no overtime pay. The workers chose to go on strike and demanded union recognition. The strike lasted over four weeks, and was well publicized throughout the Korean community. The strike also attracted considerable support among forces with no prior union experience. Workers from Korean communities across the country learned of the strike and sent letters of solidarity.

The Legal Aid Foundation filed a wage and hour claim on behalf of the workers, one of the first legal actions of this kind within the

Korean American community. The station's management refused to negotiate or recognize the union. Instead, it retained a union-busting law firm, cut side deals with some of the workers, and encouraged enough workers to cross the line to break the strike. The failure of the strike reflected the need to have bilingual organizers who could gauge the pulse of the workers and management every step of the way.

Although the strike ultimately failed to unionize Radio Korea this round, the campaign publicized the tremendous exploitation and abuse Asian immigrant workers face, and led to the longest strike in Koreatown history. Already, other promising developments have occurred within the Korean community. In 1992, a new organization, the Korean Immigrant Workers Advocates (KIWA), was established in Los Angeles to set the foundation for future labor organizing among Korean American workers.

## BUILDING THE ASIAN PACIFIC AMERICAN LABOR ALLIANCE

Perhaps one of the most important contributions AAPL has made to the national labor movement has been in helping to establish the national Asian Pacific American Labor Alliance (APALA). Through AAPL's work in Los Angeles, we realized that in spite of many local accomplishments, we still had to influence the national AFL-CIO in order to organize a significant number of Asian American workers.

Upon the invitation of AFL-CIO Regional Director David Sickler, I attended the 1989 national AFL-CIO Convention to lobby for establishing a nationwide Asian American labor organization. In March 1990, I met with AFL-CIO President Lane Kirkland to discuss the idea, especially in view of the growing Asian work force and organizing potential. At the following meeting of the AFL-CIO Executive Council, Kirkland appointed a committee of seven international presidents, chaired by ILGWU Presi-

dent Jay Mazur, to establish a national steering committee, comprised of thirty-seven Asian Pacific labor activists, convened in June 1991. It met for over a year to plan the Asian Pacific American Labor Alliance. The response from Asian Pacific union leaders and rank and file members exceeded all expectations. Five hundred delegates participated in the founding convention in May 1992. At the convention, we honored seven Asian Pacific labor pioneers: eighty-seven-year-old Filipino farmworker and former vice-president of the United Farm Workers Union, Philip Vera Cruz; AAFUM founder George Wong of the Graphic Communications Union; AAPL founder Art Takei of the United Food and Commercial Workers; Morgan Gin of the Newspaper Guild; Sue Embrey of the American Federation of Teachers; and Ah Quan McElrath and Karl Yoneda of the Longshoremen and Warehousemen's Union.

During APALA's first year, it has launched two national campaigns. With the first campaign, APALA is working with the AFL-CIO Organizing Institute to recruit a new generation of Asian Pacific labor organizers. At a local level, chapters are actively involved in working with the labor movement to forge labor-community alliances.

The second national campaign involves building a civil rights agenda for Asian Pacific workers. APALA is one of the few national Asian Pacific organizations based in Washington, D.C. It will play an important role in advancing a national agenda to support civil rights legislation, oppose anti-Asian violence, ensure fair representation for Asian Pacific Americans at all levels of politics, and promote Asian Pacific political power. While APALA will pay particular attention to the concerns of Asian Pacific workers, it hopes to build multiracial unity.

In spite of APALA's accomplishments to date, the task of organizing Asian Pacific workers continues on a daily basis, and unions are needed now more than ever. The challenge that lies ahead is to promote multiracial unity within the ranks of the labor movement and to build on the successes of a community-based organizing model for unions. The goals of the labor movement and the Asian American community are one and the same—justice, equality, and empowering workers. The Asian Pacific American Labor Alliance, the AFL-CIO, and other Asian American labor organizations will continued to play an important role in shaping the future for Asian Pacific American workers throughout the country.

# 4.4

# America's First Multiethnic 'Riots'

*Edward T. Chang*

〜〜〜〜〜〜〜〜〜〜〜〜〜〜〜〜〜〜〜〜〜〜〜〜〜〜〜〜〜〜〜〜

After the first verdict in the Rodney King trial, a Korean merchant was notified by a "regular customer" that if he wanted to live he should leave his store as soon as possible. He immediately closed the store and went home. On the way, he tuned into the Korean radio station and heard of the mayhem in his business area. His store on the corner of Normandie and Florence was being looted and set on fire. Little did he know that by the end of the rioting,[1] his losses combined with those of 2,700 other Korean businesses would total around $460 million—more that half the city's total property damages.[2] Never in their lives did Koreans feel so much rage and injustice at the American system.

The events were a culmination of years of neglect, abandonment, hopelessness, despair, alienation, injustice, isolation, and oppression that exploded in the wake of the King verdict. Suspicion, fear, and distrust between different ethnic and racial groups turned into the massive destruction of the Los Angeles.

Chang, Edward T. "America's First Multiethnic 'Riots'." In *The State of Asian Pacific America: Activism and Resistance in the 1990s*, Karin Aguilar-San Juan, ed. (Boston: South End Press, 1994), 101–17. Reprinted with permission.

All of sudden, residents of Los Angeles were forced to confront the myth of Los Angeles as a model multiethnic city. Promoting itself as a "world city" and a shining example of a multiculturalism, Los Angeles is in fact a sad collection of "separate and unequal" communities. In their landmark 1989 study of widening inequality in Los Angeles, urban planner Paul Ong and others documented that "to achieve full integration, over three-quarters of all blacks and over half of all Chicanos would have to move into Anglo neighborhoods."[3]

During the riots, I was forced to wear three different hats: a scholar engaged in "objective" research, a community advocate for the Korean victims, and a member of the Black Korean Alliance trying to bridge the gap between the two communities. I soon realized that wearing three hats was an impossible task. I had to choose between scholarly research and assuming a partisan role by serving as a spokesperson for the Korean American community.

Reporters kept my phone busy fifteen hours a day for almost two weeks after the riots. They wanted to know if Korean-African American tensions contributed to the riot. They also wanted to hear Korean American reactions to the riot. One of the most common complaints of the reporters was that they could not find Korean American spokespeople who could articulate their feelings in English. I had to play the role of voicing the anger, rage, betrayal, resentment, and abandonment of Korean American victims who lost everything they owned.

The purpose of this chapter is twofold. First, I analyze the riots from a multiethnic perspective by tracing its causes. To what extent did racial and class inequality contribute to the explosion of the city? Second, I ask what lessons can we learn from the riots and what are their implications for the Asian American movement?

## BEYOND BLACK AND WHITE

The 1968 Kerner Commission Report concluded that America was divided into two separate and unequal nations—one black, one white. This is how the experts used to describe race relations in America. In the past, the race problem meant a "black" problem. The demographic composition of urban cities has undergone rapid changes during the past twenty years, however, and that has profoundly altered our ways of life. As a nation, we can no longer define race relation as a black/white issue.[4] Existing race relation theories are no longer viable or relevant since they cannot fully explain our society. There is an urgent need to develop new theories that will adequately reflect the rapidly changing demography of the United States.[5]

The demographic shift of South Central Los Angeles has been even more dramatic during the past two and half decades. In 1965, South Central Los Angeles was largely known as a "black area" with 81 percent African American residents. "Black flight" to the suburbs accelerated during the 1980s, changing the face of South Central Los Angeles. The African American population declined 20 percent from 369,504 to 295,312 between 1980 and 1990. At the same time, the African American population in nearby Inland Empire of

Riverside and San Bernardino County increased 99 percent and 134 percent.[6] Today, 48 percent of South Central's population is Latino. And in Los Angeles as a whole, whites constituted less than half of the city's population as of 1980 (48 percent).

Such demographic shifts have increased tensions and polarization among different ethnic and racial groups in the United States. The tensions have reached a potentially explosive point. African Americans feel that the increasing numbers of immigrants from Latin America and Asia are squeezing them out. Latin American immigrants often compete with African American residents for affordable housing, jobs, education, health, and social welfare programs. Highly publicized confrontations at South Central Los Angeles construction sites have occurred, including Danny Bakewell and the Brotherhood Crusade chasing away Latino workers and proclaiming, "If black people can't work, nobody works."

African Americans are also worried that they are losing political and economic "gains" they made during the 1960s civil rights struggle. South Central Los Angeles is now a multiethnic community, and African Americans are concerned that they are losing influence and control in what used to be their "exclusive" domain. They are understandably suspicious of the growing numbers of Latino immigrants and Korean shop owners in "their neighborhoods." In fact, fights already have occurred between the Latino and African American communities over the redistricting for the city council. Latinos are demanding proportional representation to reflect population changes, while African Americans argue that they are entitled to retain their share of gains to compensate for past injustices. And Asian Americans are now beginning to participate in the political process. For example, the Korean American Victims Association staged daily protests at City Hall for a month to demand compensation for Koreans who lost their businesses during the riots.

If this "politics of race" continues to dominate city politics, Los Angeles will suffer from polarization along racial boundaries, pitting one minority group against another. Obviously the system has failed to provide "justice" for all. Where did it go wrong?

## LOS ANGELES RIOTS: 1965 AND 1992

Is there a difference between the Watts riots of 1965 and the Los Angeles "riots" of 1992? What took place in Los Angeles for a few days in April 1992 showed a remarkable resemblance to Watts in 1965. We could easily mistake the following description of the Watts riot for the Los Angeles riots of 1992.

> They looted stores, set fires, beat up white passersby whom they hauled from stopped cars, many of which were turned upside down and burned, exchanged shots with law enforcement officers, and stoned and shot at firemen. The rioters seemed to have been caught up in an insensate rage of distruction.[7]

Gun sales tripled as citizens armed to protect themselves during and shortly after the Los Angeles riots. During the Watts riot of 1965, we witnessed a similar reaction; "some pawnshops and gun stores have been robbed of firearms and gun sales reportedly have tripled since the riots."[8]

Was there a conspiracy to riot before the King verdict? Many believed that gang members organized and planned the civil unrest. However, both the Kerner Commission report of 1968 and the FBI investigation of the 1992 Los Angeles riots could not find any concrete evidence to support these suspicions. Charles J. Parsons, head of FBI Special Agent in Charge said, "I am not ruling out the possibility that there was a pre-rioting plan, but we don't have any hard evidence of that."[9]

The similarities end here however. Several important differences exist between 1965 and 1992. As I discussed earlier, the 1992 Los Angeles riots involved a multiethnic uprising whereas the Watts riot was primarily an African American revolt against injustice and racism. The Watts riot was confined to geographical areas largely known as South Central Los Angeles, whereas the riots of 1992 spread north of South Central Los Angeles into Koreatown, Hollywood, Pico-Union, and other middle-class neighborhoods.

In the 1960s, the Civil Rights Movement had gained momentum, and many Americans, including whites, were sympathetic to the minority (i.e., black) issues of poverty, racism, unemployment, and injustice. Whites were willing to pay for and provide assistance to improve the quality of life for African Americans and other disadvantage minorities. As I will discuss later, though, the rise of the neo-conservative movement during the late 1970s and 1980s has left white Americans less willing to "pay for" social and economic programs to aide the underprivileged.

In the 1960s, many African Americans felt optimistic. They hoped to improve their lives by actively participating in electoral politics, and they believed they could attain the "American Dream." Today, however, despair, hopelessness, and a sense of abandonment are widespread in the African American community. The gap between the haves and the have-nots has widened, and many African Americans lost their "American Dream" as they dropped out of the labor market.[10] "In the 1960s, racial disorder was about rising expectations; today it is about diminishing expectations."[11]

The Los Angeles riots seemed a cry for help. One woman explained that "this was the first time she could get shoes for all six of her children at once." No doubt, the social, economic, and political conditions of South Central Los Angeles, and the ideological shift to the right, were the main causes of the Los Angels riots. The riots told us that we have ignored these problems for too long.

## DEINDUSTRIALIZATION AND SOUTH CENTRAL LOS ANGELES

The restructuring of the economy—plant closings, runaway shops, and domestic disinvestments—has deepened racial and class inequality in U.S. cities. Deindustrialization, or the structural realignment of the American economy during the 1970s and 1980s, was the U.S. corporate response to the economic crisis created by increasing global competition. "Runaway shops" and overseas investment were an aggressive tactic by capitalists to regain competitiveness and increase profits. "By the beginning of the 1980s," wrote economists Barry Bluestone and Bennett Harrison in *The Deindustrialization of America* "every newscast seemed to contain a story about a plant shutting down, another thousand jobs disappearing from a community, or the frustrations of workers unable to find full-time jobs utilizing their skills and providing enough income to support their families."[12] Although some politicians blamed the increase of imports from Asia for the loss of American jobs, the deindustrialization of the U.S. economy caused the plant closures. In fact, during the decade of the 1970s, private disinvestment in plants and equipment probably eliminated at least 32 million jobs in the United States, Bluestone and Harrison estimate.[13]

Suddenly, unemployment was no longer the poor's problem. Many companies simply decided to pick up and move to other areas where wages were lower, unions weaker, and the business climate better. The middle-class workers in traditional manufacturing industries such as steel, rubber, and auto were the hardest hit as they experienced permanent displacement with no prospect of finding equivalent employment. "The lower-middle and middle rungs of the American occupational structure are at risk: the top and the bottom grow," wrote Michael Harrington in *New American Poverty* in 1980.[14] In other words, deindustrialization polarized class inequality in the United States: High-tech industries and low-paying unskilled jobs grew, and traditional middle-class jobs declined. For example, while New York City lost 400,000 jobs between 1970 and 1980, white-collar industries increased

their employment by 17 percent[15] and the number of sweatshops rose.

Meanwhile, on the West Coast, deindustrialization also took its toll. General Motors, Goodyear, Firestone, and Bethlehem Steel used to provide jobs and economic security to the residents of South Central Los Angeles, but by the 1980s, they had vanished. In a study of racial inequality in Los Angeles, Ong and other researchers found that "in the late seventies and early eighties alone, Los Angeles lost over 50,000 industrial jobs to plant closures in the auto, tire, steel, and non-defense aircraft industries. Since 1971, South Central Los Angeles, the core of the African American community, itself lost 321 firms."

Despite the warning of the Watts riot of 1965, the socioeconomic conditions of South Central Los Angeles continued to deteriorate. South Central Los Angeles has suffered from chronic poverty, high unemployment, inferior schooling, and soaring high-school drop-out rates. Various studies have found that one in four black men in their twenties is in jail or otherwise involved in the criminal justice system, black men in poor neighborhoods are less likely to live to age sixty-five than men in Bangladesh, and the majority of black babies are born in single-parents households.[16]

In fact, 1990 census data shows that the status of African Americans has in fact deteriorated since the 1960s. The 1990 poverty rate was over 30 percent, higher than at the time of Watts riot (27 percent). Per capital income of South Central Los Angeles in 1990 was a mere $7,023, compared with $16,149 for Los Angeles County as a whole. More importantly, half of those sixteen years and older were unemployed and not looking for a job. These statistics clearly show the failure of "trickle-down" economics; the economic recovery and boom of 1980s did not improve socioeconomic conditions of South Central Los Angeles residents. Instead, African Americans who live in the inner city often must endure the burden of the "black tax"—higher insurance and mortgage rates, abusive police patrols, and lower quality education.

The future prospects are even more gloomy, since African Americans are grossly underrepresented in the growing high-tech related industries. According to Edward Park, high-technology managers are using race and ethnicity to mitigate a class-based consciousness. Rather than hire the "traditional industrial labor force" (i.e. white and black), these managers are fostering ethnic rivalry by employing Asian immigrant workers over African Americans because Asian immigrants are perceived as docile, diligent, and easily exploitable.[17]

## 1980S: ERA OF NEO-CONSERVATISM

The Los Angeles riots exposed the failure of the 1980s neo-conservative policies. Since the passage of the 1965 Civil Rights Act, the Republican Party has dominated the presidency of the United States through its strong support from white middle-class votes. The only exception came when the Watergate scandal forced former President Nixon to resign. Beginning with the landmark 1975 Bakke decision (when Allan Bakke, a white applicant to a California medical school, charged the school with "reverse discrimination"), the attitudes of white Americans began to shift from progressive (willing to support social and economic programs to aid minorities) to conservative view (emphasis on morality, strong family values, law and order, and lowering taxes).[18]

The resurgence of the neo-conservatism has hurt minority groups during the 1980s as the federal government cut funding for social programs for inner cities. White Americans were willing to spend more tax dollars for a military build-up than to address so-called black problems. Most white Americans now believe that "blacks have been given more than a fair chance to succeed" with the passage of the Civil Rights Act and the implementation of the affirmative action programs. In fact, many whites believe that liberals and Democrats "gave in" too much to the demands of black Americans at the expense of whites.

The resurgence of neo-conservatism ensured the election of conservative presidential candidate Ronald Reagan in 1980, his landslide reelection in 1984, and the election of George Bush in 1988. These Republican administrations implemented a "politics of race" by blaming victims and scapegoating immigrants and minorities for societal problems. Although no concrete proof exists to suggest that the state has promoted or justified the recent waves of anti-Asian activities, a correlation does seem to exist between the Republican Party's policies of scapegoating and the increase of anti-Asian violence. As a result, during the 1980s, we have witnessed the sudden increase of inter-minority conflicts such as Korean/African American and Latino/African American tensions and the rise of anti-minority violence. By looking back at the history of the majority/minority relationship, we see that the power structure has a way of blaming the victims for social and economic problems in this country.

## POLICE BRUTALITY AND THE JUSTICE SYSTEM

Police brutality is nothing new to African Americans living in the inner city. The Los Angeles Police Department (LAPD) has had a reputation for brutalizing African American suspects. In fact, police mistreatment of an African American suspect triggered the Watts riot of 1965. Los Angeles has learned little from its history; little has changed. Although the King videotape shocked most Americans, for African Americans it simply confirmed the reality they face on a daily basis. Young African American men are often stopped just because they fit a "description" or are in the wrong neighborhood. African Americans are often treated as "guilty" until proven innocent, although the U.S. Constitution supposedly guarantees otherwise.

A white person appalled and disgusted by the tape of the Rodney King beating probably feels sympathy and compassion for King. In contrast, a black feels threatened and alarmed that "it could have been me." White Americans cannot even begin to grasp what it is like to be harassed by police or denied a job just because of the color of their skin. Many Asian Americans also felt shock and dismay over the brutal beating of King.

The Latasha Harlins and Rodney King verdicts added to perception that the justice system does not serve the interests of African Americans. A Korean immigrant grocer, Soon Ja Du, shot and killed a fifteen-year-old African American girl, Latasha Harlins, on March 18, 1991. Mrs Du was found guilty of voluntary manslaughter and sentenced to five years probation. Such lenience exacerbated tension between Korean American and African American communities and underlined the justice system's racist double standard.

## INTER-ETHNIC RELATIONS: KOREAN–AFRICAN AMERICAN TENSIONS

The media has continued to portray the 1992 riots as an extention of the ongoing conflict between Korean merchants and African American residents, despite the fact that more than half the looters arrested were Latinos.[19] Indeed, Korean-African American conflict has surfaced as one of the most explosive issues facing many cities in the United States since the early 1980s.[20] Despite many efforts to alleviate tension, the situation has only worsened.

In January 1990, the Red Apple boycott—which lasted a year-and-half in the Flatbush section of Brooklyn, New York—focused national attention on growing tensions between African Americans and Korean Americans. The relationship between the two communities suffered further when Korean American merchants in Los Angeles shot and killed two African American customers within a three-month period, March to June 1991. Led by Danny Bakewell of the Brotherhood Crusade, African Americans boycotted Korean-owned stores. During the boycotts,

Bakewell was seen on TV almost daily making highly charged remarks against Korean Americans. This certainly heightened the tensions and helped further polarize the two communities.

One of the most common complaints by African Americans against Korean Americans focuses on "rudeness." Some merchants are indeed rude to their customers, although the majority are kind and courteous. Korean Americans are exceptionally family-oriented, and that affects their attitudes in dealing with people they don't know. Korean Americans themselves complain that they too have experienced "rudeness" from fellow Korean merchants. In general, Korean Americans are nice to people they know but "rude" to strangers. Part of this "rudeness" is prejudice, but part is misunderstanding. Therefore, while it is wrong for Korean Americans to deny they are prejudiced, it is also wrong for African Americans to accuse all Korean merchants of being "rude."

Interethnic tensions in African American neighborhoods have historical roots. Jewish merchants and African Americans clashed during the 1960s. During the Watts riots, rioters looted and burned down many Jewish-owned stores; they destroyed 80 percent of the furniture stores, 60 percent of the food markets, and 54 percent of the liquor stores.[21] Korean immigrants are perceived as part of "a long line of outsiders who came into African American neighborhoods to exploit the community." Although over the years the conflicts in Los Angeles have shifted from one racial group to another, the class-based nature of the struggle had remained consistent. It is not, therefore, a racial issue, but a class issue involving small business and residents.

In the eyes of the underclass who have nothing to lose, the merchant class represents wealth. But Korean Americans perceive themselves as simply trying to make a living. Korean Americans often complain that life in the United States is a life of making payments. Although Korean merchants are able to make some profits from their stores, many can barely keep up with their monthly bills, such as mortgage, car, utility, and merchandise payments. These different perceptions of the status of Korean merchants have exacerbated the tensions and polarized the two communities.

In addition to believing that Korean merchants behave rudely, African Americans believe that they fail to contribute economically to the community. They complain that Korean merchants overcharge for inferior products and do not hire African American workers or contribute profits back to the community.

In any colonial situation, the middleman is inevitably a target of oppressed people. For example, Korean independence fighters saw Koreans who collaborated with the Japanese colonial government as an enemy of Korean people. Japanese-collaborators were protecting the interests of the colonial government in Korea. Therefore, Koreans had to eliminate Japanese-collaborators in order to achieve independence for Korea. That's how some African Americans perceive Korean Americans—as a "layer" that protects the interests of white America and preserves the status quo. Korean Americans have become a "symbol of oppression."

Why are African Americans unable to attain the same level of class power as Jews, WASPs, and Asians? Historically, non-African American merchants have dominated the economy of African American communities. Despite many attempts by African American leaders who advocate economic self-help, the African American community still suffers from a lack of African American-owned businesses.

African American-owned businesses fail because they are often undercapitalized, lack sufficient skills, and face stiff competition from well-financed white-owned corporations. In particular, African American leaders charge that African American capitalism has not materialized because of the discriminatory lending practices by financial and banking institutions.

## LESSONS FOR THE ASIAN AMERICAN COMMUNITY

What do the Los Angeles riots mean to the Asian American community? Although many Asian American-owned businesses were damaged or destroyed during the "riots," very few people were aware of the extent of this tragedy (see table 4.4a). The riots raised some serious questions about the viability of Asian American coalitions. One *Los Angeles Times* article argued that "Asian Americans had widely diverse reactions to the upheaval in Los Angeles highlighting strains exacerbated in recent decades."[22] Furthermore, the same article claimed that the Asian American activists and community leaders questioned the timing and intention of the *Los Angeles Times* article. Although many condemned it as divisive, I strongly believe that we must show courage and acknowledge our problems, and begin to build "common agendas" to unite Asian Americans groups.

Historically, Asian American Studies played a critical role defining and uniting

### Table 4.4a    Damage to Asian American-Owned Businesses

| | | |
|---|---|---|
| Korean American | 2,300 | $400.0 million |
| Chinese American | 262 | $53.0 million |
| Japanese American | 10 | $3.2 million |
| Filipino American | 25 | $7.5 million |
| Total | 2,597 | $463.7 million |

*Note:* Shinyodo survey did not include other Asian Americans, such as Vietnamese, Cambodian, Thai, and Laotian American-owned businesses. If we include these figure, the total damage would be much higher.
*Source:* Shinyodo Marketing Survey.

Asian American groups. Asian American Studies grew out of student activism and a desire to link students and academics with grassroots communities. During the early stage of its development, Asian American Studies primarily concerned itself with the issue of reclaiming what historian Yuji Ichioka called our "buried past." Issues of identity, history, and racism dominated research topics as Asian Americans felt it important to reaffirm their roots and re-establish an identity.

However, immigration has drastically changed the Asian American community during the past twenty years. Today, the number of immigrants outnumbers native-born Asian Americans. The real challenge for our community is to truly represent the interests of all Asian Americans, especially the majority of foreign-born. So far, Asian American Studies has failed to bring different communities together by creating common agendas for all Asian American groups. There is an absolute urgency to build networks between Asian American Studies and new immigrant and refugee communities.

For Korean Americans, the riots raised the important question of what it means to be "Korean American." The 1992 riots will be remembered as a turning point in Korean American history, similar to the internment of Japanese Americans. They opened the eyes of Korean immigrants to the problems of institutional racism, social and economic injustice, and the shortcomings of the "American Dream." Some Korean Americans felt a deep sense of disappointment at how other Asian Americans deserted them during and after the riots. Similarly, many in the Southeast Asian community are asking whether Asian American Studies is relevant to the issues of community. How long can we continue to play an advocacy and consciousness-raising role without input from new immigrant and refugee communities? These are important and difficult questions that those in Asian American Studies must address as we move to the twenty-first century.

After the riots, we often heard from community advocates including Reverend Cecil Murray, John Mack of the Los Angeles Urban League, and Danny Bakewell of the Brotherhood Crusade that "they can understand why some African Americans have participated n the violent destruction of properties and community. We understand where they are coming from. It does not justify the violence, but we certainly can understand and explain their behaviors." African American have suffered from years of racism, poverty, abandonment, betrayal, and racial injustice. Thus, community advocates have shown an extraordinary degree of patience, compassion, sympathy, and understanding toward those who looted and burned down stores.

These same individuals have shown a very little understanding, compassion, and sympathy toward Korean immigrants however. They show impatience with Korean immigrants who are struggling to learn the American language, culture, and customs.

Furthermore, some Asian American activists show a similar lack of compassion, implying that Korean Americans were responsible for their own suffering and that they "deserved it." I agree that some Korean immigrants were responsible for exacerbating conflict between the Korean American and African American communities, but we cannot blame the majority of Korean Americans for the events of April 1992. Recently, at the National Association for Asian American Studies conference in San Jose, California, I expected the Association to hold a general meeting to discuss the implication of the riots for the Asian American community. But the association failed to reach out to the Korean American community. If Asian American Studies cared about Korean American and other Asian American victims, they would have shown the same degree of compassion and understanding as many African American academics showed toward their own communities during and after the "riots."

The real challenge for Asian American Studies is to expand our agenda to include immigrant and refugee issues. It is our responsibility to reach out to immigrant and refugee populations whether we agree with their perspective or not. If new members of our community need to be educated about U.S. history, culture, and racism, we should provide educational programs. Many newcomers are naïve and ignorant about life in the United States. We must show that we care!

It is important to acknowledge that some in Asian American Studies have sincerely tried to reach out to the immigrant and refugee community. The efforts have not been successful, however. The traditional approaches, whatever they may have been, did not work. It is time for change. Fortunately, I see signs of improvement. For the first time, I witnessed the inclusion of many panels on refugees, Filipinos, Pacific Islanders, and the Korean American community during the May 1992 association meetings at San Jose. We are moving in the right direction.

But we must do more. Some Asian American Studies academics have forgotten their roots. During the past twenty years, Asian American Studies has tried to gain legitimacy and acceptance in the university community. In the process, some academics lost their connection to the community they are supposed to represent. Because of the lack of institutional supports, many Studies scholars felt forced to choose between either playing the role of the community activist or engaging in traditional academic research. One way to overcome this institutional barrier is to seek research topics that are relevant to the Asian American community. I strongly believe that relevancy is the key to reestablishing the connection between Asian American Studies and the community. If Asian American Studies wants to grow, our agenda must broaden to include the concerns of new immigrant and refugee communities.

## CONCLUSION

The 1992 riots were a turning point in Asian American history. They provided us with a unique opportunity to reexamine our ways of life and ideas. It awakened us to the new American reality: the end of the era of black/white relations and the beginning of a multiethnic and multiracial community.

Peaceful coexistence for different racial, ethnic, and national groups cannot be accomplished without more educational, social, and political efforts. How can we promote understanding, harmony, and trust between different racial, ethnic, and religious groups? We must learn to appreciate our differences. I propose an "Ethnic Studies" requirement for all school-age children in the United States. More importantly, our teachers, professors, and corporate executives must learn the real lessons of living in a multiethnic and multiracial community.

## NOTES

1. In this chapter, I chose to use the term "riots" over other terms, such as upheaval, civil unrest, rebellion, uprising, or insurrection to reflect the view of Korean Americans.

2. *The Korea Times,* July 4, 1992. It is also important to note that 48 percent of victims of the riots were not insured, according to the Department of California Insurance survey.

3. Paul Ong et al., *The Widening Divide: Income Inequality and Poverty in Los Angeles* (Los Angeles: UCLA Urban Planning Department, 1989).

4. *Los Angeles Times,* May 21, 1993 reported that 12,545 arrests were made between 6 P.M. April 29, 1952 and 5 A.M. May 5, 1992—the period of civil disorder. The Racial breakdown of those arrested was 45.2 percent Latinos, 41 percent blacks, and 11.5 percent whites.

5. Edward T. Chang, "New Urban Crisis: Intra-Third World Conflict," Shirley Hune et al., eds., *Asian Americans: Comparative and Global Perspectives* (Pullman: Washington State University Press, 1991), 169–78.

6. *Los Angeles Times,* August 13, 1992. According to the 1980 and 1990 U.S. Census, the African American population increased from 30,088 to 59,966 in Riverside County, and 46,615 to 109,162 in San Bernardino County.

7. *Violence in the City—An End of a Beginning? A Report by the Governor's Commission on the Los Angeles Riots,* December 2, 1965.

8. National Advisory Commission on Civil Disorders (New York: Bantam Books, 1969), 153.

9. *Los Angeles Times,* July 25, 1992.

10. According to the 1990 U.S. Census, 41.8 percent of residents of South Central Los Angeles have dropped out of the labor force.

11. Kevin Phillips, *Politics of Rich and Poor,* (New York: Random House, 1991).

12. Barry Bluestone and Bennett Harrison, *The Deindustrialization of America* (New York: Basic Books, Inc., 1982), 4.

13. Bluestone and Harrison, *The Deindustrialization of America*, 35.

14. Michael Harrington, *New American Poverty* (New Jersey: Princeton University Press, 1981), 166.

15. Saskia Sassen-Koob, "Recomposition and Peripheralization at the Core," *New Nomads* (San Francisco: Synthesis Publication, 1982).

16. *Los Angeles Times,* August 1, 1992:1.

17. Edward Park, "Asian Immigrants and the High Technology Industry in Silicon Valley," Ph.D. dissertation, U.C. Berkeley, Department of Ethnic Studies, 1992.

18. For more information on the Allen Bakke case, see Nathan Glazer, *Affirmative Discrimination: Ethnic Inequality and Public Policy* (New York: Basic Books, 1975).

19. *Los Angeles Times,* May 21, 1992.

20. Edward T. Chang, "New Urban Crisis: Korean-Black Conflicts in Los Angeles," Ph.D. dissertation, U.C. Berkeley, Department of Ethnic Studies, 1990.

21. Sholmo Katz, ed., *Negro and Jew: An Encounter in America* (London: The MacMillan Company, 1966), 76.

22. *Los Angeles Times,* July 13, 1992.

# 4.5

# Asian Pacific Americans and Redistricting Challenges in 2001

*Leland T. Saito*

〰〰〰〰〰〰〰〰〰〰〰〰〰〰〰〰〰〰〰〰〰〰〰〰〰〰

After each decennial census, political districts are reconfigured to reflect population changes because districts are required by the U.S. Constitution to be equal in population. Redistricting is critical for the political interests of racial groups because it creates local (e.g., City Council, Supervisorial), state (Assembly and Senate), and federal (congressional) districts from which officials are elected. Historically, geographic concentrations of racial minorities have been fragmented and placed in separate districts, diluting their political influence. Since these districts typically remain in place for a decade, that is, until the next census, their effects are long-lived.

The Voting Rights Act of 1965, which President Lyndon B. Johnson mentioned (at a press conference as he was leaving office) was his greatest accomplishment, prohibits practices that interfere with the exercise of the right to vote or result in vote dilution (Davidson 1992, 7). First enacted to remedy

Saito, Leland T. "Asian Pacific Americans and Redistricting Challenges in 2001." In *2001–02 National Asian Pacific American Political Almanac* (Los Angeles: UCLA Asian American Studies Center Press, 2001), 130–40. Reprinted with permission.

the egregious disenfranchisement of African Americans in the southern United States, the Voting Rights Act has been used to address issues of disenfranchisement across the United States, and in 1975, the Voting Rights Act was amended to cover language minority groups, including Asian Pacific Americans, Latinos, and Native Americans.

Research on the Voting Rights Act and the struggle to gain political enfranchisement has delineated four stages (Davidson and Grofman 1994; Guinier 1994). The first involves gaining the right to vote, that is, removing barriers—such as literacy tests, poll taxes, and physical and economic intimidation—that prevent eligible citizens from registering to vote and casting a ballot. The second stage addresses election systems (such as at-large versus district elections) and gerrymandered districts that result in vote dilution and hinder the ability of racial minority voters to elect representatives of their choice. Third and fourth stage issues involve the integration of elected officials into the political system and the ability of these officials to participate effectively in the formation of policies and distribution of resources on behalf of their constituents.

The dramatic rise in the number of African American (from less than 100 in 1965 to over 3,000 in 189 in the seven states originally targeted by the Voting Rights Act) and Latino (from 1,280 in 1973 to 3,592 in 1990 in six states with large numbers of Latinos) elected officials is evidence of the importance and effectiveness of the Voting Rights Act (Davidson 1992, 43). Despite these electoral achievements, however, critical third and fourth stage issues remain. For example, racial minority elected officials on a governing body, such as a city council or in a state legislature, may lack the numbers or support from white colleagues to pass legislation. Or, once minorities are elected, the procedures may be altered to limit their participation. For example, if a minority is elected to a previously all-white city council, the practice that any one member could add an item to the agenda might be changed to require two members of the council (Grofman and Davidson 1992).

Research on politics and Asian Pacific Americans has focused on the methods necessary to gain power in the electoral arena, such as the need for naturalization to increase levels to citizenship (especially critical considering that the majority of Asian Pacific Americans are immigrants), voter registration, voter turnout, voting patterns, and running for office (Cho and Cain 2001; Erie and Brackman 1993; Lien 1997; Nakanishi 2001; Ong and Lee 2001; Ong and Nakanishi 1996). These are critical issues in the first stage of political enfranchisement.

In terms of second stage issues, Asian Pacific Americans increased their involvement in redistricting in the 1990s. In part motivated by their extreme fragmentation in previous plans, they have worked to consolidate their populations in such areas as the San Gabriel Valley of Los Angeles County and the Chinatown area of New York City. Voting rights cases won by Latinos and African Americans in the 1980s and early 1990s, such as the 1990 *Garza v. Los Angeles County Board*

*Supervisors* case, also encouraged participation. Dramatically demonstrating the importance of redistricting for electoral success, as a result of the Garza decision, and with a redrawing of the supervisorial district lines and the consolidation of Latinos in the eastern region of Los Angeles County, Gloria Molina was elected, the first Latino in 116 years (Kousser 1999, 134).

These gains, however, suffered a potentially serious setback by a number of U.S. Supreme Court decisions in the 1990s (including the 1993 *Shaw v. Reno* and 1995 *Miller v. Johnson* cases), which ruled that race could not be a "predominant factor" when creating districts. As a result, Asian Pacific Americans working on redistricting must give increased emphasis to a wide range of social, economic, and political factors in addition to race (such as populations served by school districts, economic level of neighborhoods, and common interests created by such issues as transportation patterns or availability of community services).

The electoral successes of African Americans and Latinos demonstrate another issue for Asian Pacific Americans. One method of diluting the voting power of racial minorities with large populations is through packing, that is concentrating large numbers of a group within a district, as opposed to distributing them among a number of districts in which they could exert an influence. However, for Asian Pacific Americans, with their much smaller and more dispersed populations (Asian Pacific Americans tend to be less residentially concentrated than African Americans and Latinos), even if concentrations of Asian Pacific Americans are kept whole within districts, they generally still remain a minority (except in Hawaii) of the voters and may be unable to elect candidates of their choice. This has happened in the state assembly elections in the San Gabriel Valley of Los Angeles County and the New York City Council elections in the 1990s (Saito 1998, 2001).

## NEW YORK CITY: CHARTER REFORM, REDISTRICTING, AND THE 1991 CITY COUNCIL ELECTIONS

The past decade has seen a major leap forward in terms of community efforts to address stage two issues, that is, the ability of Asian Pacific Americans to elect officials. To elevate the political power of the rapidly growing Asian Pacific American population, there have been organized efforts to increase the number of voters and candidates and attempts to address gerrymandering. There remains, however, a number of structural impediments that seriously hinder their ability to elect representatives. I will discuss New York City's 1989 charter reform, 1990–1991 council redistricting, and 1991 city council elections, to illustrate these barriers, including the absence or low number of Asian Americans (the New York City population is primarily Asian American with few Pacific Islanders) on commissions that create policy; the decision to expand the number of city council districts to fifty-one, despite requests by Asian Americans to increase it to a minimum of sixty; inadequate incorporation of Asian American input in public hearings; and the census undercount.

In the November 5, 1991, New York City Council elections, in a district specifically crafted by the city's Districting Commission around Lower Manhattan's Chinatown to maximize the political strength of the city's largest concentration of Asian Americans, the Asian American candidates lost by wide margins to a white candidate. The defeat occurred despite overwhelming Chinatown voter support for the Asian American candidates (AALDEF 1992), continuing the city's history of never electing an Asian American to the council. In contrast, the number of African Americans and Latinos on the council increased dramatically from nine to twenty-one (26 to 41 percent).

Preceding the elections, a number of lawsuits charging the city with discrimination against African American and Latino voters and violation of the U.S. Constitution were filed in the1980s and won. As a result of the lawsuits, two charter reform commissions were established, the first in 1986, chaired by Richard Ravitch, and the second in 1989, chaired by Frederick A. O. Schwarz Jr. As the Charter Revision Commission Report (NYC-CRC 1990, 2) states, "The charter is New York's basic governing document. It sets forth the institutions and processes of the City's political system and defines the authority and responsibilities of elected officials and most city departments." The second commission recommended a number of significant changes, including an increase in the number of city council districts from thirty-five to fifty-one to improve the political representation of minorities. A 1989 city vote approved these recommendations.

## THE CHARTER COMMISSION AND EXPANSION OF THE NUMBER OF CITY COUNCIL DISTRICTS

The Charter Commission's decision in 1989 to expand the number of council districts from thirty-five to fifty-one, despite strong requests for a substantially larger number, was a key issue which shaped redistricting and limited efforts to address the disenfranchisement of Asian Americans. Such groups as the Asian American Legal Defense and Education Fund (Fung 1989), Chinatown Votre Education Alliance (Chen 1989), and the Puerto Rican Legal Defense and Education Fund (1988) submitted testimony and proposals that suggested a minimum of sixty to decrease district population size, thus improving the chances of creating districts that would recognize and enhance the political influence of minority communities. The number of council members has varied greatly in New York City's history, with a much greater number, seventy-three, from 1902–1917 (then called Board of Aldermen) (Muzzio and Tompkins 1989, 89). The Charter Commission's Final Report (NYC-CRC 1990, 11–12) stated that the council size was determined by an attempt to "balance four goals": "(1) to enhance opportunities for minority voters to elect candidates of their choice, (2) to increase the number of minority Councilmembers, (3) to maintain a Council of manageable size in which all members can meaningfully participate and (4) to increase Councilmembers' responsiveness by making their constituencies smaller, without making those constituencies so small as to foster parochialism."

Asian Americans protested the exclusionary character of the charter reform process in letters from community organizations (Fung 1989; Kong 1989) and reiterated in a group letter (Asian American Community 1989) addressed to Chairman Schwarz and signed by thirty-one Asian American Community members, "the exclusion of Asian American communities from this process is exacerbated by the absence of any Asian American representative on the Charter Revision commission, the lack of any translated materials until very recently, and the continued lack of outreach materials to our community organizations until the very end of this process."

## RACIAL COMPOSITION OF THE REDISTRICTING COMMITTEE

Another major issue for the Charter Commission was the racial composition of the proposed city council redistricting committee. Commissioner Amalia V. Betanzos (1989, 135), former president of National Association for Puerto Rican Civil Rights, voiced her thoughts on the configuration of the future redistricting commission membership, noted the importance of race, and suggested that the members should be "reflective of the ethnic and racial composition of the City, because I think the lines would be very different if it were that rather than nine white men." The requirement was approved by the commissioners.

In 1990, however, Richard Ravitch, Chair of the first Charter Commission who had resigned to run for mayor in 1988 (Finder 1989), successfully filed a law suit, *Ravitch et al. v. City of New York*, challenging the use of "racial and ethnic quotas," stating that

appointments should be made "on the basis of merit and of politics, not on the basis of ethnicity" (Solomon 1990, 12). The District Court Judge ruled 1922 that the requirement was unconstitutional, in part because it "does cause harm to innocent third parties" or as Alan Gartner (1998, 368) interpreted the ruling, "had the potential to harm innocent people who might be precluded by race from serving" (Gartner 1998, 368). Resonating with these concerns, in a landmark redistricting decision, *Shaw v. Reno* (1993), Supreme Court Justice Sandra Day O'Connor (Kousser 1999, 270), in her discussion of the Court's decision against a majority African American district in North Carolina, explained that creating such districts supports stereotypes "that members of the same racial group—regardless of their age, education, economic status, or the community in which they live—think alike, share the same political interests, and will prefer the same candidates at the polls."

The commentaries offered by Ravitch and O'Connor are part of the liberal legal and political ideology that emphasizes individualism and minimal government regulation (Ancheta 1998). O'Connor, by emphasizing differences among individuals, ignores the historic and contemporary practices that have created common experiences and interests for these individuals as groups. This type of analysis omits the inequality and discrimination embedded in U.S. society that racialize experiences, generate common interests among a heterogeneous population and contribute to a long history of panethnic and multiracial organizing around such issues as employment discrimination, electoral politics, distribution of government resources and services, hate crimes, and police violence, both locally in New York City and nationally (CAAV Vocie 1996; Espiritu 1992; Lowe 1996; Vo 1996).

## CHINATOWN, REDISTRICTING, AND THE 1991 ELECTION

The 1990 Census placed the Chinatown population at 62,895, which fell far short of the district requirement of approximately 143,579. While community groups agreed on the general boundaries of Chinatown, and that the area should be kept whole within one district, the groups held widely conflicting views on which areas should be added to reach the required population.

Asian American for Equality (AAFE), a Chinatown-based social service provider, emphasized descriptive representation (Pitkin 1967)—electing Asian American candidates, and proposing that Chinatown should be linked with areas to the west and south—that is, SoHo, City Hall, Tribeca, and Battery Park City.

In contrast, recognizing that no single ethnic or racial group in the area was large enough to constitute 50 percent or more of a district, area residents formed an organization, Lower East Siders for a Multi-Racial District, and stressing substantive representation (Hero and Tolbert 1995)—support of issues by an elected representative—proposed a plan that would create a majority Latino, Asian American, and African American district based on the needs and interests of low-income and working-class residents (Chan 1991). A range of community activists and organizations, including ADLDEF, the Community Service Society, and the Puerto Rican Legal Defense and Education Fund (PRLDEF) supported this plan.

Ultimately, the redistricting commission concluded that AAFE provided the strongest case and Chinatown was joined with areas to the west. "The Commission hoped that a strong Asian American candidate, with the support of the white, liberal areas surrounding Chinatown, could be elected" (Gartner 19993, 68).

Uniting Chinatown with areas to the west created District 1, in which Asian Americans were the largest group at 39.2 percent of the population, but with only 14.2 percent of the voters. In contrast, whites comprised 37.2 percent of the population but 61.5 percent of the registered voters. Latinos comprised 17.4 of the population and 8.8 percent of the voters. Although over 80 percent of the Asian American voters in Chinatown

supported the Asian American candidates, and there was some crossover voting by whites, ultimately, whites controlled the 1991 city council election and elected the white candidate (Saito 2001).

## CENSUS UNDERCOUNT

Before the 1990 Census data, community members estimated that based on the number of housing units and average occupancy, Chinatown contained between 100,000 to 150,000 inhabitants, a population sufficient to create an Asian American majority district. However, racial minorities, immigrants (especially the undocumented), non-English speakers, and low-income residents of urban areas tend to be undercounted by the largest margin, a highly partisan issue in the battle over methods to improve the accuracy of the census, since the undercounted tend to be Democrats (Anderson and Fienberg 1999).

According to the 1990 census, the city's population was 7,322,564 and each of the fifty-one districts required a population of approximately 143,579 and the census counted only 62,895 in Chinatown, as mentioned above. A high undercount in Chinatown meant that other areas (in this case, white neighborhoods) had to be added to meet minimum population requirements for a district.

Feelings of betrayal about the Census Bureau and the undercount were expressed at a public forum. Responding to criticism that ethnic communities should have taken greater responsibility to ensure an accurate census, Esmeralda Simmons (Santiago n.d., 32)—former member of the Districting Commission and Director for the Center of Law and Social Justice at Medgar Evers College—cited U.S. government actions that stifled community efforts. Simons stated that "our communities were geared up to get involved until the INS [Immigration and Naturalization Service] decided to undo their commitment and do those raids immediately as the Census started . . . When they started doing raids, that was the end of the Census, and it was, in my opinion, deliberately timed. No one's going to sign up and say that they're here illegally and risk being deported."

## CONCLUSION

The vast majority of the Asian American voters in Chinatown supported the Asian American candidates in the 1990 city council election, but the impact of those votes was limited by the aggregate effects of the configuration of the district and its demographic profile, population requirements for districts (fifty-one rather than sixty), census undercount, and a range of other factors—such as the demographic and ideological makeup of commissions—that framed electoral politics. Since the earliest history of the United States, when voting rights were limited to white men of property, political practices have had racial consequences, particularly in the way such practices have been rooted in privileged access to power, rewards, and opportunities for whites (Lipsitz 1998; Kousser 1999). Because of these procedures, political access and power are shaped by the structure of political institutions, that is, these institutions are not simply neutral instruments through which interests are contested and expressed (Crenshaw et al. 1995). The New York City case demonstrated that the actions of the Charter and Districting Commissions to enhance the political power of racial minority groups were constrained by the commission members' limited recognition of the historical and current institutional barriers that actively worked to privilege whites over minorities in politics.

As a way of electing representatives, single member districts have been very effective for large populations of hypersegregated African Americans and whites, but in the case of New York City and much of the United States, the more dispersed population of Asian Pacific Americans—and to a lesser degree, Latinos—make such districts problematical. As Lani Guinier (1994) points out in her discussion of the problems

associated with single member districts, group interests may not coincide with district boundaries; gerrymandering is an "inevitable" part of redistricting; and the dominance of the majority voters can lead to a "tyranny of the majority" in which the votes of the minority are unproductive and "wasted." To counter these problems, alternative election systems have been suggested, such as cumulative voting. In this election procedure, voters can cast as many votes as there are open seats and can strategically use their votes by spreading them among the candidates or use all of their votes for one candidate, and voters can more readily form alliances with other voters based on shared interests (Reed 1992).

The members of the Districting Commission emphasized racial boundaries and labels for Asian Americans and Latinos, and past white support for Asian American candidates. Implied in the commission's analysis is that whites would recognize the merits of Asian American candidate. However, this viewpoint does not adequately consider the "racial" identity of whites and the active support of white racial privilege through the historic and contemporary practices of political exclusion employed by whites against racial minorities. Certainly whites have joined with racial minorities to elect minorities, but this scenario primarily occurs when progressive whites need allies to supplant an entrenched group (Browning, Marshall, and Tabb 1984; Sonenshein 1993), not when they are a voting majority, such as in District 1.

Clearly, Asian Pacific Americans have achieved electoral success with the help of white voters, and the 1996 election of Chinese American Gary Locke as governor of the state of Washington is a notable example. I would suggest, however, that Asian Pacific American candidate in areas with low numbers of Asian Pacific Americans face a different set of circumstances than racially diverse communities such as New York City. In Washington, Locke's personal qualifications (such as his college degrees and experience in elected offices) were strong, and his Asian American heritage was correlated with such positive characteristics as "hardworking, family-oriented, [and] strongly supportive of education" (Yu and Yuan 2001, 357). I suggest, however, that the racial identity of a candidate gains added importance, and its meaning changes, when a minority population becomes significant. At this "tipping point," the political salience of race is amplified when political interests overlap with race, such as concern over racial profiling by police, economic redevelopment plans that displace low-income minority communities, or inadequate funding for urban public schools servicing minorities. As a result, I would argue that whites "see" a minority candidates as linked to his or her ethnic community, and unable or unwilling to represent all residents, while at the same time, ignoring the history of discriminatory policies and practices and viewing white candidates as viable representatives for everyone.

The history of politics in the United States demonstrates the need for multiple strategies to work for the enfranchisement of Asian Pacific Americans. Efforts to increase rates of citizenship, voter registration, voting, and running for office are important. Equally significant are efforts to address structural barriers that limit the effectiveness of such efforts, and the support and development of organizations that can pursue institutional change. Some communities have allowed noncitizens to vote on issues that directly affect them, such as parents voting in school board elections. Mobilizing people and working toward social change requires tremendous amounts of resources and calls for the support of organizations and community efforts working toward these goals. This is one of the key areas for Asian Pacific Americans seeking increased political power, elevating the strength of organized efforts working toward issues of political equality and social justice. As the U.S. Supreme Court redistricting decisions clearly demonstrated, gains can be reversed and progress is not inevitable.

## REFERENCES

AALDEF (Asian American Legal Defense and Education Fund). 1992. Outlook Spring.

Ancheta, Angelo N. 1998. *Race, Rights, and the Asian American Experience.* New Brunswick, N.J.: Rutgers University Press.

Anderson, Margo J., and Stephen E. Fienberg. 1999. *Who Counts? The Politics of Census-Taking in Contemporary America.* New York: Russell Sage Foundation.

Asian American Community Letter. July 18, 1989. Letter addressed to Frederick A. O. Schwarz Jr. Chair, New York City Charter Revision Commission. Appendix X, 10–11.

Betanzos, Amalia V. 1989. Minutes of the New York City Charter Revision Commission, May 6. N.Y.C. Mayor. C.R.C. Submission under Sec. 5 of the Voting Rights Act. Appendix V, 7–8.

Browning, Rufus P., Dale Rogers Marshall, and David H. Tabb. 1990. *Racial Politics in American Cities.* New York: Longman.

*CAAAV Voice.* 1996. Newsletter of the Committee against Anti-Asian Violence. Winter 8(1): 3.

Chan, Elaine. 1991. Oral testimony delivered to the New York City Districting commission. March 21. Appendix III, Volume 7, 182.

Chen, Pauline. 1989. Testimony of Pauline Chen, President of the Chinatown Voter Education Alliance before the New York City Charter Revision Commission. June 6, 1989. Appendix X, No. 9 (Item 14).

Cho, Wendy Tam and Bruce E. Cain. 2001. "Asian Americans as the Median Voters: An Exploration of Attitudes and Voting Patterns on Ballot Initiatives." In Gordon H. Chang, ed., *Asian Americans and Politics: Perspectives, Experiences, Prospects,* 133–52. Stanford: Stanford University Press.

Crenshaw, Kimberle, Neil Gotanda, Gary Peller, and Kendall Thomas, eds. 1995. *Critical Race Theory.* New York: The New Press.

Davidson, Chandler. 1992. "The Voting Rights Act: A Brief History." In Bernard Grofman and Chandler Davidson, eds., *Controversies in Minority Voting: The Voting Rights Act in Perspective,* 7–51. Washington, D.C.: The Brookings Institution.

Davidson, Chandler and Bernard Grofman. 1994. *Quiet Revolution in the South.* Princeton, N.J.: Princeton University Press.

Erie, Steven P. and Harold Brackman. 1993. *Paths to Political Incorporation for Latinos and Asian Pacifics in California.* Berkeley: California Policy.

Espiritu, Yen L. 1992. *Asian American Panethnicity: Bridging Institutions and Identities.* Philadelphia: Temple University Press.

Finder, Alan. 1989. "Charter Panel Tilted Scales Toward Minorities and Away From Boroughs." *New York Times,* May 16: B1.

Fung, Margaret. 1989. Testimony of Margaret Fung, Executive Director, Asian American Legal Defense and Education Fund, before the New York City charter Revision Commission. June 7, 1989. Appendix X, 9, #136.

Gartner, Alan. 1993. "Drawing the Lines: Redistricting and the Politics of Racial Succession in New York." Unpublished monograph. The City University of New York: The Graduate School and University Center.

Gartner, Alan. 1998. New York City Redistricting: A View from Inside." In Bernard Grofman, ed., 367–73. *Race and Redistricting in the 1990s.* New York; Agathon Press.

Grofman, Bernard and Chandler Davidson. 1992. *Controversies in Minority Voting: The Voting Rights Act in Perspective* Washington, D.C.: The Brookings Insitution.

Guinier, Lani. 1994. *The Tyranny of the Majority.* New York: Free Press.

Hero, Rodney E. and Caroline J. Tolbet. 1995. "Latinos and Substantive Representation in the U.S. House of Representatives: Direct, Indirect, or Nonexistent?" *American Journal of Political Science* 39(3): 640–52.

Kong, Gail. 1989. Testimony of Gail M. Kong before the New York City Charter Revision commission. June 8, 1989. Appendix X, No. 9. No page number.

Kousser, J. Morgan. 1999. *Colorblind Injustice: Minority Voting Rights and the Undoing of the Second Reconstruction.* The University of North Carolina Press: Chapel Hill and London.

Lien, Pei-te. 1997. *The Political Participation of Asian Americans: Voting Behavior in Southern California.* New York: Garland Publishing.

Lipsitz, George. 1998. *The Possessive Investment in Whiteness: How White People Profit from Identity Politics.* Philadelphia: Temple University Press.

Lowe, Lisa. 1996. *Immigrant Acts: On Asian American Cultural Politics.* Durham, N.C.: Duke University Press.

Muzzio, Douglas and Tim Tompkins. 1989. "On the Size of City Council: Finding the Mean." In Frank J. Mauro, ed., *Restructuring the New York City Government: The Reemergence of Municipal Reform,* 83–96. New York: Academy of Political Science.

Nakanishi, Don. 2001. "Beyond Electoral Politics: Renewing a Search for a Paradigm of Asian Pacific American Politics." In Gordon H. Chang, ed., *Asian American and Politics: Perspectives, Experiences, Prospects,* 102–129. Stanford: Stanford University Press.

NYC-CRC (New York City. Charter Revision Commission). March 1990. *Final Report of the New York City Charter Revision commission: January 1989–November 1989.* Frederick A. O. Schwarz Jr., Chair.

Ong, Paul M. and David E. Lee. 2001. "Changing of the Guard: The Emerging Immigrant Majority in Asian American Politics." In Gordon H. Chang, ed., *Asian American and Politics: Perspectives, Experiences, Prospects,* 153–72. Stanford: Stanford University Press.

Ong, Paul and Don Nakanishi. 1996. "Becoming Citizens, Becoming Voters: The Naturalization and Political Participation of Asian Pacific Immigrants." In Bill Ong Hing and Ronald Lee, eds., *Reframing the Immigration Debate,* 275–305.

Pitkin, Hanna Fenichel. 1967. *The Concept of Representation.* Berkeley: University of California Press.

Puerto Rican Legal Defense and Education Fund. 1998. Letter to Richard Ravitch, Chair of the Charter Reform Commission, April 1. Appendix IX, #2. Page number not legible.

Reed, Judith. 1992. "Of Boroughs, Boundaries and Bullwinkles: The Limitations of Single-Member Districts in a Multiracial Content." *Fordham Urban Law Journal* 19: 759–80.

Saito, Leland T. 1998. *Race and Politics; Asian Americans, Latinos, and Whites in a Los Angeles Suburb.* Urbana and Chicago: University of Illinois Press.

Saito, Leland T. 2001. "Asian Americans and Multiracial Political Coalitions: New York City's Chinatown and Redistricting, 1990–1991." In Gordon H. Chang, ed.,

*Asian Americans and Politics: Perspectives, Experiences, Prospects,* 383–408. Stanford: Stanford University Press.

Santiago, John, ed. N.d. *Redistricting, Race and Ethnicity in New York City: The Gratner Report and its Critics.* New York City: Institute for Puerto Rican Policy.

Solomon, Alisa. 1990. "Ravitch Sues Districting Panel." *Village Voice,* November 13, 1990: 12.

Sonenshein, Raphael. J. 1993. *Politics in Black and White: Race and Power in Los Angeles.* Princeton, N.J.: Princeton University Press.

Vo, Linda Trinh. 1996. "Asian Immigrants, *Asian Americans,* and the Politics of Economic Mobilization in San Diego." *Amerasia Journal* 22(2): 89–108.

Yu, Judy and Grace T. Yuan. 2001. "Lessons Learned from the 'Locke for Governor' Campaign." In Gordon H. Chang, ed., *Asian Americans and Politics: Perspectives, Experiences, Prospects,* 354-66. Stanford: Stanford University Press.

# Index

# About the Contributors

~~~~~~~~~~~~~~~~~~~~~~~~~~~~~~~~~~~~~~~~~~~~~~~~~~~~~~~~~~~~~~~~~~~~~~~~~~~~~~~~~~~~~~~~~~~~~

**Harold Brackman** is a consultant on intergroup relations for the Museum of Tolerance in Los Angeles. His recent publications include "'A Calamity Almost beyond Comprehension': Nazi Anti-Semitism and the Holocaust in the Thought of W. E. B. Du Bois," *American Jewish History* (2000); and "African Americans as a Cultural Group," in Mary Kupiec Cayton and Peter W. Williams, eds., *Encyclopedia of American Cultural and Intellectual History* (2001).

**Edward T. Chang** is associate professor of ethnic studies and a former director of the Center for Asian Pacific America (CAPA) at the University of California–Riverside. He earned his B.A. (1982) in sociology and a Ph.D. (1990) in ethnic studies at UC–Berkeley and M.A. (1984) in Asian American studies at UCLA. He is the author of several books, including *Ethnic Peace in the American City: Community Building in Los Angeles and Beyond* (with Jeannette Diaz-Veizades) (1999); *Following the Footsteps of Korean Americans*; and *Who African Americans Are*. In addition, he coedited two volumes about Los Angeles civil unrest and its aftermath: *Los Angeles: Struggles toward Multiethnic Community* (1995) and *Building Multiethnic Coalitions* (1995). Chang was invited as special guest editor of the *Korean and Korean American Studies Bulletin*: "Emerging Generation of Korean Americans" (1999), "The Korean Diaspora in the USA: Challenges and Evolution" (2000), and "Korean Diaspora in China: Ethnicity, Identity, and Change" (2001).

**Elaine L. Chao** is the nation's twenty-fourth secretary of labor, representing a new generation of American leadership. She was confirmed by the U.S. Senate on January 29, 2001. When President George W. Bush nominated Elaine L. Chao, the first Asian-American woman appointed to a president's cabinet in U.S. history, he described her as an individual with "strong executive talent, compassion, and commitment to helping people build better lives."

Before coming to the Labor Department, Secretary Chao was a Distinguished Fellow at The Heritage Foundation, a Washington-based public policy research and educational institute. Previously she served as president and chief executive officer of United Way of America. Secretary Chao received her M.B.A. from the Harvard Business School and her undergraduate degree in economics from Mount Holyoke College. She also studied at MIT, Dartmouth College, and Columbia University. Active in many volunteer activities, Secretary Chao has received numerous awards for her professional accomplishments and community service. She is the recipient of eleven honorary doctorate degrees from colleges and universities across the country. Secretary Chao is married to Senator Mitch McConnell of Kentucky.

**Wendy K. Tam Cho** is associate professor of political science and of statistics at the University of Illinois at Urbana–Champaign. Her research interests focus on racial and ethnic politics, electoral behavior, and statistical methodology. Her work has appeared in numerous scholarly journals and edited volumes, including the *American Political Science Review*, the *Journal of Politics*, and *Political Analysis*.

**Steven P. Erie** is director of UC–San Diego's Urban Studies and Planning Program, an associate professor of political science at UCSD, and a senior fellow at USC's Southern California Studies Center. His book *Rainbow's End: Irish Americans and the Dilemmas of Urban Machine Politics* won the Best Urban Politics Book award from the American Political Science Association and the Robert Park Award from the American Sociological Association. Dr. Erie's current policy research addresses the demographic, trade, and infrastructure linkages between Southern California, Mexico, and the Pacific Rim. He is the author of two California Policy Research Center studies on these subjects: *Paths to Political Incorporation for Latinos and Asian Pacifics in California* (1993) and *International Trade and Job Creation in Southern California: Facilitating Los Angeles/Long Beach Port, Rail, and Airport Development* (1996). He is completing a book project, *Globalizing L.A.: The Politics of Trade, Infrastructure, and Regional Development*.

**Kim Geron** is assistant professor of political science at California State University–Hayward. He is conducting research on Latino and Asian Pacific Islander elected officials and their policy priorities. His research interests also include labor and social movements.

**Bill Ong Hing** is a professor of law and Asian American studies at the University of California–Davis, where he teaches constitutional law, judicial process, Asian American history, and Asian Americans and the law. Professor Hing is the author of several books, including *To Be an American: Cultural Pluralism and the Rhetoric of Assimilation* (1997); and *Making and Remaking Asian America through Immigration Policy* (1993). He co-counseled the precedent-setting asylum case *INS v. Cardoza-Fonseca* in the Supreme Court. He is the founder of the Immigrant Legal Resource Center, a national immigrant rights support group.

**Thomas P. Kim** is an assistant professor of politics at Scripps College and a member of the Intercollegiate Department of Asian American Studies at the Claremont Colleges. His publications include "Clarence Thomas and the Politicization of Candidate Sex," *Legislative Studies Quarterly* (1998); and, with Paul Frymer and Terri Bimes, "Party Elites, Ideological Voters, and Divided Party Government," *Legislative Studies Quarterly* (1997). His current research interests include urban political economy, the political construction of race, and racial and ethnic political strategies.

**Harry H. L. Kitano** is professor emeritus of social welfare and sociology in the School of Public Policy and Social Research at UCLA. He was the first to hold the endowed chair of Japanese American Studies. He is the author of numerous scholarly articles and books, including *Japanese Americans: The Evolution of Subculture* (1976), *Generations and Iden-*

*tity* (1993), and *Race Relations* (1998), now in its fifth edition. He spent his teenage years in the Topaz Concentration Camp in Utah. He continues to teach and conduct research on the Asian American experience.

**James S. Lai** is assistant professor at Santa Clara University. He holds a joint appointment in the Department of Political Science and the Ethnic Studies program. He is the coeditor of the *National Asian Pacific American Political Almanac,* a biannual publication by the UCLA Asian American Studies Press. Recent articles include "The Symbolic Politics of Affirmative Action" (coauthored with Michael B. Preston) in *Racial and Ethnic Politics in California,* vol. 2 (1997); "Asian Pacific Americans and the Pan-Ethnic Question" in Richard Keiser and Katherine Underwood, eds., *Minority Politics at the Millennium* (2000); and "Transforming Racial Politics: The Electoral Paths and Policy Priorities of Asian Pacific American and Latino Elected Officials" (coauthored with Kim Geron), forthcoming in *Asian Law Journal.*

**Taeku Lee** is assistant professor of public policy at Harvard's Kennedy School of Government. Lee is a political scientist who specializes in public opinion, racial politics, social movements, and social policy. He is author of *Mobilizing Public Opinion* (2002). He has written on issues of ethnic identity, language, stereotypes, discrimination, and partisanship involving Asian Americans and Latinos and is a collaborator on the first-ever national survey of Asian American political opinion. In the areas of health and social policy, Lee is currently at work on projects that examine the politics of obesity, AIDS policy, and public support for health care reform.

**Pei-te Lien** teaches political science and ethnic studies at the University of Utah. Her primary research interest is the political participation of Asian and other American racial and ethnic groups. She is the author of *The Political Participation of Asian Americans: Voting Behavior in Southern California* (1997) and *The Making of Asian America through Political Participation* (2001). She also publishes widely on issues of race, gender, and Asian American politics and behavior in professional journals and edited book volumes.

**Gary Locke** was elected Washington's twenty-first governor in 1996, making him the first Chinese American governor in U.S. history. In 2000 he was reelected to his second term. Born into an immigrant family in 1950, he spent his first six years in Seattle's Yesler Terrace, a public housing project for families of World War II veterans. Gary received his bachelor's degree in political science from Yale University in 1972. He was elected to the Washington State House of Representatives in 1982, where he served on the House Judiciary and Appropriations committees, with his final five years as chairman of the House Appropriations Committee, and was elected chief executive of King County in 1993. As governor, he has worked to make Washington a better place to live, work, and raise a family. Believing that education is the great equalizer, he has made it his top priority.

**Lee A. Makela** is associate professor of East Asian history and coordinator of the Asian Studies Program at Cleveland State University. His current research interests revolve around aspects of urban cultural history in Japan during the Tokugawa period between 1600 and 1868. His Web site, "Teaching (and Learning) about Japan," at www.csuohio.edu/history/japan/index.html, was selected by the National Endowment for the Humanities (NEH) as one of the thirty best educational Web sites for 1999 and is listed among the NEH EDSITEment "Best of the Humanities" Web sites currently recommended to educators throughout cyberspace.

**Mitchell T. Maki** is associate dean of the College of Health and Human Services at California State University–Los Angeles. Prior to this appointment, Dr. Maki was a professor in the UCLA Department of Social Welfare. He is the lead author of the award-winning book, *Achieving the Impossible Dream: How Japanese Americans Obtained Redress*, which is a case study of the passage of the Civil Liberties Act of 1988. Additionally, Dr. Maki has authored numerous articles about multicultural social work issues. Dr. Maki is active in several community groups and serves on the advisory board for the California Civil Liberties Education Project. He is a sought-after presenter on issues ranging from the Japanese American redress movement to contemporary community issues.

**Norman Y. Mineta** became the fourteenth secretary of transportation in 2001. Prior to joining President Bush's administration as secretary of transportation, Secretary Mineta served as secretary of commerce under President Clinton, becoming the first Asian Pacific American to serve in the cabinet. He is the first secretary of transportation to have previously served in a cabinet position. From 1975 to 1995, Secretary Mineta served as a member of the U.S. House of Representatives, representing the heart of California's Silicon Valley. While in Congress, he was the driving force behind passage of H.R. 442, the Civil Liberties Act of 1988, which officially apologized for and redressed the injustices endured by Japanese Americans during World War II. He cofounded the Congressional Asian Pacific American Caucus and served as its first chair. Secretary Mineta served as San Jose mayor from 1971 to 1974, becoming the first Asian Pacific American mayor of a major U.S. city. In 1995, George Washington University awarded the Martin Luther King Jr. Commemorative Medal to Secretary Mineta for his contributions to the field of civil rights.

**Don T. Nakanishi** is the director and a professor of the UCLA Asian American Studies Center, the nation's largest and most comprehensive research, teaching, publications, and policy program on Asian Pacific Americans. He has written extensively on ethnic and racial politics and has authored seminal contributions like "Asian American Politics: An Agenda for Research," "A Quota on Excellence? The Debate on Asian American Admissions," and "The Next Swing Vote? Asian Pacific Americans and California Politics." A former national president of the Association of Asian American Studies, he cofounded *Amerasia Journal*, the leading scholarly journal in the field of Asian American Studies, and is the coeditor of the *National Asian Pacific American Political Almanac*.

**Glenn Omatsu** is a staff member of the UCLA Asian American Studies Center and part-time faculty at California State University–Northridge and Pasadena City College, and works with community and labor groups and solidarity networks. At UCLA, he serves as associate editor of *Amerasia Journal*, the nation's leading research publication in Asian American Studies, and as editor of *CrossCurrents*, the news magazine of the UCLA Asian American Studies Center. At UCLA, he teaches classes in Asian American social movements, community education/youth empowerment, and Asian American labor, as well as other classes relating to students and community activism. At California State University–Northridge, he teaches classes in service learning, Asian American contemporary issues, and developmental reading; he also serves as faculty mentor coordinator for the Educational Opportunity Program. At Pasadena City College, he teaches an introductory sociology course focusing on the Asian American experience. He is coeditor (with Steve Louie) of *Asian Americans: The Movement and the Moment* (2001).

**Elena Ong** is a public affairs and public policy consultant recognized by *Who's Who among American Women* and *Who's Who in Research*. She is the first vice chair of the California Commission on the Status of Women, a board member of LA 80-20, past state director of the National Women's Political Caucus–LA/Metro, and past president of the Los Angeles Women's Appointment Collaboration. She pursued ethnic studies at UC–Berkeley prior to attending the Kennedy School of Government and earning a master's degree in health policy and management at Harvard.

**Paul M. Ong** is professor at UCLA's School of Public Policy and Social Research, affiliated faculty with Asian American Studies, and director of UCLA's Lewis Center for Regional Policy Studies. He has done extensive research on immigration, racial inequality, and welfare reform. His publications include *The New Asian Immigration in Los Angeles and Global Restructuring* (1994), *Impacts of Affirmative Action: Policies and Consequences in California* (1999), and *Transforming Race Relations: The State of Asian Pacific America* (2000). He has served on the Race and Ethnic Advisory Committee for the U.S. Bureau of the Census.

**Leland T. Saito** is associate professor of sociology at the University of Southern California. His research focuses on urban politics, economic redevelopment, and race relations in Los Angeles, New York City, and San Diego. He is the author of *Race and Politics: Asian Americans, Latinos, and Whites in a Los Angeles Suburb*. He was the vice chair of the 2000 San Diego City Council Redistricting and a cofounder of the Southwest Center for Asian Pacific American Law.

**Sandhya Shukla** is an assistant professor of anthropology and Asian American studies at Columbia University. She has published articles on migration, race, and diaspora, and has held fellowships at UCLA's Asian American Studies Center and Cornell University's Society for the Humanities. She recently completed a book entitled *India Abroad: Postwar Diasporic Cultures of the US and UK* and is currently working on two projects, one on transnational cultures of Harlem and the other on cross-culturality in the Caribbean.

**Okiyoshi Takeda** is assistant professor at Aoyama Gakuin University in Tokyo, Japan. Before receiving a Ph.D. at Princeton (his dissertation addressed bill passage in the House of Representatives), he taught a course in Asian American politics at the University of Pennsylvania, New York University, and Columbia University. His research interest includes legislative politics, minority political representation in the United States, and pedagogical issues. He has published in the *Journal of Asian American Politics* and contributed a chapter to *Representation of Minority Groups in the U.S.: Implications for the Twenty-First Century* (2001).

**Spencer K. Turnbull** was born in Santa Barbara, California, and grew up in the nearby Santa Ynez Valley, where he attended public schools. Turnbull attended Stanford University, graduating in 1996 with a B.A. in international relations, with an emphasis on Latin American studies. In 2001 he earned his J.D. from the UCLA School of Law. A former U.S. Army J.A.G. Corps intern, Turnbull currently practices law at the Los Angeles office of Latham & Watkins.

**L. Ling-chi Wang** was born and reared in Xiamen, Fujian, China, and Hong Kong. He received his B.A. (music) from Hope College, Holland, Michigan; his B.D. (Old Testament) from Princeton Seminary; and his M.A. (Semitic languages and literature) from UC–Berkeley. Wang is the author of "Lau vs. Nichols: History of a Struggle for Equal and Quality Education," in *Counterpoint: Perspectives of Asian America,* edited by Emma Gee (1976). His contributions also include *Educational Experience of Asian Americans: A Sourcebook for Teachers and Students,* edited by Don T. Nakanishi (1994), "Meritocracy and Diversity in Higher Education: Discrimination against Asian Americans in the Post-Bakke Era," *Urban*

*Review* (1988), and "Racism and the Model Minority: Asian Americans in Higher Education," in *The Racial Crisis in American Higher Education,* edited by Philip G. Altbach and
Kofi Lomotey (1991) (coauthor Sucheng Chan). His research interests include Asian American history, Asian American civil rights issues, overseas Chinese, U.S. foreign policies in
Asia, bilingual education, and Asian Americans in higher education.

**Janelle S. Wong** is an assistant professor in the Department of Political Science and Program in American Studies and Ethnicity at the University of Southern California. Her
research focuses on racial and ethnic politics in the Unites States. She has published articles in *Political Behavior* and the *American Journal of Sociology* and is currently working
on a book manuscript on political participation and incorporation among Asian American
and Latino immigrants. She is also part of the research team led by Pei-te Lien that conducted the Pilot National Asian American Political Survey, the first multi-city, multiethnic, multilingual survey of Asian American political attitudes and behavior in the United
States.

**Kent Wong** is director of the Center for Labor Research and Education at UCLA, where he
teaches labor studies and Asian American studies. He served as the founding president of
the Asian Pacific American Labor Alliance, AFL-CIO from 1992 to 1997. Wong previously
worked as the staff attorney for the Service Employees International Union, Local 660, representing 40,000 Los Angeles County workers and worked as the first staff attorney for the
Asian Pacific American Legal Center of Southern California. Mr. Wong is president of the
United Association for Labor Education, a national organization of labor educators from
unions, universities, and the community and serves on the executive committee of the
International Federation of Worker Education Associations. Mr. Wong regularly addresses
labor, community, civil rights, university, and student conferences throughout the country. He has written extensively on labor issues for various journals and newspapers, and
recently published a book entitled *Voices for Justice: Asian Pacific American Organizers
and the New American Labor Movement.* He also coedited a book entitled *Voices from the
Front Lines: Organizing Immigrant Workers in Los Angeles.*

**David Wu,** a Congressman from Oregon, was born in Taiwan in 1955. In 1961 he and his
family moved to the United States from Taiwan after President John F. Kennedy signed an
executive order updating unfair immigration quotas. He was educated in public schools,
earned a B.S. from Stanford University in 1977, attended Harvard Medical School, and
received a law degree from Yale University in 1982. Congressman Wu is the only Chinese
American member of the U.S. House of Representatives. He was elected to a second term
and sworn in as a member of the 107th U.S. Congress in 2001. Congressman Wu represents Oregon's First District and serves as a member of the New Democrat Coalition, a
group of moderate Democrats in the House. He also serves as chair of the Congressional
Asian Pacific Caucus.

**Frank H. Wu** joined the faculty of the Howard University School of Law in Washington,
D.C., in 1995. Professor Wu's *Yellow:Race in America beyond Black and White* was pub-
lished in early 2002. His coauthored textbook, *Race, Rights, and Reparation: Law and the
Japanese American Internment,* was published in spring 2001. Mr, Wo's more than 200
articles have appeared in periodicals such as the *Washington Post, L.A. Times, Chicago
Tribune, Toronto Star, Atlanta Journal & Constitution, Chronicle of Higher Education,
National Law Journal, Legal Times, Nation,* and *Progressive.* From 1995 until 1998, he
was Washington correspondent for *Asian Week.*